Obama's Book of Lies

Obama's Book of Lies

A Legacy of Taqiyya and Fake News

James McCormack

Contact James McCormack at jmk91234@gmail.com. James McCormack is available for corporate or government policy consulting.

ISBN: 1546669183
ISBN 13: 9781546669180

Table of Contents

Introduction

"It ain't what you don't know that gets you into trouble. It's what you know for sure that just ain't so." *Mark Twain, American author and philosopher.*

ALL POLITICIANS MISLEAD the public, hedge on difficult issues, or outright lie. But no one, in the history of the presidency, has told so many blatant lies as President Barack Obama. He is a consummate liar, and has been called the "Liar in Chief" of the United States of America, the "Lord of the Lies," and the "Lying King." The lies told during his presidency were continuous and non-stop. Unfortunately, many of Obama's misrepresentations that he floated to the press and the American pubic generally went unchallenged since the mainstream media supported his agenda and did not want to make waves that could embarrass the president or impede his liberal agenda which was embraced by much of the establishment.

Some of the lies were subtle while others were heinous and mocked the intelligence of the American public. Lies were told for various reasons including protecting his presidency and political viability, advancing his domestic and international political agenda, shielding Islam and radical Islamists from scrutiny, weakening Israel's political diplomatic and military position, empowering Iran, protecting jihad, funding various radical Islamic political entities, and weakening America. Some of Obama's lies will be forgotten as America and the world become more engrossed in new political administrations, as new challenges and crises confront future American politicians with different ideas, discourses and policies.

Obama's lies started when he entered politics and increased in frequency and intensity as the political stakes increased. As time moves forward and more information is revealed about Obama's administration, Obama's lies will become more obvious and his promise to protect the Constitution and American interests will become more in doubt. A sampling of his various lies, many of which will define his presidency, include:

- "Iran, Cuba, Venezuela, these countries are tiny compared to the Soviet Union. They don't pose a serious threat to us the way the Soviet Union posed a threat to us."

- "We cannot allow Iran to obtain a nuclear weapon, it's unacceptable, and I will do everything that's required to prevent it."
- "America is determined to prevent Iran from getting a nuclear weapon and I will take no options off the table to achieve that goal."
- "Our goal is to get Iran to recognize it needs to give up its nuclear program and abide by the UN resolutions that have been in place ... the deal we'll accept is: They end their nuclear program. It's very straightforward."
- "According to their Supreme Leader, it would be contrary to their faith to obtain a nuclear weapon."
- "America's strong bonds with Israel are well known. This bond is unbreakable. It is based upon cultural and historical ties, and the recognition that the aspiration for a Jewish homeland is rooted in a tragic history that cannot be denied."
- "I would consider it a failure on my part, a fundamental failure of my presidency, if on my watch, or as a consequence of work I have done, Israel was rendered more vulnerable. That is not just a strategic failure, that would be a moral failure ... This has been as hard as anything I do, because of the deep affinities that I feel for the Israeli people and for the Jewish people."
- "Today, the United States ... has reached a historic understanding with Iran ... If this framework leads to a final, comprehensive deal, it will make our country, our allies, and our world safer."
- "My hope is they can achieve an agreement ... I've said from the start, I will walk away from the negotiations if in fact it's a bad deal."
- "If Iran violates the deal, sanctions can be snapped back into place."
- "And there's a permanent prohibition on Iran ever having a nuclear weapon."
- "They've got a chance to get right with the world ... Because if they do, there's incredible talent and resources and sophistication inside of Iran and it would be a very successful regional power that was also abiding by international norms and international rules – and that would be good for everybody."
- "The defense budget of the United States is more than $600 billion. To repeat, Iran's is about $15 billion."
- "This wasn't some nefarious deal ... We do not pay ransom for hostages. We didn't here and we won't in the future."
- "We have no information to suggest that it was a pre-planned attack. The unrest we have seen around the region has been in reaction to a video that many Muslims find offensive." *(Carney – Obama's White House press secretary discussing Benghazi)*

- "What happened in Benghazi is a tragedy. We're investigating what happened. I take full responsibility for that fact … But my biggest priority now is [to] bring those folks to justice and I think the American people have seen that's a commitment I'll always keep."
- "Gaddafi threatens a bloodbath that could destabilize an entire region."
- "First of all, ISIL is not Islamic. No religion condones the killing of innocents."
- "Al-Qaeda is on the run."
- "We've got choices about war and peace … I ended the war in Iraq, as I promised. We are transitioning out of Afghanistan. We have gone after the terrorists who actually attacked us on 9-11 and decimated al-Qaeda."
- "Our objective is clear. We will degrade and destroy ISIS."
- "I don't think they're gaining strength … What is true is that from the start, our goal has been first to contain and we have contained them."
- "As president, my first priority is the safety of the American people. And that's why even as we accept more refugees including Syrians we do so only after subjecting them to rigorous screening and security checks."
- "Turkey has been a strong partner with the United States and other member of the coalition in going after the activities of ISIL, or Daesh, both in Syria and Iraq."
- "So, there should not be a shred of doubt by now – when the chips are down, I have Israel's back. Which is why, if during this political season, you hear some questions regarding my administration's support for Israel, remember that it's not backed up by the facts."
- "And that is why my administration has consistently rejected any efforts to short-cut negotiations or impose an agreement on the parties …"
- "We have continued to insist that any Palestinian partner must recognize Israel's right to exist, and reject violence, and adhere to existing agreements."
- "I stood before the United Nations General Assembly and reaffirmed that any lasting peace must acknowledge the fundamental legitimacy of Israel and its security concerns. I said that America's commitment to Israel's security is unshakeable."
- "If you like your doctor, you will be able to keep your doctor. Period. If you like your health-care plan, you will be able to keep your healthcare plan. Period. No one will take it away. No matter what."
- "The new healthcare law will 'cut the cost of a typical family's premium by up to $2500 a year.'"
- "Under our plan, no federal dollars will be used to fund abortions."
- Obamacare is "absolutely not a tax increase."

- "I will never forget my own mother, as she fought cancer in her final months, having to worry about whether her insurance would refuse to pay for her treatment."
- "Today, I'm pledging to cut the deficit we inherited by half by the end of my first term in office … Now, this will not be easy … If I don't have this done in three years, then there's going to be a one term proposition."
- "We've got shovel-ready projects all across the country that governors and mayors are pleading to fund. And the minute we can get those investments to the state level, jobs are going to be created."
- "And, since I took office the United States has reduced the deficit by two-thirds."
- "I do solemnly swear (or affirm) that I will faithfully execute the Office of President of the United States, and will to the best of my ability, preserve, protect and defend the Constitution of the United States."
- "We all agree on the need to better secure the border and to punish the employers who chose to hire illegal immigrants. We are a generous and welcoming people here in the United States, but those who enter the country illegally and those who employ them disrespect the rule of law, and they are showing disregard to those who are following the law. We simply cannot allow people to pore into the United States undetected, undocumented, unchecked and circumventing the line of people who are waiting patiently, diligently and lawfully to become immigrants."
- "I don't want to pit Red America against Blue America. I want to be president of the United States of America."
- "I believe that marriage is the union between a man and a woman … for me as a Christian, it is also a sacred union – G-d is in the mix."
- "Not even mass corruption – not even a smidgen of corruption."
- "I had an uncle … who was part of the first American troops to go into Auschwitz and liberate the concentration camps."
- "… rather because only a more civil and honest public discourse can help us face up to the challenges of our nation in a way that would make them proud."
- "One of my core principles is that I will never engage in a politics in which I'm trying to divide people."
- "America is a nation of laws, which means I, as the president, am obligated to enforce the law. I don't have a choice about that."
- "If you actually took the number of Muslim Americans, we'd be one of the largest Muslim countries in the world."
- "I've always been a Christian … The only connection I've had to Islam is that my grandfather on my father's side came from that country [Kenya]. But I've never practiced Islam."

- "As a student of history, I also know civilization's debt to Islam. It was Islam – at places like al-Azhar University – that carried the light of learning through so many centuries, paving the way for Europe's Renaissance and Enlightenment."
- "These rituals remind us of the principles that we hold in common, and Islam's role in advancing justice, progress, tolerance, and the dignity of all human beings."
- "Today, the Security Council reaffirmed its established consensus that settlements have no legal validity." *Obama's UN Ambassador Samantha Power*
- "As you examine my commitment, you don't just have to count on my words. You can look at my deeds … As president of the United States, I have kept my commitments to the State of Israel. At every crucial juncture – at every fork in the road – we have been there for Israel. Every single time."
- "We reject the notion that somehow the US was the driving force behind this UN resolution (2334) … The United States did not draft or originate this resolution. Nor did we put it forward … It was possible that if the resolution were to be balanced… it was possible that the United States would then not block it … It was balanced and fair." *U.S. Secretary of State John Kerry speaking on behalf of Obama.*
- "One of the things that you discover as president is that there are all these rules and norms and laws … and the people that work for you are also subject to these rules and norms … I am very proud that we have been able to leave this administration without significant scandal."
- "I committed to President-elect Trump that my administration would ensure the smoothest possible transition, just as President Bush did for me."
- "The worst of the weapons are gone, but the despicable regime and the crisis it created remain and require our collective focus … [later, another declaration] … We got 100% of the chemical weapons out [of Syria]." *Obama's Secretary of State John Kerry, 2014.*
- "There will be no more illegal wiretapping of American citizens."
- "I know nothing about this. I was surprised to see reports from Chairman Nunes on that account today … can we trust the word of the White House?" *Susan Rice lied during a PBS NewsHour interview when responding to a question whether Trump or any of his associates and campaign officials were swept up in incidental intelligence collections.*

Interestingly, the press and mainstream media rarely, if ever, dissected the above statements and revealed the specifics of Obama's disingenuousness. *Fox News* and conservative bloggers were the few political observers who did not stay silent with Obama's easy disregard for the truth and safeguarding America's best interests. The lack of interest and indignation in Obama's lies proved the media's bias against Trump and conservatives in general, and that the press was not interested in shedding light on the truth but focused on advancing a liberal agenda, even if it was advanced on lies. In fact, some

Democrats called the lies Obama told to advance Obamacare - "noble lies." But from a philosophical perspective, can any lie be noble, and can ignoring and burying the truth in a contentious political world create a more unified and dignified country in the long run? Where was all these editors' and reporters' moral indignation with Obama's outright lies? Why wasn't the press ever concerned with digging for the truth during the Obama presidency? Unfortunately, the managing editors at *The New York Times, CNN, MSNBC, CBS, ABC*, and many others rarely became incensed with Obama's lies, yet when Trump voiced any statements that might be construed as being in any way inaccurate, Trump was immediately and repeatedly attacked and vilified as exemplified by:

- *Miami Herald*: "This president lies. Granted, every president tells the occasional politically expedient untruth. But this guy is different. He lies constantly. *[And not Obama?]* He lies about relatively unimportant things. He lies when the truth can be easily verified … Trump renewed his claim that he would have won the popular vote in the November election except that massive fraud cost him millions of ballots. And that's a lie, too … If we cannot trust these people to tell us the truth on minor matters that can be easily checked, what confidence can we have that they will be square with us on substantive matters where the truth is not a Google search away? What confidence can our allies and adversaries have? … That should scare you … Just a few days in, this may already be the least trustworthy regime in history."[1] ***(January 24, 2017 – only 4 days into his presidency)***
- A *Washington Post* headline, January 26, 2017: "Trump Just Gave a Remarkable News Interview. Here's a Tally of All His Lies."
- A *New Republic* article, January 23, 2017: "The Trump Administration's Lies Have Already Ruined Its Credibility"
- *The Nation* headline, January 24, 2017: "Donald Trump Intentionally Lies to Us"
- *The Atlantic* headline, January 24, 2017: "The White House Clings to False Claims of Massive Voter Fraud" and "Calling Out a Presidential Lie"
- *The New York Times* headline, January 23, 2017: "Trump Repeats Lie About Popular Vote in Meeting with Lawmakers" and "In a Swirl of 'Untruths' and 'Falsehoods,' Calling a Lie a Lie"
- A *CNN* lead article, January 26, 2017: "Booker: Trump Spreading Lies and 'Propaganda'"
- *CNN Politics* headline, March 8, 2017: "*NYT* Columnist Calls Trump a Pathological Liar." *(regarding Obama wiretapping accusation)*
- *Mika Brzezinski, MSNBC,* March 14, 2017: "Were you lying, Mr. President? Did you make it up? Was it some little spurt of activity that you had out of need to have action? I'd like to know where it came from because it's a very serious allegation. And it questions everything that you're about, and it questions whether we can ever believe you." *MSNBC, Morning Joe,*

discussing Trump's accusations concerning Obama's 'alleged' wiretapping of Trump, which was later proved true.

- *Joe Scarborough tweet,* March 13, 2017: "This is a joke right? I'm not being a smart ass here but everybody knows Trump was lying about Obama and the FBI tapping him. EVERYBODY." *MSNBC, Morning Joe.*
- "Watch: *CNN* Reporters and Anchors Call Out Trump and Spicer as Liars," *Mediaite.com headline.*
- *Fareed Zakaria, CNN interview with Don Lemon,* March 18, 2017. "I think the president is somewhat indifferent to things that are true or false. He has spent his whole life bull shitting. He has succeeded by bull shitting. He has gotten into the presidency by bull shitting. It is very hard to tell someone at that point that bull shitting doesn't work because look at the results." *Zakaria is talking about President Trump, but he could be talking about Obama. Zakaria is just plagiarizing Obama, who stated in May 2016 during the Republican presidential primaries, "He's nothing but a bull shitter." Zakaria was previously accused of plagiarizing in 2012, and was suspended from CNN when it was shown he duplicated another article concerning gun control.*
- A *CNN* lead article, March 22, 2017: "Trump's Problem with the Truth"
- *Time Magazine* cover, March 23, 2017: "Is Truth Dead?" Lead Article: "When a President Can't Be Taken at His Word."
  - "Half a century later, I suspect that about as many would say they believe in Truth, and yet we find ourselves having an intense debate over its role and power in the face of a President who treats it like a toy. The old adage that "a lie gets halfway around the world before Truth has a chance to get its pants on" was true even before the invention of Twitter. But it has been given new relevance by an early-rising Chief Executive and his smartphone. Like many newsrooms, we at *Time* have wrestled with when to say someone is lying. We can point out, as we often do, when a President gets his facts wrong. We can measure distortions, read between lines, ask the follow-up question. But there's a limit to what we can deduce about motive or intent, the interior wiring of the whopper, as opposed to its explosive impact." *(Nancy Gibbs, Time Magazine, March 23, 2017) What about Obama?*
- *Democratic Senator Chuck Schumer* at a New York restaurant raving to Mr. and Mrs. Joseph Caliphano, both Democrats and Joseph being a former advisor to President Johnson and a former U.S. Secretary of Health, Education and Welfare with President Carter: "How could you vote for Trump? He's a liar. He's a liar … He's a liar." Senator Schumer made a scene. *Where were his ethical standards during the Obama presidency?*

- *Representative Maxine Waters, (D – CA), MSNBC interview, March 31, 2017*: "[Trump] continues to go down a road where nobody is going to believe him … He wants everybody to believe that he told the truth when he said he was wiretapped … As a matter of fact, I've never heard a president of the United States been called a liar as much as he's been called a liar by practically everybody. He just does not have credibility."

- *Carl Bernstein, of Woodward and Bernstein / Watergate fame, CNN interview, "Reliable Sources," April 30, 2017*: "I wish this president well. He is the duly elected president of the United States, and he deserves respect as the duly elected president of the United States. That doesn't mean he deserves not to be called on lies. He has lied as no president of the United States in my lifetime has, day in and day out." *Is Bernstein confusing Trump for Obama?*

- *CNN commentator after Trump announced he did not tape his conversations with former FBI Director Comey after Trump tweeted that he may have taped the conversations. June 22, 2017.* "I am going to just use the L word. He lied. And there is no way around it. I went home and my kids asked me. My kids asked me 'What does the president do?' The only answer is that he lied … This was a sort of blatant lie." *Trump bluffed Comey so he would not lie during his Senate testimony.*

The journalists and politicians were incensed about Trumps "lies" concerning his questioning of the estimates of the inauguration crowd size, Obama's politicization of U.S. intelligence agencies, the number of illegal aliens voting fraudulently in the national election, and the effects of massive Middle Eastern immigration upon Sweden regarding the increased crime associated with these recent demographic shifts. The press was relentless in calling Trump a liar, even when the leader of the Sweden Democratic Party, Jimmie Akesson, wrote in *The Wall Street Journal*, "Mr. Trump did not exaggerate Sweden's current problems. If anything, he understated them."[2] There is significant proof that Obama had easy access to the monitoring of all of Trump's communications while he ran for president and during the transition phase before the inauguration. These are all topics worthy of a robust debate supported by facts and respected studies that can illuminate the real core issues comprising these subjects. These issues, which have valid various debatable perspectives, don't alter the lives of American constituents. Yet Obama's "lies" protected ISIS which enacted genocide, weakened Israel – our strongest and most reliable ally in the Middle East, fully funded Iran's worldwide Islamic terrorism operations, will allow Iran to develop nuclear weapons in at least 10 -12 years, and passed a healthcare law despised by many Americans who have seen their healthcare premiums and out of pocket deductibles skyrocket. Obama's lies helped pave the way for the rise of ISIS, increased fractures in American political leadership around the world, increased civil strife and political divisions in Europe and America, increased war and genocide in Iraq and Syria, and expanded the regional hegemony by the number one state supporter of terrorism, Iran, in the Middle East and around the world. Obama's words mattered, and the consequences were real, effecting the lives of tens of millions of individuals in the Middle East and in Europe.

With respect to Trump, the media responded to his valid insights during the first few days of his presidency with calls for impeachment and questions of mental instability, while they responded to Obama's extremely consequential misrepresentations with silence and collusion. Even Larry Elder, a very well respected award-winning nationally syndicated author wrote a column, "If Trump is 'Liar-in-Chief,' What of Obama's Lies?" and shed light on the hypocrisy of the Democrats and the anti-Trump establishment. Of course, something is not right, and the powers that be (TPTB), the swamp, RINOs, neoconservatives, Democrats, and the establishment are collectively fighting Trump's attempt to dismantle many aspects of the liberal progressive agenda that has permeated many aspects of the Western economy and society which has been moving forward for over 100 years since the era of Woodrow Wilson. This obvious contrast to the press's reactions to respective "lies" by Obama and Trump clearly justified claims of "fake news" and helped add clarity to much of the reason why Donald Trump, a political disruptor, captured the presidency with a surprising victory and mandate for change. Much of the independent thinking public could no longer tolerate the lies and private agendas emanating from the news media and the political establishment.

There are at least three major themes underlying all of Obama's lies – taqiyya, delusions, and fake news. At the very least, Obama is an Islamist, who supported jihad and viewed a large part of his political mission as the need to advance and proselytize for Islam. In his autobiography, Obama confirmed he would stand with the Muslims during politically contentious times, and during his presidency, he warned the world from the podium of the UN General Assembly in 2012 not to commit blasphemy. There were many members of his administration who were affiliated with the Muslim Brotherhood. ISIS rose and almost established a viable caliphate, the Muslim Brotherhood took over Egypt, Iran was allowed to keep its nuclear program and maintain its ability to develop nuclear weapons, Muslim immigration flooded into Europe and the United States, and Obama declared the vast majority of Jewish and Christian holy sites in Jerusalem were occupied Islamic Palestinian territory – all occurring during his presidency. To pretend Obama is not an Islamist is by itself a delusion.

Since practicing taqiyya allows Muslims to lie to infidels so that Islamic interests, the encroachment of Sharia law around world, and the establishment of an Islamic caliphate are advanced, Obama had the theological underpinnings to lie regularly to the American and Israeli public. Obvious examples of taqiyya include promising he would never endorse dividing Jerusalem, declaring he feels a deep affinity for the Jewish people, repeatedly stating the JCPOA (Joint Comprehensive Plan of Action, or the Iran nuclear agreement) will make the Middle East, Israel, and America safer, ISIS is JV, ISIS is contained, al-Qaeda is on the run, and Rouhani and his Iranian administration are moderates. This book is not a proof that Obama is a Muslim, but with Obama's infatuation and embrace of Islam, even more so than his professed Christian religion, Obama most likely incorporated and embraced taqiyya as a legitimate political tool to advance his agenda.

Delusion must be considered as a component of Obama's presentations, since he lied about his uncle liberating Auschwitz, lied about how his parents met and how he was conceived, and even how he met his wife. From an economic perspective, Obama always praised the improving economic conditions during his presidency, and discounted many signs of economic weakness which included record low home ownership rates, record high food stamp participation, record low labor participation rates, and record low economic growth rates recorded during a sustained recovery. Obama will also be remembered for revealing his delusions, or even possibly narcissism, when he stated during his 2008 presidential campaign, "I face this challenge with profound humility, and knowledge of my own limitations. But … I am absolutely certain that generations from now, we will be able to look back and tell our children that this was the moment when … the rise of the oceans began to slow and our planet began to heal." Obama believed what he was saying, and most neutral psychiatrists could consider attaching a DSM V diagnosis to this statement.

Fake news in itself are lies. Blaming the video for the Benghazi attacks was fake news, as was Obama's supervising the creation of political "echo chambers" which were needed to help win approval for the JCPOA in Congress and in the court of public opinion. As Trump started his presidency, the fake news stories alleging his collusion with the Russians continually dominated the headlines. Even *CNN* producer John Bonifield admitted "Because it's ratings … I mean it's mostly bullshit right now *[the Trump – Russia collusion story]*. Like, we don't have any big giant proof … I think the President is probably right to say, like, look, you are witch-hunting me. You have no smoking gun, you have no real proof."[3] Obama, with Clinton, may have laid the groundwork for this fake news story, hoping it could stick and eventually destroy Trump's presidency. One of Obama's final fake news stories originating from his administration at the end of his second term and which garnished many headlines was the declaration that the Obama administration was "scandal free." Not only did Obama and Valerie Jarrett reiterate this point at the end of his presidency, but so did many people in the mainstream press, including *New York Times* op-ed writer, David Brooks, who said "President Obama has run an amazingly scandal-free administration, not only he himself, but the people around him," during a *PBS NewsHour* interview in 2015. Liberal ideologues in the press wouldn't even consider Obama giving Iran $1.7 billion in untraceable cash to Iran with $400 million exchanged in the middle of the night on an Iranian airport runway as ransom for American political prisoners, as something worthy of a thorough investigation. Or a video was the root cause of the Benghazi fiasco. In what may be the biggest scandal in the history of the presidency, Obama may have spied on the opposing party's political contestants, nominee, and the President-elect in order to thwart future policies changes that would threaten his legacies, his foreign Islamic allies, and the advancement of Islam in the West. With over 600 pages of lies and related analysis, Obama must be considered as an originator of the fake news epidemic which has permeated much of the press and mass media.

As Obama fades into the history books and his legacy is reduced to politically correct soundbites and hackneyed liberal objectives, this evaluation of Obama's speeches and remarks, and its mining of Obama's misrepresentations is necessary in order to pursue a valid academic analysis of Obama's policies and motivations. Obama presented himself as an agent of change during his national political campaigns. Unfortunately, all his lies were necessary so that his pro-Islamic and radical progressive visions for the future of America would not prevent him from maintaining his political power and retaining the support of and mandate from the American people. Obama's lies, unethical behavior and constantly misleading words had real political repercussions upon the United States, which resulted in the decimation of the Democratic Party during the 2010 – 2016 election cycles, more aggressive Islamists throughout the West, the weakening of America, and the rise of an unorthodox, brash, and polarizing political phenomenon – the Trump presidency. Obama's lies also helped usher in a period of worldwide political transition and upheaval, with increasing chaos in the Middle East, the rise of Iran as a world nuclear power, increasing civil strife between Muslim communities and immigrants and their European hosts, and the increasing influence of Islam throughout the West which was supported by massive Islamic immigration. If Obama was able to present the real endpoints of his policies as political talking points while running for president, it is doubtful Obama could have achieved a national political victory without the lies shielding a harsh reality that accompanied Obama and his policies. "Obama's Book of Lies" reveals the true Obama presidency as memories fade, and is a great starting point for a thorough evaluation of most of the issues confronting Obama and his presidency. It also allows the reader to fully understand Obama's political direction and the real nature of Obama's political endpoints, while presenting opposing narratives which support the politically incorrect yet entertaining nature of this book.

Benghazi Lies / Fake News
(Including the Big Lie – "It was the video.")

"The report is a devastating account of staggering dereliction of duty and **deception by the president** and his top subordinates … In his campaign for reelection, President Obama repeatedly declared that the killing of Osama bin Laden signaled the defeat of al-Qaeda and its network of affiliates. *[taqiyya]* In reality, the terror threat still remained grave, especially in a post-Qaddafi Libya that had collapsed into chaos and provided a refuge for terrorists, *[Obama's policy endpoint]* including groups tied to al-Qaeda and ISIS … The administration has claimed that there was no time for a response, that the siege appeared to have terminated at the State Department compound – where Ambassador Stevens and State Department technician Sean Smith were attacked – before war planes or armed drones could have gotten there, and that it only later unexpectedly resumed at the nearby CIA compound. This misstates the facts … **Obama and his subordinates never even tried to relieve the Americans under attack**. It is not that rescue craft turned around once reports led them to believe it was too late to get to Benghazi; they never left the ground in the first place. The spin, though, launched immediately. Even as jihadists continued firing at Americans and torching American facilities, even as Ambassador Stevens was missing and feared dead or abducted, **Clinton and Obama went to work <u>crafting a fictional account of events</u>**. Shortly after 10 p.m., Clinton issued a statement depicting the ongoing violence as an overwrought response provoked by an anti-Muslim video. Key administration players knew from the first that this was a lie … The administration went into full damage-control mode, with White House apparatchik Ben Rhodes … counseling that the administration's "goals" included "to underscore that these protests are rooted in an Internet video, and not a broader failure of policy." … When it came time to explain themselves, <u>**administration officials lied**</u>: **Obama**, **Clinton**, **Rice**, **Rhodes**, **Carney**, and the rest – serially and systematically." *(source – "What We Do Know about the Benghazi Attack Demands a Reckoning," National Review editorial commenting on the House Select Committee on Benghazi Final Report, June 28, 2016)*

A 2012 Defense Intelligence Agency (DIA) report dated **September 12, 2012**, one day after the Benghazi attack stated, "The attack was **planned ten or more days prior to** approximately 01 September 2012. The intention was to attack the consulate and **to kill as many Americans as**

possible to seek revenge for the US killing of Aboyahiye (Alaliby) in Pakistan and in memorial of the 11 September 2001 attacks on the World Trade Center buildings." The attack was thought to have been organized by the "Brigades of the Captive Omar Abdul Rahman," whose leader Abdul Baset was "**sent by al-Qaeda leader Ayman al Zawahiri** to set up al-Qaeda bases in Libya … also responsible for past attacks on the Red Cross in Benghazi and the attack on the British ambassador, they have approximately 120 members." The report was sent directly to Secretary of State Clinton, Secretary of Defense Panetta, National Security Advisor Susan Rice, the White House National Security Council, and the Joint Chiefs of Staff. Obama and Clinton knew within 24 hours that the attack was not spontaneous, involved al-Qaeda, was not related to the Internet video, and was specifically timed to celebrate the anniversary of 9-11. Despite this intelligence briefing, Obama and his staff moved forward with multiple lies to cover up failings of his administration and save his chances for winning a second term as president. *CNN* and *CBS* also reported on the scene on September 11th that **Ansar al-Sharia** was the group behind the attack. Sidney Blumenthal, an ex-Clinton aide and longtime confidante, citing "sensitive sources," advised Clinton two days after the attack that an al-Qaeda aligned group, Ansar al-Sharia, planned the attack for one month beforehand. **Five independent sources have now confirmed the attack originated from within al-Qaeda – the DIA report**, *CNN*, *CBS*, **Sidney Blumenthal, and the president of Libya**. Was Obama protecting al-Qaeda with this cover story? This scenario must be considered since in early 2012, Secretary of State Clinton was informed by her staff in an email that "<u>**AQ is on our side** in Syria</u> … Things have basically <u>**turned out as expected**</u>."

1. "**Some have sought to justify this vicious behavior as a response to inflammatory material posted on the internet** … The United States deplores any intentional effort to denigrate the religious beliefs of others. Our commitment to religious tolerance goes back to the very beginning of our nation." *Secretary of State Hillary Clinton Memo, "Statement on the Attack in Benghazi," 10:08 PM EST, September 11, 2012, after Ansar al-Sharia used Twitter to claim responsibility for the attack and after Clinton spoke to Obama that evening.* **Interestingly, Clinton's first statement did not mention the Internet video or a protest**, **but focused on** "**heavily armed militants** [who] **assaulted the compound**." Obama told Clinton to issue a State Department memo blaming the attack on a spontaneous demonstration resulting from the anti-Islamic video. Obama later had Ben Rhodes incorporate this strategy in his talking points memo used by Susan Rice. Why didn't Obama just blame the attack on terrorists who were celebrating the anniversary of 9-11, or on an obvious lack of security? **First, Obama used this opportunity to divert attention away from his policy flaws that could hinder his chances for re-election** to the presidency less than two months down the road. **Second**, Obama had stated al-Qaeda was on the run, which was a lie. **Obama wanted to divert attention away from the situation in which the Libyan war ousting Gaddafi created a**

vacuum that was filled by Islamic extremists, including al-Qaeda. **Third**, Obama also wanted to **divert attention from the State Department and U.S. intelligence involvement with illegal arms deals that were supplying weapons and munitions to Libyan and Syrian rebels who were also affiliated with al-Qaeda**, in violation of a UN arms embargo to Libya, **and to al-Qaeda in Iraq, which later became ISIS**. Obama knew the irony that surrounded the scenario where his ambassador to Libya was murdered by militias that were backed and armed by the U.S. government. Fourth, Obama **wanted to place the blame on Western Islamophobia and the Western concept of free speech**, which he abhors as a radical Muslim, since it can be used to criticize Islam and Mohammed. **Obama is also advancing the anti-blasphemy policies of the OIC**. In their 10-Year Plan presented in 2005 in Saudi Arabia, the OIC established guidelines for Combatting Islamophobia ("Endeavor to have the UN adopt an international resolution to counter Islamophobia, and call upon all States to enact laws to counter it, **including deterrent punishments**.") Obama used the Benghazi episode to show solidarity with the OIC by attacking the irrelevant video. The Benghazi attack would also set up Obama's speech before the UN two weeks later.

a. "Benghazi has been attacked by militants. [There was no mention of a protest.] In Cairo, police have removed demonstrators." *Victoria Nuland, State Department Spokesperson, September 11, 2012.*

b. One hour before the attack on Benghazi, which commenced at 3:42 PM EST, Ambassador Stevens walked a diplomat to the gate of the consulate and there was no disturbance, because there were no protests. The conflict started with the attack on the consulate, consistent with a terrorist attack. Two intelligence reports on September 11 confirmed there were no protests and no demonstrations.

c. At 4:02 PM EST, an eye witness in the command center on the ground stated "no protest, no demonstration." **At 4:06 PM EST, a State Department operations alert warned "mission under attack**, armed men, shots fired, explosions heard."

d. Greg Hicks, the #2 man in Libya, stated that if there had been a protest, Ambassador Stevens would have reported it, which was never done.

e. An **email** that was circulated to the White House and the State Department on **September 11, 2012 at 6:07 PM**, during the attacks, had the subject line or title stating, "Update 2: **Ansar al-Sharia Claims Responsibility for Benghazi Attack**." *Obama and Clinton knew almost immediately when the attacks on Benghazi commenced that al-Qaeda has launched a pre-planned attack on the Benghazi consulate.*

f. "**Two of our officers were killed in Benghazi by an al-Qaeda-like group**." *Clinton, September 11th email to Chelsea Clinton at 11:12 PM EST found on her private server.* **This private email to her family proves that Clinton knew the Benghazi attack was not caused by the video.**

g.   "Ansar al-Sharia [affiliated with al-Qaeda] is claiming responsibility" [for the Benghazi attack]. *Clinton speaking with the president of Libya on the night of September 11.*

h.   "**We** [Obama, Clinton, defense and intelligence officials] **know that the attack in Libya had nothing to do with the film**. It was a planned attack – not a protest, we believe the group that claimed responsibility for this was affiliated with al-Qaeda." *Clinton conversation with Egyptian Prime Minister Kandil. September 12, 2015.* This revelation proves both Obama and Clinton knew that the video was not the cause of the Benghazi attack, and both subsequently lied for various political and religious reasons.

i.   "**The film's not as explosive of an issue here** as it appears to be in other countries in the region … And it is becoming increasingly clear that the series of events in **Benghazi was much more terrorist attack than a protest**, which escalated into violence ... It is our opinion that in our messaging, we want to distinguish, not conflate, the events in other countries with **this well-planned attack by militant extremists**." *State Department email from the U.S. Embassy in Tripoli, Libya, sent on September 14, 2012.* With this State Department email along with the previous supporting evidence, the Obama administration knew the video had nothing to do with the attack on Benghazi from the start of the crisis. All statements from Obama, Clinton, Rice and other Obama administration officials regarding the video as the root cause of the crisis were known lies.

j.   "Well, Anderson, according to eye witnesses up to about an hour ago he describes the situation there as frontline. **Libyan security forces were engaged in heavy clashes with** members of an armed group; that is **Ansar al-Sharia**, that is a radical militant group that is based in eastern Libya." *CNN reporter and producer Jomana Karadsheh was reporting live on AC 360 (Anderson Cooper's live CNN news show) during the Benghazi attack on the CIA annex at 9 PM on September 11, 2012.*

k.   On September 11, 2012, the night of the attack, **CBS** reported at 11:42 PM EST, "witnesses say members of a radical Islamist group called **Ansar al-Sharia** …"

2.   **Obama's and his administration's lies concerning al-Qaeda formed a major plank in his re-election campaign in 2012**. The Benghazi massacre shattered this false narrative, but Obama stuck with his talking points until he won the 2012 presidential election. Obama may also have been trying to protect al-Qaeda by continually downplaying their threat to American and western interests.

a.   "**al-Qaeda operatives** who remain are scrambling, knowing that they **can't escape the reach of the United States of America**." *Obama, State of Union Address, 2012* Al-Qaeda-linked Libya rebels held a major military parade in Benghazi within a month before the murder of Ambassador Stevens and were flying black jihadi flags and demanding Sharia law.

b. "A day after 9-11, we are reminded that a new tower rises above the New York skyline, but **al-Qaeda is on the path to defeat** and bin Laden is dead." *Obama at a campaign fundraiser **one day after Ambassador Christopher Stevens is murdered** by al-Qaeda-related terrorists on the anniversary of 9-11.* Obama slept through the night while the Benghazi compound was destroyed and Ambassador Stephens was raped and murdered, and departed the following morning for campaign fundraising, showing his brazen disregard toward the life of those who were killed in the attack.

c. "We've got choices about war and peace … **I ended the war in Iraq**, as I promised. We are **transitioning out of Afghanistan**. We have gone after the terrorists who actually attacked us on 9-11 and **decimated al-Qaeda**." *Obama at a New York fundraiser on September 14, 2012. Three lies in one short statement.*

   i. "**The Islamic State is al-Qaeda** … It is the evolution of the ruthless al-Qaeda division that grew up in Iraq under Abu Musab al Zarqawi." *Andrew McCarthy, former federal prosecutor of terrorists in New York.*

d. "We have **decimated al-Qaeda**." *Susan Rice, CBS and NBC September 16, 2012 news interview.* Either Rice is lying or she is just repeating Obama's own talking points which she heard two days earlier. Rice had received a briefing beforehand from CIA Director General Petraeus indicating al-Qaeda was behind the terrorist attacks on the consulate. Since Susan Rice is the president's national security advisor, she knows the true state of al-Qaeda, and is lying.

e. "**al-Qaeda is on the run and Osama bin Laden is no more**." *Obama, October 5, 2012.* Obama knows from CIA and State Department reports that al-Qaeda operatives played a major role in the Benghazi attacks, thus he is lying on the fresh graves of the four men who died there. Obama should have reworded his statement – "al-Qaeda is on the run … into Libya, Afghanistan, Yemen, Iraq, Syria, Mali, the Sinai, Gaza, Algeria, and Iran."

f. "**Bin Laden is dead** and General Motors is alive." *Vice President Biden at the Democratic National Convention, August 2012.*

3. "Since our founding, the United States has been a nation that respects all faiths. **We reject all efforts to denigrate the religious belief of others**." *Rose Garden address by Obama, September 12, 2012, after intelligence confirms Benghazi attack is a terrorist attack.* Obama is deceptively attacking Islamophobia instead of focusing on al-Qaeda. Is Obama protecting al-Qaeda by putting the focus on the video?

   a. Obama may have been looking for a controversial video on which to place the blame for the Benghazi attacks. Tom Fitton, the president of *Judicial Watch*, commented on some documents released under the Freedom of Information Act that "show the Obama White House rushed to tie yet another video to the Benghazi attack, even before Ambassador

Stevens was accounted for … The Obama White House evidently was confused as to which Internet video to falsely blame for the Benghazi terrorist attack." State Department documents obtained by *Judicial Watch* and dated September 11, 2012 9:11 PM EST stated the "**White House is reaching out to U-Tube to advise ramifications of posting of the Pastor Jon video**." Pastor Jon Courson is a Christian pastor who created a video "G-d vs. Allah," which Obama initially considered targeting as the cause of the riots. Obama made a quick decision to blame the attack on the "Innocence of Muslims" video, created by Basseley Nakoula, probably because Nakoula was a foreign national and an easier target. Obama chose to target Nakoula since he was born in Egypt, and Obama's decision would receive less scrutiny than if he blamed an American-born pastor. Within an hour of this memo, Clinton released her "Statement on the Attack in Benghazi" which blamed the video for the attack and set in motion the policy lies that plagued the administration for at least the next two weeks. This revelation proves that Obama used the attack on the Benghazi consulate as an excuse to advance blasphemy laws and Sharia law in America. **It is a shame that Obama used this critical time after the attack to promote the interests of Islam instead of focusing on saving the lives of the embattled Americans trapped at the consulate**.

4. "We've seen rage and violence directed at American embassies **over an awful internet video** that we had nothing to do with." *Clinton, Andrews Air Force Base, September 14, 2012.*

5. "We have **no information** to suggest that it was a **pre-planned** attack. The unrest we have seen around the region has been **in reaction to a video** that many Muslims find offensive." *Jay Carney, White House spokesperson, September 14, 2012.*

6. "Let me state very clearly, and I hope it is obvious. That **the United States government had absolutely nothing to do with this video**. We absolutely reject its content and message. America's commitment to religious tolerance goes back to the very beginning of our nation." *Secretary of State Clinton's paid advertisement in Pakistan blaming the video and its blasphemous content for the massacre when she knows that the attack in Benghazi was perpetrated by al-Qaeda extremists and their allies.*

7. **Rice**: "But let's remember what has transpired over the last several days. **This is a response to a hateful and offensive video that was widely disseminated throughout the Arab and Muslim world**. Obviously, our view is that there is absolutely no excuse for violence and that - what has happened is condemnable, but **this is a – a spontaneous reaction to a video** …"
    Gregory: "Well, let's talk – talk about – well, you talked about this as spontaneous. Can you say definitively that the attacks on – on our consulate in Libya that killed ambassador Stevens and others there – security personnel, that was spontaneous, was it a planned attack? Was there a terrorist element to it?" **Rice**: "Well, let us – let me tell you the – the best information we have at present. First of all, there's an FBI investigation which is ongoing. *[The FBI did not arrive on*

the scene until three weeks later, so credible evidence could not be collected. Obama was protecting the terrorists.] … **But putting together the best information that we have available to us today our current assessment is that what happened in Benghazi was in fact initially a spontaneous reaction to what had just transpired hours before in Cairo, almost a copycat of – of the demonstrations against our facility in Cairo, <u>which were prompted, of course, by the video</u>** … And it escalated into a much more violent episode. *[The heavy weapons were present from the beginning.]" Susan Rice being interviewed by David Gregory on Meet the Press, on September 16, 2012.* Ben Rhodes sent an email to White House staff a day before the Sunday interview shows entitled "**RE: PREP Call with Susan**: Saturday at 4:00 PM ET … Goals: **To underscore that these protests are rooted in an Internet video, and not a broader failure of policy**." Obama ignored the available evidence and formally placed the blame for Benghazi on the video for political purposes and advanced an anti-blasphemy law agenda.

a. "I think Rice was off the reservation on this one … Off the reservation on five networks!" *Senior State Department official with the Bureau of Near Eastern Affairs commenting in an email on Rice's multiple Sunday talk show performances. The response was from the deputy director of the bureau's Office of Press and Public Diplomacy. (source – 2016 Congressional Benghazi Report)*

    i. "Luckily there's enough in her language to fudge exactly what she said / meant … WH *[White House / Obama]* very worried about the politics. This was all their doing." *The bureau's senior advisor for strategic communications blamed the White House for the video lie. State Department officials acknowledge the lie started with Obama. (source – 2016 Congressional Benghazi Report)*

    ii. "I was surprised … there was some connection to the anti-Muslim video of concern that had been circulating online, that there was some connection to that." *The deputy director for the State Department's Office of Maghreb Affairs also acknowledged the cover story regarding the video as the cause of the Benghazi attack was a lie. (source – 2016 Congressional Benghazi Report)*

b. "We still don't know with any degree of certainty what motivated the attackers that night … **My analysts never said that attackers that night were motivated by the video**." *Mike Morrell, Former Deputy Director of the CIA.*

c. "It was planned, definitely, **it was planned by foreigners**, by people who entered the country a few months ago, and they were planning this criminal act since their arrival." *Libyan President Mohamed Yousef El-Magarif, CBS News interview.*

d. "The idea that this criminal and cowardly act was a spontaneous protest that just spun out of control is completely unfounded and preposterous … We firmly believe that this was a pre-calculated, pre-planned attack that was carried out specifically to attack the U.S. Consulate." *Magarif during an NPR interview.*

e.   "I am convinced that this is a terrorist attack … **a coordinated mob does not use mortars and RPGs**." *Secretary of Defense Panetta testifying before Congress.*

f.   "I thought it was a terrorist attack from the get go … I never reported a demonstration, I reported an attack on the consulate." *Gregory Hicks, former Deputy Chief of Libyan operations and foreign service officer.* In another interview, Hicks also confirmed, "I think everybody in the mission thought it was a terrorist attack from the beginning." Hicks never heard State Department officials, including Clinton, state the cause of the attack as being related to the video in his initial contact with them.

g.   "The group that conducted the attacks, **Ansar al-Sharia**, is affiliated with Islamic terrorists.*" Beth Jones, State Department official, September 12, 2012 email and with discussions with the Libyan Ambassador to the United States.*

h.   "Petraeus will acknowledge that **he knew quite quickly**, <u>immediately</u>, afterwards that it was **Ansar al-Sharia** that Libyan al-Qaeda sympathizer group that was responsible for it." *CNN reporter discussing future congressional testimony live with Anderson Cooper.* **November 16, 2012**. Obama refused to identify that al-Qaeda – Ansar al-Sharia – was behind the Benghazi attacks until after he was reelected in order to protect al-Qaeda, protect Answar al-Sharia (translation – supporters of Islamic law or Sharia law) and save his presidency. Patraeus was told by Obama or one of his senior staff members to delay his acknowledgement of the identity of the perpetrators of the Benghazi attack until after the election. Anderson Cooper seemed shocked when he heard these remarks in November, but he was informed by Jomana Karadsheh on live TV that Ansar al-Sharia was the source of the terrorism during the attacks on September 11th.

8.   "We are going to have the film maker arrested who was responsible for the death of your son." *Clinton speaking to Ty Woods' father. Woods was killed by terrorists at the CIA annex in Benghazi.*

9.   "You had **a video** that was released by somebody who lives here, sort of a shadowy character who, who made **an extremely offensive video directed at**, at **Mohammed** and Islam … Making fun of the Prophet Mohammed. And so, this **caused great offense** in much of the Muslim world … As offensive as this video was, and obviously, we denounced it, the United States government had nothing to do with it." *Obama on the **David Letterman Show**, **September 18, 2012**.* Obama is blaming America's cherished First Amendment right of free speech as the root cause of the murders at the Libyan consulate, thus lying to the public and attacking the Constitution. Incidentally, there was no mention of the video on Libyan social media, discounting the theory that the video was a motivating factor in the Benghazi attacks.

10. "… **offensive video** or cartoon directed at the prophet Mohammed …" *Obama being interviewed on **Univision**, September 20, 2012, discussing the Benghazi attack.*

11. "And that is what we saw play out in the last two weeks, **where a crude and disgusting video sparked outrage throughout the Muslim world. Now, I have made it clear that <u>the United States government had nothing to do with this video</u>, and I believe its message must be rejected** by all who respect our common humanity. It is an insult not only to Muslims, but to America *[taqiyya]* as well … We understand why people take offense to this video because millions of our *[Muslim]* citizens are among them. I know there are some *[Muslims – Obama represents the Muslims and proponents of Sharia law]* who ask why don't we just ban such a video … **<u>The future must not belong to those who slander the prophet of Islam</u>**." *Obama, Address to the **UN General Assembly**, September 25, 2012.* In the last statement, Obama is actually telling the truth, and advancing the agenda of the OIC, the Muslim Brotherhood and the Umma to the detriment of the West and freedom of speech. Two weeks after the Benghazi attack, Obama was still advancing the false video scenario, the fight against Islamophobia and blasphemy, despite knowing the truth that al-Qaeda affiliated terrorists meticulously planned the assault from defense intelligence sources as well as from the president of Libya. Obama would not let the truth stand in the way of getting re-elected, raising money for his campaign, advancing Sharia law, and attacking blasphemers. Even though the video was repeatedly mentioned by President Obama, Secretary of State Clinton, and UN Ambassador Rice for weeks after the attack, the Accountability Review Board's (ARB) report on the Benghazi debacle failed to mention the Internet video even once.

12. "Number one, make sure we are securing our personnel and **doing whatever we need to.**" *Obama's response to a reporter's question asking if pleas for help were denied by the administration or by him.* Obama did nothing. Obama certainly did not tell any military officials or national security officials "Do whatever we need to."

13. "What happened in Benghazi is a tragedy. **We're investigating** what happened. I take full responsibility for that fact. I send these folks in harm's way, I want to make sure they're always safe and when that doesn't happen, that we figure out what happened and make sure that doesn't happen again. **But my biggest priority now is** [to] **bring those folks to justice** and I think the American people have seen **that's a commitment I'll always keep**." *Obama. Up to this date, almost four years later, only one person has been arrested for participating in these Benghazi crimes.*

14. "And make no mistake, we will work with the Libyan government to bring to justice the killers who attacked our people … We will not waver in our commitment to see that justice is done for this terrible act. **And make no mistake, justice will be done**." *Obama, Rose Garden Address, Remarks by the president on the Deaths of U.S. Embassy Staff in Libya, September 12, 2012.* Ironically, the only person who was held accountable and jailed in the United States

because of the Benghazi attacks was Mark Basseley Youssef, the producer of the "Innocence of Muslims," who was arrested and imprisoned for about one year for probation violations which served as a cover for Obama's enforcement of blasphemy laws. This sentence was considered harsh for a minor probation violation, but would be an appropriate punishment for someone insulting Mohammed in Turkey.

15. **"Those talking points originated from the intelligence community** [CIA' Office of Terrorism Analysis]. **They reflect the IC's** [intelligence community's] **best assessments of what they thought had happened** … The White House and the State Department have made clear that the **single adjustment** that was made to those talking points by either of those two institutions were **changing the word** 'consulate' **to** 'diplomatic facility' because 'consulate' was inaccurate." *Obama's White House Press Secretary James Carney answering a question regarding the Benghazi talking points that Susan Rice used before going on five Sunday morning talk shows where she blamed the Benghazi attacks on a spontaneous protest that was a reaction to a hateful video on November 28, 2012.* Carney referred to the changes as only "stylistic." In reality, White House and State Department officials revised the talking points twelve times, deleted references to al-Qaeda and Ansar al-Sharia, kept the focus on the video, which was not done with the CIA's input, and deleted the CIA's earlier warnings regarding terrorist threats in Benghazi. Part of the CIA's assessment included, "The Agency has produced numerous pieces on the threat of extremists linked to al-Qaeda in Benghazi and eastern Libya. These noted that, since April, there have been at least five other attacks against foreign interests in Benghazi by unidentified assailants, including the June attack against the British Ambassador's convoy. We cannot rule out the individuals had previously surveilled the U.S. facilities, also contributing to the efficacy of the attacks … We do know that Islamic extremists with ties to al-Qaeda participated in the attack." There were over six references to Islamic extremists and al-Qaeda affiliates in the CIA's original talking points. These assessments were supported by intercepted communications after the attack between al-Qaeda operatives and eye witnesses of the attack who identified who identified participants with ties to al-Qaeda. Adjusting (or falsifying) the talking points became a White House obsession before Susan Rice appeared on the Sunday morning talk shows. Deputy National Security Advisor Ben Rhodes sent out an email saying, "We must make sure that the talking points reflect all agency equities, **including those of the State Department**, *[Clinton's and Obama's input deciding to blame the video]* and we don't want to undermine the FBI investigation. We thus will work through the talking points tomorrow morning at the Deputies Committee meeting." *Carney continued to attempt to mislead the public after twelve revisions before the talking points became public by saying,* "The CIA drafted these talking points and redrafted these talking points … **The fact that there are inputs is always the case in a process like this, but the only edits made by anyone here at the White House were stylistic**

and non-substantive. They corrected the description of the building or the facility in Benghazi from consulate to diplomatic facility and the like." CIA Director Petraeus was surprised that the talking points deleted references to al-Qaeda and jihad, and was even more surprised when the Obama administration soon after leaked details of Petraeus's affair forcing him to resign.

16. *Clinton covered for Obama while testifying before the Senate in 2013 since she wanted to secure his help and support in the 2016 presidential campaign.* "So, I saw firsthand what Ambassador Pickering and former Chairman Mullen called **timely and exceptional coordination**. No delays in decision making, **no denials of support from Washington or from our military**, *[There was a stand down order for military intervention]* ... we continue to hunt the terrorists responsible for the attacks in Benghazi and are **determined to bring them to justice**. *[Only one person has been arrested]* ... The professionals in **Washington paid close attention to Chris' judgment** based on his experience and his firsthand knowledge. *[Ambassador Stevens' multiple requests for more security were ignored and denied by Clinton. Ambassador Stevens requested that at least thirteen security personnel would be needed for "transportation security and incident response capability" in a July 9, 2012 cable. Clinton was aware of the problems when Stevens wrote in that same cable "Overall security conditions continue to be unpredictable, with large numbers of armed groups and individuals not under control of the central government, and frequent clashes in Tripoli and other major population centers." Stevens and his staff in Libya requested more security over 600 times, with his last formal request on September 11th.]* ... When I was here four years ago testifying for my confirmation, **I don't think anybody thought that Mubarak would be gone**, Gaddafi would be gone, that Ben Ali would be gone, that we would have such revolutionary change in this region. *[Obama knew, since Mubarak, Gaddafi, and Assad were the prime targets for him and the Muslim Brotherhood.]* ... I do not know. **I don't have any information on that**. *[Clinton lied and denied any knowledge of the arms transfers from Libya through Turkey to Syria to Senator Paul's question.]* " Secretary of State Clinton, Testimony at the Senate Hearing on Benghazi, January 23, 2013.

   a. Obama and Clinton stated there was no "denial of support" for a military option. But an email from Jeremy Bash, Panetta's chief of staff, said otherwise. At 7:19 PM EST, the Pentagon was ready to launch a rescue mission. The email read, "I just tried you on the phone but you were all in with S [Clinton] ... After consulting with General Dempsey, General Ham and the Joint Staff, **we have identified the forces that could move to Benghazi. They are spinning up as we speak**." Secretary of Defense Panetta also lied to Congress in 2013 when he told Congress there was not enough time to launch a military response. Panetta was informed there was an AC 130H "Spectre" gunship stationed in Sicily ready to go that was only a 45-minute flight away. Obama made the decision to have the military stand down and not engage the al-Qaeda terrorists in Benghazi, and let four Americans die. Clinton and Panetta lied to cover for their boss.

17. "There was never a recommendation from any intelligence official in our government, from any official in the State Department, or from any other person with knowledge of our presence in Benghazi, to shut down Benghazi." *Clinton, Testimony before the House of Representatives regarding Benghazi, September 23, 2015.*

   a. "(CIA) suggested that Mission personnel could co-locate to the Annex if the security environment degraded suddenly ... In the longer term, we believe formal collocation with the CIA will greatly improve our (State Department personnel) security situation." *Classified State Department cable, August 16, 2012.* Senior State Department and Obama administration officials purposely left Ambassador Stevens in a high-risk situation, where he would be more vulnerable to kidnapping or murder.

   b. "In 2010, when Secretary Clinton ordered a review of processes, there was a strong recommendation made that changes should be made about how the State Department handled security. That was rejected by Under Secretary Kennedy, and they went with the status quo, or what they call regular order. So things should have changed before this incident ever happened. And once Ambassador Stevens ... went to Libya, he went with no military assistance. He went and requested multiple times, he and other diplomatic security, to have more agents, to have more physical security, and quite frankly, it was rejected by the State Department." *Rep. Susan Brooks (R-IN) commenting on the Benghazi Select Committee Report, June 2016. Ambassador Stevens was set up.* The Obama administration's betrayal of Stevens was acknowledged in a private memo discussing Benghazi, which was obtained by Guccifer 2.0 from Pelosi's computer that stated, "State received requests for additional security at the facility in Benghazi in the months prior to the attack, ignoring some and denying others. **State had <u>recently reduced security</u> at the facility** *[immediately before the attack]*, a move which was **approved at a 'high level.'** *[Obama or Clinton]*"[4] Either Clinton or Obama, but most likely Obama, removed the security details protecting Stevens right before the Benghazi attack, in order to make him a more accessible target for the al-Qaeda terrorists on September 11, 2012.

18. "I gave **three very clear directives**. Number one, make sure we are securing our personnel and that we are doing whatever we need to. Number two, we are going to investigate exactly what happened and make sure it doesn't happen again. Number three, find out who did this so we can bring them to justice." *Obama, response to a Denver reporter regarding his directives he says he issued related to the Benghazi crisis at the time of the attack, October 2012.* The House Select Committee on Benghazi issued their final report on June 28, 2016 that indicated Obama did not issue these three directives to his staff or Cabinet level administrators at the

time of the attack. All three of these directives, if actually given, did not reflect the reality of the situation. Obama made no effort to secure the personnel in Benghazi during the attack. Obama went to sleep during the battle and never bothered to appear in the White House situation room. The remaining Americans were actually rescued by former Gaddafi loyalists. Obama promised to investigate Benghazi and find out exactly what happened, but Obama blamed a video for weeks and did not permit the FBI on the crime scene at Benghazi for almost three weeks, so he actually created a situation where he was protecting the Islamic terrorists. Obama promised to bring the perpetrators to justice, but only one person has been arrested since the Benghazi attack. Obama was never concerned about what happened at Benghazi or a future response by the United States, since he did not bother to attend the intelligence briefing on September 12, 2012.

a. "Almost eight hours after the initial attack on the mission compound, and after our brave men had moved to the annex, there were still no military assets moving directly to Benghazi. We also learned that there was a White House secure video conference that took place, we did not know that previously. That Secretary Clinton participated in, and other White House officials, although Secretary Panetta did not, the president did not, and **they had discussions for over two hours about how to go in without truly offending Libya, how to send people to Tripoli, never to Benghazi.**" *Rep. Susan Brooks (R-IN) commenting on the Benghazi Select Committee Report, June 2016.* Obama had someone at this conference stalling the decision-making process so that military personnel would not reach Benghazi before the Islamic terrorists had finished the attack.

b. "**At the same time, the State Department appeared to waste time on what our soldiers would wear**, it also **appeared to waste time and focus on the YouTube video** that the administration would later blame, falsely, for the attack. It has emerged that during an emergency call at 7:30 p.m. on the night of the attack involving Secretary Clinton and other high-level officials from the Department of Defense, State Department, and CIA that **a full five of the eleven action items from the meeting related to the video.**" *Benghazi Select Committee Report, June 2016.* The Obama administration was stalling and purposely delayed a rescue operation in order to protect the Ansar al-Sharia terrorists attacking the Benghazi compound.

19. "The day after it happened, I acknowledged that this was an **act of terrorism**." *Obama, News conference, May 13, 2013.* The day after the Benghazi attack, Obama stated in the Rose Garden on September 12, 2011, "No **acts of terror** will ever shake the resolve of this great nation, alter that character, or eclipse the light of the values that we stand for." Obama presented the "act of terror" in vague terms following a national tragedy, and continued to refuse to label the event a specific act of terrorism. During a *Univision* town hall interview

eight days later, Obama **responded to the question**, "We have reports that the White House said today that the attacks in Libya were **a terrorist attack**. Do you have information indicating that it was Iran, or al-Qaeda was behind organizing the protests?" by stating, "Well, **we're still doing an investigation, and there are going to be different circumstances in different countries**. And **so I don't want to speak** to something until we have all the information. What we do know is that the **natural protests that arose because of the outrage over the video** were used as an excuse by extremists to see if they can also directly harm U.S. interests." Obama continued to blame the video, and refused to label the episode as a specific act of terrorism.

CHAPTER 2

Family and Personal Life

"No man has a good enough memory to be a successful liar." *Abraham Lincoln*

1. Obama's biography released by his book publicist and approved by Obama stated that Obama was "born in Kenya." *Lie? Maybe, maybe not.*
2. "My father left my family when I was two years old." *Maybe before he was born.*
3. "This may come as a surprise, for some of you know, **I did not come from a particularly religious family. My father**, who I barely knew – I only met once for a month in my entire life – was said to be **a non-believer throughout his life**." *Obama, 2011 National Prayer Breakfast speech.* Obama's father was a Muslim, who believed and practiced polygamy. His whole father's family is composed of religious Muslims. His grandmother from Kenya went on a Hajj to Mecca. Obama's mother placed Barack in a religious madrassa in Indonesia, where he was enrolled in classes where he memorized the Quran in Arabic.
4. *Dreams from My Father.* The title of Obama's autobiography suggests Obama's father had great qualities. He was a communist, alcoholic, wife beater, and polygamist. He deserted his son, and was a fundamental Muslim. Obama used the title to project pro-family righteous images upon not only his father, but upon himself to get elected.
   a. Much of *Dreams* was fiction as well, although it was marketed as a relative autobiography. According to David Greenberg's article in *Politico*, "Garrow's [author of *Rising Star: The Making of Barack Obama*] debunking goes into high gear when he gets to *Dreams from My Father*. That book, whose lyrical style and affecting narrative seduced many voters after its 2004 reissue, still furnishes the version of Obama's early life that most people subscribe to. Even though Obama was candid about having altered key details of his life in *Dreams*, including creating composite characters, the book was nonetheless marketed as a "memoir" and "autobiography" and taken by readers to be a reliable account of his life. Garrow, however, dwells on the substantial amount of invented material in *Dreams* and ultimately pronounces it, maybe too severely, '**historical fiction**.'"[5]

5. "**My father was a foreign student**, **born and raised in a small village in Kenya**. He grew up herding goats, went to school in a tin-roof shack. His father, my grandfather, was a cook, a domestic servant to the British." *Obama, 2004, Democratic National Convention speech.* There are many clues in Obama's behavior that indicate this family narrative is a lie. "In his writings from 1958 to 1964, including more than 20 letters, the Kenyan Barack H. Obama makes no mention of an American wife and Hawaiian-born American son. In 2013 and 2016, on his last Father's Day in office, the president was invited to review this material but never did so. The reason is not difficult to understand. The president knows that his father is somebody else. 'My father was a college educated African-American poet and journalist. He chose to join the Communist Party and spent much of his life defending all-white Stalinist dictatorships. My father also took photos of naked women and authored a pornographic novel. But my father believed in a better world, and so do I.' Even at a Democratic Party convention in San Francisco, this would not be an acceptable introduction for anyone running for Congress, let alone President of the United States … Stanley Dunham, identified only as Gramps, 'might' say that the Kenyan looks like Nat King Cole. He doesn't look at all like Cole, but as Joel Gilbert's *Dreams from My Real Father* confirms, the president is the spitting image of Frank Marshall Davis. As the Kenyan's son Malik Obama has noted that goes right down to the spots on their faces … In 2008, Barack Obama is elected President of the United States. His closest advisors David Axelrod and Valerie Jarrett are both out of Frank's old network in Chicago. The president ignores Africa in general and Kenya in particular, making only one trip there in eight years as president. On the other hand, the president's policies bear 'remarkable similarities,' to the writings of Frank Marshall Davis, as Paul Kengor confirmed in *The Communist*. Truth is, the *Dreams from My Father* were always Frank's dreams … As Trump voter **Malik Obama** put it in 2015: 'I would be willing to do that *[undergo a DNA test with Barack Obama to see if they are related]*. I don't know how I'd deal with it, if it really came out that he really is a fraud or a con.'"[6] *(FakePrez.con, FrontPageMag.com, January 2017)*

6. "I had an uncle … who was part of the first American troops to go into Auschwitz and liberate the concentration camps." *Obama. The Russians liberated Auschwitz.*

7. "I've written two books. I actually wrote them myself." *Obama discussing Dreams from My Father and The Audacity of Hope.*

    a. "The second one *(Audacity)* was more of a political hack book … But the first *(Dreams)* book's quite good. Did you know I wrote it." *Bill Ayers commenting on Obama's two books and admitted to students at Montclair State University, in March 2011, he wrote Obama's autobiography, Dreams.* The Audacity of Hope was mostly written by a mixture of aides, advisors, and speech writers.

    b. In 2016, Malik Obama, the half-brother of Obama, released a draft of *Dreams*, which contained sticky notes that proved Obama did not write large portions of his autobiography.

c. "During the 2008 campaign, I read Barack Obama's alleged 1995 masterpiece, *Dreams from My Father*, and came to a startling conclusion. This conclusion was later confirmed by celebrity biographer Christopher Andersen, namely that "literary devices and themes [in *Dreams*] bear a jarring similarity to [Bill] Ayers' own writings." Did they ever ... At the end of the day, I found in both Dreams and in Ayers' several works the following shared words: fog, mist, ships, sinking ships, seas, sails, boats, oceans, calms, captains, charts, first mates, floods, shores, storms, streams, wind, waves, waters, anchors, barges, horizons, harbor, bays, ports, panoramas, moorings, tides, currents, voyages), narrower courses, uncertain courses, and things howling, wobbling, fluttering, sinking, leaking, cascading, swimming, knotted, ragged, tangled, boundless, uncharted, turbulent, and murky ... Obama did not copy from Ayers. He had Ayers write the damned book." *(source – "Did Someone Mention 'Obama' and 'Plagarism'?," Jack Cashill, American Thinker, July 21, 2016)* Jack Cashill, in Deconstructing Obama (2011), forwarded many convincing statistical and literary style arguments which concluded Bill Ayers authored a significant portion of *Dreams from My Father*.

d. "For all his research, Garrow refuses to ask what Bill Ayers saw in Obama. The answer may well be found in a 1994 essay that Ayers co-authored, whose title befits a former merchant seaman: "Navigating a restless sea: The continuing struggle to achieve a decent education for African American youngsters in Chicago." In "Navigating," Ayers and his nominal co-author, former New Communist Movement leader Michael Klonsky, offer a detailed analysis of the Chicago school system and a discussion of potential reforms ... Garrow cites "Navigating" twice but chooses not to see the obvious – namely, that Obama offers a nearly identical analysis in *Dreams* ... *Dreams* describes a "bloated bureaucracy" as one source of the problem and "a teachers' union that went out on strike at least once every two years" as another. "Navigating" affirms that the "bureaucracy has grown steadily in the past decade" and confirms *Dreams'* math, citing a "ninth walkout in 18 years." ... In *Dreams*, educators "defend the status quo" and blame problems on "impossible" children and their "bad parents." In "Navigating," an educator serves as "apologist for the status quo" and "place[s] the blame for school failure on children and families." ... In *Dreams*, the thoughts on educational reform are channeled through the soulful voice of two older black Americans. The first, Moran, a composite, tells Obama, "The public school system is not about educating black children. Never has been. Inner-city schools are about social control. Period." "Social control" is an Ayers obsession. "The message to Black people was that at any moment and for any reason whatsoever your life or the lives of your loved ones could be randomly snuffed out," he writes in his memoir, *Fugitive Days*. "The intention was social control through random intimidation and unpredictable violence." ... The second of Obama's educational mentors is "Frank,"

Obama's mentor in Hawaii, the Communist Frank Marshall Davis. Frank tells the college-bound Obama, "You're not going to college to get educated. You're going there to get trained. They'll train you to forget what it is that you already know." Ayers makes the identical distinction in his 1993 book *To Teach*. "Education is for self-activating explorers of life, for those who would challenge fate, for doers and activists, for citizens. Training is for slaves, for loyal subjects, for tractable employees, for willing consumers, for obedient soldiers.""[7] *(Jack Cashill, American Thinker, May 18, 2017)*

8. "This is a guy *[speaking about Bill Ayers]* who lives in my neighborhood … **He's not some-body who I exchange ideas from on a regular basis**." *Obama responding to ABC's George Stephanopoulos question during an interview in 2008* when he asked Obama, "They [Ayer's Weather Underground terrorist group] bombed the Pentagon, the Capitol, and other build-ings. He's never apologized for that. Can you explain that relationship [with him] for the voters and explain to Democrats why it won't be a problem?"

a. "But after ten years researching this book and interviewing a thousand people, he re-veals just how strong was the relationship between Ayers and Obama and how deep was the lie that protected it. Unfortunately, there is an element of that lie Garrow *(David Garrow, author of the 2017 biography on Obama called "Rising Star: The Making of Barack Obama")* himself insists on protecting. Garrow sticks to the story that state senator **Alice Palmer asked Ayers and his wife Bernardine Dohrn to host a <u>fundraiser</u> for state Senate candidate Obama** in the fall of 1995 – as if they needed to be asked. Then Garrow begins adding information. "After that gathering, **Barack and Michelle began to see a great deal more of not only Bill and Bernardine but also their <u>three clos-est friends</u>, Rashid and Mona Khalidi and Carole Travis**." Rashid Khalidi was a Palestinian native of radical bent then living in Chicago. According to Garrow, Obama did the following during the next eight years. **He organized a <u>panel on juvenile justice</u> based on a new book by Ayers. He served on the <u>Woods Fund board</u> with Ayers. He joined Ayers for a <u>panel discussion</u>, "<u>Intellectuals, Who Need Them</u>**." Up until the time of his 2004 Senate run, he and Michelle attended "the **<u>almost nightly dinners</u>**" held with Ayers, Dohrn, and the Khalidis. [The Ayers also babysat for Obama's young children regularly.] Ayers obviously meant a whole lot more to Obama than "a guy who lives in the neighborhood" might be expected to. But how much more? Khalidi did not shy from giving credit where it was due.   He began the acknowledgment section of his 2004 book, *Resurrecting Empire,* with a tribute to his own literary muse: "First, chrono-logically and in other ways comes Bill Ayers." Khalidi had no reason to be coy about this relationship. Obama obviously did. Garrow obliges him. Although he concedes that Ayers follows Obama to Chicago and both work on educational reform with the same people during the years 1987-1988."[8] *(Jack Cashill, American Thinker, May 18, 2017)* Obama probably moved to Chicago after his formal education secondary in part to his strong relationships with Bill Ayers and Valerie Jarrett.

b. Obama's domestic and foreign policies parallel Ayers' policy recommendations that he outlined in the Weather Underground's political manifesto, *Prairie Fire*. The following text is from *Unexpected Treason*, Chapter 4, and is an evaluation of *Prairie Fire* quotes.

    i. "Like people everywhere, **we are analyzing how to bring to life the potential forces which can destroy U.S. imperialism**. *[Obama's foreign policy and slashing of the military, especially with the sequester.]* We are a **guerrilla organization**. We are **communist women and men** *[Obama is surrounded by red diaper babies, including himself.]*, underground in the United States for more than four years … Our intention is to **disrupt the empire**, **to incapacitate it**, **to put pressure on the cracks** *[Obama's Cloward-Piven strategy]* … to join the world struggle *[jihad]*, to attack from the inside. *[BLM, Muslim Brotherhood plants, ISIS terrorists embedded in Syrian Muslim migrants - Obama's presidency is the ultimate inside attack with his political, economic and foreign policy initiatives.]* … to wear away at him *[continual suicidal defense budget cuts]*, to harass him *[Obama constantly criticizes America.]*, to isolate him *[Obama destroyed alliances with Israel, Great Britain, Saudi Arabia, Egypt, and the GCC.]*, to expose every weakness *[massive debt, open borders, government dependency, social engineering in military]*, to pounce, to reveal his vulnerability."

    ii. "We have an urgent responsibility: **to destroy imperialism from within**. *[Similar to the "Explanatory Memorandum of the General Strategic Goal for the Muslim Brotherhood in North America" which states "The Ikhwan must understand that their work in America is a kind of grand Jihad in eliminating and **destroying the Western civilization from within** and "sabotaging" its miserable house by their hands and the hands of the believers." The far-left and Islam have similar political goals.]*"

    iii. "Socialism is the total opposite of capitalism / imperialism. It is the **rejection of empire and White supremacy** *[Obama's "white privilege" issues, BLM]*. Socialism is the violent overthrow *[Obama's preaching of political non-violence is taqiyiya.]* of the bourgeoisie, the establishment of the dictatorship of the proletariat *[executive orders by Obama]*, and the eradication of the social system based on profit. Socialism means control of the productive forces *[massive increase of regulations by Obama, "you didn't build that"]* for the good of the whole community instead of the few who live on hilltops and in mansions. Socialism means priorities based on human need instead of corporate greed." *Reverend Wright paraphrased this last sentence from Prairie Fire in one of his sermons when he stated, "White folks' greed runs a world in need."*

iv. "**Revolution** is a fight by the people for power. It is a **changing of power in which existing social and economic relationships are <u>turned upside down.</u>**" *[Obama's attacks on and vilification of organized law enforcement, Islam is a religion of peace, importing jihad into the West while protecting the rights of radical Muslims, catch and release, reversal of U.S. alliances with respect to Iran – Israel – Saudi Arabia – Egypt, gay marriage, genderless bathrooms, prioritizing transgender rights, illegal aliens and Muslim refugees obtain more government benefits than American citizens, the military is a laboratory for social change at the expense of national security]*

v. "From its inception, **Zionism has been an imperial ideology**, presented as an alternative to communism … **the Zionist state is clearly the aggressor, the source of violence and war in the Mideast, the occupier of stolen lands** *[Obama will only refer to the West Bank and East Jerusalem as occupied territory.]* … It is racist and expansionist – the enemy of the Palestinians, the Arab people, and the Jewish people *[J Street]*. The U.S. people have been seriously deceived about the Palestinians and Israel. SELF DETERMNATION FOR THE PALESTINIAN PEOPLE! *[two-state solution]* **U.S. OUT OF THE MIDDLE EAST**! *[Obama's Middle East Policy]* END AID TO ISRAEL! *[difficult even for Obama]*" This is the only section in Prairie Fire that Ayers put in caps, which demonstrates his close emotional ties to this issue and his intrinsic anti-Semitism. Israel is the only democracy in the Middle East, and any land obtained after the 1948 partition has been as a result of defensive wars launched as a result of aggression by surrounding Arab and Muslim powers. Obama's withdrawal from Afghanistan and Iraq also reflect Ayers' view of removing U.S. influence from the Middle East, which allowed Iran, Russia, al-Qaeda and ISIS to expand their spheres of influence. Ayers' revolutionary thinking undoubtedly has helped contribute to Obama's anti-Israel and Middle East policies.

9. "I was a constitutional law professor." *March, 2007.* "I'm a law professor at the University of Chicago teaching constitutional law. I am a great admirer of our founding charter *[taqiyya]*."[9] *(2004 interview with Cathleen Falsani, Sojourners) Obama's official title at the University of Chicago Law School was senior instructor.*

10. In *The Audacity of Hope*, Obama stated, "I met Michelle in the Summer of 1988 while we were both working at Sidley and Austin." When visiting Russia in 2009, Obama stated, "I don't know if anyone will meet their future wife or husband in class like I did."

11. "This is not to say that I'm unanchored in my faith. There are some things that I'm absolutely sure about – the Golden Rule, the need to battle cruelty in all its forms, the value of love and charity, humility and grace." *- Barack Obama, The Audacity of Hope.*

12. "I appreciate the opportunity to once again meet with my friend and colleague, Prime Minister Erdogan … I find Prime Minister Erdogan to be **an outstanding partner** and an

outstanding friend on a wide range of issues … **I also appreciate the advice he gives me**, because he has two daughters that are a little older than mine – they've turned out very well, so **I'm always interested in his perspective on raising girls**." *Obama, March 2012 nuclear summit in Seoul, South Korea.*

a. Obama reached out multiple times for Erdogan's advice on raising his daughters, even though as a strict fundamental Muslim, Erdogan believes in mandatory clitorectomies for girls, arranged marriages, and forced marriages for girls under the age of 10, which occur throughout the Middle East under Sharia law. In 2016, Erdogan backed Turkey's Constitutional Court, which "ruled to annul a provision that punishes all sexual acts against children under the age of 15 as 'sexual abuse,'" which legalized sex with girls as young as twelve years old.[10] Later in the year, Erdogan supported legislation in the Turkish parliament that would pardon men who rape female children if they agreed to marry them after the sexual assault. Erdogan insulted a prominent female reporter who disagreed with some of his policies by saying, "shameless militant woman disguised under the name of a journalist … Know your place." In January 2016, the Office of Turkish Religious Affairs, which is under President Erdogan's direction as an Islamist, stated that a man's lustful kissing of his own daughter would not forfeit his marriage according to Islamic law. Erdogan was critical of working women in 2016, when he stated, "A woman who abstains from maternity by saying 'I am working' means that she is actually denying her femininity," and that she is "deficient" and a "half person." As the liberal Democratic president of the United States and a father who wants the best future for his two daughters, it does not seem that these two leaders would have much in common. There must be other issues securing the strong bond between them, such as the devotion to Allah. Or Obama, as a radical Muslim, may support these controversial sexist positions, but he cannot openly express these opinions since he is the president of the United States.

13. Obama promised transparency with his presidency, but not with his personal record. "Further, as is common knowledge, the biographical dossier we have at our disposal is radically incomplete. All Obama's vital documents are sequestered: his name change, baptism and adoption records, Noelani Elementary School records, Punahou School financial aid or school records, Occidental College financial aid records, Harvard Law School records, Columbia senior thesis, record with Illinois State Bar Association, and his law client list, medical records and passport records, among others [including the records documenting his renunciation of Indonesian citizenship and being granted U.S. citizenship when he moved back to Hawaii]. He has also suppressed the marriage license of his parents. His backdated Selective Service form remains unexplained and his Massachusetts Social Security Number appears to be invalid. Moreover, the digital copy of Obama's birth certificate released by the

White House on April 27, 2011 remains contentious; its authenticity has been disputed by many expert analysts. And there is considerably more that suggests we are dealing with a factitious personage, which would also qualify him for the title of Anti-President."[11] *(David Solway, American Thinker)* Can a politician be trusted to be the leader of the free world, with so many details of his personal history being suppressed?

CHAPTER 3

Healthcare Lies

1. "**If you like your doctor, you will be able to keep your doctor**. Period. **If you like your healthcare plan, you will be able to keep your healthcare plan**. Period. No one will take it away. No matter what." Policies that don't comply with the Affordable Care Act have been and will continue to be terminated, and many have been forced to buy health insurance through the government exchange when their private insurance policies are deemed out of compliance. Obama committed fraud with his lies about his healthcare product. *Forbes* estimated that over 93 million Americans would lose their health insurance policies with the ACA. Obama repeated this lie <u>**over 36 times**</u> (If you like your insurance plan, you can keep your insurance plan).

   a. "Since 2013 Obamacare premiums have skyrocketed. In Alaska, they went up over 200% recently … In Arizona, they've been up over 118% … Despite the promise that premiums would decrease by $2,500 on average, they've actually increased by $3,000 and even much more than that in some cases. It's crushing the middle class and the families of the middle class. It's frankly crushing our country. **Obamacare was a big lie. You can keep your doctor – <u>Lie</u>! You can keep your plan – <u>Lie</u>! <u>It was a lie directly from the president</u>. You can keep your doctor. You can keep your plan. 28 times he said that. 28 times. And it was a lie and <u>he knew it was</u>**! And now it is hurting this country irreparably." *President Trump, White House luncheon meeting with Republican senators, July 19, 2017.*

   b. "<u>**I am sorry**</u> that they are finding themselves in this situation based on assurances they got from me." ***Obama** admitted he lied regarding promises he made to Americans that they could keep their health insurance plans.*

   c. "He should've just been specific. No, **we all knew**." *Democratic Senator Gillebrand, on ABC's This Week in November, 2014, admitting that all the Democrats knew that Obama was lying when he continually stated that American would be able to keep their doctors and healthcare plans under Obamacare.*

d. "This [Affordable Care Act] was written in a tortured way to make sure CBO did not score the mandate as taxes … If CBO scored the mandate as taxes, the bill dies … In terms of risk-rated subsidies … if you had a law which said that healthy people are going to pay in, you made explicit healthy people pay in and sick people get money, it would not have passed. **Lack of transparency is a huge political advantage** … the stupidity of the American voter … was critical." *J. Gruber, chief architect / political consultant to Obamacare legislation, 2013.*

e. **Jon Lovett**, **former Obama speechwriter**: "I really like, I was very – the joke speeches is the most fun part of this. But the things I'm the most proud of were the most serious speeches, I think. Health care, economic speeches. **Jon Favreau**, **former Obama speechwriter**: Lovett wrote the line about "If you like your insurance, you can keep it." **Lovett**: How dare you! [laughing] … And you know what? It's still true. No! [not really] [laughing] *Charlie Rose interview with former Obama speechwriters Jon Lovett and Jon Favreau. May 2016.* The Obama administration thought lying to the American public was entertaining and a big joke. Obama used this line 36 times to fraudulently sell Obamacare to the American public.

f. "The **litany of lies** and disappointments delivered by the Obama administration, congressional Democrats, and their media enablers is too long to repeat here, but the highlights should be familiar: 'If you like your plan, you can keep your plan' was an **outright lie** with malice aforethought; 'doesn't add one dime to the deficit' was, at best, wishful thinking; the promise of saving the average family $2,500 a year in insurance premiums was **economic illiteracy** … There were deep and serious problems with the U.S. health-care system before Obamacare. Obamacare has made those problems worse -- that much is impossible to deny. If a 22 percent hike in premiums isn't enough to get Americans interested in consumer-driven, market-based alternatives, do not despair: It is going to get worse."[12] *(National Review editorial, October 2016)*

2. "**If you've got a health care plan that you like**, **you can keep it**. All I'm going to do is help you to **lower the premiums** on it. You'll **still have a choice of a doctor**. There's **no mandate** involved … For **my mother** … **to spend the last months of her life in the hospital room arguing with insurance companies** … there's something fundamentally wrong about that." *Obama debating John McCain in the 2008 presidential debates. Five blatant lies and a straight face.* Obama's mother had a good Cigna health insurance plan, and had minimal out of pocket expenses. In 2013, right after Obama won his re-election, over 4 million Americans had their health insurance policies cancelled.

a. "The new healthcare law will '**cut the cost of a typical family's premium by up to $2500 a year**.'" *Obama, 2007, campaign trail.* Obama repeated this outright false statement **over 22 times**. Obama also quoted that same number in February 2008 on the campaign trail. One year after the law was signed, the average premium for families rose $1500 per year. Premiums increased up to 78%. The Affordable Care Act turned out to be not that affordable. Blue Cross Blue Shield of Texas incurred massive losses in mid-2016, and planned on raising premiums on 603,000 policy holders by 57 - 60%. According to the Freedom Partners Chamber of Commerce 2016 report, the average Obamacare insurance premium was expected to increase over 22% in 2017, with fewer policy options available to subscribers. Arizona 2017 Obamacare unsubsidized insurance premiums were expected to increase by over 100%.

b. "Tennessee is ground zero for Obamacare's nationwide implosion. Late last month the state insurance commissioner, Julie Mix McPeak, approved premium increases of up to 62% in a bid to save the exchange set up under the Affordable Care Act. "I would characterize the exchange market in Tennessee as very near collapse," she said … State regulators have already approved the highest annual rise [of premiums] in the nation, a weighted average of nearly 56% … The bottom line is that Tennesseans on Obamacare must choose from fewer, and increasingly unaffordable, options … All Obamacare consumers face rising deductibles, which aren't covered by subsidies and can range up to $6,580 for the most 'affordable' family plans."[13] *(Wall Street Journal, October 2016)* Obamacare is part of Obama's intended war on the working American middle class.

3. In November 2014, Obama described and **downplayed** Obamacare consultant and MIT economics professor Jonathan Gruber as "**some advisor who never worked on our staff.**" *The Wall Street Journal* reported in June 2015, that there was frequent contact between Gruber and White House and HHS staff. Gruber discussed Obamacare policy and strategy with President Obama, the director of the Office of Management and Budget Peter Orszag, an economic advisor to President Obama, and special adviser for healthcare policy at OMB - Ezekiel Emanuel. Representative Chaffetz of Utah stated, "His proximity to HHS and the White House was a whole lot tighter than they admitted … There's no doubt he was a much more integral part of this than they've said. He put up this facade he was an arm's length away. It was a farce." Jeanne Lambrew, a senior Obama advisor who worked at HHS and the White House sent an email to Gruber stating, "Thank you for being an integral part of getting us to this historic moment … [you are] our hero."

4. "We'll have the **negotiations televised on C-SPAN** … so that people can see who is making arguments on behalf of their constituents, and who are making arguments on behalf of the drug companies or the insurance companies." *Obama lied concerning his administration's promise of transparency.* Pharmaceutical and insurance company deals were made in secret.

5. "What I am convinced of is, if we actually hope to pass universal health care this time around, **we have to bring Republicans and Democrats together … We have to have an open and transparent process so that the American people participate in the debate and**

see exactly what we're doing." *Obama*. Republicans had no input into the healthcare law. The bill was passed without one Republican vote supporting the revolutionary ACA.

   a.   "We have to pass the bill so that you can find out what is in it." *Nancy Pelosi, Democratic Speaker of the House. No transparency from Obama.*

6.   "Having differences of opinion, having a real debate about matters of domestic policy and national security – and that's not something that's only good for our country, it's absolutely essential. **It's only through the process of disagreement and debate that bad ideas get tossed out and good ideas get refined and made better. And that kind of vigorous back and forth – that imperfect but well-founded process, messy as it often is – is at the heart of our democracy** … So, yes, I want you to challenge my ideas, and I guarantee you that after reading this I may challenge a few of yours. (Laughter) **I want you to stand up for your beliefs, and knowing this caucus, I have no doubt that you will. I want us to have a constructive debate**." *Obama, January 29, 2010. Meeting with Republicans regarding healthcare law reform and the subsequent debate.* Obama pretended that the deliberations would be bipartisan. Obama refused to compromise with Republicans and increased the use of executive orders as his presidency progressed, especially with respect to the ACA, where Obama unilaterally mandated amendments and new waivers.

7.   "Under our plan, **no federal dollars will be used to fund abortions**, and federal conscience laws will remain in place." *(President Obama 2009 Address to Congress)* and "There are **no plans under health reform to revoke the existing prohibition on using federal tax payer dollars for abortions**. Nobody is talking about changing that existing provision. The Hyde amendment. Let's be clear about that. Its just not true … The best offense against lies is the truth. So, all we can do is keep on pushing the truth. *[all lies]*" *Obama. Town hall meeting. August 20, 2009.* According to the Government Accountability Office (GOA), over 1000 Obamacare plans fund abortions. **Over 1000 Obamcare plans** include abortion services. Obama repeated this lie <u>**over 12 times**</u>.

8.   "And it will slow the growth of health care costs for our families, our businesses, and our government." *Obamacare increased national spending on healthcare by up to 8% after the bill was signed.*

   a.   "Marilyn Tavenner, CEO of America's Health Insurance Plans, revealed that she expects ObamaCare premium hikes "to be higher than we saw in previous years," including last year, which saw double-digit rate increases across the country … In addition to the cost of complying with ObamaCare's insurance regulations and mandates, there's the fact that the ObamaCare exchanges have failed to attract enough young and healthy people needed to keep premiums down. Plus, two industry bailout programs expire this year, Tavenner notes … United Health Group is planning to drop out of almost every ObamaCare market it currently serves after losing $1 billion on those policies."[14] *(Investor's Business Daily editorial, April 2016).*

  b. In 2017, health insurers are planning to raise premium rates by at least 20% in New York, Pennsylvania, and Georgia.

9. "The plan I'm proposing will cost around $900 billion over 10 years." *Obama*. The Congressional Budget Office estimated the costs of Obamacare at a minimum of $1.7 trillion over 10 years and later increased the estimate to over $2.7 trillion.

10. "I will not sign a plan that adds one dime to our deficits, either now or in the future." *Obama*. The Heritage Foundation estimated that Obamacare will add over $1 trillion to the deficit.

11. "Under my plan, no family making less than $250,000 a year will see any form of tax increase." *Obama*. Obamacare was filled with fees and taxes including tanning salon and medical device taxes, that affected all tax payers. Other taxes included a 40% tax on Cadillac health insurance plans and new healthcare-related payroll taxes.

12. Obamacare is "**absolutely not a tax increase**." *Obama, former Constitutional Law Instructor at the University of Chicago Law School, 2009 interview with George Stephanopoulos.* The Supreme Court subsequently ruled that the individual mandate was legally a tax. "Under the mandate, if an individual does not maintain health insurance, the only consequence is that he must make an additional payment to the IRS when he pays his taxes … That, according to the Government, means the mandate can be regarded as establishing a condition – not owning health insurance – that triggers a tax – the required payment to the IRS. Under that theory, the mandate is not a legal command to buy insurance. Rather, it makes going without insurance just another thing the Government taxes, like buying gasoline or earning income. And if the mandate is in effect just a tax hike on certain taxpayers who do not have health insurance, it may be within Congress's constitutional power to tax … It is of course true that the Act describes the payment as a 'penalty,' not a 'tax,' … **The same analysis here suggests that the shared responsibility payment may for constitutional purposes be considered a tax, not a penalty**." *Chief Justice John Roberts.* Obama denied Obamacare was a tax, so that he could sell the legislation to the American public, but then admitted it was a tax, so that it could pass the scrutiny of the Supreme Court.

  a. "Transparent financing and also transparent spending. I mean, **this bill was written in a tortured way to make sure CBO did not score the mandate as taxes. If CBO scored the mandate as taxes the bill dies**. Okay? So it's written to do that … In terms of risk rated subsidies, if you had a law which said that healthy people are going to pay in, you made explicit healthy people pay in and sick people get money, it would not have passed. Lack of transparency is a huge political advantage." *Jonathan Gruber, chief architect of Obamacare.* Obama lied when denied the mandate was a tax.

13. During Mother's Day weekend in 2013, Obama described Obamacare as the "**largest health care tax cut for working families and small business** in our history." Obamacare actually contained over $1 trillion in tax increases which were focused on investments, medical devices, and insurance plans.

14. "It will create 4 million jobs, 400,000 jobs almost immediately … again, in the health care industry but in the entrepreneurial world as well." *Nancy Pelosi, Speaker of the House, promoting Obamacare, September 2010.*

15. "If Obamacare is repealed, the national debt could increase by $137 billion." *Obamacare Tweet, June 22, 2015.* The national debt at the time of this tweet was $18.3 trillion, and is not a major concern for Obama. When Obama became president, the national debt was $10.6 trillion.

16. "The VA is handling millions more appointments, inside and outside the VA, and delivering more care … **On average**, **veterans are waiting just a few days for an appointment**. And that's all good news." *Obama, July 21, 2015, John Stewart Show.*

    a. "Under President Obama, the VA's budget has massively increased, yet the backlog of disability claims more than doubled in his first term … wait times for health care have increased, and the department remains devoid of any sort of accountability … Even after the VA wait list scandal and another funding increase from Congress as part of the VA reform bill passed last summer, wait times for health care have continued to increase and veterans have a 'choice card' most are unable to use." *Dan Caldwell, legislative and political director of Concerned Veterans for America.* According to The Washington Post, there has been a 50% increase in the number of veterans on VA wait lists.

17. "The fact of the matter is that when Obamacare is fully implemented, we are going to be in a position to show that costs are going down. Over the last two years, health care premiums have gone up – it is true – but they have **gone up slower than any time in the last 50 years**." *Obama, Presidential debate with Mitt Romney, October 3, 2012.*

    a. "President Obama reiterated a claim that his healthcare law will reduce costs, a promise he made when he started pushing for an overhaul as a candidate four years ago. Then, Obama said he would cut family health insurance premiums by $2,500 by the end of his first term. Today, this stands as one of the president's biggest unfulfilled promises. In fact, the average employee share of an employer-provided health plan jumped from $3,515 in 2009 to $4,316 in 2012, an increase of more than 22%, according to a survey from the Kaiser Family Foundation and the Health Research & Educational Trust. The total cost of an average employer-provided family health plan - shared by the employer and the employee -reached $15,745 in 2012. When the law is fully implemented in 2014, some low- and middle-income Americans will qualify for government subsidies to help them afford health insurance … there is little evidence that the Affordable Care Act has made healthcare any more affordable for the vast majority of Americans."[15] *(Robert Pear, The New York Times)*

18. "Health care costs are rising at the slowest rate in 50 years." *Obama, Presidential Farewell Address, January 10, 2017.* According to *The New York Times*, "Premiums for midlevel health plans under the Affordable Care Act will increase by an average of 25% next year (2017), while consumers will find significantly fewer insurance companies offering coverage, the federal government said."[16] Some states had premium increases over 100%.

19. "I don't want to, in any way, pretend that we are where we need to be but we have, in fact, **fired a whole bunch** of people who are in charge** of these facilities." *Obama, CNN town hall, September 28, 2016.* The Obama administration removed only one to a maximum of six VA employees who were in charge of facilities related to the wait time scandals. "Bunch" is a very vague term.

20. "I will never forget my own mother, as she fought cancer in her final months, **having to worry about whether her insurance would <u>refuse to pay for her treatment</u>**. And by the way, this was because the insurance company was arguing that somehow she should have known that she had cancer, when she took her new job, even though it hadn't been diagnosed yet." *Obama, Portsmouth New Hampshire town hall meeting, August 11, 2009.* Obama's mother had health insurance that paid for her cancer treatments, but her disability insurance policy refused to pay her because they claimed her uterine and ovarian cancer was a pre-existing condition. Obamacare had guidelines that forced healthcare insurance companies to write policies for people with pre-existing conditions, but these criteria were not forced upon disability insurance policies.

    a. "During the campaign, Obama said: "She was 52 years old when she died of ovarian cancer, and you know what she was thinking about in the last months of her life? She wasn't thinking about getting well. She wasn't thinking about coming to terms with her own mortality. She had been diagnosed just as she was transitioning between jobs. And she wasn't sure whether insurance was going to cover the medical expenses because they might consider this a pre-existing condition. I remember just being heartbroken, seeing her struggle through the paperwork and the medical bills and the insurance forms." He also said: "For my mother to die of cancer at the age of 53 and have to spend the last months of her life in the hospital room arguing with insurance companies because they're saying that this may be a pre-existing condition and they don't have to pay her treatment, there's something fundamentally wrong about that." But ex-*New York Times* reporter Janny Scott wrote a flattering book about Obama's mom. Scott describes Obama's mom's "battle" with insurance carriers quite differently. Scott said Dunham had employer-provided health insurance that "covered most of the costs of her medical treatment. … The hospital billed her insurance company directly, leaving Ann to pay only the deductible and any uncovered expenses, which, she said, came to several hundred dollars a month." The only quarrel was over a disability policy Dunham had, but her pre-existing condition disqualified her. So much for the mean old insurance company, but Obama's tale helped get Obamacare passed."[17] *(Larry Elder, World Net Daily)*

21. "There are also those who claim that our reform efforts would insure illegal immigrants. This too is false. The reforms, **the reforms I'm proposing would not apply to those who are here illegally**. It's not true. And one more misunderstanding I want to clear up. Under our plan, no federal dollars will be used to fund abortions." *Obama, 2009 State of the Union Address.* Congressman Joe Wilson yelled during these remarks, "You lie," and he was right.

    a. "Illegal immigrants and individuals with unclear legal status wrongly benefited from up to $750 million in ObamaCare subsidies and the government is struggling to recoup the money, according to a new Senate report obtained by *Fox News*. The report, produced by Republicans on the Senate Homeland Security and Governmental Affairs Committee, examined Affordable Care Act tax credits meant to defray the cost of insurance premiums. It found that as of June 2015, "the Administration awarded approximately $750 million in tax credits on behalf of individuals who were later determined to be ineligible because they failed to verify their citizenship, status as a national, or legal presence." The review found the credits went to more than 500,000 people – who are illegal immigrants or whose legal status was unclear due to insufficient records. The Centers for Medicare and Medicaid Services confirmed to *FoxNews.com* on Monday that 471,000 customers with 2015 coverage failed to produce proper documentation on their citizenship or immigration status on time."[18] *(Fox News, February 2016)*

CHAPTER 4

Economic Lies

1. "**Increasing America's debt weakens us domestically and internationally**. Leadership means that "the buck stops here." Instead, Washington is shifting the burden of bad choices today onto the backs of our children and grandchildren. **America has a debt problem and a failure of leadership. Americans deserve better.** <u>I therefore intend to oppose the effort to increase American's debt limit</u>." *Senator Barack Obama, Congressional Record, March 16, 2006.* Obama is falsely positioning himself as a conservative while he prepares to run for the presidency in 2008, but in reality, only Democrats are allowed to spend government money. While campaigning in 2008, Obama again falsely presented himself as a fiscal conservative when he stated, "The problem is, is that the way Bush has done it over the last eight years is to take out a credit card from the Bank of China in the name of our children, driving up our national debt from $5 trillion for the first 42 presidents – #43 added $4 trillion by his lonesome, so that we now have over $9 trillion of debt that we are going to have to pay back – $30,000 for every man, woman and child. **That's irresponsible. It's unpatriotic.**" As president, Obama increased the deficit to almost $20 trillion, and disregarded his own campaign rhetoric. Obama lied.

2. "**It's not that I want to punish your success** … I want to make sure that everybody who is behind you, that they've got a chance for success, too … My attitude is that if the economy's good for folks from the bottom up, it's gonna be good for everybody. I think when you **spread the wealth around**, it's good for everybody." *Obama responding to Joe the Plumber who complained about the high level of taxation while Obama was on the campaign trail in Ohio in 2008.* In 2015, according to the Federal Reserve, the bottom 80% of the population owned less than 5% of the equity market. The average net worth of Americans was ranked fourth in the world in part because of the concentration of wealth in the top 10%. However, the median net worth of Americans ranked nineteenth in the world. The average net income and purchasing power of American workers declined precipitously during the Obama presidency. Obama's socialism significantly hurt his constituency, and empowered the elite power brokers who backed his candidacy.

3. "Today, **I'm pledging to cut the deficit we inherited by half by the end of my first term in office** … Now, this will not be easy. It will require us to make difficult decisions and face challenges we've long neglected. But I refuse to leave our children with a debt that they cannot repay, and that means taking responsibility right now, in this administration, for getting our spending under control … **If I don't have this done in three years**, **then there's going to be a one term proposition**." *Obama, Fiscal Responsibility Summit, February 2009*. Obama did not cut the deficit in half at the end of his first time, ran again for the presidency, and lied to the American people regarding his intent to reign in government spending.

4. "The stimulus package would "save or create 3.5 million jobs" … over 2 years. *Obama, February, 2009*. The economy lost more than 3 million jobs over the next year, according to Labor Department statistics.

5. "We've got **shovel-ready projects** all across the country that governors and mayors are pleading to fund. And the minute we can get those investments to the state level, jobs are going to be created." *Obama, December 2008*

    a. "The term shovel-ready, let's be honest, it doesn't always live up to the billing." *Obama, November 2009*.

    b. "There is no such thing as shovel-ready projects." *Obama in The New York Times interview, November 2010*.

6. "So here's what I've done since I've been president … we have increased oil production to the highest level in 16 years … *[Romney stated the above was not true and said Obama did his best to block oil production.]* … Very little of what Governor Romney just said is true. We've opened up public lands. We're actually drilling more on public lands than in the previous administration." *Obama, second presidential debate, October 2012*. It was later proven Romney was right and Obama was wrong. Obama lied.

7. In 2014, Obama fought for his economic policies by calling the present environment an "era of austerity" despite record high spending, deficits, and increasing the debt by a factor of two.

8. "The president has already **reduced the deficit by over $2.5 trillion**, cutting spending by over $1.4 trillion, bringing domestic discretionary spending to its lowest level as a share of the economy since the Eisenhower era. **As a result of these savings**, **together with a strengthening economy**, **the deficit is coming down at the fastest pace of anytime in American history** other than the demobilization from World War II." *Whitehouse.gov statement, 2014*.

9. "We are 15 years into this new century. Fifteen years that dawned with terror touching our shores … that saw a vicious recession spread across our nation and the world. But tonight, we turn the page … Tonight, after a breakthrough year for America, **our economy is growing and creating jobs at the fastest pace since 1999** … America, for all that we have endured; for all the grit and hard work required to come back; for all the tasks that lie ahead, know this: **The shadow of crisis has passed**, **and the State of the Union is strong**." *Obama, 2015*

State of the Union Address. In the first quarter for 2015, the GDP estimate was revised downward, with the U.S. economy contracting by an annual negative 0.7%. Although the Obama administration has called the recent period an expansion, this will be the first "expansion" with three quarters of negative GDP growth since the mid-1950s. Obama is the only president without a year of >3% GDP growth during both his terms.

10. "And, since I took office the United States has **reduced the deficit by two-thirds**." *Obama at the G7 Summit in Germany on June 8, 2015. U.S. National Debt per US Debt Clock.org – $19,056, 000,000,000 on March 5, 2016.* Once Obama passed $10 trillion, he never looked back. The national debt has never decreased since Obama became president. The present debt burden per taxpayer is $159,295.

11. "Another manifestation of irresponsibility is the large budget deficits we are inheriting. These deficits, over time, will harm economic growth and impose burdens on our children and grandchildren." *Obama, 2010 FY Budget Blueprint.* Seven years later Obama added another six + trillion dollars to the national debt, which totaled almost 20 trillion dollars.

12. "I've proposed a specific $4 trillion deficit reduction plan. ... The way we do it is $2.50 for every cut, we ask for $1 in additional revenue." *Obama, Presidential debate with Mitt Romney, Denver, October 3, 2012.*

    a. "In promising $4 trillion, Obama is already banking more than $2 billion from legislation enacted along with Republicans last year that cut agency operating budgets and capped them for 10 years. He also claims more than $800 billion in war savings that would occur anyway. And he uses creative bookkeeping to hide spending on Medicare reimbursements to doctors."[19]

13. "It's how we recovered from the worst economic crisis in generations ... Let me start with the economy, and a basic fact: the United States of America, right now, has the strongest, most durable economy in the world. We're in the middle of the longest streak of private-sector job creation in history ... Anyone claiming that America's economy is in decline is peddling fiction." *Obama, State of the Union Address, January 12, 2016.* At the time of the SOTUA in 2016, the national debt was at $18.9 trillion dollars and poised to break a record $20 trillion before the next president assumed his office. The labor force participation rate decreased to under 63%, the lowest rate in 35 years. In 2015, there were over 93 million American adults who did not have jobs. In December 2015, the CBO reported that Obamacare would reduce the number of work hours of Americans so that the equivalent of two million jobs would be lost. The median net worth of the American family decreased from $138,00 to under $83,000 during Obama's presidency. During Obama's first term, the real median household income for Americans declined by over $4000 per family. During Obama's presidency, the middle class lost about 1,000,000 workers who were earning between $32,000 and $53,000 per year. Obama's flooding of the United States with immigrants has put continual

downward pressure on American wages. Income inequality increased with Obama as president where significant assets were shifted from the middle and lower classes to the upper class. During Obama's presidency, home ownership hit 63%, a 50-year low near the end of his second term. Obama had the weakest post-recession recovery when compared to previous economic recoveries in modern American history. By 2014, after six years of an Obama presidency, the child poverty rate continued to increase and set record highs. Even UNICEF ranked the United States 36th out of 41 among wealthy countries with respect to child poverty. During Obama's presidency, economic freedom decreased dramatically since 2008, as evaluated by the *Wall Street Journal* and the *Heritage Foundation*. Insurance premiums and deductibles increased substantially with Obamacare, and devastated the finances of many middle-class families. Student loan burdens on American youth continued to increase while post-graduation job opportunities withered. Government food stamp expenditures nearly tripled during the Obama presidency.

14. "Saving the world from a great depression, that was quite good ... I'm proud. I think I've been true to myself during this process." *Obama, April 2016 statements during European tour.* "I actually compare our economic performance to how, historically, countries that have wrenching financial crises perform. By that measure, we probably managed this better than any large economy on Earth in modern history." *Obama, The New York Times Sunday Magazine, April 2016, and "President Obama Faults Himself for Failing to Sell US Economic Recovery to Voters," David Usborne, The Independent, April 28, 2016.* Obama will be the first president in U.S. history to never see one year of his presidency with economic growth at 3% or greater. Obama's record of economic growth during his presidency will rank fourth from the worst when compared to all other U.S. presidents. The following records accrued during the Obama presidency may help to explain that Obama's vision is not based in fact: record high federal debt, record high health care premiums, record high food stamp participation, record high money printing via quantitative easing (not leading to significant economic growth), record low labor force participation rate, record low home ownership percentage, decreasing median family income, increasing economic inequality between Blacks and the average American, and record high student loan burdens coupled with decreased job opportunities for college graduates.

15. *Remarks by the President on the Economy, Elkhart, Illinois, June 1, 2016:* "America's economy is not just better than it was eight years ago – it is the strongest, most durable economy in the world ... By almost every economic measure, America is better off than when I came here at the beginning of my presidency. *["This is the worst period, I recall, since I've been in public service. There's nothing like it." – former Federal Reserve Chairman Alan Greenspan, June 24, 2016]* That's the truth. *[Not quite. Record food stamp dependence. Record disability. Record $20*

trillion deficits. Record health care premiums. Record black inequality. Increasing wealth gap between the rich and the poor/middle class. 94 million American adults not working in 2016. Record low home ownership. Decreasing median family income. Record low labor participation rate.]... But I also know that I've spent every single day of my presidency focused on what I can do to grow the middle class *[shrinking the middle class]* and increase jobs, and boost wages *[real wages are decreasing with Obama's immigration policies and surges]*, and make sure every kid in America gets the same kind of opportunities Michelle and I did. *[College graduate have less opportunities now than with any previous generation. A record number of young adults are living with their parents.]* ... When Bill Clinton and I have held this job, deficits have gotten smaller ... They're [entitlements for others] not what's holding back the middle class. And, by the way, neither is Obamacare. *[Record high Obamacare premiums devastate American workers' disposable income.]* ... dramatically slowing the rate in which health care costs were going up *[recent record high increasing premiums in 2016]* ... Today, the average family's health insurance premium is $2,600 less than it would have been if premiums had kept on going up at the pace before Obamacare *[all theoretical]* ... I've issued fewer regulations than my predecessor *[The business costs associated with regulations along with the total volume of regulations are both at record highs.]* ... Right now, the number of people trying to cross our border illegally is near its lowest level in 40 years. *["We continue to have tens of thousands of people come across our border illegally, every single month ... it seems like the president's memory is short, because it was just two years ago, at this particular time, when we were dealing with that crush of young unaccompanied minors comes across the border. And now, I was actually in Washington, DC just a couple of months ago, talking with Secretary Jeh Johnson about another new crush, a large number of unaccompanied minors coming across the border. We've had that this past fall. We've had it this spring." Texas Governor Greg Abbott, Fox News Channel "The Real Story," June 23, 2016]* It's near its lowest level in 40 years. *["Refugees from Central America are pouring into the United States, a trend from 2014 that seems to be resurfacing along the U.S.-Mexican border this year. Many of them are children. ... Yuma Sheriff's Capt. Eben Bratcher said, "Many of these people are from other nations, other than Mexico. Central America, Chinese, Romanians are a big one right now, and so that's kind of a change in what we've come to expect here."... This year, the surge is already back to [record] 2014 levels with more than 27,000 children." ("New Surge of Central Americans Seen on Border," Michel Marizco, Arizona Public Media, PBS, NPR, June 6, 2016)]* ... Everybody thinks that immigrants come here and then they're getting all this stuff from the government. Immigrants pay a lot more in taxes than they receive in services. *[Lies. Studies show that immigrants receive much more in government benefits than U.S. citizens. The National Academies of Science, Engineering and Medicine released a report in September 2016 revealing that each immigrant costs state and local taxpayers a net of $1,600 after accounting for* *taxes paid by them. The annual net cost to the United States for all first-generation immigrants is $57.4 billion.[20]]* But most important, immigrants are not the main reason wages haven't gone up for middle-class families. *[Lower immigrant wages are a major cause of wage depression with the American middle class.]* … let's be honest – most Americans don't have the same benefits package or job security as their member of Congress. I'm just saying. They've got a pretty good deal. That was part of what Obamacare is all about, right? *[Congress and their staff received waivers from Obamacare.]* … Now, here's the good news: Wages are actually growing at a rate of about 3 percent so far this year. That's the good news *[The Bureau of Labor Statistics revealed on August 9, 2016 that "real hourly compensation (for the first quarter of 2016) decreased 0.4% after revision." For the second quarter of 2016, hourly wages decreased another 1.4%, which means for the first half of 2016, wages decreased by 2%. These numbers are consistent with Obama's policy to import over 2 million guest-workers and migrants annually, not counting illegal immigration, which puts steady downward pressure on all wages.]* … Have we really forgotten what just happened eight years ago? It hasn't been that long ago. And because of their reckless behavior [Wall Street bankers], you got hurt. *[Obama's class action lawsuit against Citibank helped usher in the era of subprime loans, which was at the core of the financial crisis.]*" Obama is severely misrepresenting his achievements or he is delusional.

    a.   Obama continued the lies with his 2016 Democratic National Convention speech, where he stated, "If you're really concerned about pocketbook issues and seeing the economy grow, and **creating more opportunity** for everybody, then the choice isn't even close. If you want someone with a lifelong track record of fighting **for higher wages**, and better benefits, and a fairer tax code, and a bigger voice for workers … you should vote for Hillary Clinton." *Obama. DNC speech. July 27, 2016.*

16.   "We've seen the longest streak of job growth on record, and wages have grown faster over the past few years than at any time in the past 40 … Add it all up, and last year the **poverty rate fell at the fastest rate in almost 50 years**, while the median household income grew at the fastest rate on record … And we have done all this while cutting our deficits by nearly two-thirds, and protecting vital investments that **grow the middle class.**" *Obama, White House Press Conference, December 16, 2016.* Obama's economic record was reviewed by Sean Hannity on *Hannity of Fox News* at the same time. Obama had one of the weakest economic records of any two-term American president with the lowest labor participation rate since the 1970s, 95 million Americans out of the labor force, the worst economic recovery since the 1940s with no GDP growth greater than 3%, the lowest home ownership rate in 51 years, 13 million more Americans on food stamps, over 43 million Americans living in poverty (an increase of 8 million Americans in poverty since the start of Obama's presidency), 1 in 5 American families without someone in the work force, the doubling of the national federal deficit, and the addition of more debt than all other president's combined.[21] The middle class

was decimated with increased taxes, stagnant wages, and huge Obamacare premiums, and accounted for a record low percentage of the American population. African-American and child poverty increased significantly during Obama's presidency.

a. "While the top one percent has amassed a bigger share of wealth and income, too many families, in inner cities and in rural counties, have been left behind – the laid-off factory worker; the waitress or health care worker who's just barely getting by and struggling to pay the bills – convinced that the game is fixed against them, that their government only serves the interests of the powerful – that's a recipe for more cynicism and polarization in our politics." *Obama discussed the actual bleak economic environment in his farewell address, that is being handed off to the Trump administration, which is in marked contrast to his upbeat misleading assessments of his economic performance he made during his final months as president. Obama is refuting Obama, thus at least one scenario is inaccurate.*

b. "The American middle class is losing ground in metropolitan areas across the country, affecting communities from Boston to Seattle and from Dallas to Milwaukee ... The **shrinking of the middle class** at the national level, to the point where it may no longer be the economic majority in the U.S."[22] *(Pew Research Center, May 2016)*

c. "The country faces serious economic challenges: **A steady hallowing of the middle class**, **for example**, **continued during Obama's presidency**, and **income inequality reached its highest point** since 1928."[23] *(Pew Research Center, 2017)*

d. "Their relative **standard of living has declined**. They feel shut out of opportunities. And their economic security feels jeopardized. Taken together, these forces are effectively **hollowing out the middle class**-the traditional engine of economic growth and social stability in Western nations ... But we can and we must take action to **mitigate the economic trends that are stoking unrest** in so many advanced economies and undermining people's basic sense of dignity." *Vice President Biden, Davos Summit speech, January 18, 2017.* Although he was Obama's vice president, and was awarded the Presidential Medal Freedom days earlier, Biden criticized Obama's economic performance during his eight-year presidency, and admitted that Obama's policies decimated and shrunk the American middle class. Biden disagreed with Obama's previous assessment of the economy and the growth of the American middle class, as Trump assumed power.

17. "We said working folks deserved a break, so within one month of me taking office, we signed into law **the biggest middle-class tax cut in history**, putting more money into your pockets." *Obama, Labor Day Detroit speech, September 5, 2011.* "John F. Kennedy seems to win the prize for biggest tax cut, at least in the last half century. By the same measure, the income tax provisions of George W. Bush tax cuts are more than twice as large as Obama's tax cut over the same three-year time span."[24] *(Glenn Kessler, The Washington Post)*

18. Keystone XL Job Creation: "most realistic estimates" … "maybe 2,000 jobs during the construction of the pipeline." *When Obama finally cancelled the Keystone XL Pipeline project in November 2015, IBD estimated that over 40,000 jobs were lost.*

19. "I've already said I'm happy to look at how we can increase pipeline production for U.S. oil, but **Keystone is for <u>Canadian oil</u> to send that down to the Gulf. It <u>bypasses the United States</u>** and is estimated to **create a little over <u>250, maybe 300 permanent jobs</u>**. We should be focusing more broadly on American infrastructure for American jobs and American producers, and that's something that we very much support." *Obama, WDAY Fargo, ND interview, February 26, 2015.* Obama also stated earlier, "Understand what this project is. It is providing the ability of Canada to pump their oil, send it through our land, down to the Gulf, where **it will be <u>sold everywhere else</u>**." *Obama, press conference, Rangoon, Burma, November 14, 2014.* There are at least three lies in these short statements. An HIS Energy report concluded in 2015 that 70% of the refined end products from Canadian oil transported in the Keystone XL pipeline would be consumed in the United States. It is estimate that 12% of the capacity for the Keystone XL pipeline would be set aside for oil produced in Montana and North Dakota. In 2014, the State Department estimated, "A total of 42,100 jobs throughout the United States would be supported by construction of the proposed project." The TransCanada CEO denied that the 42,000 jobs would be part-time or temporary by calling them "ongoing" and "enduring." After Trump asked TransCanada to re-apply for a permit to build the Keystone XL pipeline, TransCanada announced, "KXL **creates thousands of well-paying construction jobs** and would generate tens of millions of dollars in annual property taxes to counties along the route as well as **more than $3 billion to the U.S. GDP**." TransCanada owns the Keystone XL pipeline project. Obama wants to maintain U.S. energy dependence upon sources of oil in the Middle East, and will not support major projects that will create high paying permanent U.S. jobs. Obama purposely downplayed the strong economic impact the Keystone XL pipeline project would have upon the national economy.

20. "What we have to do is to make sure that folks are trained for the jobs that are coming in now because some of **those jobs** of the past **are <u>just not going to come back</u>** … When somebody says like the person you just mentioned who I'm not going to advertise for, that **he's going to bring all these jobs back. Well how exactly are you going to do that**? What are you going to do? There's uh-uh no answer to it. He just says. "I'm going to negotiate a better deal." Well how? How exactly are you going to negotiate that? **What magic wand do you have**? And usually the answer is, **he doesn't have an answer.**" *Obama, PBS broadcast, June 2016.* During Trump's first month as president, he added 300,000 jobs and persuaded many companies including Ford, GM, and Carrier to keeping manufacturing facilities in the United States.

21. "I think you'd have to say that we've managed the economy pretty well." *Obama, 2014*

    a. **"This is the worst period, I recall, since I've been in public service. There's nothing like it, including the crisis** – remember October 19th, 1987, when the Dow went down by a record amount 23 percent. That I thought was the bottom of all potential problems … I'd love to find something positive to say." *Former Federal Reserve Chairman Alan Greenspan, CNBC interview, June 24, 2016.* Greenspan is commenting on the general economic conditions in the United States after the British public voted for the Brexit and the Down was down 600 points the following morning.

    b. "Despite all the attention federal spending cuts and sequestration have received, our calculations suggest they are not the main contributors to this projected drag. **The excess fiscal drag on the horizon comes almost entirely from rising taxes**." *Federal Reserve Bank of San Francisco Report, 2013*

The Constitution

"The consciousness of good intentions disdains ambiguity ... (and) ... will not disgrace the cause of truth." *Alexander Hamilton, Federalist No. 1*

1. "I do solemnly swear (or affirm) that I will faithfully execute the Office of President of the United States, and will **to the best of my ability, preserve, protect and defend the Constitution of the United States**."

   a. Obama's deliberate refusal to protect the borders of the United States and refusal to enforce existing immigration statutes has resulted in an unprecedented flood of illegal migrants entering the country. Hans von Spakovsky of the Heritage Foundation stated, "When President Obama was inaugurated, he swore an oath to 'preserve, protect and defend the Constitution of the United States.' Article II, Section 3 directs the president to 'take Care that the Laws be faithfully executed.' Unfortunately, in what has become an all too common occurrence in this administration, Obama is once again bending that oath to the breaking point by specifically not taking care that immigration laws passed by Congress are faithfully executed ... But this is also another example of the contempt that the President has for the separation of powers embedded in our Constitution ... His assigned duty under the Constitution is to enforce the laws passed by Congress – not to act as a super legislator who implements his own laws when a particular bill he supports fails to pass in Congress. More than a flagrant abuse of the doctrine of 'prosecutorial discretion,' it amounts to lawlessness."

   b. "President Obama has once again abused his authority and unilaterally refused to enforce our current immigration laws." *Bob Goodlatte, House Judiciary Committee Chairman commenting on Obama using "prosecutorial discretion" when increasing the number of immigrants not subject to deportation by U.S. Immigration and Customs.*

   c. Obama failed to defend the Constitution when he chose to enforce blasphemy laws in the United States over the Bill of Rights' guarantee of free political speech. Obama has repeatedly demonstrated his allegiance to the Sharia over the American political and judicial system by arresting and incarcerating the man who produced a video that was falsely accused of being the root cause of the Benghazi attack, and by scrubbing all law enforcement manuals of references to Islam, jihad, Sharia law, inciting quotes in the Quran, and the term radical Islamic terrorism which would erroneously reinforce the notion of Islam as a religion of peace and falsely disassociate Islam from terrorism. Obama also scrubbed all references to Islam, Islamic terrorism, and al-Baghdadi's name from the Orlando massacre 911 tapes and from the transcripts of negotiations between law enforcement officials and the Orlando Muslim terrorist who was shouting "Allahu Akbar" as he was murdering dozens of young Americans. Obama views any association of Islam with violence as blasphemy and represents Obama's practicing of taqiyya to the Western world. Since Sharia law, which allows the murder of homosexuals and apostates, honor killings, bigamy, female genital mutilation, and child marriages among other crimes that are recognized as intolerable in the West, is incompatible with the U.S. Constitution, Obama committed an impeachable offense by incorporating Sharia law as central political directives within the Department of Justice and the DHS. Obama proved to the world that he supports Sharia law over the Bill of Rights and the cherished American right of freedom of speech when he announced at the UN in 2012 that he was against blasphemy by stating, "The future must not belong to those who slander the prophet of Islam."

d. **Acts of Treason**

　　i. In 1991, the **Muslim Brotherhood** published a document entitled "An Explanatory Memorandum on the General Strategic Goal for the Brotherhood in North America," which stated, "The process of settlement is a 'Civilization-Jihadist Process' with all the word means. The *Ikhwan* must understand that their work in America is a kind of grand Jihad in **eliminating and destroying the Western civilization from within** and 'sabotaging' its miserable house by their hands and the hands of the believers so that it is eliminated and G-d's religion is made victorious over all other religions." The Muslim Brotherhood directed this memo at North America, specifically the United States. The Muslim Brotherhood's goal is clearly to destroy the United States and replace it with a Sharia-compliant state that would eventually become part of an Islamic caliphate. Any action in support of the Muslim Brotherhood should be defined as treason. After Obama left the presidency, many Arab states including Saudi Arabia, Egypt, the UAE, Bahrain, and Jordan cut diplomatic and economic ties with Qatar based on its ties with Hamas, Iran **and the Muslim Brotherhood** and their being major supporters of Islamic terrorism. Coincidentally, Obama's closest ties in the Middle East were with Iran, the Muslim Brotherhood, Hamas, Qatar and Turkey – all countries and political entities that are major supporters of Islamic terrorism. These relationships clearly prove that Obama is allied with the terrorists, and committed treason as president of the United States.

(1)   Obama **supported the Muslim Brotherhood and Mohamed Morsi**, a leader in the Egyptian Muslim Brotherhood, over America's long-term Egyptian ally, Hosni Mubarak during the Arab Spring. **Obama ignored the advice of all the senior members of his national security team and immediately backed the Muslim Brotherhood at the start of the Egyptian revolution** as they took control of the Egyptian government in 2011 and 2012. In an interview with *Fox News's* Bret Baier in March 2016, former Secretary of Defense Robert Gates admitted, "Literally **the entire national security team recommended unanimously handling Mubarak differently** than we did." Obama went against the recommendations of his most seasoned and experienced national-al security advisors and quickly supported the Muslim Brotherhood because Obama is a radical Muslim and laying the groundwork for them to takeover Egypt was always part of his hidden agenda.

(2)   Obama's administration lied about and downplayed the threat of the Muslim Brotherhood to America and the West when James Clapper, Obama's National Intelligence Director testified before Congress that "The term '**Muslim Brotherhood**' ... is an umbrella term for a variety of movements, in the case of Egypt, **a very heterogeneous group**, <u>largely secular</u>, **which has** <u>eschewed violence</u> **and has** <u>decried al-Qaeda</u> **as a perversion of Islam** … They have pursued social ends, a **betterment of the political order in Egypt**, et cetera ... In other countries, there are also chapters or franchises of the Muslim Brotherhood, but there is **no overarching agenda, particularly in pursuit of violence**, at least internationally."

(3)   Obama **supported Hamas**, a **branch of the Muslim Brotherhood** in Gaza, in their 2014 war against Israel. He instituted a military and economic em-bargo against Israel and pressured Israel to accept all of Hamas's demands dur-ing ceasefire negotiations. Obama demanded Israel institute an unconditional unilateral ceasefire during the war when Hamas's inventory of rockets and missiles was nearly depleted. Obama accepted Hamas as a legitimate partner of the Palestinian Authority and financially supported both. Khaled Mashal, a Hamas leader stated in 2006, "We say this to the West … Death to Israel. Death to America." Ismail Haniya, Hamas's Prime Minister in 2008 said, "Oh Americans. The time has come for Allah to declare war on you." Obama is partnering with an organization that views itself at war with the United States

and supports Jewish genocide in its charter. Caroline Glick in *The Jerusalem Post* noted, "On both fronts, the Sunni regimes, led by Egypt under President Abdel Fattah al-Sisi, the Saudi regime and the United Arab Emirates, were shocked to discover that the Obama administration was siding with their enemies against them. If Israel went into the war against Hamas thinking that the Obama administration would treat it differently than it treated the Sunni regimes, it quickly discovered that it was mistaken. **From the outset of the battle between Hamas and Israel, the Obama administration supported Hamas against Israel**. America's support for Hamas was expressed at the earliest stages of the war when then-secretary of state John Kerry demanded that Israel accept an immediate cease-fire based entirely on Hamas's terms. This demand, in various forms, remained the administration's position throughout the 50-day war … If Israel had accepted any of Hamas's cease-fire terms, its agreement would have constituted a strategic defeat for Israel and a historic victory for Hamas … Obama and Kerry threatened to join the Europeans in condemning Israel at the UN. Administration officials continuously railed against IDF operations in Gaza, insinuating that Israel was committing war crimes by insisting that Israel wasn't doing enough to avoid civilian casualties … Washington placed a partial embargo on weapons shipments to Israel. Then on July 23, 2014, the administration took the almost inconceivable step of having the Federal Aviation Administration ban flights of US carriers to Ben-Gurion Airport for 36 hours. The flight ban was instituted after a Hamas missile fell a mile from the airport … Netanyahu asked Sisi for help in blunting the American campaign for Hamas. Sisi was quick to agree and brought the Saudis and the UAE into an all-but-declared operational alliance with Israel against Hamas … In a bid to undermine Egypt, Obama and Kerry colluded with Hamas's state sponsors Turkey and Qatar to push Sisi out of the cease-fire discussions … Netanyahu was never able to let the public know what was happening … Had he informed the public, the knowledge that the **US was backing Hamas** would have caused mass demoralization and panic."[25]

(4)   Obama has appointed or allowed numerous individuals who are members or who have been members of Islamic political groups that have been affiliated with the Muslim Brotherhood [CAIR, ICNA, MSA, ICNA, NAIT …] to serve within the defense, national security and executive office departments of the U.S. government or as administration advisors.

(a)   **Huma Abedin**, Deputy Chief of Staff to Secretary of State Hillary Clinton – Both her parents are affiliated with the Muslim Brotherhood, and during college she was active with the MSA, a Muslim Brotherhood front group. She also worked at a journal founded by an al-Qaeda financier.

(b) **Mohammed Elibiary**, a member of the Homeland Security Advisory Council, was one of the main speakers at a Dallas 2004 conference honoring Ayatollah Khomeini. Elibiary even maintained an official Muslim Brotherhood symbol on his DHS twitter account.

(c) **Arif Alikhan,** was Assistant Secretary of Homeland Security for Policy Development and has been described as a devout Sunni Muslim. Alikhan founded the World Islamic Organization, a front group for the Muslim Brotherhood.

(d) **Rashid Hussain**, was appointed by Obama as the U.S. Special Envoy to the Organization of Islamic Conference, which advocates building the Islamic caliphate, and the institution of blasphemy laws on a worldwide basis, two of Obama's major goals. Hussain has served as Special Envoy and Coordinator for Strategic Counterterrorism Communications and as a political appointee to the National Security Council. Hussain met with Sheik Abdullah Bin Bayyah at the White House, who is vice president of the International Union of Muslim Scholars. The group is headed by radical Egyptian cleric Yusuf Qaradawi, who is a spiritual leader of the Muslim Brotherhood. Qaradawi is barred from entering the United States, has supported al-Qaeda, and has publicly called for the killing of Americans and Jews. At a MSA event in 2004, he supported a convicted terrorist, Sami al Arian.

(e) **Salam al Marayati** is the co-founder of the Muslim Public Affairs Council (MPAC), which has been linked to the Muslim Brotherhood. The State Department chose Marayati to represent the United States at the Organization for Security and Cooperation in Europe's Annual Human Rights Conference.

(f) **Imam Mohamed Magid**, president of the ISNA, which is a Muslim Brotherhood front group, was appointed by President Obama as an advisor of the Department of Homeland Security (Countering Violence and Extremism working group, 2011). Magid is an Islamic scholar **from Sudan**, Obama's Arab ancestral homeland, and is on the FBIs Sikh, Muslim and Arab advisory board.

(g) **Eboo Patel** was appointed by Obama to his Advisory Council on Faith Based Neighborhood Partnerships. Eboo was also a member of the MSA and maintains close contact with the grandson of the founder of the Muslim Brotherhood.

(h) **Hesham Islam**, a native Egyptian and senior advisor for international affairs to former deputy Defense Secretary Gordon England, was instrumental in the firing of Stephen Coughlin, who as a Pentagon analyst, recommended the Pentagon discontinue outreach relations with ISNA. Islam was protecting the ISNA's political influence. Islam also advocated on behalf of Saudi Arabia, for the eventual release of Saudi nationals at Guantanamo. He was later fired for lying on his resume and meeting with a Syrian Muslim Brotherhood member at the Pentagon. Islam had a top-secret security clearance.

(i) **Louay Safi**, a leader at the ISNA, a Muslim Brotherhood front group, was lecturing U.S. troops at Fort Hood on Islam.

(j) **Dalia Mogahed** was assigned by Obama to serve on his Advisory Council on Faith Based and Neighborhood Partnerships and to the Department of Homeland Security's Advisory Council. She helped author a study published by the Leadership Group of U.S. Muslim Engagement that recommended opening up dialogue with Hamas and Egypt's Muslim Brotherhood before Mubarak resigned. She stated that Sharia law promotes "a more just society" and the "protection of human rights." She also supports CAIR and ISNA, saying that their association with the Muslim Brotherhood has been used as a "witch hunt" against them. She also stated that "terrorism is not Islamic by definition," paralleling Obama by denying any link between Islam and terrorism.

(k) At the 2015 White House Iftar Dinner celebrating Ramadan, **Riham Osman**, the communications coordinator of MPAC, a front group for the Muslim Brotherhood, was seated at the "President's Table." Osman has lobbied that Hamas and Hezbollah should not be labelled as terrorist groups.

(l) **Mehdi Alhassani**, who is the special assistant to the Office of the Chief of Staff of the National Security Office, was a recipient of an email from Ben Rhodes he sent three days after the Benghazi attacks, where Rhodes wanted to "underscore that these protests are rooted in an Internet video, and not a broader failure of policy." Alhassani was president of the MSA at George Washington University. Funding for the MSA was originally provided by the Muslim World League, which has been implicated in funding al-Qaeda operations. The MSA is a branch of the Muslim Brotherhood.

(m) **Chaplains associated with the ISNA**, a Muslim Brotherhood front group, have been hired by the military.

(n) **A professor at the U.S. Naval Academy** has been found to be instructing on behalf of a Muslim Brotherhood front group, the International Institute of Islamic Thought (IIIT), where Youssef Qaradawi is a trustee. Qaradawi is a spiritual guide for the Muslim Brotherhood and issued a fatwa in 2004 authorizing attacks of U.S. troops in Afghanistan.

(o) Security compromise at various U.S. intelligence agencies have been perpetrated by Arabic and Muslim employees who are translators or linguists. **The administration has used Muslim Brotherhood front organizations to help recruit translators** instead of employing Sephardic Jews, Coptic Christians, or Yazidis who are fluent in Arabic.

(p) The UN, the OIC, the **Muslim Brotherhood**, and other Middle Eastern Islamist organizations are pre-screening Muslim Syrian refugees for admission to the United States. This will facilitate Islamic terrorists posing as refugees to settle across the United States and set up terrorist sleeper cells.

(q) "On Dec. 14, **the White House invited CAIR officials** *[for Muslim Brotherhood input]* and other representatives tied to Brotherhood entities to join senior Obama advisor **Valerie Jarrett** and deputy national security advisor **Ben Rhodes** at a meeting to discuss anti-Muslim discrimination. The meeting was especially disturbing given that the FBI won't meet with CAIR due to its relationship with Hamas. Hundreds of newly declassified FBI documents provide overwhelming evidence of "CAIR's ties to the MB (Muslim Brotherhood) and its Palestinian affiliate Hamas." The Brotherhood infiltration has only deepened in the wake of the San Bernardino terrorist attacks, the worst on U.S. soil since 9-11." At the same time that Obama embraced the Muslim Brotherhood and its front groups to help guide U.S. policies, Great Britain designated the Muslim Brotherhood and its affiliates as terrorist organizations. A House of Common investigation concluded that, "aspects of Muslim Brotherhood ideology and tactics, in this country and overseas, are contrary to our values and have been contrary to our national interests and our national security ... [The Muslim Brotherhood and its affiliates] have deliberately incited violence." The report also concluded that the Muslim Brotherhood had significant ties with Hamas and other various Islamic terrorist groups … Obama supported the Muslim Brotherhood's ability to function as a viable political entity in Great Britain by stating "[The] **political repression** of non-violent Islamist groups *[also with Guantanamo per Obama]* has historically contributed to the radicalization of the minority of their members who would consider violence … The de-legitimization of non-violent political groups does not promote stability, and instead advances the very outcomes that such measures are intended to prevent."[26] *(IBD editorial)*

(r)   Obama appointed a former FBI agent, **Gamal Abdel-Hafiz**, as an advisor to the DHS program on "Countering Violent Extremism." Hafiz was born in Cairo and immigrated to the United States in 1990, after growing up in Egypt. As an FBI agent Hafiz refused to legally wiretap a Muslim suspect and stated, "a Muslim doesn't record another Muslim," interfered with ongoing terror investigations, was fired (which was reversed) from the FBI for inappropriate behavior, insurance fraud, and the mismanagement of 9-11 files, and has advocated for a comprehensive national gun registry. Obama is appointing a Middle Eastern Muslim, (although not a documented member of the Muslim Brotherhood), who placed the interests of potential Muslim terrorists above the well-being of the United States, as a major contributor to the national security apparatus of the United States.

(s)   Obama ordered that **counterterrorism materials be scrubbed of references to Islam when discussing terrorism.** Countering Islamic terrorism becomes **Countering Violent Extremism**. Obama reinforced this dogma at the White House Countering Violent Extremism Summit in February 2015, which was attended by many individuals representing organizations allied with the Muslim Brotherhood.

(t)   In mid-December 2015, **Valerie Jarrett met with Hassan Shibly, the chief executive director of the Florida chapter of CAIR** at the White House, as well as other members of the American Muslim community, to discuss combatting religious discrimination. CAIR is a front group for the Muslim Brotherhood and Hamas, and has been declared a terrorist organization by the United Arab Emirates. Shibly is helping the family of a suspect in the Boston marathon bombing sue the FBI. The suspect, Ibragim Todashev, was killed by the FBI when he attacked agents who were seeking to question him. CAIR was originally founded by Hamas operatives.

(u)   Secret Service White House visitor records have shown that **Esam Omeish** has met with Obama or White House officials at least nine times starting in 2011. Omeish helped hire Anwar Awlaki, a cleric who later became an al-Qaeda leader, at the Dar al-Hijrah *[immigration jihad]* Islamic Center. Omeish also led the Muslim American Society and was vice president of a mosque which were both later shown to be affiliated with the Muslim Brotherhood according to the FBI. Obama used Omeish as a trusted advisor for his Libyan policies, which resulted in the chaotic collapse of Libya along with the empowerment of al-Qaeda and ISIS in Libya. Obama later called Libya a "shit show"[27] after he deposed Gaddafi and supported the Islamist rebels that murdered him.

ii. Despite Iran's leadership regularly shouting "Death to America" and declaring the United States a real enemy, Obama approved the JCPOA (Iranian nuclear agreement), allowing **Iran** to obtain significant sanctions relief and gain access to over $150 billion in funds as part of the final agreement. This is the very definition of "**aid and comfort**." Caroline Glick, former managing editor of *The Jerusalem Post* observed the JCPOA is "a heinous act of aggression by the United States against its allies in the Middle East and against its own national security … Iran has pledged to destroy the United States, it's developing military bases throughout Central and South America for that explicit purpose, and Obama just approved a deal that all but guarantees that Iran will acquire nuclear weapons."[28] Obama also allowed Iran to continue to develop their ballistic missile program and even downplayed an illegal test fire of a new missile prototype in October 2015. In 2016, Obama advised Iran to keep their illegal missile tests 'under the radar.' Iran does not pose just a hypothetical threat. Iran was allied with al-Qaeda before the 9-11 attacks, they supplied IEDs to Iraqi insurgents who killed or maimed hundreds of U.S. serviceman fighting in Iraq, and they were partners with Hezbollah when they blew up the Marine barracks in Beirut in 1983. Did Obama commit nuclear treason by allowing Iran to become a nuclear power where they would eventually be able to build a nuclear arsenal? With Iran, Obama changed years if not decades of U.S. policy from prevention, to containment and enablement. These insights are not the result of misguided naïve policy implementation, but of a president who has intentionally placed his loyalty with the ayatollahs and has reneged on his expectations to advance America's best interests. Other issues that could be interpreted as Obama working against U.S. interests with respect to Iran include:

(1) Obama misled the Senate and the House of Representatives by not revealing the details of the side deals attached to the JCPOA that specifically defined the guidelines and criteria for future Iranian inspections to be carried out by the IAEA. This calculated and pre-planned deception benefitted Iran, an enemy of the United States, while compromised U.S. national security and that of our allies. Obama violated the Iran Nuclear Agreement Review Act of 2015, which

required him to reveal all side agreements. Obama stonewalled Congress to protect Iranian interests. Despite Iran's long history of cheating on diplomatic agreements, Obama allowed Iran to inspect its own sites, which constitutes a U.S. national security fraud.

(2) Obama wrote letters to at least the French, British, Chinese and German governments assuring them they would not be penalized for doing business with Iran if Congress continued or re-imposed sanctions. Obama supported actions strengthening the Iranian economy and military.

(3) Obama inserted a clause in the JCPOA where the United States would help secure and defend Iran's nuclear installations from cyberattacks or sabotage. Obama has, therefore, entered a formal military alliance with Iran, which seeks the destruction of America. The primary purpose of this alliance between Iran, the United States and the P5 +1 is to intimidate and threaten Israel.

(4) Obama retreated from almost all the American negotiating endpoints with Iran while Iran achieved all their negotiating endpoints with the JCPOA. Obama backed off from stating that containment was not U.S. policy, requiring anytime - anywhere inspections with all Iranian facilities, prohibiting Iranian uranium enrichment, dismantling the Fodrow facility, implementing snap back sanctions, assuring Iran would never be able to produce a nuclear weapon, and requiring a thorough investigation and complete transparency of the military dimensions of Iran's previous nuclear research.

(5) By allowing Iran to become a nuclear threshold state, Obama is permitting Iran to become more powerful and assert its hegemony over the Middle East. Iran is now in a better position to threaten U.S. allies, including Saudi Arabia, Kuwait, the UAE, Bahrain, Israel and Jordan. Obama is also putting a significant percentage of the crude oil supply to Europe, Japan and the United States at increased risk. Obama is forcing many other Middle East states to pursue nuclear weapons acquisition or development to counter the Iranian nuclear program, which puts the Middle East and the West at a much higher risk of confrontation or nuclear strikes.

(6) While Obama slashed funding and development for America's ABM systems, Obama allowed Iran to develop their intercontinental ballistic missile systems by ignoring their missile tests and allowing Iran to become significantly economically stronger so their economy can support massive advanced ballistic missile development with nuclear warhead delivery systems. These weapons will be aimed at the United States.

(7) Obama refused to bomb and destroy an advanced U.S. drone with classified stealth technology that was pirated by Iran and which landed safely at an Iranian airbase.

(8) In 2016, Obama oversaw the surrender of ten U.S. sailors to the IRGC, who then had access to advanced proprietary U.S. military technology on the high-tech, high-speed assault boats and also had access to the laptops and cell phones of all the captured Navy personnel.

(9) Obama removed Iran and its proxies from the terror section of the 2015 "Worldwide Threat Assessment of the U.S. Intelligence Community." One year later, an IRGC commander announced that, "the whole world should know that the IRGC will be in the U.S. and Europe very soon," by embedding their terrorist forces in America to continue their war against the United States. After Obama removed Iran from the Worldwide Threat Assessment, he funded their terrorist activities against America by giving them $1.7 billion in untraceable cash for four American hostages. Obama funded Iranian directed terrorism against America, and has thus committed treason.

(10) The $1.7 billion Obama gave to the Iranians in exchange for four American hostages released in January 2016 was reported to all go directly to the IRGC, the number one sponsor of terrorism in the world and an organization that has helped kill hundreds if not thousands of American troops in the Middle East. Eli Lake reported in *Bloomberg View* on June 9, 2016, "Saeed Ghasseminejad, an associate fellow at the Foundation for Defense of Democracies, spotted the budget item. He told me the development was widely reported in Iran by numerous sources including the state-funded news services. 'Article 22 of the budget for 2017 says the Central Bank is required to give the money from the legal settlement of Iran's pre- and post-revolutionary arms sales of up to $1.7 billion to the defense budget,' he said." This transfer of funds to the IRGC was also confirmed by Omri Ceren, a managing director at The Israeli Project (TIP).

(a) Obama was a knowing major funder of Iran's intercontinental ballistic missile development program, whose missiles were to be used against the United States. After "moderate" Rouhani won his re-election for the presidency in Iran in May 2017, he stated, "We need missiles and the enemy should know that we make everything we need and we don't pay an iota of attention to your words." The ransom, which went directly to the IRGC, is overseeing the development of Iran's third underground ballistic missile factory. The IRGC leader, General Amir Ali Hajizadeh commented, "We will increase our missile power. **Our enemies, the United States** and the Zionist regime, are naturally upset and get angry at our missile production, tests and underground missile facilities." With sanctions relief, asset transfers, and ransom payments, Obama funded the development and production of Iran's intercontinental ballistic missiles, which are going to be targeting the United States. Obama committed treason, and allied himself with powers that want to destroy America.

(11) Obama lied to the American public, the Israelis, and the world for years by continually stating that "all options were on the table." In 2015, he declared, "A military solution will not fix it." He used more than six years of Iranian negotiations as a stalling technique to give the Iranians enough time to develop their uranium enrichment facilities and nuclear warhead technology to the point of no return. Obama used the negotiations to empower and aid Iran to the detriment of the security interests of the United States.

(12) Amir Hossein Motaghi, a defector from the Iranian nuclear negotiating delegation, commented on the U.S. role concerning the talks with Iran by warning "The U.S. negotiating team are mainly there to speak on Iran's behalf with other members of the 5 + 1 countries and convince them of a deal."

(13) In the spring of 2016, Obama advised Iran to keep a low profile while conducting their controversial ballistic missile tests that may be capable of delivering nuclear weapons, and to keep related activities clandestine.

(14) Obama blocked legislation that would allow Iran to become legally liable for Hezbollah's bombing in Beirut, Lebanon that killed 241 Marines.

(15) Obama reestablished diplomatic relations with Cuba, and created conditions that would help their economy without obtaining any reciprocal gestures. By strengthening Cuba, Obama helped Iran expand its presence in Central and South America, since Cuba is allied with Iran.

(16) A secret side deal discovered by the *Associated Press* in July 2016, revealed that Obama allowed Iran to accelerate its uranium enrichment program up to five years before the conclusion of the JCPOA. Obama lied to Congress and the American public regarding the limits of Iran's uranium enrichment capabilities as dictated by the JCPOA.

(17) With ten days remaining in his presidency, Obama approved a transfer of nearly 130 tons of natural uranium to Iran, which is enough uranium needed to manufacture at least ten nuclear weapons. "Global powers, including the

United States, have reached an agreement to provide Iran with nearly 130 tons of uranium – which experts believe would be enough to make 10 nuclear bombs. Two diplomats involved with the deal told the *Associated Press* that the so-called P5+1 powers agreed to the transfer of Russian natural uranium in exchange for 44 tons of "heavy water" nuclear runoff, which Iran has already sent to Russia after it created more than was allowed under last year's nuclear deal. That shipment to Russia involved the second time that Iran exceeded its heavy water limit; it shipped excess heavy water to Oman last year. David Albright and Andrea Stricker of the Institute for Science and International Security criticized Iran's excess heavy water deals in a research paper (.pdf) published last month, pointing out that instead of insisting that Iran abide by the terms of the deal, "the United States tolerated and minimized Iran's violations and sought to legitimize its international standing as a commercial supplier of heavy water." Albright told the *AP* that "depending on the efficiency of the enrichment process and the design of the nuclear weapon," Iran could create more than 10 atomic bombs with the uranium it will receive."[29] *(TheTower. org, January 9, 2017)*

(18) Senior Obama officials met with former Iranian diplomats and pro-Iranian lobbyists with close ties to the Iranian government over 30 times during the JCPOA negotiations. These Iranian protagonists worked with Obama and his administration to help craft the talking points and create the echo chamber which lead to the adoption of the JCPOA by the U.S. government. Obama allied himself with pro-Iranian individuals who worked with the administration to advance an agreement in the best interests of Iran, and not the United States, which is treason.

(19) Obama withheld components of the nuclear deal with Iran from Congress and the American public when he "downplayed the release of Iranian prisoners [spies whom he presented as civilians], shut down existing Department of Justice investigation into [Iranian] individuals accused of funneling [military] technology and hardware to Iran, and dropped charges and arrest warrants against more than a dozen dangerous fugitives [associated with the Iranian military and their clandestine nuclear program] … One of them, Seyed Abolfazl Shahab Jamili, 'had been charged with being part of a conspiracy that from 2005 to 2012 procured thousands of parts with **nuclear applications for Iran** via China.' *(Politico, Josh Meyer)*" *(Republican Jewish Coalition press release, April 24, 2017) Politico* revealed how Obama misled the American

people by suppressing the details of the Iranian agents he released from U.S. custody as part of the overall JCPOA implementation. "Pres. Barack Obama lied about the **seven Iranians** who were released in exchange for five American political prisoners held by Iran, saying they were "civilians" caught up in sanctions-related offenses. Some of them were **involved in procuring technology for Iran's military development**." *(RJC press release, April 27, 2017)*

(20)   Iran is using the billions in dollars they received from the JCPOA to modernize their armed forces and to create significant offensive "forward moving" capabilities. Since the JCPOA was ratified in 2015, the Iranian defense budget has increased 145%, and much of these funds were used to support terrorism.[30] Obama is directly responsible for modernizing and funding the largest state supporter of terrorism in the world, which is also an enemy of the United States.

iii.   **Al-Qaeda** attacked Washington D.C. and New York City on 9-11-2001, and murdered over 3,000 American citizens that day. Al-Qaeda and all their partners, allies and associates are enemies of the United States of America. Any effort by any American citizen, including the president of the United States, to give aid and comfort to al-Qaeda or its associates, is treason.

(1)   Released emails published by *Wikileaks* confirmed that Obama and Clinton committed treason as president and secretary of state. **Jake Sullivan, a State Department policy advisor, sent an email to Hillary Clinton on February 12, 2012, stating, "AQ is on our side in Syria ... Things have basically turned out as expected**." Obama and Clinton knowingly allied with AQ in early 2012, and later that year, AQ attacked the Benghazi consulate and killed four Americans. Obama and Clinton did not send military help to the counter the attack since they were protecting the identify of their allies, al-Qaeda operatives, who were killing Americans. If this information was revealed immediately after the attack, Obama surely would have been impeached. Obama refused to send military relief, so all the al-Qaeda operatives who murdered four Americans and raped the ambassador, would be able to escape from the scene without the risk of death or being apprehended. Information obtained from any interrogation of captured al-Qaeda operatives may have destroyed Obama's presidency.

(2)   Obama ignored foreign intelligence warnings that by allying himself with Qatar, he was **strengthening U.S. ties with the Muslim Brotherhood and al-Qaeda**. *Breitbart* reported, "According to the source, a number of Arab

countries, including Jordan and Egypt, raised the issue of suspect **connections between Qatar and the Nusra Front, the Syrian branch of al-Qaeda**, and other jihadist organizations many times, 'but President Obama chose to ignore the warnings of the Arab countries … The **Obama** administration was prisoner to the perception that **the Muslim Brotherhood was a significant component in American interests** and Qatar is the political and regional patron of the Muslim Brotherhood, so the administration refused to confront the facts presented to it, especially with the media and economic support provided by Qatar and various Qatari funds to groups like the Nusra Front and others.'[31] Obama allied himself with Qatar over the other Gulf States and Sunni Middle East states because Obama was a big supporter of the Muslim Brotherhood and al-Qaeda.

(3)   Morsi and the Muslim Brotherhood had an alliance with al-Qaeda when they took control of the Egyptian government. Much of the original leadership of al-Qaeda originated from the Muslim Brotherhood. Obama has been a major supporter of Morsi and the Muslim Brotherhood.

(4)   Obama lied and blamed the Benghazi attack on a video, thus shielded al-Qaeda from scrutiny regarding their role with the death of four Americans, including the ambassador to Libya.

(5)   Al-Qaeda supported the overthrow of Mubarak in Egypt, and so did Obama.

(6)   Al-Qaeda supported the overthrow of Gaddafi in Libya, and so did Obama.

(7)   Al-Qaeda supported the overthrow of Assad in Syria, and so did Obama.

(8)   Obama made a "willful decision" (quote former DIA director General Michael Flynn) to support al-Qaeda elements in his attempt to overthrow President Assad of Syria. In 2012, Obama supported and helped arm the al-Nusra Front in their war against Assad. Al-Nusra was later determined to be part of al-Qaeda and subsequently merged with ISIS. Is Obama violating the National Defense Authorization Act of 2012, which makes providing material assistance to al-Qaeda a crime?

(9)   A memo received by Secretary of State Clinton in 2012 documented Obama's support (funding and arming) for al-Qaeda in Iraq (AQI), which later became ISIS. Obama also sought to establish safe havens in Iraq and Syria for these Islamic terrorists, who were attempting to depose Assad and take over Syria, which was Obama's intent.

(10) Obama supported and armed rebels in Libya who were affiliated with al-Qaeda in the war against Gaddafi. Obama bought oil from Libyan rebels, many of whom were from al-Qaeda, and allowed al-Qaeda rebels in Libya

to raid Gaddafi's arsenals during the overthrow of his regime. Al-Qaeda and ISIS subsequently obtained advanced military equipment including surface-to-air-missiles capable of shooting down civilian airliners.

(11) Al-Qaeda leader Zawahiri joined ISIS, the Muslim Brotherhood and Erdogan in their support for a future Islamic caliphate. Obama has been a strong and loyal ally to Erdogan and the Muslim Brotherhood and most likely supported the establishment of an Islamic caliphate.

(12) In 2011, the Congressional Anti-Terrorism Caucus revealed Iran had a strong working relationship with al-Qaeda leaders. By insisting on sanctions relief for Iran totaling over $150 billion dollars to Iran, Obama is enabling al-Qaeda to have access to almost unlimited funding and possibly nuclear weapons.

(13) In 2011, a federal judge found Iran, along with al-Qaeda and the Taliban were liable for the 9-11 terrorist attacks. Even though the same regime controls the Iranian policies with no change in their jihadi nature, Obama praised and comforted Iran by saying, "They've got a chance to get right with the world … Because if they do, there's incredible talent and resources and sophistication inside of Iran and it would be a very successful regional power that was also abiding by international norms and international rules - and that would be good for everybody." Obama has, by initiating sanctions relief, aided a country and its political leadership that was a willing accomplice with the 9-11 attacks and participated in an act of war against the United States.

(14) The Obama administration has awarded military contracts to al-Qaeda affiliates in Afghanistan.

(15) Obama has released many Guantanamo Bay prisoners who have had operational ties to al-Qaeda, including the five Taliban commanders who were exchanged for Private Bergdahl. American forces were still fighting the Taliban at the time of the release. Thus, Obama was aiding and abetting an enemy in their war against the United States. Obama's actions, which replenished the leadership ranks of the Taliban and al-Qaeda in Afghanistan, could have been significant factors in the delay of the withdrawal of American forces from Afghanistan during the fall of 2015 after significant military gains by the Taliban in many provinces. Did Obama purposely use the swap as cover for releasing key military Islamic radical leaders who could help consolidate a future Islamic caliphate in their region of influence? Besides committing treason, Obama may have broken another federal law by not giving Congress thirty days of advance notice for the release of these Guantanamo Bay prisoners. Obama may have violated the National Defense Authorization Act, which

makes it a felony to offer or provide assistance to terrorist organizations, including the Taliban. The Taliban commander, Mullah Omar, declared the prisoner swap a "great victory." This swap would undoubtedly lead to the needless deaths of many more American and allied soldiers in the Afghanistan military theater, which was later confirmed by a Defense Department official testifying before Congress.

(16)   Obama released Mashur al Sabri from Guantanamo Bay in 2016. Sabri was a Yemeni al-Qaeda operative who was directly involved in the planning and implementation of the bombing of the *USS Cole* which killed 17 American sailors. Even though Sabri had American blood on his hands, Obama gave him his freedom.

(17)   In 2012, under Obama's direction, the National Intelligence Estimate issued a preliminary report that concluded al-Qaeda was no longer threatening the United States. In 2011, Obama ordered government officials to minimize references to al-Qaeda. Obama altered intelligence assessments in many defense and intelligence departments in order to aid al-Qaeda.

(18)   Obama used his catch and release program to free al-Qaeda operatives who were apprehended in war zones, knowing there was at least a 30% recidivism rate.

(19)   Obama refused to acknowledge jihad as a motivational factor in the Fort Hood massacre by calling the attack "workplace violence," even though Major Hasan was in direct contact with Anwar al-Awlaki, an al-Qaeda leader. The attack on Fort Hood was an act of war by Islamic radicals on the United States, and Obama treated it as a random act of violence with no link to Islam, thus shielding the motives of those who want to destroy America.

(20)   Obama cancelled three different operations to apprehend or kill Osama bin Laden before military and intelligence officials launched the final operation without Obama's knowledge.

(21)   Obama immediately announced the killing of Osama bin Laden and the subsequent acquisition of hard intelligence, thereby giving all al-Qaeda operatives worldwide the opportunity escape future possible military action by the United States.

(22)   Obama repeatedly downplayed al-Qaeda operational capabilities by claiming that they were "on the run," which was not true.

(23)   Obama purposely adjusted intelligence assessments against ISIS so that the American public would be misled into believing that ISIS' operational capabilities were damaged much more than they were by American attacks. ISIS was formed from al-Qaeda and is allied with al-Qaeda.

(24) Obama protected ISIS with his cumbersome rules of engagement and by admitting twice he had no strategy to defeat them. When Putin entered the fight against ISIS, his airstrikes decimated ISIS positions in less than one week, proving Obama had no intention of hurting ISIS.

(25) Obama deliberately protected ISIS by defending Turkey's downing of a Russian bomber over Syria while it was bombing ISIS positions and its allies. Obama also protected ISIS when he lied saying that Turkey was a "strong partner" in the war against ISIS, when in reality Turkey has been a major ally, supporter and funder of ISIS since its inception. German intelligence deduced that Turkey was an Islamist state allied with the Muslim Brotherhood, Hamas, al-Qaeda, and ISIS.

(26) Obama has referred to the Taliban as America's "peace partners," even though they sheltered al-Qaeda while they planned and perpetrated the 9-11 terrorist attacks against the United States, and re-allied themselves with al-Qaeda during Obama's presidency. While Obama pursued the Taliban as "peace partners" in 2012, Taliban officials refused to renounce their ties with al-Qaeda.

(27) On June 13, 2013, the White House hosted secret talks with Sheik Abdullah bin Bayyah, a top aide of Yusuf al-Qaradawi, the spiritual leader of the Muslim Brotherhood, which is allied with al-Qaeda. Al-Qaradawi has supported suicide bombings and issued fatwas calling for the death of American soldiers in the Middle East.

(28) Obama invited Labib al Nahhas, the foreign affairs director of Ahrar al-Sham, an al-Qaeda affiliate in Syria, for strategy discussions in Washington in December 2015.

(29) Obama gave $1.7 billion cash to Iran in January 20116 in exchange for four American hostages despite knowing that al-Qaeda would receive some of these funds since al-Qaeda is a documented ally with Iran.

iv. Obama protected **<u>Saudi Arabia</u>** and its role in assisting al-Qaeda with its 9-11 attacks against the New York and Washington D.C. in 2011 by opposing the release of 28 pages of the 9-11 report which detailed Saudi Arabian involvement in the 9-11 terrorist jihadi attacks. Obama also ordered the House Intelligence document be altered (redacted) over 150 times so that Saudi Arabian complicity would be removed from the official record.

v. Obama hired pro-ISIS individuals for DHS positions. For example, former Obama DHS appointee Mohamed Elibiary, tweeted his support for massacre of Coptic Christians by ISIS terrorists in early 2017, by declaring "Subhanallah what goes around comes around." The translation for "Subhanallah" from Arabic is "Glory to Allah."

vi. Obama's **rules of engagement** and **catch and release programs** in Afghanistan and Iraq protected and supported Islamic terrorist forces, while putting U.S. troops at a major strategic disadvantage and leading to increased casualties among American soldiers. Over 75% of the military deaths in Afghanistan occurred under Obama's leadership. Obama applied his "catch and release" strategy to many political and military arenas including the Taliban in Afghanistan, al-Qaeda operatives in Iraq, al-Qaeda and Taliban detainees at Guantanamo Bay, Iranian spies in U.S. custody, and illegal aliens crossing the U.S.-Mexican border who were apprehended in the southern United States.

vii. Obama revealed his military strategy to the Taliban and told them his planned exit dates from Afghanistan without achieving a military victory.

viii. Obama's **massive budget cuts** to the U.S. defense establishment has rendered America unable to defend herself and her allies adequately over his two presidential terms in any future major military conflict in one or multiple fronts.

ix. Obama **kept key cabinet officials in the dark** concerning the endpoint and motives of many of his critical foreign policy initiatives. These events prove that Obama's major policy initiatives were decided without the input of his cabinet and top advisors, and major decisions were made either before formal negotiations or decision-making mechanisms were in play, or foreign input from powers who were enemies of America from the Middle East were controlling Obama's policy directives and endpoints.

(1) John Kerry, the Secretary of State and main negotiator for the United States with his Iranian counterparts regarding the JCPOA, admitted to Congress that he never saw the secret side deals.

(2) Valerie Jarrett held secret talks with the Iranians that most likely outlined the parameters of the final JCPOA years before the 2015 formal end of negotiations, without the knowledge of the American negotiating team.

(3) Obama never informed Secretary of Defense Robert Gates of his actual anticipated defense budget cut targets, which were very significant and compromised the security of the United States.

(4) Obama never informed Leon Panetta, the director of the CIA and later the secretary of defense, of letters Obama sent to Ayatollah Khamenei, that outlined America was willing to accept all of Iran's negotiating targets regarding the future JCPOA, while Obama deceived his cabinet and the American people making them believe he was negotiating in good faith and attempting to advance American interests.

(5)   Panetta admitted that he was misled by Obama into believing that a military strike against Iranian nuclear installations was always on the table. After leaving office, Panetta realized that Obama never had any intentions to launch a military strike against Iran, and that U.S. foreign policy actually was formulated to prevent Israel from launching air strikes against Iran.

(6)   After Obama had initial meetings regarding al-Qaeda's attack at Benghazi early in the evening on September 11, 2012, Obama then had a private meeting with Valerie Jarrett where they decided the best strategy to protect Obama's interests would be to remain unreachable for the remainder of the evening, and let the Islamist forces kill the occupants of the consulate and destroy evidence at the compound that may have linked Obama to supplying weapons to radical Islamic factions (al-Qaeda and ISIS) in Syria. Obama left the Secretary of State and the Secretary of Defense clueless regarding the United States response to this prolonged eight-hour terrorist attack.

x.   Obama had U.S. government officials **reading Miranda rights to captured and incarcerated Muslim terrorists** to protect their terror networks and associates. Obama immediately intervened during the interrogation of Umar Farouk Abdulmutallab, a Nigerian national, who tried to blow up flight A330 on Christmas day 2010. He had federal officials read the prisoner his Miranda rights, giving him the legal right to stop informing government national security officials of future terrorist attacks against U.S. targets. In 2009, Obama ordered the FBI to read Miranda rights to high value suspected terrorist detainees in Afghanistan, which blocked U.S. officials from obtaining needed intelligence needed to protect U.S. soldiers in Afghanistan. Mike Rogers, the senior Republican on the House Intelligence Committee and former special FBI agent commented, "The administration has decided to change the focus to law enforcement. Here's the problem. **You have foreign fighters who are targeting U.S. troops today – foreign fighters who go to another country to kill Americans. We capture them … and they're reading them their rights – Mirandizing these foreign fighters**." Obama also read Miranda rights to the Boston bomber, and used the guise of civil rights protection as a reason to halt investigations into suspected domestic foreign national terrorists.

xi.   As commander in chief of the armed forces of the United States of America, Obama has **never pursued a military victory over the enemies of the United States during wartime**. Obama's basic strategy was to declare a verbal victory, leave and let the Islamic radicals take control. Obama put hundreds of thousands of Americans at risk and wasted hundreds of billions, if not trillions, of dollars in resources to pursue strategies that would not ultimately advance American interests on the ground. Why didn't Obama pursue victory against these multiple radical Islamic forces? Because Obama is a radical Muslim, and he was protecting the interests of Islamic terrorists.

(1)   Obama never sought to retain the victory in Iraq that was handed to him by President Bush. Obama withdrew U.S. forces and created a vacuum that allowed Islamic terrorist interests to reassert themselves, eventually allowing Iran to dominate Iraq.

(2)   Obama admitted he did not see "victory" as a goal with his confrontation with the Taliban. Even though Obama called the war in Afghanistan a war of necessity and fundamental to the defense of our people, Obama never made a concerted effort to achieve a military victory.

(3)   Obama admitted twice he did not have a strategy to defeat ISIS.

(4)   Obama's overall approach to ISIS was to admit that he could not win the war by just killing them. Instead he wanted to focus on bringing jobs programs to the troubled areas in the Middle East.

(5)   The Iranians always knew Obama would never bomb their nuclear facilities. Obama admitted as much during a 2015 Israeli TV interview. Consequently, the Iranians always had an unyielding negotiating position.

(6)   Even though al-Qaeda was expanding in Iraq, Syria and Libya, DHS chief Jeh Johnson announced in 2013 that "our efforts should no longer be considered an armed conflict against al-Qaeda and its affiliates."

(7)   Russian military intervention in Syria proved Obama was protecting ISIS, when Russian forces devastated ISIS forces on the ground in Syria in less than one week of air strikes, after years of Obama's ineffectual military strategy.

xii.   Obama consistently **altered intelligence assessments** to benefit radical Islam.

(1)   CIA talking points were changed to take focus off al-Qaeda's role in the Benghazi attack. CIA director General Petraeus' acknowledgement that he knew immediately Benghazi was a terrorist attack was absent from the final intelligence assessment.

(2)   Intelligence evaluations were altered to show the American public that Obama's strategy against ISIS appeared more effective than it actually was.

(3)   Obama had military leadership testify that American allies fighting against the Taliban were doing well, when, in reality, they were suffering significant losses on the Afghan battlefield.

xiii.   Obama did not protect the interests of Americans living or travelling abroad in the Middle East.

(1)   Obama requested $1.8 billion dollars in Egyptian aid for the Muslim Brotherhood government in early 2012, without any demands for the release of Americans held by the Egyptian government for allegedly violating foreign funding laws.

(2)   Obama secured a nuclear agreement with Iran in 2015, without demanding as a precondition the release of four Americans held in Iranian jails as political prisoners. The prisoners were later released only after Obama paid Iran $1.7 billion. Obama left the whereabouts of a "missing" American Jew unaccounted for in Iran despite signing the JCPOA and transferring the astronomical fee for the four Americans' freedom.

(3)   Obama never reprimanded or threatened the Palestinian Authority or Hamas for supporting the kidnapping and / or murdering of American Jews living in the West Bank or in Israel who have dual citizenship.

(4)   Obama never changed his ineffectual strategy against ISIS, despite the beheading of James Foley by an ISIS insurgent and the murder and rape of Kayla Mueller by the leader of ISIS. Obama repeatedly delayed hostage rescue attempts for Foley. Obama allowed a witness and accomplice to the murder and rape of Mueller to be transferred to the custody of the Kurds.

(5)   Obama **ignored the knifing murder of a former Army officer, Taylor Force**, which was incited by the Palestinian leadership. Force was visiting Israel on vacation in 2016. The Palestinian Authority paid the family of this terrorist a yearly stipend for the murder of this American, where some of the funds supporting this PA policy originated from U.S. aid, which was approved by Obama. Thus, Obama is knowingly funding and supporting the murder of multiple Jewish and non-Jewish American citizens in the Israel and the West Bank.

xiv.   With ISIS admitting that over 4,000 of their fighters are already embedded in Europe, and with Obama knowing that there is a guaranteed percentage of ISIS terrorists embedded in the Middle Eastern refugees / migrants flooding into Europe and the United States, Obama is **guaranteeing that radical Islamic forces will have sufficient manpower to start an insurrection against the Western states, NATO and American allies** by continuing to advance and accelerate the resettlement of Muslim refugees / migrants in America and Europe. Obama is directly supporting a policy that will undermine the security interests of the United States, Europe and NATO.

(1)   On November 15, 2015, immediately after the Paris terrorist attacks, Obama announced at the G20 Summit that he will continue to import tens of

thousands of Syrian Muslim refugees into America despite knowing that 1-2% of these migrants are ISIS fighters and up to 25% of them support ISIS. The head of the FBI has stated that it is impossible to adequately vet these individuals. Obama is embedding Islamic terrorists into the United States so that they can continue their jihad against American infidels. Obama has been clandestinely planting Syrian Muslim refugees into states such as Louisiana without informing state and local governments, thereby ignoring public concerns about the safety of U.S. citizens. Several governors have demanded a halt of the resettlement process in their states. Governor Jindal of Louisiana wrote to Obama saying, "It is irresponsible and severely disconcerting to place individuals, who may have ties to ISIS, in a state without the state's knowledge or involvement … As governor of Louisiana, I demand information." Obama is creating Islamic terrorist sleeper cells in the United States.

(2)   "Despite a clear nexus between immigration and terrorism, and warnings from top officials in his own Administration about their inability to properly vet refugees, President Obama **remains in denial** [*Obama is purposely advancing jihad by implanting ISIS sleeper cells and transferring large groups of foreign Muslims into America, many of whom support or will support ISIS and the institution of Sharia law.*] about the dangers that his policies pose to the United States … the Obama Administration leads the United States down a dangerous path [*It is Obama's intent.*] – **admitting as many refugees as possible from areas of the world where terrorists roam freely**, and <u>**granting a temporary amnesty to Syrians living in the United States illegally**</u>. And contrary to the assertions made by many, **the potential for future terror activity is real** … This radical increase places the safety and security of the American people at risk, there will surely be consequences … these cases [*There are at least 40 proven cases since 9-11 of Muslim refugees having proven links with terrorism.*] refute the false assertion that those admitted to the United States as refugees never engage in terrorism … **he rejects his sacred oath** [*Obama committed taqiyya when he took the oath of office as he was sworn in as president. Obama advances jihad and ignores American security needs. Rejecting his sacred oath is grounds for impeachment.*] for what he perceives as **political gain** [*more Democratic voters, more jihadists*] … there is no way to properly vet these refugees … There is no doubt that this continuous, dramatic increase in refugees from areas of the world where terrorists roam freely **will endanger this nation**. [*In 2016 Obama has increased the number of Muslim Syrian refugees entering America by a factor of five (over 10,000 refugees) as compared with 2015 (1600 refugees)*]"[32]

Senator Jeff Sessions, Chairman of the Subcommittee on Immigration and the National Interest. August 10, 2016. By early August 2016, Obama had already admitted over 61,000 refugees during the first seven months of the year from jihad nations across the Middle East, **including 2,838 from Iran**. Other nations contributing to the rush of Muslim migrants include Iraq, Somalia, and Afghanistan *[not quite refugees]*, which are all states dominated by Islam and Sharia law. Obama is building support for the institution of Sharia law in America by importing huge numbers of people whose political and religious beliefs are incompatible with the political principles established by the U.S. Constitution.

xv. Obama **supported Turkey's entry into the European Union**, which would guarantee the Islamization of Europe and would accelerate the demise of Christian Europe, based on Turkish Muslims' abilities to migrate freely into other EU countries.

xvi. In 2012, Obama proposed legislation that would support the Arab Spring with $800 million in aid. Obama was actually supporting radical Islamic terrorist groups, since a large percentage of the Muslim activists were affiliated with the Muslim Brotherhood, al-Qaeda and other radical Islamic extremist organizations. When Obama requested $1.3 billion in military aid to the new Muslim Brotherhood backed Egyptian government, Obama was theoretically requesting funding for the Muslim Brotherhood (and al-Qaeda) valued at $2+ billion in 2012. Between the funds Obama gave to support the Arab Spring, the Egyptian Muslim Brotherhood, and "moderate" Syrian rebels, along with the military equipment ISIS obtained by defeating poorly trained U.S. supported forces, **Obama was able to transfer more resources to radical Islamic forces surrounding Israel, than the financial aid earmarked for Israel in the U.S. budget on an annual basis**.

xvii. **Questionable Russian Relations**

(1) Obama reneged on a 2009 promise to deliver missile defense systems to Poland and the Czech Republic under pressure from Russian demands.

(2) Obama gave Russia classified information regarding Britain's Trident nuclear missiles to secure Russia's approval for a future arms control treaty.

(3) With the New START treaty, Obama gave Russian inspectors unprecedented intimate access to U.S. military nuclear installations.

(4) In exchange for Russian cooperation with European missile defense, Obama strongly considered giving the Russians highly classified data regarding velocity at burnout for advanced U.S. interceptor missiles stationed in Europe.

(5) Obama permitted Clinton to sell over 20% of U.S. uranium reserves to Russia while she was secretary of state.

(6)   In 2012, Obama promised the Russian leadership at a Seoul meeting, "This is my last election. After my election, I have more flexibility." Did this flexibility mean handing over Syria and Iraq to Russian and Iranian forces before the end of Obama's second term? Niall Ferguson, a Harvard history professor and author, told Maria Bartiromo on *Sunday Morning Futures* on October 18, 2015, "**He's [Obama] really created an explosion of sectarian conflict right across the region. And I think now he's being check-mated by Vladimir Putin**, the Russian president who you said a moment ago has taken in the initiative. It's really the first time since the early seventies that the Russians have been in a position to play the part of power broker in the Middle East." By giving Putin more flexibility, Obama betrayed America and her allies.

(7)   Russia expanded its military bases and increased its military and political role in Syria during Obama's tenure.

(8)   Russian humiliated Obama by forcing him to back away from his red line regarding Syria's chemical weapons.

(9)   Russian bombers were less than one mile away from the *USS Ronald Reagan* aircraft carrier during American / Korean joint military exercise in October 2015. Russia could have destroyed the *USS Ronald Reagan.*

(10)   The Russian Ambassador to the United States, Sergey Kislyak, held meetings with Obama White House officials at least six times at the White House during 2010, the year Secretary of State Clinton approved the sale of over 20% of the U.S. uranium reserves to the Russian government. The uranium transfer was most likely discussed in the Obama White House, and could not have occurred without Obama's approval. The loss of control of these resources compromised the national security interests of the United States, while the Clinton Foundation reaped $145,000,000 in donations from interested parties in this deal.

(11)   "The circumstantial evidence is mounting that the Kremlin succeeded in infiltrating the U.S. government [Obama administration] at the highest levels. How else to explain a newly elected president looking the other way after an act of Russian aggression? Agreeing to a farcically one-sided nuclear deal? Mercilessly mocking the idea that Russia represents our foremost geopolitical foe? Accommodating the illicit nuclear ambitions of a Russian ally? Welcoming a Russian foothold in the Middle East? Refusing to provide arms to a sovereign country invaded by Russia? Diminishing our defenses and pursuing a Moscow-friendly policy of hostility to fossil fuels? … He [Obama] reset with Russia shortly after its clash with Georgia in 2008. He concluded the New START agreement with Moscow that reduced our nuclear forces but not theirs. When candidate Mitt Romney warned about

Russia in the 2012 campaign, Obama rejected him as a Cold War relic. The president then went on to forge an agreement with Russia's ally Iran to allow it to preserve its nuclear program. During the red-line fiasco, he eagerly grasped a lifeline from Russia at the price of accepting its intervention in Syria. He never budged on giving Ukraine "lethal" weapons to defend itself from Russian attack. Finally, Obama cut U.S. defense spending and cracked down on fossil fuels, a policy that Russia welcomed since its economy is dependent on high oil prices. Put all of this together, and it's impossible to conclude anything other than that Obama was a Russian stooge ... he asked then-Russian President Dmitry Medvedev during a hot-mic moment at an international meeting to relay to Vladimir Putin his ability to be more "flexible" after the 2012 election; he was, to put it in terms of the current Russian election controversy, "colluding" with the Russians ... When he pulled up short from enforcing his red line, an agreement with the Russians to remove Bashar Assad's chemical weapons became the fig leaf to cover his retreat. This deal was obviously deficient, but Obama officials used clever language to give the impression that it had removed all chemical weapons from Syria ... What was the Obama administration's excuse? It effectively made itself a liar for the Russians at the same time Moscow bolstered the Assad regime we said had to go, smashed the moderate opposition we were trying to create and sent a destabilizing refugee flow into Europe. This was a moral and strategic disaster."[33] *(Rich Lowry, The National Review)* And the Democrats ironically asserted that Trump colluded with the Russians without supporting evidence, while ignoring Obama's previous questionable interactions with the Russians.

xvii.   By **refusing to name radical Islam or Islamic extremists as the enemy**, Obama is severely compromising American national security, protecting enemies of the United States, and instituting Sharia law in a secular democratic republic.

xviii.   Obama has consistently **postponed or cancelled urgent military missions against Islamic extremists**.

(1)   Obama refused to launch an emergency military effort to defend and protect the Benghazi consulate attack victims.

(2)   Obama cancelled three planned raids to kill or capture Osama bin Laden.

(3)   Obama postponed multiple military raids to rescue James Foley, Steven Sotloff and Kayla Mueller – all held hostage by ISIS. All were eventually murdered.

(4)   Obama ordered the U.S. Navy in the Persian Gulf not to assist ten Navy sailors in two advance fighter boats who were taken prisoner by Iran, and not to prevent Iran from gaining access to advanced U.S. military technology built into the fighter boats.

(5)   Obama refused to launch a rescue mission to save over 300 Nigerian school girls who were kidnapped and sexually abused by Boko Haram, citing the mission was too dangerous and may not have been in American interests.

xix.   Obama purposely **sabotaged long-term U.S. alliances**, while opponents or enemies of the United States have been strengthened, and radical Islamic forces and regimes have been empowered. This has been Obama's strategy since he entered politics with his goals to destroy America's status as a superpower, to disassemble America's alliances and weaken her partners, decimate America's military and to allow radical Islamic Iranian forces to fill the voids.

(1)   Obama created such extreme hostility between himself and Netanyahu the Israelis did trust Obama's administration.

(2)   Leading Gulf states in the Gulf Cooperation Council did not trust Obama since he supported the Muslim Brotherhood and the Arab Spring riots, which both threatened to overthrow their political institutions. These countries were also against the JCPOA, which allowed Iran to exert its increased military and political power in the Gulf States to advance Iranian interests and give the Iranian Shiites an advantage in the millennial conflict between the Sunnis and the Shiites.

(3)   Obama sabotaged President Mubarak of Egypt with the Arab Spring riots and paved the way for the Muslim Brotherhood to take control of Egypt with help from al-Qaeda.

(4)   Obama has sabotaged and destabilized Christian Europe with the massive Muslim immigration from the Middle East in part caused by the chaos in Libya and Syria. Both crises were intended direct results of Obama's foreign policy interventions.

(5)   Obama sabotaged America's special relationship with Great Britain by telling them they would need to go to the "back of the que" regarding future trade agreements if they voted in favor of leaving the European Union.

(6)   Obama destroyed the political infrastructure of Iraq by prematurely withdrawing American forces and created conditions leading to the rise of ISIS and the genocide of Christian communities in Iraq and Syria. By the fall of 2015, Iraq, a previous U.S. ally, was working with Russia with their fight against ISIS.

(7)   In 2011, Obama, under pressure from China, denied Taiwan's request for 66 additional F-16 fighter aircraft. This decision weakened America's ability to project power and influence in the Far East and prevents the creation of 16,000 American jobs needed for the project.

(8)   China is slowly expanded its hegemony in the South China Sea and the Far East which threatened the vital interests of many U.S. allies in the Far East, and sent its navy off the West coast of the United States.

(9)   Obama, under Russian pressure, cancelled ABM systems scheduled for deployment in Poland and the Czech Republic early in his first term.

(10)   During the fall of 2016, the Filipino leadership announced they were distancing themselves from their alliance with the United States and establishing closer ties with China.

(11)   Radical Muslim Powers Empowered by Obama at the Expense of U.S. Interests:

(a)   Iran – received sanctions relief and the ability to build a nuclear weapons arsenal with the implementation of the JCPOA, which changes the balance of power for regional and world domination in favor of Islamist powers.

(b)   Al-Qaeda and ISIS – expanded operations in Libya, Iraq, Syria, Afghanistan, Yemen and Central Africa via Boko Haram. Gaddafi's military arsenal was disseminated to Central Africa, the Sinai, Gaza, Syria, and Iraq via Obama's support of al-Qaeda linked Libyan rebels. Obama armed al-Qaeda elements with his support of "rebel" "moderate" Islamic militias in his fight against Gaddafi and Assad.

(c)   Taliban – poised to take over Afghanistan with Obama decreasing Allied troop strength in that region.

(d)   ISIS – expands its reach into Western Europe and the United States as Obama supports massive Muslim migration into the West.

(e)   Muslim Brotherhood – threatened Egypt and Gulf states by converting itself into a nation state with Obama's political support. By allowing the Muslim Brotherhood to become a nation-state in Egypt, Obama tried to fund this terrorist group with billions of dollars disguised as economic and military aid.

(f)   Hamas, al-Qaeda and Hezbollah will have access to almost unlimited Iranian funding with sanctions relief guaranteed by the JCPOA.

(g)   Obama empowered the Muslim Brotherhood in America with his many appointments of officials affiliated with the Muslim Brotherhood and his support for organizations like CAIR, ISNA, the MSA and other Muslim Brotherhood front groups.

xx.   Obama's **domestic policies created the circumstances that directly and predictably led to the San Bernardino Christmas party massacre** in December 2015.

Obama prevented the DHS from reviewing the social media postings of visa applicants coming into the United States. Tashfeen Malik, one of the Muslim terrorists
who helped murder fourteen Americans, posted her support for violent jihad against
infidels for at least three years on Facebook before she immigrated to California.
Obama's directives prevented U.S. officials from obtaining that information during her application screening. The Obama administration also terminated a DHS
investigation into various radical mosques in America. One of those mosques was
frequented by Syed Farook, who participated in the San Bernardino terrorist attack.
Obama instituted policies that purposely allowed foreign Muslim terrorists to clear
immigration screening reviews, and when they are in the United States, the mosques
that they attend are removed from government scrutiny.

xxi.   Obama had the DHS Civil Rights and Civil Liberties Division and the State
Department **halt the investigations into foreign jihadists on U.S. soil**, under the
guise of protecting their civil liberties.

xxii. Obama ordered the DHS in 2009 to **delete and scrub the national security records of hundreds of possible Muslim terrorists**.

xxiii. Obama **betrayed all of Judaism and Christianity** at the end of his presidency by
supporting UNSC Resolution 2334, which attempted to transfer the holiest Jewish
and Christian religious sites in the East Jerusalem and the Old City to the control of
the PLO and Hamas, radical Islamic terrorist groups. Obama directed the creation
and passage of this resolution, which called the Western Wall, the Church of the
Holy Sepulchre, the Via Dolorosa, and many other Christian and Jewish holy sites –
illegally occupied Palestinian territory.

xxiv. Obama is guilty of sedition when he actively **directed and aided many of his political allies in their attempts to undermine and eventually impeach Trump
before he was inaugurated**. Obama signed an NSA directive that allowed them to
share "overseas" intercepted communications with 16 other government intelligence
agencies. This allowed the communications of many people in the Trump administration to be accessed by Obama allies, which would be used to undermine and
embarrass the new administration. With Obama's embedded allies in these agencies,
he probably had access to these classified documents, which would qualify Obama
as committing sedition and possibly treason by attempting to overthrow the new
U.S. president. He also worked with George Soros in funding and directing his
Organizing For Action, which actively supported protests, some of which turned
violent, against many of the items in the Trump agenda which would devastate
Obama's legacy.

2. "I believe in the Constitution … and **I will obey the Constitution of the United States** … We're not going to use signing statement as a way of doing an end run around Congress."

   a. Obama issued executive orders changing Obamacare, and later with immigration reform / amnesty in end runs around Congress.

   b. Obama used a signing statement excuse to exempt him from giving Congress thirty-days notice regarding the release of five senior Taliban commanders imprisoned at Guantanamo in exchange for the deserter – Bergdahl. Obama broke the law with this failure to notify Congress, thus, committing an impeachable offense.

   c. Obama did not want the Senate to review and approve his agreement / treaty with Iran. The Senate relinquished their legal responsibility under the Constitution with Obama's support by agreeing to rescind the treaty if two-thirds of the Senate voted against the agreement, rather than two-thirds of the Senate needed to approve the deal.

3. "We all agree on **the need to better secure the border** and to punish the employers who chose to hire illegal immigrants. We are a generous and welcoming people here in the United States, but **those who enter the country illegally** and those who employ them **disrespect the rule of law**, and they are showing disregard to those who are following the law. **We simply cannot allow people to pore into the United States undetected**, **undocumented**, **unchecked** and circumventing the line of people who are waiting patiently, diligently and lawfully to become immigrants." *Senator Obama, 2005.* Obama lied to the American people regarding his position concerning illegal immigration, so he could be viewed as mainstream and somewhat conservative heading into the 2008 presidential campaign. During his presidency, Obama kept a relatively open border between the United States and Mexico, which contradicted his earlier position as a U.S. senator.

4. "Even as we are nation of immigrants, we are also a nation of laws. Undocumented workers broke our immigration laws, and I believe that they must be held accountable, especially those who may be dangerous. When I took office, I committed to fixing this broken immigration system. And I began to **doing what I could to secure our borders**. But today, our immigration system is broken, and everybody knows it. There are actions I have the legal authority to take as president … **If you are a criminal**, **you will be deported**. If you plan to enter the U.S. illegally, your chances of getting caught and sent back just went up. We expect people who live in this country to play by the rules … The actions I'm taking are not only lawful, they're the kinds of actions taken by every single Republican president and every single Democratic president for the last half century." *Obama, Immigration Address, November 2014.* Obama sounds like Trump and most conservative politicians. But unfortunately, Obama lied and failed to enforce immigration laws, and kept an open southern U.S. - Mexican southern border for the remainder of his presidency.

a. "The only reason the older youth, Sanchez Milian, was in the country at all was because of the **Obama administration's catch and release policies** that allowed him to be resettled in Maryland, with few questions asked ... Eighty percent of the tens of thousands of Central American kids who were caught by the Border Patrol and released by [the Department of Health and Human Services] have been **released to other illegal aliens** ... Not surprisingly, few bother to show up for or complete their immigration court proceedings and have **joined the larger illegal alien population** ... Instead of allowing these youths to settle here, they should have been turned back at the border ... That would have stemmed the influx early on, and it would not have **created such incentives for more to come here, knowing that they would be allowed to stay** ... American communities cannot continue to absorb so many new arrivals, so many of whom unfortunately are going to contribute only problems to our schools."[34] *Jessica Vaughan, Center of Immigration Studies, Director of Policy.* Vaughan is commenting on the rape of a 14-year old girl by two illegal aliens, who are students at a public high school in Rockville, Maryland. One of the eighteen-year old illegal aliens was allowed to register as a freshman and had an outstanding warrant for his arrest.

b. Obama released not only illegal aliens who were caught in the United States, but also illegal aliens who were labeled as "criminal threats" by the federal government. In 2015, Obama officials established rules that released nearly 90,000 illegal alien criminals inside American borders. Senator Sessions commented, "By defining its 'priorities' to exclude large categories of illegal immigrants, including those who have already been ordered deported or those who illegally reenter after having been deported, PEP ensures that countless more dangerous aliens will be released into U.S. communities - allowing otherwise entirely preventable crimes, including some of the most violent and egregious, to occur." Failure to adequately protect the United States and its citizens against obvious and controllable threats is grounds for impeachment.

    i. "Congressman Lamar Smith of Texas had previously chaired the House Immigration Subcommittee and the House Judiciary Committee ... Smith's understandable outrage at the April 19th hearing became readily apparent when he stated rhetorically that he wondered if **President Obama might be an accessory to the crimes committed by illegal aliens since he has implemented policies that he knows are going to result in the loss of life to innocent Americans**, noting that the administration had released from custody some 100,000 aliens who had been convicted of committing serious crimes. He also noted that although it has been estimated that illegal aliens account for about 3% of the U.S. population, they account for 30% of all murders – making illegal aliens 10 times more likely to commit murder than anyone else ... There is no way of knowing how many additional crimes have been committed by these aliens released in Obama's-sanctioned 'prison-break.'"[35]

ii.   "At least 95 percent of convicted criminal aliens known to the Department of Homeland Security (DHS) are not detained. The fact remains that illegal immigration has consequences – it is not a victimless crime. Yet, these consequences would be largely avoidable if this Administration would just enforce the law. Alarmingly, those trying to enforce the law cannot! ... By releasing known criminal aliens and refusing to secure our border, the Administration has sent a clear message to the American people that their safety and security are far less important than ensuring that these individuals remain here. I want to see these dangerous policies stopped, and I will continue working to stand in the way of President Obama's pen and phone. The real costs of illegal immigration are something no family should be forced to pay." *Rep. Robert Goodlatte, Chairman of the House Judiciary Committee, "The Real Costs of Illegal Immigration," April 22, 2016.*

c.   "Senator Ron Johnson, chairman of the Senate Homeland Security Committee, said a whistleblower turned over Customs and Border Protection documents from 2014 detailing the 16 people who were caught cross the border. "CBP apprehended them, knew they were **MS-13 gang members**, and they processed and **disbursed them into our communities**," Mr. Johnson, Wisconsin Republican said."[36] *(The Washington Times, May 24, 2017)* Obama deliberately embedded lethal MS-13 gang members into American communities throughout the United States, which contradicted his promise and oath to protect America.

5.   "I believe in the Second Amendment. I will not take your shotgun away. **I will not take your rifle away. I won't take your handgun away ... But I am not going to take your guns away.** So, if you want to find an excuse not to vote for me, don't use that one because it just ain't true. It ain't true." *Obama 2008 campaign speech.*

a.   In July 2015, Obama stated his intent to deny gun ownership to Social Security recipients who cannot manage their own affairs due to "marked subnormal intelligence, mental illness, incompetency, **condition**, **or disease**." This could force the confiscation of firearms from millions of Americans, since "condition or disease" is very vague.

b.   In an interview with *GQ* on November 16, 2015, Obama addressed gun control with executive actions by stating he "wants **to make sure that there's a <u>sustained attention paid to it</u>**."

c.   Obama immediately called for strict gun control after the Orlando massacre was perpetrated by a radical Muslim extremist. Attorney General Lynch stated on *Meet the Press*, "We want to be able to have the tools we need to stop individuals from obtaining guns who should not have them. *[which may include political opponents of Obama]*" Homeland Security Secretary Johnson stated on *CBS This Morning* that, "We have to face the fact that meaningful gun control has to be a part of homeland security." Obama is turning the focus of the DHS away from Islamic terrorists and upon law abiding American citizens. Obama's official statements after the massacre reflected his desire to institute harsh gun control measures when he stated, "We are also going to have to have to make sure that we think about the risks we are willing to take by being so lax in how we make very powerful firearms *[most firearms]* available to people in this country … we ignore the problems with easy access to firearms … we also have to make sure that it is not easy for somebody who decides they want to harm people *[Obama wants to take away the gun-owning rights of American citizens as protected by the Second Amendment secondary to his suspicions that they may cause harm in the future without any further fact to substantiate this claim. Thus, gun ownership in America would no longer be a legally protected right for all law abiding citizens and the government could unilaterally decide who could not own firearms without due process or proven criminal intent.]* in this country to be able to obtain weapons."

    d.   Obama wants to prevent people on the no-fly list from owning firearms. The government can put any individual on the no-fly list without due process and with the suspicion or rumor you might be connected with terrorism. The Obama administration has labelled groups such as Orthodox Jews, evangelical Christians, veterans, libertarians, Mormons, Catholics, and members of the Jewish Defense League as potential terrorists. The Department of Defense also labelled the founding fathers as radicals. Thus, Obama would be able to forcibly disarm many law abiding conservative Americans who are his political opponents.

6.   "America is a nation of laws, which means I, as the president, am **obligated to enforce the law. I don't have a choice about that**. *[Obama chose not to enforce immigration laws.]* … But I can advocate for changes in the law so that we have a country that is both respectful of the law but also continues to be a great nation of immigrants … **With respect to the notion that I can just suspend deportations through executive order, that's just not the case**, because there are laws on the books that Congress has passed … we've got three branches of government. **Congress passes the law. The executive branch's job is to enforce and implement those laws** … There are enough laws on the books by Congress that are very clear in terms of how we have to enforce our immigration system that **for me to simply through executive order ignore those congressional mandates would not conform with my appropriate role as president**." *Obama, March 28, 2011. Obama lying to a Univision audience in 2011 regarding his future use of executive orders concerning immigration reform and amnesty.*

Obama pretended to support the law with another presidential election campaign in 2012. Before his final 2012 presidential victory, Obama lied to the country over 22 times when he stated he could not institute amnesty with executive action.

a. In 2015, less than 1% of foreign nationals who overstayed their visas were actually deported by ICE officials.

b. "We're releasing basically everybody as long as you're not from the country of Mexico. And even if you're from the country of Mexico and you claim that you have a credible fear and you're asking for asylum for one reason or another – we're still releasing those individuals … at least 80 percent of the individuals that the United States Border Patrol arrests at the border qualify for this catch and release program and in essence we are just letting them come into the United States … If you are an unaccompanied minor we will not only release you, but will escort you to your final destination. If you are a family unit, we will release you. If you claim credible fear, we will release you. If you are a single male and we do not physically see you cross the border and you claim that you have been in this country since 2014, we will release you."[37] *Brandon Judd, President of the National Border Patrol Council, testifying before the Senate Judiciary Subcommittee on Immigration and the National Interest, May 2016.* Obama has instituted de facto amnesty and has bypassed Congress and the will of the American people.

c. "The Department of Homeland Security (DHS) is quietly transporting illegal immigrants from the Mexican border to Phoenix and releasing them without proper processing or issuing court appearance documents, Border Patrol sources tell *Judicial Watch.* The government classifies them as Other Than Mexican (OTM) … A security company contracted by the U.S. government is driving the OTMs from the Border Patrol's Tucson Sector where they were in custody to Phoenix, sources said … Outraged Border Patrol agents and supervisors on the front lines say illegal immigrants are being released in droves … "They're telling us to put them on a bus and let them go … Just move those bodies across the country." *("DHS Quietly Moving, Releasing Vanloads of Illegal Aliens Away from Border," Judicial Watch, June 3, 2016)* **Obama now has the DHS enforcing a catch and release policy, but also is actively involved in smuggling illegal aliens away from the southern border into the United States.**

d. An Obama interview days before the 2016 Presidential Election: **Rodriguez:** "Many of the Millennials, DREAMers, **undocumented citizens – and I call them "citizens" 'cause they contribute to this country – are fearful of voting.** So if I vote, will immigration know where I live? Will they come for my family and deport us?" **Obama:** "Not true. And the reason is – first of all, **when you vote, you are a citizen yourself,** and there is not a situation where the voting rolls somehow are transferred over and people start investigating, et cetera. The sanctity of the vote is strictly confidential in terms of who you voted for. If you have a family member who maybe is undocumented, then you have an even greater reason to vote." Obama is encouraging voter fraud and criminal activity in the election process by supporting an illegal alien's right to vote. Obama lied when he took his presidential oath promising to preserve, protect and defend the Constitution. Neil Cavuto of *Fox News* responded, "I can't believe how blithely the President of the United States, the keeper of our Constitution, and all the rights that come with it, including the right to vote, legal citizens having the right to vote, blithely dismissing that. In other words, he is advocating for an illegal act here. That you are not a citizen of the United States, whatever your preferences or sympathies, you are not yet a citizen of the United States. So somehow, you got away with … getting into a voting booth when you shouldn't have. And now **you have the man who protects our United States Constitution** … **Saying**, **don't worry**, **we're not going to chase you down**. **As you're doing this illegal act**!"[38]

    i.   During Obama's December 16th 2016 press conference, Obama attacked the Electoral College as a relic by stating, "**The Electoral College is a vestige**, it's a car-ryover from an earlier vision of how our federal government was going to work that put a lot of premium on states … going to disadvantage Democrats." Obama wants presidential elections determined by popular vote, and supports the right of illegal aliens to vote in federal elections, which would guarantee Democratic victories in all future presidential elections. Obama knows by allowing illegals to vote combined with eliminating the Electoral College would ensure Democratic dictatorial control over the United States.

7.   "I guarantee that there is **no political influence in any investigation conducted by the Justice Department**, **or the FBI**, not just in this case, but in any case … Guaranteed. Full stop. Nobody gets treated differently when it comes to the Justice Department, because **nobody is above the law** … I continue to believe that she has not jeopardized America's national security." *Obama interview with Chris Wallace on Fox News Sunday. April 10, 2016.* Commenting on the Department of Justice and FBI investigations into the issues surround-ing Hillary Clinton's private email server and pay to play allegations regarding her relation-ship between the State Department and the Clinton Foundation.

    a.   Former President **Bill Clinton met with Attorney General Lorretta Lynch aboard a private plane at an airport in Phoenix**, **Arizona** in June 2016, allegedly to discuss the DOJ investigations into Hillary Clinton's private email server and the Clinton Foundation. There is a good chance that Clinton told Lynch that she could keep her job as Attorney General if Hillary Clinton was cleared of wrong doing regarding these pertinent issues, which were hurting Hillary Clinton's chances of winning the 2016 presidential election.

    i.   Catherine Herridge reported on *Fox News* on May 4, 2017, "What we heard today for the first time were details about a document that related to Attorney General Loretta Lynch that had been obtained by Russian hackers. And that **the document indicated that <u>Lynch would do whatever it took to prevent criminal charges to be brought against Hillary Clinton</u> in the email probe** …On several of the questions referring to Loretta Lynch the FBI director said he couldn't discuss it in an open unclassified setting … in light of the Arizona [airport] tarmac meeting with Loretta Lynch … The FBI director said today he felt boxed in by Lynch and kind of a victim of circumstances." Obama and the Justice Department were protecting Hillary Clinton, as well as Huma Abedin, who had many classified documents on her husband's (Anthony Weiner) laptop.

  b. On June 8, 2017, during testimony before the Senate Intelligence Committee, former FBI Director James Comey, revealed that Obama's Attorney General Loretta **Lynch asked him to refer to Hillary Clinton's email investigation as a "matter" and not an "investigation."** Lynch sought to downplay Clinton's problems surrounding the email server, which would protect the political futures of both Clinton and Obama, since Obama corresponded with Clinton on her private server concerning classified national security issues. Comey also testified before the Senate Judiciary Committee on May 3, 2017, that "a number of things had gone on which I can't talk about yet, that made me worry that **the department leadership could not credibly complete the investigation and decline prosecution without grievous damage to the American people's confidence in the justice system** … her meeting with President Clinton on that airplane was the capper for me. And I then said, you know what? **The [Justice] Department cannot by itself credibly end this**." Obama had politicized the FBI via Lynch. On the same day as the Senate hearings, former US Attorney General Michael Mukasey summarized on *Newsmax TV*, "What makes it egregious is the fact, and I think it's obvious that it is a fact, that the Attorney General of the United States was adjusting the way the department talked about its business so as to coincide as to the way the Clinton campaign talked about that business. In other words, **it made the Department of Justice essentially an arm of the Clinton campaign**. That is really a betrayal of the department and its independence. Clearly the Attorney General was clearly in the tank for Secretary Hillary Clinton."

    i.   With the above information, the Senate Judiciary Committee asked Lynch to testify before the committee with bipartisan support. The June 22, 2017 Senate letter to former Attorney General Lynch stated, "On April 22, 2017, *The New York Times* reported that during the investigation of Russian hacking against political organizations in the United States, the FBI "received a batch of hacked documents" from U.S. intelligence agencies that had access to stolen materials stored on Russian networks. One of the documents provided to the FBI reportedly appeared to have implications on the then-ongoing Clinton email investigation. Specifically, **the FBI is reported to have obtained an email or memo "written by a Democratic operative who expressed confidence that Ms. Lynch would keep the Clinton investigation from going too far**." According to anonymous government officials cited in the report, **the discovery of the document "complicated" how FBI and the Justice Department would interact in the investigation** because "[i]f Ms. Lynch announced that the case was closed, and Russia leaked the document, Mr. Comey believed it would raise doubts about the independence of the investigation." ... On May 24, 2017, *The Washington Post reported* that in early March 2016 the FBI had received "what was described as **a Russian intelligence document**" that "**cited a supposed email describing how then-Attorney General Loretta E. Lynch had privately assured someone in the Clinton campaign that the email investigation would not push too deeply into the matter**." More specifically, the Russian intelligence document reportedly "referred to **an email supposedly written by the then-chair of the Democratic National Committee, Rep. Debbie Wasserman Schultz**, and sent to Leonard Benardo, an official with the Open Society Foundations." According to the article: "[i]n the supposed email, Wasserman Schultz claimed **Lynch had been in private communication with a senior Clinton campaign staffer named Amanda Renteria during the campaign**. The document indicated **Lynch had told Renteria that she would not let the FBI investigation into Clinton go too far** ..."

c. "Ex-FBI Director James Comey has privately told members of Congress that he had a **frosty exchange** with Obama Attorney General Loretta Lynch last year when he confronted her about possible political interference in the Hillary Clinton email investigation after showing Lynch a sensitive document she was unaware the FBI possessed ... Comey said "the attorney general looked at the document then looked up with a **steely silence** that lasted for some time, then asked him if he had any other business with her and if not that he should leave her office," said one source who was briefed."[39] *(Circa, June 2017)*

d. According to *The Wall Street Journal*, Department of Justice officials repeatedly told FBI agents to "stand down" and halt all **investigations regarding the Clinton Foundation**, despite the agents' having credible witnesses available and other substantial evidence that would warrant further investigation and possible criminal charges against Hillary

Clinton. After FBI Director Comey cleared Clinton of criminal wrong doing in mid-2016, multiple FBI agents handed in their resignations, which helped Comey decide to reactivate the investigation two weeks before the 2016 presidential election, which was revealed in a letter to Congressional leaders.

e. The DOJ gave Heather Samuelson and Cheryl Mills, both top aides to Hillary Clinton, immunity as they testified regarding their knowledge of the issues surrounding the Clinton's private email server. The DOJ instructed the FBI to destroy laptops from the witnesses, which was not done.

f. A PAC run by Terry McAuliffe, governor of Virginia and good friend of Hillary Clinton, gave $650,000 to the state Senate campaign of the wife of Andrew McCabe, second in command at the FBI, and the official in charge of the investigations regarding Hillary Clinton.

g. Peter Kadzik, the Assistant Attorney General in charge of the DOJ investigation of Hillary Clinton, is good friends with John Podesta, Hillary Clinton's campaign chairman. Podesta was also chief of staff to President Bill Clinton and legal counselor to President Obama. Senator Grassley, chairman of the Senate Judiciary Committee, raised legitimate concerns when he wrote to the DOJ Inspector General, "The Justice Department has failed to appoint a special counsel to ensure that these inquiries are insulated from the appearance that decisions are being made based on political considerations rather than on the merits … The American people deserve to know whether political considerations have improperly affected the handling of this inquiry and understand why key officials failed to recuse themselves to protect the public's confidence in a fair and impartial inquiry based on merits and the evidence rather than on politics." Concerns over Kadzik's impartiality have been raised with, "Mr. Kadzik represented Mr. Podesta during the Monica Lewinsky investigation … Mr. Kadzik lobbied Mr. Podesta for then-President Bill Clinton to pardon Marc Rich … Mr. Podesta emailed Obama campaign officials to recommend Mr. Kadzik for a role in the Obama campaign and called Mr. Kadzik a "fantastic lawyer" … Mr. Kadzik met with Mr. Podesta for dinner one day after Secretary Clinton's Benghazi testimony … Mr. Kadzik's son asked Mr. Podesta for a job on the Clinton campaign."[40]

h. "Look, it started with **the New Black Panther case** that, you remember, I was involved in, and there, politics and ideology affected law enforcement. The ideological opposition to using the Voting Rights Act against people like the New Black Panthers led to that case getting scuttled after we brought it during the Bush administration, after the inauguration in 2009 … It's ideological allies in positions of power, like this clown who's the Assistant Attorney General for Legislative Affairs [Kadzik] tipping off the Clinton campaign of a pending pleading being filed … This wasn't tipping them off about a hearing.

Yeah, that's no big deal. But this was a piece of confidential information that a lawyer had, as a lawyer, and he gave it away unethically to the Clinton campaign."[41] *J. Christian Adams, former Justice Department official. November 2016.*

i. Susan Rice, Obama's national security advisor, whose office was adjacent to the Oval office, unmasked Trump and Trump's associates in incidentally collected phone calls for about one year, that were followed by the U.S. intelligence community for "alleged" national security interests. Rice did not unmask any officials affiliated with the Clinton campaign although the Clinton Foundation received donations from Russian affiliated institutions, Bill Clinton received $500,000 for a speech given to a Russian investment banking conference, Hillary Clinton oversaw the sale of over 20% of U.S. uranium reserves to Russia, John Podesta lobbied on behalf of a bank owed by the Russian Central Bank, and John Podesta's brother received significant compensation from being on the board of a Russian company. Senator Ron Johnson, chairman of the Senate Homeland Security Committee, said, "What we do know about Susan Rice is you can't believe what she says, and that is pretty obvious, so we need to get her under oath … **It doesn't surprise me in the slightest that the former administration would utilize the awesome power of the government – they did it with Lois Lerner and the IRS, using the IRS as a political weapon against their political opponents**." Susan Rice used her role as national security advisor to the president in order to undermine the Trump administration and his previous political campaign. In 2016, a major presidential election year, the Obama administration unmasked over 1900 individuals from intelligence reports and performed over 30,000 searches. Obama was desperate to find incriminating and embarrassing information on Clinton's political opponents.

j. Obama's Former FBI Director Comey, before he was fired, released private conversations he had with President Trump to a friend who forwarded the information to *The New York Times*, so that the Justice Department could have enough information to hire a special council who would investigate the fake news accusations that Trump had colluded with the Russians during the 2016 presidential campaign. Former CIA Director James Woolsey commented on *CNN's Fareed Zakaria*, "It's just amazing … Not all leaks have to be classified … I just found it stunning that he [Comey] would give up the secrecy of a conversation with the President of the United States." Comey is hoping to entrap President Trump in a process crime. Comey is working with Obama to destroy the Trump presidency.

8. "I taught constitutional law for ten years. I take the Constitution very seriously. The biggest problems that we're facing right now have to do with [the President] trying to bring more and more power into the executive branch and not go through Congress at all, and that's what I intend to reverse when I'm President of the United States of America." *Obama, 2008*

campaign. When Obama became president, he used executive orders to bypass Congress when Congress would not support his legislative agenda regarding amnesty for illegal aliens, amending Obamacare, and attacking the Second Amendment. Obama instituted regulations issued by the EPA in order to bypass Congress, when Congress would not pass laws supporting his green and climate change agendas.

9. "There will be **no more illegal wiretapping of American citizens**." "No more tracking citizens who do nothing more than protest a misguided war." "We will again set an example for the world that **the law is not subject to the whims of stubborn rulers** and justice is not arbitrary." *Obama, 2007.* Obama used the fake fears and fake concerns of Trump's non-existent political relationship with the Russians in order to obtain a FISA warrant in order to spy on the Trump campaign. Their initial request was initially rejected by the FISA court, and with their subsequent surveillance of the Trump campaign, Obama found nothing. Obama was trolling the Trump campaign with U.S. intelligence resources looking for an anti-Trump "October surprise" so Hillary Clinton would have an assured electoral victory. Obama may not have directly ordered the wiretaps, but he did coordinate the operation and was briefed on its findings. Obama would be at least aware of any FISA warrant issued against Trump or any of his associates, and the Obama administration went to the FISA court twice.

    a. "Two separate sources with links to the counter-intelligence community have confirmed to Heat Street that the FBI sought, and was granted, a FISA court warrant in October, giving counter-intelligence permission to examine the activities of 'U.S. persons' in Donald Trump's campaign with ties to Russia."[42] *(HeatStreet, November 7, 2016)*

    b. "Terrible! Just found out that Obama had my 'wires tapped' in Trump Tower just before victory. Nothing found. This is McCarthyism! ... Is it legal for a sitting President to be 'wire tapping' a race for president prior to an election. Turned down by court earlier. A NEW LOW! ... How low has President Obama gone to tap my phones during the very sacred election process. This is Nixon / Watergate. Bad (or sick) guy!" ***Trump tweets***, *March 4, 2017.*

    c. **Brett Baier:** "There's a report that June 2016 there's a FISA request by the Obama administration from a communications court to monitor communications to monitor Donald Trump and several campaign officials. They get turned down. Then in October (immediately before the election) they renew it. And they do start a wiretap at Trump Tower with some computer and Russian banks and it doesn't show up anything. Have you heard that?" **Paul Ryan:** "Again as I said none of us in Congress or anybody I know in Congress has been presented with evidence to the contrary to what you just said." *On March 4, 2017. Speaker of the House Paul Ryan confirms the Obama administration wire tapped Trump Towers and the Trump campaign.*

d. **Former Obama speechwriter**, **Jon Favreau**, confirmed there were wiretaps directed against Trump and his campaign when he tweeted, "I'd be careful about reporting that Obama said there was no wiretapping. Statement just said that neither he nor the WH ordered it." *March 4, 2017.* Obama did not give the direct order, but he did give his approval and accessed the wiretap transcripts.

e. "This is huge! I mean, dare I say this is Soviet level wrongdoing … The Obama Administration was taking on the form using their version of the FSB, or the KGB, to go and target a candidate. Let me be very clear on this for your audience, simply because you don't like someone does not give you the right as the sitting President to do something like this…." ***Lt. Col. Tony Schaffer***, *previous presidential national security briefer, Fox and Friends, March 4, 2017.*

f. **The Obama administration has a history of inappropriate wiretaps**: House of Representatives cloak room in 2013[43], James Rosen and *Fox News*, *AP* reporters and editors, *CBS News* reporter Sharyl Attkinson (hacking her computer), UN Secretary General Ban Ki-Moon and German Chancellor Merkel, Chief of Staff of UN High Commissioner for Refugees, Director of the Rules Division of the World Trade Organization, EU and Japanese trade ministers, Italy's ambassador to NATO, Italian diplomatic cables referring to Israel, French President Sarkozy / Merkel / Berlusconi meeting. Why not Trump and his campaign team?

g. "In my communications with you and other top officials in the national security community, **it has become clear that you possess explosive information about close ties and coordination between Donald Trump**, **his top advisors**, **and the Russian government** – a foreign interest openly hostile to the United States, which Trump praises at every opportunity … I wrote to you months ago calling for this information to be released to the public … and yet, you continue to resist calls to inform the public of this critical information." ***Senator Harry Reid***, *Minority Leader, writing to FBI Director Comey, March 30, 2017.* Democratic Senator Reid knew about the wiretaps on Donald Trump and was telling Comey to release any damaging information that could hurt Trump's campaign. One day later, Hillary Clinton also revealed she was aware of the wiretaps.

h. **Hillary Clinton** was aware of the Obama administration's wiretapping of Trump and his campaign officials when she tweeted on October 31, 2016, "Computer scientists have apparently uncovered a cover server linking Trump Organization to a Russian-based bank." Was Clinton informed of this eavesdropping by people in the Obama administration or by her husband, who met with Attorney General Loretta Lynch on the tarmac at a Phoenix airport in June 2006, right before the Department of Justice submitted their first request to tap Donald Trump via a FISA warrant – which was refused.

i. "Today Hillary **Clinton's former campaign manager (Robby Mook)** told *Fox* he **had knowledge of wiretaps being used during the campaign** but he suggested they were targeted at Russian officials, not directly at Trump Tower." *Fox News, March 7, 2017.* Hillary Clinton may have had access to the wiretaps.

j. "They did spend time listening to conversations between then - **Senator Jeff Sessions** and the ambassador to Russia while he was in his Senate office ... If that were to take place - which supposedly did take place - what other conversations did they listen in on from the American public? ... Is it possible that that previous administration was listening to the conversations that took place in Trump Tower from their political opponents? If that is the case, and what Donald Trump alludes to is accurate, then that's very, very disturbing for our future going forward." *Corey Lewandowski, former Trump campaign manager, March 4, 2017, Fox News interview.* The Obama administration had wiretapped Jeff Sessions since early 2016.

k. "**Former Attorney General Michael Mukasey** on Sunday said that President Trump is likely correct that there was surveillance on Trump Tower for intelligence purposes, but incorrect in accusing former President Barack Obama of ordering the wiretapping. "I think he's right in that there was surveillance and that it was conducted at the behest of the attorney general – at the Justice Department," Mukasey told *ABC's* "This Week." ... Mukasey, who served as the attorney general under former President George W. Bush, said he believes there was surveillance on Trump Tower."[44] *(The Hill, March 5, 2017)*

l. "Three intelligence sources have informed *Fox News* that **President Obama went outside the chain of command**. He didn't use the NSA. He didn't use the CIA. He didn't use the FBI, and he didn't use Department of Justice. **He used GCHQ.** What the heck is GCHQ? That's the initials for **the British spying agency.** They have 24 / 7 access to the NSA database. So, by simply having two people go to them saying, 'President Obama needs transcripts of conversations involving candidate Trump, conversations involving president-elect Trump,' he's able to get it, and there's no American fingerprints on this ... It's not a wiretap ... Everything is done electronically now via computer. The NSA has 24 hour 365 day access ... and they share that with various intelligence agencies, including the Brits." *Judge Andrew Napolitano, Fox and Friends, March 14, 2017.* Obama may have obtained the transcripts of all of Trumps communications before and after the election from British intelligence.

   i. "The Guardian adds to our knowledge of how the Obama administration and its allies overseas tried to discredit Donald Trump ... 'Britain's spy agencies played a crucial role in alerting their counterparts in Washington to contacts between members of Donald Trump's campaign team and Russian intelligence operatives, the Guardian has been told. GCHQ first became aware in late 2015 of suspicious "interactions" between figures connected to Trump and known or suspected Russian agents, a source close to UK intelligence said. This intelligence was passed to the US as part of a routine exchange of information, they added. Over the next six months, until summer 2016, a number of western agencies shared further information on contacts between Trump's inner circle and Russians, sources said. The European countries that passed on electronic intelligence – known as sigint – included Germany, Estonia and Poland. Australia, a member of the "Five Eyes" spying alliance that also includes the US, UK, Canada and New Zealand, also relayed material, one source said. Another source suggested the Dutch and the French spy agency, the General Directorate for External Security or DGSE, were contributors.' So just about every Western intelligence service was collaborating with the Obama administration in trying to elect Hillary Clinton. Yet, amazingly enough, they failed. The blindingly obvious point that the Guardian tries to obscure is that the combined assets of all of these agencies failed to find any evidence of collaboration between the Trump campaign and Russia. We know this, because the Democrats have pulled out all the stops. Both before the election, and especially after the election, they have leaked furiously to try to discredit President Trump. If there were any evidence of collusion between Trump (or even obscure, minor "advisers" like Carter Page) and Russia, there would have been nothing else in the *Washington Post* or the *New York Times* for the past five months? But they have nothing."[45] (*Powerline, John Hinderaker*)

m.   "**Former Rep. Dennis Kucinich** (D-Ohio) is defending President Trump's claims about being wiretapped by the Obama administration, saying during an appearance on *Fox News's* "The O'Reilly Factor" that **his own phone had been tapped**. Kucinich told Bill O'Reilly Monday night that a phone call to his congressional office from a foreign leader was tapped in 2011. Kucinich said he listened to the recording after leaving office in 2015. "I had a resolution in the House to try to stop the war and [Saif al-Islam Gadhafi, a high-ranking official in Libya's government and son of President Moammar Gadhafi] called me to talk about it," Kucinich said. "I cleared the discussion with House attorneys, and a member of Congress is not supposed to be listened to by the executive branch," he continued. "The director of national intelligence under President Obama was tracking my resolution, and I didn't find out until two years after I had left Congress.""[46] (*The Hill, March 14, 2017*) The Obama administration wiretapped members of Congress for political reasons. Why not wiretap candidate and President-elect Trump for political reasons?

n.   "**The work that <u>has already been discovered</u>, that was done**, in order to have Trump, should be followed up … I think there is a trail. And, I think that **<u>the Obama</u>**

administration has done everything that it can possibly do, and that's probably been verified somewhat by *The New York Times.*" *Congresswoman Maxine Waters admitted Obama spied on Trump before he became president so that he could collect evidence for grounds for impeachment, while talking with Chris Hayes on MSNBC, March 2017.*

o. "I recently confirmed that on numerous occasions **the intelligence community incidentally collected information about U.S. citizens involved in the Trump transition. Details about U.S. persons associated with the incoming administration details with little or no apparent foreign intelligence value were widely disseminated in intelligence community** reporting. Third, I have confirmed that additional names of Trump transition team members were unmasked. And fourth and finally I want to be clear, none of this surveillance was related to Russia or the investigation of Russian activities or of the Trump team. *[Reporter: Can we rule out senior Obama officials were involved in (wiretapping the Trump Team)]* ... No we cannot." *Representative Devin Nunes, Chairman of House Intelligence Committee, March 23, 2017.*

   i. "There was high drama last week when Rep. Devin Nunes announced at the White House that he had seen evidence that the communications of the Donald Trump campaign people, and perhaps even Trump himself, had been "incidentally collected" by the US government. If true, this means that someone authorized the monitoring of Trump campaign communications using Section 702 of the FISA Act ... First there is Section 702 itself. The provision was passed in 2008 as part of a package of amendments to the 1978 FISA bill. As with the PATRIOT Act, we were told that we had to give the government more power to spy on us so that it could catch terrorists. We had to give up some of our liberty for promises of more security, we were told. We were also told that the government would only spy on the bad guys, and that if we had nothing to hide we should have nothing to fear. We found out five years later from Edward Snowden that the US government viewed Section 702 as a green light for the mass surveillance of Americans. Through programs he revealed, like PRISM, the NSA is able to collect and store our Internet search history, the content of our emails, what files we have shared, who we have chatted with electronically, and more. That's why people like NSA whistleblower William Binney said that **we know the NSA was spying on Trump because it spies on all of us**!"[47] *(Former Congressman Ron Paul, Ron Paul Institute, Weekly column, March 27, 2017)*

p. "The president had a very legitimate case to make [about **being 'surveilled'**] ... I would say, from all I know, you're at least 99-and-a-half percent accurate, and probably 100 percent." *Representative Peter King, House Intelligence Committee, March 23, 2017.*

q. "Inside NSA there are a set of people who are – and we got this from another NSA whistleblower who witnessed some of this – they're inside there, they are targeting and looking at all the members of the Supreme Court, the Joint Chiefs of Staff, Congress, both House and Senate, as well as the White House. And all this data is inside the NSA in a small group where they're looking at it. The idea is to see what people in power over you are going to – what they think, what they think you should be doing or planning to do to you, your budget, or whatever so you can try to counteract before it actually happens." ***NSA Whistleblower, former NSA chief, William Binney***, *Fox News interview, Tucker Carlson Tonight, March 24, 2016.* These intelligence officials reported to Obama throughout his whole presidency, and probably still are loyal to Obama's agenda.

r. "As I have written in this *Newsmax* blog and elsewhere particularly of late, my client, former NSA and CIA contractor Dennis Montgomery, holds the keys to disproving the false claims of those representatives and senators on the House and Senate intelligence committees, reportedly as well as FBI Director James Comey, that there is no evidence that the president and his men were wiretapped. Montgomery left the NSA and CIA with 47 hard drives and over 600 million pages of information, much of which is classified, and sought to come forward legally as a whistleblower to appropriate government entities, including congressional intelligence committees, to expose that the spy agencies were engaged for years in systematic illegal surveillance on prominent Americans, including the chief justice of the Supreme Court, other justices, 156 judges, **prominent businessmen such as Donald Trump**, and even yours truly. Working side by side with Obama's former Director of National Intelligence (DIA), James Clapper, and Obama's former Director of the CIA, John Brennan, Montgomery witnessed "up close and personal" this "Orwellian Big Brother" intrusion on privacy, likely for potential coercion, blackmail or other nefarious purposes. But when Montgomery came forward as a whistleblower to congressional intelligence committees and various other congressmen and senators, including Senator Charles Grassley, Chairman of the Senate Judiciary Committee, who, like Comey, once had a reputation for integrity, he was "blown off;" no one wanted to even hear what he had to say … After Montgomery was turned away as a whistleblower, he came to me at *Freedom Watch* … **he laid out how persons like then-businessman Donald Trump were illegally spied upon by Clapper, Brennan, and the spy agencies of the Obama administration**. He even claimed that these spy agencies had **manipulated voting in Florida during the 2008 presidential election**, which illegal tampering resulted in helping Obama to win the White House."[48] *(Larry Clayman, founder of Judicial Watch and Freedom Watch, Newsmax, March 19, 2017)* Dennis Montgomery is a CIA / NSA whistleblower who is claiming the CIA and the NSA spied on Trump and many other senior government officials. Brennan, Obama's ally and suspected radical

Muslim, was a leading figure in these various wiretapping schemes. It can be assumed that Iran and the Muslim Brotherhood have access to all this CIA documentation with Brennan and Obama being involved in these intelligence activities.

s. "Fingerprints that are now gonna start coming out that will show that **the Obama administration was heavily listening to what was going on in the Trump campaign**. They (Democrats) do not want the Trump administration to start looking in at the violation of the Espionage Act by Hillary Clinton with her rogue server and by **the President who used a pseudonym on her rogue server and they are both in violation of the Espionage Act**. They do not want this to come out so they brought up all these other facts out about Russia … the unmasking (of Trump people) is another criminal offense … the special prosecutor should start looking at Hillary's rogue server." *Retired Lt. General Thomas McInerney, Air Force Commander, Iran Policy Committee member, Fox Business News, March 27, 2017.*

t. "Frankly speaking, the people on The Hill … get as much information as you can. Get as much intelligence as you can before President Obama leaves the administration because I had a fear that somehow that information would disappear with the senior people who left so it would be hidden away in the bureaucracy … Ummm that **the Trump folks if they found out how we knew what we knew about the Trump staff dealing with Russians that they would try to compromise the sources and methods** meaning that we would no longer have access to that intelligence … I became very worried because not enough was coming out into the open and I knew that there was more. We have very good intelligence on Russia. So then, **I had talked to some of my former colleagues and I knew they were trying to also get information to the hill**. (leaks from former Obama officials.)" *Evelyn Farkas, former Obama administration Asst. Secretary of Defense, admit the Obama administration spied on Donald Trump. MSNBC interview, March 28, 2017.*

u. "Eli Lake from *Bloomberg* set off a firestorm in the US this week with his revelation on Monday that in the last six months of the Obama administration, Susan Rice, former president Barack Obama's national security adviser, requested that the US intelligence community enable her to use foreign intelligence collection as a means of gathering information about Donald Trump's advisers. According to Lake's story, during the course of the US presidential campaign, and with steadily rising intensity after President Donald Trump won the November 2016 election, Rice used her access to intercepted communications of foreign intelligence targets to gather information on Trump's advisers. Some of those reports were then leaked, injuriously, to the media in violation of US criminal statute. Whereas in the normal course of events, the identities of American citizens whose conversations with foreigners are intercepted by the US intelligence community are shielded, in the final months of the Obama administration, Rice repeatedly – on "dozens of occasions" – asked that the identities of Americans who conversed with foreigners be exposed. The Americans in question were Trump's advisers ... This week's discovery that Rice played a central role in the intelligence collection regarding Trump's advisers brings Nunes's allegations that the outgoing Obama administration conducted surveillance of the Trump team to the highest reaches of the administration. Now that Rice has been exposed, it is impossible to claim that in the event such surveillance occurred, it did not reflect the Obama administration's concerted policy ... In the latest iteration of the Obama White House's abuse of intelligence data, administration officials collected and leaked information about members of the incoming Trump administration to undermine its ability to chart a new course in foreign affairs ... Due to their efforts, Trump's national security adviser Lt.-Gen. (ret.) Mike Flynn *[anti-Iran, anti-Sharia]* was forced to resign in a cloud of controversy just three weeks after Trump took office ... This brings us to 2015, and the fight in Washington and throughout the US about Obama's nuclear deal with Tehran. In the 2015 operation, the White House allegedly used intercepted communications between US citizens and Israeli diplomats and between Israeli diplomats in Washington and Jerusalem to defame opponents of the nuclear deal. Lawmakers and private citizens were repeatedly subjected to condemnations in the media where unnamed administration sources questioned their loyalty, alleged that they were serving the interests of a foreign power against the US, and that in the case of lawmakers, they were bought and paid for by rich Jewish donors."[49] *(Caroline Glick, The Jerusalem Post)*

v. "The accusation that the Obama administration used information gleaned from classified foreign surveillance to smear and blackmail its political opponents at home has gained new traction in recent days, after reports that former National Security Adviser Susan Rice may have been rifling through classified transcripts for over a year that could have included information about Donald Trump and his associates ... But what if Donald Trump wasn't the first or only target of an Obama White House campaign of spying and illegal leaks directed at domestic political opponents? In a December 29, 2015 article, *The Wall Street Journal* described how the Obama administration had conducted surveillance on Israeli officials to understand how Prime Minister Benjamin Netanyahu and other Israeli officials, like Ambassador Ron Dermer, intended to fight the Iran Deal. The *Journal* reported that the targeting "also swept up the contents of some of their private conversations with U.S. lawmakers and American-Jewish groups." ... I believe the spying was real and that it was done not in an effort to keep the country safe from threats – but in order to help the White House fight their domestic political opponents. "At some point, the administration weaponized the NSA's legitimate monitoring of communications of foreign officials to stay one step ahead of domestic political opponents," says a pro-Israel political operative who was deeply involved in the day-to-day fight over the Iran Deal. "The NSA's collections of foreigners became a means of gathering real-time intelligence on Americans engaged in perfectly legitimate political activism – activism, due to the nature of the issue, that naturally involved conversations with foreigners. We began to notice the White House was responding immediately, sometimes within 24 hours, to specific conversations we were having. At first, we thought it was a coincidence being amplified by our own paranoia. After a while, it simply became our working assumption that we were being spied on." This is what systematic abuse of foreign-intelligence collection for domestic political purposes looks like: Intelligence collected on Americans, lawmakers, and figures in the pro-Israel community was fed back to the Obama White House as part of its political operations. The administration got the drop on its opponents by using classified information, which it then used to draw up its own game plan to block and freeze those on the other side. And – with the help of certain journalists whose stories (and thus careers) depend on high-level access – terrorize them … In spying on the representatives of the American people and members of the pro-Israel community, the Obama administration learned how far it could go in manipulating the foreign-intelligence surveillance apparatus for its own domestic political advantage. **In both instances, the ostensible targets – Israel and Russia – were simply instruments used to go after the real targets at home** … During the long and contentious lead-up to the Iran Deal the Israeli ambassador was regularly briefing senior officials in Jerusalem, including the prime minister, about the situation, including his meetings with American lawmakers and Jewish community leaders. The Obama administration would be less interested in what the Israelis were doing than in the actions of those who actually had the ability to block the deal – namely, Senate and House members. The administration then fed this information to members of the press, who were happy to relay thinly veiled anti-Semitic conceits by accusing deal opponents of dual loyalty and being in the pay of foreign interests."[50] *(Lee Smith, The Tablet)*

w. On May 5, 2017, **Senator Rand Paul** of Kentucky, announced that secondary to multiple independent sources, the **Obama** administration wiretapped his communications during the 2016 presidential campaign, in which he was a Republican presidential candidate. One week later Paul revealed that Obama was **spying on multiple Republican candidates** when he told *Fox News*, "When I have **two different reporters calling me saying they have multiple sources** saying the Obama administration was either unmasking or querying presidential **candidates** my ears do perk up."

x. **Obama** may have **spied on the Supreme Court**. Judge Andrew Napolitano revealed on the *Fox Business Network* on May 15, 2017, that "**Justice Scalia told me that he often thought the court was being surveilled**. And he told me that probably **four or five**

years ago … [and with reference to the above quote] … If they had to unmask Senator Paul's name to reveal a conversation he was having with a foreign agent and the foreign agent was hostile to the United States they can do that. That's not what he's talking about. They're talking about unmasking him when he's having a conversation with his campaign manager when he's running in the Republican primary."

y. "Evidence shows that John Roberts, Chief Justice of the United States Supreme Court, was "hacked" by a Deep State surveillance operation overseen by Obama administration CIA director John Brennan and Obama director of National Intelligence James Clapper … Tapes released by Federal Judge G. Murray Snow – preserved on a Whistleblower Soundcloud page – show real estate billionaire Timothy Blixseth explaining Brennan and Clapper's surveillance program to Maricopa County Sheriff Joe Arpaio and detective Mike Zullo. **The existence of this surveillance program has been corroborated by Wikileaks' "Vault 7" release and by <u>the public comments</u> of former CIA and NSA contractor Dennis Montgomery**, who says he worked on the program for Brennan and Clapper … Montgomery has gone public with his claims exposing how **the program was used to spy on President Donald Trump when he was a private citizen**. On the explosive tapes, Blixseth walks Arpaio and Zullo through the details of the program on a computer screen. At one point, the three begin pulling up specific names of targeted individuals. "You know who that guy is? That's the head of the FISA court they hacked into, Reggie Walton," Blixseth tells the investigators. "**John Roberts**, **the Chief Justice of the Supreme Court**, **was hacked**," Blixseth tells Arpaio and Zullo."[51] *(Big League Politics, July 12, 2017)*

z. **Obama illegally spied on Americans for years**, **which was confirmed by the Foreign Intelligence Surveillance Court**. According to *Circa News (May 2017)*, "The National Security Agency under former President Barack Obama routinely violated American privacy protections while scouring through overseas intercepts and failed to disclose the extent of the problems until the final days before Donald Trump was elected president last fall, according to once top-secret documents that chronicle some of the most serious constitutional abuses to date by the U.S. intelligence community. More than 5 percent, or one out of every 20 searches seeking upstream Internet data on Americans inside the NSA's so-called Section 702 database violated the safeguards Obama and his intelligence chiefs vowed to follow in 2011, according to one classified internal report reviewed by Circa. The Obama administration self-disclosed the problems at a closed-door hearing Oct. 26 before the Foreign Intelligence Surveillance Court that set off alarm. Trump was elected less than two weeks later. The normally supportive court excoriated administration officials, saying the failure to disclose the extent of the violations earlier amounted to a "**institutional lack of candor**" and that the improper searches constituted a "**very serious Fourth Amendment issue**," according to a recently unsealed court document dated April 26, 2017. The admitted violations undercut one of the primary defenses that the intelligence community and Obama officials have used in recent weeks to justify their snooping into incidental NSA intercepts about Americans. Circa has reported that there was a three-fold increase in NSA data searches about Americans and a rise in the unmasking of U.S. person's identities in intelligence reports after Obama loosened the privacy rules in 2011. Officials like former **National Security Adviser Susan Rice have argued their activities were legal** under the so-called minimization rule changes Obama made and that the intelligence agencies were strictly monitored to avoid abuses. *[Rice lied again.]* **The intelligence court and the NSA's own internal watchdog found that not to be true**. "Since 2011, NSA's minimization procedures have prohibited use of U.S. - person identifiers to query the results of upstream Internet collections under Section 702," the unsealed court ruling declared. "The Oct. 26, 2016 notice informed the court that **NSA analysts had been conducting such queries in violation of that prohibition, with much greater frequency than had been previously disclosed to the Court**.""[52]

aa. "The **National Security Agency and Federal Bureau of Investigation** violated specific civil liberty protections during the Obama years by **improperly searching and disseminating raw intelligence on Americans or failing to promptly delete unauthorized intercepts**, according to newly declassified memos that provide some of the richest detail to date on the spy agencies' ability to obey their own rules. The memos reviewed by *The Hill* were publicly released on July 11 through Freedom of Information Act litigation by the American Civil Liberties Union. They detail specific violations that the NSA or FBI disclosed to the Foreign Intelligence Surveillance Court or the Justice Department's national security division during President Obama's tenure between 2009 and 2016."[53] *(The Hill, July 25, 2017)*

10. **Susan Rice**, Obama's former national security advisor, lied during a *PBS NewsHour* interview when she stated, "**<u>I know nothing about this</u>. I was surprised to see reports from Chairman Nunes on that account today … <u>can we trust the word of the White House</u>**," in responding to a question whether Trump or any of his associates and campaign officials were swept up in incidental intelligence collections. Eli Lake, reporting on *Bloomberg* that "White House lawyers last month learned that the **former national security adviser Susan Rice requested the identities of U.S. persons in raw intelligence reports on dozens of occasions that connect to the Donald Trump transition and campaign**, according to U.S. officials familiar with the matter. The pattern of Rice's requests was discovered in a National Security Council review of the government's policy on "unmasking" the identities of individuals in the U.S. who are not targets of electronic eavesdropping, but whose communications are collected incidentally. Normally those names are redacted from summaries of monitored conversations and appear in reports as something like 'U.S. Person One.'"[54]

This information was confirmed by two other reliable independent sources. Rice may be a major source of some leaks.

a. "Susan Rice, who served as the National Security Adviser under President Obama, has been identified as the official who requested unmasking of incoming Trump officials, *Cernovich Media* can exclusively report. The White House Counsel's office identified Rice as the person **responsible for the unmasking after examining Rice's document log requests**. The reports Rice requested to see are kept under tightly-controlled conditions. Each person must log her name before being granted access to them."[55] *(Medium, April 2, 2017)*

b. "**Computer logs that former President Obama's team left behind in the White House indicate his national security adviser Susan Rice accessed numerous intelligence reports** during Obama's last seven months in office that contained National Security Agency intercepts **involving Donald Trump** and his associates, *Circa* has learned. Intelligence sources said the logs discovered by National Security Council staff suggested Rice's interest in the NSA materials, some of which included unmasked Americans' identities, appeared to begin last July around the time Trump secured the GOP nomination and accelerated after Trump's election in November launched a transition that continued through January. The intelligence reports included some intercepts of Americans talking to foreigners and many more involving foreign leaders talking about the future president, his campaign associates or his transition, the sources said. Most if not all had nothing to do with the Russian election interference scandal, the sources said, speaking only on condition of anonymity given the sensitive nature of the materials."[56] *(Circa, April 3, 2017)*

c. "Former President Barack Obama's **national security adviser Susan Rice ordered U.S. spy agencies to produce "detailed spreadsheets" of legal phone calls involving Donald Trump and his aides** when he was running for president, according to former U.S. Attorney Joseph diGenova. "What was produced by the intelligence community at the request of Ms. Rice were detailed spreadsheets of intercepted phone calls with unmasked Trump associates in perfectly legal conversations with individuals," diGenova told *The Daily Caller News Foundation* Investigative Group Monday. "The overheard conversations involved no illegal activity by anybody of the Trump associates, or anyone they were speaking with," diGenova said. "In short, the only apparent illegal activity was the unmasking of the people in the calls." Other official sources with direct knowledge and who requested anonymity confirmed to The DCNF diGenova's description of surveillance reports Rice ordered one year before the 2016 presidential election. **Also on Monday**, *Fox News* and *Bloomberg News*, **citing multiple sources reported that Rice had requested the intelligence information that was produced in a highly organized operation**."[57] *(The Daily Caller, April 3, 2017)*

d. "The **foundation of the United States' unrivaled global leadership rests only in part on** our military might, the strength of our economy and the power of our ideals. It is also grounded in **the perception that the United States is steady, rational and fact-based**. To lead effectively, the United States **must maintain respect and trust**. So, when a White House deliberately dissembles and serially contorts the facts, its actions pose a serious risk to America's global leadership, among friends and adversaries alike."[58] *(Susan Rice, "When the White House Twists the Truth, We are all Less Safe," The Washington Post, Opinions, March 21, 2017. Rice is attacking Trump regarding the insinuation that Obama was eavesdropping on the Trump campaign and Trump Tower.)* Susan Rice is delusional if she believes the world leaders are not aware of all the lies documented in this book regarding Obama and her role in supporting Obama's most flagrant and unpatriotic misrepresentations. Rice advances the concepts of respect and trust during her political surveillance of the Trump campaign and transition period using the resources of the U.S. intelligence community. The following list contains **examples of <u>Rice's other lies</u> she has told over the years** to protect her liberal bosses, including President Barack Obama. All of these lies were approved for dissemination by Presidents Obama and Clinton.

i.   "Newly obtained emails on Benghazi show then-U.N. **Ambassador Susan Rice was <u>coached by a key White House aide to lie</u> and ignore the facts known and reported on the ground** to make the administration look good … That email, with the subject line: "RE: PREP Call with Susan: Saturday at 4:00 p.m. ET," was sent to other key White House staffers such as then-Communications Director David Plouffe and Press Secretary Jay Carney the day before now-National Security Adviser Susan Rice made her whirlwind tour on five Sunday news show appearances to specifically and emphatically blame an Internet video for the Sept. 11, 2012, attack on the American diplomatic mission in Benghazi, Libya, in which U.S. Ambassador Christopher Stevens and three other nationals were killed. **One of the goals listed in the emails was the need for Rice** "to underscore that these protests are rooted in an Internet video, and not a broader failure or policy." She was also to "reinforce the President and Administration's strength and steadiness in dealing with difficult challenges." Her job was not to tell the truth, but to put lipstick on the Obama administration's Benghazi pig … **The terms "al-Qaida" and "attack" were stripped out** by 4:42 p.m., and shortly afterward Vietor thanked colleagues for revisions and said they would be vetted "here," as in the White House. He then forwarded "edits" from John Brennan, the current CIA chief who then was a White House counterterrorism adviser. In a White House meeting on Saturday morning, Sept. 15, the CIA, at the direction of the State Department and White House, drafted the final version of the talking points from which **all references to al-Qaida and security warnings in Benghazi before the attack were deleted**."[59] *(IBD editorial, April 29, 2014)* Rice stated on *ABC News 'This Week'*, on September 16, 2012, "First of all, **<u>let's be clear about what transpired here</u>**. What happened this week in Cairo, **in Benghazi,** in many other parts of the region ... was a result -- **a direct result of a heinous and offensive video that was widely disseminated**, that the U.S. government had nothing to do with, which we have made clear is reprehensible and disgusting. We have also been very clear in saying that there is no excuse for violence, there is -- that we have condemned it in the strongest possible terms." The Select Committee on Benghazi Releases Proposed Report from the House of Representatives stated, "**Susan Rice's comments on the Sunday talk shows were met with shock and disbelief by State Department employees** in Washington. The Senior Libya Desk Officer, Bureau of Near Eastern Affairs, State Department, wrote: "I think Rice was off the reservation on this one." The Deputy Director, Office of Press and Public Diplomacy, Bureau of Near Eastern Affairs, State Department, responded: "Off the reservation on five networks!" The Senior Advisor for Strategic Communications, Bureau of Near East Affairs, State Department, wrote: "**WH [White House] very worried about the politics. This was all their doing.**"

ii.   Rice declared that **Sergeant Bergdahl**, the Muslim convert who deserted his fellow soldiers to find the Taliban and was later exchanged for five Taliban and al-Qaeda leaders, **served with** "**honor and distinction**." Bill Kristol responded on national TV, "There's a lot of reporting that he wasn't taken in battle. He seems to have deserted or at least gone AWOL. He may have cooperated with the enemy after they captured him. Soldiers have died trying to find him. His own platoon and his own battalion, company and battalion, seem to have come under a lot more attacks after he was taken. The degree of anger amongst soldiers, on email and on listservs, is unbelievable. And that needs to be taken seriously. Those are the people who fought, who fought in the same company in some cases, and who feel like they sacrificed to get this guy back who may have **behaved at best irresponsibly and at worst worse**."

iii. Rice was also an integral part of the "**echo chamber**" that advanced Obama's lies that supported the JCPOA with Iran.

iv.   "We were able to **find a solution** that didn't necessitate the use of force **that actually removed the chemical weapons that were known from Syria**, in a way that the use of force would never have accomplished. Our aim in contemplating the use of force following the use of chemical weapons in August of 2013 was not to intervene in the civil war, not to become involved in the combat between Assad and the opposition, but **to deal with the threat of chemical weapons by virtue of the diplomacy** that we did with Russia and with the Security Council. **We were able to get the Syrian government to voluntarily and verifiably give up its chemical weapons stockpile.**"[60] *Rice interview with NPR Morning Edition host Rachel Martin, January 16, 2017.* In early April 2017, Assad attacked Syrian civilian population centers with Sarin gas which led to Donald Trump ordering a cruise missile attack on a Syrian air base. Rice knew that Obama's agreement with the Russians and the Syrians to remove Assad's chemical weapons was a sham since Obama's Director of National Intelligence James Clapper testified before Congress in February 2016 that there were "gaps and inconsistences in Syria's declaration," that they did not possess chemical weapons. If Obama's agreement with the Syrians and the Russians turned out to be worthless, what can we expect from the JCPOA, that was negotiated between Obama and Iran?

v.   "My responsibility is **to execute the most responsible, comprehensive, effective transition** that we possibly can. That is the direction that President Obama has given and that's what we're doing." *Rice interview with NPR Morning Edition host Rachel Martin, January 16, 2017.*[61] Rice unmasked Trump and Trump officials from intelligence transcripts in order to sabotage the Trump campaign and his future presidency.

vi. In 1998, after Madeline Albright, Secretary of State for President Clinton refused requests for additional security for the U.S. embassy from the U.S. ambassador to Kenya, "the American embassies in Tanzania and Kenya were simultaneously attacked with car bombs. In Kenya, 12 American diplomats and more than 200 Africans were killed. As in Benghazi, requests for more security were denied, warnings were issued, prior incidents were ignored and Susan Rice went on TV to explain it all. Within 24 hours, Rice, then assistant secretary of state for African affairs, went on *PBS* as spokesperson for the administration – just as she was regarding Benghazi when **she parroted the administration's false narrative on five Sunday talk shows** on Sept. 16, 2012, that Benghazi was caused by a flash mob enraged by an Internet video … Also then, as now, she went on TV to claim, falsely, that we "**maintain a high degree of security at all of our embassies at all times**" and that we "had no telephone warning or call of any sort like that, that might have alerted either embassy just prior to the blast." There were plenty of warnings and our East African diplomats were begging for help as Ambassador Chris Stevens was in Benghazi. Eerie similarities between Benghazi and Nairobi are many. A review of the attacks showed the CIA repeatedly told State Department officials in Washington and in the Kenya embassy that there was an active terrorist cell in Kenya connected to Osama bin Laden, who masterminded the attack. The CIA and FBI investigated at least three terrorist threats in Nairobi in the year before the bombing. Gen. Anthony Zinni, commander of the U.S. Central Command, had visited Nairobi on his own and warned that the Nairobi embassy was an easy and tempting target for terrorists. For Susan Rice and her defenders to claim that she had "nothing to with Benghazi," that she was an innocent victim of altered talking points, is completely bogus."[62]

(IBD Editorial, November 30, 2012) Rice has a history of lying for her bosses in order to protect their legacies and bury their policy failures.

vii. **Susan Rice**: "The investigations that are underway as to the Russian involvement in our electoral process are very important. They're very serious. And every American ought to have an interest in those investigations going where ever the evidence indicates they should. I have an interest in that as an American citizen …" **Andrea Mitchell, MSNBC News**: Do you regret that the Obama White House did not decide earlier to blow the whistle on the Russians? **Rice**: We did blow the whistle on October 7th. And that came as soon as **the intelligence community and all of its component parts**, <u>17 agencies</u>, **came to a consensus conclusion**, that we took the extraordinary step of making public that the Russian government at the highest levels was involved in an effort to play in our electoral process. That information was put out to the American people in a statement from the Director of National Intelligence and the Secretary of Homeland Security." *Rice interview with Andrea Mitchell, MSNBC News, April 4, 2017.* Only four agencies made the above conclusion and the *New York Times* was forced to retract its story. As Obama's National Security Advisor, Rice always knew only four agencies were involved with that assessment.

(1) *The New York Times* issued a correction on June 29, 2017 stating, "A White House Memo article on Monday about President Trump's deflections and denials about Russia referred incorrectly to the source of an intelligence assessment that said Russia orchestrated hacking attacks during last year's presidential election. The assessment was made by four intelligence agencies – the Office of the Director of National Intelligence *[Clapper – Muslim Brotherhood is not violent]*, the Central Intelligence Agency *[Brennan – jihad is not violent, clandestine Muslim convert, politicized intelligence reports for Obama]*, the Federal Bureau of Investigation *[Comey – admitted he is source of leaks from FBI, Clinton ally, redacted FBI transcripts of Orlando terrorist attack]* and the National Security Agency. **The assessment was not approved by all 17 organizations in the American intelligence community.**"

(2) Even the *AP* issued a clarification stating, "In stories published April 6, June 2, June 26 and June 29, The Associated Press reported that all 17 U.S. intelligence agencies have agreed that Russia tried to influence the 2016 election to benefit Donald Trump. That assessment was based on information collected by three agencies – the FBI, CIA and National Security Agency – and published by the Office of the Director of National Intelligence, which represents

all U.S. intelligence agencies. <u>**Not all 17 intelligence agencies were involved in reaching the assessment**</u>."

(3) "Well, it is hard not to reach that conclusion that, exactly so. First of all, on the number of components in the international community, yes, there are 17; the 16 components by law plus the Office of the Director of National Intelligence. When then president-elect Trump was briefed on this on the 6th of January, there were four of us – meaning the directors of NSA, FBI and CIA and myself. That's all. And we explained who did the report. **So how this narrative got out there about 17 components being involved**, I don't know. But the report itself makes it clear that it was the three agencies plus the Office of the Director of National Intelligence that put this intelligence community assessment together." *Former Director of National Intelligence James Clapper, CNN's "The Situation Room," July 6, 2017.* Rice lied about the number of assessments to hurt Trump.

11. "No President can order a wiretap. Those restrictions were put in place to protect citizens from people like you (Trump)." *Ben Rhodes tweet, responding to Trump tweet, March 4, 2017.* Former National Security Advisor Rice also stated on a PBS NewsHour interview with Judy Woodruff, "No president, no White House can order the surveillance of another American citizen."

a. "(1) **Notwithstanding any other law, the President, through the Attorney General, may authorize electronic surveillance without a court order** under this subchapter to acquire foreign intelligence information for periods of up to one year if the Attorney General certifies in writing under oath that …" *Chapter 36 of Title 50 of the US Code, War and National Defense, Subchapter 1, Section 1802.*

b. "Besides the FISA court, "wiretapping" or electronic surveillance can also be done under Title III authority. The government used this authority, for example, in the Justice Department's secret Fast and Furious "gunwalking" case. **Additionally, U.S. presidents have the power to issue secret presidential directives that can authorize otherwise illegal acts** (theoretically in the country's best interests). These directives may come with pre-planned cover stories to be used in the event the operation is exposed, and they come with indemnity for those involved, giving them permission to lie about the operation or their involvement without fear of prosecution. The public will rarely know about such presidential directives since most who see them must sign agreements that promise non-disclosure and consent to polygraphs. [snip] There are "back-door" ways to collect and report on a target without Title III or FISA court authority. If it's for political purposes or blackmail, this may consist of "inventing" an excuse to surveil the target. If the work of targeting an individual cannot be accomplished by government intel officers, it can be contracted out to third parties or to foreign parties who aren't bound by U.S. law. Incidental collection of a U.S. citizen target may be "orchestrated" for political reasons by those who have tools and tradecraft available to them because of their positions of power. There are ways to do it with no fingerprints." *(Sharyl Attkisson website, April 12, 2017 posting)*

CHAPTER 6

Politics

"In a time of universal deceit, telling the truth is a revolutionary
act." *George Orwell*

OBAMA'S QUESTIONABLE LYING was initially pushed into the headlines in 2009 by Joe Wilson, a five-term congressman from South Carolina. Wilson twice called out "You Lie" when Obama stated that the new health care law would not "insure illegal immigrants," and "the reforms I'm proposing would not apply to those who are here illegally." In retrospect, there are two lies here. First, the new law would give benefits to those individuals who are in the United States illegally. Obama always knew that the status of the illegal aliens would be changed either through legislation signed with his approval, or by amnesty via an executive order. Either way, illegal aliens would not be illegal in the near future. Thus, by being on the fast track to citizenship, they would be eligible for the insurance benefits. Obama would later call illegal aliens "Americans in waiting." Obama knew the nomenclature of illegal aliens was changing and the present nomenclature did not represent anyone in his presentations. Obama was putting forward the "hoodwinking and bamboozling" strategy advanced by Malcolm X. By June 2016, eighteen states were already offering healthcare subsidies through the ACA for undocumented children and pregnant women.

A Senate report released in 2016 also proved that Obama blatantly lied to the country, as *Fox News* reported, "Illegal immigrants and individuals with unclear legal status wrongly benefited from up to $750 million in ObamaCare subsidies … The report, produced by Republicans on the Senate Homeland Security and Governmental Affairs Committee, examined Affordable Care Act tax credits meant to defray the cost of insurance premiums. It found that as of June 2015, 'the Administration awarded approximately $750 million in tax credits on behalf of individuals who were later determined to be ineligible because they failed to verify their citizenship, status as a national, or legal presence.' The review found the credits went to more than 500,000 people – who are illegal immigrants or whose legal status was unclear due to insufficient records."[63]

The above Congressional incident was a landmark event early in Obama's presidency. Regarding immigration reform, Obama repeatedly stated he did not have the constitutional authority to advance his agenda by executive orders. He stated, "The problem is that I'm the president of the United States, I'm not the emperor of the United States," and also "believe me, the idea of doing things on my own is very tempting ... But that's not how our system works. That's not how our democracy functions. That's not how our Constitution is written." Obama repeated this line over twenty times, emphasizing he did not have the executive authority to implement a unilateral fundamental change to our immigration laws. Listening to Obama during these recourses, one would tend to believe these statements coming from someone who taught constitutional law at the University of Chicago Law School and who was president of the Harvard Law Review. Yet, he signed controversial executive orders, reversing his original position, and showed a blatant disregard for the Constitution of the United States.

Obama told another major lie to the national press regarding Hillary Clinton's private email server. In a March 2015 interview with *CBS News* correspondent Robert Plante, Obama stated he first heard about Clinton's email problems in the daily newspaper. Obama declared, "The same time everybody else learned it through news reports ... The policy of my administration is to encourage transparency, which is why my emails, the BlackBerry I carry around, all those records are available and archived." Later, the White House Press Office declared that Obama had corresponded with Clinton via email with her private address and her private server. It would have been impossible for Obama not to know he was sending the emails to a non-government server and a private address. In September 2016, the FBI, via admissions by Huma Abedin, revealed that Obama often corresponded with Clinton with a pseudonym, which also showed he did not want third parties to realize he was communicating with a cabinet member via an unsecured unapproved server. By using a pseudonym, Obama also lied about wanting to maintain an acceptable level of transparency. Abedin also revealed during an FBI investigation that she was instructed to update the White House records at least six times whenever Clinton changed her email address, including those addresses used on her private server. Even Clinton's staff knew the president was lying. Cheryl Mills, Clinton's chief of staff and counselor as secretary of state, wrote to John Podesta, Clinton's presidential campaign manager in March 2015, stating, "We need to clean this up – he has emails from her – they do not say state.gov."[64] Obama lied to *CBS News* and protected Clinton's illegal use of a private server for communicating on matters regarding national security, thus he knowingly compromised U.S. national security and intelligence sources, which could be viewed as grounds for impeachment. FBI investigators admitted that at least five foreign intelligence agencies had hacked Clinton's private server. Obama's denial of knowing about Clinton's private server followed his Selma speech, which brought back memories of Obama's first presidential campaign, when he stated, "There was something stirring across the country because of what happened in Selma, Alabama, because some folks are willing to march across a bridge. So they got together and Barack Obama Jr. was born." This was yet another lie told by Obama, as the Selma march occurred in 1965 and he was born in 1961.

After seven to eight years of endless lies, the American public started to wise up to Obama and his antics. A *Fox News* poll in early 2015 showed a record low of 43% of respondents saying they felt that Obama was honest, and a majority of Americans (54%) believing the president was dishonest. But to Obama, these sentiments are a moot point, since polls go up and down and Americans have such a short memory span. The amount of distrust leveled at this president by the American public is unprecedented. As long as Obama advanced his radical policies without being impeached, he always moved "forward" with his agenda, and used lies to secure his political goals.

1. "If I am the Democratic nominee, I will aggressively pursue an agreement with the Republican nominee to preserve a publicly financed general election." *Obama, 2008 presidential campaign trail.* Obama presented himself as a candidate with stellar ethics, yet backtracked on this promise by blaming a broken system abused by the Republicans. One of Obama's first major lies on the presidential campaign trail. **A harbinger of things to come**.

2. "With an endless parade of distractions, political posturing and **phony scandals**, Washington has taken its eye off the ball." *Obama, Knox College economic address, 2013.* "One of the things that you discover as president is that there are all these rules and norms **and laws** … **and the people that work for you are also subject to these rules and norms** … I am very proud that we have been able to leave **this administration without significant scandal** … I will put this administration against any administration in history." *Obama, one week after Trumps election victory, mid-November 2016.* And … "The president prides himself on the fact that **his administration hasn't had a scandal and he hasn't done something to embarrass himself**. That's because that's who he is – that's who they are – and I think that's what really resonates with the American people." *Valerie Jarrett, senior Obama advisor, CNN interview, January 1, 2017.* Former White House Press Secretary Jay Carney repeated the same theme during *CNN's* "New Day," on January 10, 2017, saying Obama's presidency was "**scandal-free** beyond his personal life." Scandals (a) – (y) should be considered among the top 25.

    a. Obama **purged the U.S. military** of hundreds of senior experienced and well-respected officers and leaders during his first term, **at the same time** Prime Minister Erdogan of Turkey and President Morsi of Egypt were purging their respective military forces of officers who were considered not loyal to their radical Islamic agenda. It was a coordinated effort between Morsi, Erdogan and Obama.

    b. Obama **allowed Afghan soldiers to rape young Afghan boys on U.S. military bases** in Afghanistan, and prosecuted U.S. military personnel who attempted to prevent these atrocities.

    c. Obama **refused to send military help** to assist the U.S. ambassador to Libya, Christopher Stevens and his associates, while they were being attacked by al-Qaeda forces for eight hours **in Benghazi**. Obama then lied to the American public when he blamed the **Benghazi attack** on an internet video. Obama disappeared and **went to sleep early** in the White House, while Ambassador Stevens was **raped** and murdered, and three other Americans were killed.

d.   Seventeen members of the Obama administration **met with IT specialist Abid Awan at the White House for 7 hours on November 23, 2013**. Abid is the younger brother of **Imran Awan**, who was **arrested for bank fraud** at Dulles airport while he was **attempting to flee the United States** after **wiring** $**300,000 to Pakistan**. Imran also worked as an IT specialist for Congresswoman Debbie Wasserman Schultz, who was also head of the DNC. The three Awan brothers (Abid, Jamal and Imran) were previously arrested for accessing unauthorized computers and worked with multiple Congressmen who were members of many committees involved with defense and national security issues including the House Permanent Select Committee on Intelligence, the Committee on Homeland Security, and the House Committee on Foreign Affairs. The three brothers were relieved of their jobs the day after the Navy SEALs launched a raid against al-Qaeda positions **in Yemen** resulting in the **death of one Navy SEAL officer**. Reports immediately surfaced that the al-Qaeda operatives knew the American forces were attacking their positions beforehand, and were prepared for the fight. It is suspected that these defense and intelligence "leaks" originated from Obama appointments (i.e. - plants) to key and sensitive areas in the defense and intelligence establishments, which may have included the Awans. It was alleged that **smashed computer drives** were found at a property owned by Imran Awan, which were later possessed by the FBI. **Seth Rich**, a DNC staffer who may have been cooperating with the FBI regarding illegal activity at the DNC, attended a party of DC IT staffers, including Imran Awan, just hours before he was murdered on the streets of DC. Congresswoman Wasserman **Schultz kept Awan on her payroll** after he was relieved of his other congressional related jobs and after he planned on living in Pakistan for at least six months (? hush money). Imran was also hired by Andre Carson, a Muslim congressman who was the ranking member of the Emerging Threats Subcommittee and the Intelligence Committee. Carson has many documented **ties to the Muslim Brotherhood**, including ISNA, ICNA, CAIR, and MPAC. The Awan brothers also reportedly owed $100,000 to an Iraqi politician with **links to Hezbollah**. Obama may have helped plant Muslim IT experts with connections to the Muslim Brotherhood and other Middle Eastern terrorist groups with various congressional staff whose computers had access to sensitive materials regarding defense, intelligence, and homeland security. Obama may have helped place these congressmen on sensitive committees and then had IT specialists loyal to enemies of the United States handle their IT needs, which would lead to a significant compromise of United States' interests. These possible agents could have transferred sensitive national security documents to these terrorist organizations and other enemies of the United

States, which is treason. Retired U.S. Army Lt. Col Tony Shaffer stated on *Fox News* with Laura Ingraham on *Tucker Carlson Tonight*, "They had massive access to all databases to include e-mail of members of Congress, super-user access to the system itself, and most importantly the sensitive information being held by the House Foreign Affairs Committee and other committees that they had access to ... And then they dumped – then there's evidence some of the information they had access to dumped off into a third database that's actually being called a breach ... Now the FBI has rolled in and let me give you the big take away here, **it looks like a foreign intelligence service may be the recipient of all this. Something called the Muslim Brotherhood.**" Andre Carson may have brought the Awan brothers on board into his network and allowed them access sensitive information which he knew would be transferred to the Muslim Brotherhood and various Islamic terrorist groups. The meeting held at the White House must be thoroughly investigated. Who attended the meeting with Abid Awan? Was Obama present? Did Valerie Jarrett attend? What was discussed during the seven-hour meeting. Why were White House officials meeting with low level congressional IT technicians until midnight? Obama may have helped lay the groundwork for these alleged spies to compromise U.S. congressional records and U.S. national security interests at least on behalf of the Muslim Brotherhood, an organization to which Obama has been very supportive throughout his presidency.

e. **IRS targeting and political persecution** of conservative political and religious groups and Obama's political adversaries. Many of the IRS's records related to its abuses and political targeting have been lost, which implies a significant cover-up has been instituted.

f. Obama was **briefed by the CIA in mid-2016 concerning Russia's hacking and interference in the 2016 election cycle, and did nothing** to halt this unacceptable intervention except to ask Putin to "cut it out." Obama, along with the Clinton campaign, then created the fake news accusation that Trump colluded with the Russians and attempted to create a scenario where a special prosecutor would advance charges that would lead to the impeachment of President Trump, despite no evidence of collusion.

    i. According to *The New York Times*, "Around mid-August, Mr. Johnson said [during senate testimony], federal officials began hearing reports of "scanning and probing" of some state voter database registries. In the weeks after, intelligence officials became convinced the Russians were behind those efforts ... **Asked why former President** <u>Barack Obama</u> **did not make his own announcement that a foreign power was meddling in the election process**, Mr. Johnson suggested administration officials believed just his involvement would inherently politicize the facts. "We were very concerned that we not be perceived as taking sides in the election, injecting ourselves into a very heated campaign or taking steps to delegitimize the election process and undermine the integrity of the election process," he said."[65] *Obama did* *nothing because he thought Hillary was going to win the election. If Obama had any evidence of Trump colluding with the Russians, the information would have been released before the election, guaranteeing a Clinton victory.*

ii.   "Well I just heard today for the first time that Obama knew about Russia a long time before the election, and he did nothing about it. But nobody wants to talk about that. **The CIA gave him information on Russia a long time before they even -- before the election**. And I hardly see it. It's an amazing thing. To me -- in other words, the question is, **if he had the information**, **why didn't he do something about it**? He should have done something about it. But you don't read that. … That doesn't leak out, no. They're very selective leaks." *Trump, Fox and Friends, June 26, 2017.* Trump answered his own question hours later in a tweet saying, "The reason that President Obama did NOTHING about Russia after being notified by the CIA of meddling is that **he expected Clinton would win** … and did not want to 'rock the boat.' He didn't 'choke,' <u>**he colluded or obstructed**</u>, and it did the Dems and Crooked Hillary no good." Obama doing nothing when Russia was interfering in the U.S. presidential election is a major scandal. The collusion and obstruction investigation by the special prosecutor targeting Trump, should be directed at Obama and Lynch.

g.   **Obama payed a $1.7 billion-dollar cash ransom**, which he denied was a ransom, for four American hostages held by Iran, which was most likely used to fund the IRGC and Islamic terrorism. Charles Krauthammer concluded on *Fox News' Special Report* on August 3, 2016, "It was illegal. It isn't only the optics. It isn't only that they are just looking ridiculous in denying that it was a quid pro quo. Obviously, it wasn't a coincidence. The reason that it was objected to by Justice, **there is a statute that prohibits us from engaging in Iran dealing with dollars**. So, they had to print the money here, ship it over to Switzerland, turn it into Swiss francs and euros and ship it over to Iran. If a private company had done this, this is called **money laundering**. The CEO would be in jail right now … The reason **it was concealed is because it's illegal**. That's why Congress wasn't notified, because <u>**it's scandalous**</u> for the administration to explicitly defy a law that says you can't deal in American currency. And the second thing is, it isn't only that it encourages terrorism in the future, it's that the money is in cash. **Why in cash**? *[The Swiss francs and Euros will also be used to fund the immigration jihad of Muslim migrants invading and 'fundamentally changing' Europe. The cash can be dispersed very easily to the groups supporting hijrah and terrorism, and will not leave a paper trail.]* **Because that you can't trace it. It's going to go straight to Hezbollah, straight to Hamas, straight to terrorists in Iraq** [ISIS and al-Qaeda]." It wasn't just illegal. It's treason. There are federal laws that prohibit the **funding of terrorist groups by the American government**,

and Obama broke that law as well by knowingly financing Hamas and Hezbollah.
One week after this story broke, the Obama administration confirmed they had transferred the remainder of the $1.7 billion payment to Iran.

i. "The exportation, reexportation, sale, or supply, directly or indirectly, from the United States, or by a United States person, wherever located, of any goods, technology, or services to Iran or the Government of Iran is prohibited." *U.S. Federal law, Section 560.204.* Obama's deal broke federal law, and is illegal. Violations of these laws is a felony and punishable with up to twenty years in prison.

ii. "Evasions: attempts; causing violations; conspiracies: … any transaction … that evades or avoids, has the purpose of evading or avoiding, causes a violation of, or attempts to violate any of the prohibitions set forth in this part is prohibited … Any conspiracy formed to violate any of the prohibitions set forth in this part is prohibited." *U.S. Federal law, Section 560.2014.* Obama violated another aspect of the federal code. Obama broke his oath to uphold the laws of the United States, especially when those laws are in place to protect the national security interests of the United States.

iii. "The clearing of U.S. dollar- or other currency-denominated transactions through the U.S. financial system or involving a U.S. person remain prohibited." *Treasury Department Guidelines concerning the JCPOA.* Obama knowingly violated the JCPOA guidelines in order to infuse Iran with massive amounts of cash divided between multiple foreign currencies, a transaction that was hid from Congress and the American public. The fact that Obama transgressed the JCPOA agreement which he helped write and approve, proves he committed fraud against the United States and sacrificed the national security interests of America.

iv. Section 2339A of the federal penal code makes it illegal to provide material support to terrorists or terrorist organizations. Since both John Kerry and Susan Rice have admitted that a percentage of these funds will finance Islamic terrorism associated with the Iranian government (the IRGC Quds organization, Hezbollah, Hamas, al-Qaeda), Obama violated another federal statute and broke the law.

v. "The second law involved money laundering, criminalized by Congress in Section 1956 of the penal code. There are several prohibited varieties of money laundering. It can be a crime, for example, to conduct a financial transaction involving money used to facilitate unlawful activity. And if money is transferred outside the United States, it can be illegal to use it to promote criminal activity."[66] *Andrew McCarthy, The National Review*

vi. "Obama has clearly admitted that he knew about the planeload of cash … He chose to use foreign currency from foreign banks in an attempt to knowingly evade restrictions on sending money to Iran. As former prosecutor Andrew McCarthy however has pointed out, the law criminalizes efforts to evade sanctions, stating "any transaction . . . that evades or avoids, has the purpose of evading or avoiding" is prohibited. Furthermore "any conspiracy formed to violate any of the prohibitions set forth in this part is prohibited."[67] Obama and his administration represent a criminal conspiracy to violate the laws of this country. Even if these regulations were not in place, funding Iran directly funds terrorism. And that's a crime. The latest State Department report found that Iran, "continued its terrorist-related activity in 2015, including support for Hezballah, Palestinian terrorist groups in Gaza, and various groups in Iraq and throughout the Middle East." It found that, "Iran increased its assistance to Iraqi Shia terrorist groups, including Kata'ib Hezballah (KH), which is a U.S. designated Foreign Terrorist Organization." It even noted that, "Iran remained unwilling to bring to justice senior al-Qa'ida (AQ) members it continued to detain and refused to publicly identify the members in its custody. Iran previously allowed AQ facilitators to operate a core facilitation pipeline through Iran since at least 2009, enabling AQ to move funds and fighters to South Asia and Syria." By aiding Iran, Obama is aiding a whole range of Islamic terrorist groups from Hezbollah to Al-Qaeda … **When you are reduced to funneling cash from foreign banks to a state sponsor of terrorism in an unmarked cargo airplane**, **then your presidency has become a corrupt criminal enterprise** … Funneling $400 million in cash to Iran is the opposite of strictly maintaining sanctions. It's the sort of thing that smugglers do when they are violating sanctions. Iran's chief smuggler *[because Obama is an Iranian agent]* is now a man living in the White House. And that is unacceptable … It's the sort of thing people go to jail for. It's the sort of thing that presidents **ought to be impeached** for."[68] *Daniel Greenfield, Frontpage Magazine, 2016*

h. Obama conducted official government business related to U.S. national security and foreign affairs with Secretary of State Clinton via an **unsecured email system**, on Hillary Clinton's private server. Obama knowingly allowed his privileged communications to be conducted in a network that he knew was compromised and would be monitored by competing and antagonistic foreign powers, which is why Obama used an alias instead of his real name. In January 2016, the State Department announced that there were at least 18 email exchanges between President Obama and Secretary of State Clinton. At the very least, Obama allowed Clinton to use a network that was vulnerable and compromised. Obama also knew that information and intelligence that pertained to Iran would be in Clinton's communications and Iran would be able to obtain this classified information with much less effort. Iran was able to identify one of their nuclear scientists,

Shahram Amiri, who was giving U.S. officials data regarding Iran's nuclear program, and later executed him based on Clinton's unsecure email communications. At least five foreign intelligence agencies hacked into Clinton's private server, and Obama allowed them to access critical classified documents and communications that were exchanged between the Oval Office and Clinton's private server.

i.   The Obama administration **requested a FISA warrant in order to tap the phones and computer servers of Donald Trump and his campaign team weeks before the presidential election**, under the guise of investigating fake concerns that he was colluding with Russia during the 2016 presidential campaign.

j.   Obama unofficially sponsored **UNSC Resolution 2334**, which declared that the Western Wall in Jerusalem in the Jewish Quarter of the old city was "occupied Palestinian territory." Days later Kerry gave moral equivalence to Israeli independence and the Palestinian "Naqba" (catastrophe) Day [establishing the state of Israel was a catastrophe], thus Kerry and the Obama administration may feel that the creation of a Jewish state in the Middle East was a diplomatic and ethical mistake.

k.   Obama failed to notify Congress thirty days before **the Bergdahl-Taliban prisoner exchange**, as required by National Defense Authorization Act, which by itself was an act of treason that would validate grounds for Obama's impeachment.

l.   **Supporting BLM**, whose leaders and followers publicly called for the murder of policemen at various rallies. BLM officially accused Israel of committing genocide. Obama invited BLM officials, who were felons, to the White House.

m.   Obama **conspired against American interests with Russian President Medvedev**, when Obama **promised him** "**more flexibility**" concerning nuclear missile negotiations and other issues. Obama was caught on an open microphone saying, "On all these issues, but particularly missile defense, this can be solved, but it's important for him to **give me space** … This is my last election. **After my election, I have more flexibility**." Obama presented false foreign policy positions during the 2012 presidential campaign regarding policies affecting Russian interests, which would not represent his true positions after he won his second term. Obama may have colluded with the Russians.

n.   Obama **gave security clearances to Huma Abedin and a huge number of other individuals all who were affiliated with the Muslim Brotherhood**, which has formally dedicated itself to destroying the United States "from within."

o.   Obama's **failed to have one year of annual real GDP growth surpassing 3%** during his eight-year presidency, which is the worst economic record since the Great Depression in the early 1930s. *The Wall Street Journal* reported in July 2016, "Even seven years after the recession ended, the current stretch of economic gains has yielded less growth than much shorter business cycles."[69] Obama **increased the national debt by over $10**

trillion, yet for every year of his administration, the economy grew at unexpectedly low anemic GDP growth rates. Where did the money go?

p. **Obama lied** when he promised **Obamacare** would decrease the cost of healthcare premiums and that Americans could keep their doctors. Obama gave waivers for Obamacare to his political supporters including federal employees and Muslims. Obama illegally rewrote and amended the law by executive action. Obamacare's billion-dollar website had many flaws and functioned poorly.

q. **Reaching out to enemies of the United States,** like Cuba, Iran and Hamas, while alienating allies of the United States, like Israel and Great Britain. Obama **interfered in domestic British elections** by going to Great Britain and campaigning against a Brexit, and threatened the British with economic retaliation if they voted against his wishes.

r. Obama may have broken the law by **<u>violating the Logan Act</u>**, which prohibits private citizens negotiating with foreign governments against United States interests. "The Logan Act (18 U.S.C.A. § 953 [1948]) is a single federal statute making it a crime for a citizen to confer with foreign governments against the interests of the United States. Specifically, it prohibits citizens from negotiating with other nations on behalf of the United States without authorization." *(The Free Dictionary)* Obama met with Chancellor Merkel within days of her meeting with President Trump, and likely discussed topics including NATO and climate change, where his views were divergent from the United States' administration. Months later, Obama also flew to South Korea to meet with President Moon, where he was briefed by the South Koreans on their meeting with President Trump just days earlier. Obama most likely wanted to have input into the diplomatic situation regarding North Korea, which fired their first intercontinental ballistic missile just hours after Obama's meeting. With North Korea demonstrating their ability to strike the United States with nuclear weapons just hours after Obama's meeting, Obama's actions may be threatening the welfare of the United States.

s. Backed down from his **Syrian red line** with respect to Syrian use of chemical weapons.

t. A trillion-dollar **stimulus program** early in his first term created minimal private-sector jobs. The bill created many government jobs and supported unions and Obama's political allies. The cost for each job created by Obama's stimulus program ranged from $196,000 to $562,000, according to the CBO, estimating there were 1.4 million to 4 million full-time equivalent jobs created.

u. Obama's speeches have **incited violence and murderous acts against law officers** throughout the United States, including the heinous assassinations of five Dallas officers and three Baton Rouge officers in July 2016. A class action lawsuit has been filed against Obama by a former Department of Justice U.S. attorney.

v. Obama may be considered to be an **accomplice in multiple war crimes** by being an active proponent of massive Muslim immigration into Europe and America, when he knew that increased **Islamic terrorism** and a statistically increased number of **rapes** against non-Muslims would be a direct result of his policies. Obama has repeatedly asked for additional funding to accommodate these Muslim migrants, who have been committing these barbaric crimes. **Being a party to war crimes is grounds for impeachment**. Since George Soros has funded organizations that have assisted Obama's policies as an independent third party enabler, he too, should be held accountable and be charged with war crimes and crimes against humanity. By advancing policies that have led to the genocide of Christians in Iraq and Syria, Obama has committed another war crime.

  i. "The UN Commission of Experts identified 1,600 actual cases of rape in the Bosnian War that took place in the former Yugoslavia over a period of years. In Germany, 2,000 Muslim migrants sexually assaulted 1,200 women in a single night in cities across Germany. The former was considered one of the worst war crimes of the decade. Its perpetrators were bombed and then faced war crimes trials."[70] *(Daniel Greenfield, FrontPage Magazine)* The number of rapes and sexual assaults committed by Muslim migrants across Europe over the past few years may total in the tens of thousands, since just 1,200 were committed in Germany alone on one night. This would signify that Muslims pursing jihad have already committed horrendous war crimes where the migrants and their enablers (Obama, Merkel, Soros) should be tried for war crimes and crimes against humanity. The systematic rape and abuse of women in a society by a single political and religious entity should be treated with the same seriousness as crimes that occurred in Bosnia or in Nazi Germany, which resulted in the Nuremberg trials.

w. Obama **infiltrated the FBI with pro-Islamist leadership** that purposely jeopardized U.S. national security interests and who may have cleared the path for multiple heinous domestic terrorist attacks.

  i. "Before he bombed the **Boston Marathon**, the FBI interviewed Tamerlan Tsarnaev but let him go. Russia sent the Obama Administration a second warning, but the FBI opted against investigating him again …

  ii. The FBI had possession of emails sent by Nidal Hasan saying he wanted to kill his fellow soldiers to protect the Taliban -- but didn't intervene, leading many critics to argue the tragedy that resulted in the death of 31 Americans at **Fort Hood** could have been prevented.

  iii. During the Obama Administration, the FBI claimed that two private jets were being used primarily for counterterrorism, when in fact they were mostly being used for Eric Holder and Robert Mueller's business and personal travel …

iv.   The father of the radical Islamist who detonated a backpack bomb in **New York City** in 2016 alerted the FBI to his son's radicalization. The FBI, however, cleared Ahmad Khan Rahami after a brief interview.

v.   The FBI also investigated the terrorist who killed 49 people and wounded 53 more at the Pulse Nightclub in **Orlando**, **Florida**. Despite a more than 10-month investigation of Omar Mateen -- during which Mateen admitting lying to agents -- the FBI opted against pressing further and closed its case.

vi.   *CBS* recently reported that when two terrorists sought to kill Americans attending the "Draw Muhammad" event in **Garland**, **Texas**, the FBI not only had an understanding an attack was coming, but actually had an undercover agent traveling with the Islamists, Elton Simpson and Nadir Soofi. The FBI has refused to comment on why the agent on the scene did not intervene during the attack."[71]

vii. **FBI Director Comey colluded with Obama to protect the Islamic terrorist**, Muhammad Yousef Abdulazeez, when Comey declared that he did not know the motivations behind the killing of the four Marines in **Chattanooga**, **Tennessee**, five months after the attack, despite the significant proof that Abdulazeez was committing jihad. Comey stated, "**We're still trying to make sure we understand Abdulazeez**, **his motivations** and associations, in a really good way ... **We don't want to smear people**." Comey is protecting the terrorists at war with the United States. Firing Comey should have been Trump's first official act as president.

x.   Obama allowed ISIS to perpetuate genocide against the Christians in Iraq and Syria, and then attempted to purge government records of the evidence that he knew that genocide directed against the Christians was in progress. The American Center for Law and Progress reported at the end of July 2017, "In a startling revelation, news is breaking this week that Obama holdovers within the State Department are actively attempting to scrub its records to remove any mention of the ISIS genocide against Christians."

y.   Obama **withheld components of the nuclear deal with Iran** from Congress and the American public when he "downplayed the release of Iranian prisoners [spies whom he presented as civilians], shut down existing Department of Justice investigation into [Iranian] individuals accused of funneling [military] technology and hardware to Iran, and dropped charges and arrest warrants against more than a dozen dangerous fugitives [associated with the Iranian military and their clandestine nuclear program]." *(Republican Jewish Coalition press release, April 24, 2017)* Politico revealed how Obama misled the American people by suppressing the details of the Iranian agents he released from U.S.

custody as part of the overall JCPOA implementation. Valerie Lincy, the executive director of the Wisconsin Project on Nuclear Arms Control declared, "**This is a scandal**. The cases bear all the hallmarks of exactly the kinds of national security threats we're still going after. It's stunning and hard to understand why we would do this." *[Because Obama advanced Iranian interests over U.S. interests, and is an agent for Iran.]*

z. Obama **distributed the TARP funds to various distressed banks under the condition that they donate a portion of their government funding to Democratic politicians and their PACs** (political action committees). According to documents obtained from the Clinton Foundation computers hacked by Guccifer 2.0, recipients of government funds included former House Speaker Nancy Pelosi, Barney Frank, James Clyburn, Chris Van Hollen, Luis Gutierrez, and Steny Hoyer – all Democratic Congressional leaders. Obama ensured that the U.S. government taxpayer TARP funds were clandestinely and illegally recycled back to the Democratic Congressional leadership. Theoretically, this is an impeachable offense since it involved kick-backs and bribery at the highest levels of the federal government and the executive branch. The banks may have been coerced to donate to Democrats in order to receive funding, or the banks may have bribed the Democratic Congressional leadership in order to receive government bailouts. Either way, the law was broken and individuals on both sides of the fence should be indicted and if found guilty, go to jail. As head of the Democratic Party, Obama is ethically and legally responsible, and his role in these illegal activities needs to be fully investigated.

aa. The total **U.S. national debt almost surpassed $20 trillion** at the end of Obama's second term.

bb. Over **95 million adult Americans were not in the workforce** as Obama left the presidency.

cc. According to Bloomberg, **only 62.9% of Americans owned their own homes** in the second quarter of 2016, which is over a **50-year record low** statistic.

dd. Obama presided over the **greatest gap in income inequality** since the 1920s.

ee. The Obama administration oversaw the **weakest growth in personal income** since data started being collected in 1960. After 2009, the average annualized growth rate was 3.9%, which is a record low for a respective ten-year period.

ff. During the transition period in Egypt when the state leadership was being transferred from Mubarak to the Muslim Brotherhood, **Morsi's political allies whom Obama supported, raped at least three Western journalists**, and used rape and torture as weapons against political opponents.

gg. **Refused to say "Islamic terrorism"** or even "radical Islamic terrorism."

hh.   Obama armed Mexican drug cartels in an ATF operation called "**Fast and Furious**." The **guns were used in the murder of two federal agents** and hundreds of Mexican citizens. "Fast and Furious" firearms supplied by the Obama administration were used also in the ISIS Paris nightclub attack.

   i.   Members of a congressional committee at a public hearing Wednesday blasted former President Barack Obama and his attorney general for allegedly **covering up an investigation into the death of a Border Patrol agent killed as a result of a botched government gun-running project known as Operation Fast and Furious**. The House Oversight Committee also Wednesday released a scathing, nearly 300-page report that found Holder's Justice Department tried to hide the facts from the loved ones of slain Border Patrol Brian Terry – seeing his family as more of a "nuisance" than one deserving straight answers – and slamming **Obama's assertion of executive privilege to deny Congress access to records** pertaining to Fast and Furious. Terry's death exposed Operation Fast and Furious, a Bureau of Alcohol, Tobacco, Firearms and Explosives (ATF) operation in which the federal government allowed criminals to buy guns in Phoenix-area shops with the intention of tracking them as they were transported into Mexico. But the **agency lost track of more than 1,400** of the 2,000 guns (including 50 caliber rifles) they allowed smugglers to buy. Two of those guns were found at the scene of Terry's killing."[72] *(Fox News, June 7, 2017)* Obama blocked the Congressional investigation into the Fast and Furious operation with various strategies as documented in *The Washington Times*. "The details of Operation Fast and Furious in the nearly five years since the Terry murder have been documented through congressional investigations, committee hearings and Office of the Inspector General reports revealing government retaliation against whistleblowers, lies, stonewalling, cover-ups, email and document scandals, President Obama's assertion of executive privilege, and the first-ever citation for contempt of Congress levied against a sitting U.S. attorney general."[73]

   ii.   **Attorney General Holder was <u>held in contempt of Congress</u>** during the "Fast and Furious" investigation, for lying to Congress under oath and for not turning over documents requested by Congress. As Investor's Business Daily revealed, "**<u>Holder lied to Congress</u>** on May 2, 2011, when he was asked about when he knew about the Bureau of Alcohol, Tobacco, Firearms and Explosives' Fast and Furious gun-running operation. He told House Oversight Committee Chairman Darrell Issa he was 'not sure of the exact date, but I probably learned about Fast and Furious over the last few weeks.' Holder learned of the operation as early as July 2010 in a memo from the director of the National Drug Intelligence Center informing him of an operation run by the Organized

Crime Drug Enforcement Task Force out of the Phoenix ATF office, under which 'straw purchasers are responsible for the purchase of 1,500 firearms that were then supplied to Mexican drug cartels.'"[74]

jj.   Obama **withdrew U.S. forces from Iraq**, creating a geopolitical / military vacuum which paved the way for the rise of ISIS and the subsequent Christian genocide in Iraq and Syria.

kk.   The Justice Department was **spying on journalists**.

ll.   Abuse of **executive orders**.

mm.   Obama **released hundreds of al-Qaeda operatives from the Guantanamo** Bay detention center knowing that about 30% of these terrorists would return to the battlefield, and attempt to kill more American and our allies.

nn.   **Obama invited Bill Ayers**, former head of the Weather Underground terrorist group, and **Louis Farrakhan**, head of the anti-American Nation of Islam, **to the White House** multiple times. Both Barack and Michelle Obama also honored other criminals and revolutionaries with White House visits and policy discussions on a semi-regular basis.

oo.   **JCPOA** related lies including anytime anywhere inspections, all options are on the table, the agreement makes Israel more safe, Obama's policies are not containment of Iran's nuclear program, and Iran would not be allowed to enrich uranium.

pp.   Obama created **JCPOA secret side deals**, whose detail were withheld from Congressional oversight and the Secretary of State.

qq.   Obama had the **JCPOA approved by the UN** before it was presented to the Senate. The Senate changed the rules so the JCPOA did not need to be ratified as a treaty.

rr.   **Solyndra** bankruptcy and Obama's payback to his campaign fundraising bundlers.

ss.   President Obama and Secretary of State Clinton **approved the sale of 20% of the U.S. uranium reserves to Russia**, while the Clinton Foundation received millions of dollars of donations and Bill Clinton received massively inflated speaking fees from foreign Russian parties involved with this deal.

tt.   Obama sent American community organizers to Israel to **work with liberal political groups to defeat Netanyahu** in Israel's national elections for prime minister. **Obama interfered in the Israeli national elections** and targeted the leader of an ally of the United States for political defeat so the Palestinians, Hamas, and Iran could gain control of half of Jerusalem. With the Democrats demanding Trump's impeachment for "alleged" Russian interference in the U.S. 2016 presidential election and Trump team's alleged collusion with Russian operatives during the election, Obama's proven tampering in Israeli domestic politics should be considered as grounds for impeachment. Obama also actively intervened in the Egyptian (actively supported the Muslim Brotherhood),

French (CIA spied on Le Pen, hacked her website in 2011 and 2012) and British (against Brexit) elections.

uu. Obama **continually underestimated the capabilities and reach of ISIS and al-Qaeda**. Obama lied when he stated, **ISIS** is "JV" and "contained."

vv. Obama lied to Fareed Zakaria in a CNN interview on December 7, 2016, when he admitted, "**The ability of ISIL** to not just mass inside of Syria, but then to initiate major land offensives that took Mosul, for example, that **was not on my intelligence radar screen**" and "**took me by surprise**," when multiple intelligence reports warned Obama than an Islamic state could be created by the terrorists in major parts of Iraq and Syria. Obama has always supported radical Islamic interests, and with respect to ISIS, Obama was supportive of their expansion since it might lead to the formation of an Islamic caliphate stretching between Turkey and Iran, would create the military forces that could lead to the overthrow of the secular leader of Syria, and would mobilize a radical Islamic army along Israel's northern border, which would eventually be used to invade Israel.

ww. Obama **helped create the condition in Iraq and Syria that led to the massive refugee crisis** that has plagued Turkey, Europe, and the United States, with massive social welfare burdens, increasing civil strife, along with the increased risk of implanted clandestine ISIS terrorists infiltrating the West.

xx. **VA policies** repeatedly led to the premature death of veterans seeking care at VA medical facilities.

yy. **Iran's kidnapping of ten U.S. sailors and commandeering of two high-tech naval attack boats** in international waters, which Obama ignored during his 2016 State of the Union address days later.

zz. China actively expanding its hegemony over the South China Sea.

aaa. Obama's **incessant criticism of America** throughout his presidency.

bbb. The first African-American president oversaw a **significant deterioration in race relations and African-American economic opportunities**. Obama's embarrassing performance as president to help the black community was reviewed in *The Atlantic's* "How Barack Obama Failed Black Americans," in December 2016, a liberal publication.

ccc. **Obama awarded himself the Department of Defense Medal for Distinguished Public Service** on January 4, 2017, at the end of his presidency. Secretary of Defense Ash Carter, pinned the military medal on Obama's chest.

ddd. Obama spent over **$85 million of tax payers' money for his family vacations**.

eee. Before the 2016 presidential elections, Obama violated his presidential oath to protect the constitution by **encouraging and publicly supporting the right of illegal aliens to vote** in the U.S. national elections.

fff.   Intelligence officials in the Obama administration released private conversations between General Michael Flynn and the Russian ambassador to the United States, in order to derail Flynn heading the NSA. The Obama official / officials committed crimes when they **unmasked Flynn** as a participant and instigated a **significant national security leak**. Obama wanted Flynn removed as head of the NSA since Flynn was vocally anti-Iran and viewed radical Islamic terrorism as a major threat to America and the West.

ggg.   Obama **bypassed a Congressional freeze on Palestinian aid**, **by authorizing the transfer of** $221 **million to the Palestinians just hours before the end of his presidency**. Obama had also authorized funds up to $500 million to be transferred to Hamas and the PA earlier in January 2017. With Hamas being a recognized Islamic terrorist group dedicated to the genocide of the Jews, and an organization allied with ISIS, Obama was knowingly financing Islamic terrorism. Funds going to the PA would be used in part to support the families and terrorists who had spearheaded attacks against Israel during the recent knife intifada that killed many Americans, which was subtly supported by Obama.

hhh.   Obama **undermined Congress's ability to give advice and consent to treaties** when he submitted the JCPOA to the UN Security Council before Congress had the opportunity to review the JCPOA. He labeled the JCPOA as an executive agreement instead of a treaty which could constitute diplomatic fraud.

iii.   Obama fraudulently treated the **Paris Agreement on climate change**, negotiated in December 2015, as an executive agreement with which the United States will become a party, after it is ratified in the United Nations. **Obama is labelling treaties which will not be able to pass the required two-thirds majority in the Senate**, **as executive agreements**, **thus entering the United States into legally binding and diplomatic relationships that do not have the support of the American public or its representatives**. Even the UN views these relationships as treaties since, the UN Treaty collection website acknowledges that its guidelines, "grants states the necessary time-frame to seek the required approval for the treaty on the domestic level and to enact the necessary legislation to give domestic effect to that treaty." Both the Paris Agreement and the JCPOA should be challenged before the Supreme Court, since neither agreement, which are actually treaties, obtained the required two-thirds approval of the Senate, as required by Article 2, Section II of the Constitution.

jjj.   Obama **ignored the War Powers Act** when he deployed U.S. forces to fight a war against Gaddafi in Libya.

kkk.   Obama **released the name of a senior U.S. intelligence officer serving overseas**, thus violating the Intelligence Identity Protection Act.

lll.   Obama appointed over **30 "czars"** to help oversee federal agencies, who were **not vetted by Congress** as required by law.

mmm.   Obama's role in the **redistribution of TARP funds to the Congressional leadership and their PACs,** needs to be fully investigated. As head of the Democratic Party, Obama's oversight or acquiescence in these activities should be grounds for impeachment since it involves the illegal distribution of taxpayer dollars to Democratic Party officials and their lobbying organizations.

nnn.   The **very poor performance of the Obamacare website**, and Obama's awarding these huge contracts for building the website to political allies, validating the concept of "**crony capitalism**." The actual cost of the website may be over $2 billion. "As you may remember, back in May we were told by the Department of Health and Human Services (HHS) secretary Sylvia M. Burwell that the cost of building HealthCare.gov totaled $834 million, glitches and all. HHS's Office of the Inspector General (OIG) provided its own estimate of $800 million. However, that $800 million price tag is roughly 40 percent of the actual cost of the defective website. According to a new report produced by Bloomberg Government (BGOV), **the cost of HealthCare.gov is closer to $2,142 million than $834 million.**"[75] *(The National Review, October 2014)*

ooo.   **Funding al-Qaeda and ISIS forces in Syria and Iraq** under the guise of supporting "moderate" Syrian rebels.

ppp.   Obama **funding the Muslim Brotherhood in Egypt** with over $2 billion in military and financial aid.

qqq.   **Meeting with aides of Yusuf Qaradawi**, the spiritual leader of the Muslim Brotherhood and recognized terrorist, at the White House.

rrr.   Granting **U.S. visas to known al-Qaeda** members.

sss.   Obama **equating Orthodox Jews and Evangelical Christian with al-Qaeda terrorists** by placing them on high risk terrorist watch lists.

ttt.   **Advocating for the building of an Islamic mega mosque at the site of the 9-11 Islamic terror attacks in lower Manhattan** and over the remains of dead Americans despite overwhelming domestic opposition.

uuu.   **Siding with Hamas**, a genocidal Muslim terrorist group, by forcing Israel to abide by a unilateral ceasefire in their war against Hamas which was proposed by Turkey and Qatar, two pro-ISIS and pro al-Qaeda countries, while closing down Ben Gurion airport to US air traffic and instituting an arms embargo against Israel.

vvv.   **Advocating for strict gun control multiple times immediately after Islamic terrorists murdered scores of Americans** on American soil.

www.   Forcing Obamacare through Congress without any Republican votes.

xxx.   Obama **diverted billions of dollars from Fannie and Freddie profits** that were deposited in the Treasury Department's general fund to help fund Obamacare.

yyy.   Susan Rice, Obama's national security advisor **unmasked dozens of instances of Trump associates having conversations with foreign individuals**, and kept highly detailed spreadsheets of these episodes, and most likely used her office **to spy on the domestic political operations** of Obama's and Clinton's presidential opponents.

zzz.   **Loretta Lynch**, Obama's attorney general, committed perjury by **submitting misleading affidavits to the FISA court** under the pretext to spy on foreign targets, when the real targets were people associated with the Trump campaign. Susan Rice, Obama's national security advisor then unmasked the Trump officials in intelligence reports, which were then used to advance the political fortunes of Obama, Hillary Clinton, and his progressive administration.

aaaa.   Obama received reports from multiple foreign intelligence agencies detailing the political activities of Trump during the 2016 campaign and during the transition period. Obama could still be receiving these intelligence briefings as a private citizen after Trump was inaugurated so he could orchestrate the strategy from his base in Washington, D.C., which could either lead to the embarrassment of President Trump, the paralysis of his administration, or eventually to his impeachment, so that Obama could protect his far left-wing legacy and his pro-Islamist anti-American agenda.

bbbb.   **Seth Rich**, who worked at the DNC and was suspected of leaking tens of thousands of DNC (Democratic National Committee) emails to *Wikileaks* during the 2016 presidential campaign, was **murdered in Washington**, D.C. Rich was shot in the back of the head and nothing was stolen. Obama, who was head of the Democratic Party as president, was intimately involved in the operations of the DNC.

cccc.   **Huma Abedin**, Clinton's top aide at the State Department and a woman who was continually praised by Obama, allowed her husband, **Anthony Weiner**, a former Congressman and convicted sex offender, to have **access to highly classified top-secret State Department documents on her home computer network**, where he downloaded these files to his personal laptop.

dddd.   **Obama does nothing**. Any patterns? But Obama verbally threatened Israel on a regular basis.

   i.   **North Korea develops its nuclear / EMP capabilities** and becomes a lethal threat to the U.S. homeland. Obama ignored the threat and left the United States increasingly vulnerable to this lethal threat. **In 2012**, according to Peter Vincent Pry, a former CIA analyst and executive director of the EMP Task Force on National and Homeland Security, "North Korea now has an intercontinental ballistic missile (ICBM) capable of delivering a nuclear weapon to the United States, as demonstrated by their successful launch and orbiting of a satellite on Dec. 12 … North Korea has already successfully tested and developed nuclear weapons. It has also already miniaturized nuclear weapons for ballistic missile delivery and has armed missiles with nuclear warheads … Any nuclear weapon detonated above an altitude of 30 kilometers will generate an electromagnetic pulse that will destroy electronics and could collapse the electric power grid and other critical infrastructures – communications, transportation, banking and finance, food and water – that sustain modern civilization and the lives of 300 million Americans. All could be destroyed by a single nuclear weapon making an EMP attack … So, as of Dec. 12, North Korea's successful orbit of a satellite demonstrates its ability to make an EMP attack against the United States – right now …Iran will certainly be inspired by North Korea's example to persist in the development of its own nuclear weapon and ICBM programs to pose a mortal threat to the United States. Indeed, **North Korea and Iran have been collaborating all along**. If North Korea and Iran both acquire the capability to threaten America with EMP genocide, this will destroy the foundations of the existing world order, which has since 1945 halted the cycle of world wars and sustained the global advancement of freedom."[76] *(The Washington Times, December 2012)* Obama advanced Iranian interests with the JCPOA, thus advancing North Korean interests would also be part of his agenda. Obama kept Iran's nuclear enrichment program intact, knowing they were working with the North Koreans, whose nuclear program is dedciated to destroying the United States. Obama has known about this threat for most of his eight-year presidency.

ii. Benghazi al-Qaeda attack.

iii. Afghan officers rape Afghan children on U.S. military bases.

iv. Assad's use of chemical weapons and crossing Obama's red line.

v. Russian interference in the 2016 U.S. elections.

vi. Multiple Iranian violations of the JCPOA and missile testing guidelines.

vii. Hamas, allied with PA, kidnaps and murders American teens.

viii. Hamas fires hundreds of missiles at Israeli civilians.

ix. North Korea detains and eventually murders an American, Otto Warmbier.

x. ISIS kidnaps and eventually beheads Americans, despite Obama knowing where the Americans are located.

xi. The Palestinian Authority (PA) violates the Oslo Accords by petitioning many international bodies as a sovereign state.

xii. Obama funds the PA after they give stipends to the families of terrorists who murder Americans and Israelis.

xiii. Eric Holder, Obama's attorney general, is held in contempt of Congress.

xiv. Iran takes over two U.S. Navy vessels in international waters.

xv. Iran commandeers a high tech advanced U.S. stealth drone, and Obama has options to destroy it before Iran can reverse engineer advanced U.S. military technology.

xvi. Students initiate a "green" revolution in Iran and have the opportunity to overthrow the ayatollahs.

xvii. Obama's wars in Libya and Syria lead to massive Muslim immigration into Europe.

eeee.   And many more.

3. "I don't want to pit Red America against Blue America. I want to be president of the United States of America." *Obama, campaign speech, November 10, 2007.*

4. "I believe that marriage is the union between a man and a woman … **for me as a Christian**, it is also a **sacred union** – G-d is in the mix." *Obama voicing opposition to same sex marriage in a conversation with Pastor Rick Warren in 2008, portraying himself in the political midstream. Later in his presidency he supported same sex marriage, when he said his political position had "evolved." He also used the term "sacred union" with "me as a Christian" to portray himself as a religious Christian which are two lies. On May 12, 2015 Obama lectured the Catholic leaders at Georgetown University to spend less time and resources on issues like gay marriage and abortion. Obama said what needed to be said to win the 2008 election. Evolving or lying?*

   a. Obama projected the LGBT colors on the White House at night after the Supreme Court legalized gay marriage. Obama also tweeted the same day on June 26, 2015, "Today is a big step in our march toward equality. Gay and lesbian couples now have the right to marry, just like anyone else." Obama lectured America and the West on the sanctity of gay marriage, but he never broached the subject with Islamic leaders from the Middle East. Obama later refused to light the White House blue which would show solidarity with murdered police officers.

   b. "Today is a big step in our march toward equality. Gay and lesbian couples now have the right to marry, just like anyone else." *Obama Tweet after the Supreme Court legalized same sex marriages, June 26, 2015. If you like your traditional marriage, you can keep your traditional marriage.*

   c. At the end of 2015, Obama listed the legalization of gay marriage as one of the major accomplishments of his presidency.

5. "I favor legalizing same sex marriages, and would fight efforts to prohibit such marriages." *Obama, 1996. Or maybe Obama had evolved twice?*

a. "Opposition to gay marriage was particularly strong in the black church, and as he ran for higher office, he grudgingly accepted the counsel of more pragmatic folks like me, and modified his position to support civil unions rather than marriage, which he would term a 'sacred union.'" *David Axelrod, chief Obama strategist for his 2008 and 2012 presidential campaigns.* While discussing Obama's presidency, he admitted Obama lied in his memoirs.

6. "The fact that since 2007, they have filibustered about 500 pieces of legislation that would help the middle class just gives you a sense of how opposed they are to any progress." *Obama, Democratic Congressional Campaign Committee dinner, Los Angeles, May 7, 2014.* "A filibuster generally refers to extended debate that delays a vote on a pending matter, while cloture is a device to end debate. Filibusters are used by opponents of a nominee or legislation, while cloture is filed by supporters. Since 2007, there have been 527 cloture motions that have been filed, according to Senate statistics. This is apparently where Obama got his figure. But this tells only part of the story, as many of those cloture motions were simply dropped, never actually voted on, or "vitiated" in the senatorial nomenclature. Obama is assuming every cloture motion can be counted as a filibuster."[77]

7. "Let me say it as simply as I can. **Transparency and the rule of law** will be the touchstones of this presidency." And, "Transparency promotes accountability and provides information for citizens about what their government is doing … public engagement enhances the government's effectiveness and improves the quality of its decisions." *Obama statement during the 2008 campaign (first quote), and the White House website (second quote).*

    a. During the first two years of his presidency, Obama went as long as 10 months without a press conference. Obama often gave elongated and rambling answers at his press conferences, which limited the number of questions to which he could respond.

    b. "The suspicion has to be that maybe these leak investigations are less about deterring leakers and more about intimidating the press." *Wall Street Journal editorial.*

    c. "Obama administration routinely makes a mockery of its long-ago pledge to establish itself as the most transparent administration in U.S. history."[78] *Washington Post editorial.*

    d. Obamacare was negotiated in secret, especially with the pharmaceutical and hospital corporations.

    e. DOJ subpoenaed telephone records of over twenty *AP* telephone lines regarding investigations of the CIA operations in Yemen.

    f. DOJ investigated *Fox News's* James Rosen for his investigation of the North Korea Nuclear program and threatened prosecution under the Espionage Act. Was Obama protecting North Korea?

    g. "President Obama will surely pass President Richard Nixon as the worst president ever on issues of national security and press freedom … President Obama wants to criminalize the reporting of national security information." *James Goodale, First Amendment lawyer / specialist, "Only Nixon Harmed a Free Press More," The New York Times Op Ed page, July 31, 2013.*

h.   Obama won't reveal **secret** **side deals** to the public regarding the inspection of Iran's military nuclear site with the July 2015 Iranian nuclear agreement.

i.   Other JCPOA **secret side deals**.

j.   Obama won't reveal the identity of Syrian Muslim immigrants or their locations to the governors of states where Obama has resettled high risk pro-ISIS, pro-Jihad migrants.

k.   In 2015, Obama set a record where the White House could not find documents requested by citizens or journalists under the Freedom of Information Act. The Obama administration responded to 77% of all requests under the FOIA with censored or no records. "The Obama administration 'set a record' for failing to provide information requested by the press and the public under the Freedom of Information Act."[79]

l.   "We cannot have a healthy democracy in the digital age, in the modern age without more transparency in our government … **He has, factually been, the least transparent administration, probably in this nation's history, certainly in modern time**. And it comes at a time when people are demanding to have more transparency in their government …. And when you have something like this, where the administration is clearly lying, it's clearly hiding documents that belong to us, not them … we really have a problem." *National Journal Senior Political Columnist Ron Fournier discussing the Fast and Furious scandal on Fox News with Bret Baier, Special Report, April 13, 2016.*

m.   "Federal health officials refuse to give Congress hundreds of subpoenaed documents on Obamacare's failed co-ops so that people will continue enrolling in the deeply troubled program, a congressional leader said Tuesday. Twelve of the 23 co-ops created in 2011 under Obamacare at a cost of $2.4 billion have failed, and another eight of the remaining 11 are likely to go under this year."[80] *(Kathryn Watson, The Daily Caller)* The failed co-ops have cost the federal government billions of dollars, and over 800,000 paying customers have lost their health insurance coverage while doctors and hospital have not been paid. The HHS may be involved in fraud and a Ponzi scheme.

n.   Obama initially **altered the 911 and police transcripts from the Orlando Islamic jihad massacre in 2016** and removed all references to jihad, Sharia law, and Allah. Obama is enforcing Sharia law and practicing taqiyya in America by pretending that Islam, the "religion of peace," had nothing to do with this religiously motivated terrorist attack.

o.   Obama **censored the video of French president Francois Hollande** when his statement blaming Islamic terrorism at the root of terrorism was deleted from the official White House version.

p. Obama flew $400,000,000 *[foreign currencies from foreign banks to terrorists = money laundering to fund Islamic terrorism]* to Iran in the **middle of the night** via an **unmarked chartered airplane** in exchange for the release of the four Americans held hostage by Iran. Obama **refused to notify Congress** *[like with the Bergdahl exchange]* and **exchanged the dollars for foreign currencies before giving this down payment** on the $1.7 billion.

q. "At the time, I said that that $1.7 billion payment was a ransom itself, but **the administration has consistently stonewalled Congress and the American people**. We didn't know the cash payment, for instance. **We didn't know that it was paid for with bills that can be easily laundered and used for terrorism or support for Iran's allies** throughout the region. And **we didn't know the Department of Justice opposed it**. I think it's really shocking to most Americans that the United States government was acting like a drug cartel or a third-world gun runner might, stacking cash in a pallet and wrapping it in cellophane and flying it in an unmarked aircraft to give to the world's worst state sponsor of terrorism."[81] *Senator Cotton (R-AR), discussing Obama's clandestine $400 million cash payment to Iran in early August 2016.* Transparent legal U.S. government operations / transactions do not occur in the middle of the night via unmarked chartered aircraft with recently exchanged dollars for untraceable foreign currencies that can be easily distributed to Iran's terrorist allies and accomplices without leaving a paper trail. Obama refused to notify Congress about this transaction for almost half a billion dollars. One reason why Obama hid this deal from the American public and Congress was because he violated federal laws by breaking sanctions and enabling Iran to obtain this huge windfall payment and knowingly funding Islamic terrorist groups (Hamas, Hezbollah, IRGC – Quds, al-Qaeda) with U.S. government funds. Obama used the hostage release as an excuse to fund Islamic terrorist groups throughout the Middle East. The almost $2 billion transfer in cash to Iran almost matches annual U.S aid packages to the Israeli defense budget. In order to obtain U.S. aid, Israel must agree to significant constraints on dollars received from America, but with Obama's untraceable foreign cash, Iran can spend the money freely and easily distribute it to its terrorist proxies.

r. "New documents obtained through Freedom of the Press Foundation's lawsuit against the Justice Department reveal that the Obama administration - the self-described "most transparent administration ever" - aggressively **lobbied behind the scenes in 2014 to kill modest Freedom of Information Act reform** that had virtually unanimous support in Congress … But these new documents show it went well beyond that: the Justice Department vehemently objected to both House and Senate members on nearly all aspects of the bill from the very start, and made clear: "The Administration strongly opposes passage of [the FOIA Act]." … The Obama administration's specious objections to

FOIA reform were manifold. They were against codifying the Obama administration's "presumption of openness" policy that Obama declared upon his first month in office, they were against Congress mandating that the federal government create a unified on-line portal to process FOIA requests, they were against mandating discipline for FOIA redactors who break any of rules or regulations for processing FOIA requests, and they were against providing more reporting and oversight to Congress to make sure FOIA was being complied with ... Most importantly, the administration was vehemently opposed to the "foreseeable harm" provision, also known as the "presumption of openness" standard. During President Obama's first few weeks in office, Attorney General Holder made clear that the Justice Department would defend an agency's decision to withhold information from the public "only if (1) the agency reasonably foresees that disclosure would harm an interest protected by one of the statutory exemptions [in the FOIA], or (2) disclosure is prohibited by law." The FOIA Act would have simply made this policy the law: An agency may not withhold information under this subsection unless such agency reasonably foresees that disclosure would cause specific identifiable harm to an interest protected by an exemption [in the FOIA], or if disclosure is prohibited by law ... Multiple investigations have shown that the Obama administration has been the most secretive ever when it comes to FOIA. Requests can often take years to be fulfilled if at all, and the only way to get results is to sue, like we were forced to. (We did not receive any documents for over a year from our first requests, and only received these documents after filing a lawsuit)."[82] *Freedom of the Press Foundation, 2006.*

s. "As I mentioned the other day to a liberal lawyer friend of mine, the worst thing ever accused concerning Nixon was about using private resources to try to illegally spy on people. **Here you had Obama's people using the NSA to spy on his adversaries, and apparently include the CIA, the FBI, and members of the Department of Justice in that loop, in a manner that was not approved of by any court, that was not approved by even a FISA court – the special court that monitors certain kinds of surveillance** ... Just because a conversation involves a foreign official doesn't allow you **to illegally tape it, illegally monitor it,** or **illegally record it when a U.S. citizen is on there, particularly when it's your political adversary** ... I'm sure the liberals would go nuts if Trump tomorrow started listening in on every conversation Obama had with anybody that's foreign, or that Bill Clinton had with anybody that's foreign, or that Hillary Clinton had with anybody that's foreign. So it's a dangerous, precarious path that Obama has opened up, and hopefully there is a full investigation into that activity ... You clearly also have **lots of illegal leaks going on**, particularly as it related to the recent Yemen issue involving the widow of the Navy SEAL who passed way, that became a big issue at the State of the Union. There you had people reporting that no intelligence was gathered. Well, that's an illegal leak. It turns out that they're *wrong,* they were lying about what intelligence developed or the fact that intelligence *did* develop, but they shouldn't have been out there saying anything like that … There are people willing to leak the most sensitive national security secrets about any particular matter, solely to have a one-day political hit story on Trump. These are people who are violating their oath, and violating the law. Hopefully there *is* **ultimately criminal punishment.**" *Sirius XM radio interview with attorney Robert Barnes, Breitbart, March 3, 2017.* Obama authorized the illegal wiretapping of Trump officials and future cabinet level appointees while president and guided branches of the U.S. government to sabotage and attempt to destroy the Trump presidency.

t.   "WASHINGTON (AP) — The Obama administration in its final year in office **spent a record $36.2 million on legal costs defending its refusal to turn over federal records under the Freedom of Information Act**, according to an *Associated Press* analysis of new U.S. data that also showed poor performance in other categories measuring transparency in government. **For a second consecutive year**, **the Obama administration set a record for times federal employees told citizens**, **journalists and others that despite searching they couldn't find a single page of files that were requested**. And it set records for outright denial of access to files, refusing to quickly consider requests described as especially newsworthy, and forcing people to pay for records who had asked the government to waive search and copy fees."[83] *(AP, March 14, 2017)* The Obama administration refused to turn over public requests for government records for greater than 75% of inquiries during 2016.

u.   Obama transferred the official White House and NSC records that detailed the unmasking of Trump officials by Susan Rice and other Obama personnel during the 2016 campaign and during the transition period in the Obama presidential library. The National Security Council responded to a Judicial Watch subpoena by stating, "**Documents from the Obama administration have been transferred to the Barack Obama Presidential Library**. You may send your request to the Obama Library. However, you should be aware that under the Presidential Records Act, Presidential records **remain closed to the public for five years** after an administration has left office." Obama placed official government records, that could have implicated Susan Rice and possibly himself in illegal spying activities, under his control in his presidential library, where they would be inaccessible for at least five years. Obstruction of justice?

8.   "When there is a bill that ends up on my desk as president, you will have five days to look online and find out what's in it before I sign it." *Obama violated this campaign pledge numerous times.*

9. "I do think at a certain point you've made enough money." *Obama, Quincy, Illinois 2012 speech*. And "I did not run for office to be helping out a bunch of fat-cat bankers on Wall Street." *Obama, 2009 "60 Minutes" interview*. In 2017, Obama is getting paid $400,000 for a one-hour speech at a Cantor Fitzgerald investment banking conference, after signing a book deal reported to guarantee Obama at least $60 million. At the very least, Obama proves he is a hypocrite.

10. "I am running to tell the lobbyists in Washington that their days of setting the agenda are over … They will not run my White House, and they will not drown out the voices of the American people when I am president." *Obama, Remarks at the Democratic National Committee Fall Meeting, November 30, 2007*.

11. "We need to close the revolving door that lets **lobbyists** come into government freely." *Obama, January 2009*. On his second day of his presidency, Obama signed two executive orders and three presidential directives that established strict guidelines and limits regarding the role of former lobbyists working in his administration, especially in policy-level positions.

    a. "President Obama has hired more than 100 lobbyists in his administration, a new academic study reports. This doesn't match Obama's campaign promise to exclude lobbyists, or his pretenses of having kept that promise. "President Obama's public rhetoric on contact with lobbyists does not always accord with his private actions," lobbying scholar Conor McGrath writes in the latest issue of the Journal of Public Affairs … McGrath finds 119 former lobbyists in the Obama administration. The administration employs former in-house lobbyists from Microsoft, Fannie Mae, insurance giant Wellpoint, AT&T, Verizon, Sprint, Monsanto, Yahoo, Google, Microsoft, Raytheon, and Goldman Sachs. Obama has hired from the ranks of K Street firms Cassidy & Associates, Covington & Burling, Heather Podesta & Partners, Akin Gump, Arnold & Porter, Winston & Strawn, Timmons & Co., and others."[84] *(Timothy Carney, The Washington Examiner, 2013)*

    b. In August 2014, Obama rolled backed his legal guidelines restricting the role of lobbyists in the federal government.

12. "No political appointees in an Obama-Biden administration will be permitted to work on regulations or contracts directly and substantially related to their prior employer for two years. And no political appointee will be able to lobby the executive branch *[but not Congress]* after leaving government service during the remainder of the administration." *Obama ethics plan*. Obama granted waivers and recusals for lobbyists working within his administration. Senator Grassley wrote to Obama in 2009 requesting, "**The American people deserve a full accounting** of all waivers and recusals to better understand who is running the government and whether **the administration is adhering to its promise to be open**, **transparent**, **and accountable**."

13. "**Rogue agents**" operating out of the Cincinnati IRS office were responsible for the IRS's targeting of conservative groups.

   a. "The heart of the effort to target tea-party and other conservative groups, we are learning, occurred in Washington, and that is likely why **five D.C.-based IRS officials** who are connected to the targeting have retired, resigned, been replaced, or been put on administrative leave, since news of the scandal broke in mid-May. They include **Holly Paz**, who last week, according to an IRS source, was replaced as **director of Rulings and Agreements**, the division that oversaw the targeting of conservative groups; Washington **lawyer Carter Hull**, who is accused of micromanaging the processing of tea-party cases, and who, according to IRS sources, requested his retirement package on March 12; **the commissioner of the agency's Tax Exempt and Government Entities division**, **Joseph Grant**, who retired on June 3; **former IRS commissioner Steven Miller**, who resigned days after news of the scandal broke; and the **director of the IRS's Exempt Organizations division**, **Lois Lerner**, who was placed on administrative leave only after refusing to tender her resignation, according to Iowa's Chuck Grassley."[85] *Eliana Johnson, The National Review, 2013.*

14. "Not even mass corruption – **not even a smidgen of corruption**." *Obama **downplaying the IRS targeting of conservatives with the Bill O'Reilly interview on Fox News before the Super Bowl, 2015.*** On July 21, 2015, during a Jon Stewart interview, **Obama again denied that the IRS targeted the Tea Party** or other conservative groups, and blamed Congress for passing "crummy laws" and requested more funding for the IRS as a remedy.

   a. "(Washington, DC) – Judicial Watch announced today that it has obtained documents from the Internal Revenue Service (IRS) that confirm that the IRS used donor lists to tax-exempt organizations to target those donors for audits … The IRS produced the records in a Freedom of Information lawsuit seeking documents about selection of individuals for audit-based application information on donor lists submitted by Tea Party and other 501(c)(4) tax-exempt organizations (Judicial Watch v. Internal Revenue Service (No. 1:15-cv-00220))."[86] *The IRS targeted the Tea Party where over 10% of its donors were audited, along with hundreds of conservative organizations, pro-life groups, pro-Israeli groups, constitutional groups, organizations that criticized Obama, and many others. All the 501(c)(4) groups that were audited were conservative.*

   b. In June 2016, the IRS released the names of 426 conservative organizations that were targets of extra scrutiny, delaying their tax-exempt status and audits. In May 2013, the IRS had only identified 298 groups that were targeted for their political beliefs or for having certain names in their titles including – "patriot," "tea," "liberty," or "Constitution." Tea Party Patriots co-founder Jenny Beth Martin stated, "**The IRS has once again admitted**

     to targeting Americans for their political views, including Tea Party Patriots and over 70 groups that include the word 'tea' **in their name."**

  c. Lois Lerner illegally transmitted a massive 1.25 million pages of unrequested tax returns of conservatives and Tea Party personnel to the Justice Department for review for prosecution in 2010. Dan Epstein, the executive director of Cause of Action stated, "**The IRS**, in the midst of its political targeting of groups **engaged in policy advocacy**, was engaging in the disclosure of millions of records aimed at ginning up prosecutions of these groups without going through the legally required channels." *The National Review* broke this story in late June 2016.

  d. The IRS, with the approval of the Obama administration, targeted conservative and religious groups and other political opponents of Obama for tax audits and harassment to marginalize their political effectiveness. In a March 2016 ruling against the IRS, which admitted to harassing over 400 conservative organizations, **Judge Raymond Kethledge** ruled, "Among the most serious allegations a federal court can address are that **an Executive agency has targeted citizens for mistreatment based on their political views**. No citizen – Republican or Democrat, socialist or libertarian – should be targeted or even have to fear being targeted on those grounds."

  e. Lois Lerner, the former director of the IRS's Exempt Organizations Unit, refused to testify before Congress, and took the Fifth Amendment.

15. "There's **not a smidgen of evidence for it** *[that I am anti-Semitic]*, other than the fact that there have been times where I've disagreed with a particular Israeli government position on a particular issue." *Obama is responding in an interview with Forward.com in August 2015 questioning whether he is anti-Semitic.* Of course, when Obama uses the word "smidgen," he is lying.

16. "The Fast and Furious program was a field initiated program begun under the previous administration." *Obama lying again. When in doubt, blame it on Bush.*

17. Obama is **incredulously out of the loop** on major controversies regarding his administration or are his admissions lies. "It's a remarkable irony: the same U.S. president whose administration has gone to great lengths to monitor journalists, whistleblowers and the public, claims to be oddly in the dark regarding basic information on some of his biggest controversies." *(source – Sharyl Attkisson blog, Untouchable Subjects, Fearless Reporting, March 9, 2015)*

  a. "It was something that, uh, we found out about, uh, **along with all of you**." *Obama. Air Force One makes an unscheduled flyover near the Statue of Liberty on April 27, 2009.*

  b. "I heard **on the news** about this story, that, uh, Fast and Furious." *Obama responding to the breaking Fast and Furious scandal.*

c. "I first learned about it **from the same news reports** that I think most people learned about this. I think it was on Friday." *Obama responding to the IRS targeting conservative groups in May 2013.*

d. "We don't have any independent knowledge of that, [President Obama] found out about the news reports uh yesterday **on the road**." *Obama press secretary, Jay Carney responding to reporters regarding the Obama's administration seizing the phone records of AP reporters.*

e. "I can assure you that **I certainly did not know anything** about the IG report before the IG report **had been leaked through the press**." *Obama responding to the Inspector General's report concerning his administration's spying on foreign leaders in October 2013.*

f. "You mean the specific allegations that I think were reported first by your news network out of Phoenix, I believe. We learned about them **through the reports**. I will double check if that is not the case. But that is when we learned about them and that is when I understand [V.A.] Secretary Shinseki learned about them, and he immediately took the action that he has taken." *Jay Carney responding to Obama being out of the loop concerning the VA waiting list scandal.*

g. Obama told Bill Plante of *CBS News* during an interview, that he found out about Hillary Clinton using a private email server for official government business "the same time everybody else learned it **through news reports**." His press secretary, Josh Earnest said, "I wouldn't be surprised, however, if he had learned about that **by reading the newspaper**."

18. "And we also recognize that most of the guns used to commit violence here in Mexico come from the United States." *Obama, Mexican speech, May 2013, criticizing America abroad like with previous apology tours.* Obama was trying to use the Fast and Furious program to advance gun control in the United States.

19. *Obama, 2004, Keynote Address at the Democratic National Convention in Boston where Obama laid out his trap of lies to a gullible American public, since everything Obama did was planned for years if not decades in advance. -* "We can participate in the political process without fear of retribution *[IRS scandal and targeting of conservatives]* ... John Kerry believes in an America where all Americans can afford the same health coverage our politicians in Washington have for themselves. *[exemptions from Obamacare for federal employees and many constituencies supporting Obama]* ... And John Kerry believes that in a dangerous world, war must be an option sometimes *[not with Iran expanding and developing their nuclear capabilities]* ... When we send our young men and women into harm's way, we have a solemn obligation not to fudge the numbers or shade the truth about why they are going *[Obama altered ISIS intelligence reports]*, to care for their families while they're gone, to tend to the soldiers upon their return *[VA scandal]* and to never, ever go to war without enough troops to win the war *[Afghanistan retreat and declared victory, created Iraq vacuum, with ISIS Obama feels we can't win by killing them, near the end of his term Obama sends 50 then 250 American troops to the Middle East to*

fight ISIS], secure the peace *[withdrawal from Iraq created geopolitical vacuum leading to ISIS empowerment, chaos and terrorism has increased exponentially under Obama's tenure, especially in Libya and Iraq where U.S. military victories were followed by Islamic radical takeovers.]* and earn the respect of the world *[not Israel, the GCC, Russia, China, Egypt, Jordan, Germany, Syria, Poland, Cuba, and Vietnam]* … It's what allows us to pursue our individual dreams *[lowest percentage of small business owners in recent history because of taxes and regulations]* … Now even as we speak, there are those who are preparing to divide us *[war on women; Holder calling us a nation of cowards, Black-White friction getting worse with Trayvon Martin, Ferguson, arrest of Harvard professor, BLM, incitement against police officers; unisex bathrooms for children]* … there's not a liberal America and a conservative America; there's the United States of America. *[Obamacare passed without Republican input or support. IRS attack on conservatives. Obama importing record number of immigrants to make America a one-party system. Obama wanted to secure an Iranian nuclear arms agreement without Senate consent, by not calling it a treaty].* There's not a Black America and White America and Latino America and Asian America; there's the United States of America *[Obama promotes conferences for the military and federal employees disparaging "white privilege," and continually calls America "racist" at home and abroad]* … There are patriots who opposed the war in Iraq, and there are patriots who supported the war in Iraq *[But you are a traitor if you are a senator who opposes the Iranian nuclear agreement].* We are one people, all of us pledging allegiance to the stars and stripes *[apology tour, releases Taliban and al-Qaeda commanders for the deserter Bergdahl, vetoed rescue mission to help Benghazi compound fight back against 8+ hour al-Qaeda attack, lets Iran kidnap ten U.S. Navy sailors, omnipresent criticism of America, implementing Muslim Brotherhood and OIC hijrah agendas],* all of us defending the United States of America *[Went to sleep while four Americans including the ambassador, were murdered and raped in Benghazi. Obama issued a stand down order to the military to prevent any intervention and possible rescue, unprecedented slashing of the military budget, the sequester, rules of engagement to prevent defeating enemy forces in the Middle East and Afghanistan, catch and release of al-Qaeda, let Iran kidnap 10 U.S. sailors in international waters]* … Hope in the face of difficulty, hope in the face of uncertainty, the audacity of hope" *[The "Audacity of Hope" was the name of a Reverend Wright sermon that inspired his second book, which he did not write. In that sermon Wright preached, "white folks greed runs a world in need ," which accurately reflects Obama's core values].* This speech includes nonstop lies. Obama needed to make a very positive impression upon the American public and set up his run for the presidency four years later. Obama deceived America by presenting himself as a middle of the road Democrat and an American patriot, while always being on the far-left and despising America and its history.

a.   Obama presented himself as a post-racial presidential candidate during his 2004 DNC speech where he stated, "There is not a liberal America and a conservative America – there is the United States of America. There is not a Black America and a White America and Latino America and Asian America – there's the United States of America." But as a law school student he wrote a book manuscript with Robert Fischer that was never published that declared, "**Racism against African Americans continues to exist throughout American society**, an admittedly **racist culture** … Precisely because **America is a racist society** we cannot realistically expect white America to make special concessions toward blacks over the long haul." Obama lied to the American public and hid his anti-American, racist points of view.

20. "The truth of the matter is that my policies are so mainstream that if I had set the same policies that I had back in the 1980s, I would be considered a moderate **Republican**." *Obama, responding to criticisms that he is socialist in Florida, December 2012.* He is the most liberal president in the history of the United States, and was ranked as the most liberal senator during his tenure as an Illinois senator.

21. "The arc of the moral universe is long, but it bends towards justice." *Obama quoting Martin Luther King repeatedly.* Obama colluded with the PLO to pass UNSC Resolution 2334 which labels all the Jewish and Christian holy sites, including the Western Wall and the Jewish Quarter, "illegally occupied Palestinian territory." Obama supported and held meetings at the White House with Black Lives Matter, whose members publicly advocated for the killing of police officers at their rallies. Obama traded five al-Qaeda and Taliban leaders for a Muslim convert Army deserter, who fled his Army comrades in Afghanistan.

    a. "The American abstention on UN Security Council Resolution 2334 *[which was organized, promoted, and passed with Obama's guidance and collusion]*, which enabled the anti-Israel resolution to pass, demonstrates **a loss of the moral clarity and sense of justice** that had always filled me and "every American heart" with pride. And I know that almost all of Congress and a high percentage of Americans agree with my embarrassment over this decision. The resolution blames Israel – the one law-abiding democracy in the Middle East – and its "settlement activity" for failing to implement the two-state solution. It doesn't blame the Palestinian leadership, which has refused all of Israel's generous offers for peace. It doesn't blame the Palestinian Authority incitement, which inspires its children to butcher Jewish children in their beds. It doesn't call out the Palestinian leadership for naming schools and public squares after murderous terrorists. No, it is Israel – the only party in this conflict that condemns terrorism and prosecutes any Israeli who carries out an act of terrorism – which is the obstacle to peace. The one sentence that condemns "all acts of violence against civilians, including acts of terror, as well as all acts of provocation, incitement and destruction" without naming and outright blaming the Palestinian leadership is **an embarrassment to anyone who seeks truth**. This is a **complete lack of moral clarity**."[87] *(Dov Lipman, The Jerusalem Post, December 29, 2016)*

22. "But at a time when our discourse has become so sharply polarized – at a time when we are far too eager to lay the blame for all that ails the world at the feet of those who happen to think differently than we do – **it's important for us to pause for a moment and make sure that we're talking with each other in a way that heals, not in a way that wounds** ... let's use this occasion to expand our moral imaginations, **to listen to each other more carefully, to sharpen our instincts for empathy and remind ourselves of all the ways that our hopes and dreams are bound together** ... And if, as has been discussed in recent days, their death **helps usher in <u>more civility in our public discourse</u>**, let us remember it is not because a simple lack of civility caused this tragedy – it did not – but rather because **<u>only a more civil </u>and honest public discourse can help us face up to the challenges of our nation in a way that would make them proud ... We can question each other's ideas without questioning each other's love of country** and that our task, working together, is to constantly widen the circle of our concern so that we bequeath the American Dream to future generations." *Obama, Memorial Services, Tucson, Arizona, Gabby Giffords shooting, January 2011.* Obama also preached civility for others during his 2011 Notre Dame Commencement address where he told the newly minted graduates *(regarding his healthcare law and birth control issues)* "Each side will continue to make its case to the public with passion and conviction. **But surely, we can do so without reducing those with differing views to caricature. Open hearts. Open minds. <u>Fair-minded words</u>**."

   a. "It's one of the few regrets of my presidency– that the rancor and suspicion between the parties has gotten worse instead of better. There's no doubt a president with the gifts of Lincoln or Roosevelt might have better bridged the divide, and I guarantee I'll keep trying to be better so long as I hold this office." *Obama, State of the Union Address, January 12, 2016. Obama admits he did not live up to his earlier promises of promoting political civility.*

   b. Obama **mocks handicapped individuals** and the Special Olympics on *The Tonight Show* with Jay Leno in in 2009, when the president discussed his bowling skills and stated, "No. No. I have been practicing ... I bowled a 129 ... It was like Special Olympics or something."

   c. "What we witnessed in Ferguson, in Baltimore, and in Baton Rouge was a collapse of social order. So many of the actions of the Occupy movement and Black Lives Matter transcend peaceful protest, and violates the code of conduct we rely on. I call it anarchy." *Milwaukee County Sheriff David Clarke, speaking at the Republican National Convention,*

July 18, 2016. Obama has supported and mentored the BLM leadership and activists with his rhetoric and with meetings at the White House. Clarke had previously observed, "Every time he opens his mouth he fans the flames of anti-police sentiment … he reminds me of a pyromaniac who sets a fire, calls 911, and then returns to the scene to watch."

d.   "Iran agreed to a political framework with the other P5+1 nations … Iran has its own politics around this issue. **They have their own hardliners. They have their own countervailing impulses as to whether or not to go forward with something. Just as we have in our country**" *Obama compares Republicans and Democrats who oppose or question the nuclear framework agreement to the Iranian hardliners who are responsible for the murder of gays, who advocate for wiping Israel off the map, and who back Hamas and Hezbollah and other revolutionary terrorist groups like those who overthrew the U.S.-backed government in Iran. Summit of the Americas Conference, April 11, 2015.*

e.   "**Vote for revenge**." *Obama*

f.   "If they bring a knife to the fight, **we bring a gun**. Because from what I understand folks in Philly like a good brawl." *Obama, 2008 campaign, Philadelphia fundraiser*

g.   "If you get hit, we will **punch back twice as hard**." *Jim Messina, Obama Deputy Chief of Staff, 2009 advice to senators supporting Obama's healthcare agenda.*

h.   "What we're not for is negotiating with people with a bomb strapped to their chest. We're not going to do that." *Obama's senior advisor Dan Pfeiffer compared Republicans to suicide bombers when they tried to put conditions on their agreeing to increases in the national debt ceiling in September 2013.*

i.   "I don't want the folks that created the mess. I don't want the folks that created the mess doing a lot of talking. I want them to **get out of the way** so we can clean up the mess." *Obama, 2008 campaign trail.*

j.   "Go out and talk to your friends. Talk to your neighbors. I want you to talk to them whether they are independent or whether they are Republican. **I want you to argue with them and get in their face**." *Obama 2008 campaign trail.*

k.   "We talk to these folks because they potentially have the best answers so I know **whose ass to kick**." *Obama, 2008 campaign trail.*

l.   "If Latinos sit out the election instead of saying, "**We're gonna punish our enemies** and we're gonna reward our friends."" *Obama, Univision Radio interview, 2012 presidential campaign.*

m.   Obama uses **Al Sharpton** as his point man for race relations.

n.   Rasheen Aldridge, a 20-year-old Ferguson activist, was invited to the White House to discuss the Ferguson race issues, and was later arrested for assault against a security guard.

o. Obama is a **follower of Black Liberation Theology** and a supporter of Islam.

p. Obama and DOJ ignored funerals of Brian Terry, a U.S. agent killed with **Fast and Furious** guns, and an American general assassinated in Afghanistan, yet sends administration representatives to attend the funeral of Michael Brown, who was killed by a police officer after assaulting a local merchant and a police officer, grabbing for the officer's gun and then charging him despite orders to stop.

q. In 2014, a high-ranking Obama administration official (or Obama himself) called Netanyahu "**chicken-shit**."

r. Leon Panetta tells Israel "to **get to the damned table**," with respect to talks with the Palestinians in 2011.

s. "Racism, we are not cured of it. **And it's not just a matter of it not being polite to say n*gger in public**." *Obama, June 2015. Not too civilized or graceful.*

t. "… figuring out how we are going to **deal with the crazies in terms of managing some problems**." *Obama calls Republican opponents of the JCPOA, Obama's healthcare and immigration policies, crazy, for disagreeing with him. August 24, 2015.*

u. Anti-Semitism instigated by the executive branch entered the congressional debate over the passage of the JCPOA during the summer of 2015.

v. Obama **supports Black Lives Matters**. At Dartmouth University in November 2015, BLM protesters verbally accosted undergraduate students studying in the library by screaming, "**F**k you**, **you filthy white f**ks!**" "**F**k you and your comfort!**" "**F**k you**, **you racist sh*ts!**" Deray Mckesson, a Black Lives Matters leader, declared that the French police efforts to find the ISIS terrorists were a "witch hunt." BLM has allied itself with ISIS. A rational deduction is that Obama is allied with ISIS. Obama supported BLM and has helped them construct and implement their political strategy at the White House. A BLM political platform accused Israel of committing genocide against the Palestinians.

w. After a campaign speech in Omaha on January 13, 2016, **Obama met with anti-gun activist professor Amanda Gailey** who posted on her Facebook page, "F**k the society that has allowed itself to become so saturated in guns … F**k the laws that allow toy makers to make toys that look like real guns … **F**k the racists** who think black children look like adults … **F**k the police officers** who think … any perceived risk to them whatsoever justifies instantaneous lethal force … And F**k the NRA."

x. In December 2015, a poll conducted by *NBC / The Wall Street Journal* demonstrated that race relations were at a 30-year low heading into the last year of the Obama administration.

y. "There probably has not been a more racially divisive, economically divisive president in the White House since we had presidents who supported slavery … It's a part of the Democratic Party's campaign strategy to divide Americans based on skin pigmentation and to try to collect the votes of everybody who is a non-white on the basis that whites are discriminatory and the reason you are where you are in the economic ladder is because of racism." *Rep. Mo Brooks (R - AL), The Dale Jackson Show interview, January 13, 2016.*

z.   **Obama mocks Republicans** in Manila, a foreign country, regarding their opposition to his policy that would let Muslim Syrian refugees into America. Up to one-third of these migrants may support ISIS and up to 2% of the migrants may be ISIS fighters. Obama derided Republicans before foreign leaders stating, "When people say we should have a **religious test**, and only Christians, proven Christians, should be admitted, **that's offensive and contrary to American values**. These are the same folks often times that say they're so tough that just talking to Putin or staring down ISIL or using some additional rhetoric will solve the problem – and **they're scared of widows and three-year-old orphans**." Protecting the lives of Americans is not offensive and contrary to American values, especially when a vast majority of American politicians and its citizens are against the entry of these migrants to America. Coincidentally, Obama mocked the Republicans' false fear of widows right before a female suicide bomber attempted to murder Parisian policemen as she blew herself up during a gun battle immediately following the Paris massacre. Former Senator Santorum commented on Obama's remarks by saying, "It was despicable. You wonder how low this president can go in his mischaracterization, **his depiction of anyone who opposes him, and taking the most extreme and lowest form of rhetoric …**"

   i.   Obama lied about religious tests not being part of the process where asylum is granted. The U.S. code states that an alien "must establish that ... **religion … was or will be at least one central reasons** for persecuting the application." The U.S. code also states, "The term 'refugee' means (A) any person who is outside any country of such person's nationality … and who is unable or unwilling to return to … that country **because of persecution or a well-founded fear of persecution on account of … religion**." Since ISIS is targeting Christians for genocide with beheadings, crucifixions, and mass murder – and Sharia law legalizes the subjugation and harassment of non-Muslims in Islamic societies – the U.S. government has every right to use religion as a criterion for granting asylum.

aa. In mid-April 2016, **Obama invited rapper William Leonard Roberts II to the White House**, where his **ankle monitor began beeping**. Roberts was recently arrested for "alleged" **kidnapping, assault, and pistol whipping**. Why did Obama invite a street thug and felon to the White House as his honored guest? Apparently, Obama is not too concerned about civility at the White House or at official D.C. functions.

bb.   At the **White House Correspondent's Dinner**, on April 30, 2016, **Larry Wilmore** who was the host of the function mocked Dr. Ben Carson's defense of keeping Andrew Jackson on the twenty-dollar bill by stating, "What did the **jigaboo** say?" At the end Wilmore stated, "Mr. President, I'm going to keep it 100. Yo Barry, you did it, my **n*gger**," as he was thumping his chest. Obama gave a nod of approval and smiled as he **thumped his chest** as well. Earlier in the evening, Wilmore mocked CNN's Don Lemon by calling him an "alleged journalist," and Lemon responded by giving Wilcox **the middle finger** in front of the president, as the president laughed and **enjoyed the vulgarity** before the nation.

cc.   Pro-Obama anti-Trump demonstrators routinely verbally harass and assault Trump supporters at their political rallies during the 2016 Republican primary season.

dd.   Obama invited **Deray Mckesson, a Black Lives Matter leader** who was instrumental in leading violent protests in Ferguson (riots, looting) and Baltimore, to the White House on May 17, 2016, to lecture on race-related issues.

     i.   "**Black Lives Matter is endangering the fairness of our legal system**. Because they're rooting for outcomes based on race. Started a long time ago. Started with the O.J. Simpson case … African Americans wanted an acquittal without regard to the evidence [O.J. Simpson]. Now many want convictions [Freddie Gray death] without regard to the evidence." *Alan Dershowitz, Harvard Law School Professor, Fox News, The Kelly File, May 24, 2016.* Obama is supporting groups and individuals who want race-based justice.

ee.   **Charles Wade**, a **Black Lives Matter activist** who also founded a social justice charitable organization named Operation Help or Hush which was formed after the death of Michael Brown, was arrested in April 2016 on seven counts of **prostitution and felony human trafficking**, which involved a **minor** girl. **In May, one month later, Obama invited him to the White House** as a guest for a movie screening, where Obama was watching movies with other Black Lives Matter activists. Obama views prostitution and human trafficking as civil endeavors.

ff.   In mid-July 2016, after five Dallas police officers were murdered during a Black Lives Matter rally, and after **McKesson was arrested in Baton Rouge** during BLM protests, **Obama invited McKesson to the White House** for a three-hour meeting to discuss future strategies for the BLM movement. This meeting followed many violent protests across the country. Within one week of Obama's meeting with McKesson, multiple black activists gunned down and **murdered three Baton Rouge police officers**, and wounded four others. Since 2015, BLM activists have killed eleven police officers.

i. Two weeks after Obama met with one of the leaders of BLM at the White House for strategy sessions, a BLM spokesperson rejected an invitation from the Oakland Police Department to join officers in a community barbeque and stated, "I eat pigs, I don't eat with them." BLM supporters at the Democratic National Convention at the end of July rudely interrupted a moment of silence commemorating police officers who were killed in the line of duty. Obama's direct input into BLM policy is leading to increasing violence and discord.

ii. During the first half of 2016, there was a 76% increase in the shooting deaths of police officers when compared to the first half of 2015. This was accompanied by a **300% increase in ambush-style murders** of police officers during the same time-period. *(source – National Law Enforcement Officers Memorial Fund report)* This significant increase in police murders followed Obama's increasingly public support of BLM, along with his criticism of and incitement against law enforcement officials, whom he repeatedly called racist. Immediately after the murder of five Dallas police officers in Dallas, Obama stated, "We're here to honor the memory, and mourn the loss ... [but] police departments will acknowledge that, just like the rest of us, they are not perfect; that **insisting we do better to root out racial bias** is not an attack on cops, but an effort to live up to our highest ideals."

iii. In August 2016, **BLM** announced a political agenda which included the **release of killers of police officers**. (Obama is a mentor to BLM.) BLM demanded, "We are calling for the release of all political prisoners held in the U.S. and the removal of legitimate freedom fighters from international terrorist lists" and the halting of investigations of various black activists wanted for murder. BLM is more comfortable presenting itself as a revolutionary racist anti-American organization after multiple meetings with Obama.

gg. On July 14, 2016, Obama held a town hall meeting in Washington, D.C., where he **invited Rasheen Aldridge**, who has previously been **indicted for assaulting a security guard** in St. Louis. Obama also **invited Lesley McSpadden**, Michael Brown's mother, who had **incited a riot and arson** in Ferguson, Missouri after yelling to a crowd, "Burn this b*tch down!"

hh. In early October 2016, Black Lives Matter activists vandalized the new Trump International Hotel in Washington D.C. by spray-painting the slogans "Black Lives Matter" and "No Justice No Peace" around the entrance. Obama continues to mentor these activists.

ii. In October 2016, Black Lives Matter supporters attacked a high school student in Alabama after he posted "Blue Lives Matter" on his Facebook page. He suffered multiple skull fractures with a brain bleed, and was listed in critical condition. Obama has held multiple BLM strategy meetings with its leaders at the White House.

jj. During President-elect Trump's first meeting with Obama at the White House on November 10, 2016, Obama **refused to be photographed with Donald Trump and his wife** and ignored an American tradition that accompanies the first step leading to the transition to a Trump administration. Just days before, despite losing the election, Hillary Clinton refused to give a concession speech during the night of her election defeat and told her campaign workers to go home. She did not give a formal concession speech until almost ten hours after her defeat. Both Obama and Clinton showed inappropriate disrespect to the man who achieved an unprecedented uncontested election victory and landslide. The final electoral vote count was 332 to 206.

kk. Obama encouraged his supporters to continue protesting the election of Donald Trump during a press conference with German Chancellor Merkel in Berlin in 2016, when he stated, "I've been the subject of protests during the course of my eight years … So I would not advise people would feel strongly or are concerned about some of the issues that have been raised during the course of the campaign, **I wouldn't advise them to be silent**." The following are examples of Obama and Clinton supporters violently attacking Trump supporters while both Clinton and Obama remained silent. Cory Cataldo was assaulted and choked for wearing a pro-Trump Make America Great Again hat on the Bronx subway. A BLM gang attacked Feras Jabro, a Trump supporter wearing a similar hat in El Cajon, California. David Wilcox, a pro-Trump 49-year-old, was dragged from his car and beaten by pro-Clinton supporters in Chicago, Obama's home town. Pro-Clinton high school supporters assaulted a 15-year-old pro-Trump supporter during school hours. Jade Armenio, a high school student was assaulted by pro-Clinton supporters at school. She was struck and multiple assailants pulled out her earrings and some hair. In Connecticut, a 45-year-old man was assaulted in public by multiple men for displaying a pro-Trump poster and the American flag. Clinton supporters assaulted a homeless woman who was protecting Donald Trump's star on the Hollywood Walk of Fame after it was vandalized. A 74-year-old Trump supporter was assaulted by a BLM activist outside Trump Tower in Manhattan. Obama talks about unity and civility when implying violence and racism originates from the right, while his silence condones the violence originating from the left. These protests, encouraged by Obama, only widen the divide and increase the animosity between supporters of the left and the right.

ll. President-elect Trump was critical of Obama's supervision of the transition period leading to his inauguration when he tweeted, "**Doing my best to disregard the <u>many</u>**

inflammatory President O statements and roadblocks. Thought it was going to be a smooth transition – NOT!" Obama disregarded the American tradition of maintaining a smooth non-controversial transition period when he betrayed Israel at the UN with his support for UNSC Resolution 2334, increased Russia sanctions and expelled 35 Russian diplomats in response to Russia's alleged interference in the U.S. presidential election thus creating a new Cold War with Russia, engaged in a public argument with Britain over his UNSC strategy of blaming Israeli settlements as the major reason for a lack of a peace agreement, accelerated his executive implementation of governmental regulations and the settlement of Muslim refugees, permanently banned oil and gas drilling in large areas of the Atlantic and Arctic Oceans, accelerated the release of Muslim terrorists from Guantanamo, and eliminated the National Immigration Registry which was needed to help vet Muslim immigrations from terror-prone regions in the Middle East.

mm. Over 50 Democratic congressmen, lending support to the narrative of an upcoming illegitimate Trump presidency which was advanced by President Obama, his wife and his politicized intelligence services, formerly announced that they were boycotting the Trump inauguration ceremonies on January 20, 2017.

nn. "Our rights are being assailed, being trampled on and even being rolled back. I know that this is a time of great fear and uncertainty for so many people. I know it's a time for concern for people, who see our rights being assailed, being trampled on and even being rolled back. **I know that this is difficult**, **but I remind you that this has never been easy** … It has been people, individuals, who have banded together, **ordinary people who simply <u>saw what needed to be done</u>** and came together and supported those ideals who have made the difference. They've marched, **<u>they've bled</u> and yes**, **some of them have died**. This is hard. **<u>Every good thing is</u>**. **We have done this before**. <u>**We can do this again**</u>." *Former Obama Attorney General Loretta Lynch, March 4, 2017.* Lynch is encouraging left-wing protestors against Trump to be violent up to the point of dying or killing others in order to advance their political agenda. Lynch is a long-term confidante of Obama. Three months later, a Bernie Sanders supporter attacked a group Republican congressman practicing for a charity softball game, and seriously wounded Representative Scalise.

oo. On May 20, 2017, **the Democratic leadership at the California state convention** in Sacramento led the crowd with **chants of** "**F**k Donald Trump**" while the chairman, John Burton, **help up both middle fingers** for the crowd. **Rep. Nancy Pelosi**, the House minority leader, was laughing at the spectacle while supporting the obscenities shouted by the state leadership.

pp. During the presidential campaign, *Joe Biden*, Obama's vice president, threatened to beat up Trump by saying, "**I wish I were in high school, I could take him behind the**

gym." Biden is threatening violence against the future president weeks before the national election.

qq. Months after her presidential loss, *Hillary Clinton*, Obama's former secretary of state, may have aligned herself with violent factions against a sitting president by stating, "I'm now back to being an activist citizen, and **part of the Resistance**." Clinton's words and those of others may have encouraged many Hollywood elites *(including Madonna [blow up the White House], Kathy Griffen [ISIS beheading], Johnny Depp [encourages an actor to murder Trump like with Lincoln], Robert DeNiro [wants to punch Trump in the face])* to threaten the life of President Trump.

rr. Rep. Nancy Pelosi, the Speaker of the House during Obama's presidency stated in reaction to Trump's firing of his chief advisor Steve Bannon on August 18, 2017, "Steve Bannon's firing is welcome news, but it doesn't disguise where President Trump himself stands on **white supremacists and the bigoted beliefs they advance**. President Trump's growing record of **repulsive statements** is matched by his **repulsive policies.** Personnel changes are worthless so long as President Trump continues to advance policies that **disgrace our cherished American values**. The Trump Administration must not only purge itself of the remaining **white supremacists on staff**, but abandon the **bigoted ideology** that clearly governs its decisions."

23. "One of my core principles is that **I will never engage in a politics in which I'm trying to divide people**." *Obama POTUS Tweet, June 1, 2015.* Days before Obama left the presidency he commented on race relations in a Chicago ABC7 interview on January 5, 2016, "You know I think that in some ways, like everything else it's gotten better and in some ways, we have surfaced tensions that were already there but are getting more attention … **I promise you**, **for the most part**, **race relations have gotten better**." Obama taught **Alinsky Methodology** at the University of Chicago, and applied the "Rules for Radicals" to all his campaigns and political fights. It's core tenets include: Rule #1 – "Power is not only what you have, but what the enemy thinks you have." Rule #5 – "Ridicule is man's most potent weapon." Rule #12 – "Pick the target, freeze it, personalize it, and polarize it." **Race relations have deteriorated significantly** since Obama became president. Obama incessantly campaigned on themes such as the **war on women**, war on the elderly, discrimination against minorities, and Islamophobia while continually calling Americans and police racists. Obama supported ACORN, which morphed into Occupy Wall Street, which morphed into Black Lives Matter, the latter two being funded by George Soros. After the Dallas police massacre, the Black Lives Matter organization evolved into a domestic terrorist organization. **Obama enacts executive orders to bypass Congress and institute laws and regulations that are opposed by the majority of Americans**.

a. Obama admitted his presidency and his policies caused significant sociological, racial and economic divisions when he stated during his last press conference two days before

Trump's inauguration, "I worry about inequality, because I think that if we are not investing in making sure everybody plays a role in this economy, the economy will not grow as fast, and I think it will also **lead to further and further separation between us as Americans -- not just along racial lines**. There are a whole bunch of folks who voted for the President-elect because they feel **forgotten and disenfranchised**. **They feel as if they're being looked down on**." *Yes. Looked down upon by Obama.*

b.   A Gallop poll released on April 11, 2016 revealed that 35 percent of Americans surveyed worried "a great deal" about domestic race relations. This percentage has doubled over the past two years, and is the highest value recorded since Gallop started asking about races relations in 2001.

c.   "It's fair to say that President Obama entered office as chief executive of a divided country, and he's done nothing noticeable to heal those divisions in his seven years." *William Galston, former advisor to President Clinton and senior fellow at the liberal Brookings Institution*

d.   *The New York Times* revealed the extreme deterioration in race relations in 2016, in the article "Race Relations Are at Lowest Point in Obama Presidency, Poll Finds." The article stated, "Sixty-nine percent of Americans say race relations are generally bad, one of the highest levels of discord since the 1992 riots in Los Angeles during the Rodney King case, according to the latest *New York Times / CBS News* poll. The poll, conducted from Friday, the day after the killing of five Dallas police officers, until Tuesday, found that six in 10 Americans say race relations were growing worse, up from 38 percent a year ago. Racial discontent is at its highest point in the Obama presidency and at the same level as after the riots touched off by the 1992 acquittal of Los Angeles police officers charged in Mr. King's beating … Despite President Obama's insistence at a memorial service for the fallen officers that the races in the United States are 'not as divided as we seem,' the poll found that black and white Americans hold starkly different views on race."[88] "The proportion of Americans who believe race relations are generally good has declined over all since 2009,"[89] with over 63% believing relations are good just after Obama's 2009 inauguration to slightly over 20% by July 2016.

e.   "The [Obama] administration's directive – citing Title IX in telling school to give transgender students access to all activities and facilities consistent with their gender identity – effectively touched off a national debate."[90] (*Fox News*) Obama threatened all American public school districts that don't comply with his directive by withholding federal funds and initiating lawsuits against them. Obama's unilateral actions affect over 100,000 public schools and 55 million American children. Many state leaders felt that Obama's threats constituted blackmail and that these directives run counter to the moral values of the vast majority of American citizens, who don't want boys (or young men) presenting themselves as girls to be in the same rest rooms or playing on the same athletic teams as their daughters. Even liberal Supreme Court Justice Ginsberg stated in a *Washington Post* article in 1975, "Separate places to disrobe, sleep, perform personal bodily functions are permitted, in some situations required, by regard for individual privacy," when arguing the Equal Rights Act would not "require unisex restrooms in public places." Certain constituencies are so incensed that the Oklahoma legislature filed a resolution recommending the impeachment of Obama along with the U.S. attorney general and the secretary of education. Obama is more concerned with Marxist social engineering in U.S. public schools, which will be a significant distraction for the students, instead of improving their academic performance. Obama is disrupting the traditional fabric of society across the country for a group of individuals that comprise less than 0.3% of the population.

f. Obama formally pushed his gun control agenda within 24 hours of the 2016 Orlando night club massacre, which was committed by a radical Muslim ISIS supporter.

g. After the shooting deaths of two African-Americans by police on July 7, 2016, Obama immediately stated on Facebook, "All Americans should be deeply troubled by the fatal shootings of Alton Sterling (career criminal, registered sex offender, resisting arrest, grabbing for the gun of the police officer with the intent to kill before being shot) in Baton Rouge, Louisiana and Philando Castile in Falcon Heights, Minnesota ... these fatal shootings are not isolated incidents. They are symptomatic of the broader challenges within our criminal justice system, **the racial disparities that appear across the system year after year** *[incitement]*... we can and must do better to institute the best practices that reduce the appearance or reality of **racial bias in law enforcement** *[incitement]*... all Americans should recognize the anger, frustration, and grief that so many Americans are feeling – feelings that are being expressed in **peaceful protests** *[not quite]* and vigils." **Later that day, a Black Lives Matter protest in Dallas produced a gunman who shot eleven police officers, killing five of them**. Obama has invited Black Lives Matter leaders to the White House many times in order to discuss strategies that will advance their objectives. Obama is a mentor to Black Lives Matter leaders.

i. "This paper takes first steps into the treacherous terrain of understanding the nature and extent of racial differences in police use of force. On non-lethal uses of force, there are racial differences ... Yet, on the most extreme use of force – officer-involved shootings – we are unable to detect any racial differences in either the raw data or when accounting for controls ... It is plausible that racial differences in lower level uses of force are simply a distraction and movements such as Black Lives Matter should seek solutions within their own communities rather than changing the behaviors of police and other external forces."[91] *(Roland G. Fryer, Jr, PhD, Professor of Economics,* **Harvard University***)* In a *New York Times* interview, Fryer, an African-American

Harvard professor, stated, ""It is the most surprising result of my career."[92] Obama lies about racial bias with police shootings, as proved by a Harvard study that reviewed data from ten major police departments and over 1,000 shootings.

ii.   Obama has been inciting against police officers throughout his presidency. He stated that police "acted stupidly" when they arrested Harvard professor Henry Louis Gates. Obama lamented that the shooting of Michael Brown "stains the heart of black children." After Freddie Grey died in police custody, Obama stated, "This is not new, and we shouldn't pretend it's new."

h.   Larry Klayman, a former Department of Justice prosecutor and founder of Judicial Watch, filed a **class action lawsuit against President Obama**, former Attorney General Holder, Black Lives Matter founders (invited by Obama for strategy meetings at the White House), Al Sharpton (at the White House over 50 times), Nation of Islam leader Louis Farrakhan (close associate of Obama's spiritual mentor – Reverend Wright), and others **seeking to "redress the incitement, threats and killings provoked by the defendants**." The law suit accuses the defendants of "inciting the imminent serious bodily injury and killing of police officers and other law enforcement persons of all races and ethnicities, Jews, and Caucasians by convincing their supporters and others that there is a civil war between blacks and law enforcement, thereby calling for immediate violence and severe bodily injury or death in response to that non-existent and fictitious threat." The plaintiffs are seeking damages for over $2 billion. The lawsuit directly accused Obama of inciting the violence in Dallas that led to the murder of five police officers by stating, "Obama directly incited early in the day the murders that occurred much later that same day in Dallas, Texas … Obama's War on the Police is directly endanger the public safety of all Americans, but particularly placing in danger law enforcement." Obama has close political alliances with mentors and associates who have openly advocated for the killing of police officers. Bill Ayers dedicated his book, *Fugitive Days*, to the murderers of policemen. Obama launched his political career at Ayers' home and Ayers' wrote most of *Dreams from My Father*. Ayers has been a guest at the White House many times. Louis Farrakhan incited his followers to "rise up and kill those who kill us." Obama has been honored with Farrakhan on the same stage while he was living in Chicago, and Obama was fully supportive of the National of Islam during his early years in Chicago. Farrakhan, like Ayers, has been a guest at the White House. In 2007, Obama marched with Malik Shabazz, head of the New Black Panther party, at a civil right function in Selma, and the two men spoke at the same podium. Just days after the Baton Rouge murders, Shabazz said he could understand why some people called the murderer of three police officers, a hero. Obama allowed the New Black Panther party to officially endorse his candidacy on his 2008 campaign website, until a public outcry forced him to remove the webpage. In 2015 Shabazz stated, "Build up an army. Right now it's time for us to build up those corps, those troops." As a radical Muslim and as a politician and student who has been allied with radicals for decades, Obama may quietly support the murder of police officers. As Obama escalated his verbal attacks which labelled police officers as racists, the number of officers murdered by gun violence on the job throughout the United States in 2016 more than doubled when compared to similar statistics compiled in 2015.

i.   "I grew up at the beginning of the civil rights movement. **I really thought we would be a different country by now**. [since] We have elected an Africa American president … But **the hostility out there is really unsettling to me**. And it's based on pigmentation. People are making judgments based on the color of skin. Bang like that." *Tom Brokaw, former liberal NBC Nightly News anchor, July 17, 2016.* Brokaw is acknowledging that race relations have significantly deteriorated during the Obama presidency.

j.   "You've had 7 1/2 years of a black president. 7 1/2 years of a black attorney general. **Gallup report race relations are worse than any time in the last 17 years**. Why? Because [look] how often has he hit the police. He hit the police in Cambridge and he was wrong. He hit the police in Ferguson, he was wrong. He hit the police about Florida, he was wrong. At what point does the president have some obligation to say – you know there are two parts of this … in places like Chicago where 3,200 people have been killed in the Obama presidency … 7 1/2 years into his presidency, he began to realize now that we've had two massacres of policemen that maybe as president of the United States and leader of law and order in America, he should say something on behalf of law and order. I mean, that's fairly pathetic." *Former Speaker of the House Gingrich, Morning Joe, MSNBC, July 19, 2015.*

k.   "Under President Obama, many black folks think racial division has increased, not decreased … **the state of racial affairs seems to have gotten worse under him** … How did we get to a spot where black and white perceptions on race are so divergent, and we are more divided than ever? It starts with how you view our country … **I believe that when President Obama thinks of America**, **more so than a place of hope or opportunity**, **he thinks of a place where racist white Christian fundamentalists came here from Europe**, committed genocide against Native Americans, enslaved and segregated black people, denied women, gays, and other minorities their rights, and used capitalism and a rigged legal system to oppress poor people for centuries. He also believes this is still continuing today. *[The author's arguments are deficient since he has neglected to couch these them through the viewpoint* *of a radical Muslim with a traditional Middle Eastern Arab political viewpoint which is dominated by the advancement of Sharia law and the ultimate establishment of the Islamic caliphate. All of Obama's political policies are directed toward making America and the West vulnerable to jihad so that Islam will eventually dominate the West.]* **Given this view of America as an evil place in need of forceful justice for her sins, the president's overarching goal has been to eliminate what he sees as the structural, institutionalized discrimination that defines America***. [i.e., Obama hates America.]* He has done this by taking every opportunity to see disparities between groups as evidence of discrimination, then using all available resources to fight this perceived discrimination by going to war against the Americans he believes are responsible for it, who are almost always whites, men, police, and Christians. *[Obama uses these political excuses as a liberal to target these demographics since he is a radical Muslim, and he views them as enemies of an expanding Islamic caliphate and the natural targets of jihad. Obama uses the political expediency of liberalism to advance jihad and hijrah, while empowering Islam and the Sharia via political correctness and inclusivity.]* A small sampling of the ways he has done this are: accusing whites of "white privilege," which means having an unfair advantage due to being white, an advantage built upon oppressing minorities; accusing the police and justice system at large of racism; blaming pay differences between men and women on discrimination; **and casting Islamic radicalism as a legitimate response to discrimination** (ostensibly by white Christians). *[Obama supports radical Islam through the arguments of moral equivalence and downplaying, and protects jihad through the prism of freedom of religion with its constitutional protections.]*" (source – ***How Obama Left Us More Racially Divided than Ever****," John Gibbs, The Federalist, July 13, 2016)*

l. "He's spent most of his life trying to stay as far away from working people as he could. And now this guy is going to be the champion of working people. I mean, he wasn't going to let you on his course. He wasn't going to let you buy in his condo. And now suddenly this guy's going to be your champion." *Obama accuses Trump of discriminating against the working class, poor people, and minorities. September 13, 2016.*

m. After a black police officer shot and killed Keith Scott, an African-American who refused to drop his gun when confronted by multiple police officers and was told ten times to drop his weapon, racial riots broke out in Charlotte, North Carolina in September 2016. During the first two nights of chaos and riots, a dozen cops were injured, multiple white individuals were assaulted because they were white, a news person was thrown into a fire, multiple stores were looted, a rioter shot and murdered an innocent bystander, interstate highways were shut down, and state troopers and the National Guard were needed to reinforce local police. Scott was an ex-convict who had a previous conviction for assault with a deadly weapon, and was wearing an ankle bracelet at the time of the shooting. Obama commented on these incidents and stated, "The overwhelming majority of the people [are] doing it the right way," despite the wide spread destruction of private and public property and violent civil disobedience. The riots were supported by Black Lives Matter, an Obama ally. The majority of the protesters (70%) were from out of state, and were probably paid by Soros front groups, who are allies of Obama. Obama supported the riots since he was trying to rally the black vote before the November 2016 presidential election.

n. "I think there's a reason attitude about my presidency among whites in northern states are very different from **whites in southern states** … Are there folks whose primary concern about me has been that **I seem foreign** – the other? Are those who **champion the birther movement** feeding off of bias. Absolutely" **Obama**, *during a CNN interview with Fareed Zakaria on December 7, 2016, **called southern whites racists** while reviewing his presidency and expressed some disdain towards them.* In 2008, Obama criticized whites in the rust belt and the bible belt by commenting in his bitter clingers speech, "You go into these small towns in Pennsylvania and, like a lot of small towns in the Midwest, the jobs have been gone now for 25 years and nothing's replaced them … And it's not surprising then **they get bitter, they cling to guns or religion or antipathy toward people who aren't like them or anti-immigrant sentiment or anti-trade sentiment** as a way to explain their frustrations." These two comments demonstrate that even after eight years as president, Obama is still playing the race card and is advancing the politics of division. The only whites Obama has not criticized are the elitists on the East and West coasts who support Obama's progressive and Islamist agenda.

o. *Time Magazine* described the America that Trump inherited from Obama as the "**Divided States of America**," when *Time* named Donald Trump "Person of the Year" during the first week of December 2016. Obama created the political conditions during his presidency that led to a very divided electorate in 2016.

p. In early December 2016, Obama ordered American intelligence agencies to investigate the possibilities that Russia ordered cyber-attacks upon or interfered with the American presidential electoral process. Following Obama's lead – politicians, liberal reporters and academics advanced the proposition that Russia interfered in the American electoral process with the intent to make Donald Trump president and that Trump may have been aware and may have been allied with those Russian efforts. According to *The Washington Post*, CIA officials informed senators at a behind closed doors briefing that, "It is the assessment of the intelligence community that Russia's goal here was to favor one candidate over the other, to help Trump get elected … That's the consensus view,"[93] according to a U.S. official present at the meeting. Liberals insisted that the intelligence agencies brief Electoral College delegates of their findings before they voted for their presidential candidate in mid-December, thus attempted to overturn Trump's presidential election victory by converting Trump delegates to Clinton delegates. The consensus that the Russian interference was directed toward electing Trump originated from the CIA. John Brennan, the CIA director, who is in favor of jihad and is believed to be a Muslim convert incognito, took orders from President Obama to have the CIA release information that the Russians, an adversary to the United States, supported Donald Trump and actively intervened on his behalf, which is another example of fake news originating from the Obama administration. The net effects of this action would be to undermine the credibility of Trump's decisive election victory, hope for the possibility of interfering with and changing the electoral vote count in favor of Clinton, and **sewing deep divisions between the left and right in the American political arena**. Both Obama and Brennan are very concerned that Trump will put a halt to Obama's accelerated immigration jihad strategy of infiltrating the United States with Middle Eastern Muslims who are either pro-Sharia law or are outright terrorists who would be forming radical Islamic terrorist sleeper cells throughout America. Obama, who knows that Trump will dismantle and erase his political legacy, is implementing any strategy to prevent Trump from ascending to the presidency. Obama politicized the CIA in order to attempt to instill Clinton as president against the will of the American public, even though she lost clearly lost the election, which could be viewed as a coup engineered by Obama and the Democrats. Obama knows that if Clinton were to win the Electoral College vote secondary to Electoral College delegates switching their allegiance, a permanent division between liberal and conservatives would be created, which would lead to the most divisive period in American history. William Jacobson, professor of law at Cornell University, surmised on his blog, *Legal Insurrection*, "The one thing you must understand about the unfolding media – Democratic Electoral College coup attempt … We are witnessing nothing short of an attempt to steal the election by some Democrats [Obama and Clinton] and a very supportive mainstream and left-wing media, by causing electors in the Electoral College to go rogue and vote for Hillary, or at least not vote for Trump." Since the electoral recount request in Michigan, Wisconsin and Pennsylvania headed by Jill Stein of the Green Party failed, Obama is pursuing the Russian interference strategy heading into the formal Electoral College voting. Incidentally, the Director of National Intelligence, James Clapper, "refused to endorse the CIA's assessment 'because of a lack of conclusive evidence' that Moscow intended to boost Trump over Democratic opponent Hillary

Clinton."[94] In November 2016, Clapper stated, "As far as the *Wikileaks* connection, the evidence there is not as strong and we don't have good insight into the sequencing of the releases or when the data may have been provided." In a briefing before the House Permanent Select Committee on Intelligence, an FBI counterintelligence official did not support the CIA's assessment that the Russians actively intervened in the presidential election to support Trump. The difference between the conclusions of the various U.S. intelligence agencies may be based on the fact that the CIA is headed by James Brennan, an Islamist who probably takes his marching orders from Obama. Thus, Obama probably politicized the CIA to such an extent that it was disseminating information with the intention of upsetting a domestic presidential election which had already been decided. From a different perspective, Obama may have tried to instigate a major conflict between the United States and Russia secondary to this false flag – fake news story since both Russia and the United States are the two remaining major powers in the world that actively support Judeo – Christian ethics, and Christianity over Islam. If war broke out between Russia and the United States, Islam would be the only party that would undoubtedly benefit from this conflict. Putin is also leading a successful campaign in the Middle East to defeat ISIS, and Obama is advancing any strategy during his last months as president to interfere with Russia's assault on the Islamic caliphate. Since Putin knows Obama would institute policies that might lead to a military conflict between Russia and the United States, Putin kept a low profile after these taunts from Obama since he knew Obama would no longer be president in about one month. Obama may have earlier arranged for a Turkish jet to shoot down a Russian fight jet near the Turkish – Syrian border in order to initiate a military conflict between Russia and NATO. This latest episode where Obama accused Russia of interfering in the U.S. elections was devised in order to create a similar response. Obama even publicly threatened Russia when he stated during an NPR interview, "I think there is no doubt that when any foreign government tries to impact the integrity of our election that **we need to take action and we will** at a time and place of our own choosing." At the very least, Obama is a hypocrite since he actively interfered in Israeli, British, Egyptian and French elections.

q.   "Well, **that's not the way policy should be made**. **To get even** in the lame duck period when there are no checks and balances. And you don't have to worry about an election. It is **the most undemocratic thing** a president can do, to tie the hands of his successor during the lame duck period. And **what he did was so nasty**. He pulled a **bait and switch**. He said to the American public – this is all about the settlements deep in the West Bank. And yet he allowed his representative to the UN to abstain ... Jews can't pray at the Western Wall." *Attorney Alan Dershowitz commenting on Obama's support for UNSC Resolution 2334. Fox and Friends, December 26, 2016.*

r. Thomas Perez, Obama's former Assistant Attorney General for Civil Rights and former Secretary of Labor, stated that white individuals were not entitled to legal protection with the Voting Rights Act. According to the Department of Justice, "CRT AAG Perez stated that interpreting Section 5's retrogressive-effects standard to not cover White citizens was consistent with the Division's longstanding practice, as well as case law interpreting the provision and the intent behind its enactment." Perez was also instrumental in dropping charges of voter intimidation against Black Panther members, who brought weapons to a polling place in 2008. In early 2017, Perez was elected chairman of the Democratic National Committee.

s. Since Obama's politics were so divisive and alienated so many people from his political ideology and political platform, the Democrats suffered their worst electoral losses during Obama's presidency when compared to any other presidential administration since WWII. "**Over 8 years of Obama's presidency the Democratic Party lost more combined seats in the US Senate, US House, Governorships, State Legislative Seats and State Chambers than any president since FDR** … Democrats surrendered the White House to non-politician President Donald J. Trump … US Senate seats slipped from 58 to 46 … US House seats fell from 256 to 194 … Democratic state legislative seats decreased by 959 … Democratic governorships slid from 28 to 16 … State legislatures plunged from 27 to 14 … States with Democratic governors and both legislative chambers cratered from 17 to 6."[95] *(Joe Hoft, The Gateway Pundit)* Although Obama presented himself as a likable politician, the country thoroughly rejected his political platform, his political messages, and his legacy.

24. "Today border security is stronger than it ever has been." *White House statement, 2014, while unaccompanied illegal alien minors are flooding the border with the anticipation of future amnesty.*

a. "In a shocking reversal of policy, U.S. Customs and Border Protection agents are being told to release illegal immigrants and no longer order them to appear at deportation hearings, essentially a license to stay in the United States, a key agent testified Thursday. What's more, the stand down order includes a requirement that the whereabouts of illegals released are not to be tracked. "We might as well abolish our immigration laws altogether," suggested agent Brandon Judd, president of the National Border Patrol Council … "The willful failure to show up for court appearances by persons that were arrested and released by the Border Patrol has become an extreme embarrassment for the Department of Homeland Security. It has been so embarrassing that DHS and the U.S. attorney's office has come up with a new policy," he testified before the immigration subcommittee of the House Judiciary Committee. The biggest change: Undocumented immigrants are no longer given a "notice to appear" order, because they simply ignore them. Judd said that border agents jokingly refer to the NTAs as "notices to disappear." (*"Border Agent: We Might as Well Abolish Our Immigration Laws Altogether," Paul Bedard, The Washington Examiner, February 4, 2016*). Obama is extending his "catch and release" policy to the domestic illegal immigration issue. The Obama administration does not believe in borders, even when open borders leads to significantly increased risk for the citizens of America. Obama and his administration are globalists. Obama never had any intention to enforce immigration law and border security laws as president. Open borders make it easier for jihadi terrorists to infiltrate the United States, thus Obama, as a radical Muslim, supports an open global borderless society.

25. In *The New Yorker* in 2014, Obama stated, "The way I've thought about this issue is, **I have a solemn duty and responsibility to keep the American people safe**. That's my most important obligation as President and Commander-in-Chief." *Taqiyya*. Yet in spite of his pledge to protect America, and knowing that the Iranian leadership regularly chants "Death to America," Obama paved Iran's path to acquiring nuclear weapons while weakening our own military defense. Obama also demonstrated his disregard toward this sacred obligation by not responding to the seven-plus hour terrorist attack on the Benghazi diplomatic consulate that left four people dead, including Ambassador Stevens. Poorly vetted Syrian Muslim immigrants being settled throughout America during Obama's tenure also pose a substantial security risk to America. In 2014, Obama settled many MS-13 gang members illegally crossing the southern border throughout the United States.

    a. "I am the only major candidate who opposed this war from the beginning and as president I will end it. Second, I will cut tens of billions of dollars of wasteful spending. *[taqiyya – actually hundreds of billions from the defense budget]* **I will cut investments in unproven missile defense systems**. *[ABM systems]* **I will not weaponize space. I will slow our development of future combat systems … Third, I will set a goal of a world without** *[American]* **nuclear weapons. To seek that goal, I will not develop new nuclear weapons. I will seek a global ban on the production of missile material**. *[not with Iran, Iranian intercontinental ballistic missile restrictions were not linked to the JCPOA]* And I will negotiate with Russia to take our ICBMs off hair trigger alert **and to achieve deep cuts in our nuclear arsenal**."[96] *Obama, 2008 campaign speech, YouTube video*. This strategy is not meant to strengthen American defenses.

    b. "I've never seen more threats to our country at any one time in my 33 years in the business … I think in the history of our country … These are very dangerous times … I think we are at risk of another attack here, and I want Americans to know that." *Former CIA Deputy Director Mike Morell, Fox News Special Report, May, 2015*.

    c. "Members of the Muslim Brotherhood, CAIR, and MPAC have sinister goals that are not in support of the US Constitution or The Bill of Rights. They have become a very dangerous "Fifth Column" in the United States, appointed by Obama to very high and sensitive positions in the US Government agencies. For nearly 8 years Obama has been filling the Washington bureaucracy including DHS, the CIA, DOD, the National Security Council, the White House, the State Department, every US Intelligence Agency, and the US Armed Forces with thousands of members of the CAIR, MPAC, the Muslim Brotherhood, and other Muslim Brotherhood front groups."[97] *Retired USN Capt. Joseph John, the Chairman of Combat Veterans for Congress PAC*

d. Obama **deleted the security files of radical Islamists** and increased the risk of America to terrorism. "After leaving my 15-year career at DHS, I can no longer be silent about the dangerous state of America's counter-terror strategy … Just before that Christmas Day attack, in early November 2009, **I was ordered by my superiors at the Department of Homeland Security to delete or modify several hundred records of individuals tied to designated Islamist terror groups like Hamas from the important federal database**, the Treasury Enforcement Communications System (TECS). These types of records are the basis for any ability to "connect dots." Every day, DHS Customs and Border Protection officers watch entering and exiting many individuals associated with known terrorist affiliations, then look for patterns. **<u>Enforcing a political scrubbing of records of Muslims</u> greatly affected our ability to do that. Even worse, going forward, my colleagues and I were prohibited from entering pertinent information into the database** … And I was well aware that, as a result, it was going to be vastly more difficult to "connect the dots" in the future – especially before an attack occurs. As the number of successful and attempted Islamic terrorist attacks on America increased, **the type of information that the Obama administration ordered removed from travel and national security databases was the kind of information that, if properly assessed, could have prevented subsequent domestic Islamist attacks** like the ones committed by Faisal Shahzad (May 2010), Detroit "honor killing" perpetrator Rahim A. Alfetlawi (2011); Amine El Khalifi, who plotted to blow up the U.S. Capitol (2012); Dzhokhar or Tamerlan Tsarnaev who conducted the Boston Marathon bombing (2013); Oklahoma beheading suspect Alton Nolen (2014); or Muhammed Yusuf Abdulazeez, who opened fire on two military installations in Chattanooga, Tennessee (2015). It is very plausible that one or more of the subsequent terror attacks on the homeland could have been prevented if more subject matter experts in the DHS had been allowed to do our jobs back in late 2009."[98] *(Phillip Haney, DHS 15 year employee, The Hill, 2016)* Obama is protecting Islamic terrorists in America.

e. In early 2014, DHS Secretary Jeh Johnson continued a policy that **prevented immigration personnel from reviewing social media content** of foreigners seeking to obtain U.S. visas.

Charles Krauthammer commented on *Fox News* on December 17, 2015, "it's also incomprehensible … The argument against it, which apparently prevailed a few years ago *[with Muslim Brotherhood input]*, within DHS, is ridiculous … it's absurd to say that looking at a public posting, as an invasion of privacy, and it's doubly absurd if that's done in the case of a non-American, outside the country, who possesses zero constitutional rights." Tashfeen Malik posted on Facebook her desire to support and participate in violent jihad as early as 2012. *The New York Times* reported Malik "made little effort to hide [and] talked openly on social media about her views on violent jihad." Johnson followed policies under the guidance from Obama, that directly led to the San Bernardino Christmas party massacre. Obama is implementing rules that will allow radical Islamic jihadis to enter the United States without proper vetting so that Islamic terrorist sleeper cells can be established throughout America.

f. Obama shielded foreign Islamists and future terrorists from investigation by domestic intelligence and national security agencies by halting investigations under the guise of protecting their civil rights as guaranteed by the Constitution. Haney revealed, "after more than six months or research and tracking; over 1200 law enforcement actions and more than 300 terrorists identified; and a commendation for our efforts; **DHS shut down the investigation at the request of the Department of State** *[Clinton and Abedin]* **and DHS' own Civil Rights and Civil Liberties Division** *[Muslim Brotherhood appointee or Islamist policy recommendations from DHS committees]*. They claimed that since the Islamist groups in question were not Specially Designated Terrorist Organizations (SDTOs) **tracking individuals related to these groups was a violation of the travelers' civil liberties**. These were almost exclusively foreign nationals: When were they granted the civil rights and liberties of American citizens?"[99] *Haney, The Hill, February 5, 2016.* Obama and DHS officials shut down investigations including the one targeting the San Bernardino jihadists and paved the way for the San Bernardino Christmas party massacre. The *Washington Free Beacon* confirmed, "The DHS removed the names of nearly 1,000 individuals suspected of terrorism ties from the U.S. terrorist watch list, according to newly released documents … At least 1,000 names were scrubbed from the U.S. Terrorist Screening Database as part of an [Obama] administration effort to protect the civil rights of suspected individuals."[100] Tom Fitton, president of *Judicial Watch* commented, "These new documents bolster allegations that the Obama administration may have removed information from a terrorist watch list that could have prevented the San Bernardino terrorist attack … Philip Haney risked his career to blow the whistle on how the Obama administration created a "hands off" list of over 1,000 foreign nationals with potential terrorist ties."[101] Obama committed treason.

g. Over 500,000 foreign nationals who visited the United States in 2015 have overstayed their visas. Immigration and Customs Enforcement (ICE) investigated about 0.05% of visa overstays during this period. This lack of enforcement is supervised by Obama's DHS.

h. In August 2015, an investigation by the inspector general determined that **72 individuals employed by the Department of Homeland Security were on terror watch lists**.

i. In 2015, **James Clapper**, **Director of National Intelligence**, presented a report to the Senate that **did not include Iran or Hezbollah as terror threats** to the United States. Both Iran and Hezbollah were listed as terror threats one year previously. Iran is viewed as the world's leading supporter of terrorism and has proxy forces destabilizing Yemen, Lebanon, Syria, Iraq, and Israel.

j. In February 2016, it was revealed that U.S. military analysts informed the director of national intelligence (Office of the Director of National Intelligence – ODNI) that their **formal intelligence reports were manipulated and altered** by their superiors for political reasons, so their intelligence assessments would support Obama's claim that his policy was effectively damaging and weakening ISIS operations. Analysts at the U.S. Central Command raised similar complaints about the manipulation of their intelligence reports to CENTCOM intelligence operations in 2015.

k. Obama hired **Laila Alawa**, a 25-year-old Muslim **Syrian immigrant**, to serve on the **Homeland Security Advisory Council's Subcommittee on Countering Violent Extremism** in 2015. Alawa had just obtained her American citizenship. She had just contributed to a report that recommended the DHS avoid using Muslim terminology such as "Sharia," "jihad," "takfir," or "umma." Alawa is probably a perfect reflection of Obama's and Johnson's political philosophy. Some of the comments she has posted on internet include:

   i. The 9-11 attacks in New York City and Washington D.C. "changed the world for good, and there's no other way to say it." *She supports the al-Qaeda terrorists.*

   ii. Even after she obtained her American citizenship, she stated, "I will always be Syrian. I will always be from Syria. I will always be of Syria." She refers to Syria as her "homeland." *Not quite loyal to America.*

   iii. After Kerry announced that the U.S. was admitting 85,000 Syrians in 2016 and over 100,000 Syrians in 2017, Alawa commented, "Salty white tears all over my newsfeed." *Supporting hijrah.*

   iv. "I can't deal with people saying America is the best nation in the world. Be critical. Be conscious. Don't be idiots." *Obama doesn't like America either.*

   v. "We are living in a country that deems it 'freedom of speech' to spew absolutely hateful ish about Muslims. That's not freedom of speech." *Against the First Amendment and the Bill of Rights. In support of blasphemy laws and Sharia law, like Obama.*

vi. "Ya know, @TheBachelor, white people of America. They're not gonna be dominant majority for much longer." *She supports Obama's fundamental change of America.*

vii. "There's nothing Islamic about the mass shooting in Orlando." *Taqiyya.*

l. At the end of Obama's presidency, officials from the State Department and Homeland Security admitted in testimony before the House Oversight Committee, that **the U.S. government lost track of over 122,000 immigrants who had their visas revoked, including 9,500 individuals who had documented links to terrorism**. Obama allowed thousands of terrorists to become clandestinely embedded throughout the United States, just as he allowed ISIS operatives to be distributed throughout America under the guise of being legitimate Middle Eastern immigrants.

m. The **Obama administration publicly identified the Kabul CIA station chief** in a press release when Obama visited Afghanistan in 2014, thus severely compromising intelligence operations in that theater. The CIA chief's name in any country is always a deeply guarded secret.

n. The *Associated Press* **(through administration leaks) exposed a U.S. operative in al-Qaeda in Yemen**. This operative discovered plans to blow up commercial airlines with improved underwear bombs.

o. On December 29, 2009, under the cover his Hawaii vacation, Obama signed Executive Order 13526 dealing with Classified National Security Information. The order significantly raised the standards used for determining if government information should remain classified, which will lead to the **declassification of huge numbers of government and national security related documents, thus compromising U.S. security interests**.

p. In June 2009, **the Obama administration** "accidentally" **released** a "highly confidential" 266-page report revealing details about the civilian nuclear programs and identifying the **locations of the nuclear weapons fuel storage sites**, which could later be targeted by ISIS operatives.

q. In 2010, Obama initiated a **full revision of the national security strategy** that **removed all connections between Islam and violence, and Islam and terrorism.** There would be no such thing as militant Islam, Islamic radicalism, or Islamic terrorism in American political and military doctrine.

i. "In October 2011, the DHS Civil Rights and Civil Liberties division released government guidelines forbidding reference to Islam in presentations and related work product. In keeping with the **OIC's Ten Year Programme of Action** [adopted in 2005], "Countering Violent Extremism Training Guidance & Best Practices" formalized the CRCL's aggressive campaign to counter Islamophobia. [354] … Today, the

Muslim Brotherhood dictates who does and does not do threat analysis for the government on War on Terror issues. The Brotherhood also dictates what can and cannot be discussed. This certainly fulfills key elements of any long-term campaign oriented toward *jihad fi sabilillah* [*jihad* in the Cause of Allah]. We ignore these realities at our peril. This is ignorance that kills. [p. 367]"[102] *(Stephen Coughlin, Catastrophic Failures)* Obama has subjugated the national security interests of the United States to formal doctrine established by the OIC and the Muslim Brotherhood.

r.   Obama encourages **immigration jihad** by **preventing the State Department from asking prospective Muslim immigrants their views on jihad or Sharia law**. And those Muslims who support Sharia law will support the creation of a worldwide Islamic caliphate, which they hope will replace the American republic.

s.   In September 2009, Obama spoke at the UN and declared that **global warming** was the greatest threat to Americans. In 2014, the **Pentagon identified** climate change **as the major national security risk**.

t.   Obama **protected thousands of domestic terrorists**, just as he protected the Taliban with the **rules of engagement and assigning them Miranda rights**.

u.   Obama has paralyzed the military with **rules of engagement that cancel or prevent most U.S. military attacks that may endanger civilians**. Most Islamic and ISIS terrorists operate in civilian districts, thus rendering them immune from U.S. strikes.

v.   **Obama is emptying Guantanamo to replenish the leadership and ranks of al-Qaeda to assist in their war against the West**. Treason. Obama has a very low threshold of criteria that are used to help guide the release of Islamic terrorists held by the United States.

w.   Obama is purposefully **weakening and degrading the military** according to Retired Army Major General Robert Dees, who stated in September 2015 at the Values Voter Summit "Not only are **we losing physical readiness to fight**, we have to fix the problem of **moral readiness** … [which is] more important than physical readiness, which **is very low**. The moral readiness is degraded by **social experimentation** within our military … It's a top driven mandate for social agendas **that occurs by this administration within the military**, which is a captive audience. It is not enhancing our readiness, it declines our readiness … **It's not an accident** … [which is producing] a rash of poor leaders, and in many cases **toxic leaders within the military** … the very best of our officers are the ones who leave first."

x.   Part of Obama's strategy to defeat ISIS was announced by Attorney General Lynch immediately after the ISIS-inspired Orlando massacre. Lynch stated in June 2016, "We stand with you to say that the good in this world far outweighs the evil, that our common humanity transcends our differences, and that **our most effective response to** terror and to hatred is compassion, it's unity, and it's love." Soon after Lynch made this statement, she also admitted that she lost track of the whereabouts of Mateen's wife who was an "alleged" co-conspirator with this Islamic terrorist attack, and declared that the true motivation of Mateen "may never be known."

   y.   Obama's **domestic anti-terrorism strategy** has been a documented **failure**. According to a study by the Triangle Center on Terrorism and Homeland Security at **Duke University** released in February 2016, the number of domestic Muslim-American terrorism related incidents has increased every year since 2012, with the number of incidents in 2015 doubling those recorded in 2014.[103]

26. "As Commander-in-Chief, I have no more solemn obligation than leading our men and women in uniform. **Making sure they have what they need to succeed.**" *Obama's Memorial Day Weekly Address, May 27, 2016.* Blatant lies from Obama, especially with his significant defense budget cuts.

   a.   "Our Air Force today is the oldest and smallest it has ever been. In January 2015, then-Army Chief of Staff Gen. Ray Odierno testified that the Army was as unready as it had been at any other time in its history. Chief of Naval Operations Adm. Jonathan W. Greenert testified similarly that, "Navy readiness is at its lowest point in many years." Nearly half of the Marine Corps' non-deployed units – the ones that respond to unforeseen contingencies – are suffering shortfalls, according to the commandant of the Corps, Gen. Joseph F. Dunford Jr. For the first time in decades, American supremacy in key areas can no longer be assured."[104] *Former Vice President Dick and Liz Cheney, Wall Street Journal, September 2016.*

   b.   "We've cut the military to its lowest levels. Yet we are facing a world that is the most complex environment that we have faced since at least the end of WWII. *[as a result of Obama's policies]* … The United States of America is in a less strong position today because of the readiness and the size of our armed forces … I think that he sees the military actually as something that is more dangerous to the world … I think that he looks at the U.S. military and sees it as a threatening application *[a threat to Iran and the Muslim world in the Middle East]* around the world than actually as a useful tool. *[Obama views the U.S. military as harming the well-being of the world.]*" *Retired three-star General Michael Flynn, former director of the DIA, 2012 - 2014. Interview with Fox News, Brett Baier, 2016.* Flynn's direct, anti-Obama, and anti-Islam insights probably helped contribute to the early termination of his role as Trump's first national security advisor.

   c.   "From 2010 to 2014, annual defense spending was estimated to decrease from $721 billion to $566 billion. With the sequester budget cuts, the Navy will lose two carrier battle groups, strategic bombers will decrease from 153 to 101, and the air force will lose over 50% of its fighter aircraft. Obama's budget projections cut just under $500 billion from the military budget over the next decade and, along with a $500 billion cut in the sequester, Obama defense budget cuts over the next 10 years are estimated at about $1 trillion dollars. This total is the equivalent of the lifetime costs of the amnesty program for illegal aliens, authorized by Obama by executive action. **Defense spending was 4.8% of GDP in 2010, and will drop to 2.9% of GDP in 2017**, at the end of Obama's presidency. With such severe austerity within the military budget, many military programs were going to be terminated. Besides wanting to cancel anti-ballistic missile defense systems, Obama also had many other projects in his sights for termination including Virginia Class submarines, the V-22 Osprey, and the F-22 Raptor. Besides weakening America, these savings would be redirected to help fund social programs and expanding the entitlement state. On November 12, 2014, **105 retired U.S. admirals with Navy Now published a letter to Congress stating**, 'We are concerned that if the Department of the Navy is required to continue to respond to crisis after crisis without the funding needed to build new ships, repair old equipment and provide routine maintenance to existing equipment, the nation risks permanent damage to our national defense and negative impacts on the domestic and international economies that rely on the safety and security that U.S. sea power provides … we write to express our concern that the United States Department of the Navy is underfunded and overextended, placing our national defense, our Sailors and Marines, and the stability of the global economy at risk.'[105]" *(Unexpected Treason, James McCormack)*

d. "For fiscal 2017, President Obama has requested $551 billion for the base defense budget, plus funding for ongoing operations, for a total of $610 billion. That sounds like a lot of money – but only if you overlook a couple of very important points. One is that these amounts, historically speaking, are extraordinarily low. Few people will be surprised that the U.S. spent more on defense in the Reagan years (the same investment of gross domestic product would be $1.1 trillion annually, on average). But it was $917 billion annually during the Carter years, and $761 billion when George W. Bush was in office. The military's budget was even higher during the Clinton years: $624 billion. Now we're talking about lowering it to $610 billion. As defense expert Justin Johnson recently pointed out, "As a percent of the government spending or total economy, the U.S. has not spent so little on national defense since the end of World War II." These progressively smaller budgets have taken their toll. Our shrinking military is stretched thinner than it's been in years. It's had to forgo modernization efforts repeatedly. The four branches have been forced to make aging ships, planes and other vehicles last well beyond their intended life spans."[107] *(Ed Feulner, The Washington Times, 2016)* Despite massive budget deficits and uncontrolled government spending, Obama is decimating the U.S. military with draconian budget cuts

e. Other Obama miscellaneous defense budget cuts.

    i. During Obama's first term, **over 50 major weapons programs have been delayed or terminated**. Obama decommissioned an entire class of fighting Navy frigates. In 2014 the Army terminated the class of Kiowa armed reconnaissance helicopters. Other programs that have been terminated including the combat search and rescue helicopter, the Navy's next generation cruiser, multiple anti-missile defense systems including systems that were to defend Poland and the Czech Republic, and the Army's future combat vehicle program.

    ii. In June 2009, the Obama administrated announced plans **to terminate a DHS spy satellite program**, initiated by the previous Bush administration.

    iii. **The** "**Sequester**": "In the summer of 2011, House Republicans insisted that actual spending cuts go along with an increase to the debt limit … The closed-door negotiations fell apart … Republicans and Democrats came to a less ambitious agreement to raise the debt limit through the Budget Control Act of 2011. The law found approximately $1.2 trillion in budget cuts spread over 10 years. But it also directed Congress to find another $1.2 trillion through a Joint Select Committee on Deficit Reduction, which came to be known as "the super-committee." The super-committee was supposed to meet and agree on a deficit reduction package by Nov. 23, 2011. Their proposal – which could include tax increases, spending reductions or both – would then get a filibuster-proof, up-or-down vote in Congress. … If the super-committee couldn't agree on a package, or if Congress voted it down, then automatic, across-the-board cuts would go into effect, with **half of those cuts hitting defense**. These automatic cuts are referred to as 'sequestration.'"[107] **Obama hoodwinked Congress**, and ensured the implementation of crippling defense budget reductions. In August 2012, Defense Secretary Panetta commented on the sequester, "I've made clear, and I'll continue to do so, that **if sequestration is allowed to go into effect**, **it'll be a disaster for national defense** and it would be a disaster, frankly, for defense communities as well … It was never designed to be implemented … It was designed to trigger such untold damage that it would force people to do the right thing." The sequester added $500 billion in military spending cuts in addition to the $487 billion in spending reductions already in place.

    iv. In 2012, Obama anticipated during the next decade, over **500,000 military personnel would have to be fired and four nuclear submarines decommissioned** due to budget pressures, while the civilian federal government grew along with their increasing benefit packages.

v.   In 2012 and 2013, Obama eliminated the **primary heavy armor force in in Europe** by deactivating two U.S. Army heavy brigade combat divisions, that were positioned inside Germany.

vi. In 2013, the Obama administration **decreased domestic bombing prevention funding by 45%**.

vii. In July 2015, the **army planned to reduce the number of soldiers by 40,000** and the number of civilian employees by 17,000, over the next two years, because of budget constraints. This is equivalent to a 10+% cut in army personnel. **Sequester cuts in the fall of 2015**, will force an estimated **addition 30,000 layoffs** among the army's soldiers. Even though Obama was publicly against the sequester, he created an uncompromising negotiating position so the sequester would be implemented with its disastrous effects on the military. The army numbered at 566,000 in 2011, and in 2015 there were less than 500,000 Army personnel. By March 2016, the Army numbered 479,000 active troops, which is the lowest number since 1940. Obama is targeting to cut the Army to an inadequate 420,000 by the end of his second term, which is the lowest number of troops since before WWII.

viii. During the last five years of the Obama administration, **the gap between the Department of Defense's requested budget and the actual DOD spending has increased exponentially**. In 2015, the Defense Department requested $619 billion but only received $515 billion under the Obama administration.

ix. In the 2017 budget, Obama proposed decreasing **counterterrorism** funding to the **Urban Area Security Initiative** by nearly $300 million dollars.

x.   In March 2015, General John Paxton. Assistant Commandant of the **Marine Corps**, testified before the Senate Armed Services Committee that, "I worry about the capability and the capacity to win in a major fight somewhere else right now … In the event of a crisis, these degraded units (intelligence and communications) could either be called upon to deploy immediately at increased risk to the force and the mission, or require additional time to prepare thus incurring increased risk to mission by surrendering the initiative to our adversaries." Paxton also mentioned that there have been a significant higher number of accidents in the aviation units that were probably secondary to budget cuts.

xi. In their annual 2016 report, the Heritage Foundation downgraded their assessment of the **U.S. Army** from "marginal" to "weak," secondary to major cuts in the defense budget, training, personnel and equipment.

xii. "The **U.S. Air Force** is now short 4,000 Airmen to maintain its fleet, short 700 pilots to fly them and short vital spare parts necessary to keep their jets in the air. The shortage is so dire that some have even been forced to scrounge for parts in a remote desert scrapheap known as "The Boneyard." ... about half of the 28th Bomb Wing's fleet of bombers can fly ... Since the end of the Gulf War, the U.S. Air Force has 30 percent fewer airmen, 40 percent fewer aircraft and 60 percent fewer fighter squadrons. In 1991, the force had 134 fighter squadrons; today, only 55." ("'*Wiped Out': Air Force Losing Pilots and Planes to Cuts, Scrounging for Spare Parts," Jennifer Griffin, FoxNews.com, May 14, 2016)* The Air Force has been decimated with the Obama administration's budget cuts and the sequester.

    xiii. By June 2016, **only four of the Navy's ten carrier air wings are fully functional**, and cannibalization of spare parts has impaired the readiness of U.S. armed forces in all spheres in the defense establishment.

27. Obama **lied about the origins of the "sequester."**

    a. "If President Obama has an enemies list, Bob Woodward is probably at the top of it. After all, it was Woodward who started the unraveling of the president's "sequestration apocalypse" mantra by confirming it was the White House's idea in the first place. [**During the 2012 presidential debates with Mitt Romney, when President Obama said the "sequester is not something that I proposed**. It's something that Congress has proposed. It will not happen ... The budget we are talking about is not reducing our military spending."] **he lied**. His then-OMB Director Jack Lew, recently confirmed as Treasury Secretary, and White House Legislative Affairs Director Rob Nabors pitched the idea to Senate Majority Leader Harry Reid, D-Nev., who pushed it, according to Woodward's book, *The Price of Politics."* ... "So we now have the president going out (saying), '**Because of this piece of paper and this agreement**, I can't do what I need to do to protect the country.' *[taqiyya - Obama falsely asserted he wanted to protect the country, since he wanted to cripple the military so the United States cannot fight a multi-front war, confront our adversaries when needed, and will be unable to fully fight against the rise of Islamic terrorism and jihad.]* That's **a kind of madness** that I haven't seen in a long time," Woodward told MSNBC."[108] Obama planned and implemented the sequester as a method to slash the defense budget so the military would be devastated during his administration and he could fraudulently blame Congress. In June 2017, Trump's Secretary of Defense General Mattis testified before the Senate appropriations committees and the House Armed Services Committee stating, "**No enemy in the field has done more to harm the combat readiness of our military than sequestration**." The idea of sequestration started with Obama, and became a legitimate vehicle to decimate the U.S. military establishment, which was Obama's intent.

28. Lies from Obama's "Remarks by the President on the Administration's Approach to Counterterrorism" on December 6, 2016.

a. "The **most solemn responsibility for any President is keeping the American people safe**." Poor vetting techniques, Obama's refusal to review social media postings of Middle Eastern immigrants, and Obama's order to delete databases of high risk Muslim terrorism suspects from intelligence files led to the San Bernardino Christmas party attack. The FBI had numerous warnings concerning the perpetrator of the Orlando nightclub massacre, but chose not to intervene.

b. "I believe that the United States military can achieve any mission; that **we are, and must remain, the strongest fighting force** the world has ever known." Obama decimated U.S. military forces with massive budget cuts, which resulted in a major decrease in Army and Marine forces, along with generational low operational capacities for U.S. naval ships and military aircraft. Vice President-elect Pence noted in a speech before the Heritage Foundation in December 2016 per *Breitbart* that "since 1991, America's active duty armed forces has decreased from 2 million to 1.3 million members, the Navy has shrunk to 272 ships from 500, the Air Force is roughly one-third smaller since that period of time and our standing army is the smallest it has been since WWII."[109] Obama greatly accelerated this contraction during his eight years as president.

c. "Instead, it has been my conviction that even as **we focus relentlessly on dismantling terrorist networks like al-Qaeda and ISIL**, we should ask allies to do their share in the fight … **So the campaign against ISIL has been <u>relentless</u>**." *Obama*. Despite fighting ISIS for four years – the length of WWII, ISIS still controls significant sections of Iraq and Syria, has metastasized throughout the Middle East and North Africa, has infiltrated thousands of fighters throughout Europe under the guise of refugees, and recruits "lone wolfs" throughout the West. ISIS is still a viable and formable terrorist organization, despite Obama's pretense of being relentless and promising to destroy and degrade ISIS.

d. "Today, by any measure, **core al-Qaeda -- the organization that hit us on 9-11 – is a shadow of its former self**." *Obama*. Al-Qaeda, along with ISIS, has spread throughout the Middle East, during his presidency.

e. "By 2011, Iraqis wanted our military presence to end, and **they were unwilling to sign a new Status of Forces Agreement** to protect our troops from prosecution if they were trying to defend themselves in Iraq." *Obama* refused to sign the Status for Forces Agreement, so that ISIS could fill the geopolitical vacuum in Iraq that was created by Obama's actions. At the same time, Obama funded and armed early ISIS forces who were disguised as moderate Syrian rebels and U.S. allies who were fighting Assad in Syria. Obama ordered Clinton to transfer weapons from Gaddafi's arsenals to Syrian Islamic radicals via Benghazi and then Turkey.

f. "In addition, **maintaining American troops in Iraq at the time could not have reversed the forces that contributed to ISIL's rise** -- a government in Baghdad that pursued a sectarian agenda, a brutal dictator in Syria who lost control of large parts of the country, social media that reached a global pool of recruits, and a hollowing out of Iraq's security forces, which were ultimately overrun in Mosul in 2014." *Obama.* By abandoning Iraq, Obama gave ISIS the opportunity to expand and grow in vulnerable territories where a missing U.S. military presence could not thwart and intimidate pro-Islamic State forces.

g. "And in Yemen, where **years of targeted strikes have degraded al-Qaeda in the Peninsula**." The Houthi rebels and al-Qaeda have led a sustained military assault against Saudi forces along the Yemenite – Saudi Arabian border for years. Obama released a senior al-Qaeda leader in Yemen (AQAP) from Guantanamo.

h. "**No foreign terrorist organization has successfully planned and executed an attack on our homeland.**" *Obama.* Fort Hood. San Bernardino. Orlando.

i. "I can tell you, during the course of my eight years, **that I have never shied away from sending men and women into danger where necessary**." *Obama.* Benghazi. The capture of American Naval sailors in international waters in the Persian Gulf by Iran. Obama cancelled at least two operations to capture and / or kill Bin Laden.

j. "And I always remind myself that as Commander-in-Chief, I must protect our people, but **I also swore an oath to defend our Constitution**." *Obama* bypassed Congress with unprecedented use of executive orders. Obama ignored immigration laws on the books by allowing unlimited immigration across the U.S. southern border.

k. "We are fighting terrorists who claim to fight on behalf of Islam. But **they do not speak for over a billion Muslims around the world**." The majority of Muslims around the world support Sharia law and the establishment of an Islamic caliphate / an Islamic state in the Middle East.

29. "The Obama Administration "grossly misrepresented" the number of crimes the criminal aliens it released from custody in FY 2014 subsequently committed by nearly tenfold … According to FAIR (Federation for American Immigration Reform), Immigration and Customs Enforcement (ICE) records the Immigration Reform Law Institute (IRLI) obtained via a Freedom of Information Act (FIOA) request on FAIR's behalf reveal that the 30,558 criminal aliens ICE released in FY 2014 committed 13,288 additional crimes. The number of subsequent convictions contained in FIOA documents is far higher than the 1,423 additional offenses ICE reported to the House Judiciary Committee last July." *("Report: Released Criminal Aliens Committed Nearly Ten Times More Crimes than Obama Admin. Told Congress," Caroline May, Breitbart, June 21, 2016)*

30. "When I took office, I committed to fixing this broken immigration system. **And I began by doing what I could to secure our borders**. Today, we have more agents and technology deployed to secure our southern border than at any time in our history. And over the past six years, **illegal border crossings have been cut by more than half**. Although this summer, there was a brief spike in unaccompanied children being apprehended at our border, the number of such children is now actually lower than it's been in nearly two years. Overall, **the number of people trying to cross our border illegally is at its lowest level since the 1970s**. Those are the facts … Even as we are a nation of immigrants, we're also a nation of laws. Undocumented workers broke our immigration laws, and **I believe that they must be held accountable**, **especially those who may be dangerous**. That's why, over the past six years, deportations of criminals are up 80 percent. And that's why we're going to keep focusing enforcement resources on actual threats to our security. Felons, not families. Criminals, not children." *Obama, Remarks by the President in Address to the Nation on Immigration, The White House, November 20, 2014.*

31. "This kind of **mass violence** does not happen in other **advanced** countries." *Obama, June 18, 2015.* Obama politicized the heinous murder of nine Black church goers by a White assailant in Charleston, South Carolina in order to advance his gun control agenda. Other examples of mass shootings / killings include:

    a. August 18, 2017 – An 18-year-old Moroccan Muslim asylum seeker **stabbed** 8 individuals in **Turku, Finland** – killing two and wounding six. One of the deaths was a 15-year-old Finnish girl. Four other Muslim migrants were arrested as being part of the operation.

    b. August 17, 2017 – Muslim terrorists from North Africa perpetrated **a van attack** on a popular tourist attraction in **Barcelona**, **Spain** where 14 individuals were killed and over 90 persons were injured.

    c. June 3, 2017, Saturday night – **During Ramadan** three Islamic terrorists in a van rammed into multiple people on **London Bridge**, and then exited the van where then stabbed many people, slashed the throats of pedestrians, and fired weapons. Seven people were killed and over 24 individuals were hospitalized.

    d. May 26, 2017 – **During Ramadan**, Muslim insurgents reported to be affiliated with ISIS murdered at least 24 Coptic Christians in **Egypt** by attacking their bus with assault rifles.

    e. May 22, 2017 – **At the start of Ramadan**, Salman Abedi, the son of Muslim immigrants from Libya, killed 22 people, including an 8-year-old girl, and injured over 50 others, after he blew himself up at an Ariana Grande concert in **Manchester**, Great Britain. Two weeks after this attack, both Jewish kosher restaurants in Manchester were firebombed, and the Muslims' slow motion ethnic cleansing and jihad continued in a major British city.

f. March 2017 – An Islamic terrorist attack near the **Parliament in London** led to the death of 6 people with over 50 other people injured.

g. On July 14, 3016, during Bastille Day celebration in **Nice, France**, a Muslim terrorist drove a heavy van through a thick crowd on the Promenade des Anglais, leading to the murder of 86 people. ISIS later claimed responsibility.

h. November 13, 2015 – ISIS operatives some who gain entry to Europe posing as Muslim Syrian refugees, murdered about 130 civilians in **Paris, France**.

i. January 7, 2015 – 12 people are murdered in **Paris, France** at the *Charlie Hebdo* offices by an Islamist who is retaliating for the publication of Mohammed cartoons.

j. June 26, 2015 – About one week after Obama makes the above statement, a radical Islamic extremist guns down and murders 38 people on a beach in **Tunisia**, a bomb kills multiple people at a mosque in Kuwait, and a radical Muslim extremist bombs an American factory in France, beheads a supervisor, and places his head on a fence.

k. November 20, 2015 – Islamic al-Qaeda terrorists murder over 20 tourists at a Western **Mali** hotel.

l. March 13, 1996 – 16 kindergarten children and their teacher are killed by a 43-year-old shooter in **Dublane, Scotland**.

m. November 7, 2007 – 9 people are killed by Pekka Eric Auvinen at his high school in **Tuusula, Finland**.

n. July 22, 2011 – 77 individuals killed by Ander Breivik in Norway with a bombing in downtown **Oslo**, and a shooting attack at a youth camp.

o. The United States (0.15) ranks fourth in mass shooting fatalities per 100,000 with Norway (1.3), Finland (0.34), and Switzerland (1.7) having a higher number.

32. "So it is worth reminding ourselves of how lucky we are to be living in **the most peaceful** *[? – ISIS, Nice, Orlando, Paris, Brussels, Boston marathon, Fort Hood, San Bernardino, 9-11, collapse of Syria – Iraq – Yemen – Libya, Chinese expansion in South China Sea, increasing Iranian hegemony, Turkish failed coup and subsequent purges, Palestinian third intifada – knife attacks – car rammings, North Korean nuclear threats, record amount of fear of domestic U.S. terror attacks leading to the rise of Donald Trump]* most prosperous, **most progressive era in human history** *[True – Socialism is the dominant political force in America, Canada, and Europe.]* … **Because the world has never been less violent** *[Orland, Nice, and Turkish airport attacks within the past month]*, healthier, better educated, **more tolerant** *[European rape epidemics]*, **with more opportunity for more people** *[less opportunities for American college graduates, record number of young adults living with parents, worst economic recovery in U.S. modern history]*, and more connected than it is today." *Obama, White House Summit on Global Development, July 21, 2016.*

33. "What I have done, and this is unprecedented … is I've said to each agency … look at regulations that are already on the books and if they don't make sense, let's get rid of them." *Obama interview, June 29, 2011.*

    a. The American Action Forum determined that since Obama became president, he has issued over 600 major regulations, which cost $743 billion. George Bush issued 426 major regulations.[110]

34. Obama **manipulated and falsified climate data** in order to advance his climate change agenda. According to the *Daily Caller*, "Former Energy Department Undersecretary Steven Koonin told *The Wall Street Journal* Monday that bureaucrats within former President Barack Obama's administration spun scientific data to manipulate public opinion. "What you saw coming out of the press releases about climate data, climate analysis, was, I'd say, misleading, sometimes just wrong," Koonin said, referring to elements within the Obama administration he said were responsible for manipulating climate data. He pointed to a National Climate Assessment in 2014 showing hurricane activity has increased from 1980 as an illustration of how federal agencies fudged climate data. Koonin said the NCA's assessment was technically incorrect."[111]

35. "**Don't tell me words don't matter**. I have a dream. Just words. We hold these truths to be self-evident and that all men are created equal. Just words. We have nothing to fear but fear itself. Just words. Just speeches." *Obama, 2008 presidential campaign trail.* **Obama actually plagiarized this phrase** from Deval Patrick, who used these words while he was campaigning for governor of Massachusetts in 2006. Deval's original words were, "All I have to offer is words. Just words. We hold these truths to be self-evident. Just words. Just words. We have nothing to fear but fear itself. Just words. Ask not what your country can do for you. Ask what you can do for your country. Just words. I have a dream. Just words."

    a. Days before the 2016 presidential election, Obama voiced his support for the right of illegal aliens to vote in U.S. elections, during an interview with Gina Rodriguez, and would ignore voter fraud.

    b. Obama ignored the hateful, belligerent and genocidal statements originating from Iran and is willing to allow them to fund their international terrorist activities with sanctions relief, and allowing them to continue developing their nuclear and ballistic missile programs. Millions of Iranians and their leaders were chanting "Death to America" and "Death to Israel" on Al Quds Day. In November 2014, Ayatollah Khameini tweeted, "there is no cure for Israel other than annihilation" and has publicly called Jews "dogs." To Obama these words, the ayatollah's words don't matter, since as a radical Muslim, he probably agrees with the ayatollah and lying (taqiyya) is a legitimate strategy. The Obama administration never made any future negotiations with Iran dependent on them toning down or eliminating their genocidal rhetoric.

c.   During the heat of a close Israel election in 2015, Netanyahu stated there would be no Palestinian state with his future government. Considering the Palestinian Authority was partners with a genocidal Hamas organization backed by Iran, Netanyahu was addressing legitimate security concerns, since Hamas would likely take over half of Jerusalem and the West Bank under Iranian guidance. Obama commented, "We take him at his word when he said that it [Palestinian statehood] wouldn't happen during his prime ministership," and threatened a reassessment of the U.S. / Israeli relationship while his press secretary warned of significant consequences, since "words matter." It appears that words do matter to Obama, but only when they originate from the prime minister of Israel. **When an individual does not apply the same standards to other people that are applied to Jews**, **that is called anti-Semitism**, or a double standard. Why isn't Obama incensed with Iran's genocidal words? But then again, a radical Muslim would be incensed when Jews stand and fight for their security and their lives in the face of continual non-stop Arab and Muslim aggression.

d.   Obama is making the West and America less secure when he refuses to associate Islam with terrorism and when he refuses to identify terrorists motivated by the Quran, Sharia law and Mohammed as "Islamic terrorists." Obama responded to Donald Trump and issued a tense and emotional appeal to the country why Islam should not be part of defining process of terrorism after the Orlando attacks. Obama argued, "The main contribution of some of some of my friends on the other side of the aisle have made in the fight against ISIL is to criticize the administration and me for not using the phrase "radical Islam." That's the key, they tell us. We cannot beat ISIL unless we call them radical Islamists. What exactly would using this label accomplish? What exactly would it change? Would it make ISIL less committed to try to kill Americans? Would it bring in more allies? Is there a military strategy that is served by this? The answer is none of the above. Calling a threat by a different name does not make it go away." *[But properly identifying the threat saves lives and makes our free society more secure.]* Trump responded to Obama's tirade by stating, "Political correctness is deadly. They [Obama] don't want to talk about the problem. And as I watched President Obama today and **he was more angry at me than he was at the shooter** … The level of anger is the kind of anger that he should have for the shooters and these killers." Obama is emotionally opposed to Trump since Trump has proposed a temporary ban on Muslim immigration into America, until all immigrants can be properly vetted.

i.   "Mr. President. When you instruct the State Department to not inquire of Muslim immigrants if they believe in jihad and the institution of Sharia law around the world with the establishment of an Islamic caliphate – words matter. When you ignore the genocidal rants of the ayatollah and his senior leadership – words matter. When you continually praise Islam as a religion of peace, yet ignore the racism and incitement to violence and murder originating from the Quran – words matter. When you ignore the religious motivations of violent jihadists who dream of killing Americans and destroying the United States – words matter. When you refuse to properly identify the enemies who are dedicated to destroying America – words matter. When you do not permit law enforcement to use Islam as a criterion for identifying high risk individuals who subsequently engage in terrorism, like in San Bernardino and Orlando, and countless innocent Americans are slaughtered – then words really do matter, especially when those policies instituted by you lead to the infliction of harm upon our country and its citizens." *(source – Author's parody of Obama's landmark "words matter" speech during his 2008 campaign)*

ii. In the Fort Hood, San Bernardino, Boston Marathon, and Orlando Islamic terrorist attacks, political correctness and Obama's pro-Islamist policies allowed future terrorists to escape the scrutiny of fellow workers, State Department employees, and law enforcement officials who could have prevented future terrorist attacks by actively intervening in these terrorists lives so they would be unable to commit future heinous crimes. As *The New York Post* noted in an editorial on June 18, 2016, "Years before Omar Mateen's bloodbath at Pulse, the FBI had him on its watch list – twice. He also made two trips to Saudi Arabia … But Orlando was hardly an isolated failure. The bureau also had the Tsarnaev brothers on its radar screen before the Boston Marathon bombing. It probed Elton Simpson before he took part in the hit on the "Draw Mohammed" event in Garland. Tashfeen Malik made it through a Homeland Security screening and later joined Syed Farook in the San Bernardino shooting. Agents cleared Maj. Nidal Hasan prior to his Fort Hood rampage … they all operate under real constraints – including not just proper regard for civil liberties but also orders from a White House that obsessively fears seeming anti-Muslim … **James Brennan**, **then deputy national security adviser for Homeland Security and Counterterrorism**, **in late 2011** *[under orders from Obama]* **ordered a purge of all federal law-enforcement "training materials that contain cultural or religious content, including information related to Islam or Muslims**." In other words, the FBI's political overseers [Obama] ordered it [FBI …] not to husband expertise on Islamist self-radicalization – and the bureau's bureaucrats, **from Comey** *[therefore Comey should not have been part of the Trump administration]* on down, complied. The same idiocy rules the entire Obama effort at "countering violent extremism." Bad as it is that **President Obama** refuses to use the words "Islamist terror," it's far worse that **he's put blinders on everyone who's supposed to be keeping America safe**." *(source – "How Obama's Blackout on 'Radical Islam' Leads to Dots Going Unconnected," New York Post editorial, June 18, 2016)*

iii. As a radical Muslim, Obama did his best to help establish Islam as a major force in America, and incessantly worked on misrepresenting its teachings and its cultural manifestations so it will be in a position to eventually control America and the West. For Obama, not equating Islam with violence goes beyond standard political correctness, where people are fearful that associating violence and terrorism with Islam or the potential for violent jihad with individual Muslims, will cause them to be labelled racists and bigots, be discredited in their communities, and possibly lose their ability to make a living for their families. By refusing to implicate Islam's role in the Orlando attack, as well as with its incitement to violent jihad, Obama has already instituted Sharia law as major United States policy directives, since he considers the criticism of Mohammed or Islam as blasphemy. Obama again demonstrated his allegiance to Sharia law days after the Orlando massacre by having Attorney General Loretta Lynch scrub all references to Islam, ISIS and al-Baghadadi from the partial transcripts of the 911 calls and of the discussions between the terrorist and police negotiators. In this case, it is the lack of words and improper descriptions that matter. Obama attempted to remove all references to Islam from the historical record of this massacre so he can continue to misrepresent Islam as a religion of peace. And if Obama acknowledged we were at war with radical Islam, he wouldn't have been able to give Iran $150 billion in sanctions relief since he would be telling the world he was funding radical Islamic terrorist organizations, such as Hamas, Hezbollah and the IRGC – all enemies of the United States. Obama wouldn't have been able to support Morsi and the Muslim Brotherhood by giving them over $1 billion in aid and F-16s, if his foreign policy labelled "radical Islam" as an enemy of the United States and the West. Obama, as a radical Muslim, will advance any policy to promote, strengthen, and protect the Islamic terrorists and jihad, and weaken and hurt America and the West.

Foreign Policy

"He's nothing but a bull shitter." Obama describing Trump after Trump's November 2016 presidential election victory according to People magazine. But what about Obama?

1. "I take a wait and see approach … **It's not productive**, given the history of U.S. - Iranian relations, **to be seen as <u>meddling</u> in Iranian <u>elections</u>**." *Obama in 2009 is giving an excuse not to support the insurrection against the ayatollahs, where numerous young protesters were killed in the street by the Iranian government thugs.* Obama did not interfere with the Iranian political process since he was allied with the ayatollah and his radical Islamic theocracy which have consistently been the number one state supporter of terrorism in the world during Obama's presidency.

   a. Obama was happy to interfere in **<u>Egyptian politics</u>**, which led to the overthrow of Mubarak and the rise of the Muslim Brotherhood. Obama interfered in Egypt so that the radical Islamic terrorist group, the Muslim Brotherhood, which Obama misrepresented as a peaceful moderate political party, could gain power and ally themselves with Iran and al-Qaeda, with the help of U.S. aid provided by the American president.

   b. **During the <u>Israeli national elections</u> in 2015, Obama sent his best political operatives, who helped run his winning presidential campaigns, to assist the Arabs and the liberal Israelis attempt to defeat Netanyahu**. The Arabs committed voting fraud, and Obama funded the opposition with money, supplies and volunteers, yet Netanyahu scored a major victory. Obama wanted to oust Netanyahu so that a liberal Israeli government would be in control, which would support a two-state solution and give the PLO, Hamas, and their allies (al-Qaeda, IRGC) - East Jerusalem and the West Bank. Obama was attempting to create a radical Islamic terror state in the heart of Israel and its capital.

   c. In **<u>Great Britain</u>**, Obama actively campaigned there in 2016 to keep them in the European Union, **and against the Brexit political movement**. Obama wanted to keep Great Britain in the European Union since its bureaucrats supported unlimited Islamic immigration in Europe and Great Britain, and Obama wanted to continue unlimited and unfettered Islamic immigration into Great Britain, which would accelerate England's political transition to an Islamic Sharia compliant state.

d. In 2017, documents were released by Wikileaks that revealed that Obama and the CIA were **spying and interfering in the 2012 <u>French national elections</u>**. The February 16, 2017, *Wikileaks* press release stated, "All major French political parties were targeted for infiltration by the CIA's human ("HUMINT") and electronic ("SIGINT") spies in the seven months leading up to France's 2012 presidential election. The revelations are contained within three CIA tasking orders published today by *WikiLeaks* as context for its forth coming CIA Vault 7 series. Named specifically as targets are the French Socialist Party (PS), the National Front (FN) and Union for a Popular Movement (UMP) together with current President Francois Hollande, then President Nicolas Sarkozy, current round one presidential front runner Marine Le Pen, and former presidential candidates Martine Aubry and Dominique Strauss-Khan." Obama was interfering in the French election via the CIA, in order to ensure the socialists would win and Islamic immigration would continue in France unimpeded. Obama is laying the groundwork for civil strife and an eventual Islamic revolution in France and Europe.

e. In May 2017, Obama campaigned for Chancellor Merkel in **<u>Germany</u>** in order to support her progressive pro-Islamic immigration party, while delivering anti-Trump remarks.

f. "It's pretty clear that **the Obama administration sent their people over to Israel to work against Prime Minister Benjamin Netanyahu**, pretty much openly, significant dollars invested in that campaign over there … I just came back not that long ago from the Balkans where I sat in a place like Macedonia, and there I learned that **the United States government**, borrowing money from China and Saudi Arabia, had to be **handed over somewhere <u>at least five million dollars</u>** in contracts transferred through **USAID <u>into George Soros organizations</u> that were <u>used to manipulate elections in the Balkans</u>**, and that's just particularly Macedonia, not including the neighboring countries that are there and **some of that money was <u>used to translate Saul Alinsky's "Rules for Radicals" into Macedonian to distribute the books</u> and the rules for radicals and the actions of radicals were <u>manifested within the election efforts</u>** in that part of the world, so I would say that **the Obama administration is a long ways from clean on this as far as being involved in elections in other countries**, not to mention little comments like the British if you vote Brexit you're going to have to go to the back of the queue, so that's the taxpayer dollars piece of this, but the long string that we should be looking at with this investigation and special counsel that at our request here." *Representative Steven King, addressing Congress regarding FBI Director Comey issues, July 27, 2017. Obama illegally interfered in the Balkan elections via his Soros connections.*

2. **"Gaddafi threatens a bloodbath that could destabilize an entire region."** *Pure taqiyya.* Obama advanced this lie to pave the way for an Islamic fundamental takeover of Libya, so the caliphate being created by ISIS in Iraq and Syria could eventually expand to North Africa. Libya would later play a significant role in the Muslim war on Europe by being the jumping board for illegal Muslim immigrants travelling to southern Europe.

a. "If we waited one more day *[extreme urgency – Obama must keep to the planned schedule of Islamist revolutions in the Middle East]*, **Benghazi, a city nearly the size of Charlotte, could suffer a massacre** that would have reverberated across the region and stained the conscience of the world. *[Obama intervened to save the Libyans from a mythical massacre in Benghazi, but refused to help Ambassador Stevens who was raped and murdered in real time in Behghazi.]* It was **not in our national interest** to let that happen. **I refused to let that happen."** *[but Obama did not interfere with ISIS, al-Qaeda, or Iranian terrorism, and Obama did refuse to save Ambassador Stevens] Obama's address to the nation regarding Libya, March 28, 2011.* Obama started a war with less than 300 people being killed in Libya, who were mostly radical Islamic combatants, aligned with al-Qaeda and the future ISIS. Obama was looking for any excuse to bring down the <u>secular</u> Libyan government and create a chaotic political scenario in which the radical Islamists would thrive. Obama led from behind because he did not want his fingerprints on the main political motivations of this action that would **pave the way for the expansion of an Islamic caliphate in North Africa**, which has been one of Obama's main objectives of his presidency. The rebellion was initially suppressed by Gaddafi, but thousands more were killed on both sides after NATO intervened, which led to Gaddafi's rape and murder. Al-Qaeda and ISIS subsequently took control of vast sections of Libya. Libyan weapon stockpiles subsequently went to ISIS in Syria, Boko Haram in Africa, and various al-Qaeda-affiliated groups. If Obama was so concerned about a potential massacre in Benghazi against Muslim residents, why has he been so reluctant to intervene to thwart the genocide of non-Muslims by ISIS in Syria and Iraq? Because Obama is a radical Muslim. Obama was looking for an excuse to destabilize Libya and kill Gaddafi so the Islamic radicals could take control of vast stretches of Libya and gain control of their weapons stockpiles. Obama may have killed Gaddafi so a future Libyan government would not interfere with the future planned mass migration of Muslims that would be invading Europe. If the Muslim Brotherhood, which Obama supported, retained control of Egypt, then the Islamic radicals would have controlled all of North Africa.

b. A 2016 House of Commons Foreign Affairs Committee report[112] shed much light on the Libyan situation which proves Obama lied concerning the reasons why he helped initiate the military action to overthrow Gaddafi.

    i. "The proposition that Muammar Gaddafi would have ordered the massacre of civilians in Benghazi was not supported by the available evidence. The Gaddafi regime had retaken towns from the rebels without attacking civilians in early February 2011 …. Gaddafi regime forces targeted male combatants in a civil war and did not indiscriminately attack civilians. More widely, Muammar Gaddafi's 40-year record of appalling human rights abuses did not include large-scale attacks on Libyan civilians." *Obama lied*.

    ii. "Subsequent investigation revealed that when Gaddafi regime forces retook Ajdabiya in February 2011, they did not attack civilians. Muammar Gaddafi also attempted to appease protesters in Benghazi with an offer of development aid."

    iii. "An Amnesty International investigation in June 2011 could not corroborate allegations of mass human rights violations by Gaddafi regime troops. However, it uncovered evidence that rebels in Benghazi made false claims and manufactured evidence."

    iv. "Abdelhakim Belhadj and other members of the al-Qaeda affiliated Libyan Islamic Fighting Group were participating in the rebellion in March 2011 … There is a close link between al-Qaeda, Jihadi organizations, and the opposition in Libya." *Obama was allied with al-Qaeda in the war against Gaddafi.*

    v. "Libyan weapons and ammunition were trafficked across North and West Africa and the Middle East." *Obama and his al-Qaeda allies used the war against Gaddafi to gain control of much of the country, and to raid his advanced military arsenals, which were later distributed to Islamic terrorist groups in Africa and the Middle East. Gaddafi's advanced anti-aircraft missiles were distributed to ISIS and Hamas.*

3. "Meanwhile, yesterday marked the definitive end of the Gaddafi regime in Libya. And there, too, **our military played a critical role in shaping a situation on the ground in which the Libyan people** *[taqiyya – Obama means Islamic terrorists]* **can build their own future**. Today, **NATO is working to bring this successful mission to a close**." *Obama, October 21, 2011.* Obama's policies ultimately allowed ISIS and al-Qaeda to control large sections of Libya, and the ensuing chaos helped create the environment that led to the massive Islamic migration that overwhelmed Europe in 2015 and 2016.

a. "Even as we helped the Libyan people bring an end to the reign of a tyrant, our coalition could have and should have done more to fill a vacuum left behind." *Obama is pretending to apologize at the UN in September 2015, for leaving a vacuum and allowing ISIS and al-Qaeda to control large sections of Libya.* Obama is also responding to Putin's comments where Putin correctly analyzed "Instead of the triumph of democracy and progress, we got violence, poverty and social disaster … **Do you realize what you have done**?"

4. "In a world of new threats and new challenges, you can choose leadership that has been tested and proven. Four years ago, **I promised to end the war in Iraq**. *[U.S. troop levels in Iraq have increased in 2014, 2015, and again in 2016. In 2016, Iran is establishing multiple missile bases in Iraq after Obama invited Iran into Syria and Iraq to help fight ISIS. Obama is paving the way for Iran to control the crescent between Iran and Lebanon, and eventually attack northern Israel.]* We did. We blunted the Taliban's momentum in **Afghanistan** and **in 2014 our longest war will be over**. *[There are over 10,000 U.S. troops in Afghanistan in 2015 and 2016, and the Taliban, ISIS and al-Qaeda are all gaining strength and waiting to take over the country after the U.S. military evacuates its positions per Obama's plans. In June 2016, due to the increasing strength of the Taliban and al-Qaeda in Afghanistan, Obama permitted the military to initiate limited air bombing campaigns against the Taliban, but with strict rules of engagement criteria limiting their effectiveness. With the Trump presidency, troop levels were increased in Afghanistan.]* <u>**Al-Qaeda is on the path to defeat**</u> and Osama bin Laden is dead. *[Five days later, a branch of al-Qaeda – Ansar al Sharia – attacked the American consulate in Benghazi and killed four Americans including the U.S. ambassador. In Cairo just hours earlier, Islamist protestors invaded the U.S. embassy in Cairo, took down the American flag and raised the al Qaida flag. Al-Qaeda has been getting stronger since 2012.]*" *Obama, Democratic National Convention,* <u>***September 6***</u>*,* <u>***2012***</u>

5. **Reporter** (August 2014): "Mr. President, Do you have any second thoughts about pulling all ground troop out of Iraq? **Obama**: You know what, what I find interesting, the degree to which this issue keeps on coming up, <u>**as if this was my decision**</u>." Obama is backtracking on his scores of promises, after ISIS has taken over large parts of Syria and Iraq secondary to Obama withdrawing U.S. forces from Iraq, and Obama arming "moderate" Syrian rebels, who were usually al-Qaeda fronts. Obama is responding to a reporter's questions whether he regrets leaving Iraq, which is now under attack from ISIS. Obama never signed a status of forces agreement with Iraq and insisted on pulling all troops from Iraq, leaving it relatively defenseless against growing terrorist forces in the region. Obama even lied about events surrounding the status of forces agreement by stating, "Well, keep in mind, that wasn't a decision made by me. That was a decision made by the Iraqi government." In the 2012 presidential debate with Governor Romney, Obama denied that he wanted a status of forces agreement. Romney stated during the debate, "With regards to Iraq, you and I agreed, I believe, that there should have been a status of forces agreement." Obama countered, "That's not true."

    a. "For the first time in nine years, there are no American fighting in Iraq." *Obama, 2012.*

    b. "Four years ago, I promised to end the war in Iraq, we did."

    c.   "Four years ago, I promised to end the war in Iraq, and I did."

    d.   "I told you I'd end the war in Iraq and we did."

    e.   "In 2008, I promised we'd end the war in Iraq, we've ended it."

    f.   "I ended the war in Iraq as I promised."

    g.   "The war in Iraq is over."

    h.   "For the first time in nine years, there are no Americans fighting in Iraq."

6.   "We're leaving behind a sovereign, stable and self-reliant Iraq." *Obama. In 2010, Iraq suffered ten car bombings per month, which increased to 71 in 2013, as Obama's policies became fully implemented.*

    a.   "Our invasion created the atmosphere for a Jordanian to start a Muslim sectarian war, which ultimately created ISIS [during Obama's term] … [but the situation] worsened after U.S. troops left Iraq [during Obama's first term via his refusal to sign the status of forces agreement], helping quickly deteriorate the situation further." *Mike Ryan, Policy Director for the Democratic Congressional Campaign Committee, ISIS Backgrounder memo, October 2, 2014.*

7.   "Over the next two months, our troops in Iraq – tens of thousands of them – will pack up their gear and board convoys for the journey home. The last American soldier will cross the border out of Iraq with their heads held high, **proud of their success** …. That is how America's military efforts in Iraq will end." *Obama speech, October 21, 2011. Obama is creating a political and military vacuum in Iraq that was filled by al-Qaeda, ISIS, and Iran.*

    a.   "It'd mean that we'd be risking mass killings on a horrific scale. It'd mean we'd allow the terrorists to establish a safe haven in Iraq to replace the one they lost in Afghanistan. It'd mean we'd be increasing the probability that American troops would have to return at some later date to confront an enemy that is even more dangerous." *President Bush arguing against Democratic opposition to the surge. July 2007.*

    b.   "Now we are at the end of President Obama's term; yet, when 99% of President Obama's advisors told him to keep 10,000 troops in Iraq to stop the rise of radical terrorism; he did not listen. *[Obama only listens to the Muslim Brotherhood, Valerie Jarrett, and Erdogan regarding Middle Eastern matters. All the other foreign policy and defense advisors are just for show.]* He made a political decision rather than a decision for our national security. This is a weakness in his leadership style."[113] *Former Director of the DIA and former Assistant Director of National Intelligence Lt. General Michael Flynn. July 2016.* Obama did not pay attention to his U.S. military and national security advisors because his true partners and the ones guiding U.S. policy in the Middle East and elsewhere were the Muslim Brotherhood, Erdogan, the theocracy in Iran, and Valerie Jarrett. Obama's weakness wasn't based solely on choosing the wrong political approach to difficult issues, because as a radical Muslim, he purposely weakened America's standing in Iraq and was advancing the interests of enemies of the United States. Obama's allies were able to engineer the firing of Flynn from Trump's national security team, as retribution to his anti-Obama sentiments.

c.   "*[Without a U.S. presence]* Iraq would serve as the base of a new Islamic caliphate to extend throughout the Middle East, and which would threaten legitimate governments in Europe, Africa and Asia." *Former Bush Defense Secretary Donald Rumsfeld, 2005. Prescient. Obama already knew this and Rumsfeld's concerns were a major policy endpoint for Obama's administration and led to waves of massive Islamic immigration targeting Europe.*

8.   "We have been very clear to the Assad regime, but also to other players on the ground … that's **a red line for us is we start seeing a whole bunch of chemical weapons moving around or being utilized** … That would change my equation." *Obama, 2013.* Assad crossed that red line with supposed chemical weapons usage, yet Obama did nothing. Obama feigned a strategic devastating military assault against Assad, but backed down when confronted with Russian, congressional, and British opposition. If Obama was truly serious about striking Syria, it would be to enable Islamic radicals such as ISIS, al-Qaeda, or the Muslim Brotherhood to fill the political vacuum. In 2016, it was reported that ISIS was still using chemical weapons on the battlefield in Syria, and Obama still did nothing.

a.   In the summer of 2014, the Obama administration announced that the chemical weapons disarmament of Syria had been completed, but **during the summer of 2015, *The Wall Street Journal* revealed that much of Assad's chemical weapons arsenal remained intact**. Ex-Obama officials admitted that Obama lied. "Antony J. Blinken, a former deputy secretary of state, recently said, 'We always knew we had not gotten everything, that the Syrians had not been fully forthcoming in their declaration.'"[114] Dan Shapiro, Obama's former U.S. ambassador to Israel tweeted on April 7, 2017, "**We always knew Syria likely squirreled away some residual undeclared stocks and / or production capability**, now proven by Idlib strike." The fact that Syria retained its chemical weapons stockpiles was confirmed when the Syrian air force bombed civilian targets with chemical weapons in northern Syria in early April 2017, for which Trump retaliated with a cruise missile strike upon the Syrian air force base that launched the WMD attacks. **The Obama administration**, **including Kerry and Rice**, <u>lied repeatedly</u> about the chemical weapon stockpiles and WMD capabilities of the Assad regime in Syria.

i.   *Obama declared in his 2014 State of the Union Address* that "American diplomacy backed by the threat of force is why **Syria's chemical weapons** are **being eliminated**."

ii. "We're getting chemical weapons out of Syria without having initiated a strike." *Obama, April 28, 2014.*

iii. "**Today we mark an important achievement** in our ongoing effort to counter the spread of weapons of mass destruction by **eliminating Syria's declared chemical weapons stockpile**." *Obama, August 18, 2014.*

iv. *Kerry stated in 2014,* "**the worst of the weapons are gone**, but the despicable regime and the crisis it has created remain and require our collective focus." Ironically, the nuclear agreement with Iran allowed them to keep their nuclear enrichment program intact as well. A result of these strategies is the increased risk to Israel where Israel's enemies do not relinquish their weapons of mass destruction programs.

v. *In July 2014, Kerry stated,* "**We got 100% of the chemical weapons out** [of Syria]."

vi. *John Kerry testified before the Senate Foreign Relations Committee* on February 24, 2015 that, "**We got, as you know, last year, all the chemical weapons out of Syria**."

vii. "That was an important step, because it reduced, or **essentially eliminated, the proliferation risk from that declared chemical weapons stockpile**, that we could essentially destroy those chemical weapons and **ensure that terrorists would not be able to get their hands on them** and use them in other places." *Josh Earnest, White House press secretary, January 6, 2015.*

viii. The "declared **chemical weapons** stockpile that Assad previously denied existed has now been acknowledged, **rounded up**, **removed from the country** [Syria] **and destroyed** precisely **because of the work of this administration** and our successful efforts to work with the Russians to accomplish that goal." *Josh Earnest, White House press secretary, June 17, 2015.* But the Obama administration knew one month earlier that the Syrians had violated the agreement. In May 2015, *Bloomberg* reported that, "The U.S. government was informed months ago that an international monitoring body found traces of chemical weapons that President Bashar al-Assad had promised to turn over, including sarin gas – a clear violation of the deal he struck with President Obama after crossing the administration's 'red line' two years ago. Officials from the Organization for the Prohibition of Chemical Weapons told the Obama administration early this year that its inspectors had found traces of two banned chemical weapons during an inspection of the Syrian government's Scientific Studies and Research Center in the district of Barzeh near Damascus, two administration officials told us. A report by *Reuters* May 8 said that OPCW inspectors had found traces of sarin and VX nerve agent at the site in separate inspections in December and January."[115] Obama and his administration continued to lie.

ix. "There's a fact-check outfit out there called *PolitiFact*, and it's like all the other fact-check outfits. *The Washington Post* has one; the *AP* has one. These fact-check outfits exist only to discredit and impugn Trump. Well, the ***PolitiFact* has had to**

retract a story they categorized as "mostly true" three years ago, and this story is big. Three years ago, Barack Obama and his Regime were an abject disaster. But they were claiming success after success after success, particularly in the Middle East. One of the things that **the Obama administration was celebrating was that they had completely removed chemical weapons from Syria**. Obama drew that red line and the Syrians and everybody else realized the bad actor they were dealing with, and they cowered in fear, and they did remove 100% of their chemical weapons. There's a problem now, though. Those chemical weapons were just used in an attack in Syria on Syrian citizens. So how could the Obama administration have gotten rid of all of these? … The Obama administration – now the dire enemy of the Russians, victimized by the Russians – gave the chemical weapon stocks in Syria to the Russians. Which means the Russians probably gave it right back to the Syrians. But the *PolitiFact* story retracts a 2014 article that said it was "mostly true" that the Obama administration "helped broker a deal that successfully removed 100% of chemical weapons from Syria." So, a story that was a lie backed up by *PolitiFact* for three years has been retracted, and the upshot is the Obama administration did not succeed in successfully removing all of Syria's chemical weapons, as we now know because those weapons were used recently." *Rush Limbaugh, April 6, 2017.*

b. In mid-August 2015, German and allied troops confirmed that ISIS used chemical weapons against Kurdish forces. Unlike Obama's forceful and emotional reaction to Assad's alleged use of chemical weapons resulting in Obama's desire to destroy Assad's military with the full fury of American forces, Obama ignored this assault on the Kurds, and issued no warnings to ISIS. Within the month before ISIS' use of WMDs, Obama reached an agreement with Erdogan to target all terrorists in the region, which allowed Erdogan to conduct military strikes against the Kurds. Could it be that part of Obama's hidden agenda involved defeating the Kurds, so that ISIS could become a permanent political and military feature in the Middle East, which would help lead to the creation of an Islamic caliphate?

9. "With respect to Israel, **the interests of Israel in stability and security are actually very closely aligned with the interests of the Sunni states … What's preventing them from entering into even an informal alliance** [against Shia-run Iran] **with at least normalized diplomatic relations is not that their interests are profoundly in conflict but the Palestinian issue, as well as a long history of anti-Semitism that's developed over the <u>course of decades</u> there**, and anti-Arab sentiment that's increased inside of Israel based on seeing [Jewish] **buses** being blown up." *Obama interview with The New Yorker magazine, 2014.* Obama is practicing taqiyya by implying Islamic anti-Semitism only started when the State of Israel was created, or during the 1967 war when Israel united Jerusalem and captured

the West Bank, when it has been in existence since the inception of Islam. Obama is ignoring the anti-Semitism embedded in the Quran, which states Jews are the worst enemies of the believers. He is also white-washing the Islamic pogroms throughout the history of the Middle East and Islam's alliance with Hitler during WWII. Maimonides stated in the 1100's, "never did a nation molest, degrade, debase and hate us as much as they … Although we were dishonored by them beyond human endurance … our sages instructed us to bear the prevarications and preposterousness of Ishmael [Muslims] in silence." Obama accidentally exposed his true thought process regarding the Middle East. Obama, as a radical Muslim, hates Israel, and one of his top priorities as president is to destroy the Jewish state. Knowing that the Sunni states have informal unofficial aligned interests with Israel, Obama has directed his foreign policy to undermine those Sunni states – Libya, Egypt, Jordan, Syria, Saudi Arabia, Yemen, and the UAE, and attempt to build the Islamic caliphate from Iran across the Middle East to North Africa, while empowering Iran. Obama wanted to destabilize and / or overthrow any Muslim / Arab nation that has any positive contacts with Israel.

a. "All the childhood memories of the man who rules the White House are **Shiite** memories … that is why he is so anxious for Iran to emerge victorious." *Syrian writer Muhydin Lazikani, March 25, 2015, Hiwar TV Interview, London.*

b. "Barack Hussein Obama is the **son of a Shiite father** … Some people call **him the Iranian lobby** in America." *Iranian opposition activist Abu Muntasir Al-Baloushi, Saudi 4Shbab TV channel, April 10, 2015.* Everyone in the Middle East knows Obama is a Muslim, a Shiite Muslim, and most of the world knows Obama is a Muslim. Only in America does the majority of the population believe that Obama is a Christian, and that group is concentrated in the Democratic Party. The conclusion that Obama is a Shiite Muslim put sunlight on the obvious affinity and support that Obama showed Iran with the nuclear negotiations and most other aspects of foreign policy.

c. "By attacking Yemen, the Saudis have made a mistake and created an evil and contemptible *bid'a* [i.e., forbidden innovation in Islam] in the region. **The Saudi government is currently carrying out crimes in Yemen identical to those committed by the Zionists in Gaza. The operation against the Yemeni nation is a crime and a massacre** … Killing children, razing homes, and destroying the infrastructure and national wealth of a state are a great crime … The coming defeat of the Saudis is clear, and stems from the fact that the Zionists, who have many times the military capability of the Saudis, could not defeat a small territory like Gaza, [let alone] Yemen, which is a large country with a population of tens of millions." *Iranian Supreme Leader Ali Khamenei, April 9, 2015, discussing the April 2, 2015 Iranian Nuclear Framework Agreement presented in Lausanne, Switzerland.* The Ayatollah Khamenei and Obama are basically stating the same political concepts, that the Israelis and the Saudis are allies, and both are making war on Islamic entities. Obama is allying himself and his policies with Shiite Iran in the millennial Shiite-Sunni conflict. The ayatollah is laying the political framework for the overthrow and destruction of the Saudi regime, just as they have advocated for the annihilation of Israel. He compares the Saudi military action against the Iranian-backed rebels in Yemen to the Israeli military strikes against Hamas in Gaza, both of which were initiated for self-defense purposes. The ayatollah uses the same politically slanted arguments against the Saudi Arabians, using descriptions of their actions like massacres, crimes, unacceptable attacks on children, and wanton destruction of the fabric and resources of the Yemeni nation, as he would use them against Israel in its wars with Gaza. Whenever Israel counter-attacked, children were used as human shields, and most of their actions resulted in accusations of war crimes and massacres. Of course, Iran wants its allies to control Yemen, and they want to protect their proxies in Gaza. Yet, Iran treats Saudi Arabia as an enemy and a mirror image of Israel, so that in the war for the heart of the Arab and Islamic world, the Muslim street will back and support Iran as it expands its hegemony in the Middle East and seeks to dominate a future Islamic caliphate. Unfortunately for Israel, America, and the West, Obama is clearly on the same page as Iran and its radical leaders.

d. When Muslims go to war and they are on the verge of major losses, they will generally seek a hudna or a ceasefire. When Hamas was firing thousands of missiles into Israel in 2014, there were no major international cries calling for an immediate halt to Hamas's shelling of civilian targets. Fortunately, the Iron Dome anti-missile defense system kept Israeli casualties to a minimum. But when Hamas was sustaining heavy losses at the hands of Israeli air power and their 10,000 missile inventory was being rapidly depleted, Obama and other Hamas allies insisted on an immediate ceasefire, to which Israel agreed, since Israel did not want to face further significant international repercussions. On May 7, 2015, it was reported that Obama and Secretary of State Kerry were pushing for a ceasefire between Saudi Arabia and the Iranian-backed Houthi rebels, which materialized a few days later. Yet within that week, Saudi Arabia sent ground forces into Yemen, and the Houthi rebels shelled a girls' school, a hospital, and a residential neighborhood. The Saudi Arabian air campaign also caused significant damage to rebel forces. There is no logical reason for Saudi Arabia to consider restraining their military strategy at this time with the war being advanced inside their territory and their air campaign being effective within Yemen. Still, Obama called for a ceasefire, even if only for five days. Again, Obama was backing Iran's regional and military interests by allowing the Houthis to regroup, assess their strategy, protect their military and leadership assets, and receive supplies from Iran, under the guise of alleviating a "humanitarian crisis." If Obama was truly an ally of Saudi Arabia, he would have let the Saudis continue weakening the Houthis and advance toward securing an uncontested victory against the Iranian proxies with their military forces. Like the situation between Israel and Hamas, where an Obama-backed ceasefire allowed Hamas to restock their missiles and prepare for the next conflict, Obama also backed a ceasefire in the Arabian Peninsula to the advantage of the Houthis. Obama was using parallel strategies of hudnas aiding the radical Islamic extremist groups, while hindering the military advancement of his "traditional allies," i.e., Israel and Saudi Arabia. The Obama administration lied when they said in the press release that Saudi Arabia initiated the truce. When Mohammed's forces were the weaker party in an ongoing conflict, he generally sought hudnas lasting ten years, giving him time to rebuild his forces so that he could prevail when the military conflict resumed in the future. **Obama is seeking a 10-year period for the inspections with Iran within the nuclear framework agreement, which realistically is a Mohammed-inspired hudna, giving Iran ten years to continue to build up its military forces, and expand its nuclear capabilities without a war with the West.** After this 10-year period of inspections, it is very likely that Iran will seek to initiate a significant military conflict with the West and its allies. The American military approach to hudnas is another major reason why Obama wants to fundamentally transform the U.S. military culture. In the tradition of Generals Patton and Sherman, the United States very rarely employs ceasefires in major military conflicts, a strategy which would be to the detriment of Muslims if the United States became fully committed in another Middle East war. In order to be victorious against Islamic military powers, allied forces must forgo any ceasefires, obtain a complete unconditional military surrender, and dismantle the Islamic network of hate, supremacy, and Sharia law by banning the Quran and making Islam in its present state illegal, even in the Middle East. Otherwise Islamic societies use periods after their military defeats as opportunities to regroup, rebuild, and prepare for the next military conflict.

e. On May 10, 2015, Saudi Arabia's King Salman withdrew from participating in an Obama-sponsored summit with the Gulf Cooperative Council, which was voicing real concerns over the developing Iranian nuclear framework agreement with the United States and other major world powers. With Obama paving Iran's way to becoming a major nuclear power and supporting a truce allowing the Houthis to rearm and regroup, the King of Saudi Arabia expressed his extreme displeasure with Obama by diplomatically skipping the summit after U.S officials were under the impression he would attend. With increasing Iranian hegemony in the Middle East, the Gulf States were also pushing for a NATO-like treaty with the United States that would commit America to fight against Iran or its proxies under well-defined circumstances. Obama balked at this alliance, since his personal true loyalties are with Iran.

f.   Iran's state press, *Press TV*, released a report that falsely accused the Saudi King of financing the re-election campaign of Israeli Prime Minister Netanyahu with $80 million. The government of Iran is using the same strategy that Obama previously advanced, which was to alienate and ostracize the Saudi royal family from the Arab world by portraying them as allies with the Israelis. Iran and Obama are also attempting to turn the Saudi Arabian population against the royal family so when internal strife increases in the Saudi kingdom (via internal revolt or an external attack as planned by Iran and / or Obama), the Saudi regime has an increased risk of collapsing.

10. On April 3, 2009, **Obama bowed to King Abdullah of Saudi Arabia**, **making the world think he was showing his utmost respect to the keeper of Mecca**. It raised the question of whether Obama was a Muslim, and whether he violated diplomatic protocol and the honor of America by having a president bow and subjugate himself to another world leader. Obama was hoodwinking the King of Saudi Arabia and the Sunni world, making them believe that Obama had their interests at heart and would be a credible ally with Saudi Arabia in the future. Obama clandestinely supported Iran in their conflict with Saudi Arabia, and their goals to destabilize and replace the Saudi Arabian monarchy with a pro-Iranian regime.

11. "The Armenian Genocide is not an allegation, a personal opinion, or a point of view, but rather a widely documented fact supported by an overwhelming body of historical evidence … As president, **I will recognize the Armenian Genocide** … **America deserves a leader who speaks truthfully about the Armenian Genocide** and responds forcefully to all genocides. I intend to be that president." *Obama, 2008, campaign trail.* For seven years during his presidency, and on the 100th anniversary of this state sponsored terrorism, Obama failed to link the killing of the Armenians to genocide. Of all world leaders, Obama has the closest relationship with Turkey's President Erdogan, and Obama would not advance this emotional issue against the wishes of Erdogan. Even Pope Francis called the slaughter of 1.5 million Armenians at the hands of the Turks, "the first genocide of the 20th century." As Aram Hamparian, executive director of the Armenian National Committee of America, stated, "This is a betrayal of the truth, a betrayal of trust, a disgraceful national surrender to a foreign gag order being imposed by the government of Turkey." *The New York Times* published an editorial by Peter Baker on April 21, 2015 stating, "The president's continued resistance to the world stood in contrast to a stance by Pope Francis, who recently called the massacres 'the first genocide of the 20th century' and equated them to mass killings by the Nazis and Soviets. The European Parliament, which first recognized the genocide in 1987, passed a resolution last week calling on Turkey to 'come to terms with its past.'"

12. "People don't remember, but when I came into office, the United States in world opinion ranked below China and just barely above Russia, and today once again, **the United States is the <u>most respected country on earth</u>**. Part of that I think is because of the work we did

to reengage the world and say we want to work with you as partners with mutual interests and mutual respect. It was on that basis **we were able to end two wars** *[not quite true with Iraq and Afghanistan]* **while still focusing on the very real threat of terrorism and try to work with our partners in Iraq and Afghanistan**. It's the reason why we are moving in the direction to **normalize relations with Cuba and the nuclear deal** that we are trying to negotiate with Iran." *Obama, June 1, 2015.* One month before leaving the presidency, Obama reiterated his beliefs at his final 2016 press conference by stating, "**And almost every country on Earth sees America as <u>stronger and more respected</u>** *[Just hours before Obama attended his final press conference, China stole an underwater military drone that was adjacent to an American ship in international waters. At the same time, Putin told Obama and the American intelligence community to release the intelligence that allegedly implicated him in the DNC and Podesta hacking scandals or stop talking, i.e. – put up or shut up.]* **today than they did eight years ago**." Obama withdrew support from President Mubarak of Egypt, who was a stable and dependable ally of the United States, and supported the Muslim Brotherhood, which created an Islamo-fascist dictatorship in **Egypt**. Just one month previously, King Salman of **Saudi Arabia** refused to attend a GCC Summit at Camp David with Obama as a protest against the JCPOA. Four of six heads of state from the Gulf States boycotted the meeting. **Brazil** and **Germany** are upset with Obama over U.S. spying on their internal affairs. **Russia** and **China** are becoming more aggressive in their spheres of influence based on their perception of Obama's weakness. Russia annexed Crimea and invaded **Ukraine**. China expanded its military footprint in the South China Sea. ISIS has grown under Obama's watch, and Yemen rebels are at war with Saudi Arabia. **Iraq** lost control of a significant part of their country to ISIS after Obama withdrew U.S. forces, and the Taliban are poised to take over Afghanistan. When Obama landed in Havana on March 20, 2016, which was the first time a U.S. president visited **Cuba** in 90 years, neither Fidel or Raul Castro met Obama at the airport nor was Obama provided with a red carpet, unlike when the Iranian foreign minister visited Cuba five months later. The Cuban leadership greeted the Pope and the president of Iran when they landed in Cuba, but not Obama. Obama enjoyed subjugating himself to the Cuban leadership and showed his perceived inferiority by allowing his wrist to go limp when Raul Castro raised his arm at a press conference. Raul Castro just laughed at Obama. The United States may be respected, but Obama certainly is not.

a.   "Every time this happens, we hear from people in this administration and other governments as well that we will not accept North Korea as a nuclear armed state. And, yet it is. You also say this about other things too. *[including Secretary of State Kerry stating that Obama brought "peace and security" to Syria as a major policy achievement of his presidency]* You say you will never accept Crimea as a part of Russia. And, yet it is. **Isn't it time to recognize these things for what they are and not live in this illusion or fantasy**

where you pretend that things are, **are not**? *[fantasyland or taqiyya?]" Matt Lee, AP reporter questioning the State Department spokesman concerning North Korea's alleged detonation of a hydrogen bomb. January 6, 2016.*

b. When Obama landed in **Saudi Arabia** on April 20, 2016, King Salman did not greet Obama as he exited his plane, nor did any other member of the Saudi royal family. Obama was met by an insignificant regional governor. The Saudi's are upset with Obama in part due to his pro-Iranian policies.

c. On May 22, 2016, **Vietnamese leaders** were not present when Obama stepped off Air Force One at the start of his first trip to Vietnam.

d. When Obama landed in **China** for the G20 conference on September 3, 2016, the Chinese refused to roll out a moving staircase with a red carpet to Air Force One, and forced Obama to exit the "ass" of the plane. The leaders of Russia, Brazil, South Korea, India, and Great Britain all had respectful red carpet receptions. *The New York Times* commented, "The reception that President Obama and his staff got … was bruising, even by Chinese standards."

e. After the Chinese humiliated Obama as he arrived at the 2016 G20 Summit, Rodrigo Duterte, president of the **Philippines**, warned Obama in China not to discuss the extrajudicial killing of drug dealers in his country. Duterte stated, "Who does he think he is? I am no American puppet. I am the president of a sovereign country and I am not answerable to anyone except the Filipino people, nobody but nobody. You must be respectful. … **Son of a bitch I will swear at you** … We inherited this problem from the United States (Muslim insurgency and drugs)." Days later, Obama cancelled his meeting with Duterte. Yet, Obama has never shown his indignation at Iran when the ayatollah insulted him or proclaimed, "Death to America." Duterte is agitated with Obama since many of the victims of the extrajudicial killings are probably linked to the Abu Sayyaf Islamic terrorist group, which has launched many recent lethal terrorist attacks in the Philippines, and Obama's criticisms of Duterte's policies would protect the Islamic terrorists. Duterte probably knows Obama is a radical Muslim and is demonstrating significant public resistance to Obama's input, since the Islamic terrorists have been a plague upon the Philippines for years. Duterte knows that Obama uses the mantra of promoting human rights as a strategy to protect the Islamic terrorists. Duterte witnessed Obama protecting the civil rights of high risk Muslim immigrants and radicals only to watch Americans get slaughtered in Orlando, San Bernardino, and Paris. Duterte commented in November 2016, "they [ISIS] will come here and we have to prepare for that … Remember, these guys, they do not have an iota of what is human rights, believe me. I will not just simply allow my people to be slaughtered for the sake of human rights [unlike Obama in America]; that's bullshit … [on] some parts of the islands of Mindanao,

there are white people. I suppose they are Arabs, and they are here as missionaries. …
They are here for indoctrination … We have problems with Muslim insurgency."[116]
Duterte is protecting his people from immigration jihad, while Obama is importing
hijrah into the United States.

f.   Immediately after the 2016 G20 Summit, Robert Mugabe, the dictator of **Zimbabwe**,
     publicly mocked Obama by challenging him to prove that he is not the **son of a whore**.

g.   Obama former best friend among world leaders, Recip Erdogan of Turkey, leveled
     significant public criticism at Obama during a November 2016 *60 Minutes* interview.
     Erdogan accused Obama of not taking Turkey's concerns regarding the war in Syria
     and the resultant refugee crisis seriously, and attacked Obama by stating, "We have
     addressed these issues; discussed them with President Obama and Vice President
     Biden. **They failed to rise to the occasion and handle these issues seriously**. This
     is quite upsetting for us … Let me be very frank in my remarks. I've been known for
     my candor. I wouldn't speak the truth if I said I was not disillusioned, because **I am
     disillusioned**." At the end of Obama's presidency, there was a significant deteriora-
     tion in the interpersonal relationship between Obama and Erdogan. Analysts may
     place the blame on different approaches to the Syrian refugee crisis and the Syrian
     civil war, but Obama may have turned against Erdogan when Turkey reinstated full
     diplomatic relations with Israel and ambassadors were exchanged between Ankara
     and Jerusalem. As Obama lost control of an Egyptian attack along Israel's south-
     ern border when Sisi overthrew Morsi and subsequent relations between Egypt and
     the United States deteriorated, Obama again lost the ability to control united Arab
     armies along Israel's northern border when Erdogan reestablished full diplomatic
     relations with Israel. As with Egypt, when various Muslim countries improved rela-
     tions with the Jewish state, Obama relations with those corresponding states and
     their respective leaders deteriorated significantly. Although Turkey is a member of
     NATO, Erdogan drifted away from the American sphere of influence, and moved
     towards allying itself with Russia and purchasing its advanced S-400 long-range air
     defense missile system. Obama's policies and deteriorating personal relationship with
     Erdogan is leading to the dissolution of NATO's southern flank, which is probably
     Obama goal since it weakens NATO, and diminishes U.S. influence in the Middle
     East as Turkey aligns its military and defense interests with Russia. Coincidentally,
     days after Erdogan reestablished full diplomatic relations with Israel and repaired
     relations with Russia, Islamic terrorists attacked the major Istanbul airport, at the
     same time Obama was clearly dissatisfied with Erdogan's rapprochement with Israel
     and Russia. Were the radical Islamists and their supporters sending Erdogan a mes-
     sage to reverse his diplomatic advances?

h. "Every country needs a strong leader in order to progress. A country without a strong leader will go down." *Erdogan, interview with Israel's Channel 2 News, November 2016, after Trump's election victory.* Erdogan insinuates Obama is a weak leader.

i. "And so, in early September (2016) when I saw President Putin in China, I felt that the most effective way to ensure that that did not happen *[Russian hacking into and interfering with the American electoral process]* was to talk to him directly and **tell him to cut it out, there were going to be some serious consequences if he did not**." Putin ignored Obama and his innocuous red line, since he knew that the American president would not back up his threats. With one month remaining in his presidency, Obama again threatened Putin during a December 2016 *NPR* interview by stating, "I think there is no doubt that when any foreign government tries to impact the integrity of our elections that **we need to take action. And we will – at a time and place of our own choosing**. Some of it may be explicit and publicized; some of it may not be … we have been working hard to make sure what we do is proportional. *[Obama admits his actions will be insignificant.]*" Days later, Obama left Washington to enjoy his last Christmas vacation in Hawaii before he vacated the presidency, and Donald Trump was inaugurated. Ironically, Obama ignored the Russian hacking into White House emails and the Joint Chiefs of Staff, and the Chinese hacking into the OPM and intelligence files. Obama did not take action sooner since he was more than happy to let America's adversaries compromise our national security, intelligence, and military operations earlier in his administration. Regarding the 2016 election related leaks, there was not a consensus that the Russians were undeniably the source of the released documents, and the leaks may have originated from sources inside those respective operations or from the CIA which has a unit to disguise their computer hacking as originating from adversarial foreign sources. Even Julian Assange, the editor-in-chief of *Wikileaks*, revealed the Russians were not the source of the DNC / Podesta document release.

    i. "**The conclusions of the intelligence community with respect to the Russian hacking were not conclusive** as to whether *WikiLeaks* was witting or not in being the conduit through which we heard about the DNC emails that were leaked." *Obama's final press conference, January 18, 2017.* Obama admitted there is no substantial proof that the Russians were responsible for the leak of DNC documents which were hacked by an unknown source. The U.S. government has no proof how *Wikileaks* obtained the DNC documents, and a leak instead of a hack could have been the source. Thus, the charges against the Russians for interfering in the 2016 U.S. presidential election and against Trump that asserted he was allied in some capacities with the Russians against the Clinton campaign were **fake news**. Obama's last-minute sanctions against the Russians and his concomitant expulsion of Russian diplomats were based on his desire to complicate President-elect Trump's future dealings with the Russians and not a response to proven Russian interference in the American presidential election.

j.   A spokesperson for British PM Theresa May reflected her strong disagreement with the tone of Kerry's anti-Israel speech and announced a strong disagreement with the Obama administration over their harsh criticism of Israel and the settlements being the major cause of a lack of progress in the Middle East peace process. May's spokesperson stated at the end of December 2016, "**We do not … believe that the way to negotiate peace is by focusing on only one issue**, in this case the construction of settlements, when clearly the conflict between the Israelis and Palestinians is so deeply complex … And **we do not believe that it is appropriate to attack the composition of the democratically elected government of an ally** … The Government believes that negotiations will only succeed when they are conducted between the two parties, supported by the international community … we are also clear that **the settlements are far from the only problem in this conflict**. In particular, the people of Israel deserve to live free from the threat of terrorism, with which they have had to cope for too long." The British government realized that Obama was too biased against Israel when he blamed the settlements for the lack of a peace agreement.

k.   The Australian Prime Minister, Malcolm Turnbull, called UNSC Resolution 2334, crafted and supported by Obama, "**one-sided**" and "**deeply unsettling**," and indicated that Australia would have voted against this resolution. Turnbull also stated, "**Australia stands with Israel**. We support Israel, the only democracy in the Middle East," as an opposing position to that staked out by Obama.

l.   Russia responded to new sanctions and massive diplomatic expulsions issued by Obama against it in response to unproved Russian interference in the 2016 presidential elections by issuing a tweet calling him "**hapless**" and mocked him with a picture of a baby duckling with the word "**lame**" over the photo. Maria Zakharova, the Russian Foreign Ministry spokesperson responded by stating, "**The outgoing US administration has not given up on its hope of dealing one last blow to relations with Russia, which it has already destroyed**. Using obviously inspired leaks in the US media, it is trying to threaten us again with expansion of anti-Russian sanctions, "diplomatic" measures and even subversion of our computer systems. Moreover, this final New Year's "greeting" from Barack Obama's team, which is already preparing to leave the White House, is being cynically presented as a response to some cyber-attacks from Moscow. **Frankly speaking, we are tired of lies about Russian hackers that continue to be spread in the United States from the very top**. The Obama administration launched this misinformation half a year ago in a bid to play up to the required nominee at the

November presidential election and, having failed to achieve the desired effect, has been trying to justify its failure by taking it out with a vengeance on Russian-US relations. However, the truth about the White House-orchestrated provocation is bound to surface sooner or later. In fact, this is already happening. On December 8, US media quoted Georgia's Secretary of State Brian Kemp as saying that the local authorities tracked down the origin of a hacker attack on his voter registration database after the election. The attack was traced to an IP address of the Department of Homeland Security. This was followed by an attempt to quickly cover up this information by a flood of new anti-Russian accusations that did not contain a single piece of evidence." Obama may have been trying to create a false flag diplomatic and / or military confrontation with Russia during his final days as president in order to complicate Trump's relationship with Russia and "box" him in a corner by setting up circumstances where he could be viewed as aiding an enemy of the United States, if he rolled back Obama's last-minute sanctions.

m. During Trump's May 2017 trip to Israel, multiple Israeli leaders insinuated criticism at former President Obama's Middle Eastern foreign policy. Israel's liberal President Rivlin stated during joint remarks with President Trump, "Mr. President. We are happy to see that **America is back in the area**. **America is back again**. You remarked, the defeating of ISIS as one of your top missions. This is a most important objective." Rivlin implied that Obama reneged on continuing America's leadership role in Middle East politics and stability and purposely created multiple geopolitical vacuums that opened the doors to the rise of ISIS and chaos across the region. Rivlin also implied that Obama had no intentions to defeat ISIS and there would be a pro-Israeli president in office. Netanyahu later reiterated similar points by declaring, "I want you to know how much **we appreciate the change in American policy on Iran** … I wanted to tell you also how much we appreciate the **reassertion of American leadership** in the Middle East." Netanyahu has finally realized that Obama was allied with Iran, and also makes a similar statement concerning American leadership as President Rivlin. The Israeli leadership was not aware until late in the game that Obama was implementing Mulsim Brotherhood policy and Bill Ayers' foreign policy declarations which were stated very clearly in the Weather Underground manifesto *Prairie Fire*, "U.S. OUT OF THE MIDDLE EAST!," which synchronized well with Obama's and Ayers' pro-Ayatollah and pro-radical Muslim policies.

13. "I believe in a **smarter kind** of American leadership." *Obama, 2015 State of the Union Address.* Failed or detrimental Obama policies include the Russian reset, failing to respond to the attack on Benghazi, supporting the Muslim Brotherhood in Egypt while removing U.S. support from Mubarak, allowing Iran to keep their nuclear program and enrichment capabilities while removing significant sanctions, allowing North Korea to minitiarize their

nuclear warhead capabilities and to develop their EMP capabilities to destroy America, calling ISIS "JV," recognizing Cuba with no reciprocal gestures from the Castros, not recognizing "Islamic" terrorism, and withdrawing American leadership from the Middle East while Russia, Iran, and Turkey expand their influence in Syria and Iraq. Obama described ISIS as "contained" just days before they attacked multiple targets in Paris and killed 132 civilians. Obama may have consulted or even coordinated with Erdogan when he decided to shoot down a Russian bomber over Syria that was targeting ISIS forces and their allies. Obama and Erdogan may have been instigating a war between NATO and Russia. North Korea allegedly tested a hydrogen bomb during Obama's last year as president. Obama remains silent as Turkey bombs Kurdish forces with embedded American troops and advisors.

a. "There's a shared assessment that the European security architecture is falling apart in many ways … There is a growing sense that this U.S. administration is focused on establishing a legacy on what has already been achieved rather than trying to achieve anything more. Yet the problems can get much worse." *Camille Grand, director of the Foundation for Strategic Research in Paris, 2016 Munich Security Conference.*

b. "The question of war and peace has returned to the continent … We had thought that peace had returned to Europe for good." *German Foreign Minister Frank-Walter Steinmeier, 2016 Munich Security Conference.*

c. In late February, Norwegian Prime Minister Erna Solberg commented on the European mass immigration debacle by, "It is force majeure proposals which we will have in the event that **it all breaks down**." Luxembourg's foreign minister Jean Asselborn stated, "The outlook is gloomy … We have no policy any more. We are **heading into anarchy**." These leading European politicians are commenting on Obama's policy of supporting mass illegal Muslim immigration into Europe. In 2016, the European continent is expecting the arrival of over one million new Muslim migrants.

d. The Kurds, which are backed by the Pentagon, initiated fighting with Syrian rebels which are backed by CIA operations, in mid-February 2016. At the same time, Turkey, a member of NATO, started shelling the Kurds, backed by the United States in Aleppo, after Syrian rebels were losing ground to Russian, Hezbollah and Syrian forces. Thus, American supported proxies are fighting among themselves in Syria, and a member of NATO is shelling American allies.

e. In an interview with David Goldberg in *The Atlantic* in March 2016, Obama blamed British Prime Minister Cameron and other European allies for the diplomatic disaster and chaos that followed the overthrowing of Gaddafi in Libya. Obama stated, "When I go back and I ask myself what went wrong there's room for criticism, because I had more faith in the Europeans, given Libya's proximity, being invested in the follow-up." Obama's comments created a diplomatic uproar in Britain and on the European continent. Obama also questioned the existence of the special relationship between the United States and Great Britain.

f.   "The fact is the Middle East and North Africa are literally melting down. If you look at the actions of the Saudis and other coalitions going into Yemen and whatnot, on the one hand that's good. On the other hand, it signals a lack of or a concern that America's not doing what we used to do. So in reality it's important we re-establish a level of legitimacy and credibility that we are going to help stabilize that region because we can't ignore it."[117] *Retired four-star Army General Stanley McChrystal. Leading from behind and strategic patience are not working out well for President Obama's foreign policy.*

g.   "Later, the president would say that he had failed to fully appreciate the fear many Americans were experiencing about the possibility of a Paris-style attack in the U.S." *"The Obama Doctrine"*

h.   "He understands that Russia's overall position in the world is significantly diminished. And the fact that he invades Crimea or is trying to prop up Assad doesn't suddenly make him a player. You don't see him in any of these meetings out here helping to shape the agenda. For that matter, there's not a G20 meeting where the Russians set the agenda around any of the issues that are important."[118] *("The Obama Doctrine"). Obama greatly underestimates Putin's role in the world and the Middle East. Obama is somewhat naïve downplaying Putin's significance because he doesn't attend Obama's climate change meetings.*

i.   "American alliances are not in good shape these days, with many countries worrying that **President Obama does not value the alliances**, their own role in those alliances, or the commitments our alliances imply to the safety of states that are to some degree dependent on the United States. It is therefore mysterious why the president decided to inflict further damage in interviews with *The Atlantic* … Words have consequences. In these recent interviews, **the president undermined trans-Atlantic relations and relations with Saudi Arabia and other Gulf allies**. … What does the president have to say to calm their fears? Nothing. Instead, he builds them, and suggests that **he looks upon growing Iranian power** with indifference, or even **with approval**. *[Because Obama is an agent for Iran.]* To those comments, he added criticisms of the United Kingdom and France, as if he were concerned lest any key allies be left out *[Obama is purposely trying to destroy America's alliances and its role as a superpower.]* … In fact they rely on the words of the top officials with whom they interact; for them, in this sense the president IS the United States. Mr. Obama's deprecation of presidential credibility is alarming for Americans, and dangerous for our friends."[119] *Elliott Abrams, a top foreign policy advisor to Presidents Reagan and George W. Bush, responding to "The Obama Doctrine."* Maybe certain sections of "The Obama Doctrine" should not have been published since Obama may have violated one of his own tenets emphasized in the article, which was "Don't do stupid shit."

j. Obama called the **Libyan political environment** after his failed intervention and policies there as a "**shit show**" while discussing the "Obama Doctrine" with Jeffrey Goldberg. *Not quite "a smarter kind of American leadership."*

k. "Advisers recall that Obama would cite a pivotal moment in *The Dark Knight*, the 2008 Batman movie, to help explain not only how he understood the role of ISIS … . "There's a scene in the beginning in which the gang leaders of Gotham are meeting," the president would say. "These are men who had the city divided up … Everyone had his turf. And then the Joker comes in and lights the whole city on fire. ISIL is the Joker."[120] *(The Obama Doctrine). Obama relates to ISIS and its threats via cartoons and comic book characters at national security meetings. Should Americans expect more from their president?*

l. "In *The New York Times Sunday Magazine, ("The Aspiring Novelist Who Became Obama's Foreign Policy Guru," May 5, 2016),* Samuels details how Ben Rhodes, a script writer, author of the *Beloit Journal* fiction piece titled "The Goldfish Smiles, You Smile Back," and brother of CBS president David Rhodes, **a man with zero foreign policy experience, shaped and promoted the president's foreign policy initiatives**. Samuels observes, "His lack of conventional real world experience of the kind that normally precedes responsibility for the fate of nations – like military or diplomatic service, or even a master's degree in international relations, rather than creative writing – is startling." The article details how these two shaped and **spun make-believe** about the facts and their policies and with the aid of a supine press … helped **propagate the false narratives** these two wove out of their **fantasies**."[121] *(Clarice Feldman, AmericanThinker.com)* Rhodes helped Obama craft the lies surrounding the JCPOA, which enabled Obama to have it approved by Congress while deceiving the American people.

m. "The persistent **disconnect between White House expectations and reality** is nothing new. It's the defining characteristic of Obama's **delusional and failed foreign policy**, perfectly encapsulated by his visit to Asia … That foreign policy has always favored stagecraft over substance … When it comes to the specifics of nuclear security – the key focus of this visit – President Obama's immense stagecraft also betrays a weak record. His signature foreign-policy accomplishment is a diplomatic farce that pays Iran tens of billions of dollars to destabilize Iraq, and to develop ballistic-missile capabilities that are only useful as a delivery system for nuclear weapons. The threat posed by America's most capable nuclear adversary, Russia, has grown exponentially during his time in office, and then there's North Korea, which has not posed a more serious threat since the Korean War … While the president and his sidekick Ben Rhodes have spent the past seven years heaping disdain upon their critics, their hubris has become all-encompassing.

Tomorrow, in failing to defend Harry Truman's decision to use the bomb, the leader of the free world will disregard the responsibility of his office to the men and women of the U.S. military."[122] *(Tom Rogan, National Review, May 2016)*

n. "Last week, Russian officials warned the Obama administration about the installation of a new anti-ballistic missile system in Romania and talked of a possible nuclear confrontation … Such apocalyptic rhetoric follows months of Russian bullying of nearby neutral Sweden, harassment of U.S. ships and planes, warnings to NATO nations in Europe, and constant threats to the Baltic states and former Soviet republics. China just warned the U.S. to keep its ships and planes away from its new artificial island and military base in the Spratly archipelago … Iranian leaders routinely threaten to close down the key Strait of Hormuz. North Korea and the Islamic State are upping their usual unhinged bombast to new levels – from threatening nuclear strikes on the U.S. homeland to drawing up hit lists of Americans targeted for death … After the abject pullout from Iraq in 2011 and the subsequent collapse of the country eroded U.S. credibility, after the fake Syrian red lines, the failed reset with Russia, the Benghazi fiasco, and the **slashing of the military, America has lost its old deterrence** … And given that there are only eight months left to take advantage of this global void, Russia, China, Iran, North Korea, and Islamic terrorists are beginning to believe that the U.S. will not do anything to stop their aggressions once they change global realities by force."[123] *(Victor Davis Hanson, Hoover Institution, Stanford University, National Review)* Obama, the radical Muslim, has accomplished his goals which include destroying the old world order with the United States as the sole superpower, changing the balance of power around the world and especially in the Middle East, creating multiple conflicts on multiple fronts around the world so the United will be unable to ably defend its allies, and to create a worldwide political environment where Islamist interests can rapidly assert their political and military power in vacuums and weakened geopolitical regional systems so that the creation of an Islamic caliphate and the spreading of Sharia law can be accomplished.

o. "In a shockingly non-politically-correct outburst, Patrick Calvar, chief of the Directorate General of Internal Security, told members of the French parliamentary commission that **thanks to the increasing frequency of sexual assaults by Islamic migrants**, 'Extremism is growing everywhere … **We are on the brink of civil war.**' [Mr. Calver also noted] 'There will be a confrontation between the far right and the Muslim world … **Europe is in great danger**, extremism is growing everywhere.'"[124] Obama supports massive Muslim immigration, which is tearing Europe apart. For Europe, this policy is not smart. But for Obama, as a radical Muslim, his jihad against Europe is moving forward as planned.

p. In response to the overwhelming unexpected high costs of the "**<u>Affordable</u>**" Care Act or Obamacare, Hillary Clinton is campaigning against Obama's landmark health insurance reforms by stating, "It is finally time for us to deal with the skyrocketing out-of-pocket health costs." Obama lied when he declared on the day that the ACA became law, "Once this reform is implemented, health insurance exchanges will be created, a competitive marketplace where uninsured people and small businesses will finally be able to purchase **affordable**, quality insurance." In 2016, insurance premiums in some states are increasing by 60%. In 2017, insurance premiums are estimated to be increasing 10 - 65%. The *Motley Fool* reported in August 2016, "One standout is Arizona, where the two largest insurers in the state, Blue Cross Blue Shield (BCBS) of Arizona and Phoenix Health Plans, which insure 113,400 of the state's 152,600 Obamacare members, are requesting respective premium increases of 64.9% and 60%. In Tennessee, BCBS of Tennessee, which enrolled roughly 222,800 of Tennessee's 304,300 Obamacare members in 2016, is requesting a 62% premium hike in 2017. Once more, BCBS of Illinois, which controls 70% of the Illinois Obamacare market, is asking for a 50.2% premium hike Humana isn't much better, either, with a 46.3% rate hike request on the table in Illinois."[125]

q. Aetna announced in August 2016 that it was decreasing its participation in state exchanges for Obamacare policies from fifteen states to four states, secondary to significant losses. Aetna announced a $200 million loss for the second quarter of 2016. For similar reasons, Humana and United Healthcare have also decreased their participation in state exchanges. Mark Bertolini, the CEO of Aetna recognized major flaws in Obamacare from its inception and warned Obama administration officials. An *IBD* editorial stated, "At an investor conference in late 2012, Bertolini warned that 'in some markets,' Obamacare premiums could 'go as high as 100%. And we've done all that math. We've shared it with all the regulators. We've shared it with all the people in Washington that need to see it. And I think it's a big concern.' … In 2014, he complained that Obamacare is 'not an affordable product' for many people and that it didn't fix the underlying problems driving high health care costs … 'Providing affordable, high-quality health care options to consumers is not possible without a balanced risk pool.'"[126]

r. "The people are out there busting it, sometimes 60 hours a week wind up with **their premiums doubled and their coverage cut in half**. It's the **craziest thing in the world** … The people that are getting killed in this deal are small business people and individuals who make just a little too much to get any of these subsidies." *Former President Bill Clinton* is very critical of Obamacare, Obama's primary domestic achievement as president, while campaigning for his wife. Even the Democratic leadership is publicly recognizing Obamacare as an unmitigated disaster. *Early October 2016.*

s.   **"During the eight years of the Obama administration**, **half a million Christians**, **Yazidis and Muslims were slaughtered in the Middle East** by ISIS and other Islamic jihadists, in a genocidal campaign waged in the name of Islam and its G-d. Twenty million others were driven into exile by these same jihadist forces. Libya and Yemen became terrorist states. **America** - once the dominant foreign power and anti-jihadist presence in the region – **was replaced by Russia**, *[Obama, not Trump, colluded with Russia]* an ally of the monster regimes in Syria and Iran, and their terrorist proxies. Under the patronage of the Obama administration, Iran - the largest and most dangerous terrorist state, with the blood of thousands of Americans on its hands - emerged from its isolation as a pariah state to re-enter the community of nations and become the region's dominant power, arming and directing its terrorist proxies in Lebanon, Syria, Gaza and Yemen. *[Obama also colluded with Iran, an enemy of the United States.]* These disasters are a direct consequence of the policies of appeasement and retreat of the Obama administration. …
[First] At the time of Obama's election, America and its allies had won the war and subdued the terrorists by turning the Sunnis in Anbar province against them. But the new commander-in-chief refused to use American forces to secure the peace, and instead set out to withdraw all American military personnel from Iraq. This was a fatal step that **created a power vacuum**, which was **quickly filled by Iran and ISIS**. Obama's generals had advised him to maintain a post-war force of 20,000 troops in country along with the military base America had built in Baghdad. But Obama had made military withdrawal the centerpiece of his foreign policy and ignored his national security team's advice. Had he not done so, American forces would have been able to effectively destroy ISIS at its birth, saving more than 500,000 lives and avoiding the creation of nearly 20 million refugees in Syria and Iraq. **Obama surrendered the peace**, **turning Iraq over to Iran and the terrorists**, and betraying every American and Iraqi who had given their lives to keep them out. … **Second** among the causes of the Middle East's human tragedy was Obama's **support for the Syrian dictator Bashar al-Assad** whom his secretaries of state, Clinton and Kerry both endorsed as a democratic reformer on the very eve of his savage war against his own people. This was followed by Obama's **refusal to enforce the red line he drew** to prevent Assad from using chemical weapons on the Syrian population. When Assad did use them, Obama averted his eyes and papered over his culpability by arranging a **phony deal with Russia to remove Assad's chemical arsenal**. *[Obama lied.]* … The **third cause** of the Middle Eastern morass was Obama's **failure**, early on in his Obama administration, **to support the green revolution in Iran**, when its brave citizens poured into the streets in 2009 to protest a rigged election and the totalitarian regime. Obama's silence was in effect support for the Jew-hating and America-hating regime, into whose ruling group Secretary of State Kerry's daughter soon married. Obama's betrayal of the Iranian people was a reiteration of his signature message to the region. *[Obama was an ally / agent of the Ayatollahs, enemies of*

America, and rose to the presidency so that he could make Iran a major nuclear power, give them hegemony over the Middle East, and allow them to ultimately take over Mecca. Obama sabotaged the student rebellion in part by cutting off their CIA support when he became president.] … The **fourth cause** of the Middle Eastern morass was Obama's intervention in Egypt - **his overthrow of an American ally, Hosni Mubarak, and his open support for the Muslim Brotherhood, the spawner of al-Qaeda and Hamas and the chief sponsor of the Islamic *jihad* against the West**. *[Obama became the largest funder of Islamic terrorism in world history.]* … The **fifth cause** of the terrorist upsurge that has shattered the peace of the Middle East was Obama's **unauthorized, illegal intervention in Libya and murder of its ruler Gaddafi** – a ruthless dictator no doubt – but a dedicated enemy of al-Qaeda with whom he was actively at war. *[Libya became the springboard for the Islamic invasion of Europe – part of Obama's plan. Obama protected and supported al-Qaeda in Libya in part by deposing Gaddafi.]* … The **sixth reason** the Middle East is now in flames is Obama's policy of what he calls "**strategic patience**" but is in effect strategic cowardice **and worse**. *[Obama helped create and was an ally of ISIS.]* Obama's **failure to act decisively against ISIS** – to take only one example - allowed the Islamic State (which Obama has even refused to concede is Islamic), **to become the largest terrorist force ever**, and to provide its armed missionaries with **a free hand to destroy the oldest Christian community in the world** in Iraq, exterminating 200,000 members of the faith, while driving many more into exile. *[Obama supported ISIS and the subsequent Christian genocide]* … The **seventh cause** of the humanitarian crisis in the Middle East – and the one with the most long-lasting consequences - is Obama's **embrace of the terrorist regime in Iran**. Iran has killed more Americans than any other enemy of this country. *[Obama committed treason.]* Its kill list goes back to the Marine bombing of 1983 and includes the supply of every I.E.D. in Iraq used to blow up several thousand American soldiers." *(David Horowitz, "**The Root Cause of Disasters** in the Middle East," Front Magazine Magazine, July 31, 2017)*

t. Fomer Obama National Security Advisor Susan Rice admitted on *CNN* on August 10, 2017 that Obama's North Korean policy was a failure when she clearly stated, "**You can call it a failure** … I accept that characterization of the efforts of the United States over the last two decades *[the latter half were during Obama's presidency]* … The fact of the matter is, that despite all of those efforts, the North Korean regime has been able to succeed in progressing with its program, both nuclear and missile. **That's a very unfortunate outcome**. But we are where we are."

14. "Assad must go." *Obama, 2011.*

a. "I think sadly, but inevitably, he is. [Assad needs to be part of the diplomatic solution.] Realistically, **Assad is not going to be overthrown**. This becomes more clear with every day that passes. Western analysts have been indulging in wishful thinking for five years; it's time to get real, we owe it to the Syrian people to be much more realistic and hard-headed about this. The West [**Obama**] **has to stop propping up the so-called 'moderate opposition,' which is not moderate** at all. *[Obama focuses on supporting the radical Muslims, so they could take control of Syria.]* … we should have backed off, we should have not tried to overthrow the regime … In Afghanistan, Iraq, Libya, *[Egypt as well, but Sisi regained power after the Muslim Brotherhood took power with Obama's planning and assistance.]* like a dog returning to vomit *[A British view of Obama's foreign policy in the Middle East.]*, we go back to, we *[**Obama**, the radical Muslim president]* **never saw a secular Arab regime that we didn't want to overthrow**." *Ambassador Peter Ford, UK's ambassador in Syria from 2003 – 2006, discussing Obama's foreign policy during a BBC interview on February 14, 2016.* A veteran British foreign affairs expert acknowledges Obama supports the radical Muslim extremists and targets the secular Middle Eastern regimes for destruction with the unchecked power of the presidency.

15. "I do not foresee a situation in which we can end the civil war in Syria while Assad remains in power." *Obama, end of November 2015.*

    a. "The United States and our partners are **not seeking so-called regime change** … there is no policy of the United States, per se, to isolate Russia." *Secretary of State Kerry, Moscow, December 15, 2015.* Obama evolved, lied, or was blackmailed by the Russian president, who may have presented Obama with evidence of his treasonous activities.

16. "That's not who we are. **We don't have religious tests** to our compassion." *Obama responding on February 2, 2016, to a reporter's questioning if he will take Syrian Christian refugees as a priority over Syrian Muslim Sunni refugees, with Syria being a majority Sunni state.* Obama does have a religious test regarding immigration requirements, and he almost always favors Muslim migrants. Since 2011, the United Stated has accepted 2098 Muslim refugees (96%) from Syria vs. only 53 Christian Syrian refugees (2.4%). Syrian Christians make up about 20% of all Syrian refugees who have fled Syria, and Christians make up about 10% of the total Syrian population. Obama disfavors the Syrian Christians by almost a factor of ten when comparing the relative numbers of Syrians among displaced Syrians vs. how many are allowed by the United States immigration authorities.

17. "North Korea is an example where direct, tough diplomacy that lays out clear choices to rogue regimes for good and bad behavior can lead to change … As President, Barack Obama will work with diligence and determination with our friends and allies **to end the threat of North Korea** and to secure a lasting peace on the Korean peninsula." *Obama's 2008 "Change We Can Believe In," campaign literature.* In 2016, Obama promised a missile defense shield to protect America from North Korean nuclear armed ballistic missiles, yet

he has cut anti-missile defense funding and research drastically during his two presidential terms.

18. "We may not be able to eliminate man's capacity to do evil *[Obama calls America evil]*, so nations and the alliances that we form must possess the means to defend ourselves. But among those nations like my own that hold nuclear stockpiles, we must have the courage to escape the logic of fear and **pursue a world without them**." *Obama, Hiroshima remarks, May 27, 2016*. Obama really wants a world without American nuclear weapons, so he can pave the way for increasing Iranian, Russian, and Chinese hegemony. The Chinese are developing hypersonic nuclear MIRVs. The JCPOA has guaranteed Iran's right to enrich and their freedom to produce nuclear weapons when the JCPOA expires, if not sooner. Obama promised Russian President Medvedev in 2012 – more "flexibility" after the election – with respect to nuclear issues. North Korea has accelerated their nuclear weapon and ballistic missile testing during the Obama administration and is partnering with Iranian scientists and military officials. By weakening America' deterrent capabilities, Obama is purposely allowing the tyrants of the world to become more aggressive, which will create more overall chaos that allows the Islamic world to advance its agenda to build the caliphate and institute Sharia law in the Middle East and the Western hemisphere. Obama also advanced a similar lie in Prague, 2009, when he stated, "So today, I state clearly and with conviction America's commitment to seek the peak and security of **a world without nuclear weapons** … The United States will take concrete steps towards a world without [American] nuclear weapons."

19. "President Obama **did not come into office preoccupied by the Middle East**. He is the first child of the Pacific to become president – born in Hawaii, raised there and, for four years, in Indonesia – and he is fixated on turning America's attention to Asia. For Obama, Asia represents the future."[127] *(The "Obama Doctrine")* Not true – taqiyya. Obama is trying to shift the reader's attention away from his Middle East failures. Obama was much more engaged in the Middle East than the Far East throughout his presidency. Why were so many of Obama's political appointments Muslims or pro-Islamist policy experts, rather than having administrators with significant backgrounds rooted in Far East exposure if Obama truly had significant interests in the Far East?

    a.   "There will be a great temptation to do something in the final year … For a president who **came out faster and more aggressively on the Middle East than any of his predecessors**, there is a gnawing sense of incompletion and perhaps even failure."[129] *(Aaron David Miller, Vice President, Woodrow Wilson International Center for Scholars, The New York Times, March 2016)* A foreign policy expert predicted Obama's support for UNSC Resolution 2334 before the end of his presidency (as did this author in *Unexpected Treason*).

Iran Lies, Pre – JCPOA

"Iran will become a nuclear power. The only mystery over how that will happen is whether Obama was inept or whether **he <u>deliberately</u> sought to make the theocracy some sort of strategic power**. The Middle East over the next decade may see three or four additional new nuclear powers."[129] *Professor Victor Hanson, Senior Fellow, Hoover Institute, Stanford University, September 15, 2015*

1. "**Iran**, Cuba, Venezuela, these countries are **tiny** compared to the Soviet Union. They **don't pose a serious threat to us** the way the Soviet Union posed a threat to us." *Obama, 2008 presidential campaign, Oregon.* Obama is lying to the American public about the potential threat Iran poses to the United States and the West, and attempted to put America at ease, while he **prepares to deliver a diplomatic sucker punch** to the country he swore to defend. Obama, as a radical Muslim advancing Iran's best interests, planned on implementing the JCPOA, which will eventually allow Iran to develop nuclear intercontinental ballistic missiles and will fully fund their position as the number one state sponsor of (Islamic) terrorism in the world and underwrite their developing nuclear and ballistic missile programs.

2. "The way in which most Americans have heard **the story of the Iran deal** presented – that the Obama administration began seriously engaging with Iranian officials in 2013 in order to take advantage of a **new political reality** in Iran, which came about because of elections that brought **moderates** to power in that country – **was largely manufactured** for the purpose for selling the deal … The idea that there was a new reality in Iran was politically useful to the Obama administration …Not from …any particular optimism about the future course of Iranian politics and society … It derived from his [Obama / Rhodes] own sense of the urgency of **radically reorienting American policy in the Middle East** in order to make the prospect of American involvement in the region's future wars a lot less likely."[130] *(David Samuels, The New York Times Magazine – interview with Ben Rhodes, advisor and speechwriter to President Obama)* David Samuels misinterpreted Obama's intentions. Obama radically

reoriented American policy in the Middle East in order to support the radical Muslims and American's enemies.

a.   "If we sign this nuclear deal, we strengthen the hand of those more moderate forces inside Iran … in fact, the Rouhani administration – the forces that are more moderating." *Obama, NPR interview, April 2015. Taqiyya. Obama lied about fictional Iranian moderates to NPR and the American public.*

b.   "Those who believe Obama risked American interests to take a cheap shot at allies from the pedestal of the Oval Office ("The Obama Doctrine, *The Atlantic*, April 2016) will be appalled to see **Rhodes dancing in the end zone to celebrate the well-packaged misdirections and even lies** – what Rhodes and others call a "narrative" – that won Obama his signature foreign policy initiative … For the last seven years the American public has been living through a **postmodern narrative crafted** by an extremely gifted and unspeakably cynical political operative whose job is to wage digital information campaigns **designed to dismantle a several decade old security architecture while lying about the nature of the Iranian regime**. No wonder Americans feel less safe – they are."[131] *(Lee Smith, The Weekly Standard)*

c.   "Why on earth was such conduct remotely acceptable *[lies and misrepresentations surrounding the JCPOA]*? Because Samuels made clear, Rhodes and Obama believe they're the only sensible thinkers in America and that **there's no way to get the right things done other than to spin them** *[to lie]* … What the Samuels piece shows is that the Obama administration chose to attempt to get its way not by winning an argument but my bringing an almost fathomless cynicism to bear in **manipulating its own clueless liberal fan club**."[132] *(John Podhoretz, The New York Post)*

d.   "The profile of Ben Rhodes … contains the admission that **the deal was based on a lie** and that the real agenda was radically different from the one that Americans were told about. For one thing the whole "moderate" Iranian government vs. the hardliners nonsense … was a lie *[confirmed by CIA director Panetta]* manufactured to sell the deal … It was never about "peace" or Iran abandoning its nuclear program. It was never about backing moderates. Rhodes admits that's nonsense. It was the ongoing obsession of the administration with "reorienting" American foreign policy to make deals with the enemy in order to weaken us, strengthen them and prevent us and our allies from being able to check their aggression."[133] *(Daniel Greenfield, FrontPage Magazine)* Obama switched sides and is playing for the other team as evidenced by Obama backing a deal that strengthens our enemies, weakens our allies, and puts U.S. interests in jeopardy.

e.   "Does the fact that **the White House lied to the American people when it was selling the Iran nuclear deal** to the media, Congress and the public matter? *[Obama committed fraud with a major national security issue against the Congress and the American people in* *favor of an enemy that has sworn to destroy us should be viewed as treason and is grounds for impeachment.] …* It's also true that much of the mainstream media … bought the administration's party line *[taqiyya]* about the rise of Iranian moderates providing the opening for a nuclear deal. … [**set up Obama's lie** that new Iran administration would] … "**get it right with the world**." … But the lie is of lasting importance because, if there are no real Iranian moderates, [then it] … strengthens and empowers a dangerous regime. As the *Foundation of Defense of Democracies'* Mark Dubowitz noted … "As a result of sunset clauses in the deal that see most of the key restrictions disappearing over an 8-15 year period, Iran will be left with an industrial-size nuclear program with near-zero nuclear breakout, easier advanced centrifuge-powered clandestine sneak out, an ICBM program and a more powerful economy increasingly immunized against sanctions. If the Iranian regime has not moderated by then … Rhodes may have made war with Iran more not less likely." … Obama and his mind-meld partner Rhodes endangered the security of the United States, Israel, and the West. *[Rhodes was used by Obama because he was a master at advancing propaganda, manipulating the press, and controlling the omnipresent talking points.]* That it was **done on the strength of a falsehood** and with the help of credulous, feckless Washington press corps is less important than the catastrophic nature of the mistake they have made."[134] *(Jonathan Tobin, Commentary Magazine) The deal threatens the stability of the Middle East, and puts the United States and Israel at increased risk of a nuclear attack by Iran or by one of its terrorist proxies.*

f. **George Soros**, was instrumental in disseminating the "misleading," "manufactured," and "false" narratives surrounding the JCPOA by having the Ploughshares Fund finance various media outlets, journalists, lobbies, and think tanks who created the "**echo chamber**" that helped push the deal upon Congress and the American public. The Ploughshares Fund receives a large block of its funding from George Soros' Open Society Institute. Rhodes and Obama relied on Ploughshares to effectively disseminate misleading talking points surrounding the JCPOA. Organizations that received funding from Ploughshares includes NPR ($700,000 since 2005), J Street ($576,000), a reporter at *The Nation*, the Brookings Institute, the Arms Control Association, and the National Iranian American Council. In March 2015, *The Wall Street Journal* reported that Ploughshares was working with a former Iranian government spokesperson. Thus, an organization that was allied with Iranian government officials was funding media outlets and reporters to support the White House narrative of the JCPOA. Soros has also been implicated in helping to fund other radical Obama policies or allies, including the massive wave of Muslim immigration that has descended upon Europe, the overthrow the Ukrainian government where a state department approved successor rose to power, and giving over $33 million to Black Lives Matter, which has advocated the killing of police officers and whose political rhetoric helped lead to the sniping and murder of five Dallas police officers on July 7, 2016. Soros must be considered Obama's main source of funding, originating from outside the U.S. government, for many of his radical policies that lead to revolution, instability in the West, and the support of pro-Islamist policies. Regarding the European refugee crisis, Soros has stated, "Our plan treats the protection of [Muslim] refugees as the objective and national borders as the obstacle." Soros has been supporting Obama throughout his whole presidency.

g. "A turning point came in June of 2013, when Hasan Rouhani won the Iranian election by a healthy margin, **pledging a more moderate course** *[a lie told so Obama could substantiate one of the main misleading talking points used to support the JCPOA]* towards engagement with the West … Iran's approach to its nuclear program has changed, but thus far, **its broader foreign policy – and the nature of its regime – has not**." *Remarks by Deputy National Security Advisor Ben Rhodes at the Iran Project, Washington, D.C., June 16, 2016.* Rhodes is now reverting back to the original lie after his *New York Times Magazine* interview, but admits later in the speech that the nature of the Iranian regime never changed.

3. "**The issue of negotiating with the Americans is related to the term of the previous [Ahmadinejad] government** [2011 or sooner], and to the dispatching of a mediator to Tehran to request talks. At the time, a respected regional figure came to me as a mediator [referring to Omani Sultan Qaboos] and explicitly said that **U.S. President [Obama] had asked him to come to Tehran and present an American request for negotiations. The Americans told this mediator:** 'We want to solve the nuclear issue and lift sanctions within six months, <u>while recognizing Iran as a nuclear power</u>.' I told that mediator that I did not trust the Americans and their words, but after he insisted, I agreed to reexamine this topic, and negotiations began." *Ayatollah Khamenei, Iranian speech, June 23, 2015.* Almost from the beginning of the Obama administration, the Iranians knew Obama would allow them to keep their nuclear program and lift sanctions. Obama's threats of military action, maintaining sanctions, not permitting uranium enrichment, or not allowing Iran to develop nuclear weapons were all lies for American and Western European consumption. Ambassador Ali Khorram, an advisor to Iranian Foreign Minister Zarif, revealed Obama had sent a letter to Ayatollah Khamenei over three years prior to the 2015 Vienna agreement accepting Iran's right to enrich uranium. Obama, from the outset, was negotiating for Iran and ensuring all their interests would be protected and their demands met. The talks began with the Ahmadinejad regime and not with the Rouhani regime. Valerie Jarrett held secret talks with Iran regarding the nuclear deal and the terms of the final agreement were probably decided during Obama's first term, if not sooner. Just as Kerry admitted he did not know what details were in the side deals between the IAEA and Iran after the nuclear

deal was concluded, Kerry did not know Obama and the Iranians had already agreed to the terms of the final agreement before he became secretary of state. Thus, as the Iranian team or the lead Iranian negotiator already knew the end point of the discussions, Obama slowly directed Kerry to the final agreement, pretending that real negotiations were occurring for two and a half years. Another possibility is that both negotiating teams did not know that the final deal was already determined, and that Obama and his senior Iranian counterparts used the negotiations for show and domestic political consumption. Obama knew if details of the final agreement were released before the 2012 presidential election or before the 2014 congressional midterm elections, the Democrats would incur major losses, so Obama delayed the release of the final agreement until the second half of his final term. Former Iranian Security Minister Ayatollah Moslehi concluded that Obama delayed the nuclear negotiations to calm domestic opposition. *[taqiyya]* Obama needed to announce the agreement early in his final two years, so Iran would have time to establish economic relationships with other major world powers, so if a Republican president reinstituted sanctions in 2017, the world would be unwilling or unable to fully implement snap back sanctions, as promised by Obama.

a.   "'Go tell them that these are our demands. [Salehi speaking to a mediator] Deliver [the note] during your next visit to Oman.' On a piece of paper I wrote down four clearly-stated points, one of which was [the demand for] official recognition of the right to enrich uranium … All the demands presented in this letter were related to the nuclear challenge. [They were] issues we had always come up against, like the **closing of the nuclear dossier, official recognition of [the right to] enrichment**, and **resolving the issue of Iran's past activities under the PMD [possible military dimensions] heading [and sanctions relief]. After receiving the letter, the Americans said, 'We are definitely and sincerely willing, and we can resolve the issues that Iran mentioned.'"** *Iranian Vice President Ali Akbar Salehi and head of Iran's Atomic Energy Organization, Interview with "Iran" daily newspaper, August 4, 2015.* Salehi is discussing secret negotiations that started in 2011. Obama informed the Iranian political leadership, headed by radical Mahmoud Ahmadinejad, that the United States would allow them to keep their nuclear program intact with the right to enrich uranium. Obama never had Israeli interests in mind, and was predetermined to make Iran a major nuclear power, regardless of who was in control of the Iranian government, even a radical who threatened to wipe Israel off the map. **Obama may even have decided in 2009, or before, to allow Iran to pursue nuclear weapons** with Secretary of State Clinton stating on July 20, 2009, "We want Iran to calculate what I think is a fair assessment that, if the United States extends a defense umbrella over the region, if we do even more to support the military capacity of those in the Gulf, it's unlikely that Iran will be any stronger or safer because they won't be able to intimidate and dominate as they apparently believe they can, **once they have**

<u>a nuclear weapon</u>." If this is the case, **all the political posturing by Obama over the Iranian nuclear program for six and a half years as president was a fraud, a scam perpetrated upon the American public and all allied negotiating parties**.

b. "After **two years** of negotiations ..." *Obama's speech announcing the Iranian nuclear agreement, July 14, 2015*. Obama should have stated – "after four or even seven plus years." Even Ben Rhodes admitted that negotiations started with the Ahmadinejad regime in his May 2016 interview with *The New York Times Magazine*.

    i. "In truth, Obama was so intent on reaching a deal with Iran at any price that **senior members of his administration had started serious discussions with Iranian hardliners a year before Rouhani's election**. "Obama's closest advisers always understood him to be eager to do a deal with Iran as far back as 2012, and even since the beginning of his presidency," David Samuels concluded after speaking with key members of the administration including Rhodes, who were part of Obama's inner circle. Indeed, three months before Rouhani's election, Deputy Secretary of State Bill Burns and Jake Sullivan, a close aide to then Secretary of State Hillary Clinton, worked out the details of an "interim" agreement with their Iranian counterparts that became the basis of the JCPOA."[135] *(Joseph Klein, FrontPage Magazine)* In *The Iran Wars*, author Jay Solomon stated as a reason for Obama not supporting the 2009 Iranian student revolt, was that he was involved in secret negotiations with the Iranians over their nuclear program in 2009. Thus, Obama was dealing with the Iranians through clandestine channels (Valerie Jarrett – grew up in Iran with strong political ties to the radicals) over six years before the approval of the final JCPOA.

c. "A report from the Middle East Media and Research Institute (MEMRI) has apparently brought to light the existence of a secret letter revealing that the Obama Administration secretly approached the Iranian leadership in 2011, offering to recognize Iran's alleged right to uranium enrichment – a right that does not exist under the Nuclear Nonproliferation Treaty, which Iran signed in return for Iran negotiating a resolution of the Iranian nuclear issue. If true, this means that President Barack **Obama brazenly lied to the American public when his Administration continued stating, after that date, that the U.S. demands an end to Iranian uranium enrichment activities ... In light of all these apparent lies and deceptions** *[after 2 years of negotiations]* - **most recently falsely claiming in his speech at the American University that this nuclear deal 'permanently' prevents Iran develop nuclear weapons – how can we trust anything President Obama or Secretary Kerry say about this Iran deal**, especially since we know nothing of the secret side deals made, which Secretary Kerry says he hasn't even read." *Zionist Organization of America, August 12, 2015*.

d. **During the 2008 presidential campaign, Obama dispatched Ambassador William Miller to Iran**, **and let them know that they should not sign a nuclear agreement with President Bush, since Obama would give them better terms**. Obama undercut President Bush's diplomacy and compromised American national security interests by allowing Iran to wait out for a deal that would secure all their major nuclear goals. **In 2008, Obama already knew that his endgame was the creation of a major nuclear power in Tehran**. Thus, all the rhetoric and all the negotiations were a scam to seduce the American public into believing Obama had their best interests at heart. Even in 2008, Obama knew a deal would be signed in 2015, since he had to maximize the duration of negotiations yet give the Iranians time after a deal was signed to reap the benefits of sanctions relief and have economic relations develop between Iran and the West, Russia, and China before the next president took office.

4. "If Iran does not take steps in the near future to live up to its obligations, then **the United States will not continue to negotiate indefinitely ... Our patience is not unlimited**." *[Actually, it is.] Obama, October 1, 2009, Washington, D.C.* Four years later, the Obama continued to lie when Secretary of State Clinton warned in Saudi Arabia, "Iran's window of opportunity ... will not remain open forever."

a. "I'm unconvinced ... that the Iranians will not try to drag it out ever further, because the message that they have internalized since 2009 is the longer they remain at the table, the more concessions they make, that **the administration has said repeatedly that the window for opportunity will not remain indefinitely open, but it's never really closed. I'm not sure it's a window. And the Iranians have taken notice of that** ... They also may conclude that they're getting so many benefits from the negotiations, for example, they've had their – they've gained legitimacy for their nuclear program. Even beyond that, they've gained recognition of their right to enrich uranium, which is not in the Nuclear Non-Proliferation Treaty. They've gotten recognition for their aspirations, their regional aspirations. All of this, so far without paying any price. Why would they want to start paying a price? Because of sanction relief, but maybe they're banking on the fact that the sanctions will begin to unravel [or be part of the final agreement]." *Michael Oren, former Israeli Ambassador to the United States, July 2015, the "Hugh Hewitt Show."* On June 30, 2015, Obama extended negotiations past an official deadline for the fifth time. Besides the above points, Obama is giving Iran space and time to develop their nuclear infrastructure past the point of no return, along with the opportunity to build a nuclear bomb, which will fundamentally change the balance of power in the Middle East and the world.

b. "We have no time limit in order to reach a good deal." Iranian negotiation position, Vienna, July 9, 2015. Iranian stalling during the nuclear negotiations generally lead to more American concessions.

5. **"We cannot allow Iran to obtain a nuclear weapon, it's unacceptable, and I will do everything** that's required to prevent it." *Obama, October 7, 2008.*

6. "Developing a strategy to **use all elements of American power** to prevent Iran from developing a nuclear weapon." *Obama, February 28, 2009.* Obama would never use military force against Iran, with whom he is allied as a radical Muslim. He is providing diplomatic cover for Iran until the final nuclear agreement is officially signed. Obama falsely threatened military action against Iran to keep America off guard while Iran moves forward with its nuclear program. With the American National Intelligence Estimate declaring in 2007 that the Iranian nuclear program had abandoned its quest to obtain nuclear weapons, Obama had the backing of the U.S. intelligence community to support a position of never initiating military action against Iran. Astute diplomats and politicians would have known that Obama's military threats against Iran were a lie.

    a. "And **we don't take any options off the table** in terms of how we operate with Iran." *Obama, October 13, 2011.*

        i. "**The President says all options are on the table. Nobody believes him. The Iranians don't believe him. The Israelis don't believe him. He doesn't believe it.** So the spot light is on Israel." *Former UN Ambassador John Bolton, Bloomberg Politics, April 17, 2015.*

        ii. "I can, [I] think, demonstrate, not based on any hope but on facts and analysis, that **the best way to prevent Iran from having a nuclear weapon is a verifiable tough agreement. A military solution will not fix it**, even if the United States participates. It would temporarily slow down an Iranian nuclear program but **it would not eliminate it**." *Obama interview, Free Republic, June 1, 2015.* Obama finalized a deal that did not allow U.S. inspectors in Iran, and authorized side deals between Iran and the IAEA, the details of which are unknown even to the secretary of state and some members of Congress. Obama admitted he never believed a military strike would fix the Iranian nuclear dilemma, thus his threats of military action against Iran were all lies.

        iii. "We should thank Obama for refreshing us by referring to **his 'options on the table,' including the military one; we just relax and laugh at such ridiculous words ... The military option that the Westerners speak of constantly is ridiculous** and they know that if the military option could have produced any result, they would have already used it many times." *Brigadier General Mohammad Ali Asoudi, Islamic Republic's Revolutionary Guard Corps (IRGC).*

        iv. "He [Panetta, Obama's former secretary of defense] understands the president's pivot toward Iran as the logical result of a deeply held premise about the negative effects of use of American military force on a scale much larger than drone strikes or Special

Forces raids. "I [Panetta] think the whole legacy that he was working on was, 'I'm the guy who's going to bring these wars to an end, and **the last g-ddamn thing I need is to start another war**,'" he explains of Obama. "If you ratchet up sanctions, it could cause a war. If you start opposing their interest in Syria, that could start a war, too." *(source – "The Aspiring Novelist Who Became Obama's Foreign – Policy Guru," David Samuels, The New York Times Magazine, May 5, 2016 – interview with former Obama Secretary of Defense Leon Panetta.)* Obama was never going to bomb Iran's nuclear program or initiate any military confrontation with Iran under any circumstances according to Panetta. **Panetta even admitted in this interview that in retrospect he doubted Obama was serious when he threatened military action** against Iran's nuclear facilities when asked by Samuels, "Would you make that same assessment now?" Panetta responded, "Probably not." While Panetta was part of the administration, Obama misled him into believing he would bomb Iran's nuclear facilities if there was evidence proving they were developing nuclear weapons, but only so Panetta could allay Israeli fears so Israel would not take military action against Iran.

b.   "America is determined to prevent Iran from getting a nuclear weapon **and I will take no options off the table** to achieve that goal." *Obama, January 24, 2012, State of the Union Address.*

i.   "When I hear some, like Sen. McCain recently suggest that **our Secretary of State John Kerry,** who served in the United States Senate, a Vietnam veteran who has provided exemplary service to this nation, **is somehow less trustworthy in the interpretation of what's in a political agreement than the Supreme Leader of Iran**, that's an indication of the degree to which partisanship has crossed all boundaries. And we're seeing this again and again. We saw it with the letter by the forty-seven senators who communicate directly to the Supreme Leader of Iran, the person that they say can't be trusted at all, **warning him not to trust the United States government** … And now we have a senator suggesting that our secretary of state is purposely misinterpreting the deal and giving the Supreme Leader of Iran the benefit of the doubt in the interpretations. You know that's not how we're supposed to run foreign policy, regardless of who's president or secretary of state. We can have arguments and there are legitimate arguments to be had. I understand why people might be mistrustful of Iran. I understand why people might oppose the deal. Although the reason is not because this is a bad deal per se but they just don't trust any deal with Iran and **may prefer to take a military approach to it**." *Obama at Summit of the Americas Conference, April 11, 2015.* If Obama had John Kerry and leaders of the Iranian delegation sign a joint declaration of basic principles on the framework agreement supposedly agreed to in Switzerland, discrepancies between the American and Iranian interpretations of the agreement would not have occurred. The Republicans are just taking the ayatollah at his word that sanctions would be lifted immediately and that military sites would not be inspected. Why wouldn't Obama lie in order to lessen public and political opposition to the nuclear agreement? The second major point is that Obama, for years, always said a military option was on the table. Now that there is significant opposition to the agreement with the Iranians, Obama is accusing the opposition of only wanting a military confrontation and another major war in lieu of a diplomatic resolution, even though no one in the opposition including Netanyahu or the Republican leadership, has specifically mentioned military options, only a better agreement. Isn't it ironic that Obama, for years, threatened Iran with military action to maintain his credibility with the American voters and Congress, but now uses this threat as a counterargument against the opposition and paints them as warmongers? Obama changed positions since the original position helped him get elected and re-elected to the presidency, and now as a radical Muslim, he must protect Iranian interests during the final phases of the negotiations.

(1)   "I have to be honest with you, the more I hear from the administration and its quotes, the more it **sounds like talking points that come straight out of Tehran**. And it feeds to the Iranian narrative of victimization when they are the ones with original sin." *New Jersey Democratic Senator Robert Menendez, Senate Foreign Relations Committee on January 21, 2015.* Menendez was later indicted on corruption charges by Eric Holder for questioning the sincerity of Obama's negotiating position with the Iranians, and doubting Obama's ability to represent American interests.

(2)   "The **U.S. negotiating team are mainly there to speak on Iran's behalf** with other members of the 5+1 countries and convince them of a deal." *Amir Hossein Motaghi, defecting Iranian journalist, who was a public relations manager for President Rouhani during his 2013 campaign for the Iranian presidency.*

7.   "As Iran's leaders continue to ignore obligations, there should be no doubt, **they too will face growing consequences. That is a promise**." *Obama, State of the Union Address, January 27, 2010. Taqiyya by the playbook.*

8.   "The United States and the international community are determined to **prevent Iran from obtaining nuclear weapons**." *Obama, July 1, 2010*

a.   "**No single nation should pick and choose which nations hold nuclear weapons**. That is why I strongly reaffirmed America's commitment to seek a world in which no nations hold nuclear weapons." *Obama, Cairo University speech, June 2009.* **Since Obama**

is confirming his belief that the United States does not have the right to unilaterally decide that Iran should not have nuclear weapons, the 2015 agreement would not have been such a major surprise to Israel or Republicans. But Obama immediately contradicted himself by saying he was against expanding the number of states with nuclear weapons and that he wants a world without nuclear weapons. Yet, the result of the Iranian negotiations will be a massive expansion of states with nuclear arms with Iran guaranteed to have nuclear weapons within ten years. If Obama was truly interested in a world without nuclear weapons, he would have insisted on at least closing the Fordow reactor and "anytime, anywhere" inspections of suspected Iranian military facilities, which would have severely hampered Iran's quest for a domestic nuclear weapons program. So, the only true statement Obama forwarded in this section in Cairo was his castigation of America dictating to others about nuclear arms control, thus confirming his disdain for American power and influence, especially in the Middle East. With Obama's massive cuts in America's nuclear arsenal, and the expansion of nuclear arsenals in the Middle East, Obama's real goal is emasculating American power and deterrence, and ensuring that Islamic powers in the Middle East, if united, may control a large contingent of nuclear weapons so that they can influence world events to a greater degree. An alliance between North Korea, Iran and Pakistan could create a significant nuclear arsenal which would be formidable when compared with future contracting American and Western arsenals. Thus, Obama is purposely creating the military – political conditions that could force the West to be subservient to radical Islamic powers in the near future. Obama wants America, but not the world, to be free from nuclear weapons.

b. With about one week remaining in his presidency, Obama approved the transfer of 116 metric tons (130 tons) of natural uranium to Iran in exchange for 70 metric tons of heavy water, which Iran produced in excess of the limits delineated in the JCPOA. Heavy water is needed for the production of weapons – grade plutonium. The natural uranium delivered to Iran was enough to produce at least 10 nuclear weapons. In February 2016, Obama had purchased excessive heavy water from Iran for $8.6 million in early 2016.

9. "When it comes to preventing Iran from obtaining a nuclear weapon, I will **take no options off the table** … That includes all elements of American power: a political effort aimed at isolating Iran, a diplomatic effort to sustain our coalition and ensure that the Iranian program is monitored, an economic effort that imposes crippling sanctions **and, yes, a military effort to be prepared for any contingency.**" *Obama, Speech to pro-Israel lobbying group AIPAC, March 4, 2012. Taqiyya to the Jews – a time tested successful Islamic strategy.*

10. "**My policy here is not going to be one of containment. My policy is prevention** of Iran obtaining nuclear weapons." *Obama, March 5, 2012. By 2015, it was obvious Obama's policy was containment with the introduction of the Iranian Nuclear Framework Agreement in April.*

a. **"Iran is not going to simply dismantle its program because we demand it to do so."** *Obama, April 2, 2015.* Obama is **defending Iran's right and ability to enrich uranium**, and is reciting talking points originating from Tehran. Which side does he represent? Obama's true intentions are clear.

11. "We're going to keep on seeing if we make progress. Now, the clocking is ticking and I've been very clear to Iran and to our negotiating partners that **we're not going to have these talks just drag out in a stalling process** … But so far at least **we haven't given away anything**." *Obama, April 2012. In 2015, after three years of stalling, Obama gave everything away.*

12. "Our goal is to get Iran to recognize **it needs to give up its nuclear program and abide by the UN resolutions** that have been in place … **the deal we'll accept is: They <u>end their nuclear program</u>**. *[One of Obama's most flagrant lies occurred during the presidential debates, where he had an extremely large captivated audience.]* **It's very <u>straightforward</u>**." *Obama, October 2012, presidential debates with Mitt Romney, and Obama lies to win the election.*

a. "**Now, let's be <u>clear</u>. The international sanctions were put in place precisely to get Iran to agree to <u>constraints</u> on its program**. That's the point of sanctions. Any negotiated agreement with Iran would involve sanctions relief." *Obama, American University speech, August 5, 2015.* Do sanctions exist to end the Iranian nuclear program or to constrain the nuclear program? It appears Obama changed his position after his election win. **Now let's be <u>clear</u> and very <u>straightforward</u>** – Obama lied.

13. *Obama lied again on October 22, 2012 in __another presidential debate__. Obama never had any intentions to end Iran's nuclear program.* "To the issue of Iran. **As long as I am president of the United States, Iran will not get a nuclear weapon**. I made that clear when I came into office. We then organized the strongest coalition and the strongest sanctions against Iran in history. And it is crippling their economy. Their currency has dropped 80%. Their oil production has plunged to the lowest level since they were fighting a war with Iraq 20 years ago. Their economy is in a shambles. **And the reason that we did this is because a nuclear Iran is a threat to our national security and it is a threat to Israel's national security. We cannot afford to have a nuclear arms race in the most volatile region of the world. Iran is a state sponsor of terrorism**. And for them to be able to provide nuclear technology to non-state actors, that is unacceptable. And they said they want to see Israel wiped off the map. So, the work that we've done with respect to sanctions now offers Iran a choice. **They can take the diplomatic route and <u>end their nuclear program</u>**. *[Romney folded, did not call Obama out on this lie, and lost the election.]* Or they will have to face a united world and a United States president who said **we are not going to take any options off the table**."

a. *Later, Obama **admits to a major change in policy**, and supports the talking points for Iran.* "In a perfect world, Iran would say, 'We won't have any nuclear infrastructure at all,' but what **we know is that this has become a matter of pride and nationalism for**

Iran. Even those who we consider moderates and reformers are supportive of some nuclear program inside of Iran, **and given that they will not capitulate completely, given that they can't meet the threshold that Prime Minister Netanyahu sets forth, there are no Iranian leaders who will do that.** And given the fact that this is a country that withstood an eight-year war and a million people dead, they've shown themselves willing, I think, to endure hardship when they considered a point of national pride or, in some cases, national survival." *Obama interview with Thomas Friedman, The New York Times, March 5, 2015, supporting the Iranian Nuclear Framework Agreement.* Obama is arguing for Iran's right to have a nuclear program and why it is inappropriate to attempt to dismantle Iran's nuclear weapons program, **a complete reversal of his previous positions.** *[Bait and switch right before Obama presents the JCPOA.]* Obama is basically acting as the public relations agent and the defense attorney for Iran. Why not for the United States? Where does Obama's real loyalty lie?

i.   "For 20 years, three presidents of both major parties proclaimed that an Iranian nuclear weapon was contrary to American and global interests – and that they were prepared to use force to prevent it. **Yet negotiations that began twelve years ago as an international effort to prevent an Iranian capability to develop a nuclear arsenal are ending with an agreement that concedes this very capability.**"[136] *Henry Kissinger and George Shultz, previous Secretaries of States, The Wall Street Journal.* Instead of eliminating or diminishing Iran's nuclear capabilities, the final nuclear agreement is actually expanding Iran's nuclear capabilities, which is a complete reversal of formal U.S. policy towards Iran without any real reciprocal policy changes originating from Tehran. Just two weeks after the agreement was finalized in Vienna, Iran announced its plans to build two new nuclear power plants on the coast of the Indian Ocean at a cost of $10 billion. With Iran's sanction relief and the release of frozen assets estimated in value at over $150 billion, Obama is actually paying for Iran's expanding nuclear program. In 2016, Iran announced they will have seven functioning nuclear reactors by 2020.

ii. "The Security Council demands … that **Iran shall suspend all enrichment related and reprocessing activities**, including research and development, to be verified by the IAEA." *UN Security Council Resolution 1696, July 31, 2006. Obama independently ignored UN Security Council resolutions and policy directives.*

15. *Obama agrees with Netanyahu that at the very least, Iran's nuclear enrichment program must stop.* "What I also shared with the Prime Minister is that, because of the extraordinary sanctions that we have been able to put in place over the last several years, the Iranians are now

prepared, it appears, to negotiate. We have to test diplomacy. *[Obama is transitioning to the bait and switch.]* We have to see **if, in fact, they are serious about their willingness to abide by international norms and international law and international requirements and resolutions** [six UN Security Council resolutions that demand Iran **to halt all nuclear enrichment programs**]. And we in good faith will approach them, indicating that it is our preference to resolve these issues diplomatically." *Obama's remarks after meeting with Israeli Prime Minister Netanyahu at the White House on September 30, 2013.* Netanyahu demanded that Iran dismantle their nuclear program, and Obama did not disagree. A CBS news report stated, "**President Obama and Israeli Prime Minister Benjamin Netanyahu emerged from a meeting Monday <u>united on the fact</u> that Iran** must show concrete proof that it **is <u>dismantling</u> its nuclear program in order for the U.S. to lift any economic sanctions.**" Obama lied to Netanyahu to help prevent Israel from launching a surprise attack on Iran's nuclear infrastructure. Obama's number one foreign policy objective throughout his presidency was to prevent Israel from bombing Iran's nuclear facilities.

16. "But I don't think that any of us thought that we were imposing these sanction for the sake of imposing them, we did it because we knew that it would hopefully **help Iran dismantle** its nuclear program. That was the whole point … **There is no right to enrich in the NPT.**" *John Kerry, Secretary of State, December 10, 2013.* Kerry is not aware of Obama's shifting negotiating end points and / or is lying.

    a. "We came to the [secret] negotiations [with the United States in 2011] after **Kerry wrote a letter** and sent it to us via [mediator Omani Sultan Qaboos], **stating that America officially recognizes Iran's rights regarding the [nuclear fuel] enrichment cycle.**" *Hossein Sheikh Al-Islam, senior Iranian government official, interview with Iran's Tasnim news agency, (source – MEMRI).* Obama always planned to allow Iran to keep its nuclear program and to enrich uranium. Obama had Kerry, who was then head of the Senate Foreign Relations Committee, write the letter in 2011 to ensure Kerry was loyal to Obama's strategy before he appointed him as secretary of state.

17. "We know that **they don't need to have an underground fortified facility like Fordow in order to have a peaceful nuclear program.**" *Obama, December 7, 2013. Fordow remained intact with the final agreement.*

    a. "Our facilities will continue. **We will continue enriching and we will continue the Fordow facility.**" *Iranian Foreign Minister Mohammad Zarif, April 2, 2015.*

18. "A comprehensive solution that would constrain Iran's nuclear program over the long term, provide verifiable assurances to the international community that **Iran's nuclear activities will be exclusively peaceful,** and ensure that **any attempt by Iran to pursue a nuclear weapon would be promptly detected.**" *Obama White House 2013 Fact Sheet.*

a.   "We have gone from preventing Iran having a nuclear ability to managing it … We have uranium enrichment deep inside of a mountain. That doesn't happen for a peaceful civilian program." *Senator Menendez, ABC News Sunday morning talk show, July 12, 2015.*

b.   **"Tehran has developed technical expertise in a number of areas – including uranium enrichment, nuclear reactors, and ballistic missiles – from which it could draw if it decided to build missile-deliverable nuclear weapons.** These technical advancements strengthen our assessment that **Iran has the scientific, technical, and industrial capacity to eventually produce nuclear weapons.** This makes the central issue its political will to do so. Of particular note, Iran has **made progress during the past year that better positions it to produce weapons-grade uranium (WGU) using its declared facilities and uranium stockpiles,** should it choose to do so." <u>***2014***</u> *Worldwide Threat Assessment of the U.S. Intelligence Community.*

19. "We will not countenance Iran getting a nuclear weapon. **My policy is not containment. My policy to prevent them from getting a nuclear weapon because if they get a nuclear weapon, that could trigger an arms race in the region, it would undermine our non-proliferation goals, it could potentially fall into the hands of terrorists. And we have <u>been in close consultation with all our allies including Israel</u> in moving this strategy forward.** At this stage it is my belief, that we have a window of opportunity where this can be resolved diplomatically." *Obama press conference, March 18, 2013.* Obama is misleading Israel so they won't proceed with a military strike against Iran's nuclear facilities. Obama lied about his close coordination with Israel since he initiated secret negotiations with Iran without Israel's knowledge.

20. "**Iran must accept <u>strict limitations</u> on its nuclear program** that make it **impossible** to develop a nuclear weapon," *[And negotiations must produce]* "fully verifiable agreements *[But Americans are not allowed in Iran to perform nuclear inspections]* that make Iran's pursuit of nuclear weapons impossible." *Obama, 2013.* Iran announced in 2016 that they plan to build the world's first fusion nuclear reactor by 2020. In 2015, Iran revealed plans to build four new nuclear reactors – two with Russia and two with China. Iran will also be cooperating with Japan and South Korea with their nuclear research. With the JCPOA, Iran will be keeping its basic nuclear infrastructure and 5000 advanced centrifuges. Although Iran is shipping uranium out of their country as part of the JCPOA, they are simultaneously receiving equivalent amounts of uranium ore that can produce enriched uranium in months. With Iran's expansion of its nuclear program and facilities in the near future along with unlimited funding for their nuclear program guaranteed by $150 billion in sanctions relief, Iran will be able to easily produce nuclear weapons at its own convenience – legally at the end of the agreement. *(source – "The Iran Nuclear Construction Deal," Investor's Business Daily editorial, January 20, 2016) Not quite strict limitations.*

21. "As we gather here tonight, Iran has begun to eliminate its stockpile of higher levels of enriched uranium *[False – Iranian stockpiles of enriched uranium have slowly increased under the Obama administration.]* It's not installing advanced centrifuges *[False]*. Unprecedented inspections help the world verify every day that Iran is not building a bomb *[False – Iran has blocked access to multiple sites including military sites by IAEA inspectors, and refuses to answer a majority of the questions presented to them by the IAEA.]*… But these negotiations don't rely on trust. Any long-term deal we agree to must be based on verifiable action that convinces us and the international community that Iran is not building a nuclear bomb *[U.S. inspectors will not be allowed.]* … The sanctions that we put in place helped make this opportunity possible. But let me be clear: **If this Congress sends me a new sanctions bill now that threatens to derail these talks, I will veto it** *[Obama is protecting the Iranian economy, so it stays viable and will continue to advance its nuclear program, fund terrorism, and decrease the risk of internal dissent.]* For the sake of our national security, we must give diplomacy a chance to succeed. **If Iran's leaders do not seize this opportunity, then I will be the first to call for more sanctions, and stand ready to exercise all options** *[taqiyya]* to make sure Iran does not build a nuclear weapon." *Obama, State of the Union Address, January, 2014.* Obama will never re-issue sanctions. Russia has also stated they will not support snap back sanctions after a deal is reached. Obama pretends military options are still on the table, but he will never attack Iran. In 2015, he took Iran and Hezbollah off the U.S. terror threat list.

22. "Our diplomacy is at work with respect to Iran, where, for the first time in a decade, **we've halted the progress of its nuclear program and reduced its stockpile of nuclear material**." *Obama, State of the Union Address, January 20, 2015.*

    a. "As the June 30th deadline approaches for a nuclear deal with Iran, **a UN report shows that Iran's nuclear fuel has increased by 20 percent during the last 18 months of negotiations.** The finding undercuts President Obama's claim that progress has been 'halted' and stockpiles 'reduced' during the course of negotiations … Israel's Prime Minister Benjamin Netanyahu has been an outspoken critic of the Obama administration's nuclear negotiations with Iran for several months. He pointed out that under the terms of the deal, '**thousands of centrifuges' would continue to spin enriching uranium**, while thousands more would be "temporarily disconnected, but not destroyed." His overall assessment was that it is a "bad deal" that "doesn't block Iran's path to the bomb; it paves the way to Iran's path to the bomb."[137] *(Western Journalism, 2015).*

    b. Olli Heinonen, who headed the IAEA's safeguards section during the 2003-2005 talks between Iran and three European powers (United Kingdom, France and Germany), said "it is true that 20-percent enriched uranium stocks have decreased, but Iran is still producing uranium enriched up to 5-percent uranium. The latter stocks have actually increased when you talk about stocks of UF6 [uranium hexafluoride] and other chemical compounds. Moreover, while there has been no installation of new centrifuges, "it appears that the production of centrifuge components continues. Same with the Arak reactor. No new nuclear components have been installed, but it does not mean that the production of those came to halt … The JCPOA is just a step to create negotiation space; nothing more. It is not a viable longer term situation."[138]

23. "President Obama and I are both extremely welcoming and grateful for the fact that **Supreme Leader [Khamenei] has issued a fatwa** [prohibiting nuclear weapons]." *John Kerry, March 2014. Khamenei never issued a fatwa. Kerry is practicing taqiyya.*

24. "According to their Supreme Leader, it would be **contrary to their faith to obtain a nuclear weapon.**" *Obama, Press Conference with Merkel, German Chancellor, February 2015.* Obama is covering for the lies presented by the Iranian Supreme leader, and proselytizing for Islam. But Khamenei's faith compelled him to hold an AK-47 on stage while declaring "Death to America" when discussing the final nuclear agreement four days after its conclusion.

    a.   The Iranian military views an attack on the United States with a nuclear electromagnetic pulse device as a legitimate strategic option, according to a translated Iranian military handbook – as with North Korea. This attack could devastate the U.S. electrical grid for over one year, killing up to 90% of Americans. The attack could originate from satellites, offshore container ships, and in the near future – ICBMs.[139] Is Obama putting America's survival at risk because of a reported fatwa issued by the ayatollah, who has been leading chants of "Death to America" for years?

25. "What we will be doing even as we enter this deal, is sending a clear message to the Iranians and to the entire region that if anyone messes with Israel, America will be there … I have been very clear that Iran will not get a nuclear weapon on my watch … They should understand that we mean it **… <u>I would consider it a failure on my part</u>, a fundamental failure of my presidency, if on my watch, or as a consequence of work I have done, <u>Israel was rendered more vulnerable</u>.** That is not just a **strategic failure**, that would be a **moral failure** … This *[the policy disagreement over Israel]* has been as hard as anything I do, because of the <u>**deep affinities that I feel for the Israeli people**</u> and for the Jewish people … **It has been personally difficult for me to hear expressions that somehow this administration has not done everything it could to look out for Israel's interests** … We do not have a greater ally than Israel in the Middle East. I have instructed my team to work with the Israelis to build on the already unprecedented military intelligence cooperation that is in place … **Our core interests (in the Middle East) are, that everyone is living in peace** *[in contrast to Obama creating vacuums that allowed the rise of ISIS in Syria and Iraq, Iran-backed rebels in Yemen, Libya in chaos, and the expansion of the Iranian sphere of influence in the Middle East which has created unprecedented terrorism and chaos]*, that it is orderly, that our allies are not being attacked, that children are not having barrel bombs dropped on them *[Obama's*

pediatric human shields] and that massive displacements are not taking place. *[Obama supports massive Muslim immigration to Europe.]* Our interests are just making sure that the region is working." *Obama's interview with Thomas Friedman, The New York Times, March 5, 2015.* Why didn't Friedman bring up the recent release by the Obama administration of classified details of the Israeli nuclear program, his administration recently calling Netanyahu "chickenshit," his administration not standing by the Oslo accords when Abbas went to the International Criminal Court, and Obama closing down Ben Gurion Airport during the last Hamas Gaza war in 2014? Obama also refused to acknowledge the Jewish religion of some of the victims at the Paris kosher supermarket murder site, and his pro-Muslim statement during his Cairo speech in 2009 that Israel was born out of the ashes of the Holocaust and failed to acknowledge its long historical ties to the Holy Land. In June, during an interview with *Channel 2 News Israel*, Obama threatened Israel by considering withholding a U.S. veto regarding establishing a Palestinian state if Israel does not follow his agenda regarding the two-state solution.

a.   A survey released by the World Zionist Organization in January 2016 showed that 25% of Israelis believe that another Holocaust is a realistic future possibility.

b.   **Leon Panetta** tells Israel to "reach and mend fences" with the Muslim Brotherhood leadership in Egypt and with President Erdogan of Turkey, both of whom are very anti-Semitic. He also tells Israel "to **get to the damned table**," with respect to talks with the Palestinians.

c.   **Kerry** called Israel at risk to becoming an "**apartheid state**" if they don't accept a two-state solution based on suicidal "Auschwitz" 1967 borders.

d.   "What is a more relevant fear would be that in Year 13, 14, 15, they have advanced centrifuges that enrich uranium fairly rapidly, and at that point, **the breakout times would have shrunk almost down to zero** … The option of a future president to take action if in fact they try to obtain a nuclear weapon is undiminished." *Obama NPR interview, April 2015*. **Obama admits that in 13 years**, at the very most, **Iran will have the capabilities to almost instantaneously produce a nuclear weapon and create another Holocaust**. That is certainly not in Israel's best interests and does not reflect a deep affinity or concern for the Jewish state. In 13 to 15 years, Iran will have nuclear weapons, and a military strike to block Iran's path to the bomb would be ludicrous.

e.   "President Obama has made clear that **we need to take a hard look at our approach to the conflict**. We look to the next Israeli government … to demonstrate, through policies and actions, a genuine commitment to a two-state solution." *Susan Rice, U.S. National Security Adviser, April 29, 2015*. Obama is setting the stage to abandon Israel in the international diplomatic arena. A two-state solution is code for giving the PA, Hamas, ISIS, and the Iranians half of Jerusalem.

f. **"If the new Israeli government is seen as stepping back from its commitment to a two-state solution, that makes our jobs in the international arena a lot tougher** because our ability to push back on efforts to internationalize the conflict … has depended on our insistence that the best course is in achieving a two-state solution." *Wendy Sherman, U.S. Under Secretary of State, April 27, 2015.* High level government officials are coordinating their talking points before a diplomatic assault on Israel, which will occur after the Iranian nuclear agreement is finalized, since Obama needs the Democrat and Jewish support for the Iranian agreement.

g. "We did it. **All our goals materialized**." *Former Iranian President Rouhani, after the nuclear agreement is announced in July 2015.* Including the future annihilation of Israel? Governor Huckabee had the same thought by stating, "This president's foreign policy is the most feckless in American history. It is so naive that he would trust the Iranians. **By doing so, he will take the Israelis and march them to the door of the oven**." How many times has Iran's leadership publicly stated that annihilating Israel was a major state policy goal? Hitler was also very clear with his stated intention to kill all the Jews before he initiated the Holocaust. **As Ayatollah Khomenei has said,** "The fake **Zionist regime will disappear** from the landscape of geography," and "**Israel has no cure but to be annihilated**," and "It is the mission of the Islamic Republic of Iran **to erase Israel from the map of the region**," and many other similar statements.

h. "We have been seeing an **expansion of Iranian deployment around Israel** *[even before sanctions relief]*." *Israeli Foreign Ministry Director Dore Gold, July 2015.*

i. On August 17, 2015, Ayatollah Khamenei released the following statement to social media, "We spare no opportunity to support anyone #FightingTheZionists." At the same time, **the Iranian regime released a video showing tens of thousands if not hundreds of thousands of IRGC troops amassing outside of Jerusalem with Qassam Brigades and Palestinian forces for an assault on the capital of Israel**, with the goal of destroying Israel and killing the Jews. Obama is enabling Iran to carry out this mission with sanctions relief and is allowing Iran to build its military infrastructure as well as to support its terror proxies surrounding Israel. **The individuals or organizations who have now publicly stated their goal to recapture Jerusalem via a military invasion include Iran, Morsi, the Muslim Brotherhood, Erdogan, Hamas, Hezbollah, ISIS, and al-Qaeda. Obama empowered all these groups and individuals** during his presidency, such that all these radical Islamic and Arab forces will combine their assets and form a military alliance that could invade and destroy Israel, which is Obama's ultimate goal, being a radical Muslim.

j. "**The world is a much more dangerous place today than it was yesterday** … In the coming decade, the deal will reward Iran, the terrorist regime in Tehran, with hundreds of billions of dollars. **This cash bonanza will fuel Iran's terrorism worldwide, its aggression in the region and its efforts to destroy Israel, which are ongoing** ... While the negotiators were closing the deal in Vienna, Iran's supposedly moderate president chose to go to a rally in Tehran and at this rally, a frenzied mob burned American and Israeli flags and chanted 'Death to America, Death to Israel!' ... Iran's Supreme Leader, the Ayatollah Khamenei, said on March 21 the deal does not limit Iran's aggression in any way. He said: 'Negotiations with the United States are on the nuclear issue and on nothing else ... The United States ... **embodies global arrogance**, *[Obama agrees with the ayatollah's description of the U.S., i.e. – the apology tour and his repeatedly calling America a bully.]* and the battle against it will continue unabated *[Obama empowered Iran despite its leadership declaring it is at war with America.]* even after the nuclear agreement is concluded.' Here's what Hassan Nasrallah, the head of Iran's terrorist proxy Hezbollah, said about sanctions relief, which is a key component of the deal. He said: 'A rich and strong Iran will be able to stand by its allies and friends in the region more than at any time in the past.' Translation: **Iran's support for terrorism and subversion will actually increase after the deal** ... The bottom line of this very bad deal is exactly what Iran's President Rouhani said: 'The international community is removing the sanctions and Iran is keeping its nuclear program.' By not dismantling Iran's nuclear program, in a decade this deal will give an unreformed, unrepentant and far richer terrorist regime the capacity to produce many nuclear bombs, in fact an entire nuclear arsenal with the means to deliver it. **What a stunning historic mistake**!" *Israeli Prime Minister Netanyahu, July 14, 2015. Statement after the Iranian nuclear deal is announced.*

k. "I think no one has ever opened the door to more harm of Jewish people in the history of the world than Mr. Kerry and Mr. Obama. And **there is some kind of deep-seated physiological drama being played out here for them to hurt Israel this much**." *Ben Stein, former White House speechwriter and author. July 29, 2015. The deep-seated drama is that Obama is a radical Muslim who hates Israel.*

l. "The Israeli position is that this is an irrational regime. **This is about our survival as a people**. It's about our children and grandchildren. **What may look like an academic debate here in America is for us in Israel a matter of life and death**." *Michael Oren, former Israeli Ambassador to the United States.* In an Israeli poll taken during the debate of the Iranian nuclear agreement, 73% of Israeli's voiced concern that Obama does not have Israeli interests in mind.

m. "What we increasingly can't stomach-and feel obliged to speak out about right now – is the **use of Jew-baiting and other blatant and retrograde forms of racial and ethnic prejudice as tools to sell a political deal, or to smear those who oppose it**. Accusing Sen. Schumer of loyalty to a foreign government is bigotry, pure and simple. Accusing

senators and congressmen whose misgivings about the Iran deal are shared by a majority of the U.S. electorate of being agents of a foreign power, or of selling their votes to
shadowy lobbyists, or of acting contrary to the best interests of the United States is the
kind of naked appeal to bigotry and prejudice that would be familiar in the politics of the
pre-Civil Rights Era South." *"Crossing a Line to Sell a Deal," Tablet Magazine, August 7,
2015.* A mainstream Jewish publication accuses Obama of employing many historically
anti-Semitic tactics to build support for his Iranian nuclear agreement.

n. "The **Islamic Revolution** will continue enhancing is preparedness until it **overthrows
Israel and liberates Palestine** … We will continue defending not just our own country,
but also all the oppressed people of the world, especially **those countries that are standing on the forefront of confrontation with the Zionists**." *Brigadier General Mohsen
Kazzemeini, Tehran province commander of the IRGC, September 1, 2015. The official
Iranian reaction upon hearing that the Senate will not be able to override an Obama veto
of the congressional rejection of the deal.* With the initial $150 billion in sanctions relief,
and with Iran set to become a major regional power armed with nuclear weapons, the
Iranians may have a set time schedule for the destruction of Israel. For Israel to survive,
it must adopt proactive policies instead of reactive policies concerning regional and international events. Israel must be willing to destroy all Iranian proxies in their sphere of
influence and be prepared to permanently take control of Gaza and southern Lebanon
devoid of any supporters of Iranian objectives. If the Muslims are able to keep waging
wars against Israel without any significant negative repercussions, then Israel, no matter how many times they are able to survive life-threatening conflicts, will never have a
real peace. In the next major war, the Israelis must keep fighting until they can obtain
an unconditional surrender, and any local Muslim populations that support the terrorists should be transferred from territories adjacent to Israel. Otherwise, Hamas, the PA,
Hezbollah, and the IRGC will slowly deploy more advanced missiles and munitions in
the territories they control to eventually overwhelm Israeli defenses and cause irreparable
harm.

o. "With the clock ticking on two terms that incalculably damaged the cause of peace in
the Middle East, President Obama is reportedly planning to dictate terms of an Israeli-
Palestinian settlement through the United Nations. He must not go further down this
path of ego, **hubris**, and **vengeance**. *[and another attempt to destroy Israel]* He will not
validate the Nobel Peace Prize awarded to him in 2009 and never earned. **Undercutting
the Jewish state**, he will only make negotiations more impossible than they already are.
Plainly, the President blames Israel in the person of Prime Minister Benjamin Netanyahu
for the failure of Obama's attempts to broker a peace deal … The President's **destructive asymmetry dismembered decades of American policy in the Middle East** …

Posturing again as a tribune of peace, the President would repay Netanyahu's truculence with a **middle-fingered fiat** as he scoots out the door … His job is over. **He needs to leave bad enough alone.**" *(source – "<u>**No More, Mr. President: Obama Has Done Enough Damage to Israel Already**</u>," The New York Daily News [a liberal pro-Obama New York newspaper], March 10, 2016).* The New York Daily News identified Obama's hatred for the Jewish state, but would not comment on the cause of that hatred [Obama is a radical Muslim]. Editors of the New York Post foresaw Obama's support for UNSC Resolution 2334.

p.   "I fear that what could happen is that, **if Congress were to overturn it, our friends in Israel could actually wind up being more isolated. And more blamed**. And we would lose Europe and China and Russia with respect to whatever military action we might have to take. Because we will have turned our backs on a very legitimate program that allows us to put their program to the test over the next few years." *Kerry, Council of Foreign Relations presentation, July 24, 2015*. **Is Kerry being anti-Semitic by blaming and threatening Israel for a congressional rejection of a poorly negotiated treaty** that is not in America's interest?

i.   "First, we took the military option off the table by publicly declaring that we were not militarily capable of permanently ending Iran's nuclear weapons program. Second, we took the current tough sanction regimen off the table by acknowledging that if we did not accept a deal, many of our most important partners would begin to reduce or even eliminate sanctions. Third, and most important, we took off the table the option of rejecting the deal by publicly acknowledging that if we do so, we will be worse off than if we accept even a questionable deal. Yes, the president said he would not accept a "bad" deal, but by repeatedly watering down the definition of a bad deal, and by repeatedly stating that the alternative to a deal would be disastrous, he led the Iranians to conclude we needed the deal more than they did. These three concessions left our negotiators with little leverage and provided their Iranian counterparts with every incentive to demand more compromises from us … As Danielle Pletka of the American Enterprise Institute put it: "The deal itself became more important than what was in it." President Obama seems to have confirmed that assessment when he said: "Put simply, no deal means a greater chance of more war in the Middle East." But one thing is clear: By conveying those stark alternatives to Iranian negotiators, we weakened our bargaining position. We could have stuck to the original redlines – non-negotiable demands – from the beginning. These included on-the-spot inspections of all facilities rather than the nearly month-long notice that will allow the Iranians to hide what they are doing; shutting down all facilities specifically designed for nuclear weapons production; maintaining the embargo on missiles and other sophisticated weapons rather than allowing it to gradually be lifted; and most crucially, a written assurance that the international community will never allow Iran to develop a nuclear arsenal. Instead, we caved early and often because the Iranians knew we desperately need a deal to implement President Obama's world vision and to enhance his legacy. **This approach to the deal – surrendering leverage from the outset – violated the most basic principles of Negotiation 101**."[140] (*Alan M. Dershowitz, liberal Harvard Law professor, Jerusalem Post, originally published in the Boston Globe*) It's either this, or Obama allowed himself to be out-negotiated since Iran's objectives were his objectives. If Obama truly had U.S. interests at heart, would he have made such basic mistakes with his negotiating strategy?

q. "I think that some of it *[$150 billion in Iranian sanctions relief]* will end up in the hands of the IRGC or other *[anti-West, anti-Israel, Islamist]* entities, some of which are labelled terrorists." *Kerry, Davos Economic Forum, January 21, 2016.* Kerry acknowledges the JCPOA funds terrorist groups that are dedicated to destroying Israel and the United States. Treason? Kerry is admitting that Obama is funding Islamic terrorism and violated federal law.

r. "The Obama administration's appraisal on the Israeli-Palestinian conflict is, according to Ross, that "if you **distance yourself from Israel**, you'll gain with the Arabs." … Ross, a veteran diplomat who worked on Israeli-Palestinian peace negotiations under the Reagan, George H.W. Bush, Clinton, and Obama administrations, said that this White House [**Obama**] **is operating under the premise that** '<u>Israel is more of a problem than it is a partner</u>.'"[141] *(Deborah Danan, Breitbart)* Obama has always viewed Israel (and not the Islamic terrorist groups – Hamas, Hezbollah, Iran, Fatah …) as the main problem and instigator in the Middle East. His expression of affinities for Israel and its citizens are taqiyya. Dennis Ross is a former Obama foreign policy aide who witnessed first-hand Obama's true feelings and affinities, which he revealed while speaking at *The Jerusalem Post* annual conference in New York City in May 2016.

s. In 2017, Iran, the IRGC, and Hezbollah have built reinforced subterranean missile factories that are impervious to Israeli bunker busting bombs, and allowed Hezbollah to manufacture long-range highly accurate advanced missiles that can strike targets throughout Israel and can also strike Israeli naval forces. These military installations were undoubtedly in part funded by the JCPOA and the $1.7 billion in cash Obama gave the Iranians in exchange for four American political prisoners. Obama is personally funding the Islamic terrorists' war against Israel.

t. "The ability of the Iranians to do what they are doing now in Syria and Iraq [to maintain a permanent presence in Iraq and Syria with a cease fire agreement], and be involved in both Syria and Iraq, and their relations with Hezbollah, it is all built on the legitimacy they gained from this [nuclear] agreement … **The agreement is the source of all the problems**. It is even **more dangerous than we imagined when signed**."[142] *Former Israeli National Security chief Yaakov Amidror, Begin-Sadat Center for Strategic Studies fellow, Netanyahu security advisor, July 16, 2017.* Knowing the lethal threat to Israel's security, Obama invited Iran into Iraq and Syria under the guise to fight ISIS, and then strengthened their political position with the JCPOA and its sanctions relief. The end result is a series of direct threats to Israel with IRGC troops much closer to Israel's northern border, with the possibility of permanent Iranian bases [land and naval] in Syria and Iraq, with Iran controlling the land corridor between Iran and the Mediterranean, and with Iran eventually becoming legitimately armed with nuclear weapons at the end of the term of the JCPOA.

26. "Today, the United States … has reached a **historic understanding** with Iran … If this framework leads to a final, comprehensive deal, it **will make our country, our allies, and our world safer** *[Obama lying for Iran.]* … Nothing is agreed to until everything is agreed. *[Why does Obama oppose this strategy being applied to Israeli-Palestinian negotiations? Double standards? Anti-Semitism?]" Obama White House Statement on the Iran Nuclear Framework Agreement "Non-Agreement," April 2, 2015.* Obama pretends to have an agreement with Iran with this major announcement, but there is no agreement. For weeks after this announcement, Iran, France, and the United States could not agree upon the major talking points. There was no signed agreement and each country released conflicting fact sheets. A resulting nuclear arms race in the Middle East as a result of a weak Iranian nuclear deal, strengthening Iranian hegemony in the region, and Iran having a two- to three-month breakout period to build a nuclear weapon with their present capabilities, will not make our world safer.

   a. "Here is the paper which bears his [Adolf Hitler's] name upon it as well as mine … We regard the agreement signed last night … as symbolic of the desire of our two peoples never to go to war with one another again … I believe it is peace for our time." *Neville Chamberlain, September 30, 1938*

   b. "**We welcome war with the U.S.** as we do believe that it will be the scene for our success to display the real potentials of our power." *Islamic Revolutionary Guard Corps Lt. Commander General Hossein Salami, May, 2015.*

   c. "And Rouhani, the president, was really elected on the hope that he would bring economic relief to the Iranian people. But yes, it is real, it is possible, and, in fact, **we should expect that some portion of that money would go to the Iranian military and could potentially be used for the kinds of bad behavior** that we have seen in the region up until now." *On July 15, 2015, National Security Advisor Susan Rice admits that a significant amount of the $150 billion that Iran obtains from sanctions relief will fund* *their military and terror proxies.* Much of that money will be funding Islamic terrorism against the West and Israel. Both Rice and Kerry have now admitted that Obama is a major funder of Islamic terrorism. **The nuclear agreement has also been called the Jihadi stimulus package. <u>With this deal, Obama has become the leading financier of state-sponsored Islamic terrorism in the world</u>**. The $1.7 billion dollars given to Iran in exchange for the four American hostages only confirmed that funding Islamic terrorism is a major priority in the Obama White House. Rice confirmed that Obama broke federal law.

d.   "The final agreement on Iran's nuclear program, the JCPOA, has potentially grave strategic implications that directly threaten to undermine the national security of the United States and our closest regional allies. By allowing Iran to become a nuclear threshold state and enabling it to become more powerful and expand its influence and destabilizing activities – across the Middle East and possibly **directly threatening the U.S. homeland** – the JCPOA will place the United States in far worse position to prevent a nuclear Iran … The JCPOA will not prevent a nuclear Iran … The JCPOA will give Iran the means to **increase support for terrorist and insurgent proxies**, **aggravate sectarian conflict** and trigger both nuclear and conventional proliferation cascades. It will provide the expansionist regime in Tehran with access to resources, technology and international arms markets required to bolster offensive military capabilities in the vital Persian Gulf region, acquire long-range ballistic missiles and develop other major weapons systems … **Our long-standing allies feel betrayed** – even angry – with the JCPOA, seeing it as a weakening of U.S. security guarantees and **reversal of decades of U.S. regional security policy** *[Obama switched sides.]* … Simultaneously, sequestration *[Obama's idea]* is diminishing the ability of the United States to respond to Iranian aggression, mitigate security threats emanating from Iran and protect U.S. regional allies. Leaving it with fewer and older ships and planes as well as fewer and less well-trained troops, these cuts will severely damage the U.S. military's ability to project power in the region, even as the Iranian threat grows … The strategic environment will grow much more treacherous in the next 15 years. Comparatively, Iran will be economically stronger, regionally more powerful and militarily more capable, while the United States will have a smaller, less capable fighting force, diminished credibility and fewer allies."[143] *(JINSA Iran Strategy Council, September 2015)*

e.   "You heard '**Death to Israel**,' '**Death to the U.S.**' You could hear it. **The whole nation** was shaken by these slogans. It wasn't only confined to Tehran. **The whole of the nation**, you could hear, that was covered by **this great movement**. **So we ask Almighty G-d to accept these prayers by the people of Iran** … The Islamic Republic of Iran **will not give up support of its friends in the region** *[al-Qaeda and the Muslim*

Brotherhood] — the oppressed people of Palestine, of Yemen [Houthi rebels, al-Qaeda of the Arabian Peninsula (AQAP)], the Syrian and Iraqi governments, the oppressed people of Bahrain *[looking to overthrow Gulf states]* and sincere **resistance fighters in Lebanon and Palestine** *[Hezbollah and Hamas whose goal is to kill all Jews and destroy Israel]* … **Our policy will not change with regards to the arrogant U.S. government.**" *Ayatollah Khamenei, Sermon after Friday prayers after the nuclear agreement was announced in Vienna, July 17, 2015.*

i.   "I've said many times that Iran is an **extraordinarily gifted country**. It is an ancient culture **… It has incredibly smart and talented people. And I wish those people well** … **by virtue of its size**, talent, resources, <u>immediately rise in its influence and its power in the eyes of the world … And that's what I hope can happen</u>." *Obama interview with mic.com, August 10, 2015.* Obama's loyalty lies with the leadership of Iran. Obama supported the ayatollahs when their leadership was threatened by revolution in 2009. Obama ignored their daily chants calling for the destruction of America and annihilation of Israel. He ignored their political and military alliances with al-Qaeda, Hezbollah, and Hamas and disregards their threats to our long-term ally, Saudi Arabia. And now **Obama admits his goal is to empower Iran**, only now it is with over $150 billion and nuclear weapons.

f.   "**Israel's security will not be ensured** whether there will be a nuclear agreement or not." *Ayatollah Khamenei's tweet (July 20, 2015) after the announcement of the nuclear agreement.* The tweet was accompanied by a video of a simulated missile attack against Israel. When the ayatollah made his first public statement concerning the agreement, he had his hand on an AK-47. So much for Islam being a religion of peace.

g.   "As long as America exists, we will not rest … In revealing the truth about America and the Zionists, **we must raise public hate against the despotic powers and create the environment for the destruction of America**." *Brigadier General Mohammad Naqdi, commander of Iranian Basij militia, 2012. Farrakhan has expressed similar views and visited Iran after the JCPOA was approved.*

h.   In March 2016, Iran test fired two intermediate range ballistic missiles designed to strike Israel. The Iranians wrote in Hebrew on the missiles, "Israel must be wiped off the face of the earth." Iranian Defense Minister Dehgan previously stated in July 2015, that the "missile related issues have never been on agenda of the nuclear talks and the Islamic system will resolutely implement its programs in this field." In mid-2017, Iran fired test missiles at targets marked with large stars of David.

i.   "We have two million Iranians there. Be certain that **I will raise a guerilla army from amongst them against you** *[the United States].* You know this well. Look how vulnerable you were on 9-11 when four Arabs who don't know how to fight managed to endanger your foundations." *Hassan Abbasi, IRGC Commander, February 2017.* Obama's sanctions relief and multiple multi-billion dollar cash transfers to Iran has helped fund Iran's embedding of terror cells in America and its potential purchase of huge quantities of uranium, which will ultimately be used to manufacture nuclear weapons. The same month, Iran announced it is seeking to purchase over 950 tons of uranium concentrate from Kazakhstan.

  j.   By mid-2017, Iran had three functioning domestic underground ballistic missile factories, all funded by the JCPOA.

27. "I want to return to this point: we want Iran not to have nuclear weapons precisely because **we can't bank on the nature of the regime changing** … If suddenly Iran transformed itself to Germany or Sweden or France, then there would be a different set of conversations about their nuclear infrastructure." *Obama, NPR interview, April 2015.* Obama could have had an Iranian regime change in 2009, but chose to not support the student rebels, and let them get murdered in the streets and tortured and raped in prison. Obama even instructed the U.S. intelligence services not to help the protest movement. Later in his administration, Obama protected Iran, its Islamic terrorist allies and their networks, which is just the opposite of what one would expect from the president of the United States. According to *The Washington Free Beacon*, "David Asher, who previously served as an adviser to Gen. John Allen at the Defense and State Departments, told the House Foreign Affairs Committee Thursday (June 7, 2017) that top officials across several key law enforcement and intelligence agencies in the Obama administration "systematically disbanded" law enforcement activities targeting the terrorism financing operations of Iran, Hezbollah, and Venezuela in the lead-up to and during the nuclear negotiations with Tehran … The United States squandered the chance "at a very low financial cost" to take apart Hezbollah's finances, its global organization, and the Iran proxy's ability to "readily terrorize us, victimize us, and run a criminal network through our shores, inside our banking systems – and in partnership with the world's foremost drug cartels – target our state and society," he said. "We lost much of the altitude we had gained in our global effort, and many aspects including key personnel, who were reassigned, budgets that were slashed – many key elements of the investigations that were underway were undermined," he said."[144] Obama continually undermined key U.S. intelligence and legal efforts to thwart Iran's attempt to project its counterproductive influence around the world and Iran's backing of terrorism. Obama eventually backed the totalitarian regime, supported their fraudulent elections, worked to relieve sanctions, and protected their nuclear program and terrorist allies. Obama represented the interests of the Iranian regime and had no plans to initiate policies that would put pressure on the stability of the ayatollah's government.

28. "Iran has also agreed to **the most robust and intrusive inspections** and **transparency** regime ever negotiated for any nuclear program in history." *Obama, April 2, 2015.* There is

minimal transparency since the only people who know the side deals that outline the inspection protocols are Obama, Jarrett, Wendy Sherman, the Iranians, some briefed members of Congress, some IAEA officials, and a handful of officials who are members of the P5+1 negotiating teams, at most. The inspections are neither robust or intrusive.

29. "We can envision an end state that gives us an assurance that **even if they have some modest** *[downplaying by Obama]* **enrichment capability** it is so **constrained** and the inspections are **so intrusive**, that they as a practical matter **they do not have breakout capacity**." *Obama, December 7, 2013*. Obama is arguing for Iran to keep their nuclear enrichment capabilities, which he had earlier wanted to deny, and is shifting [evolving] his position to a more pro-Iranian stance.

30. "In the first place **we will have <u>anytime, anywhere access</u> to the nuclear facilities … the whole supply chain … if there is a suspicious site, for instance somewhere in a military base in Iran, and we want to seek access to that**, we will be able to go to the IAEA and get that inspection because of the additional protocol of the IAEA that Iran will be joining and some of the additional transparency and inspections measures that are in the deal … **Iran <u>will never be permitted</u> to build a nuclear weapon**." *Ben Rhodes speaking to Channel 2 News, Israel, April 5, 2015, trying to support the unsigned framework agreement.* The latter statement is very misleading, since, when Rhodes states Iran will never be permitted to build a nuclear weapon, it sounds as if the United States will do all in its power to prevent that feat. But in reality, Rhodes stated Obama will never give permission for Iran to build a nuclear weapon, but whether Iran builds a nuclear weapon without his permission, it is not Obama's concern. Like Obama, Rhodes has a history of lying. He most likely wrote the Susan Rice talking points memo (with Obama's approval), where she blamed the Benghazi massacre on an anti-Islamic video on the Sunday morning talk shows after Ambassador Stevens was murdered by Islamic insurgents on September 11, 2012. Rhodes also created the echo chamber that created the fake news stories that supported the acceptance of the JCPOA.

    a. "Rhodes said in April 2015, in response to a reporter's question, that under the nuclear deal, "you will have anywhere, anytime, 24 / 7 access as it relates to the nuclear facilities that Iran has." When the JCPOA turned out to contain serious qualifications on inspection rights, Rhodes shamelessly claimed, "We never sought in this negotiation the capacity for so-called anytime, anywhere where you can basically go anywhere in the country, look at whatever you wanted to do, that had nothing to do with the nuclear program …" Rhodes' attempt to wiggle out of what he had previously promised was misleading. He left out the fact that the Obama administration ended up making major concessions on the inspection issue in the face of Iran's demands, including that its military sites were off limits to outside inspectors unless Iran agreed otherwise. The JCPOA provides Iran with the means to delay any inspections of undeclared suspected sites requested by the International Atomic Energy Agency. Iran can raise objections to inspections of suspected sites, which would then have to be assessed by a commission that includes Iran itself as a member."[145] *(Joseph Klein, FrontPage Magazine)*

b. "What is a more relevant fear would be that **in Year 13, 14, 15**, they have advanced centrifuges that enrich uranium fairly rapidly, and at that point, **the breakout times would have shrunk almost down to zero** … The option of a future president to take action if in fact they try to obtain a nuclear weapon is undiminished." *Obama, NPR interview, April, 2015.*

   i. "I've been very clear that Iran will not get a nuclear weapon **on my watch**." *Obama, New York Times interview, April 4, 2015.* Obama's only concern is producing any agreement that will not allow Iran to produce a nuclear weapon during his presidency, which ends in 19+ months. He has no concern for what happens to the United States or Israel when a new president takes over.

   ii. "This deal actually pushes Iran further away from a bomb. **And there's a <u>permanent prohibition</u> on Iran <u>ever</u> having a nuclear weapon**." *Obama's weekly address, July 18, 2015.* Obama may be a psychotic liar when comparing this statement to what he revealed in the NPR interview in April. He knew the agreement would expire in ten years.

   iii. "It has been personally difficult for me to hear … has not done everything … to look out for Israel's interest … **this has been as hard as anything I do because of the deep affinities that I feel for the Israeli people and for the Jewish people**." *Obama - Friedman New York Times Interview. Pure taqiyya.*

   iv. "The government of the Islamic Republic of **Iran has <u>divine permission</u> to destroy Israel** … the noble **Koran permits** the Islamic Republic of Iran to destroy Israel." *Mojtaba Zolnour, Ayatollah Khamenei representative in the Iranian Revolutionary Guards, 2015. Is Obama ushering in a second Holocaust?*

c. "Iran's **Defense Minister Brigadier General Hossein Dehqan categorically rejected as a 'lie' a Guardian report alleging that Tehran has granted access to its military facilities** under the recent framework agreement with the world powers. '**No such agreement has been made**; principally speaking, **visit to military centers is among our red lines and no such visit will be accepted**,' General Dehqan, rejecting 'the report by foreign media outlets, such as the Guardian' as 'untruthful allegations.'"[146]

d. "A tour of military facilities by foreign inspectors is to be equated with the occupation of a country. Iran will not become a paradise for spies. We will not roll out the red carpet for the enemy … They will not even be permitted to inspect the most normal military site in their dreams." *General Hossein Salami, Iranian Revolutionary Guards, April 18, 2015, Army Day, Iran.*

    i.   "We expect to have **anywhere, anytime access** ..." *Energy Secretary and nuclear physicist Moniz, lead negotiator for the technical nuclear details of a future agreement responding to General Salami's comments, April 20, 2015, Bloomberg Politics.*

        (1)   "In the spring of last year, legions of arms control experts began popping up at think tanks and on social media, and then became key sources for hundreds of often clueless reporters. [Ben Rhodes] 'We created an echo chamber *[i.e., any-time, anywhere]* ... They were saying things that validated what we had given them to say.'"[147] *(David Samuels, The New York Times Magazine)*

e.   "We reiterate that the **permission will definitely never be issued for any kind of access** to the military centers, **even if it runs counter to the acceptance of the additional protocol** (to the NTP)." *Brigadier General Jazzayeri, Deputy Chief of Staff of the Iranian Armed Forces, June 14, 2015.* Iran admits that they may agree to inspections of their military sites in a final nuclear agreement, but they will never be permitted, thus making any Iranian promises worthless. Iran admits they will probably violate any future agreement.

f.   Iran **will not agree to** "unconventional inspections, interrogating certain Iranian individuals and **inspecting military sites.**" *Ayatollah Khamenei, June 23, 2015.*

g.   "We call on the negotiating sides to avoid stepping into this realm; because **access to military centers will not be allowed under any condition**." *Brigadier General Jazzayeri, July 2015.*

h.   "The IAEA, which is a highly respected international organization, will field an international team of inspectors. And those inspectors will in all likelihood come from IAEA member-states, most of whom have diplomatic relationships with Iran. We of course are a rare exception ... **No Americans will be part of the IAEA inspection teams ... There are not going to be independent American inspectors separate from the IAEA**. The IAEA will do the inspections on behalf of the United States and the rest of the international community." *Obama's National Security Advisor Susan Rice admits on CNN on July 16, 2015 that **the United States will not be part of any inspection teams that will evaluate Iranian compliance** with the nuclear deal.* The United States will be relying on inspectors from countries having good relations with the Iranian government, from governments that are allies with the ayatollahs, from governments wanting to increase business with Iran now that sanctions are being removed, or who are religious Muslims. Will the inspectors be trustworthy?

    i.   "The physical magnitude of the effort is daunting. Is the International Atomic Energy Agency technically, and in terms of human resources, up to so complex and vast an assignment? In a large country with multiple facilities and ample experience in nuclear concealment, violations will be inherently difficult to detect. Devising theoretical models of inspection is one thing. Enforcing compliance, week after week, despite competing international crises and domestic distractions, is another."[148] *Henry Kissinger and George Shultz, previous Secretaries of State, The Wall Street Journal.*

i.   In mid-August 2015, one of the leaked side deals between Iran and the IAEA allows **Iran to inspect the Parchin nuclear site with only its own inspectors**. Inspectors from the IAEA will not be allowed to visit that site, which has been suspected of developing nuclear triggers. The White House National Security Council spokesman, Ned Price, commented that **Obama was "confident in the agency's technical plans for investigating the possible military dimensions of Iran's former program** … The IAEA has separately developed the most robust inspection regime ever peacefully negotiated."

j.   "I think this is one of those circumstances where **we have all been rhetorical from time to time … The phrase, anytime, anywhere, is something that became popular rhetoric**, but I think **people understood that if the IAEA felt it had to have access, and had a justification for that access**, that it would be guaranteed, and that is what happened." *Wendy Sherman, chief negotiator for the United States with Iran, admits that **the Obama administration lied to the American people concerning Obama's true final position** with respect to Iranian nuclear facility inspections. Jerusalem Post, July 17, 2015.*

k.   "This deal is not built on trust; it is **built on verification** … Because of this deal, **inspectors will also be able to access any suspicious location** … [Inspectors] will have **access where necessary**, when necessary." *Obama, July 14, 2015.*

    i.   "**We never sought in this negotiation the capacity for so-called anytime, anywhere**," *Ben Rhodes, July 14, 2015, after the final deal is announced. Rhodes said just the opposite to Channel 2 News Israel on April 5, 2015.*

        (1)   "Well, Jake, first of all, under this deal, **you will have anywhere, anytime 24/7 access** as it relates to the nuclear facilities that Iran has." *Ben Rhodes, April 6, 2015, interview with Jake Tapper. Rhodes reversed his position again, i.e. - lied.*

l.   "There is no such standard within arms control inspections … **We never had a discussion about 'anywhere, anytime' managed access**." *John Kerry interview with Fox News Sunday on July 19, 2015.*

    i.   "Iran will face strict limitations on its program, and Iran has **also agreed to the most robust and intrusive inspections and transparency regime ever negotiated for any nuclear program in history** … International inspectors will have unprecedented access not only to Iranian nuclear facilities, but to the entire supply chain that supports Iran's nuclear program – from uranium mills that provide the raw materials, to the centrifuge production and storage facilities that support the program." *Obama, Rose Garden address, April 2, 2015.* More lies.

31. "If you can diplomatically and peacefully resolve the nuclear issue in a way that **prevents Iran from obtaining a nuclear weapon** … we believe that will lead to **a much _more_ stable region** … there will be **no need to see [a] regional arms race**." *Deputy National Security Advisor Ben Rhodes with National Security Advisor Susan Rice, March, 21, 2015 press conference.* **On April 28, Iran seized a cargo ship registered in the Marshall Islands**, and was forced to pay a $163,000 fine before it was released one week later. The United States signed a treaty with the Marshall Islands guaranteeing the safety and protection of their registered ships. Obama did nothing to support this ally. **On May 14, Iran's navy fired machine guns at a Singapore-based oil tanker in the Straits of Hormuz**. In May, it was reported that Saudi Arabia will purchase nuclear weapons from Pakistan. So far, not a more stable region …

    a. "The Persian enemy is Enemy No. 1, and the Zionist enemy is [only] Enemy No. 2. We must present this truth directly, flattering no one, to all those [who try] to extort us with the tale that Israel is the Arabs' Enemy No. 1 and that Iran supports us on the Palestinian issue … Moreover, let me say this bluntly: Any citizen of any of the five Gulf states who prioritizes the Israeli danger over that of the Persian enemy, whether from a pan-Arab or an Islamist perspective, is sacrificing his homeland, its security, its stability, and perhaps its very existence for his neighbor's cause. By any national standard, this is absolute treason." *Saudi daily newspaper Al Jazirah, Muhammad Al Sheikh, March 8, 2016.* The risk of war between Saudi Arabia and Iran is increasing secondary to Obama's policies, including the JCPOA.

    b. "**Whatever the Iranians have, we will have, too**." *Former Saudi intelligence head Prince Turki bin Faisal, April, 2015.* Obama is guaranteeing a nuclear arms race in the Middle East with his policies, an outcome that is the exact opposite of his stated goals with the Iranian nuclear negotiations.

    c. Saudi Prince Turki bin Faisal spoke at The Washington Institute for Near East Policy concerning the Iranian nuclear threat and stated, "all options" are being considered by the Saudi government including the "acquisition of nuclear weapons … to face whatever eventuality might come from Iran." *Early May 2016.*

    d. In June 2017, Saudi Arabia put in place a naval blockade of Qatar, secondary to its support of terrorism projected through the Muslim Brotherhood and its alliance with Iran.

32. "**It's no secret that the Israeli prime minister and I don't agree about whether the U.S. should move forward with a peaceful resolution** to the Iranian issue." *Obama statement at White House Rose Garden, April 2015.* Obama intentionally misrepresented

Netanyahu's position as a warmonger, even though he has repeatedly requested just a better deal. Does Obama ever portray Iran as being a warmonger in public? A better deal could be obtained by just continuing and increasing sanctions until terms of an agreement were palatable to Saudi Arabia, Israel and the Republican majority in Congress. One of Obama's main talking points regarding the final agreement is calling opponents of the deal "warmongers." Obama again repeated this theme in his speech at American University on August 5, 2015, when he stated, "Congressional rejection of this deal leaves any U.S. administration that is absolutely committed to preventing Iran from getting a nuclear weapon with one option, another war in the Middle East. I say this not to be provocative, I am stating a fact." Yet Obama threatened war and stated "all options are on the table" for years.

33. "Now, what you might hear from Prime Minister *[Benjamin]* Netanyahu, which I respect, is the notion, 'Look, Israel is more vulnerable. We don't have the luxury of testing these propositions the way you do,' and I completely understand that. And further, I completely understand Israel's belief that given the tragic history of the Jewish people, they can't be dependent solely on us for their own security. But what I would say to them is **that not only am I absolutely committed to making sure that they maintain their qualitative military edge**, and that they can deter any potential future attacks, but **what I'm willing to do is to make the kinds of commitments that would give everybody in the neighborhood, including Iran, a clarity that if Israel were to be attacked by any state, that we would stand by them**." *Obama, Friedman New York Times Interview, April 2015.* Israel is a one-bomb country. These assurances mean nothing when a nuclear device explodes near the vicinity of Tel Aviv. Iran has attacked Israel via Hamas, its proxy forces in the Gaza strip, and Obama basically sided with Hamas. Kerry also sided with Hamas when he stated, "that is one hell of a pinpoint strike" when describing Israeli counterattacks. And during ceasefire negotiations, when Hamas was running low on missiles, Obama adopted Hamas' talking points when pushing Israel to end the blockade so Hamas could rearm and rebuild its attack tunnels expeditiously. Obama forced a ceasefire agreement on Israel, when Hamas's missile inventory was nearly depleted. Hezbollah now has over 100,000 missiles in southern Lebanon, which, if used effectively, could destroy the infrastructure of the whole country during the next war, in violation of UN resolutions put forth at the end of the last Lebanese war. What has Obama done to mitigate this threat? Sanctions relief approved by Obama will also ensure potentially unlimited funding for Hamas and Hezbollah.

a. "If the Supreme Leader's orders [are] to be executed, with the abilities and the equipment at our disposal, **we will raze the Zionist regime in less than eight minutes**." *Ahmad Karimpour, senior advisor to the IRGC al Quds Force.* Karimpour made this statement at about the same time Iran successfully tested an extremely accurate medium range ballistic missile capable of striking Israel. *May 2016.*

b. "According to Leon Panetta, **he has questioned why the U.S. should maintain Israel's so-called qualitative military edge**, which grants it access to more sophisticated weapons systems than America's Arab allies receive."[149] *("The Obama Doctrine") Obama lied to Thomas Friedman in their New York Times interview.*

34. *AP* question in 2013: "What's the U.S. intelligence assessment at this point *[regarding Iran's breakout time to building a nuclear weapon]*? **Obama's response**: "**Our assessment continues to be a year or more away … and so we now have the time** *[to continue negotiations]*." U.S. intelligence estimates in 2013 showed that Iran's breakout time was two to three months to build a nuclear weapon. Obama was **downplaying** Iran's breakout time to ease public fears regarding Iranian threats. He was giving Iran more time for negotiations so they could advance their nuclear program, spread out their installations and harden their facilities to protect against military strikes by Israel.

35. In an NPR interview in April 2015, Obama admitted that the **present breakout time** was "about two to three months by our intelligence estimates" without an agreement, and with an agreement the breakout period would be extended to over one year. **Obama stated if Iran "decided to break the deal, kick out all the inspectors, break the seals and go for the bomb, we'd have over a year to respond**." Obama shortened his estimated present breakout period for an Iranian nuclear weapon to build his case for an agreement.

a. In an editorial published in *The New York Times* entitled "The Iran Deal's Fatal Flaw" on June 23, 2014, Alan Kuperman stated, "Based on such realistic assumptions, Iran's breakout time under the pending deal actually would be around three months, while its current breakout time is a little under two months. Thus, **the deal would increase the breakout time by just over a month, too little to matter. Mr. Obama's main argument for the agreement – extending Iran's breakout time – turns out to be effectively worthless**. By contrast, Iran stands to gain enormously. The deal would lift nuclear-related sanctions, thereby infusing Iran's economy with billions of dollars annually. In addition, the deal could release frozen Iranian assets, reportedly giving Tehran a $30 billion to $50 billion 'signing bonus.'" Even with the agreement, Iran can build a nuclear weapon in three months, which has been the intelligence estimate for the past three years. Their nuclear capabilities have not been curtailed, and their economy gets the much-needed relief from the end of many economic sanctions. If Iran, with an expanding nuclear program, has had a **three-month window to build a nuclear weapon over the past three years**, and they have been partnering with North Korea and Pakistan, who are already nuclear powers, statistics indicate that under the Obama administration, Iran may already have nuclear weapons. Obama's negotiating delays and postponing the final agreement signatures have given Iran's three-month window more than enough time to produce a nuclear bomb. Considering Iran's secrecy and lack of transparency surrounding their nuclear program, their insistence that military sites are not inspected, and the inability of the IAEA inspectors to have complete access to all sites, the odds favor Iran having nuclear weapons.

36. "They've got a chance to get right with the world … Because if they do, **there's incredible talent and resources and sophistication inside of Iran** and it would be a **very successful regional power** that was also <u>**abiding by international norms and international rules**</u> *[taqiyya]* - and that would be **good for everybody** *[except Israel, the Gulf Cooperation Council, the West, and the United States].*" *Obama, December 8, 2014, Interview with NPR News.* Obama is smitten with Iran. His descriptive adjectives are very positive, and you would never know from Obama's outlook that they are the number one backer of global terrorism in the world today and one of the primary forces that keeps the Middle East on the verge of war and chaos. An Iran with ICBMs and nuclear warheads will be a **global power** (not regional) with a nuclear umbrella to support its terrorist proxies around the world. Again, Obama is downplaying Iran's ultimate goals and trying to seduce the American public and the rest of the free world with a false narrative.

   a. Members of Gulf States' royal families were kidnapped in Iraq by Shia militias backed by Iran and al-Qaeda affiliates. Over $700 million was paid to Iran and their militias, and $300 million were paid to Syrian militias (ISIS). Besides receiving $1.7 billion for American political prisoners, in mid-2017 Iran was paid $700 million for the release of kidnapped Gulf State royalty. Iran is actively involved in kidnapping, ransoms and terrorism, despite Obama's misleading platitudes.

   b. "We know that **deception is part of the [Iranian] DNA**." *Wendy Sherman, Senate hearings, November 2013.* Iran has violated over twenty international agreements in the recent past.

      i. On August 5, 2015, in testimony before the Senate, Wendy Sherman admitted **that the Iranians will provide soil samples to the IAEA inspectors without the inspectors being able to access suspected nuclear sites.** *Obama approved a deal that facilitated Iranian cheating so that they could expand their nuclear program illegally under the guise of abiding by the nuclear agreement.*

      ii. "If you have a centrifuge that's operating 20 times faster than the IR-1 centrifuge that is currently used … you could build a clandestine enrichment facility that is relatively small, but its output would be extremely impressive because it could enrich the same amount of uranium as one of the big plants like Natanz. Once you get smaller enrichment at undeclared sites – the same is true with weaponization – the sites can be the size of a room in a school." *Israeli Foreign Ministry Director General Dore Gold, July 22, 2015.*

c.   "Most people that I know believe that **Iran will continue to be a revolutionary country**, and that's what **bothers all of the others in the region**, that this is going to **continue the expansion of power**, that they will be at a disadvantage, and they **can't count on the United States**." *Former Secretary of Defense William Cohen with the Clinton Administration, June 2015, Bloomberg interview.*

d.   The Ayatollah and Iranian leaders continue to chant "**Death to America**" and "**Death to Israel**" on a regular basis in public and throughout the time period encompassed by the nuclear negotiations.

  i.   "I think they have a policy of opposition to us and of great enmity, but I have no specific knowledge of a plan by Iran to actually destroy us." *John Kerry testifying before the House as he expresses a lack of concern regarding Iranian threats stated above during hearings regarding the Iranian nuclear agreement.*

  ii. "Just because Iranian hardliners chant "**Death to America**" [or "Death to Israel"] does not mean that that's what all Iranians believe." *Obama, American University speech, August 5, 2015. Obama is running interference for Iran.*

e.   Former Iranian President Ayatollah **Akbar Hashemi Rafsanjani** stated on July 6, 2015, during the final stages of the Vienna nuclear negotiations, the "presence of the forged **Israeli regime is temporary**, as eventually one day this alien existence, that has been urged into the body of an ancient nation and a historical region, **will be wiped off the map**."

f.   **Iranian AEOI spokesman** Behrouz Kiamalvandi **threatened UN IAEA Director General Amano** by stating, "In a letter to Yukiya Amano, we underlined that if the secrets of the agreement (side deals between Iran and the IAEA) are revealed, we will lose our trust in the Agency; and **despite the U.S. Congress's pressures, he didn't give any information to them … Had he done so, he himself would have been harmed**." *Obama is downplaying and shielding Iranian coercion and blackmail.*

g.   "Moderate" Iranian President Rouhani threatens war if the JCPOA is rejected by Congress or the P5+1 by stating, "The first line is diplomats and the second line is generals. **Diplomats should be backed by generals. If they fail, it is the generals' turn to come forward**." *August 2015.*

h.   In January 2016, the IRGC captured two high speed high tech Navy patrol boats, and humiliated the United States by releasing pictures of U.S. soldiers on their knees with their hands in the air at gunpoint. Obama admits he is not embarrassed by these photos via White House officials.

i.   In February 2016, Director of Intelligence Clapper testified before the Senate Armed Services Committee stating, "Iran probably views the Joint Comprehensive Plan of Action (JCPOA) as a means to remove sanctions while preserving some of its nuclear capabilities, as well as the option to eventually expand its nuclear infrastructure. … Iran's perception of how the JCPOA helps it achieve its overall strategic goals will dictate the level of its adherence to the agreement over time."

j.   In February 2016, Iran announced via its ambassador to Lebanon that they would pay $7000 to the family of any Palestinian terrorist who was killed while attempting to kill Israelis. They would also pay $30,000 to any Palestinian family who subsequently had their home destroyed in response to the anti-Israel terrorism. This funding was more readily available after Obama lifted sanctions on Iran with the JCPOA. Obama's sanctions relief and cash transfer to Iran are being used to directly fund the killing of Jews.

k.   The Iranians test fired ballistic missiles capable of carrying nuclear weapons in the fall of 2015 and the spring of 2016 in violation of UNSC resolutions, and inscribed on the missiles, "Israel does not have the right to exist."

l.   Domestic Iranian recruiting videos released in April 2016 are aimed at Iranian boys who will carry on Iran's war against Israel. They state, "Let's rise up to save the sacred shrine. I have joined Hossein's army division [IRGC] … On my leader [Ali Khamenei's] orders I am ready to give my life. The goal is not just to free Iraq and Syria. My path is through the sacred shrine [in Syria], but **my goal is to reach Jerusalem**." The Iranian leadership admits that their goal in sending troops to Syria and Iraq, with the blessing of Obama, is to eventually capture Jerusalem from Israel. Obama has already invited Iran into Syria and Iraq.

m.   An Iranian woman who was accused of having an extramarital affair in 2012 was publicly flogged 100 times in the Iranian state of Isfahan in late April 2016.

n.   Presenting the Iranian leadership as moderate was "politically useful to the Obama administration."[150] *Ben Rhodes, 2016 New York Times Magazine interview.* Obama lied.

o.   "Americans should learn from recent historical truths *[IRGC taking control of two U.S. Navy vessels in the Persian Gulf]* … If the Americans and their regional allies *[Saudi Arabia included]* want to pass through the Strait of Hormuz and threaten us, **we will not allow any entry** … If the Americans level threats against us, we can be very dangerous … We have increased and expanded our naval might in order to overcome the military might of the superpowers like America … We have no other enemy in the region except for America." *General Hossein Salami, Deputy Commander of the IRGC, May 5, 2016.* Iran threatens the world it will close down the Strait of Hormuz and block one-third of the world's oil supplies that is shipped through that passage daily. The Iranians were responding to a tentative Republican bill that would threaten Iran with economic reper-cussions if they continued inappropriate behavior (kidnapping American sailors, firing rockets near U.S. aircraft carriers, flying military drones over US warships …). How could a president of the United States agree to strengthen and empower a declared enemy of the United States if he was truly interested in watching out for America's best interests?

p.   "The Americans are aware that if they make even the slightest mistake, their naval vessels will be sunk in the Persian Gulf, the Hormuz Strait, and the Sea of Oman." *IRGC Navy Commander Ali Fadavi, May 10, 2016, IRINN Iranian TV interview.*

q.   "I thought some of the things the White House was saying in terms of believing that lifting the sanctions could, over time, lead the regime in Iran to change its stripes and be-come a normal country, if you will, I always thought that was a stretch." *Former Defense Secretary Robert Gates on Face the Nation, May 15, 2016.*

r.   "Today, only in Lebanon, *[not counting missiles in Syria, Iraq, and Iran – Iran admitted they control tens of thousands of other long-range missiles stationed in many other Middle Eastern countries]* more than 100,000 Qasem missiles are ready for launch … [to] come down on the heart of the Zionist regime and be the prelude for a big collapse in the mod-ern era." *IRGC Brigadier General Hossein Salami, early July 2016.* Obama empowered Iran with sanctions relief and increased its hegemony from Iraq to Lebanon so that it could be in a position to destroy Israel.

s.   "I am concerned that those ballistic missile launches are not consistent with the con-structive spirit demonstrated by the signing of the [JCPOA]." *UN Secretary General Ban Ki-Moon criticizes and doubts Iran's intentions surrounding its provocative ballistic missile tests which are a violation of the JCPOA and Security Council Resolution 2231 as stated in a 2016 UN Security Council report.* **Obama sided with Iran and not the secretary general when U.S. Ambassador Powers told the UN Security Council**, "**The United States strongly disagrees strongly with elements of this report**, including that its con-tent goes beyond the appropriate scope." Obama works for and represents the interests of Iran, regardless of the consequences to the West and the United States.

t.   In mid-July 2016, about one year after the JCPOA was approved by the Congress and **in direct violation of the JCPOA**, Ali Larijani, chairman of the Iranian parliament, sought to reopen Iranian facilities dedicated to nuclear enrichment. Larijani stated, "It is necessary for the [Iranian] Atomic Energy Organization to act in compliance with the law passed on the reopening of the nuclear plant to enrich uranium proportionate to the country's needs."

u.   "Iran has more executions than any country except the People's Republic of China, **in-cluding for homosexuality**; exercises legal brutality against women; supports religious intolerance; has committed violations of the Geneva Conventions against American sailors; provides military support to Bashar Assad as he commits war crimes against the Syrian people; violates UN bans on weapons import and export and ballistic missile testing; and censors information going into Iran and coming out. That's only a partial list."[151] *(Shoshana Bryen, American Thinker, August 2016)*

v.   In August 2016, Iran confirmed it executed a native nuclear scientist, Shahram Amiri, who forwarded information regarding Iran's nuclear program to U.S. government officials.

w.   On August 24, 2016, four IRGC military speed boats, practiced a "high-speed intercept" against a U.S. destroyer in the Strait of Hormuz, and came within 300 yards of the *USS Nitze*. The Iranians may have incorporated stolen technology from the two U.S. Navy high speed boats *[Obama instructed them to surrender to the IRGC in order to facilitate the military technology transfer]* that were commandeered by them in January 2016 into these IRGC vessels, and the Iranians were testing how close they could approach the U.S. ships. In the future, these high-speed Iranian boats will be equipped with anti-ship missiles, which will be able to sink the American vessels. Obama may have ordered the Navy captains not to fire directly upon approaching Iranian ships, unless the Iranians have initiated active hostilities, which will allow the Iranians to fire their missiles at close range before the Americans can return fire. Obama will be applying similar rules of engagement to the Navy that were mandated to America's fighting forces in Iraq and Afghanistan, which may again will lead to significant American losses. Obama directly funded the IRGC with the $1.7 billion for the American hostages, and now the IRGC is using these funds to harass and practice destroying U.S. warships in the Middle East. The following day, multiple IRGC high speed ships were swarming a U.S. destroyer, and came within 200 yards, before the U.S. ship fired warning shots in self-defense. The State Department responded, "We assess the **actions were unsafe**, they were **unprofessional … that behavior is unacceptable** as our ships were in international waters … They unnecessarily escalate tensions." Two weeks later, the IRGC practiced the same swarming techniques upon another U.S. warship and came within 100 yards.

x.   "If America wants to try its luck against us, [it should know that] we are completely capable of mobilizing nine million fighters … The IRGC's ground forces are perhaps five times better than the American army … We have warehouses full [of missiles] in Tehran, Zanjan [in northwest Iran] and Oshnavieh [in Western Azerbaijan Province in northwest Iran] that can strike Tel Aviv. If only a single [Israeli] shell would strike anywhere in this country, so that we can flatten Tel Aviv."[152] *Mofhen Rafighdoost, previous minister of the IRGC. Early October 2016.*

y.   "The whole world should know that **the IRGC will be in the U.S.** and Europe **very soon.**" *Salar Abnoush, deputy coordinator of Iran's Khatam-al-Anbia Garrison, an IRGC command front.*[153] *Early November 2016.* Obama's 2016 $1.7 billion cash payment to the IRGC for the American hostages is funding Iran's infiltration of the United States and Europe with its elite terrorist forces.

z.   "**It is now time for the Islamic conquests**. After the liberation of Aleppo, **Bahrain's** hopes will be realized and **Yemen** will be happy with the defeat of the enemies of Islam." *IRGC General Hossein Salami, December 16, 2016.* Iran states they are building the caliphate and that they are targeting Bahrain and America's gulf allies, including Saudi Arabia, next for defeat. With these statements, Iran is targeting Mecca for a takeover, since Bahrain is adjacent to Saudi Arabia and the Yemenite Houthi rebels fighting Saudi Arabia are supported by Iran. Since one of Obama's major policy objectives during his whole presidency has been to empower Iran (pathway for nuclear weapons / JCPOA, sanctions relief, billions in untraceable cash for American hostages, Boeing deals …), Obama is supporting the downfall of one of America's long-term allies in the Middle East and the creation of an Islamic caliphate dominated by Iran.

aa. The world as we speak is united in **horror at the savage assaults by the Syrian regime and its Russian and Iranian allies on the city of Aleppo** … Responsibility for this brutality lies in one place alone, with the Assad regime and its allies, Russia and **Iran**, and **this blood and these atrocities are on their hands**. *Obama, Press Conference, December 16, 2016. Too little, too late.* With one month left in his last term and for the first time in his presidency, Obama openly recognizes the true nature of the Iranian regime, but only after he has paved their path to obtaining a nuclear arsenal, allowed them to expand their influence throughout the Middle East, and rewarded them with over $150 billion in sanctions relief. Obama evaluated Iran critically only to document for the historical record that he was aware of the negative aspects of the Iranian regime. Obama always supported Iran since he was one of the world leaders who welcomed them to insert their troops into Iraq and Syria under the guise to help fight ISIS. Obama ultimately wants IRGC troops on Israel's northern border.

bb. According to *The Jerusalem Post* in early 2017, Iran most likely **violated terms of the arms embargo sanctioned by the UNSC.** "The United Nations chief expressed concern to the Security Council that Iran may have violated an arms embargo by supplying weapons and missiles to Lebanese Shi'ite group Hezbollah, according to a confidential report, seen by *Reuters* on Sunday. The second bi-annual report, due to be discussed by the 15-member council on Jan. 18, also cites an accusation by France that an arms shipment seized in the northern Indian Ocean in March was from Iran and likely bound for Somalia or Yemen … In a televised speech broadcast by Al Manar TV on 24 June

2016, Hassan Nasrallah, the Secretary-General of Hezbollah, stated that the budget of Hezbollah, its salaries, expenses, weapons and missiles all came from the Islamic Republic of Iran," Ban wrote in the report. "I am very concerned by this statement, which suggests that transfers of arms and related material from the Islamic Republic of Iran to Hezbollah may have been undertaken contrary (to a Security Council resolution)," Ban said."[154]

cc.   In early February 2017, Mojtaba Zonour, a former IRGC official and member of Iran's National Security and Foreign Policy Commission, stated that Iran would strike Israel with its missile arsenal if the Trump administration attacked Iran in any capacity. He stated, "If the enemy makes a mistake … **only seven minutes is needed for the Iranian missile to hit Tel Aviv**." Iran is holding Israel hostage to counter a tougher American foreign policy advanced by the new Trump administration. An Israeli policy to counter Iranian threats should make it very clear to the Iranians that if one missile is launched that targets any Israeli territory, especially Tel Aviv, then Israel has the right to strike Iran with any weapons (including nuclear weapons) in its arsenal that will ensure Iran will never threaten the Jewish state again for at least one to two generations. All nuclear sites, military installations, political command and control centers should be targeted. If Iran makes any attempt to destroy the Jewish state, Israel has the right to destroy Iran, which means Israel must target multiple major cities and military installations with a counter strike. Iran must be decimated to the extent that parallels the German and Japanese states at the end of World War II which forced them to sign unconditional surrenders in order to ensure the survival of their countries. As Iran is holding Israel hostage in order to deter Trump, Israel must hold Gaza, the PA, and Hezbollah hostage, so that any unprovoked attack by Iran against Israel will lead to the destruction of Hamas, the PA, Hezbollah with Israel's subsequent seizure of their respective territories and concomitant population transfers so that these societies can never threaten Israel again. Since Hamas and Hezbollah are embedded in the Gaza and Lebanese civilian populations, all of Gaza and southern Lebanon are fair targets. Israel has every right to pursue this aggressive strategy since the Hamas, Hezbollah, and the PA are all formal Iranian allies, and any attack by Iran against Israel is an uncontestable declaration of war against Israel by Iran and its partners. It is interesting to note that Iran called its recent provocative ballistic missile tests "defensive in nature," and then threatened Israel with an unprovoked first strike against Tel Aviv, a major civilian target, which is a war crime.

dd.   "[a] Tehran Revolutionary Court has sentenced the poets Fatemeh Ekhtesari and Mehdi Moosavi to 9 years and 6 months and 99 lashes, and 11 years and 99 lashes, respectively, on charges of 'insulting the sacred' for the social criticism expressed in their poetry." The flogging sentences were as a result "of their shaking hands with strangers (a person of the opposite sex who is not one's immediate kin or spouse) [.]" Thus, "[t]hese sentences show that 'repression in Iran is intensifying,' said Hadi Ghaemi, executive director of the International Campaign for Human Rights in Iran. 'Hardliners aren't just going after political activists, they are determined to stamp out any social or cultural expression with which they disagree.'"[155] *(American Thinker, April 2017)*

ee. "If the ISIS territory is occupied by Iran's Revolutionary Guards or Shia forces trained and directed by it, **the result could be a territorial belt reaching <u>from Tehran to Beirut</u>**, which **could mark the emergence of an <u>Iranian radical empire</u>**." *Henry Kissinger, "Chaos and Order in a Changing World," Capx.co, August 2, 2017.* Iran controls Lebanon since Hezbollah controls Lebanon and Iran controls Hezbollah. Obama invited IRGC troops into Iraq and Syria under the guise of fighting ISIS. As ISIS is being destroyed during the Trump presidency, IRGC troops remain and Iraninan bases are being established in the heart of the Middle East. Even though Iranian leaders boasted of the high number of Americans killed with their IEDs in Iraq, Obama allowed them to expand their hegemony in the crescent between Tehran and Beirut, which supported Iranian interests over American, Western, Gulf State and Israeli interests. Kissinger's fears of an Iranian radical empire, which was created as a direct result of Obama's policies, are already a reality. This was confirmed in *The Jerusalem Post* which stated, "Iran is moving in to fill vacuums in regions in the Middle East created by the retreat of Islamic State, Mossad head Yossi Cohen told the cabinet on Sunday at the weekly cabinet meeting. The Mossad head warned that Iran's expansion in the region through its proxies in Syria, Lebanon, Iraq and Yemen is currently the central development in the Middle East."[156] Iran continues to threaten to destroy Israel and the United States, and has their sights set on destabilizing Saudi Arabia and the Sunni Gulf states. Iran is not abiding by international norms. With Iran on the path to becoming a major nuclear power and sanctions relief moving forward, Kissinger knows there are major problems on the horizon.

37. Regarding Iran agreeing to nuclear negotiations, Obama stated that we are on "a new path toward a world that is more secure – **a future in which we can verify that Iran's nuclear program is peaceful and that it cannot build a nuclear weapon**." *November 2013.*

   a. "Let's get something straight so we don't kid each other … **They already have paved a path to a bomb's worth of material. Iran could get there now if they walked away in two to three months without a deal**." *Vice President Joe Biden (late April 2015) admits that Iran can presently build up to eight nuclear warheads within two to three months.* A deal is necessary as a policy of containment and not to prevent Iran from going nuclear.

   i. "This deal actually pushes Iran further away from a bomb. **And there's a permanent prohibition on Iran ever having a nuclear weapon**." *Obama's weekly address, July 18, 2015.* In the best-case scenario, Iran will be building nuclear weapons in

10 years, when the agreement expires. The president and the vice president need to make sure their talking points are in synch. Obama lied.

b. An Iranian purchase of advanced nuclear enrichment technology was blocked by the Czech Republic after concerns of misrepresentation after the JCPOA was finalized.

c. On June 21, 2015, the Iranian Parliament passed a bill that stated, "The IAEA, within the framework of the safeguard agreement is allowed to carry out conventional inspections of nuclear sites … **access to military, security and sensitive non-nuclear sites, as well as documents and scientists, is forbidden**." Lawmakers were chanting "death to America" while voting.

38. **Future Obama Lie**: "I am **reaffirming our iron-clad commitment to the security of our Gulf partners** … The United States will stand by our GCC partners against external attack and will deepen and extend cooperation that we have … The United States is **prepared to work jointly** with GCC member states to deter and confront an external threat to any GCC state's territorial integrity that is **inconsistent with the U.N. Charter**. In the event of such aggression, or the threat of such aggression, the United States stands **ready to work with our GCC partners** to urgently determine what actions **may be appropriate**, using the means at **our collective disposal**, including the **potential use of military force** *[all options are on the table – again?]*, for the defense of our GCC partners. And let me underscore, **the United States keeps our commitments**. *[Obama practicing taqiyya with the guardians of Mecca. Now that's chutzpah.]*" *Obama's remarks after meeting with the six-nation Gulf Cooperative Council (GCC) at Camp David on May 14, 2015, after trying to pacify moderate Arab fears over the upcoming nuclear agreement with Iran, which will strengthen Iran by paving their way to nuclear weapons and relieving economic sanctions.* The Gulf leaders remembered Obama's failed commitments to Mubarak, Ukraine, Poland, the Czech Republic, Israel, Iraq, Yemen, and the Marshall Islands. Obama also supported the Arab Spring elements in the Gulf States during his first term, where a successful revolution would have turned those countries into Muslim Brotherhood political entities.

a. "He is clearly irritated that foreign-policy orthodoxy compels him to treat Saudi Arabia as an ally. And of course, he decided early on, in the face of great criticism, that he wanted to reach out to America's most ardent Middle Eastern foe, Iran." *("The Obama Doctrine")* The fact that Iran invaded the U.S embassy in Tehran and took its personnel hostage, continually threatens to initiate a second Holocaust, is allied with al-Qaeda, participated in the 9-11 terror attacks in New York City and Washington, and is the number one state sponsor or terrorism in the world, are not issues for Obama.

b. "Since the signing of the deal, little has changed in the field of the United States' dialogue with the Gulf States on Iran-related issues, mainly the Syrian, Iraqi and Yemeni conflicts … Since the signing of the deal with Iran, the White House failed to give the other camp [GCC] security guarantees that would alleviate the dangers that the deal ushered in … Meanwhile, Iran has pursued its efforts to take over the region. … It is inconceivable that the United States would open up to Iran and at the same time allow them to threaten the interests of other countries in the region, and demand that they be generous with them to boot … **Whatever Obama says, he is clearly not interested in a special alliance with the Gulf States and doesn't see them as allies** … Obama's hands-off approach has failed – it led to anarchy and to the rise of al-Qaeda and the Islamic State."[157] *Abdulrahman Al Rashed, leading Saudi Arabian columnist with close ties to the Royal Saudi family. Former editor-in-chief of Asharq al Awsat newspaper and the Al Arabiya news network.* Al Rashed is commenting on the relationship between Saudi Arabia and the United States after Obama's visit in April 2016. The Saudi leaders realized that Obama views them as an enemy and is allied with Iran. Obama has destroyed the special relationships that the United States has had with Israel, Great Britain and Saudi Arabia – and has reached out to Iran, the Muslim Brotherhood and Cuba. Coupled with the fact that the empowerment of al-Qaeda and ISIS have occurred during Obama's presidency, these events prove Obama is allied with radical Muslims.

c. "Today, Islam in Indonesia is much more Arab in orientation than it was when he lived there, he said. "**Aren't the Saudis your friends**?" Turnbull asked. **Obama smiled**. "**It's complicated**," he said. **Obama's patience with Saudi Arabia has always been limited**. In his first foreign-policy commentary of note, that 2002 speech at the antiwar rally in Chicago, he said, "You want a fight, President Bush? Let's fight to make sure **our so-called allies in the Middle East – the Saudis** and the Egyptians – stop oppressing their own people, and suppressing dissent, and tolerating corruption and inequality." In **the White House** these days, one occasionally hears Obama's National Security Council officials pointedly **reminding visitors that the large majority of 9-11 hijackers were not Iranian**, but Saudi – and **Obama himself rails against Saudi Arabia's state-sanctioned misogyny**, arguing in private that "a country cannot function in the modern world when it is repressing half of its population." In meetings with foreign leaders, Obama has said, 'You can gauge the success of a society by how it treats its women.'"[158] *("The Obama Doctrine")* Obama does not like Saudi Arabia, and would not be upset if the Saudi royal family was overthrown like Mubarak or was eliminated by surrounding political and military powers. A clue that Obama does not like a country is seen when he complains about their human rights records. Saudi Arabia does not treat its women well; Egypt abused its protestors; Israel is an apartheid country; Europe has treated its immigrants poorly. And America is racist – racism is part of America's cultural DNA. Obama's end game in the Middle East is to have Saudi Arabia overthrown by pro-Iranian powers, so Iran and the ayatollahs, and not the Saudi Royal family, will be the guardians of Mecca. Since Islam is the fastest growing religion in the world, Iran's new status as the guardian of Mecca, accompanied with a nuclear arsenal, would make her the true world Islamic superpower, which is Obama's intention.

d.   "The King of Jordan, Abdullah II – already dismayed by what he saw as Obama's illogical desire to distance the U.S. from its traditional Sunni Arab allies and create a new alliance with Iran, Assad's Shia sponsor – complained privately, "I think I believe in American power more than Obama does." The Saudis, too, were infuriated. They had never trusted Obama – he had, long before he became president, referred to them as a "so-called ally" of the U.S. "Iran is the new great power of the Middle East, and the U.S. is the old," Jubeir, the Saudi ambassador in Washington, told his superiors in Riyadh."[159] *("The Obama Doctrine")*

e.   In a 2016 interview with Jeffrey Goldberg, Obama told Saudi Arabia to "share the neighborhood" with Iran when exerting political influence in Iraq and Syria.

39. "America is pursuing a diplomatic resolution to the Iranian nuclear issue, **as part of our commitment to stop the spread of nuclear weapons and pursue the <u>peace and security of a world without them</u>**." *Obama, UN Address, September 24, 2014.* Less than one year later, sources in the Middle East reported that Saudi Arabia would purchase nuclear weapons from Pakistan to counteract the protection of Iran's nuclear infrastructure with a nuclear framework agreement. A former U.S. defense official stated in the *Sunday Times* of Great Britain, "For the Saudis the moment has come … There has been a longstanding agreement in place with the Pakistanis and the House of Saud has now made the strategic decision to move forward."[160] The nuclear arms race in the Middle East is underway, with Egypt and Turkey soon entering the arena, making the Middle East a much more dangerous place.

a.   "Nuclear weapons programs are extremely expensive and there's no question that a lot of the funding of Pakistan's nuclear weapons program was provided by Saudi Arabia … **Given their close relations and close military links**, **it's long been assumed that if the Saudis wanted**, they would call in a commitment, moral or otherwise, **for Pakistan to supply them immediately with nuclear warheads**." *Lord David Owen, England's former foreign secretary, 1977-1979, Sunday Times, May 2015.*

b.   "The administration's intent was to have a counter-proliferation program. And the irony is, it may be just the opposite." *Former Secretary of Defense William Cohen with the Clinton Administration, June 2015 Bloomberg interview.*

c.   Within 24 hours after the Iranian nuclear agreement was announced, Saudi Arabia announced they will work with France to build two nuclear reactors.

d.   In October 2015, the United Arab Emirates signed a contract with Russia that allows the UAE to purchase enriched uranium for their nuclear power program.

e. "We see signs that [Sunni] countries in the Arab world are preparing to acquire nuclear weapons, that they are not willing to sit quietly with Iran on brink of a nuclear or atomic bomb." *Israeli Defense Minister Moshe Ya'alon, February 14, 2016.*

40. "I've said that, in exchange for some **modest** *[downplaying]* relief in sanctions, that **Iran is going to have to freeze its nuclear program, roll back on its stockpiles of very highly enriched uranium, the very stockpiles that Prime Minister Netanyahu had gone before the United Nations, with his picture of the bomb and said that was proof of how dangerous this was** … At that time, everybody said 'this isn't going to work! They're going to cheat, they're not going to abide by it.' And yet, over a year and a half later, **we know that <u>they have abided by the letter</u>** of it." *Obama, Israel Channel 2 Interview, "Uvda," June 2, 2015.* Obama is defending Iran before an Israeli audience with Tehran's talking points. According to an International Atomic Energy Agency (IAEA) report, Iranian nuclear fuel stockpiles have increased 20% over the past 18 months, and 8% since Obama stated a deal was "achieved" with Iran. Obama is lying to the Jews, again.

   a. "U.S. officials announced **Iran conducted another ballistic missile test in defiance of U.N. sanctions on Sunday**, test-firing a Khorramshahr medium-range missile from the test site in Semnan, 140 miles east of Tehran. The missile flew about 600 miles before exploding, according to *Fox News*, which **quotes the relevant U.N. resolution banning such tests by Iran**: U.N. **resolution 2231** – put in place days after the Iran nuclear deal was signed – calls on the Islamic Republic not to conduct such tests. However, this is **at least Iran's second such test since July**. The resolution bars Iran from conducting ballistic missile tests for eight years and went into effect July 20, 2015. Iran is 'called upon **<u>not to undertake any activity related to ballistic missiles designed to be capable of delivering nuclear weapons</u>**, including launches using such ballistic missile technology,' according to the text of the resolution."[161] *(Breitbart, January 30, 2017)* This was Iran's 12th ballistic missile test since the implementation of the JCPOA.

   b. "Recent Iranian actions involving a **provocative ballistic missile launch** and **an attack against a Saudi naval vessel conducted by Iran supported Houthi militants** underscore what should have been clear to the international community all along about Iran's **destabilizing behavior** across the Middle East. The recent ballistic missile launch is also **in defiance of UN Security Council Resolution 2231**, which calls upon Iran 'not to undertake any activity related to ballistic missiles designed to be capable of delivering nuclear weapons, including launches using such ballistic missile technology.' These are just the latest of a series of incidents in the past six months in which **Houthi forces that Iran has trained and armed have struck Emirati and Saudi vessels, and threatened U.S. and allied vessels transiting the Red Sea**. In these and other similar activities, Iran continues to threaten U.S. friends and allies in the region. **<u>The Obama Administration</u>**

failed to respond adequately to Tehran's malignant actions - including weapons transfers, support for terrorism, and other violations of international norms." *Michael Flynn, National Security Advisor to President Trump, February 1, 2017.*

c.   "Members of the National Council of Resistance of Iran (NCRI) presented satellite imagery and intelligence, said to be provided by informants working covertly inside the Iranian military, that indicates the **Iranian regime is far from complying with the terms of the nuclear deal**. Alireza Jafarzadeh, the deputy director of NCRI's Washington office, presented the findings in a presentation covered by major media outlets. He said the People's Mojahedin Organization's network within Iran acquired the information. "We are talking about an **extensive covert operation** by the Iranian regime," Jafarzadeh said. "Our information shows that their activities have been continuing in full gear despite the JCPOA," he said using the acronym for the Joint Comprehensive Plan of Action, the formal name for the nuclear deal. "**The engineering unit that is charged and tasked with actually building the bomb in a secret way for the Iranian regime is called the Organization of Defensive Innovation and Research**," Jafarzadeh said. It is known by its Persian acronym SPND (which is *Sazman-e Pazhouheshhaye Novin-e Defa'i* in Farsi). It has seven subdivisions, each of which carries out a certain portion of Iran's nuclear program … On Thursday, President Donald Trump accused the Iranian regime of cheating on the nuclear agreement during a joint news conference with Italian Prime Minister Paolo Gentiloni: "They are not living up to the spirit of the agreement; I can tell you that." … Jafarzadeh noted that NCRI's satellite imagery was also **focused on the Parchin military base**. Parchin and other facilities were **deemed "off-limits" to IAEA inspectors**. These locations were the sites where the Iranian regime had previously developed its nuclear program, and it is believed the Iranian regime is using the Parchin site to develop their nuclear weapons program covertly."[162] *(Breitbart, April 22, 2017)*

d.   During the summer of 2017, photographs were released proving that **Iran was transferring their soldiers and militants to Syria via Iran Air**, **an Iranian commercial airline carrier**, in violation of international agreements and the JCPOA. Iranian forces are supporting President Assad and are opposed to American allies in the region. These illegal troops transfers started during the Obama administration, and Obama was probably briefed on these illegal activities, yet did nothing. Iran is building its forces and cementing its influence from Beirut to Tehran, and is increasing its ability to harm Israel.

41. "The deal we are negotiating will take a nuclear bomb **off the table for the next twenty years** … **A military solution will not fix it**. Even if the United States participates, it would temporarily slow down an Iranian nuclear program but it will not eliminate it … **Sanctions won't do it**, **a military solution is temporary**, the deal we are negotiating **will take a nuclear bomb off the table for the next <u>twenty years</u>**." *Obama is discussing the Iranian*

nuclear framework agreement with Channel 2 News, Israel, **June 2, 2015**. This is the first time Obama has mentioned that the agreement would stipulate that Iran would not be able to manufacture weapons for twenty years. Earlier, he had mentioned thirteen years as the time frame with the preliminary agreement. He is now adamant that a military attack will not work, thus he will not use American forces against Iran, no matter what. He also admits sanctions won't work, even though within the past few weeks, Obama had been advocating snap back sanctions as an effective tool to coerce Iran to abide by any agreements. Sanctions had been working up until 2013, when Obama saved the Iranian economy by significantly easing them. **Obama discarded sanctions and military action as effective policy options, the two most effective policies that kept Iran at the negotiating table, and thus, Obama is protecting Iran from the two major potential sources of harm to their nation**. Obama proved that his talk of "all options are on the table" was a lie. Obama is working for Iran, and blatantly lying about a twenty-year prohibition.

a. "A final agreement will have to specifically address concerns about a potential covert nuclear weapon program. If we reach an agreement and Iran ends up flouting its obligations, we will know, and **we will have preserved all our options – including <u>economic</u> and <u>military measures</u>** – to make sure that Iran can never acquire a nuclear weapon … if Iran violates its commitments, we will have the full capability to snap sanctions back into place and reverse the relief … **No administration has done more for Israel's security than this one**." *Jacob Lew, Obama's Secretary of the Treasury, speaking at the annual Jerusalem Post Conference in New York City,* <u>**June 6, 2015**</u>. Apparently Secretary Lew did not pay attention to Obama's Israeli interview less than one week earlier. Lew was jeered and heckled throughout his speech by a predominantly Jewish audience, who were shocked by Lew's dishonesty or naiveté.

b. "We have sent a clear message to the Iranians – though we closed the deal, we still have not closed the account. I hope that solutions will be reached diplomatically, but if necessary, **there is also a military option**." *Obama, in an interview with the BBC on July 24, 2015,* ***reverses his position*** *and reconfirms the potential of a military option.* In Israel, in June, Obama stated, "A military solution will not fix it." Even the Iranian Foreign Minister Zarif mocked Obama and Kerry's threats by bringing the attention to the "**uselessness of such empty threats** against the nation of Iran and the resistance of the nation of Iran" after the deal was concluded.

42. "So, it is true, that in these first six months, we have not shut down all of their production of **any ballistic missile** that could have anything to do with delivery of a nuclear weapon but that is indeed **is going to be part of something that has to be addressed, as part of a comprehensive agreement**." *Wendy Sherman, Under Secretary of State, Lead Negotiator with Iran, February 4, 2014.* Ballistic missiles will not be part of any nuclear agreement with Iran.

Relief of sanctions will fund the development of these missiles that will deliver future nuclear weapons to Europe, the United States, and Israel. Sherman lied. In October 2015, Iran test fired an advanced surface-to-surface ballistic missile in violation of the JCPOA. Obama did nothing. On November 21, 2015, Iran test fired a medium range ballistic missile capable of carrying a nuclear warhead in violation of two UNSC resolutions. The Obama administration addressed this issue by stating they had "no further comment."

43. "**U.S. sanctions** on Iran for terrorism, human rights abuses, and **ballistic missiles will remain in place under the deal**." *April 2, 2015 Lausanne, U.S. factsheet regarding the future Iran nuclear framework agreement.* Obama planned on delisting 23 out of 24 Iranian banks that have been on the sanctions list, including the Central Bank of Iran, which is critical for funding Iran's ballistic missile development program, its military operations, and its foreign proxies involved in terrorism including Hamas, Hezbollah, and the Houthi rebels fighting against Saudi Arabia.

44. "**Today, the United States -- together with our allies and partners -- has reached a historic understanding with Iran**, which, <u>**if fully implemented, will prevent it from obtaining a nuclear weapon**</u>." *Obama, Statement by the President on the Framework to Prevent Iran from Obtaining a Nuclear Weapon, April 2, 2015. Preliminary Agreement for the JCPOA.* Iran kept thousands of functioning advanced centrifuges, and will be able to produce nuclear weapons in ten years, at the end of the agreement. Other lies in Obama's Rose Garden announcement include:

   a. "**As President and Commander-in-Chief, I have no greater responsibility than the security of the American people. And I am convinced that if this framework leads to a final, comprehensive deal**, it will make our country, our allies, and our world safer." A nuclear armed Iran with an intact ballistic missile program funded with $150 billion in sanctions relief and $1.7 billion in cash for four American hostages is a major threat to America, its allies, and Israel. Funding Iran, the number one state sponsor of terrorism with the above resources, does not make the world safer. Even Kerry and Rice admitted that the JCPOA would be funding Islamic terrorism.

   b. "**Iran has met all of its obligations. It eliminated its stockpile of dangerous nuclear material**." Obama is defending Iran. Since Iran was able to keep its nuclear program intact, it still possessed significant quantities of dangerous nuclear materials.

   c. "**And it is a good deal, a deal that meets our core objectives**. This framework would cut off every pathway that Iran could take to develop a nuclear weapon. **Iran will face strict limitations on its program, and Iran has also agreed to** <u>**the most robust and intrusive inspections and transparency**</u> **regime ever negotiated for any nuclear program in history**. So this deal is not based on trust, it's based on **unprecedented verification**." No anytime anywhere inspections. Iran can produce nuclear weapons at the end of the agreement, thus the JCPOA paved the way for Iran to produce nuclear weapons. American inspectors are not allowed in Iran, and the IRGC clears all inspectors entering Iran. No access to military sites. Iran self-inspects contentious sites. Obama's promise of "strict limitations on its program," was a lie. Obama allowed Iran to have the ability to restart its production of 20% enriched uranium almost instantaneously, which was confirmed by Iran's atomic chief and vice president, Ali Akbar Salehi, who stated in August 2017 in response to Trump's threat of more sanctions or challenging the JCPOA, "If there is a plan for a reaction and a challenge, we will definitely surprise them … If we make the determination, **we are able to resume 20% enrichment in at most five days.**" Twenty percent enriched uranium is the threshold for producing nuclear weapons.

d. "If Iran cheats, the world will know it. **If we see something suspicious, we will inspect it**. Iran's past efforts to weaponize its program will be addressed." *Obama*. All lies.

e. **"If there is backsliding on the part of the Iranians, if the verification and inspection mechanisms don't meet the specifications of our nuclear and security experts, there will be no deal.**" Obama would never walk away from his landmark nuclear deal with Iran. It's his legacy.

f. **"Given the importance of this issue, I have instructed my negotiators to <u>fully brief</u> Congress and the American people on the substance of the deal, and I welcome a robust debate in the weeks and months to come.**" Obama withheld the secret side deals from Congress and the American public. Obama spied on political opponents of the JCPOA, and harassed pro-Israel politicians with anti-Semitic insinuations. With these actions, and his 'echo chamber' disseminating fake news, Obama stifled any robust debate in the public forum.

g. **"Since Iran's Supreme Leader has <u>issued a fatwa against the development of nuclear weapons</u>, this framework gives Iran the opportunity to verify that its program is, in fact, peaceful. It demonstrates that if Iran complies with its international obligations, then it can fully rejoin the community of nations, thereby <u>fulfilling the extraordinary talent and aspirations of the Iranian people</u>. That would be good for Iran, and it would be good for the world.**" Obama advances the interests of Iran over those of the United States. There is no official Iranian fatwa prohibiting the development of nuclear weapons.

h. **"It's no secret that the Israeli Prime Minister and I don't agree about whether the United States should move forward with a peaceful resolution to the Iranian issue.**" Obama lies about the intentions of the Israeli prime minister by insinuating that Netanyahu wants the United States to engage in a war with Iran.

i. **"I want to express my thanks to our tireless -- and I mean tireless -- Secretary of State John Kerry and our entire negotiating team. They have worked so hard to**

make this progress." Valerie Jarrett [and Obama] negotiated the details of the JCPOA and the secret side deals – not John Kerry. Kerry even admitted before Congress that he did not know about the existence of the secret side deals.

45. "What I want to emphasize is **this negotiation was intentionally restricted to the nuclear issue**, get the nuclear bomb issue off the table, we hope, for a long time. That has other implications. For example, **things like arms embargoes, ballistic missile sanctions, those stay in place, strictly focused on the nuclear issues**." *U.S. Energy Secretary Ernest Moniz, one of the lead negotiators with the Iran nuclear agreement, April 3, 2015.*

   a. "Even if it works [keeping Iran one year away from a nuclear breakout], is it worth the cost? – This is the debate over the list of gifts the Obama administration had to give to the Iranians to induce them to accept the deal. This part of the debate includes: giving Iran a $150 billion windfall, **dropping the conventional arms embargo, shredding the sanctions regime against Iran including ballistic missile** and terrorism sanctions, obligating the international community to perfect Iran's nuclear program, and – now – lifting restrictions on Iran's nuclear weapons proliferation network [and removing sanctions against most of the individuals involved in building Iran's nuclear and ballistic missiles program]. It also includes endangering the international financial system by delisting toxic Iranian banks, eroding domestic separation of powers by having the President do an end-run around Congress."[163] *(Jay Solomon, The Wall Street Journal, July 2015)*

46. "They have to do it. It will be done. **If there is going to be a deal, it will be done ... It will be part of a final agreement. It has to be.**" *Secretary of State Kerry with Leslie Stahl interview discussing **the need to have Iran disclose its past military nuclear activities**. April 8, 2015.*

   a. "Iran specifically accounting for what they did at one point in time or another. We know what they did. We have no doubt. We have absolute knowledge with respect to certain military activities they were engaged in. **What we're concerned about is going forward**." *Secretary of State Kerry, June 2015.* Kerry lied just two months earlier.

   b. The United States is "**not fixated on Iran specifically accounting for what they did** at one point in time or another ... What we're concerned about is going forward." *Kerry, June, 2015.* Kerry backtracked on the administration's promise to obtain transparency on Iran's military involvement with their nuclear program.

   c. "World powers are prepared to accept a nuclear agreement with Iran that doesn't immediately answer questions about past atomic weapons work, U.S. and Western officials said, even though Washington had previously declared such concerns must be resolved in any final deal."[164] *(Bradley Klapper, Associated Press, June 2015)*

47. "My hope is they can achieve an agreement ... I've said from the start, **I will walk away from the negotiations if in fact it's a bad deal** ... *[if the Iranians don't agree on proper*

inspections and guidelines] … Then we're not going to get a deal." *Obama, June 30, 2015, after the fifth major negotiation extension.* Obama's threat to walk away from the negotiations is cut from the same cloth as "the United States will not continue to negotiate indefinitely … Our patience is not unlimited." and "we cannot allow Iran to obtain a nuclear weapon, it's unacceptable, and I will do everything that's required to prevent it." All of Obama's talking points since 2008 have been lies, and so is his promise to walk away from a bad deal. As in all of Obama's policy initiatives, whether it is Obamacare or Obamatrade, an agreement is always finalized amid sensational headlines and the high possibility of failure. Unfortunately, these headlines are for American and world consumption, so that the public feels Obama has been negotiating in good faith and with American interests at heart. Valerie Jarrett's secret Iranian negotiations most likely finalized the Iranian agreement before Kerry and State Department officials commenced the final round of talks. Since Obama's goals are to relieve the economic sanctions and allow Iran to become a major nuclear military power, Obama will approve any agreement that will give Iran space to continue their nuclear development program, while simultaneously building their economy. With Obama's semantics, any deal that is approved by him is "not a bad deal."

a. "It is becoming increasingly difficult to accept that the Obama administration conducted negotiations with Iran in good faith … Indeed, one can think of nothing else that would undermine US credibility more than acceptance of the deal. It not only vacates a string of UN resolutions, which, as Henry Kissinger pointed out in an appearance before the Senate Armed Services Committee, were designed "to deny Iran the capability to develop a military nuclear option," but makes a mockery of previous robustly declared objectives of the administration itself. After all, Obama himself pledged during his 2012 election campaign: "The deal we'll accept is they end their nuclear program. It's very straightforward."[165] *(Martin Sherman, The Jerusalem Post, September 2015)*

b. "We know that in five to eight years, respectively, the international ban on conventional weapons and ballistic missiles will be lifted. We know that in 10 to 15 years, most limits on Iran's ability to enrich uranium and reprocess plutonium—two key steps in building a nuclear weapon – will expire. And we know that, once most of these constraints are gone, we'll have nothing more than a promise from the mullahs that they won't build a bomb. Meanwhile, an Iranian regime buoyed by a $150 billion windfall will be free to revamp its nuclear weapons program under the guise of international legitimacy. The administration can spin it any way it likes but **this was a bad deal**." *Speaker of the House Paul Ryan, 2016*

c.   **"Every promise made to the American people about the Obama nuclear agreement has been broken**. We were promised a "world-class" verification process. Instead, the Iranians are allowed in key instances to verify themselves. We were promised the agreement would "block every pathway" to an Iranian nuclear weapon. Instead, the Obama-Clinton agreement virtually guarantees an Iranian nuclear weapon, gives them access to the latest in centrifuge technology … We were promised that non-nuclear sanctions, including those that block Iran's access to hard currency and our financial systems, would remain in place. Instead, the Obama administration has paid the mullahs at least $1.7 billion in cash … which was ransom for the release of American hostages. **In case there is any doubt that the regime will use these funds to support terror, Iran's parliament recently passed Article 22 of its 2016-2017 budget**, **mandating that all such funds be transferred directly to the Iranian military** … America's commander in chief has become the **money launderer in chief** *[because Obama is an agent for Iran]* for the world's leading state sponsor of terror."[166] *Former Vice President Dick Cheney, The Wall Street Journal*

48.   "Skeptics argued Iran would cheat, that we could not verify their compliance, and the interim agreement would fail. Instead, it has succeeded exactly as intended … <u>**Iran has met all of its obligations**</u>. **It eliminated its stockpile of dangerous nuclear material**." *Obama, Statement by the President on the Framework to Prevent Iran from Obtaining a Nuclear Weapon, April 2, 2015.* Obama discussing Iran's progress in honoring interim agreements and sounding like the ayatollah's press secretary advancing Tehran's negotiation talking points. The Obama administration also sounded like attorneys representing the Iranians when they backtracked on gaining access to suspected Iranian military sites engaged in nuclear activity by stating, "the United States of America wouldn't allow anybody to get into every military site, so that's not appropriate."

a.   "… the United States revised its criteria for Iran meeting its obligations." *Washington's Institute for Science and International Security.*

b.   "Once you say they are allowed to enrich, the game is pretty much up in terms of how do you sustain an inspection regime in a country that has **carried on secret programs for 17 years** and is **still determined to maintain as much of that secrecy as possible**." *Former Defense Secretary Cohen who served under Democratic President Clinton.*

c.   "Two reports regarding Iran's attempts to illicitly and clandestinely procure technology (industry computers, high-speed cameras, cable fiber, and pumps) for its nuclear and ballistic missile programs have recently been published. They show that Iran's procurement continues apace, if not faster than before the Joint Plan of Action was signed in November 2013. But fear of potentially embarrassing negotiators and derailing negotiations has made some states reluctant to report Tehran's illegal efforts. If these countries have hesitated to expose Iran during the negotiations, it is more likely they will refrain from reporting after a deal is struck."[167] *(Benjamin Weinthal and Emanuele Ottolenghi, The Weekly Standard, July 2015).*

d. During the summer of 2015, satellite photos documented that Iran was sanitizing the grounds surrounding the Parchin military facilities before nuclear inspections.

e. "Startling new evidence from **German intelligence** reports shows **the Tehran regime is working to illegally obtain technology and know-how to advance its nuclear weapons and missile programs**, despite the 2015 agreement to curb its nuclear program. A report from the state of Hamburg showed that "there is no evidence of a complete about-face in Iran's atomic polices in 2016" [after the Islamic Republic signed the JCPOA deal with Western powers in 2015, aimed at restricting Tehran's nuclear program in exchange for sanctions relief]. Iran sought missile carrier technology necessary for its rocket program.""[168] *(The Weekly Standard, July 7, **2017**)*

49. "**International inspectors will have unprecedented access not only to Iranian nuclear facilities** *[not American inspectors, not IAEA inspectors at Parchin whose facilities have been sanitized multiple times in the past and where Iran says they will do their own inspections, and unknown secretive side deals between the IAEA and Iran make inspections undependable and non-verifiable]*, but to the entire supply chain that supports Iran's nuclear program, from uranium mills that provide the raw materials to the centrifuge production and storage facilities that support the program. I am confident that we can show that **this deal is good for the security of the United States, for our allies, and for the world** *[taqiyya - Israel, Saudi Arabia, the GCC, Egypt, and a majority of Americans disagree]*."[169] *Obama, April 2, 2015.* In 1994, President Clinton declared with the North Korean nuclear agreement, "This is a **good deal** for the United States. North Korea will **freeze** and then dismantle its nuclear program. South Korea and our other **allies will be better protected**. The entire **world will be safer as we slow the spread of nuclear weapons**. The United States and international **inspectors will carefully monitor North Korea** to make sure it keeps its commitments." Despite Clinton's assurances, North Korea developed, tested, and produced nuclear arms. Will history repeat itself, like the speeches?

a. "American and Canadian inspectors cannot be sent to Iran … *[and IAEA inspectors will not see]* "**sensitive and military documents**." *Deputy Foreign Minister Abbas Araghchi, July 30, 2015.* Inspections may be a farce since sensitive and military documents may pertain to almost all aspects of the Iranian nuclear program. These conditions guarantee Iranian non-compliance.

CHAPTER 9

Iran Lies, Post - JCPOA

"One can hardly imagine a more grossly misleading representation of the [Iranian nuclear] deal – so much so that it is difficult not to find it strongly **reminiscent of the Muslim tactic of taqiyya** (the religiously sanctioned deception of non-Muslims)." *Martin Sherman, Op Ed page Jerusalem Post, "Into the Fray: Iran – Reaping the Storm that Barack Sowed …" July 17, 2015.*

1. **"If Iran violates the deal, sanctions can be snapped back into place**." *Obama, April 2015, warning Iran of snap back sanctions if Iran does not comply with the terms of any future deal. Obama also threatened that if Iran cheats,* "**sanctions that have helped cripple the Iranian economy will snap back in place**." *Obama repeated this misleading and inaccurate position during his weekly address on July 18, 2015,* "If Iran violates this deal, the sanctions we imposed that have helped cripple the Iranian economy [which he rescued in 2013 with the interim agreement], **the sanctions that helped make this deal possible**, **would snap back into place <u>promptly</u>**."

    a. "There can be **no automaticity, none whatsoever**." *Russian UN Ambassador Vitaly Churkin, May 2015. Why not?* There is too much money at stake with respect to military sales, nuclear support, and increased trade with a resurgent Iranian economy. A stronger nuclear Iran will diminish American influence in the Middle East, which is another undeclared goal for Obama, Russia, and China.

    b. "**The arms embargo is not tied to snapback … It is tied to a separate set of obligations**. So, they are not in material breach of the nuclear agreement for violating the arms piece of it." *Kerry, August 2015.* There are sections of the Iranian nuclear agreement where violations by Iran are not subject to the re-imposition of sanctions.

    c. "**Since November 2013**, when the Obama administration – largely on its own – negotiated an **interim deal with Iran that suspended key sanctions provisions immediately, made a commitment not to pass new sanctions during negotiations, and promised to remove sanctions once a deal was reached, U.S. proclamations**

about sanctions have gradually lost credibility. Tehran does not believe the Obama administration can re-impose sanctions. America's allies do not believe Washington will even try to roll back the **business stampede that the demise of sanctions will unleash**. And with signals from both Tehran and European capitals that **sanctions are unlikely to ever be reinstated, global business corporations don't believe it either ... Russia and China have shown no desire to expand sanctions further** ... what the Obama administration did prior to November 2013 to undermine the Iranian economy was unprecedented. By September 2012, Iran's currency was in free fall. Its foreign currency reserves were depleted. Inflation and unemployment spun out of control ... Its ability to trade and transact business was crippled. With such swift and devastating results, Washington was in a position to dictate terms of surrender ... The overarching goal was to force Iranian concessions that, without sufficient leverage, Tehran would be unwilling to make. **Yet as soon as the interim nuclear agreement was reached ... the goal of sanctions was to return Iran to negotiations**, **not to extract a set of non-negotiable parameters for a deal** ... After all, **sanctions enforcement is a cumbersome process. It costs money and takes time**. It hinders trade. It was never very popular. Why would members of the international community rush to report Iranian cheating, when they suddenly get no reward for doing so? ... **Since the interim deal was signed, the foreign ministers of Australia, Austria, Greece, Italy, Hungary, Latvia, Poland, Spain, and Sweden, among others, have all visited Tehran**. They were joined by high-profile parliamentary and business delegations, chambers of commerce ... Where diplomacy goes, business follows ... But in 2015, Tehran knows that a president who said 'Assad must go' in 2011 can no longer be believed ... What they [the Ayatollahs] see are **empty threats** ... They will treat the U.S. threat of snap-back sanctions with the same utter contempt."[170] *(Emanuele Ottolenghi, Senior Fellow, Foundation for Defense of Democracies)*

d. "In the later years of the agreement, international companies may have invested tens of billions of dollars back into Iran and will likely be less willing to forgo their business interests because of Iranian nuclear violations."[171] *(source –Foundation for the Defense of Democracies, June 2015).*

e. "These [sanctions] **cannot be 'snapped back' if Iran were to violate the deal**, as its defenders contend, but **reinstated only after a lengthy international process** that **excludes all the contracts signed by Iran before it were to cheat** ... As such, the deal serves as an incentive for foreign companies to sign a great number of short- and medium-term contracts with Iran ... The windfall is estimated to reach $700 billion, according to Israeli government sources."[172] *Former Israeli Ambassador Oren.* Obama is infusing almost $1 trillion into the Iranian economy over a multi-year period.

f.   "But any inspections at Iranian military facilities to which Iran objects, and the 'snap-back' re-imposition of UN sanctions would require the United States government to win the unanimous support of Germany, the United Kingdom, France, and the High Representative of the European Union for Foreign Affairs and Security Policy – all of them. This would be necessary to have the five votes required under the agreement's Dispute Resolution Mechanism to override objections from Iran, Russia, and China. (See Articles 36-37 and Annex I Article 78). And, under the Treaty of Lisbon rules controlling the EU's 'Common Foreign and Security Policy,' key decisions on the CFSP require unanimous approval by all 28 members of the European Union. It may be true that 'No one country could block a snap-back of sanctions,' as Secretary of Energy Ernest Moniz said, but no one country – not even the United States – could re-impose them either unless all of Europe went along." *Steven Rosen, Director, Middle East Forum, "Obama Gave Europe Control of the Iran Sanctions "Snap Back" Mechanism," July 20, 2015.*

g.   Re-imposition of sanctions must go through the UN Security Council, an international joint commission, and an international advisory board. If sanctions are put back in place, Iran has the option to abrogate its commitments under the signed agreement, and can immediately commence building nuclear weapons after benefiting from the initial financial benefits of sanction relief. Most of the countries that would be doing business with Iran after the agreement is finalized will not rejoin an effort to reinstitute sanctions led by the United States. **Obama will never torpedo the signature foreign policy achievement of his administration by walking away from a signed agreement with Iran**.

h.   "The structure of the sanctions that the US had built based on the UN Security Council's resolutions was destroyed, and like the 1990s, when no other country complied with the US sanctions against Iran, no one will accept the return of the sanctions." *Iranian Foreign Minister Zarif Speaking at Iran's Strategic Council on Foreign Relations, Fars New Agency, July 2015.*

    i.   During the summer of 2015, **Obama wrote letters to at least the French, British, Chinese, and German governments assuring them that they would not be penalized for doing business with Iran if Congress continued or re-imposed sanctions**.

2.   At an **Obama press conference** concerning the Iranian nuclear deal on July 15, 2015, one day after the final deal was presented to the public, Major Garrett, the *CBS* White House correspondent asked: "As you well know, there are four Americans in Iran – three held on trumped-up charges and according to your administration and one whereabouts unknown. Can you tell the country, sir, **why you are content with all the fanfare around this deal to leave the conscience of this nation, the strength of this nation unaccounted for in relation to these four Americans? And last week the chairman of the Joint Chiefs of Staff**

said under no circumstances should there be any relief for Iran in terms of ballistic missiles or conventional weapons. It is perceived that that was a last-minute capitulation in these negotiations. Many in the Pentagon feel you've left the Joint Chiefs of Staff hung out to dry." **President Obama responded**, "The notion that I'm content as I celebrate with American citizens languishing in Iranian jails - Major, that's nonsense, and **you should know better**. I've met with the families of some of those folks. **Nobody is content, and our diplomats and <u>our teams are working diligently to try to get them out</u>** [taqiyya]... That's why **those issues are not connected** [because Obama did not link them], but **we are working every single day to try to get them out and won't stop until they are out and rejoined with their families**." Obama could have easily requested the Iranians release the four Americans before he lifted sanctions on the ballistic missiles or the conventional weapons, but he did not. He could have demanded the four Americans be freed as a sign of good faith before any concessions were agreed to. Precedents in Obama's own policies and actions demonstrate his insistence on releasing prisoners held by opposing parties in difficult negotiations. Obama was adamant upon freeing Bergdahl from the Taliban, even though he deserted his country and colluded with the enemy. Obama used the excuse that it was his responsibility to bring Bergdahl home at almost any cost, but, then again, Bergdahl was a Muslim and worked with the Taliban. Obama pressured General Sisi and demanded that he release imprisoned Muslim Brotherhood leaders and even obtained the release of an Egyptian American, Mohamed Soltan, who colluded with the Muslim Brotherhood and allegedly helped organize violent protests. Obama forced Netanyahu to release hundreds of imprisoned Palestinians who had blood on their hands [Islamic terrorists many whom were affiliated with Hamas] during the peace negotiations with Palestinian Authority as a sign of good faith, without quid pro quo concession from Abbas. Obama has been dedicated to freeing radical Muslim terrorists and activists, and made their release a top priority when entering into the above negotiations and with his Guantanamo Bay release policy. Who are the men that Obama kept behind bars? An Iranian-American pastor who committed apostasy and blasphemy, an Iranian-American and former Marine who was arrested for spying for the CIA, a *Washington Post* bureau chief, and a missing former FBI and DEA agent. All these men are Christians or Jews, and pro-American, and are not a priority for Obama. Obama agreed to give the leading state sponsor of terrorism $150 billion and removed sanctions from IRGC Quds Force commander Qassem Suleimani, who is still on the U.S. terror list. Obama also released a top Iranian nuclear scientist in April 2015, who was arrested in America for attempting to obtain prohibited nuclear equipment, as part of the negotiating process. Obama could have easily insisted the Americans be set free as a counterpoint to the above Iranian demands. **But, Obama purposely waited to release the hostages after the JCPOA was finalized, so he could transfer to Iran an additional $1.7 billion**. Obama, as a radical Muslim, is definitely not going fight for a Christian convert who committed blasphemy, and will always be advancing Iranian, Islamic, or jihadi interests at the expense of America's and its citizens' welfare. Iran eventually released some of the Americans, but only after Obama gave Iran an additional $1.7+ billion, and Obama let the missing Jewish American remain in Iran unaccounted for. Theoretically, Obama paid an unbelievable ransom of at least $400,000,000 for each prisoner released, probably the largest ransom ever paid in the history of man, which went directly to the IRGC.

    a.   "**Every single meeting, everywhere in the world that ever took place with the Iranians**, we have raised the issue of the American citizens ... And we are working on the issue of the American citizens even now." *Kerry backing Obama in a Fox News interview on July 19, 2015. Either Kerry is lying or he is a terrible negotiator.*

3.   "We have had **extraordinarily close consultation with Israel**. Experts from Israel have been **essential in the development** of this deal." *Under Secretary of State for Political Affairs Wendy Sherman, July 15, 2015. Lies.*

    a.   "From the initial reports, we can already conclude that this agreement is an **historic mistake** for the world." *Prime Minister Benjamin Netanyahu.*

    b.   "The Cabinet unanimously rejected the major powers' nuclear agreement with Iran and it determined that Israel is not bound by it ... I expressed Israel's two major concerns ... One, the agreement allows Iran to develop extensive capabilities that will serve it in arming itself with nuclear weapons whether at the end of the period of the agreement in another 10-15 years, or earlier if it violates the agreement. Two, the agreement channels hundreds of billions of dollars to Iran's terrorism and war machine, a war that is directed against us and against others in the region." *PM Netanyahu's statement after the Security Meeting regarding the Iranian nuclear agreement, July 14, 2015.*

    c.   "The deal announced today in Vienna is **breathtaking in its concessions to an Iranian regime** ... There is no linkage whatsoever between the removal of these restrictions and Iran's behavior. In 10 years, Iran could be even more aggressive toward its neighbors, sponsor even more terrorism around the globe and **work even harder to destroy Israel, and the restrictions on Iran's nuclear program would still be automatically removed**." *Ron Dermer, Israeli Ambassador to the United States*

    d.   "The Iranians suddenly have a **cash windfall of $150 billion** *[plus the $1.7 billion hostage ransom]* ... And we would **expect a major escalation of the insurgent and terror threat against the State of Israel, along most of our border**[s]. And that's a direct result of removing sanctions and having this money that results from [it] go to Iran, first for Iran's own military buildup and secondly for Iranian surrogates [Hamas and Hezbollah], which surround the State of Israel." *Israeli Foreign Ministry Director General*

Dore Gold, July 22, 2015. Obama will be creating a terrorist superpower with practically unlimited funding.

i. "If they [the Jews] all gather in Israel, it will save us the trouble of going after them worldwide." *Hassan Nasrallah, leader of Hezbollah, based in Lebanon, commander of over 100,000 missiles directed at Israel.*

ii. "Iran, through Hezbollah, continues trying to establish terror cells in the **Golan Heights area** and we can already talk about a '**forward command**' of the **Iranian Revolutionary Guards' Al-Quds Force**." *Yossi Melman, intelligence reporter, Jerusalem Post, August 17, 2015.*

iii. Iranian officials posted a video on the Internet entitled, "**Preparation of the Complete Destruction of Israel by the Iranian Revolutionary Guards Islamic Revolution in Iran**." *The video showed hundreds of thousands of troops from the IRGC, Hamas, and Hezbollah preparing to invade Jerusalem, August 17, 2015.* Now that Iran has unlimited funding for the IRGC via sanctions relief provided by Obama, they can move toward their goal of destroying Israel. Obama will now try to give Iran a base of operations in East Jerusalem by insisting Israel agree to his two-state diplomatic solution.

iv. In February 2016, Hamas revealed that Iran was providing critical funding for the **rebuilding of their sophisticated underground tunnel network** in the Gaza strip, with some of the tunnels extending into Israeli territory. Hamas is preparing for another war with Israel with Iran's full financial support.

v. In 2017, Iran revealed that it was funding subterranean missile and firearm manufacturing facilities in Lebanon which would be under the full control of Hezbollah. These advanced missiles can strike anywhere throughout Israel and can also target Israel's naval ships.

e. The nuclear agreement contains a provision where the West (and Obama) will help train Iranian officials to protect their nuclear installations from all types of sabotage, including cyberattacks. Ari Yasher, writing in *Israel National News* stated, "**Israeli officials responded with outrage** on Monday to a **detail hidden** in the back of the Iran nuclear deal signed last Tuesday, according to which **the West will train Iran to defend its nuclear facilities from sabotage**."

i. "Well I think that would be **an enormous mistake. A huge mistake with grave consequences for Israel** and the region, and I don't think it's necessary." *Kerry, in an interview with Matt Lauer of NBC News on July 24, 2015.* Kerry is **threatening Israel** with very serious and life-threatening consequences if they attempt to thwart the development of the Iranian nuclear program or bomb their nuclear facilities.

Obama and Kerry have entered into an informal alliance with Iran against Israel.

f.   "Contrary to promises, Israel has not yet received all the written supplements to the agreement signed between Iran and the world powers." *Yossi Cohen, Israeli national security advisor testifying before the Knesset, July 29, 2015.*

g.   "Under the Iran Deal – the unthinkable would happen, what you and I would never dream would be possible in our lifetime. We would stand with all the anti-Semites in the world … and been an enemy to Israel." *Representative Louis Gohmert of Texas discussing the JCPOA in 2015.*

h.   "So many friends in Israel. They don't know what happened. [regarding the JCPOA] They actually think Obama hates Israel. I think he does … Honestly I think Israel is in a massive amount of trouble because of the agreement." *Donald Trump, Republican nominee for the 2016 presidential election speaking in Reno, Nevada while campaigning. Late October 2015*

i.   Israeli Ambassador to the United States Ron Dermer told Stuart Eizenstat, a U.S. diplomat that, "**The [Obama] administration is 'tone deaf' about the 'existential threat' to Israel from Iran**." This quote was discovered during the Wikileaks' release of emails from John Podesta's, Hillary Clinton's campaign manager. Dermer made this comment two weeks before the JCPOA was finalized in mid-July 2015.

4.   "So, this deal actually pushes Iran further away from a bomb. *[Iran is always three months to one year away from a nuclear weapon.]* And there's a **permanent prohibition** on Iran **ever having a nuclear weapon**. *[The agreement ends in ten years and Iran can do whatever they want with their nuclear program]* … **That they're inevitably going to cheat**. *[Iran has always cheated, and they just recently cheated by trying to obtain prohibited nuclear technology from Europe.]* **Well, that's wrong, too**. *[Obama is Iran's public relations agency and defense attorney.]* With this deal, we will have **unprecedented, 24 / 7 monitoring of Iran's key nuclear facilities**. *[Military instillations will not be readily available for inspection and there is at least a 24 day waiting period for inspectors to visit a requested site.]* … **If Iran violates this deal**, the sanctions we imposed that have helped cripple the Iranian economy – **the sanctions** that helped make this deal possible – **would snap back into place promptly**. *[Worldwide sanctions will never be reinstituted. American inspectors are prohibited.]* … Because we refused to accept a bad deal. *[Obama did not obtain the freedom of four Americans held in Iranian prisons and terminated the sanctions of their ballistic missiles and conventional weapons, despite their strong continued ties to terrorism.]* We held out for a deal that **met every one of our bottom lines**. *[U.S. bottom line lies – U.S. policy not containment, anytime anywhere inspections, only nuclear issues approached, continuation of conventional arms and ballistic missile sanctions, no right to enrich in NPT, underground reinforced Fordow facility not needed for a peaceful*

program, halting progress or dismantling of their nuclear program, protecting Israeli interests, making the world a safer place but not with $150 billion in sanctions relief for terrorists ...] And we got it ... Other countries in the region might race to do the same. *[Saudi Arabia, Egypt, Turkey will go nuclear with this deal.]* **And we'd risk another war** in the most volatile region in the world. *[Iran controls five capitals in the Middle East with wars being waged in Yemen, Syria, Iraq, Lebanon, Saudi Arabia, Gaza, Israel, and Libya, all with Iran's fingerprints on them.]* That's what would happen without this deal ... I fear no questions. *[Except by Major Garrett concerning abandoning the four American prisoners in Iran.]*" *Obama weekly address, July 18, 2015. All lies.*

a. "There's nothing in the deal that says they're not allowed to develop nuclear weapons *[after a decade when the deal expires. Although Iran signed the Nuclear Nonproliferation Treaty, they can opt out at any time.]* ... **I challenge** *[President Obama]* **to point to anything in this deal** *[that prevents Iran from pursuing the nuclear weapons]* **other than that preliminary statement** *[the preamble states "Iran reaffirms that under no circumstances will Iran ever seek, develop or acquire any nuclear weapons" – which is not legally binding]* **which says that Iran will not be allowed to develop a nuclear weapon after the deal expires ... He cannot do it**. So he's not telling the American people the truth about the deal ... **The sanctions are dead. They will not ever snap back**. They will never be as powerful as they once were." *Liberal Democrat and Harvard law professor Alan Dershowitz, Times of Israel interview, August 18, 2015.*

b. "President Obama was right on Tuesday to hail his nuclear agreement with Iran as historic, though not because of his claim that it will 'prevent Iran from obtaining a nuclear weapon.' The agreement **all but guarantees that Tehran will eventually become a nuclear power**, while limiting the ability of a future president to prevent it ... this means that the deal **leaves Tehran as a nuclear-threshold state** even if it adheres to the terms, able to continue its nuclear research and retain its facilities while it waits for U.N. supervision to end. The other nations of the region will take that point, no matter Mr. Obama's assurances. Instead of eliminating a revolutionary regime's nuclear ambitions, the Vienna accord **promises to usher in a new age of nuclear proliferation**." *Wall Street Journal editorial, July 15, 2015.*

c. "Far-reaching concessions have been made in all areas that **were supposed to prevent Iran from obtaining nuclear weapons capability**. In addition, Iran **will receive hundreds of billions of dollars with which it can fuel its terror machine and its expansion** and aggression throughout the Middle East and across the globe ... One cannot prevent an agreement when the negotiators are willing to make more and more concessions to those who, even during the talks, keep chanting: 'Death to America.'" *Israeli Prime Minister Netanyahu, July 14, 2015.*

i.   "**Let's stipulate that some of that money will flow to activities that we object to**. We have no illusions about the Iranian government or the significance of the Revolutionary Guard and the Quds Force. **Iran supports terrorist organizations like Hezbollah**." *Obama, American University speech, August 5, 2015*. **Obama admits he is funding terrorism**, **which is an impeachable offense and treason**. Not only did sanctions relief go the IRGC, but also the $1.7 billion untraceable cash ransom Obama paid for the four American political prisoners held in Iran. Obama used the four Americans held hostage in Iranian prisons as an excuse to give the Iranians, the largest state sponsor of terrorism in the world, more cash to fund their terrorist activities.

d.   "The final agreement on Iran's nuclear program, the Joint Comprehensive Plan of Action (JCPOA), has potentially **grave strategic implications that directly threaten to undermine the national security of the United States and our closest regional allies**. By **allowing Iran to become a nuclear threshold state** and enabling it to **become more powerful and expand its influence and destabilizing activities** – across the Middle East and possibly directly threatening the U.S. homeland – **the JCPOA will place the United States in far worse position** to prevent a nuclear Iran."[173] *JINSA's Iran Strategy Council, September 2015*. Now Obama, Kerry, and Rice have all publicly admitted that the JCPOA will fund Islamic terrorism in violation of U.S. law.

e.   "I hereby declare to the great Iranian people that their prayers have been answered. **Today, we are at an important stage in the history of our state and of our [Islamic] Revolution** … The page has been turned over, and **a new page has begun** … In the negotiations we sought to achieve four goals. The first goal was to continue the nuclear capabilities, the nuclear technology, and even the nuclear activity within Iran. The second goal was to lift the mistaken, oppressive, and inhumane sanctions. The third goal was to remove all the UN Security Council Resolutions that we view as illegal. The fourth goal was to remove the Iranian nuclear dossier from Chapter VII of the UN Charter and from the Security Council in general. In today's agreement, in the Joint Comprehensive Plan of Action, **all four goals have been achieved** … Today I declare before the honorable Iranian nation that according to the agreement, on the day of its implementation, **all the sanctions – even the embargo on weapons, missiles, and [dual-use technology] proliferation – will be lifted**, as is stated in a [Security Council] resolution. All the financial sanctions, all the banking sanctions, and all the sanctions pertaining to insurance, transportation, petrochemical [industries], and precious metals, and all the economic sanctions will be completely lifted, and not frozen. Even the arms embargo will be stopped. There will be a kind of restriction [on arms] for five years, after which it will be lifted … **This is the most important day in the past 12 years**. Historically, this is the day on which all the large countries and the superpowers in **the world have officially recognized Iran's nuclear activities**." *Iranian President Rouhani, July 14, 2015.* Obama has personally ushered in the creation of Iran as a nuclear power and sanctioned the acquisition of nuclear weapons by a jihadi state sponsor of terrorism, and initiated a nuclear arms race in the Middle East.

f.   "We have told them [the P5+1 world powers] in the negotiations that **we will supply arms to anyone and anywhere necessary and will import weapons from anywhere** we want and we have clarified this during the negotiations." *Iranian Deputy Foreign Minister Abbas Araqchi, Times of Israel, July 21, 2015.* This proves that one of Obama's major goals of this deal was to fund terrorism, which is contrary to the interests of the United States.

g.   "The Obama administration **collapsed from seeking anytime, anywhere inspections to accepting an inspection regime that allows Iran to block the IAEA for 24 days at a time**. White House officials are claiming that "environmental sampling" technology can make up for the lack of robust access. David Albright, a former weapons inspector and now president of the Institute for Science and International Security, told to Bloomberg View that the technology is **inadequate to catch cheating because a large number of secret facilities are doing work that doesn't involve radioactive isotopes** [a] … that technology is also **inadequate to catch cheating because the cheating will occur in small facilities that can be fully sanitized within the 24 day time frame** [b]. In any case the Iranians don't have to fully evade detection of nuclear activity. They just have to dismantle enough of a facility to prevent the IAEA from determining with certainty what kind of nuclear activity occurred, and the **resulting doubt will be sufficient to prevent any country from calling them out** and blowing up the deal."[174] *(Jay Solomon, The Wall Street Journal)*

h.   "The **access of inspectors** from the International Atomic Energy Agency or from any other body **to Iran's military centers is forbidden** … The AEOI and the IAEA do not have any separate agreement on visiting the Parchin military site." *Ali Akbar Velayati, Ayatollah Khamenei's Adviser for International Affairs, interview with Al Jazeera and the Iranian state-controlled ICANA News. July 24, 2015.*

i.   "The remarks by the Western officials are ambiguous comments which are merely **uttered for domestic use** and therefore we should say that there is no ambiguity in this (nuclear) agreement … [Obama is lying to] … **calm opponents in the Congress and Zionist lobbies to soothe the internal conditions prevailing over debates on the nuclear agreement** in that country." *Hamid Baeidinejad, Iranian foreign ministry official, July 2015. Iran admits Obama is practicing taqiyya.*

j. *The Washington Free Beacon* on August 17, 2015 reported in Adam Kredo's article "All Nuke Inspectors Require Approval From Iran's Intelligence Agency," that Sayyed Abbas Araqchi, one of Iran's leading nuclear negotiators and deputy foreign minister stated, **"Any individual, out of IAEA's Inspection group, who is not approved by the Islamic Republic of Iran cannot enter the country as the agency's inspector."** *These guidelines may or may not be part of a secret side deal, and pave the way to Iranian cheating.*

k. "There was a time when enemies would not accept even a single centrifuge inside Iran, but **they** [Obama] **finally <u>surrendered</u>** in the face of Iran's nuclear might." *Ayatollah Khamenei, Iranian Press TV interview, May 2016.*

l. "Key restrictions on Iran's nuclear program imposed under an internationally negotiated deal will start to ease years before the 15-year accord expires, advancing Tehran's ability to build a bomb even before the end of the pact, according to a document obtained Monday by *The Associated Press* … an add-on agreement to the nuclear deal in the form of a document submitted by Iran to the International Atomic Energy Agency outlining its **plans to expand its uranium enrichment program after the first 10 years** of the nuclear deal … as of January 2027 – **11 years after the deal was implemented – Iran will start replacing its mainstay centrifuges with thousands of advanced machines** … From year 11 to 13, says the document, Iran will install centrifuges up to **five times as efficient** as the 5,060 machines it is now restricted to using … they would **reduce the time Iran could make enough weapons grade uranium to six months or less** from present estimates of one year … And that time frame could shrink even more. While the document doesn't say what happens with centrifuge numbers and types past year 13, U.S. Energy Secretary Ernest Moniz told *The AP* that **Iran will be free to install any number of advanced centrifuges beyond that point**, even though the nuclear deal extends two additional years."[175] *(George Jahn, Associated Press, July 18, 2016)* One year after the JCPOA was implemented, previously secret documents that were released, show that Iran will be able to significantly increase its number of advanced centrifuges four years before the deal expires, and will be able to make significant quantities of weapons-grade uranium in shorter periods of time. **Obama mislead the country concerning the limitations the JCPOA placed on the Iranian nuclear program and allowed an enemy of the United States to obtain massive sanctions relief while retaining its ability to produce nuclear weapons <u>during</u> the time frame of the agreement**. Iran will be able to manufacture nuclear weapons four years before the end of the agreement in a much shortened breakout time frame. Iranian Foreign Minister Zarif commented on the secret document after it was made public by confirming that Iran's "negotiators and experts" created the document and that expanding their nuclear enrichment program before the JCPOA expires was a "matter of pride." Treason.

i.   "I challenge those who are objecting to this agreement ... to explain specifically **where it is that they think this agreement does not prevent Iran from getting a nuclear weapon, and why they're right** [*The proof was partly in the secret side deals that Obama withheld from Congress.*] and people like (Energy Secretary) Ernie Moniz, who is an MIT nuclear physicist and an expert in these issues, is wrong." *Obama, July, 2015.* Obama is lying to Congress about Iran's inability to build a nuke during the full course of the JCPOA while withholding the secret side deals that prove he is wrong. Obama used Moniz's credentials and reputation to advance his lies.

ii. "President Obama's deal with Iran was supposed to keep that nation's mullahs from creating a nuclear weapon with which it could intimidate and dominate the Mideast and much of Europe. Instead, it actually makes it more possible – and in shorter time. The *Associated Press* obtained a copy of a secret side deal that, in the words of the normally circumspect *AP*, advances: 'Tehran's ability to build a bomb even before the end of the pact.' The accord as agreed to by the U.S. and five other nations was supposed to last 15 years. This is the **<u>latest of the shocking lies</u> to emerge from our White House** about the Iran deal ... **the deal as signed all but guarantees that Iran will someday get a nuclear weapon** with which to terrorize its neighbors ... The so-called "add-on" agreement lets Iran expand its uranium enrichment program after 10 years – not 15 years ... **Moniz** [*Moniz lied when he lobbied for the JCPOA*] told *AP* this week that Iran can put any number of advanced centrifuges in place after 13 years. "That **will give Iran a huge potential boost in enrichment capacity, <u>including bomb-making</u>** should it choose to do so," said the *AP*. Please remember that the next time **Obama** uses someone's credentials, as he did with Moniz last year, to bolster a **false claim** ... President Obama has signed off on an Iranian nuke. He either doesn't care what the result of his poor diplomacy was, or **actually wants to see a radicalized [nuclear] Iran** [*Obama is an agent for Iran as substantiated by a major respectable American newspaper – Investor's Business Daily, and argued by this author in Unexpected Treason*] – a nation that our own government agrees supports terrorism – dictate events in the Mideast, **to the detriment of the U.S.** and the rest of the West [*Obama committed treason*] ... the White House held secretive talks with **promises that Iran will never get a bomb**, only for the rest of us to discover that far from keeping Iran from getting a nuke to terrorize the world with, **the so-called "deal" with Iran actually speeds it up.**"[176] (*Investor's Business Daily editorial, July 19, 2016*)

m.   "Iran is the world sponsor of terrorism all over the place, and they are really **committed to the destruction of the United States** ... North Korea may be. Russia and China, especially Russia I think is a matter of some substantial concern. But I'd put North Korea and Iran right up there at the top … *[Iran does]* Not yet *[have the capability to destroy America]* with a nuclear weapon, but **I don't think they are many years away from a nuclear weapon** … I think they may be a **relatively short time away** … And in terms of their attacks through terrorism, through the Revolutionary Guard and elsewhere throughout the Middle East and throughout other parts of the world, Iran is a very serious problem already – **and will be a much bigger one <u>very shortly</u>.**" *James Woolsey, former CIA director during the Clinton administration, CNN interview February 13, 2017.* The fruits of JCPOA may be a real existential threat to the United States before the Iranian nuclear deal expires.

5. "Without a deal, we risk even more war in the Middle East, and other countries in the Middle East would feel compelled to develop their own nuclear weapons … [leading to a nuclear arms race] … in the most dangerous region in the world." *Obama, July 15, 2015.*

    a. "I think Saudi Arabia would **seriously try to get the [nuclear] bomb if Iran did**. It's just like India and Pakistan. The Pakistanis said for years they didn't want one, but when India got it, so did they." *Jamal Khashoggi, head of Saudi Al Arab News, which is owned by the Saudi royal family, July 22, 2015.* Khashoggi is a confidante of Prince Turki al Faisal of Saudi Arabia. One week after Obama announced the Iran deal, Saudi Arabia declared it will go nuclear. Obama wants a nuclear arms race in the Middle East between the Arab countries, since if pro-Western countries are overthrown by Islamic extremists, then they will have obtained an arsenal of nuclear weapons to use against the West and Israel, which is one of Obama's objectives.

    b. "President Obama made his decision to go ahead with the Iran nuclear deal fully aware that the strategic foreign policy analysis, the national intelligence information, and America's allies in the regions intelligence all predict not only the same outcome of the North Korean nuclear deal but worse – with the billions of dollars that Iran will have access to. **It <u>will wreak havoc</u> in the Middle East which is already living in a disastrous environment, whereby Iran is a major player in the destabilization of the region … People in my region now are** relying on G-d's will, and **consolidating their local capabilities and analysis with everybody else <u>except</u> our oldest and most powerful ally.**" *Lebanon Daily Star, July 21, 2015. Former Saudi Arabia Ambassador to the United States Prince Bandar bin Sultan bin Abdulaziz al-Saud* announced that the Iranian deal sponsored by Obama will "wreak havoc" throughout the Middle East. This statement contradicts the first part of Obama's two-part lie above. The Saudi prince announced that the alliance between the United States and Saudi Arabia has been severely damaged or is irreparably harmed. Obama has destroyed America's alliances with our three strongest allies in the Middle East, namely Israel, Egypt and Saudi Arabia while strengthening

America's ties to the Muslim Brotherhood, Erdogan, and Iran. This policy outcome would be expected from a radical Muslim in control of U.S. policy.

   i. According to Debka intelligence, Iran placed an order to **buy 100 Russian long-range refueling tanker aircraft, enabling Iran's air force to reach any target in the Middle East**, including Israel and Egypt. This could be interpreted as a violation of the conventional arms embargo, which will be in effect for 5 years, although the planes won't be delivered until 2020 or later.

c. "The nuclear deal with Iran does not block Iran's path to the bomb, it paves Iran's path to the bomb. [After the deal expires] **Iran's breakout time will be practically zero** ... By keeping the deal, Iran will become a threshold nuclear-weapons power ... the deal makes it far easier for Iran to build dozens, even hundreds of nuclear weapons in a little over a decade [with the buildup of their nuclear infrastructure] ... **The countries in the region threatened by Iran have already made clear that they will work to develop atomic bombs of their own.** The deal that was supposed to end nuclear proliferation will actually trigger nuclear proliferation ... **Iran will use this cash** [$150 billion from sanctions relief] **to fund its aggression in the region, and its terrorism around the world ... It will spark a nuclear arms race in the region and it will feed Iran's aggression – that will make war, perhaps the most horrific war of all.**" *Israeli Prime Minister Netanyahu, early August 2015.*

   i. "I've gone through this backwards and forwards a hundred times and I'm telling you, **this deal is as pro-Israel, as pro-Israel's security, as it gets.**" *Kerry, August 2015.* Either Kerry and Obama are blind to the genocidal intentions of the Iranians toward Israel, or they wish to support Iran's goals.

      (1) Iran "rejects the existence of any Israeli on this earth." *Hussein Sheikholeslam, senior advisor to the Speaker of Parliament in Iran, mid-August 2015.* Iran informed the P5+1 parties of their intentions during the nuclear talks.

d. "There is only one thing the ayatollahs in Tehran want more than a nuclear bomb: that is for their regime to survive. Thanks to the agreement announced on July 14, they will get both. The deal will strengthen their tyrannical, revolutionary and fundamentalist regime, and **they will have the bomb within a matter of years ... Sooner or later the West will have to confront Iran – only later it will face an emboldened, better prepared, modernized and richer Iran** that will do its best to attain the goals we've always tried to prevent."[177] *Jose Maria Anzar, former president of Spain, The Wall Street Journal, August 5, 2015.*

e. "After negotiations, in Zionist regime they said they had no more concern about Iran for next 25 years; I'd say: Firstly, **you will not see next 25 years**; G-d willing, **there will be nothing as Zionist regime by next 25 years. Secondly, until then, struggling, heroic**

and jihadi morale will leave no moment of serenity for Zionists." *Iran's Supreme Leader Ayatollah Khamenei, September 9, 2015.*

f. "I'm deeply concerned about this deal because of the Iranian track record ... I think there is the possibility that they will try and cheat on this deal, and we need to know if they do. The second point is, we're dropping a golden shower of money on them, 100 to 150 billion dollars, a significant portion of that, in my view, will be used to facilitate wars, proxy wars, terrorism through Hezbollah. We're going to see Iran as **an imperial power moving through the region**, whether or not they have a nuclear weapon, **so buckle up**." *Admiral James Stavridis, former Supreme Allied commander at NATO, Fox News Radio "Kilmeade and Friends" interview, January 14, 2016.* In 2008, Obama called Iran a tiny country and not a serious threat. As Obama fundamentally transformed America, he also purposely helped transform Iran from a tiny threat to a major regional imperial power, which threatens the viability of Iraq, the Gulf States, and Israel.

g. "If nuclear weapons become established [in the Middle East], **a catastrophic outcome is nearly inevitable**." *Henry Kissinger, "A Path Out of the Middle East Collapse," The Wall Street Journal, October 16, 2015.*

6. "But what I said to our negotiators was, given that Iran has breached trust and the uncertainty of our allies in the region about Iran's activities, let's press for a longer extension of the arms embargo and the ballistic missile prohibitions. And we got that ... We got five years in which, under this new agreement, arms coming in and out of Iran are prohibited, and **we got eight years for the respective ballistic missiles**." *Obama press conference, July 15, 2015. The UN Security Council passed a resolution relating to the Iranian agreement stating,* "Iran is **called upon** [non-binding] **not to undertake any activity related to ballistic missiles designed to be capable of delivering nuclear weapons**, **including launches using such ballistic missile technology**, until the date eight years after the JCPOA Adoption Day or until the date on which the IAEA submits a report confirming the Broader Conclusion, whichever is earlier." *Iran claims they can work on ballistic missile technology as long as it is not related to delivering nuclear weapons, thus Obama's declared restrictions for eight years don't apply to them. Either the Iranians hoodwinked Obama, or Obama hoodwinked America.*

a. "Regarding the continuation of the prohibition on Iran's development of missiles designed to be capable of delivering nuclear weapons, President Obama made a misleading statement on the day the deal was announced. He indicated that the restrictions related to ballistic missiles and conventional weapons would remain in place and be enforced: "Iran must complete key nuclear steps before it begins to receive new sanctions relief. And over the course of the next decade, Iran must abide by the deal before additional sanctions are lifted, including five years for restrictions related to arms, and eight years for restrictions related to ballistic missiles. All of this will be memorialized and endorsed in a new United Nations Security Council resolution. And if Iran violates the deal, all of these sanctions will snap back into place." **This too turned out to be a lie**. The UN Security Council resolutions that had contained clear prohibitions on conventional arms and ballistic missiles along with sanctions for violations were swept away when the JCPOA was implemented. The Security Council resolution that replaced it was far weaker. Iran has conducted tests of ballistic missiles since the JCPOA was finalized. It has suffered no snap back of any sanctions, nor any other punitive action by the Security Council." *(source – "Obama's Master of Deceit on the Iran Nuke Deal," Joseph Klein, FrontPage Magazine, May 11, 2016)*

b. "The next redline was **refusal to allow inspection or refusal to accept any restrictions in the defense and missile spheres, which has been fully achieved through the deal**. This is even stipulated in a UNSC resolution in an acceptable form … has turned into a **non-binding restriction**." *Iranian Foreign Minister Mohammad Javad Zarif, July 21, 2015*

    i. "The missile issue has not been raised in the negotiations and Iran's missile power will never be an issue for negotiations with anyone." *Zarif, August 2014.* Zarif knew that Obama would fold on the ballistic missile issue since chief U.S. negotiator Wendy Sherman called the ballistic missile issue "almost irrelevant" in February 2014.

c. "I want to make it clear to you. **Iran is not building these ICBMs to hit Israel. They already have missiles that can hit Israel everywhere. They are building these ICBMs to hit you. To hit the United States** … You are the Great Satan … We are just a small Satan." *Israeli Prime Minister Netanyahu, July 2015 after the nuclear agreement is announced. Obama's ultimate goal.*

d. "Amir Ali Hajizadeh, commander of the Iranian Revolutionary Guard Corps' Aerospace and Missile Force, said in recent remarks that the Obama administration does not want Iran to publicize its ongoing missile tests, which have raised questions about the Islamic Republic's commitment to last summer's comprehensive nuclear agreement. "At this time, the Americans are telling [us]: 'Don't talk about missile affairs, and if you conduct a test or maneuver, don't mention it,'" Hajizadeh was quoted as saying during a recent Persian-language speech that was translated by the Middle East Media Research Institute."[178] *(The Washington Free Beacon, May 2016)* Obama is advising Iran how to subtly continue testing their ballistic missile program, so Iranian antagonists cannot use these activities to rally against the JCPOA. Obama, despite his numerous statements promising to halt Iranian ballistic development, is working to advance Iran's ballistic missile program. Obama's collaboration with an enemy of the United States should be viewed as treason.

e. "The Obama administration misled journalists and lawmakers for more than nine months about a **secret [side] agreement to lift international sanctions on a critical funding node of Iran's ballistic missile program**, as part of a broader "ransom" package earlier this year that involved Iran freeing several U.S. hostages, according to U.S. officials and congressional sources apprised of the situation. The administration agreed to immediately lift global restrictions on Iran's Bank Sepah – a bank the Treasury Department described in 2007 as the "linchpin of Iran's missile procurement" – eight years before they were to be lifted under last summer's comprehensive nuclear agreement. U.S. officials initially described the move as a "goodwill gesture" to Iran."[179] *(The Washington Free Beacon, October 2016) Obama lied about maintaining sanctions on Iran's missile program and related financial institutions.*

7. While discussing the Iranian nuclear agreement with officials from the IAEA in Vienna, Senator Tom Cotton discovered there were <u>**at least two secret non-public side deals**</u> relating to the agreement that Obama hid from all other parties, including Congress. National Security Advisor Rice confirmed their existence. Cotton stated, "I had a meeting in Vienna with the International Atomic Energy Agency (IAEA), during which the agency conveyed to the lawmakers that **two side deals** made between the Islamic Republic of Iran and the IAEA as part of the Joint Comprehensive Plan of Action (JCPOA) will remain **secret** and will not be shared with other nations, with Congress, or with the public. One agreement covers the **inspection of the Parchin military complex**, and the second details how the IAEA and Iran will **resolve outstanding issues on possible military dimensions of Iran's nuclear program**." Representative Pompeo added, "Not only does this violate the Iran Nuclear Agreement Review Act, it is asking Congress to agree to a deal where not all Congressmen including the American public are privy to the specific details. The failure to disclose the content of these side agreements begs the question, 'What is the Obama administration hiding?' Even members of Congress who are sympathetic to this deal cannot and must not accept a deal we aren't even aware of." *July 22, 2015.* By purposely withholding key element of the agreement from Congress and the American / world public, **Obama intentionally lied concerning the true nature of the final agreement to all other parties. Submitting an incomplete clandestine treaty / agreement to Congress for review / ratification is an impeachable offense, especially a treaty which benefits an enemy of the United States and may result in a nuclear attack on the United States.** Obama is protecting the most dangerous aspects of Iran's nuclear program, its military dimensions.

a. John Kerry stated on July 23, 2015 after two days of Congressional hearings that "**there are no side deals.**" Even Susan Rice confirmed that side deals existed. But in discussions with Representative Pompeo, Pompeo revealed that **Kerry** "confirmed that there were in fact side deals and **himself had not seen the agreement**." Kerry admitted before the Senate Armed Services Committee on July 29, 2015 that he had not seen the side agreements, nor did he know their contents. It appears that Obama and Valerie Jarrett left the United States Secretary of State John Kerry out of the loop of the final Iranian nuclear agreement. It is believed that Iranian-born Valerie Jarrett or one of Obama's national security aides wrote the side agreement under Obama's guidance, thus guaranteeing that Iran would maintain the secrecy of the military dimensions of its nuclear program. Obama later declared the side deals were classified, so only selected members of Congress would have access to the details, although they would not see the specific documents. The director general of the IAEA, Yukiya Amano, refused to testify before Congress regarding the contents of the side deals. This may be due to Iranian intimidation and threats against the IAEA and its members. Iranian AEOI spokesman Behrouz Kiamalvandi was quoted in Iran saying, "In a letter to Yukiya Amano, we underlined that if the secrets of the agreement (side deals between Iran and the IAEA) are revealed, we will lose our trust in the Agency; and despite the U.S. Congress's pressures, he didn't give any information to them ... Had he done so, **he himself would have been harmed**." It is apparent that Iran will control the complete inspection process at their nuclear sites. **Is it possible that there are other side deals that have not been presented** to Congress, or "understandings" between the IAEA and Iran, that will allow Iran to cheat without American knowledge of any potential violations? If Americans are not allowed to be involved with inspections and the classified side deals are between Iran and the IAEA, then the United States will be a paralyzed third party with respect to ensuring Iranian compliance with the deal, and monitoring their ability to build a nuclear weapon. If members of the IAEA don't like America, or are Muslims who believe Iran has the right to develop its own nuclear program, or have struck their own private lucrative side deals with Iran, then these inspectors may become complicit partners in Iran's cheating on the agreement. Ali Akbar Salehi, chief of the Atomic Energy Organization of Iran, has already revealed that any issues or disagreements with the IAEA have already been settled on a "political level." Obama's promise of transparency was a lie with Obamacare and Obamatrade, and he is repeating this pattern with the Iranian nuclear agreement, most likely because **the hidden details are not palatable with the American public, and may demonstrate that Obama perpetuated a national security fraud upon America and the free world**.

b. "The United States and its negotiating partners **agreed 'in secret'** to allow Iran to evade some restrictions in last year's landmark nuclear agreement in order to meet the deadline for it to start getting relief from economic sanctions, according to a think tank report published on Thursday. The report, which was released by the Washington-based Institute for Science and International Security, is based on information provided by several officials of governments involved in the negotiations … 'The exemptions or loopholes are happening in secret, and it appears that they favor Iran,' David Albright [former UN weapons inspector] said … Among the exemptions were two that allowed Iran to exceed the deal's limits on how much low-enriched uranium (LEU) it can keep in its nuclear facilities, the report said. **LEU can be purified into <u>highly enriched, weapons-grade uranium</u>.**"[180] *Reuters, September 2016.* Obama allowed Iran to bypass JCPOA mandated restrictions on enriched uranium levels, since Iran had failed to comply with the original JCPOA. This secret addendum allowed Obama and the Europeans to proclaim Iran had complied with the agreement, and sanctions could be lifted. Kerry lied on January 16, 2016, the day Iranian sanctions were lifted, when he stated that Iran "has fully implemented its required commitments … assuring continued full compliance" [with the JCPOA]. "The Obama administration not only well knew that Iran was not in compliance; it also colluded with Iran, through the secretive JCPOA device known as the "Joint Commission," in order to exempt Iran's multiple violations from compliance requirements … it appears that this was yet **another secret side arrangement** that Congress has been kept in the dark about."[181] The IAEA would no longer be supervising inspections, and there were no independent experts monitoring Iranian compliance with the JCPOA. Obama structured the JCPOA agreement, so he could exempt Iran from any violations of the agreement, which is diplomatic fraud and treason.

c. As part of the JCPOA, Obama signed legal waivers that **allowed Iran to receive over $10 billion in cash and gold during the JCPOA negotiations**. This transfer of funds and assets was not revealed to Congress or the American public, and must be considered as **another secret side deal** that was kept hidden. Obama kept these transactions hidden, since Iran, the #1 sponsor of Islamic terrorism in the world, greatly benefitted. Obama structured the deal so that it could not be traced back to his administration, even though he was the person who authorized and set up a series of complex transactions that greatly rewarded Iran and evaded existing sanctions. **These series of money transfer <u>allowed Obama to lie</u> when he denied that his administration had a "direct" role** in the payments. According to *The Blaze*, "According to *The Wall Street Journal*, the cash and gold were moved through third-party countries in the Middle East and Europe after Asian nations unfroze Iranian oil revenues and wired the funds to various banks, including in Oman, Switzerland and Turkey. U.S. lawmakers and Middle East allies worry, due to the highly liquid nature of cash, the payments could be used to fund terror regimes. The money was converted to currency and bars of gold, U.S. officials said. The White House put a single restriction on the transactions: They could not include U.S. dollars … Some of the payments were previously reported; however, others went unreported. One unreported payment included $1.4 billion to Iran in the time period between when the

Iran deal was finalized in July 2015 and when it went into effect ... The Obama administration says it played no role in the $10 billion cash and gold payments to Iran, contending that the countries that unfroze the oil revenues and made the banking transfers acted of their own volition."[182] Iran was clandestinely paid a minimum of $700 million per month over 18 months of negotiations, which was approved by Obama. According to the *The Washington Free Beacon*, "Iranian Foreign Ministry spokesman Bahram Ghasemi confirmed last week a recent report in the *Wall Street Journal* detailing some $10 billion in cash and assets provided to Iran since 2013, when the administration was engaging in sensitive diplomacy with Tehran aimed at securing the nuclear deal ... **The $10 billion figure is actually a 'stingy' estimate**, Ghasemi claimed, adding that **a combination of cash, gold, and other assets was sent by Washington to Iran's Central Bank and subsequently 'spent.'** 'This report is true but the **value was higher**,' Ghassemi was quoted as saying.'"[183]

8. The Iran Nuclear Agreement Review Act of 2015 required President Obama to submit to Congress "any additional materials related thereto, including ... **side agreements, implementing materials, documents, and guidance, technical or other understandings, and any related agreements, whether entered into or implemented prior to the agreement or to be entered into or implemented in the future.**" *Obama promised that all side agreements related to the JCPOA would be available for review by the Congress.* Obama had a legal obligation to release the documents since by signing the "Act" it was a matter of law. **By withholding the side agreements, Obama not only lied to Congress, but broke the law.** The secretive side agreements are critical for a full understanding of the Iranian nuclear agreement since it addresses Iran's past military dimensions of their nuclear program and gave important technical details regarding the inspection processes at their nuclear facilities. As Representative Mike Pompeo stated in *The Washington Post* in early September 2015, "Congress must now confront the grave issues of constitutional law prompted by the **president's failure to comply with his obligations under the act**. This is not the first time this administration **has disregarded clear statutory requirements** ... The fact that this has happened again in the context of a national security agreement vital to the United States and its allies makes the situation all the more serious. For Congress to vote on the merits of the agreement without the opportunity to review all of its aspects would both effectively sanction the president's unconstitutional conduct and be a major policy mistake. Instead, both houses should vote to register their view that **the president has not complied with his obligations under the act by not providing Congress with a copy of an agreement between the IAEA and Iran**, and that, as a result, the president remains unable to lift statutory sanctions against Iran." It may also be grounds for treason, since Obama is "aiding and abetting" Iran, an enemy of the United States, by helping protect

and shield their nuclear program that may produce nuclear weapons that could devastate America.

9. "Our nuclear experts, including one of the best in the world, Secretary of Energy Ernie **Moniz, worked tirelessly on the technical details**…" *Obama, American University speech, August 5, 2015.*

    a.   "**I personally have not seen those documents** *[side deals on inspections]."* *Secretary of Energy Moniz, early August 2015. Moniz responding to Senator McCain's questions.*

10. "I do think it is important to acknowledge another more understandable motivation behind the opposition to this deal, or at least skepticism to this deal. **And that is a sincere affinity for our friend and ally Israel. An affinity that**, as someone who has been a stalwart friend to Israel throughout my career, I deeply share." *Obama, American University speech, August 5, 2015.*

    a.   One day earlier, while meeting with American Jewish leaders, Obama warned them that should the Iranian nuclear agreement be rejected by Congress then "rockets will rain on Tel Aviv." The president stated that in response to an American strike against Iranian nuclear reactors that it is "**not going to result in Iran deciding to have a full-fledged war with United States** … You'll see more support for terrorism. You'll see Hezbollah rockets falling on Tel Aviv. **I can assure you that Israel will bear the brunt of the asymmetrical response that Iran will have to a military strike on its nuclear facilities**." <u>**Is Obama delivering a message from Iran to Israel? Is Obama threatening Tel Aviv if Jewish input contributes to defeating the agreement before Congress**</u>? Is Obama paving Iran's path for possible retaliation? Obama also warned pro-Israeli lobbyists to "stick to the facts." If Obama had a sincere affinity for Israel, he would have given assurances that he would consider any attack on Tel Aviv by Iran or their proxies, as an attack on the United States. Obama also admitted that congressional rejection of the agreement would not result in a war between the United States and Iran, which contradicts many of his previous arguments touting war as the ultimate consequence of Congressional rejection. If the JCPOA is rejected by Congress, Tel Aviv will be attacked by Hezbollah forces armed with advanced Iranian missiles. If the JCPOA is approved by Congress, Tel Aviv will probably be attacked with nuclear weapons at some point in the future. Obama is presenting scenarios with no viable options for Israel.

    b.   "Well, all you have to do … [is] go to Israel, and talk to average people, on all ends of that spectrum. **And I couldn't find a single person there who didn't feel that this administration had turned their back on Israel** … I think **anything is anti-Semitic that is against the survival of a state** that is surrounded by enemies, and by people who want to destroy them. And to sort of ignore that, and **to act like everything is normal there, and that these people are paranoid, I think that's anti-Semitic**." *Dr. Ben Carson,*

Republican candidate for the U.S. presidency, August 2015, Fox News Sunday interview. Dr. Carson called Obama anti-Semitic. Obama is America's first African-American Muslim Arab *[Obama's paternal family is from Sudan.]* openly anti-Semitic president.

    c.   After Obama invited Iran to help confront and battle ISIS in Iraq and Syria, by April 2017, Iran now commands over 25,000 soldiers who can quickly be deployed to Israel's northern border. These troops include members of the IRGC, Shiite militias from Iraq, and volunteers from Pakistan and Afghanistan.[184] Not only did the Obama's JCPOA increase the Iranian nuclear and ballistic missile threats to Israel and increase funding to Hamas and Hezbollah, but Obama's strategy to allow the Iranian military to gain a foothold in Syria now directly threatens Israel's northern border. If Israel allowed Obama to implement his two-state solution, Iran would have controlled Eastern Jerusalem including the Jewish holy sites, and the West Bank via its Hamas proxies. Obama's main foreign policy objective in the Middle East has been to harass and ultimately destroy Israel.

11.   "Those who adhere to the ideology of rejecting Israel's right to exist, they might as well reject the earth beneath them or the sky above, because Israel is not going anywhere … And today, I want to tell you – particularly the young people – so that there's no mistake here, so long as there is a United States of America – *Atem lo levad.* **You are not alone**." *Obama, Jerusalem speech, March 2013.*

    a.   "Because this is such a strong deal, **every nation in the world that has commented publicly, with the exception of the Israeli government, has expressed support** … The United Nations Security Council has unanimously supported it. The majority of arms control and nonproliferation experts support it. Over 100 former ambassadors … support it." *Obama, American University speech, August 5, 2015.* **Obama initially tells Israel they are not alone in 2013**, and then is publicly condescending to Israel and tells them they are alone in 2015.

    b.   "I want there to be no confusion on this point … Israel will not allow Iran to get nuclear weapons. **If Israel is forced to stand alone, Israel will stand alone**." *Netanyahu, October 2013 UN General Assembly speech.*

    c.   Obama helped formulate and pass UNSC Resolution 2334, which declares all Israeli settlements outside the pre-1967 borders as illegal, and labelled the Western Wall and the Jewish Quarter in East Jerusalem as "occupied Palestinian territory." Obama declared to the world, Israel is alone, with the UNSC vote at 14 to 0, with one U.S. abstention.

12.   "At no point have I ever suggested, for example that someone is a warmonger meaning they want war." *Obama is defending his strategy of calling opponents of the JCPOA "war mongers."*

    a.   "Congressional rejection of this deal leaves any U.S. administration that is absolutely committed to preventing Iran from getting a nuclear weapon with one option, another war in the Middle East. I say this not to be provocative, I am stating a fact." *Obama, American University speech, August 2015.*

13. "The **defense budget** of the United States is more than $600 billion. To repeat, **Iran's is about** $15 **billion**." *Obama, speech at American University, August 2015.* Obama repeated the $15 billion estimate of Iran's military budget in an interview with *The Forward* in August 2015. Obama is **downplaying** the depth of Iran's real military budget, which is significantly higher, so that Congress will view Iran as an inconsequential minimal military threat as they are voting on the JCPOA. The real budget of the Iranian military may be between $100 - $200 billion per year. There are over 500,000 active soldiers in their armed forces. Iran has spent over $100 billion on its nuclear program and is planning on building many new reactors. Iran is financing Hezbollah, Hamas, the Houthi rebels in Yemen, as well as Shiite forces in Syria and Iraq. The IRGC has recently moved forces into Iraq and Syria. Iran is funding a global terror network that extends into Southeast Asia and South America and has an advanced domestic weapons program, which includes ballistic missiles, drones, and fighter aircraft production. The IRGC controls up to one-third of the Iranian economy and the Iranian defense budget. It is inconceivable that $15 billion would cover the costs of all these activities in a given year. As Obama downplays ISIS, al Qaeda, and the Muslim Brotherhood, Obama is downplaying the Iranian military budget to protect the mullahs and their revolutionary, expansionary, and genocidal goals. Obama may have been in favor of sanctions during the early stages of his presidency so that the IRGC could gain control of a larger part of the Iranian economy during its sanctions-induced economic downturn, thus guaranteeing that the organization in charge of Iran's terror network would also be in control of Iran's economy when the JCPOA was approved and sanctions ended. Since Iran has been engaged in the Syrian conflict, Iran has spent over $100 billion alone on their operations in Syria according to the *Daily Mail*, which proves Obama's Iranian defense budget estimates as utterly inaccurate. If the $15 billion figure is accurate, then Obama financed the entire Iranian military for one year with clandestine payments via the hostage ransom and the monthly gold / asset transfers that were established via secret side deals and a possible signing bonus.

a. "Iran recently passed a law requiring that the $1.7 billion U.S. payment be directed to the Iranian military. Previous AAF research reported that Iran reports spending **65 percent of its military budget on the Islamic Revolutionary Guard Corps (IRGC)**, the Iranian elite paramilitary force. The IRGC actively supports terrorist organizations throughout the Middle East, spending millions of dollars every year to support the Houthis in Yemen, Hezbollah in Lebanon, and Hamas in Gaza."[185] *(American Action*

Forum, September 2016) With his $1.7 cash ransom payment to Iran, Obama may have funded up to 10% of the annual Iranian military budget and / or a majority of the annual operating budget of the IRGC, according to Obama's numbers.

    b. "Oh, I don't have any question that Iran wants the money *[$1.7 billion cash payment for the release of U.S. hostages held by Iran]* in cash because they wanted it faster than what a wire transfer would be and it's fungible … **They announced pretty quickly afterward that they were expanding their defense and their military budget by $1.7 billion dollars**, **an exact amount that we had just sent over to them. So, I don't think that was accidental** … But when you give cash, we can't track … Did that go to Hezbollah? Did that go to the Russians? Did that go to the coup in Yemen? There's no way to be able to track that."[186] *Senator James Lankford, Politico, September 2016.* Obama not only funded a significant portion of the Iranian military budget in cash, but he also knowingly provided massive funding for all the major Islamic terrorist groups in the Middle East. Both are impeachable offenses.

14. "I know it's easy to play on people's fears, to magnify threats, **to compare any attempt at diplomacy to Munich, but none of these arguments hold up**." *Obama, speech at American University, August 2015.*

    a. "For the Munich Pact and Iran 'deal' are afflicted by similar flaws: The unwillingness to recognize that making concessions to tyranny never satiates the appetite of the tyrant. Indeed, it only whets it – with each concession not being perceived as a gesture of goodwill but as a sign of weakness, inviting further demands for further concessions, until these can no longer be met – and violence becomes inevitable, albeit in far more disadvantageous circumstances."[187] *Martin Sherman, The Jerusalem Post, September 3, 2015.*

    b. "We cannot in all circumstances undertake to involve the whole British Empire in war simply on her *[Czechoslovakia's]* account. If we have to fight it must be on larger issues than that." *British Prime Minister Chamberlain addressing Britain on September 27, 1938.* Obama may deny the parallel, but he could easily replace Czechoslovakia with Israel knowing that he never intended to initiate any military actions against Iran. With World War II breaking out about one year later with Germany's invasion of Poland on September 1, 1939, **one can reasonably expect a major Middle East war expanding outside the confines of Iraq, Syria, and Yemen, during the first two years of the next presidency**. Likely scenarios include Iran invading Iraq, Iran attacking Saudi Arabia and the Gulf states, and / or Hezbollah and IRGC forces attacking northern Israel. Retired General David Petraeus recognized Iran's imperialistic aims in Iraq by stating in a *Washington Post* interview, "I would argue that the foremost threat to Iraq's long-term stability and the broader regional equilibrium is not the Islamic State; rather, it is Shiite militias, many backed by – and some guided by – Iran … Longer-term, Iranian-backed Shia militia could emerge as the pre-eminent power in the country, one that is outside the control of the government and instead answerable to Tehran."[188]

15. "It is no secret that the Prime Minister and I have had a strong disagreement on **this narrow issue**." *Obama told reporters on November 9, 2015 that the JCPOA was a "narrow issue" while meeting Netanyahu at the White House, despite all of the above controversy.* Obama implemented his "downplaying" strategy repeatedly.

16. In early March 2016, Colin Kahl, Vice President Biden's national security advisor informed participants at a RAND Corporation conference that the $100+ billion in sanctions relief for Iran was "being used for domestic investment, to the dismay of Qassem Soleimani [Quds forces leader]."[189] *(Rubin, Commentary)* Since the JCPOA was signed, Iran has spoken with the Chinese concerning air force upgrades, the IRGC has received the latest models of drones being used in Syria, the IRGC is ramping up Iranian recruitment for Syrian duty, and Iran plans on significantly increasing its purchasing of Russian military equipment including modernized air missile defense systems as well as joint airplane and helicopter manufacturing capabilities. Iran is building at least six underground missile production facilities in Iran and Lebanon. Iran plans on buying many advanced weapons systems from Russia after the lifting of sanctions including advanced fourth generation extremely maneuverable SU-30 multi-purpose warplanes with air-to-air and air-to-ground striking capabilities, long range S-300 air defense missiles which are capable of destroying advanced fighter aircraft and cruise missiles, modern T-90 tanks, and advanced anti-satellite missiles.

   a. The JCPOA gives the UN Security Council (Resolution 2231) power to veto conventional arms sales to Iran, but the Obama administration has refused to acknowledge that they would ever use U.S. veto power to halt any weapon sales to Iran. In testimony before Congress with respect to the SU-30 sales, Kerry stated, "Well, I don't think you have to use a veto …We'll stay in touch with you." Obama is allowing Iran to fully arm itself with advanced weapons systems funded with a significant portion of the sanctions relief, and he has no intention to use a United States veto in the UNSC to hinder Iran's quest to dominate the Middle East militarily.[190]

17. "There is no common 'deal' between the U.S. and the Islamic Republic of Iran. **The U.S. has a document of 159 pages, that it claims details the 'deal.' Iran, meanwhile, rejected that text**. Instead, the Iranian *majilis* approved their own version of the JCPOA, more than 1000 pages long, which, among other things, strips the U.S.' ability to "snapback" sanctions, forbids inspections of Iranian military sites, bars International Atomic Energy Agency (IAEA) interviews with Iranian military officers and scientists, calls on Iran to strengthen its military and missile arsenal, makes conversion of enriched uranium conditional, and calls for the dismantling of Israel's nuclear weapons program. Leader Khamenei has endorsed this

new version of the JCPOA, to which he attached some additional conditions ... According to the Obama administration, the JCPOA is a set of "political commitments" and not a treaty, an executive agreement, or even a legally binding document. That is because said document was **never signed by both parties** ... President Obama also forced an entirely fictional process on Congress to implement the 'deal.' He didn't use the one mentioned in the U.S. Constitution – the treaty process. He knew he would lose the battle to get two-thirds of the U.S. Senate vote ... The Iran Nuclear Agreement Review Act of 2015, i.e., the Corker legislation ... allowed Obama and his allies to turn the constitutional procedures on their heads, requiring opponents of the 'deal' to get a two-thirds majority in the Senate and House. ... One reason many opposition senators signed onto this **Corker legislation** was that it **required the president and his team to reveal to them the entirety of the Iran 'deal.'** ... **At least two side deals were never revealed by the administration** ... Thus, the Corker legislation was violated. "[191] *("The **Fictional** Iran Deal," Adam Turner, American Thinker)* The JCPOA is a fraud on many levels and will not prevent Iran from acquiring nuclear weapons.

18. "Given the enormous differences between the United States and Iran on so many issues – including Iran's **support for terrorism**, **its ballistic missile program**, **and its destabilizing actions** in the region – we had to simultaneously make clear that **we would not compromise on those issues**, while spending serious political capital to hold up our end of the deal ... All of that said, many other aspects of Iranian behavior – and U.S.-Iran relations – remain unchanged. Iran has **not ceased its support for terrorist organizations** *[Rhodes finally admits Iran is not a moderate regime]* like Hezbollah or its threats toward Israel. Iran has **continued to test ballistic missiles** *[capable of carrying nuclear warheads]*. From Iraq to Yemen, Iran has continued to **engage in destabilizing support for proxy** organizations." *Remarks by Deputy National Security Advisor Ben Rhodes at the Iran Project, Washington, D.C., June 16, 2016.* Iran's support and financing for terrorism has increased with JCPOA mandated sanctions relief. Iran tests its intermediate and long range ballistic missiles at will without any repercussions from Obama or the international community. The Middle East is only becoming more destabilized as Iranian forces become more active in Syria and Iraq as Obama's presidency comes to a close. The Obama administration lied when they stated that they "would not compromise on those issues."

19. "By all accounts, it has worked exactly the way we said it was going to work ... [the] **Israeli military and security community ... acknowledges this has been a game changer ...** The country that was most opposed to the deal." *Obama, Pentagon press briefing, August 4, 2016.* Obama declared that Israel now supports the JCPOA, but within 24 hours, Netanyahu and the Israeli military denied Obama's assertions. Netanyahu stated that, "Israel's view on the Iran deal remains unchanged." The Israeli Defense Ministry countered against Obama's statement by saying, "The Israeli defense establishment believes that agreements have value,

only if they are based on an existing reality, and that they have no value if the facts on the ground are completely the opposite of [the concepts] on which an agreement is based on … The Munich agreement did not prevent the Second World War and the Holocaust, precisely because their basic assumption, that Nazi Germany could be a partner to any kind of agreement, was wrong, and because the leaders of the world at that time ignored the explicit statements by Hitler and the rest of the leaders of Nazi Germany."[192] Israel was quick to expose Obama's lies.

20. "This wasn't some nefarious deal … **We do not pay ransom for hostages**. We didn't here and we won't in the future." *Obama, Pentagon press conference, August 4, 2016.* Secretary of State Kerry also commented, "The United States of America does not pay ransom and doesn't negotiate ransoms with any country – we never have and we're not going to do that now." Both men were referring to accusations that Obama gave Iran a down payment of $400 million in cash for the release of four American hostages held in Iranian prisons.

   a. Iranian hostage Saeed Abedini confirmed that his plane was not allowed to leave Iran until the $400 million arrived at the airport.

   b. *The Wall Street Journal* revealed on August 17, 2016, "New details of the $400 million U.S. payment to Iran earlier this year depict a tightly scripted exchange specifically timed to the release of several American prisoners held in Iran. The picture emerged from accounts of U.S. officials and others briefed on the operation: **U.S. officials wouldn't let Iranians take control of the money until a Swiss Air Force plane carrying three freed Americans departed from Tehran on Jan. 17**. Once that happened, an Iranian cargo plane was allowed to bring the cash home from a Geneva airport that day."[193] *Obama lied since he did pay a ransom.* The Iranian cargo plane belonged to Iran Air, a company that was sanctioned in 2011 by the United States for transporting arms and supplies belonging to the IRGC. Obama lifted the sanctions on Iran Air on January 16, one day before Obama permitted the $400 million cash exchange for the hostages. With either of the above two scenarios, Obama paid a ransom.

   c. Department of Justice attorneys were against the deal because the exchange of prisoners and the $400 million occurred simultaneously, and it would appear as if Obama paid a ransom and violated federal laws. But most importantly, the U.S. attorneys were against this transaction because it was illegal, and the Justice Department could not condone blatantly illegal activity by the president of the United States. As reported in *The Wall Street Journal*, "The head of the national security division at the Justice Department was among the agency's senior officials who objected to paying Iran hundreds of millions of dollars in cash at the same time that Tehran was releasing American prisoners, according to people familiar with the discussions. **John**

Carlin, a Senate-confirmed administration appointee, raised concerns when the State Department notified Justice officials of its plan to deliver to Iran a plane full of cash, saying it would be viewed as a ransom payment, these people said. A number of other high-ranking Justice officials voiced similar concerns as the negotiations proceeded, they said."[194]

d. After the American hostages left Iran, various Iranian officials confirmed the cash payment was ransom. Mohammad Reza Naqdi, a Basij Forces commander in Iran stated, "This **money was returned for the freedom of the U.S. spy** *[Jason Rezaian]* and it was not related to the [nuclear] negotiations."[195] *The Wall Street Journal* reported, "Iranian press reports have quoted **senior Iranian defense officials describing the cash as a ransom payment**. The Iranian foreign ministry didn't respond to a request for comment."[196] Obama is maximizing the funding of Islamic terrorism and breaking American laws under the guise of misleading false legalistic excuses.

e. "Look, for them to try to pretend this was anything other than a ransom is laughable, and I think it hurts their credibility … And then the president's defense of the use of cash as if this is, 'Well, we couldn't wire the money.' Well, why couldn't you wire it? He said because of sanctions. Well that means they were actually going around the law, going around sanctions and they had to do it illicitly, clandestinely at night the way it is done by gangsters. **That's because they were doing ransom.** They didn't want anyone to know and they had to go around the law and Congress. Congress didn't know. No, this is not old news. It is new news and it is highly embarrassing." *Charles Krauthammer, Fox News Channel's Special Report, August 4, 2016.*

f. "Consider the shady circumstances of the Obama administration's payment to the world's leading state sponsor of terrorism … If the $400 million payment were actually a straight-forward first installment on the settlement of a debt claim that Iran had filed with an international tribunal in The Hague, why not make the settlement agreement, if it exists at all, public? Why didn't the parties avail themselves of the option to request the tribunal under Article 26 of the **Tribunal Rules of Procedure**, as an interim protection measure, to facilitate a deposit of the settlement funds with a third party such as Switzerland? Such third party in turn could prepare for a phased hand-over of the settlement funds to Iran under the supervision of the tribunal. The answer is that **the Obama administration was doing all that it could to hide its ransom payment from the public**. It feared the political backlash from violation of U.S. government policy not to pay a ransom because such action would only encourage more hostage-taking *[and fund Islamic terrorism directed against America]*. And that is precisely what has happened in Iran. Three dual American-Iranian citizens have since been imprisoned by Iranian authorities, without any known charges being filed against them."[197] *(Joseph Klein, FrontPage Magazine, August 2014)*

g.   Attorney General Lynch refused to answer any questions from Congress regarding the $1.7 billion payment to Iran which led to the release of four American hostages.

21.   "The reason that we had to give them cash ($400 million) is precisely because **we are so strict in maintaining sanctions** and **we do not have a banking relationship with Iran** that we couldn't send them a check and **we could not wire the money**." *Obama, August 4, 2016 press conference.* If wiring money to Iran was illegal, it is quite doubtful that transferring untracable piles of cash in various foreign currencies in the middle of the night to Iran would make this transaction any more legitimate. If Obama was so concerned about maintaining sanctions, he would not have given Iran any cash at the start, since a significant percentage of this untraceable cash will be given to Islamic terrorist groups supported by Iran and the IRGC. Obama's State Department designated Iran as a state sponsor of terrorism and Kerry admitted in January that payments received by Iran related to the JCPOA or otherwise would partially be used to fund terrorism. Obama knew this as well. Yet, Obama gave Iran the money any-way, knowing he was breaking the law, since the United States government is not allowed by law to financially support radical Islamic terrorist groups. As a radical Muslim, Obama gave Iran the $400 million ransom not because Obama was paying a ransom or closing a business transaction that had been left in limbo for decades, but because Obama was funding Islamic terrorism with a massive untraceable cash infusion, and he was using the other talking points as a diversion for his real motive and objectives. Sanctions not only prevented Obama from sending a check or a wire transfer to Iran, but they also prohibited financial transactions be-tween the United States and Iran, whether they are in dollars or foreign currencies.

a.   "The Obama administration acknowledged late Tuesday that its transfer of $1.7 billion to Iran earlier this year was made entirely in cash, using non-U.S. currency … Treasury Department spokeswoman Dawn Selak said in a statement the cash payments were nec-essary **because of the 'effectiveness of U.S. and international sanctions**,' which iso-lated Iran from the international finance system… The money came from a little-known fund administered by the Treasury Department for settling litigation claims … **allow-ing the president to bypass direct congressional approval** to make a settlement."[198] *(Associated Press, ABC News)* Obama paid a $1.7 billion ransom in cash denominated in multiple foreign currencies in order to bypass sanctions and keep Congress uninformed. Texas Republican Senator Cruz commented, "This … only confirms what reasonable people had already concluded about the Obama administration's cash transaction with the Islamic Republic of Iran: This was a **ransom paid to a rogue regime** determined to spend it on terrorist attacks on America and our allies. The mullahs wanted cash so it would be immediately accessible and untraceable, and the administration agreed because they didn't want there to be proof the Iranians were using it for terrorism. It was, essentially, **a money laundering operation**."[199]

b. "The United States made at least **two separate payments to the Iranian government via wire transfer within the last 14 months**, a Treasury Department spokesman confirmed Saturday, contradicting explanations from President Barack Obama that such payments were impossible … In July 2015, the same month in which the U.S., Iran and other countries announced a landmark nuclear agreement, the U.S. government paid the Islamic republic approximately $848,000. That payment settled a claim over architectural drawings and fossils that are now housed in the Tehran Museum of Contemporary Art and Iran's Ministry of Environment, respectively. Then, in April 2016, the U.S. wired Iran approximately $9 million to remove 32 metric tons of its heavy water, which is used to produce plutonium and can aid in the making of nuclear weapons."[200] *(Politico, September 2016)* Obama knowingly violated Iranian financial sanctions, which establishes grounds for impeachment.

22. "The Iranians, by virtue of the agreement they made, have gone from 19,000 centrifuges that were enriching nuclear material, down to about 5,000 … they are limiting their enrichment to 3.67 percent, their stockpile is limited to 300 kg, down from 12,000 kg of enrichment material, so they have lived up to the agreement … **The agreement makes it safer for the world**." *Kerry, CNN interview, January 16, 2017.* Obama and Kerry allowed **Iran to keep their enrichment capabilities** which gives them the potential to make nuclear weapons at will. **Sanctions relief**, **hostage ransoms**, **and secret side deal asset transfers**, **gave Iran over $150 billion**, of which a significant portion was used to fund Islamic terrorism in the Middle East and throughout the world. As Iran expands its influence and hegemony, most astute politicians, diplomats, and political scientists realize that these end results of the JCPOA make the world much less safe and unstable.

23. As part of the final JCPOA deal, Obama lied (or at the very least – misled) to the American public concerning the release of seven Iranians, whom he described as people "who were not charged with terrorism or any violent offenses" and called them "civilians." Obama purposely downplayed the subversive nature and national security threats these individuals posed to the United States. A *Politico* investigation into this specific release of enemies of America proved that these individuals were a significant threat to the security interests of the United States, and that **<u>Obama may have used the JCPOA as a cover to release Iranian agents</u>** who were stealing U.S. military secrets, were instrumental in building Iran's nuclear program related to military usage and the possible construction of nuclear weapons, and were actively transferring restricted U.S. military technology and weapons to Iran and were committing espionage. Obama used the JCPOA negotiations to release Iranian agents, to dismiss criminal charges against them, and to advance the military and political interests of Iran over the

United States. Obama formally committed treason and advanced the interests of the number one state sponsor of terrorism worldwide over those of the United States. As *Politico* reported: "But **Obama, the senior official and other administration representatives weren't telling the whole story on Jan. 17, 2016, in their highly choreographed rollout of the prisoner swap** and simultaneous implementation of the six-party nuclear deal, according to a POLITICO investigation. In his Sunday morning address to the American people, Obama portrayed the seven men he freed as "civilians." The senior official described them as businessmen convicted of or awaiting trial for mere "sanctions-related offenses, violations of the trade embargo." In reality, some of them were accused by Obama's own Justice Department of posing threats to national security. **Three allegedly were part of an illegal procurement network supplying Iran with U.S.-made microelectronics with applications in surface-to-air and cruise missiles** like the kind Tehran test-fired recently, prompting a still-escalating exchange of threats with the Trump administration. **Another was serving an eight-year sentence for conspiring to supply Iran with satellite technology and hardware**. As part of the deal, U.S. officials even dropped their demand for $10 million that a jury said the aerospace engineer illegally received from Tehran. And in a series of unpublicized court filings, **the Justice Department dropped charges and international arrest warrants against 14 other men**, all of them fugitives. The administration didn't disclose their names or what they were accused of doing, noting only in an unattributed, 152-word statement about the swap that the U.S. "also **removed any Interpol red notices and dismissed any charges against 14 Iranians** for whom it was assessed that extradition requests were unlikely to be successful." **Three of the fugitives allegedly sought to lease Boeing aircraft for an Iranian airline that authorities say had supported Hezbollah**, the U.S.-designated terrorist organization. A fourth, Behrouz Dolatzadeh, was charged with **conspiring to buy thousands of U.S.-made assault rifles and illegally import them into Iran**. A fifth, Amin Ravan, was charged with **smuggling U.S. military antennas to Hong Kong and Singapore for use in Iran**. U.S. authorities also believe he was part of a procurement network **providing Iran with high-tech components for an especially deadly type of IED used by Shiite militias** to kill hundreds of American troops in Iraq. The biggest fish, though, was Seyed Abolfazl Shahab Jamili, who had been charged with being part of a conspiracy that from 2005 to 2012 **procured thousands of parts with nuclear applications for Iran via China**. That **included hundreds of U.S.-made sensors for the uranium enrichment centrifuges** in Iran whose progress had prompted the nuclear deal talks in the first place. When federal prosecutors and agents learned the true extent of the releases, many were shocked and angry. Some had spent years, if not decades, working to penetrate the global proliferation networks that allowed Iranian arms traders both to obtain crucial materials for Tehran's illicit nuclear and ballistic missile programs and, in some cases, to provide dangerous materials to other countries. "They didn't just dismiss a bunch of innocent business guys," said one former federal law enforcement supervisor centrally involved in the hunt for Iranian arms traffickers and nuclear smugglers. "And then they didn't give a full story of it." In its determination to win support for the nuclear deal and prisoner swap from Tehran – and from Congress and the American people — the Obama administration did a lot more than just downplay the threats posed by the men it let off the hook, according to POLITICO's findings. **Through action in some cases and inaction in others**, **the White House <u>derailed its own much-touted National Counterproliferation Initiative at a time</u> when it was making unprecedented headway in thwarting Iran's proliferation networks**. In addition, the POLITICO investigation found that Justice and State Department officials <u>**denied or delayed requests from prosecutors and agents to lure some key Iranian fugitives to friendly countries so they could be arrested**</u>. Similarly, Justice and State, at times in consultation with the White House, **slowed down efforts to extradite some suspects already in custody overseas**, according to current and former officials and others involved in the counterproliferation effort. And as far back as the fall of 2014, Obama administration officials <u>**began slow-walking some significant investigations and prosecutions of Iranian procurement networks operating in the U.S.**</u> These previously undisclosed findings are based on interviews with key participants at all levels of government and an extensive review of court records and other documents. "Clearly, **there was an embargo on any Iranian cases**," according to the former federal supervisor. "Of course, it pissed people off, but it's more significant that these guys were freed, and that people were killed because of the actions of one of them," the supervisor added, in reference to Ravan and the IED network. The supervisor noted that in agreeing to lift crippling sanctions against Tehran, the Obama administration had insisted on retaining the right to go after Iran for its efforts to develop ballistic missiles capable of delivering nuclear warheads and cruise missiles that could penetrate U.S. defenses, and to illegally procure components for its nuclear, military and weapons systems. "Then why would you be dismissing the people that you know about who are involved in that?" the former official asked."[201] Because Obama, as an Islamist and pro-Iranian agent, established these major goals as president - to fund and protect Iran's nuclear program, to implement policies to protect Iranian military and political interests around the world, and to release other Iranian agents from U.S. custody by downplaying their threat to America. In response to these startling and possibly treasonous revelations, "Citing a POLITICO investigation, Republican leaders of the House oversight committee said Friday [May 5, 2017] they have launched a sweeping investigation into whether the Obama administration, in trying to win support for a nuclear deal and prisoner swap with Tehran last year, undermined an ambitious U.S. counterproliferation effort to thwart Iranian weapons trafficking networks. Also in response to the POLITICO investigation, 13 Republican senators have demanded answers about whether the Obama administration jeopardized U.S. national security as a result of its protracted top-secret negotiations with Tehran, and then misled the American public when disclosing the terms of the two deals in January 2016."[202] *(Politico, Josh Meyer, May 5, 2017)* The 13 senators addressed their concerns to Attorney General Sessions in a letter stating, "We write to request your assistance in providing Congress with more information regarding the Obama Administration's decision [to drop charges or convictions in these 21 cases] … Based on new reports, we are concerned that President Obama and certain previous administration officials intentionally suppressed the seriousness of the charges against these individuals in order to garner public support for the nuclear deal with Iran, and we fear that **these individuals may still pose a threat to the national security of the United States** … [and are] **still engaging in illicit activities on behalf of the Iranian government**."

a. "In January 2016, the **Obama** administration released seven Iranian-born prisoners in what President Barack Obama called a "one-time" "**humanitarian gesture**" intended to sweeten the nuclear deal hammered out between Washington, D.C., and Tehran. The prisoners – who Josh Earnest insisted were guilty only of "sanctions violations or violations of the trade embargo" – were exchanged for five Americans, unjustly held by Iran since as early as 2011. In fact, some of the Iranian prisoners were national-security threats, and **it wasn't a straight prisoner swap**: *The Wall Street Journal* revealed that on the day of the exchange the U.S. flew $400 million in cash on an unmarked cargo plane to Iran. When it came to its negotiations with Iran, duplicity was the hallmark of the previous administration's public statements … According to an investigation by Politico, in addition to the prisoner release, the Justice Department quietly "**dropped charges and international arrest warrants against 14 other men, all of them fugitives**." Several of them were wanted for alleged roles in **helping to funnel materiel to Iran-backed terror outfits, such as Hezbollah, or for participating in the global network to procure components for Iran's nuclear program**. One was believed to have **helped supply Shiite militias in Iraq with a particularly deadly type of IED** – one that **killed "hundreds" of American troops** … **Barack Obama**, John Kerry, and the rest of the foreign-policy team that crafted the nuclear deal with Iran **grossly misled the American people.** This deal is a calamity for our national-security interests, and with this latest revelation, that is clearer than ever." *(National Review editorial, "The Obama Administration's Iran-Deal Duplicity," April 25, 2017)*

b. "In a blockbuster exposé, Politico's Josh Meyer reports that Team Obama overruled veteran prosecutors to free seven Iranians, claiming publicly they'd merely violated economic sanctions. In fact, they were charged with posing threats to US national security as **part of a weapons procurement ring**. More, the administration also dropped charges against

14 fugitives involved in **smuggling sophisticated weapons to Iran** and its terrorist subsidiaries. That move **ended the international arrest warrants** against the 14 – and Obama & Co. had been obstructing efforts to apprehend them. Time and again, top officials at the White House, Justice and State departments **denied prosecutors' requests to lure one of the fugitives to friendly countries** where he could be arrested … The president's men also **slowed down extradition efforts** against suspects in custody and began **slow-walking investigations and prosecutions** of US-based procurement. In effect, the administration **deliberately derailed its own National Counterproliferation Initiative** at a time, Meyer reports, 'when it was making significant headway in thwarting Iran's proliferation networks.'"[203] *(New York Post editorial)* This scenario goes beyond Obama capitulating to Iran in order to have them agree to the JCPOA. Obama works for Iran, and not the United States.

c. "Indeed, Barack Obama's concessions to the Iran regime, which he offered in order to secure Iran's agreement on the terms of the disastrous JCPOA, seem to have no bounds. The result is that **Iran is marching ahead with perfecting key elements of a full nuclear weapons program**, while already receiving many of the benefits of sanctions relief afforded by the JCPOA. And now evidence has surfaced that the Obama administration not only paid a ransom for the release of American citizens imprisoned unlawfully by the Iranian regime as the JCPOA was being implemented. According to an April 24th investigatory report by *Politico*, the Obama administration also agreed, as part of a prison swap, to release **seven Iranian-born prisoners** from U.S. custody, at least **some of whom could well go back to helping the Iranian regime procure components for its nuclear weapons program** … And from Obama on down, the small group of officials involved in brokering the trade-offs leading to the nuclear deal **misled the American people** in the process. For example, the Obama administration **downplayed its release of the Iranian-born prisoners**, whom were **referred to benignly as "civilians" and "businessmen."** President Obama himself described the prisoner swap with the Iranian regime as "a reciprocal **humanitarian gesture.**" His Press Secretary Josh Earnest represented that the released prisoners had been caught up in technical sanctions or trade embargo violations – what Earnest referred to as "nonviolent crimes." In fact, according to the Politico report, 'some of them were accused by Obama's own Justice Department of posing threats to national security. Three allegedly were **part of an illegal procurement network supplying Iran with U.S.-made microelectronics with applications in surface-to-air and cruise missiles** like the kind Tehran test-fired recently, prompting a still-escalating exchange of threats with the Trump administration.' … Moreover, the unambiguous language of the United Nations Security Council resolutions prohibiting Iran from procuring, developing or testing such missiles was wiped away - replaced with a wishy-washy Security Council resolution endorsing the JCPOA and simply "calling upon" Iran not to undertake such missile-related activities … even if Iran continues to abide by the uranium enrichments limits until they sunset as per the JCPOA, **the regime will be in a position within a decade or so to resume full scale production of nuclear fuel with technologically advanced centrifuges**. And at least one of the fugitives that the Obama administration let off the hook is in a position to continue helping them do just that, without an indictment and possible extradition hanging over his head."[204] *(Joseph Klein, Front Page Magazine)* Obama purposely crafted the JCPOA so that Iran's nuclear weapons program and related research would remain intact and would allow Iran to become a producer of nuclear weapons in the near future.

CHAPTER 10

ISIS

"War is deceit." *Mohammed*

1. "**We don't yet have a complete strategy** because it requires commitments on part of the Iraqis." *(Obama, June, 2015)* Ten months earlier at the White House, Obama also said, "I don't want to put the cart before the horse. **We don't have a strategy yet.**" The Pentagon gave Obama many options to defeat ISIS. Obama just ignored them, and implemented policies that would allow ISIS to strengthen and expand, and then lied to the American public about the Pentagon's input to his Middle East policy.

   a. "The fact that he would put the blame on the Pentagon has not offered him plans is exactly consistent with Obama's method which is always blame others." *Charles Krauthhammer, June 2015.*

   b. "What the F--- was that? WE have given him lots of options. He just hasn't acted on them." *Pentagon official responding to Fox News, June 2015.*

2. "But **we cannot win this war by killing them**. We cannot kill our way out of this war … We need in the medium to longer-term to go after the root causes that leads people to join these groups, whether it's a **lack of opportunity for jobs … We can help them build their economies so they can have job opportunities for these people** …" *State Department Spokeswoman Marie Harf reiterates Obama's point of view on MSNBC's Hardball with Chris Matthews, February 17, 2015, when discussing Obama's strategy regarding ISIL.* If you kill them all, you win the war.

3. "There wasn't a leader I met with in the region who didn't raise with me spontaneously the need **to try to get peace between Israel and the Palestinians**, because **it was a cause of recruitment and of street anger and agitation** that they felt – and I see a lot of heads nodding – they had to respond to … People need to understand the connection of that. And it has **something to do with humiliation and denial and absence of dignity.**" *In October 2014 Kerry insinuated that a lack of progress in the Israeli-Palestinian peace negotiations fueled*

Islamic terrorism and perhaps helped ISIS garnish popular support in the Muslim world. Obama and Kerry are blaming Israel as one of the root causes for Islamic terrorism and the rise of ISIS. Israel's Economy Minister Naftali Bennett commented, "Even when a British Muslim beheads a British Christian, someone will always blame the Jew." That is anti-Semitism.

4. "First of all, **ISIL is *not* Islamic**. No religion condones the killing of innocents." *Obama is protecting radical Muslims. Pure taqiyya.* As a radical Muslim, Obama does not view any infidels as being innocent.

   a. "**Interviewer**: Do you believe Daesh (ISIS) is a result of Islamic revivalism? **Al Kilbani**: There is no doubt about this. No doubt. **Interviewer**: In another occasion, you said that Daesh is an offshoot of Salafism. How is that? **Al Kilbani**: Daesh has adopted Salafist thought. It is not the Muslim Brotherhood's thought, Qutbism, Sufism, or Ash'ari thought. They draw their ideas from what is written in our own books, from our own principles. Who criticizes them the most does not criticize their thought, but their actions. We do not criticize the thought on which it is based, such as the concept of apostasy … We discuss the way people are executed, saying that it is brutal that it ruins our image in front of the world. **If we execute them in a way that does not show us in a bad light**, then that's fine. Therefore, the ideological origin is Salafism."[205] *(Sheikh Adel Al Kilbani is the former Imam of the Grand Mosque in Mecca).* Days after Kilbani admitted that ISIS evolved from Salafism and Saudi religious principles, ISIS militia members beheaded a fourteen-year-old boy in front of his parents for missing Islamic prayer sessions, which was interpreted as apostasy. Within two weeks after this speech, Secretary of State Kerry contradicted the Imam of the Grand Mosque in Mecca and called the ISIS terrorists "apostates," and attempted to protect the image of Islam.

   b. A leaked operational ISIS document released in December 2015, states, "Indeed the establishment of the Islamic State … it is a comprehensive system requiring the leaders of the ummah [Muslim nation] to realise its concepts … the state requires an Islamic system of life, a Qur'anic constitution … the mujahideen came in great numbers out of zeal for their religion … their principles as a shari'i [Islamically legitimate] organisation … Implanting Islamic values in society as well as sound, sharia-based societal manners and customs … A provision that the [Islamic] State should be witness to good treatment of Muslims in its lands and mutual affection with Muslims in other areas of the world … A provision that the agreement should first be in the interest of the Muslims, not in the interest of the disbelievers."

   c. "Indeed, all praise is due to **Allah** … We seek refuge with **Allah** … Whomsoever **Allah** guides, then none can misguide him; and whomsoever **Allah** leaves astray, then none can guide him. I testify that there is no G-d but **Allah** alone, who has no partner, and I testify that **Muhammad** is His slave and messenger. As for what follows: **Allah** (the Mighty and Majestic) said, {Fighting has been enjoined upon you while it is hateful to you} [Al-Baqarah: 216]. And He (the Mighty and Majestic) said, {So let those **fight** in the cause of **Allah** who sell the life of this world for the Hereafter. And he **who fights** in the cause of **Allah** and is **killed or achieves victory** – We will bestow upon him a **great reward**} [**An-Nisā': 74**]. ... And He (the Glorified) said, {And those who are **killed** in the cause of **Allah** – never will He waste their deeds ...} [**Muhammad: 4-6**]. O **Muslims**! O you who are pleased with **Allah** as your Lord, and with **Islam** as your religion, and with **Muhammad** (peace be upon him) as your prophet and messenger... O you who testify that there is no G-d but **Allah** and that **Muhammad (peace be upon him** *[Obama has used this phrase in his speeches.]*) is the Messenger of **Allah** ... commanded the performance of **jihād** for His cause ... And by He in whose hand is **Muhammad's soul**, I would **love to fight** for the cause of **Allah and be killed**, and then **fight for the cause of Allah** and be **killed again**, and then **fight for the cause of Allah** and be **killed again**." ... commanded you with **jihād and fighting** in dozens of verses? ... who spent his whole life (**peace be upon him**) as a **mujāhid** for the cause of **Allah, fighting His enemies**?" *Abu Bakr al-Baghadadi, ISIS leader, An ISIS Mission Statement, Address from the Khalīfah of the Muslims, May 2015.* Baghdadi has a BA, MA, and PhD in Islamic Studies from the Islamic University of Baghdad. In 2006, he was the general supervisor for the Sharia Committee for the Islamic State of Iraq.

d. "Islam was never a religion of peace. Islam is the religion of fighting ... No one should believe that the war that we are waging is the war of the Islamic State. It is the war of all Muslims, but the Islamic State is spearheading it. It is the war of Muslims against infidels." *Abu Bakr al-Baghadadi, ISIS leader, May, 2015.*

e. ISIL is "a **recurring pattern** in the history of **violent expansion. The model is Muhammad himself** ... Islamic State's legitimation finds its basis in the Koran and Islamic law, the Sharia ... You will find no arguments within Muslim theology that can be used to condemn Islamic State's behavior as un-Islamic ... Islam is more than a religion. It is **a cult with political and social rules and unites religion and political and social order in one. And it <u>has always been violent</u>** ... But they are confronted with Islam's central problem: when they return to Islam's origin, they come across the **war-like, expansionist Islam from Medina, the legitimacy of killing for Allah's honor and a violent Muhammad**." *Martin Rhonheimer, Professor at Pontifical University of the Holy Cross, Rome, October, 2014.*

f. A poll conducted by the Arab Center for Research and Policy Studies showed that 13% of Syrian Muslim refugees support ISIS, while 10% have a mixed possibly supportive view of ISIS.[206] **Thus, 23% or up to one in four Muslim immigrants may support the actions of ISIS or may even consider joining ISIS.** This is consistent with all polls that show **15% to 25% of all Muslims support violent Islamic extremists such as al-Qaeda and ISIS**, and favor violent jihad against infidels and the West to institute Sharia law. If ISIS was not Islamic, then there would not be this significant degree of backing of ISIS from the Islamic community.

g.   Up to 20% - 28% of Muslims in England have sympathy for those Muslim who left England to fight in Syria according to a *Mirror* poll released in 2015. With 2.7 million Muslims in England, that translates to over 500,000 Muslims who may support ISIS in England alone.

h.   "When we decide to destroy a population, we (first) send a definite order to those among them who are given the good things of this life and yet transgress; so that the word is proved true against them: then (it is) We destroy them utterly." *Quran (17:16).*

i.   In early January 2016, a poll *(Turkey's Social Trend Survey, November 2015)* of over 1500 Turkish citizens revealed that 21% of responders believed that ISIS represented Islam.

j.   "I hear so many people say ISIS has nothing to do with Islam – of course it has. They are not preaching Judaism. It might be wrong, but what they are saying is an ideology based on some form of Islamic doctrine. They are Muslims. That is a fact and we have to get our head around some very uncomfortable things." *Aaqil Ahmed, BBC religion chief, May 2016.*

5.   "So, the president **was not singling out ISIL** [Islamic State of Iraq and the Levant, another name for the group], he was talking about the very different threat that is posed by a range of extremists around the globe. Many of them do not have designs on attacking the West or attacking the United States, and that is what puts them in stark contrast to the goals and capability of the previously existing al-Qaeda core network that was led by Osama bin Laden." *Josh Earnest, White House spokesman, August 25, 2014. The Obama administration refused to acknowledge that the president called ISIS, "JV."* But Obama cannot deny he stated, "I think the analogy we use around here sometimes, and I think is accurate, is if a **JV team** puts on Lakers uniforms, that doesn't make them Kobe Bryant. I think there is a distinction between the capacity and reach of a bin Laden and a network that is actively planning major terrorist plots against the homeland versus **jihadists who are engaged in various local power struggles** *[major Obama lie]* **and disputes**, often sectarian." Obama was specifically referring to ISIS since he was discussing the takeover of Fallujah. Obama also lied when he commented that ISIS' aggressive strategy had local designs, when in reality they were building a regional Islamic caliphate, planned on causing a refugee crisis that would allow them to seed their Islamic terrorists throughout Europe and the United States, and would soon be plotting terrorist attacks against the United States directly or indirectly through "lone wolves."

6.   "And so here domestically I think it's critical in order to build our relationship and build our level of cooperation with the Islamic community here we have to say to them 'look we

understand what this depraved terrorist organization [ISIS] is doing is **no part of your religion**.'" *Jeh Johnson, Chief Department of Homeland Security, Aspen Institute Security Form, July 2015. Lying to support his boss.*

7. ISIS is a "**JV**" team. *Obama in 2014 is __downplaying__ the building of the Islamic caliphate in the Middle East, whose establishment is one of his major foreign policy goals.*

   a. In 2012, two years before his "JV" comment, Obama was warned by a Defense Intelligence Agency (DIA) report analyzing the real monumental impact ISIS would have on the region by stating, "This creates the **ideal atmosphere for AQI (Al-Qaeda in Iraq**) to return to its old pockets in **Mosul and Ramadi** ... **ISI (Islamic State of Iraq) could also declare an Islamic state through its union with other terrorist organizations in Iraq and Syria**, which <u>will create grave danger</u> in regards to unifying Iraq and the protection of its territory." *Obama knew in 2012 that ISIS joining with the remnants of al-Qaeda forces would present a "grave danger" to Iraq, yet did nothing proactively to help prevent the slaughters and massacres that would follow the ISIS victories.*

   b. "ISIS owns hundreds of millions of dollars of sophisticated weapons, including vehicles and GPS-equipped weapons. Many of these are American-made and were captured from Iraqi troops ... Fighters: 20,000-31,500 fighters, and as many as 15,000 of them are believed to be foreign recruits. Those 15,000 come from 80 different countries. Reports indicate that approximately 100 are from the United States." *Mike Ryan, Policy Director for the Democratic Congressional Campaign Committee, October 2, 2014 memo released by internet hacker Guccifer 2.0., who obtained the memo from Nancy Pelosi's computer. Official Democratic Party documents contradict Obama's dismissal of ISIS' capabilities. Obama lied.*

   c. "ISIS has said very clearly that they **intend to use the refugee program to infiltrate the West and infiltrate the United States**. They did that in Paris ... the encryption and the real challenge ... FBI Director Comey will tell you that in the next four to five years we may be completely dark as these organizations and **these terror groups move toward <u>encryption programs that we simply don't have the ability to penetrate</u>**." *Rep. Chris Stewart, House Intelligence Committee, December 14, 2015. ISIS is not quite the "JV" team portrayed by Obama.*

   d. "ISIL, including its eight established and several more emerging branches, has **become the preeminent global terrorist threat**. They've attempted or conducted scores of attacks outside of Syria and Iraq in the past 15 months. ISIL's estimated strength worldwide exceeds that of al-Qaeda. ISIL's leaders are determined to strike the US homeland – beyond inspiring homegrown violent extremist attacks ... ISIL has established one of its most developed branch outside of Syria and Iraq in Libya." *Director of Intelligence Clapper, Senate testimony, February 2016*

e. ISIS is attempting to create **dirty nuclear bombs**. In 2015, highly radioactive IR – 192 was stolen from a nuclear storage facility in Basra province, Iraq and government officials believe that the radioactive material is under the control of ISIS. A terror suspect in the Paris massacres was found to have over ten hours of surveillance video of a Belgian nuclear waste facility official, which implies ISIS planned on targeting nuclear facilities. In late September 2015, Jurgen Todenhofer, a German war journalist who was given permission to temporarily live with ISIS forces, reported ISIS was planning on obtaining nuclear weapons to facilitate nuclear attacks on Western and American targets that could result in the deaths of several hundred million people. Todenhofer wrote, "the terrorists plan on killing several hundred million people. The West is drastically underestimating the power of ISIS … [they are] preparing the largest religious cleansing in history."[207] Moshe Kantor, president of the International Luxembourg Forum on Preventing Nuclear Catastrophe surmised, "ISIS has already carried out numerous chemical weapons attacks in Syria; we know it wants to go further by carrying out a nuclear attack in the heart of Europe." [208]

f. ISIS is proficient in **chemical weapons warfare**. On February 9, 2016, James Clapper, director of U.S. National Intelligence, stated before the Senate Armed Services Committee, "[The Syrian government] has used chemicals against the opposition … ISIL has also used toxic chemical in Iraq and Syria, including the blister agent sulfur mustard." The U.S. Intelligence Community's Worldwide Threat Assessment for 2016 stated, "Use of chemical weapons in Syria by both state and non-state actors [ISIS] demonstrates that the threat of WMD is real." Hamish de Bretton Gordon, a former commander with the Joint Chemical Biological Nuclear Regiment stated, "It is very evident that ISIS are putting much time and effort into training its jihadis in the use of chlorine as a terror weapon and in particular in IEDs. Virtually every foreign jihadi who returns to the US or UK will have been exposed to training of this sort and will have a reasonable idea on how to use chlorine and other toxic chemicals as a terror weapon."[209] Obama wanted to wage war against Assad when it was reported he used chemical weapons against his enemies, but Obama is silent when ISIS has used chemical weapons against the Kurds and Syrian civilians. **Obama's immigration policies are laying the groundwork for WMD attacks against civilian targets in the United States and Europe**.

g. The *Associated Press* reported on November 19, 2015, that **ISIS is aggressively pursuing the development of chemical and biological weapons** with the help of former Iraqi and Syrian scientists. With the massive immigration of Muslim refugees into Europe and the United States, ISIS will have many willing partners to release these agents of mass destruction into the West.

h.   "ISIS is suspected of firing a shell with mustard agent that landed at the Qayyara air base in Iraq Tuesday where US and Iraqi troops are operating, according to several US officials."[210] *(CNN, September 21, 2016)*

8.   "Our objective is clear. We will **degrade and destroy ISIS**." *Obama, White House address, September 2014.* Obama's rhetoric does not match the reality in the air or on the ground. Obama's closest advisor and friend out of all foreign leaders is President Erdogan of Turkey, and Erdogan supports ISIS.

a.   "I do not differentiate between Daesh [ISIS] and America … I consider Daesh their [America / Obama] tool." *Former Afghan President Hamid Karzai, Voice of America interview, April 19, 2017.*

b.   "They were accusing us of supporting Daesh [ISIS] … Now they [the United States, Obama] give support to terrorist groups including Daesh [ISIS], YPG, PYD. It's very clear. We have confirmed evidence, with pictures, photos and videos." *Turkish President Erdogan, December 2016. Erdogan turns on Obama after Turkey reestablishes diplomatic relations with Israel, ISIS launches a terror attack against Ataturk Airport, and the Democrats suffer a huge electoral loss to Donald Trump.*

c.   "Seventy-five percent of the sorties that we're currently running with our attack aircraft come back without dropping bombs, mostly because they cannot acquire the target or properly identify the target." *Retired Army General Jack Keane testifying before the U.S. Senate, May, 2015.* Obama's rules of engagement paralyze U.S. fighter pilots against ISIS.

d.   Secretary of Defense Carter informed the Senate Armed Services Committee on July 7, 2015 that the military is currently only training about 60 fighters to combat the 20,000 to 30,000 soldiers in the ISIS militia. This program to train "moderate" Syrian rebels cost about $500 million. Obama is draining U.S. resources by backing ineffective intelligence and military programs.

e.   **Yahoo Interviewer**: "But let me just – if I hear what you're saying, the F.B.I. is just forwarding propag – prop – propagating propaganda. Amnesty International is propagating propaganda. Everybody is conspiring against the Syrian government. Why? … You're the one– you're the one making the allegation." **President Assad of Syria**: "No – no. I'm not making allegation. They supported the terrorists, and you go back to what they said. **John Kerry, few months ago said – and – by his voice – that "We were watching ISIS – advancing and we expected the Syrian president to make concessions**." What does it mean? **Obama said it in – in interview in – in one of his speeches that "The war in Iraq created ISIS**." So who supported ISIS? We didn't create it. You created it. The United States created all this mess. Who supported the rebels and called them "moderate rebels," while they became ISIS and Al-Nusra in Syria? We didn't. So it's not responsibility. These are facts. This is reality. We didn't give money, we didn't support these terrorists. Your country supported them." *Yahoo interview with President Bashar Assad of Syria and Michael Isakoff, February 10, 2017.*

    f. It appears that **Obama has allied himself against the Kurds (and with ISIS) along with Erdogan in 2015**. Con Coughlin, reporting for the *U.K. Telegraph* on July 1, 2015, revealed, "**The United States has blocked attempts by its Middle East allies to fly heavy weapons directly to the Kurds** fighting Islamic State jihadists in Iraq … High level officials from Gulf and other states have told this newspaper that all attempts to persuade Mr. Obama of the need to arm the Kurds directly [with heavy weapons] as part of more vigorous plans to take on ISIL have failed … The **U.S. has also infuriated its allies**, particularly Saudi Arabia, Jordan, and the Gulf states, by what they perceive to be a **lack of clear purpose and vacillation** in how they conduct the bombing campaign. Other members of the coalition say **they have identified clear ISIL targets, but then been blocked by U.S. veto from firing at them**." *Obama is protecting ISIS.*

9. "We've disrupted their command structure, undermined its propaganda, **taken out half of their senior leadership**, squeezed its financing, damaged its supply networks, dispersed its personnel, and forced them to think twice before they move in an open convoy." *Kerry at the Munich Security Conference, March 2015. Regarding air raids on ISIS.*

    a. In May, a report originating in Spain and presented in *Politica* stated there are **between 30,000 to 100,000 Europeans fighting on behalf of ISIS**, and they have been crossing easily between their European points of origin and the battlegrounds in Syria and Iraq. The terror threat to Europe is increasing exponentially, as these Islamic radicals return to Europe. Erdogan is allowing ISIS fighters to establish terror cells in Europe.

    b. On May 16, 2015, ISIS took control of Ramadi, Iraq, which is about one hour from Bagdad.

10. "And I am convinced that as the forces are redeployed and as the days flow in the weeks ahead, that's going to change, because overall in Iraq, **Daesh (ISIS) has been driven back** … As much as **30 to 30-plus percent of the area they once controlled they no longer control**." *Kerry's observations after ISIS routs Iraqi forces and overtakes Ramadi, and advance toward Bagdad, May 18, 2015.* On the same day, Josh Earnest, the White House Press Secretary responds to a question asking if Obama's ISIS strategy has been a success, by saying, "Overall, yes." Two days later, ISIS took control of historic Palmyra, Syria.

11. Obama, White House and State Department officials, as well as national security leaders in the Obama administration attributed multiple Islamic terrorist attacks to "lone wolves." Jeh Johnson, the Homeland Security Director, discussed his view of (Islamic) terrorism after the Garland, Texas attack when he said, "We're very definitely in **a new phase in the global**

terrorist threat, **where the so-called <u>lone wolf</u> could strike at any moment**." The White House attributed the Paris massacre and the Boston Marathon bombing to "lone wolves." Vice President Biden has stated, "perverse ideologues …may be able to inspire a single "**lone wolf**," but they can never, never threaten who we are." Obama also referred to the radical Muslim, Omar Mateen, who perpetrated the Orlando nightclub massacre as a lone wolf. Obama's State Department counterterrorism expert, Daniel Benjamin, stated, "Although the carnage is much worse, the Orlando attack looks at first glance like another variation on a familiar theme: **a lone operator** – a deeply disturbed one, to judge from the early reporting – who acted apparently without outside prompting." Even in 2011, Obama was advancing his "fake" national security threat concerning lone wolves when he commented, "The most likely scenario that we have to guard against right now ends up being more of a **lone wolf** operation than a large, well-coordinated terrorist attack … when you've got one person who is deranged or driven by a hateful ideology, they can do a lot of damage, and **it's a lot harder to trace** *[proactive excuses]* those **lone wolf** operators." Obama has also said, "We are now at a point where because we in fact have been successful at stopping a number of plots, a threat has evolved. We do see these **lone wolf actors** … troubled individuals pick up a gun and act out of this ideology." In early 2017, the liberal *New York Times*, debunked the concept of "lone wolves." As stated in *The New York Times*, "As officials around the world have faced a confusing barrage of attacks dedicated to the Islamic State, cases like Mr. Yazdani's offer troubling examples of what counterterrorism experts are calling **enabled or remote-controlled attacks**: **violence conceived and guided by operatives in areas controlled by the Islamic State whose only connection to the would-be attacker is the internet.** In the most basic enabled attacks, Islamic State handlers acted as confidants and coaches, coaxing recruits to embrace violence … For the most part, the operatives who are conceiving and guiding such attacks are doing so **from behind a wall of anonymity** … Because the recruits are instructed to use encrypted messaging applications, the guiding role played by the terrorist group often remains obscured. As a result, **remotely guided plots in Europe, Asia and the United States in recent years**, including the attack on a community center in Garland, Tex., **were initially labeled the work of "lone wolves," with no operational ties to the Islamic State, and only later was direct communication with the group discovered**."[211] Obama lied to the American public by focusing on lone wolves, since he wanted to divert attention away from their ISIS connections, and their involvement in directing horrendous terrorist attacks on American soil.

12. "**Qatar is a strong partner in our coalition to degrade and ultimately defeat ISIL**. We are both committed to making sure that ISIL is defeated." *Obama, after meeting with the Emir of Qatar at the White House, February, 2015*. Obama knows that Qatar is a **major financial backer of ISIS and has given hundreds of millions of dollars to Hamas** while its

leader, Khaled Mashaal, lives in Qatar. Qatar was against Egyptian air strikes targeting ISIS-affiliated rebels who beheaded twenty-one Egyptian Coptic Christians in Libya. Qatar also funds terrorists in the Sinai Peninsula, who are fighting Egyptian troops and who are allied with the Muslim Brotherhood and ISIS. It was not an accident that Obama forced Israel to accept Qatar as a biased mediator during Israel's 2014 war with Hamas.

a. "[**Qatar** and ? Saudi Arabia] are **providing clandestine financial and logistic support to ISIL** and other radical Sunni groups in the region." *Email from Hillary Clinton to John Podesta, counselor to President Obama, August 17, 2014.*

b. "As for the regime itself, it has massively financed jihadist groups for more than 20 years. <u>**Qatar is a major bankroller**</u> not only of al-Qaida and Hamas but of militias associated <u>with ISIS in Iraq and Syria.</u> **In a State Department cable** from 2009 published by *WikiLeaks*, US diplomats referred to Qatar as **<u>the largest funder of terrorism in the world</u>** … Qatar serves as **<u>Iran's banker and diplomatic proxy</u>** … in 2014, during Operation Protective Edge, the Obama administration's alliance with Qatar, Turkey and Iran against Sunnis [Saudi Arabia, Egypt, Jordan, UAE, Kuwait] and Israel came out of the shadows."[212] *(Caroline Glick, The Jerusalem Post, June 2017)*

c. In early June 2017, **Saudi Arabia**, **Bahrain**, **the UAE**, **Yemen**, **and Egypt cut diplomatic and economic ties with Qatar** secondary to Qatar's **ties with** the Muslim Brotherhood, Hamas, ISIS, and **Iran**. Saudi Arabia also closed its borders with Qatar and instituted a partial naval blockade. And Obama has always been a strong backer of the Muslim Brotherhood and its affiliates (CAIR, MSA, ISNA …) in the United States, despite their proven ties to many Islamic terrorist groups including al-Qaeda and Hamas. Adel al-Jubeir, the Saudi Minister of Foreign Affairs stated, "No one wants to hurt Qatar, but it must decide whether it is going in one direction or the other, and I hope that the cost of the economic damage that will be caused to Qatar will convince it to go in the right direction and stop supporting organizations like the Muslim Brotherhood and Hamas."[213] *(Breitbart, June 8, 2017)* Of course, Obama is complementing and praising Qatar, which besides being a major financier of Islamic terrorism, is also a major ally with Iran. After Saudi Arabia announced the naval blockade, Iran sent IRGC troop to protect the emir of Qatar and its capital. **Qatar is Iran's beachhead into the Gulf States**. Hezbollah and Turkey also sent elite troops to Qatar's capitol in order to protect its royal family. Saudi Arabia closed its borders with Qatar because Qatar is cooperating with Iran and possibly Hezbollah and Turkey, in order to infiltrate pro-Shiite terrorists into Saudi Arabia who will attempt to overthrow the Saudi family. These developments were backed by the Obama presidency, as predicted accurately in *Unexpected Treason*. Obama's allies (Iran and Turkey) in the Middle East are lining up against Saudi Arabia. Hezbollah takes their orders from Iran.

13. "The ability of ISIL to not just mass inside of Syria, but then to initiate major land offensives that took Mosul, for example, that was **not on my intelligence radar screen.**" *[fake news answer or otherwise known as lying]* Obama, responding to the question by Fareed Zakaria, December 7, 2016, during a CNN interview – "Let me ask you if it's possible in your position to be completely honest and say the rise of the Islamic State surprised you, **it took you by surprise [fake news question]**, it took the administration by surprise." Obama created the geopolitical vacuum in Iraq by withdrawing U.S. forces and created the conditions where ISIL could expand and control territory encompassing significant parts of Syria and Iraq, which would lead to the genocide of the regional Christians, non-Muslims, and other opponents of ISIS. Obama knew the genocide of the Christians would occur with the rise of ISIS, and as a radical Muslim, supported their demise. Obama tried to blame intelligence failures for the rise of ISIS but Obama missed over 50% of his intelligence briefings and did not pay attention to intelligence reports sent to the White House since he had his own agenda which was allied with the Muslim Brotherhood and other radical Islamic terrorist groups in the Middle East. Other sources prove Obama knew about the capabilities of ISIS throughout his tenure as president, but chose to ignore the warnings.

     a.   "I know some in Washington would like us to start leaving Iraq now. To begin withdrawing before our commanders tell us we're ready would be dangerous for Iraq, for the region and the United States. It would mean surrendering the future of Iraq to al-Qaeda. It would mean that we'd be risking mass killings on a horrific scale. It would mean we'd allow the terrorists to establish a safe haven in Iraq to replace the one they lost in Afghanistan. *President George Bush warned the future president of al-Qaeda and ISIL in 2007.*

     b.   "The General Situation: The Salafists, the Muslim Brotherhood, and AQI are the major forces driving the insurgency in Syria. The West [The United States and/or Obama], Gulf countries, and Turkey support the opposition, while Russia, China, and Iran support the [Syrian] regime … AQI supported the Syrian opposition from the beginning, *[Obama is allied with al-Qaeda]* both ideologically and through the media. AQI declared its opposition of Assad's government because it considered it a sectarian regime targeting Sunnis … regarding Syria as an infidel regime … Opposition forces *[including AQI – al-Qaeda in Iraq –which later transitioned into ISIS]* are trying to control the eastern areas (Hasaka and Der Zor) adjacent to the western Iraqi provinces (Mosul and Anbar), in addition to neighboring Turkish borders. Western countries [the United States / Obama], the Gulf states [Saudi Arabia, Qatar], and Turkey are supporting these efforts …ISI could also declare an Islamic State through its union with other terrorist organizations in Iraq and Syria … renewing facilitation of terrorist elements from all over the Arab world entering into Iraqi arena."[214] *Obama was certainly aware of this DIA (**Defense Intelligence**

Agency) memo that was sent to Secretary of State Clinton in 2012. Not only did this prove that Obama was one of the original founders of ISIS, but he knew in 2012 that they would have the capabilities to control significant parts of Iraq and Syria.

c. "When the final accounting is done, 2014 will have been the most lethal year for global terrorism in the 45 years such data has been compiled." *James Clapper, **Director of National Intelligence**, testifying before the Senate Armed Services Committee in February 2015.* ISIL and their affiliates was responsible for a significant share of these documented terrorist incidents.

d. 'We approached the State Department about ISIS before ISIS was in the headlines, and we were ignored." *Sherkoh Abbas, **chairman of the Kurdistan National Assembly of Syria**, 2014.*

e. ISIS "probably will attempt to take territory in Iraq and Syria to exhibit its strength in 2014, as demonstrated recently in Ramadi and Fallujah, and the group's ability to concurrently maintain multiple safe havens in Syria … Since the departure of U.S. forces at the end of 2011, [Islamic State] has exploited the permissive security environment to increase its operations and presence in many locations and also has expanded into Syria and Lebanon to inflame tensions throughout the region." *Lt. General Michael Flynn, director of the **Defense Intelligence Agency**, testimony before the Senate Armed Services Committee, February 2014.*

14. "This is an attack not just on Paris, it's an attack not just on the people of France, but this is an **attack on all of humanity** and the universal values that we share." *Obama statement after the November 13, 2015 ISIS terrorist attacks in Paris that left over 130 civilians dead.* Obama is lying [taqiyya] when he declares the terrorists are attacking all of humanity. They are Islamic terrorists who have **targeted non-Muslims** [infidels] in their religious war [jihad] to destroy the West and build an Islamic caliphate. Obama refuses to acknowledge that this is an Islamic religious war since he is protecting the motives of the terrorists and purposely dissociating Islam from violence.

15. "**I don't think they're gaining strength**," Obama responded. "What is true is that from the start, **our goal has been first to contain and <u>we have contained them</u>** [not in Orlando, Nice, or at Ataturk Airport]." *Obama gave an interview to ABC George Stephanopoulos just hours before the Paris ISIS attacks that killed over 130 civilians.* Obama is wrong and is deliberately lying. Obama knows his support of the migration of Syrian Muslim refugees to Europe and the United States will tremendously increase the likelihood of massive terrorist attacks against civilians by ISIS terrorists, thus Obama is purposely expanding their range of operations. **The Lebanese Education Minister estimated that 1-2% of Muslim refugees entering Europe are ISIS fighters and up to 25% of Muslim refugees support ISIS**. Obama also made this statement knowing ISIS had recently downed a Russian civilian plane over the

Sinai Peninsula and detonated bombs in Beirut, all targets outside ISIS's base of operations. Even liberal Democratic California Senator Dianne Feinstein lamented, "I have never been more concerned … **ISIS is not contained. ISIS is expanding**. They just put out a video saying it is their intent to attack this country."

a. "**We have not contained ISIL** … Strategically **they have spread since 2010**." *Joint Chiefs of Staff Chair Marine Corps General Joseph Dunford, December 1, 2015, testifying before the House Armed Services Committee. On December 9, 2015, Secretary of Defense Carter confirmed General Dunford's positon while testifying before Congress.*

b. "The president, he understands that he doesn't want to get us entangled with hundreds of thousands of troops deployed around the world again, and I understand that completely. But, we have to realize in order to stop this, we have to be aggressive in smaller numbers, work with other nations in order to solve these problems. This is becoming a global problem. **It's expanding** [**ISIS**], and that's my concern … **What is our strategy**? What is our? What is? **I don't know** … **Now it is spreading to North Africa. Now it is spreading to other areas around the world** … **It's popularity is growing**. *[during the Obama presidency]" Former Army Chief of Staff General Ray Odierno, MSNBC "Morning Joe," May 20, 2016.* With only months remaining in Obama's presidency, the former head of the Army still does not know Obama's strategy to counter ISIS's expansion and ISIS is still expanding. Obama doesn't have a strategy to defeat ISIS because he is a radical Muslim who is allied with ISIS.

c. ISIS takes credit for the Islamist terrorist attack at the Pulse nightclub in Orlando, Florida, which killed 49 Americans in June 2016.

d. ISIS carried out a bombing and terrorist attack at Ataturk Airport in Istanbul, Turkey in June 2016, which killed over 30 individuals.

e. ISIS takes credit for the 2016 Nice truck massacre during Bastille Day celebrations, which killed over 80 people.

f. ISIS too credit for the Islamic bombing at a 2017 Ariana Grande concert in Manchester, Great Britain, that killed 22 people. Later that week, ISIS forces took over a town in the southern Philippines, and executed over 100 people.

16. "At the same time all of our countries have to ensure our security and as president **my first priority is the safety of the American people**. *[taqiyya]* And **that's why** even as **we accept more refugees** including Syrians we do so only after **subjecting them to rigorous screening and security checks**." *Obama's G20 Summit statement immediately after the Paris massacres by ISIS terrorists who presented themselves as refugees about one month earlier, November 16, 2015.* Obama decreased the screening process for family reunion applications for Middle Eastern immigrants from as long as ten years to three months during 2016. The vetting process is based on input from multiple sources. The first source is from the UN High Commissioner

for Refugees (UNHCR). The UN is a Muslim-majority organization whose end goal is the institution of Sharia law around the world, including the West. The UN will maximize Muslim immigration to Western countries to further jihad. The UNHCR works with the OIC when choosing which refugees will be transferred to America. The OIC's charter dedicates itself to jihad and instituting Sharia law, and the OIC is also allied with the Muslim Brotherhood. Another source of information is from the refugee, who is interviewed by the State Department and the DHS. Since there are no databases in Syria, Iraq, Afghanistan, Libya, or most other Middle Eastern Muslim countries, an Islamic terrorist is the only source of information about himself. Even if the terrorist lies to U.S. officials, he or she is still easily admitted to the United States. There is no reliable vetting process and Obama is lying so that he can help terrorists infiltrate America. **Muslims believing in hijrah are helping to choose which Muslim immigrants come to America since the OIC and the UN are intimately involved in the screening process for Muslims "displaced" by the ISIS conflict or any Muslims claiming refugee status**. Obama is compromising an already inadequate screening process by decreasing the vetting time from over 20 months to three months, so he can maximize Muslim immigration [and ISIS infiltration] to the United States during his last year as president.

a. "**I fully support President Donald Trump's executive order** that temporarily halts admissions from the U.S. Refugee Admissions Program and bans travel from nationals of countries that potentially pose a security risk to the United States; however, I don't think the action goes far enough … As a recently retired 25-year veteran of the U.S. Department of State who served almost eight years as a refugee coordinator throughout the Middle East, Africa, Russia and Cuba, **I have seen first-hand the abuses and fraud that permeate the refugee program** and know about the entrenched interests that fight every effort to implement much-needed reform. <u>**Despite claims of enhanced vetting, the reality is that it is virtually impossible to vet an individual who has no type of an official record**</u>, particularly in countries compromised by terrorism. U.S. immigration officials simply rely on the person's **often rehearsed and fabricated "testimony."** I have personally seen this on hundreds of occasions. As a refugee coordinator, I saw the exploitations, inconsistencies and security lapses in the program, and I advocated strongly for change. Nonetheless, during the past decade and **specifically <u>under the Obama administration</u>, the Refugee Admissions Program continued to <u>expand blindly</u>, seemingly <u>without concern for security or whether it served the best interests of its own citizens</u>**."[215] *Mary Doetsch, retired State Department official, whistle-blower letter in The Chicago Tribune, February 2017.*

b. "There is no way that we can be assured that the refugees coming from Syria are not ISIS terrorists." *Rep. Peter King, United States House Committee on Homeland*

Security – Chairman of Counterterrorism and Intelligence Subcommittee, New York AM 970 interview, April 10, 2016.

c. "FBI director James Comey said during a House Committee on Homeland Security hearing on Wednesday that the federal government does not have the ability to conduct thorough background checks on all of the 10,000 Syrian refugees that the Obama administration says will be allowed to come to the U.S … "We can only query against that which we have collected … [Comey said] And so if someone has never made a ripple in the pond in Syria in a way that would get their identity or their interest reflected in our database … there will be nothing showing up because we have no record of them."[216] *(Chuck Ross, The Daily Caller, October 2015)*

d. Tasheen Malik, one of the San Bernardino jihadi terrorists who participated in murdering fourteen Americans, was screened and vetted by the FBI and the DHS when she came to the United States on a fiancé visa and was issued a green card. She later pledged allegiance to ISIS during the terrorist attacks and met with al-Qaeda operatives while in the Middle East. She also listed a fake home address on her visa application, which was not discovered by U.S. officials. Obama's vetting and screening process is purposely ineffective.

e. "Berlin (AFP) - The Islamic State group may have **stolen 'tens of thousands' of blank passports** that it could use to smuggle its fighters into Europe as refugees, a German newspaper reported Sunday … The passports could be issued to would-be attackers to enter the European Union as asylum seekers, according to the report. Moreover, IS has already launched a money-spinning operation with the fake documents, selling them on the black market where they fetch up to 1,500 euros ($1,630) each, Welt said. European authorities have repeatedly warned of the potential threat posed by refugees travelling with counterfeit documents."[217] *(AFP, December 2015)*

f. **Yahoo Interviewer**: "But the question was, 'Are some of these refugees in your view aligned with terrorists?'" **President Assad of Syria**: "Definitely. You can find it on the net. The same picture that you saw them, in some cases of course, in some instances, those **terrorists in Syria holding the machine gun or killing people, they are – peaceful refugees in – in Europe or in the West** in general. Yeah, that's true … No one – no one has any number. Nobody knows. Because nobody knows … You don't need significant number to commit atrocities. 11th of September – it happened by only 15 – terrorists out of maybe millions of immigrants in the United States. So it's not about the number. It's about the quality. **It's about the intention**." *Yahoo Interview with President Bashar Assad of Syria and Michael Isikoff, February 10, 2017.*

g. "**A review of information compiled by a Senate committee in 2016 reveals that 72 individuals from the seven countries covered in President Trump's vetting executive**

order have been convicted in terror cases since the 9/11 attacks. These facts stand in stark contrast to the assertions by the Ninth Circuit judges who have blocked the president's order on the basis that there is no evidence showing a risk to the United States in allowing aliens from these seven terror-associated countries to come in. In June 2016, the Senate Subcommittee on Immigration and the National Interest, then chaired by new Attorney General Jeff Sessions, released a report on individuals convicted in terror cases since 9/11. Using open sources (because the Obama administration refused to provide government records), the report found that 380 out of 580 people convicted in terror cases since 9/11 were foreign-born … The Center has extracted information on 72 individuals named in the Senate report whose country of origin is one of the seven terror-associated countries included in the vetting executive order: Iran, Iraq, Libya, Somalia, Sudan, Syria, and Yemen. The Senate researchers were not able to obtain complete information on each convicted terrorist, so it is possible that more of the convicted terrorists are from these countries. The United States has admitted terrorists from all of the seven dangerous countries: Somalia (20), Yemen (19), Iraq (19), Syria (4), Libya (2), Sudan (1) – Total (72). According to the report, at least 17 individuals entered as refugees from these terror-prone countries. Three came in on student visas and one arrived on a diplomatic visa."[218] *(Center for Immigration Studies, February 11, 2017)*

h. "**3 Somalian (Muslim) terrorists** would have not been allow into U.S. under Trump's plan: In 2016 alone there were 3 attacks carried about by Somalians, a country that is on President Trump's Travel Ban list. **Ohio State Attack**: … on November 28, 2016 the attack at the Ohio State campus by 20-year-old Abdul Artan from Somalia. Artan **rammed his car into a group of students** and then proceeded to **attack them with a Machete**. In all Artan severely wounded 11 students before being killed by law enforcement. **Minnesota Mall Stabbings**: … on September 19, 2016 the **stabbing rampage** at Crossroads Mall in St. Cloud, Minnesota. The attack was carried out by Dahir Adan who screamed "Allahu Akbar!" during the attack that injured 9 people. **Attack on Jewish Restaurant in Ohio**: … On February 12, 2016 the attack that an Islamic Terrorist carried out on a Jewish Restaurant in Ohio. Mohamed Barry **hacked 4 people with a machete** before being shot dead."[219]

i. "If one were truly interested in whether there is a terror threat from individuals born abroad, one would examine the totality of activity, not a narrowly constructed definition aimed to minimize it. That's what senators Ted Cruz and Jeff Sessions did last June when they examined **580 individuals successfully prosecuted on terrorism offenses from September 2001 until 2014. According to the senators**, **380 were foreign-born and at least 40 were refugees**. While not all of those cases involved successful or attempted terror attacks, all involved cases that were terrorism-related."[220] *(Kyle Shideler,*

The Federalist, January 2017) Examples include: "The Tsarnaev brothers of the **Boston Marathon bombing**, who were both born abroad. Tamerlan was born in Kyrgyzstan in 1986, and Dzhokhar was reportedly born in Dagestan … The 2015 **Chattanooga Recruiting Center shooter**, Mohammad Youssuf Abdulazeez, was born in Kuwait and lived in Jordan before migrating to the United States at the age of six. He killed five people … **Ohio State University attacker** Abdul Razak Artan, who ran over several fellow students with a car before attacking them with a butcher knife, was a refugee born in Somalia who had only been in the United States for two years … Ahmad Khan Rahimi, born in Afghanistan, **detonated a bomb near a 5K run event, then another in downtown Manhattan** in October of last year … Dahir Adan, a Somali born in Kenya who immigrated to the United States as a child, launched a **mass stabbing attack at a St. Cloud Minnesota mall** in 2016. And these are only a few recent examples."[221] (Ibid.) And many others.

j.   "One UK official made the extraordinary statement that raids were being conducted "almost daily" and that authorities believed there were between 6-10,000 potential terrorists in the country."[222] *(American Thinker, April 30, 2017)* America's chaotic and treacherous future secondary to Obama's immigration policies is now a fact of daily life in Great Britain. By May 2017, after the Ariana Grande concert massacre, the British government confirmed there were at least 23,000 jihadists in their country.

17. **"Turkey has been a strong partner with the United States and other member of the coalition in going after the activities of ISIL, or Daesh, both in Syria and Iraq".** *Obama, G20 Summit in Turkey, November 15, 2015.* <u>One week later</u>, Turkey shot down a Russian bomber targeting ISIS forces in Syria in order to protect ISIS positions and their illicit oil trade with ISIS. This illegal business, which is used to finance ISIS's infrastructure and pay for its terrorist activities, has annual gross revenues at well over $1 billion dollars. Obama will undoubtedly receive a substantial cut of this business, which will be transferred to him as donations to his future foundation or as astronomical speaking fees he will accrue as he travels throughout the Middle East and Europe after his presidency. Obama will be paid later for protecting ISIS and their oil industry now, and for implementing strategies that will enable ISIS to grow and prosper. Theoretically if Obama is compensated 5% for protecting ISIS' oil infrastructure for 3 years, Obama will be expecting at least $100-150 million as future "fees."

a.   An *Investor's Business Daily* editorial on November 30, 2015 entitled "Et Tu Turkey?" concluded, "Turkey is no ally but a state sponsor of ISIS terrorism." The editorial supported its contention that Obama's best friend and NATO ally is committing treason against the West, NATO, France, and the United States by funding ISIS with oil purchases, treating wounded ISIS soldiers, supplying ISIS with weapons and military equipment, training ISIS soldiers, and having Turkish soldiers support ISIS operations in

Syria. Turkey is allowing its country to be a gateway for foreign soldiers and volunteers joining ISIS in Syria. Turkey is also accessing sensitive military intelligence and satellite photographs via its membership in NATO and quite possibly via Muslim Brotherhood contacts in the American defense and intelligence establishments. Turkey is then passing on this information to help ISIS fight Assad and perpetuate genocide against Christians and other non-Muslims. Obama is blatantly lying to the world community and pretending that Turkey is an ally of the West when he knows that ISIS's survival is dependent upon Turkey's treasonous actions.

b. "Our reference [guide] is Islam. **Our only goal is an Islamic state**. They can never intimidate us. If the skies and the earth open up, if storms blow on us, if the lava of volcanoes flow on us, we will never change our way. My guide is Islam. If I cannot live according to Islam, why live at all?" *Erdogan speech while serving as mayor of Istanbul. December 6, 1997.* Erdogan has been looking to form a new Islamic caliphate for over twenty years. It is his life's goal.

c. "He's striving for absolute power in Turkey. **Erdogan wants a** [Islamic] **Caliphate**. We Kurds are in his way. Erdogan can't stop us politically, so he is denouncing us as terrorists."[223] *Selahattin Demirtas, head of the Kurkish HDP Party of Turkey, Der Spiegel International interview, April 19, 2016.* Demirtas is explaining partly why Erdogan is waging war against the Kurds.

d. Turkey **refuses to call ISIS a terrorist group**.

e. **ISIS has remained viable thanks to the supplies and military recruits that cross the border from Turkey to Syria**, with the consent of Erdogan, and most likely, Obama. Turkey is the main transit country for foreign fighters looking to join the ISIS army. **ISIS troops have been training in Turkey** and cross the border into Syria at will. According to Daniel Pipes in an article "**Turkish Support for ISIS**" in *The Washington Times* on June 18, 2014, Turkey "provided the bulk of ISIS's funds, logistics, training and arms." This is facilitated by the fact that Syria and Turkey share a very large border and many ISIS logistical centers are close to the Turkish border. Turkey has a similar relation with the al Nusra Front, al-Qaeda's main Syrian organization, which is also engaged against the Kurds in Syria, at the bequest of Turkey.

f. In 2014, **an ISIS fighter hospitalized in Turkey** told a Turkish reporter, "**the AKP government has helped us a lot … Turkey paved the way for us**. Had Turkey not shown such understanding for us, the Islamic State would not be in its current place … Large numbers of our mujahedeen [jihadis] received medical treatment in Turkey."[224] Turkey regularly treats wounded ISIS soldiers.

g. In October 2014, **Turkish soldiers posed for pictures with ISIS soldiers** in Kobani, Syria, adjacent to the Turkish border. The Turkish government refused to help the besieged Syrian refugees, many whom are Kurds, on their border. The Kurds requested heavy weapons to fight ISIS and asked Turkey to allow Syrian Kurds from the northwest to travel through Turkey to reinforce their troops. Both requests were refused. In 2014, Turkey prevented U.S. arms transfers to the Kurds through their territory.

h.   There is **support for ISIS in the Turkish police and army**. Police officials have been seen wearing ISIS t-shirts while working. In 2014, Turkish protestors and Turkish police have flashed pro-ISIS hand signals while attacking Kurdish political assemblies. These are the same hand signals that Obama flashed to African dignitaries at the U.S.-African Leaders' Summit held in Washington D.C. during August 2014.

i.   In early June 2015, **ISIS troops crossed into Turkey (Tal Abyad) and forced Syrian refugees back into Syria at gunpoint. Turkish troops did not intervene**. There are other reports that the Turkish troops fired warning shots and used water cannons against fleeing Syrian refugees approaching the Turkish border. It appears that Turkey has participated in three genocides within the past one hundred years: the Armenians, the Greeks (1914 - 1923), and now the Syrians.

j.   An ISIS representative admits there are **over 4000 ISIS armed operatives in Europe, many of whom gained entry into the EU via Turkey**.

k.   In February 2015, **U.S. Intelligence Chief James Clapper** testified before the Senate Armed Services Committee concerning foreign fighters transiting through Turkey to join ISIS, "I think **Turkey has other priorities** and other interests … the consequence of that is a **permissive environment** … because of their laws and the ability of people to travel through Turkey in route to Syria … somewhere in the neighborhood of **60 percent of those foreign fighters find their way to Syria through Turkey**."

l.   On November 1, 2015, **Erdogan refused to condemn ISIS for downing a Russian passenger plane**. Erdogan stated, "How can I condemn the Islamic State for shooting down a Russian plane as its passengers were returning from a happy vacation in a time **when our co-religionists in Syria are bombed by Putin's fighter jets**? … it is the natural outcome of Moscow's actions in Syria and the support for Assad." Erdogan confirms his support for ISIS.

m.   On November 15, 2015, **Turkish soccer fans booed and chanted "*Allahu Akbar*" during a moment of silence for the French victims of the ISIS Paris massacre** at the beginning of a soccer match between Turkey and Greece in Turkey. This act shows the Turkish Muslim population supports ISIS and their terrorist attacks in Europe.

n.   "We have serious doubts this was an unintended incident and believe this is a planned provocation [by Turkey] … by shooting down a Russian plane on a counter-terrorist mission of the Russian Aerospace Force in Syria, and one that **did not violate Turkey's airspace, the Turkish government has in effect sided with ISIS**." *Russian Foreign Minister Sergey Lavrov, November 25, 2015.*

o. "Turkey is either not fighting ISIL at all or very little, and does not interfere with different types of smuggling that takes place on its border, be it oil, phosphate, cotton or people." *Retired French General Dominique Trinquand.*

p. **Turkey has been buying oil from ISIS** for years. When **U.S. Special Forces raided an ISIS compound** in eastern Syria where ISIS leader Abu Sayyaf was killed in May 2015, **documents were obtained proving Turkey was the major purchaser of ISIS oil**, **and that ISIS is economically dependent on their relationship with Turkey**. Obama has not bombed the oil fields under the control of ISIS, since it would upset the cash flows to both the Turkish and ISIS treasuries. Turkey has an alliance with ISIS, where Turkey buys their oil at a discounted price, and ISIS uses the funds to finance their military, terrorist, and government operations. It is unfathomable that Turkey, as a full member of NATO, is the major financier of ISIS, and supports the genocide of Christians.

i. "I've shown photos taken from space and from aircraft which clearly demonstrate the [industrial] scale of the illegal trade in oil and petroleum products … Oil from Islamic State is being shipped to Turkey … **Islamic State gets cash by selling oil to Turkey.**" *Russian President Putin's comments after Turkey shoots down a Russian bomber over Syria.*

ii. Since Obama refused to bomb the ISIS oil industry's infrastructure, he allowed ISIS to remain a formidable well-funded terrorist organization and permitted Turkey to make huge profits on purchases of ISIS's greatly discounted oil products and crude. By protecting the ISIS – Turkey oil trade, Obama ensured that the ISIS military budget received continuous funding that has already surpassed $1 billion. Daniel Glaser, the Treasury Department's assistant secretary for terrorist financing stated, "We estimate that in 2015, ISIL made approximately USD 1 billion dollars in total revenue, USD 500 million of which came from the sale of oil."[225] Since half of ISIS' gross revenue came from oil sales, and by not bombing ISIS' oil infrastructure, Obama can be considered the largest financial enabler of ISIS worldwide.

iii. "**In the last eight months ISIS has managed to sell … $800 million worth of oil on the black market in Turkey.** This is Iraqi oil and Syrian oil, carried by trucks from Iraq, from Syria through the borders to Turkey and sold … less than 50 percent of the international oil price." *Former National Security Advisor and Iraqi MP, Mowaffak al Rubaie.*

iv. "Large quantities of oil have been smuggled across the border to Turkey from IS-controlled areas in Syria and Iraq … [The] oil is sent by tankers via smuggling routes across the border [and] is sold at greatly reduced prices, from 25 to 45 dollars a barrel," *Rystad Energy report written at the request of the Norwegian foreign ministry, December 2015.*

q. **The whole Erdogan family** [and Turkey] **is in the business of supporting ISIS.**[226] Obama is best friends with Erdogan, and as recently as November 15, 2015, Erdogan referred to Obama as "my dear friend, President Barack Obama," at the G20 Summit.

   i. **Recip Erdogan**, the father of Balil Erdogan and president of Turkey, along with the Turkish intelligence agency (MIT), has been supporting ISIS with training, men, materials, supplies, and logistics since its inception. Even Vice President Biden spoke at Harvard and commented that Erdogan was supporting ISIS with "hundreds of millions of dollars and thousands of tons of weapons." Erdogan's basic goal is to reestablish the Ottoman Empire in the Middle East extending toward China and Europe. Erdogan is sustaining ISIS as the military force whose military objective is to create an Islamic caliphate. Recip Erdogan also directed the pillage of Syria's archeological artifacts and their sale on the world market.

   ii. **Balil Erdogan**, Recip Erdogan's son, **is in charge of the sale of illegal oil ISIS has stolen from Iraqi oil wells**. These allegations are supported by photos showing Balil Erdogan with ISIS commanders. Balil Erdogan's main business, BMZ Ltd., is a maritime shipping company that facilitates the illegal oil trade, in which the Erdogan family has a significant interest. Recip Erdogan and his family greatly profit from ISIS' illegal oil trade. "**All of the oil was delivered to a company that belongs to the son of Recip Erdogan**. This is why Turkey became anxious when Russia began delivering airstrikes against the IS infrastructure and destroyed more than 500 trucks with oil already. This really got on Erdogan and his company's nerves. **They're importing not only oil, but wheat and historic artefacts as well.**" *Syrian Information Minister Omran al-Zoub, November 27, 2015*. **The Erdogan family is looting Iraq and Syria** of their natural resources and their historical artifacts, the majority of which are sold by ISIS in Turkey.

   iii. **Sumeyye Erdogan,** Recip Erdogan's daughter, runs Turkish hospitals adjacent to the Syrian border, where wounded ISIS soldiers are treated and returned to the battlefield.

r. "Let's be very clear: **ISIS** is not just a terrorist organization, it is a Sunni terrorist organization … **It's serving the interests of Turkey and Saudi Arabia** … ISIS got started through funding from our friends and allies." *U.S. Retired General Wesley Clark, former commander of NATO, November 28, 2015.*

s. At the end of November 2015, Turkish authorities arrested three journalists / editors for treason and espionage because the voiced dissent with Erdogan's pro-ISIS policies and revealed links between ISIS fighters and the Turkish military and intelligence.

t. "I think Turkey is indeed a member of NATO, but sometimes behaves as if it's more an ally of Islamic State. It removes oil from Syria which finances the Islamic State … They do not like the Kurds, which are the only ones who fought effectively with the Islamic State. That is why Turkey … should not be an EU member." *Czech President Milos Zeman arguing why Turkey should not be allowed to enter the European Union in early December 2015.*

u. In December 2015, Yazidi refugees were filmed by German crews in Turkey buying family members held in captivity by ISIS in Syria. ISIS was using Turkish territory as a base to conduct ransom negotiations for kidnapped Syrians.

v. A captured ISIS fighter told YPG authorities, "In August 2014, I was training in the Turkish town of Adana with one of ISIL's Emirs. [The training officer] spoke [only] Turkish, so another one had to translate for him. We were trained in Turkey because ISIL's command thought it was safer here than in Syria because of the bombardments."[227]

w. Israeli Defense Minister Ya'alon stated in Athens in mid-January 2016 that ISIS "enjoyed Turkish money for oil for a very, very long period of time" and that Turkey has allowed ISIS terrorists to transit between their bases in Syria and Iraq to Europe.

x. Vitaly Churkin, the Russian Ambassador to the United Nations, submitted a letter to Secretary General Ban Ki-moon in late May 21016 that stated that improvised explosive devices (IEDs) used in Iraq and Syria "were either manufactured in Turkey or delivered to that country without the right of re-export." Russia traced the chemical components of the explosives to five Turkish companies that were delivering the munitions to ISIS. Components of the bombs were also traced back to the United States.

y. **A released DIA memo** from August 2012 identified **Turkey** along with the **Muslim Brotherhood**, **Obama** (the United States, the West), and the Gulf States as the **primary benefactors of al-Qaeda in Iraq which morphed into ISIS**. ISIS was created to foment an insurrection in Syria which was intended to overthrow the secular Assad government and create an active military front on Israel's northern border.

z. In July 2016, French military intelligence estimated that over 100 foreign Muslim jihadis are crossing through Turkey and are reinforcing ISIS positions in Syria each week.

aa. "The Western calculus has been **complicated by** the emerging **transformation of Turkey**, once a key moderating influence, from a secular state **into an <u>ideologically Islamic</u> version. At once affecting Europe by its control over the flow of migrants from the Middle East** and <u>**frustrating Washington by the movement of oil and other goods across its southern border**</u> …" *Henry Kissinger, "Chaos and Order in a Changing World," Capx.co, August 2, 2017.* Kissinger admits that Turkey has become a pro-Islamist country, and has been allied with ISIS by maintaining trade with them and funding their operations by purchasing their oil, stolen from Iraq and Syria, at discounted prices.

18. "I'm told **the president did not want to take out the** [ISIS oil] **trucks because there are some concerns with the environment** … I'm still frustrated over them saying it's hard to

see the convoys when they're on the open terrain. **It's a bit disingenuous to me to say they can't take trucks out, they can take them out**. We've taken out some refineries. **What's the problem?**"[228] *Rep. Robert Pettenger, Vice-Chair of the Bipartisan Task Force to Investigate Terrorism Financing.* The problem is that Obama's major concern is protecting the financial resources of ISIS and Erdogan, and not the environment. The environment is merely an excuse to keep ISIS' oil infrastructure intact. Obama will probably be getting financial kickbacks from the Middle East for keeping the ISIS – Turkey oil trade viable for many years by refusing to bomb the ISIS oil industry infrastructure.

19. **Turkey "has a right to defend its territory and its airspace**." *Obama, November 24, 2015.* Obama lied to support Turkey's assertion the Russian aircraft violated Turkish airspace. Radar maps clearly showed that the Russian aircraft stayed within Syrian boundaries. Obama is supporting Turkey's decision to shoot down a Russian aircraft over Syria to protect ISIS. Obama and Erdogan may have discussed shooting down Russian aircraft with Turkish F-16s at the G20 Summit, and subsequently bringing NATO into the equation so that NATO would support Obama's strategies and his desire to protect ISIS by being a counterweight to increasing Russian aggression in Syria. Putin revealed on November 26 that Obama was given the coordinates of the Russian fighters beforehand, so confrontations between the allies and Russia could be avoided. Obama then gave those coordinates to Turkey. Obama knows that Germany will not join NATO with any aggression or significant policies against Russia, and thus, Obama may be planting the seeds for a major regional war in the Middle East and quite possibly the disintegration of the NATO alliance.

20. "**ISIL will not pose an existential threat to us**. *[Tell that to the families of the fourteen murdered individuals in San Bernardino who were killed solely because they were not Muslims or the fifty young Americans who were killed in Orlando.]* ... The American people should feel confident that, you know, **we are going to be able to defend ourselves** *[not with Obama's planned gun control]* and make sure that, you know, we have a good holiday and go about our lives." *Obama, CBS interview,* **just hours before** *(like in Paris) ISIS inspired Muslim terrorists murdered fourteen Christians who were attending a company Christmas party in San Bernardino, California. December 2015.*

    a. "We've said to them a hundred times, a million times ... America will pay the price in a way it cannot even imagine. **Obama the liar, the ally of the terrorists** ... I call him a liar ... the American people is our friend ... They love Egypt very much ... but I would like the Congress to send Obama to the guillotine, because three days before the San Bernardino *[and Paris]* terror attack ... he appeared and lied, like he always does, that liar. **All the allies of terrorism *[including Obama]* are liars**. He said: "There is not threat to American citizens." It is as if he was trying to cover. Today, **I suspect that Obama is connected to the terrorists who carried out the attack** [in San Bernardino]. When he says something like this, he numbs the security agencies, the military, and the intelligence agencies. If this had happened in a respectful country, Obama would have been placed on trial. The U.S. Congress should ask: How come you said that according to your information no terrorist attack was imminent? … Less than 72 hours later, a terror attack took place." *Popular Egyptian TV Host Ahmed Moussa, Sada al Balad TV, MEMRI TV, December 5, 2015.*

    b.   "I'm expecting them [ISIS] to try to put in place the operatives, the material or whatever else that they need to do or to incite people to carry out these attacks, clearly. So I believe that **their attempts** *[to launch significant terrorist attacks in America]* **are inevitable**." *CIA Director John Brennan, CBS 60 Minutes interview, February 14, 2016.* Even after Brennan's remarks, Obama is seeking to increase the number of Syrian refugees / migrants settled in the United States. Felicia Escobar, Obama's assistant for immigration policy stated, "We want to make sure that we can increase our numbers of refugees that are able to settle here." Obama knows ISIS operatives are embedded with the refugees and he wants to maximize the number of Islamic terrorist cells and their supporters in America before he leaves office.

21.   "So far we have <u>**no evidence**</u> that the killers were **directed by a terrorist organization overseas**, or that they were **part of a broader conspiracy here at home**." *Obama, Oval Office speech addressing America's concerns regarding terrorism after the San Bernardino terrorist attack. December 6, 2015.* Obama is **downplaying** the connections and support structure for Farook and Malik. Obama is also running interference for the terrorist groups.

    a.   Farook's mother lived in the same house as the terrorists that had multiple weapons, a pipe bomb / IED factory, and over 7000 rounds of ammunition. She also had GoPro packaging and practice targets in her car. She was aware of the future jihad. The mother is a member of the **Islamic Circle of North America**, which supports radical foreign jihadi imams.

    b.   Farook's father admitted his son admired and supported ISIS.

    c.   Farook's salary could not support the purchase of weapons and ammunition found in his possession, thus third parties financed his operations. $28,500 was deposited in Farook's bank account around the time of the terrorist attack.

    d.   Farook reportedly contacted Mohamed Abdullahi Hassan, an ISIS recruiter and a Muslim Somali refugee who lived in Minneapolis.

    e.   Farook's in-law, Enrique Marquez, purchased the weapons used in the terrorist attacks.

    f.   Witnesses place multiple Middle Eastern men with Farook and around his home in the weeks preceding the terrorist attacks.

g.   Roshan Abbassi, one of the Muslim clerics at the Dar al Uloom al Islamiyyah mosquee that Farook attended, texted with Farook at least 38 times before the attack. This mosque is believed to shelter Talishi Jamaat activists, who are also known as the "Army of Darkness."

22.   State Department spokesperson proclaimed that **a major achievement of Obama and Kerry in 2015 was "bringing peace [and] security" to Syria.** He also stated that the United States is "**winning** [the] **fight against violent extremists** [**ISIS – in Syria**]." During this time the Russians complained that Obama was fighting against ISIS "in word only." The Russian air force has been the most effective entity targeting and destroying ISIS military and economic resources, including oil ground tankers. Obama refused to cooperate with Russia with respect to identifying ISIS targets. This statement continued the Obama tradition of falsifying information to downplay ISIS just as he stated that ISIS was "JV" or that ISIS was "contained" just before the Paris attacks.

23.   Obama released a misleading statement after the Orlando nightclub massacre dealing with national security issues surrounding ISIS. Obama declared, "We are making significant progress ... This campaign at this stage is firing on all cylinders ... ISIL is under more pressure than ever before ... ISIL continues to lose key leaders ... ISIL continues to lose ground in Iraq ... in Syria as well ... it also continues to lose the money that is its lifeblood ... ISIL's ranks are shrinking as well. Their morale is sinking ... The flow of foreign fighters – including from America to Syria and Iraq – has plummeted." Two days later, on June 16, 2016, CIA Director John **Brennan contradicted Obama** with testimony before the Senate Intelligence Committee by stating, "despite all our progress against ISIL on the battlefield and in the financial realm, **our efforts have not reduced the group's terrorism capability and global reach** ... Moreover, the group's foreign branches and global networks can help preserve its capacity for terrorism regardless of events in Iraq and Syria. In fact, as the pressure mounts on ISIL, we judge that **it will intensify its global terror campaign to maintain its dominance of the global terrorism agenda** ... ISIL has a **large cadre of Western fighters** who could potentially serve as operatives for attacks in the West. And the group is probably exploring a **variety of means for infiltrating operatives into the West, including refugee flows, smuggling routes, and legitimate methods of travel** ... The **branch in Libya is probably the most developed and the most dangerous** ... ISIL's Sinai branch has established itself as the most active and capable terrorist group in Egypt ... **I have never seen a time when our country faced such a wide variety of threats to our national security.**" *Statement by Director Brennan as Prepared for Delivery Before the Senate Select Committee on Intelligence, June 16, 2016. Obama lied.*

a.   "NBC News has exclusively obtained a map showing the global expansion of the terror group. The map is part of a **classified briefing document received by the White**

House dated "**August 2016**" and **prepared by the National Counterterrorism Center.
It shows a stunning <u>three-fold increase</u> in the number of places around the globe
where ISIS is operating**. U.S. State Department documents indicated that in 2014,
when the U.S. military began its campaign to destroy the extremists, there were only sev-
en nations in which the fledgling state was operating … The current briefing map shows
18 countries where ISIS is fully operational. The map also displays a new category –
"aspiring branches" – and lists six countries where they're taking root: Egypt, Indonesia,
Mali, the Philippines, Somalia and Bangladesh."[229] *Obama lied to the American public
about ISIS' capabilities and downplayed its threat to the West. Obama is running interference for the terrorists. In May 2017, ISIS terrorists overran a town in the southern Philippines
and executed over 100 civilians.*

24. "Michelle and I are also ever-mindful that many of our fellow Christians do not enjoy that
right [to freely practice their faith], and hold especially close to our hearts and minds those
who have been driven from their ancient homelands by unspeakable violence and persecution … This silence [of Middle Eastern church bells] bears tragic witness to the brutal
atrocities committed against these communities by ISIL. We join with people around the
world in praying for G-d's protection *[but not America's or Obama's protection]* for persecuted
Christians …" *Obama's Statement on Persecuted Christians at Christmas, 2015.* Out of 384
Syrian refugees admitted to the United States by Obama since the Paris attacks (November
13), only one person was a Christian, and 382 were Muslims. Obama has directed the State
Department and the DHS to severely limit Christian immigration into America while they
maximize Muslim immigration, which proves Obama's sympathies and affinities lie with the
Muslims, despite his speech expressing faux Christian concerns. Since October 1, Obama
admitted only 6 Christians from Syria while 668 Muslims (99.1%) were admitted. By the
end of 2015, Obama would not label the atrocities against Christians as genocide, which
would prioritize the Christian community's ability and ease to gain entry into the United
States. During the same week that Obama delivered the above address, Justin Welby, the
Archbishop of Canterbury reflected, "They [ISIS] hate difference … because of them, the
Christians face elimination in the very region in which Christian faith began." The elimination of Christianity by radical Muslims from various sections of the Middle East occurred
during Obama's tenure, when he repeatedly praised Islam and instituted policies that allowed
massive Muslim migration to Europe and America while blocking Christian migration from
the Middle East. These are the actions and policies of a radical Muslim who is targeting the
Christian communities in Iraq and Syria for annihilation. During Obama's two terms as
president, the Christian communities in Iraq and Syria decreased by over 50-70% as a result
of murder or forced migration. An article in *The New York Post* recognized one of Obama distinct grim legacies – "Prospects of Christianity surviving in its birthplace, the Middle East,

appear as grim this Holy Week as they have at any time in the last two millennia. Persecution of the world's largest religion has intensified, especially in Muslim-dominated countries. Jihadists appear to have repeatedly carried out one of their oft-stated goals of erasing any trace of Christianity in some regions."[230]

25. "So how do we, as people of faith, reconcile these realities – **the profound good, the strength, the tenacity, the <u>compassion and love</u> that can flow from all of our faiths, operating alongside those who seek to hijack <u>religions</u> for their own murderous ends**? [*taqiyya*] Humanity has been grappling with these questions throughout human history." *Obama, National Prayer Breakfast Address, February 5, 2015.* Obama advances two false moral equivalences in one sentence. First Obama connects the love and compassion associated with Judeo-Christian ethics to Islam. Then he discusses those extremists in all religions (plural) who hijack their theological underpinnings to justify terrorism – equating ISIS extremists with those "extremists" present in all other religions.

26. "Yet what we also know is that <u>**severe drought**</u> **helped to create the instability in Nigeria that was exploited by the terrorist group Boko Haram**. It's now believed that drought and crop failures and **high food prices helped fuel the early unrest in Syria**, which descended into civil war in the heart of the Middle East." *Obama, Remarks by the President at the United States Coast Guard Academy Commencement, May 20, 2015.* Obama is blaming weather for the rise of Boko Haram and ISIS, diverting attention away from jihad and fundamental Islamic root causes as the impetus of their political and military movements. Obama helped arm Boko Haram and ISIS with weapons transfers from the Libyan military, which he helped secure by overthrowing Gaddafi. Obama was one of the founders of ISIS in Syria. Obama is running political interference for ISIS and Boko Haram.

27. "We'll constantly reaffirm through words and deeds that **we will never be at war with Islam** … [ISIS] Ideologies are **not defeated with guns, they are defeated by better ideas**, a more attractive and more compelling vision … This <u>**will not be quick**</u>, *[Obama is stalling, giving ISIS time to build a caliphate.]* this is a <u>**long-term campaign**</u> *[Obama wants a long-term conflict between Islamic terrorists and the West, so the West's will to win will be drained and its resources will be depleted. Obama followed this strategy in Afghanistan, the longest war in American history. This strategy has been outlined in al-Qaeda's war with the West.]* … I think it is important for us to recognize **the threat of violent extremism is not restricted to any one community**. *[false moral equivalence]* **Here in the United States, we've all kinds of home grown terrorism**. And tragically, recent history reminds how even a single individual can inflict horrendous harm on Americans. **So our efforts to counter violent extremism must not target any one community** *[Obama is diverting attention away from Islam.]*, **because of the patriotic Muslim Americans who are partners in keeping our country safe** *[CAIR tells Muslims not to work with the FBI.]*… We also have to acknowledge that ISIL has been

particularly effective at reaching out to and recruiting vulnerable people around the world including here in the United States and they are **targeting Muslim communities** around the world … If we try to do everything ourselves all across the Middle East *[i.e., U.S. ground troops will not be involved which guarantees the survival of the Islamic terrorists.]*, all across North Africa, we'll be playing 'Whack-a-mole' and there will be a whole lot of unintended consequences that ultimately will make us less secure. *[Obama is protecting ISIS.]*" *Obama, July 6, 2015, Department of Defense Press Conference.* Again, Obama is declaring there is no special relationship between Islam and ISIS, violence, and terrorism. Obama sees a moral equivalency between ISIS and crime in America. Obama states he will not defeat ISIS and its culture with military force, and the conflict between ISIS and the West will be a long-term event. Obama has no real plans and no intentions to defeat ISIS during his term.

    a.   "If they bring a knife to the fight, **we bring a gun**." Obama may not want to fight ISIS with a guns, but he is always willing to wage a political war [with theoretical guns] against Republicans, conservatives and Christians. Despite threatening political opponents with images of weapons, Obama will not hesitate to oppose Republicans and conservatives on guns control issues.

28. Obama called the shooter Muhammad Youssef Abdulazeez a "**lone gunman**" after the murder of four Marines in Chattanooga, Tennessee on July 16, 2015. Obama immediately described him as "lone," which means not related to Islam or ISIS, and a "gunman," who is not an Islamic radical or even a radical extremist. Abdulazeez was not a lone gunman since ISIS tweeted 11 minutes before the attack, "O American Dogs. Soon You Will See Wonders #Chattanooga." **Obama knew this with his intelligence briefing and lied to America, thus protected ISIS. Obama <u>downplayed and whitewashed this jihadi act of war against America</u> by calling this attack a "<u>heartbreaking circumstance</u>**." Obama is always trying to protect and downplay radical Islam and its warriors. The shooter travelled to Jordan one year previously, spending months in the Middle East, failed a security clearance when applying for a job at a nuclear power plant *[where he would try to instigate nuclear terrorism for ISIS]*, had a Palestinian father from Nablus (hotbed of jihad) who was under investigation for ties with foreign terrorist organizations, wrote in his diary of his desire to become a martyr, and posted on his blog: "We need … to establish Islam in the world." There could be no doubt this was jihad. After expressing his sympathies publicly (not privately) to the families of the slain Marines, Obama later went to dinner celebrating the end of Ramadan, a time when Muslims worldwide increase the number and intensity of terrorist attacks against infidels and those whom Muslims considered their enemies. Obama was not opposed to celebrating the end of Ramadan and extolling the virtues of Islam at the time of the murders. Obama did not lower the federal flags to half-mast for six days until a national uproar forced him to do it, he refused to reverse his policy of not permitting military personnel to carry arms on their bases

or at recruiting stations, and he did not call the attack terrorism. Some in the news media are questioning why Obama is so inflexible and insensitive on these issues, and the obvious answer is – because he is a radical Muslim.

29. "The overwhelming majority of victims of terrorism over the last several years, and certainly **the overwhelming majority of victims of ISIL, are themselves Muslims. ISIL does not represent Islam**. *[taqiyya]* **It is not representative in any way of the attitudes of the overwhelming majority of Muslims**. *[But a vast significant minority of Muslim worldwide support ISIS.]* … **And so to the degree that anyone would equate the terrible actions that took place in Paris with the views of Islam, those kinds of stereotypes are counterproductive. They're wrong.** *[taqiyya]* **They will lead, I think, to greater recruitment into terrorist organizations over time if this becomes somehow defined as a Muslim problem as opposed to a terrorist problem** *[Obama's weakness and tacit support of terrorism is the most important factor in accelerating the recruitment of Muslims worldwide into Islamic terrorist organizations.]*… And so I think, on the one hand, **non-Muslims cannot stereotype** *[Obama dictates to or subjugates, and criticizes non-Muslims, which is behavior one would expect from a Muslim.]*… The people who are fleeing Syria … are parents, they are **children** *[75% of Sweden's children Muslim refugees are adults as confirmed by multiple studies]*, they are **orphans** *[pediatric political human shields]*." *Obama at the G20 Summit, November 16, 2015.* Obama is proselytizing for Islam and doing his best to distance Islam from terrorism and violence. Pure taqiyya. Obama is also lecturing non-Muslims on how to think and view the terrorist attacks. Obama also misrepresented (or lied about) the situation by stating the people fleeing Syria are children, orphans, and parents, when the vast majority of the refugees are young adult males without families, many of whom are eager to wage jihad. Obama embellishes the use of children and orphans in his arguments because he wants to shield the terrorists who will infiltrate Europe and the United States via refugee programs.

30. "It is possible this is terrorist related. **We don't know**. It is also possible this was **workplace related** *[How many times can Obama use 'workplace violence' as a cover for an Islamic terror attack? As with Fort Hood.]* … **We have to search ourselves as a society.** *[Obama blames Western freedoms when the real culprit is Islam.]*" *Obama's statement concerning an Islamic terrorist attack on December 2, 2015 in San Bernardino, California that massacred fourteen people.* Obama is diverting attention away from **obvious** Islamic terrorism. Obama also denied Islam as the motivating factor of terror attacks in Orlando and Nice, immediately after they occurred. Obama proclaimed that this type of violence "has no parallel anywhere else in the world [except in the United States]." Obama needs to look at every Muslim country where violence against infidels is pandemic. Obama falsely *[taqiyya]* placed the blame on American society *[like he placed the blame for Benghazi on anti-Islamic video]* despite knowing the following facts and making his statement one day after the incident:

    a.   The perpetrators were all Muslims and the FBI was treating the massacre as terrorism.

    b.   One of the assailants, Syed Farook, had recently taken an extended trip to Saudi Arabia, and married a Pakistani Muslim, Tashfeen Malik, who also participated in the attack.

    c.   Investigators found a bomb / IED factory in Farook's home, where IEDs and remote control bombs using al-Qaeda technology were discovered. Investigators found more than a dozen pipe bombs. The terrorists left a pipe bomb at the scene of the attack.

    d.   According to the FBI, Farook was in contact with known international terrorists before the attack.

    e.   The perpetrators wore GoPro cameras, just as ISIS terrorists and other Muslim extremists have done in previous European attacks.

    f.   The assailants had 7,000 rounds of ammunition in their possession.

    g.   Neighbors noted multiple Middle Eastern men congregating around the assailants' home weeks before the attack.

    h.   The Muslims targeted a Christmas party. The Christmas party may have been offensive to these devout Muslims, as is free speech and blasphemy.

    i.   The assailants destroyed their digital footprints one day before the massacre. Cell phones were crushed, hard drives disappeared, and emails were erased.

    j.   After Obama's remarks, it was revealed the wife pledged allegiance to ISIS, and the couple may have had contacts with al-Qaeda while in the Middle East. Again, **Obama is running interference for the terrorists**. Obama knew immediately they were foreign supported Islamic terrorists since a third party had to pay for all their equipment which could not be bought on Farook's limited salary that went towards supporting his wife and baby.

31. "Although it's still early in the investigation, we know enough to say that this was an act of terror and an **act of hate** … We are **still learning all the facts**. This is an open investigation. <u>**We've reached no definitive judgment on the precise motivations**</u> of the killer. *[As in San Bernardino, Obama tries to obscure and hide the motivations of Islamic terrorists and killers, whom he supports.]* The FBI is appropriately investigating this as an act of terrorism … What is clear is that he was a person **filled with hatred** … And no act of hate or terror will ever change who we are or the values that make us Americans … This massacre is therefore a further **reminder of how easy it is for someone to get their hands on a weapon** that lets them shoot people in a school, or in a house of worship, or a movie theater, or in a nightclub. *[Obama uses jihad as an excuse to attack the Second Amendment.]* And we have to decide if that's the kind of country we want to be … In the face of **hate and violence**, we will love one another. We will not give in to fear or turn against each other." *Obama, Remarks on the Mass Shooting in Orlando, June 12, 2016, 2 PM.* A radical Islamic terrorist allied with ISIS kills forty-nine Americans at a gay nightclub while yelling "Allahu Akbar," and Obama refused to

mention Islam in his opening statement and will not associate Islam with violence, regardless of the evidence. Obama does use this emotionally distraught time immediately after the massacre to launch another crusade for gun control. A radical Muslim jihadi massacres defenseless American citizens, and Obama's response is to disarm the American population so they will be less able to defend themselves against future jihadi attacks.

32. "And when I hear folks say that, well, maybe we should just admit the Christians but not the Muslims; when I hear political leaders suggesting that there would be **a religious test** for which a person who's fleeing from a war-torn country is admitted, when some of those folks themselves come from families who benefitted from protection when they were fleeing political persecution – **that's <u>shameful</u>. That's not American. That's not who we are. <u>We don't have religious tests to our compassion</u>**." *Obama at the G20 Summit, November 16, 2015.* Obama has a solemn constitutional duty to protect American citizens, and by forcing the immigration of Syrian Muslim refugees in America, he is purposely planting a proven number of terrorists in our country. Up to 2% of Syrian refugees are ISIS fighters / terrorists, and up to 25% of these migrants support ISIS. Obama is increasing the risk of Islamic domestic terror attacks in the United States, like the ones in Nice, San Bernardino, Brussels, and Paris, where hundreds of adults and children were slaughtered by Muslim immigrants and their accomplices. At least 30 governors, including Democrats, have refused to allow the resettlement of Syrian Muslim refugees in their states in order to protect the safety of their citizens. The FBI and the Department of Homeland Security (DHS) have admitted they cannot fully vet the refugees. Obama is using the bully pulpit to harass and shame loyal Americans who do not want ISIS terrorists in their communities. Obama initially defended Islam, then transitioned to criticizing and chastising patriotic Americans – the modus operandi of a radical Muslim.

a. Obama has actively blocked Christian refugees from seeking asylum in America and has even sent some Christians back to the Middle East. Obama has refused to meet with Middle Eastern Christian leaders who were in Washington on other official business. Less than 2-3% of refugees / immigrants from the Middle East are Christians. Obama has refused to arm Christian and Yazidi fighters who are opposing ISIS in Syria and Iraq. Obama is anti-Christian and is aiding their genocide, and that is shameful and not American. *["In exclusive interviews, photos and research, The Associated Press has documented and mapped 72 of the mass graves, the most comprehensive survey so far, with many more expected to be uncovered as the Islamic State group's territory shrinks ... the known numbers of victims buried are staggering – from 5,200 to more than 15,000."231]* What is shameful is a president who refuses to help Americans under attack in Benghazi – goes to sleep and lets them die. What is shameful is an American president who abandons and ousts America's long-standing Egyptian ally Mubarak, while supporting the Muslim

Brotherhood, a worldwide terrorist group that has spawned Hamas and al-Qaeda. What is shameful is a president who wants Hamas to take over East Jerusalem, and gives an enemy of the United States – Iran – who has sworn to destroy us, the increasing ability to develop nuclear weapons and intercontinental ballistic missiles.

b. From May 1-24, 2016, Obama's State Department admitted 499 Syrian Muslim refugees and no Christian refugees to the United States. From October 1, 2015 through May 24, 2016, only 0.4% of all refugees admitted from Syria that were resettled in the United States were Christians.

c. Ninety-eight percent of the Syrian refugees admitted by Obama are Sunni Muslims, who are generally not persecuted by ISIS and al-Qaeda, since they all originate from the same sect of Islam. Thus, the Sunnis will be more sympathetic to ISIS, their policies, and jihad.

d. In June 2016, Obama accepted a record number of Syrian migrants, over 2,300. Sunni Muslims comprised over 99% of the total number of immigrants, with only eight Christians allowed entry into the United States. With the Syrian population being over 10% Christian before the start of the civil war initiated by Obama backed rebels, at least 10% of the refugees admitted into the United States should be Christian. Obama is discriminating against the Christians, and has his own religious test – immigrants accepted into America must be Muslim. With Obama's directives to speed up the vetting process and to ignore applicants' views on jihad, Sharia law, and Islamic terrorism, Obama is guaranteeing that ISIS terrorists will easily infiltrate the United States. Since ISIS is instructing its agents on how to avoid being flagged as a potential terrorist suspect, many ISIS operatives will be able to settle in the United States and establish sleeper cells, which will guarantee the repetition of horrific Islamic terrorist attacks on American soil.

33. "It's important to emphasize that we're **still at the preliminary stages of the investigation**, and there's a lot more that we have to learn *[Obama is stalling so he is increasing the chances Islam will not be part of the discussion regarding the attack in the near future. Obama will not permit Islam to be considered as contributing to the motivation of the terrorists.]* … It appears that the shooter was inspired by various **extremist** information *[Obama is pushing hard to protect Islam by not mentioning Islam. Obama is enforcing Sharia law and practicing taqiyya by not linking Islam with violence and the killing of infidels.]* that was disseminated over the Internet … It does appear that, at the last minute, he announced allegiance to ISIL *[Obama is downplaying ties to Islamic terrorism by stating "at the last minute."]*, but there is no evidence so far that he was in fact directed by ISIL. *[Obama is protecting ISIS, since ISIS announced three days before the attack that Florida would be targeted.]* And there also, at this stage, is no direct evidence that he was part of a larger plot *[taqiyya – he travelled to Saudi Arabia twice, his family was involved, he previously threatened courthouse security officials with retribution by al-Qaeda, he had been in touch with an American ISIS suicide bomber, he was investigated by the FBI multiple times]*… **homegrown**

extremism *[diverting attention away from Islam]* … that one of the biggest challenges we are going to have is this kind of propaganda **and perversions of Islam** *[taqiyya - Obama is defending Islam, and disassociates Islam from terrorism. Obama knows all too well that this attack was an act of Islamic jihad.]* that you see generated on the Internet, and the capacity for that to seep into the minds of troubled individuals or weak individuals *[Obama is diverting attention away from religious Muslims who commit terrorism after being motivated by their imams and the Quran, and blames the psycho-social conditions of the perpetrator.]* … countering this **extremist ideology** *[Still no mention of Islam as a contributing factor.]* … we ignore the problems with easy access to firearms *[Obama shifts the discussion to attacking the U.S. Constitution and the Second Amendment.]* … We have to go after these terrorist organizations and hit them hard. *[taqiyya – Obama has had no strategy to destroy ISIS.]* We have to **counter extremism**. *[Obama will use this event to focus DHS and federal law enforcement resource to go after non-Muslim extremists, i.e., his political opponents.]* But we also have to make sure that it is not easy for somebody who decides they want to harm people in this country to be able to obtain weapons to get at them *[Obama is pushing gun control, so he can start to disarm the non-Muslim society in America. Theoretically, Obama wants strict gun control for all law abiding citizens since it is nearly impossible to determine beforehand who will commit acts of terrorism. Since Sharia law is anti-gay and promotes violence against gays, why not make Sharia law illegal, and make those who support Sharia law or attend organizations advancing any aspect of Sharia law unable to legally purchase any firearms?]*… **Well, I think we don't yet know the motivations** *[taqiyya – Obama distancing Islam from jihad and is protecting the Muslim perpetrator.]*… organizations like ISIL or organizations like al-Qaeda, or those who have perverted Islam *[Obama again lies and separates Islam from terrorism.]* … And **unfortunately**, that's something that the LGBT community is subject to <u>not just by ISIL but by a lot of groups</u> that purport to speak on behalf of G-d around the world *[Obama advances false unethical moral equivalence arguments to divert attention away from Islam. Just because Christian and religious Jews frown upon homosexuality, Obama links them with ISIS and their atrocities. Obama conveniently ignores the abusive punishments and death penalties handed to homosexual in all countries and societies governed by Sharia law.]* … we have **self-radicalized** *[Self-radicalization and the redacted Department of Justice transcript is to Orlando as the video is to Benghazi.]* individuals in this country *[By only blaming the individual and self, Obama is defending the imams, the Islamic preachers, Sharia law, and the Quran – which are all sources of hate and incitement that cause young Muslims to engage in jihad and commit acts of terrorism. As Philip Haney, a former DHS official has stated, "If you know anything about the Islamic worldview, family and community is ultimately central to everything they do. The concept of operating alone is anathema to the Islamic worldview. They just don't do it." Obama is practicing taqiyya.]*… And we make it very easy for individuals who are troubled or disturbed or want to engage in violent acts to get very powerful weapons very quickly. And that's a problem. *[more gun control advocacy]*" Obama,

Remarks After Briefing on the Attack in Orlando, June 13, 2016, 11:13 AM. Thirty-six hours after the attack, Obama still does not know the motivations of the attacker, does not link Islam to the violence by using "extremism" terminology, refuses to implicate ISIS as causing the attack despite their announcement three days prior that an attack in Florida was coming, defends Islam, and attacks Judaism and Christianity for being anti-LGBT while not mentioning the racism and hatred against gays which has been an integral part of Islam since its founding. **Even Charles Krauthammer is suspicious of Obama's motivations and loyalties** when he stated, "Violent extremism is a completely empty phrase. No one has ever strapped on a suicide vest in the name of extremism. Nobody dies in the name of extremism … **Obama is deliberately trying to deny, or to hide or to disguise** *[lying]* **the connection between all of these disparate attacks and groups** *[so Islam will not be rightly blamed for or associated with the terrorist attacks]."*[232] Daniel Horowitz, the senior editor of the *Conservative Review* took the analysis of violent extremism closer to the truth where Obama uses the terminology of violent extremism to protect radical Islam with the help and guidance of the Muslim Brotherhood by stating on Sirius XM radio (June 2016), "There's something called CVE, **Countering Violent Extremism**. It's not just an Orwellian term to expunge any mention of Islamic terror and make it about a kind of generic extremism, including so called Right Wing extremism; it's a term of art. It is a very specific term **concocted by the Muslim Brotherhood** front groups like CAIR. They have successfully introduced this lexicon in our DHS [Department of Homeland Security and the Department of Justice]. These people are most commonly found in the Homeland Security Advisory Council *[Marayati, Alawa …]*, as well as the civil rights and civil liberties division of DHS." **Obama is embedding Muslim Brotherhood policy directives into U.S. intelligence and defense protocols**. Even though Obama disassociates Islam from terrorism, and refused to acknowledge Islam as the prime motivation of this jihadi terrorist, Obama should reconsider the following facts, many of which he knew before making the above statements, which would easily prove Islam's core role in promoting this terror attack. The issues that need to be discussed should not revolve around gun control but around Islam, inadequate vetting, and political correctness that is blinding law enforcement officials to real dangers in our society and muting American citizens to real threats that endanger their lives. Under the Obama administration, the FBI has been compromised and infiltrated by radical Islamists and the Muslim Brotherhood since **FBI Director Comey, who knows all the following contacts, leads and info concerning the Omar Mateen case, still stated, "I don't see anything in reviewing our work that our agents should have done differently."** Regarding Obama, there can be no doubt this attack was related to Islam, and regarding Comey, there can be no doubt that the FBI had ample evidence to conclude that Mateen was a violent high-risk suspect, who should have been arrested, watched, or at the very least, prohibited from purchasing firearms. Trump was right to fire Comey, if only for his negligent insights with this case alone.

a. Mateen attended an **Islamic school** during his early years and identified his first language as Afghani, which was spoken at home.

b. As a fourteen-year-old student, Mateen hit a classmate repeatedly on the head and was subsequently charged with **criminal battery**.

c. Classmates recall that Mateen was **cheering on September 11**, **2001**, after the Islamic terrorist attacks against New York City and Washington, D.C. On the school bus he was mimicking noises planes crashing into buildings.

d. While a student at Indian River Community College, Omar Mateen **threatened to shoot everyone at a school barbeque**, because he thought pork had contaminated some of the food on the barbeque grill.

e. While at school, Mateen **threatened other classmates** that events similar to the Virginia Tech massacre [32 students murdered by Seung Hui Cho, who had a tatoo – "Ismail AX" – which is well known in the Islamic world] could occur in their present school.

f. *The Wall Street Journal* reported that Mateen had his **car raided at college by the police**, who were searching for firearms.

g. In 2011 and 2012, Mateen **travelled to Saudi Arabia** and the United Arab Emirates **twice**, which was known by the **FBI**. These trips, where he stayed on four star hotels paid by a third party, cast doubt on Obama's claim that he was a "lone wolf." The San Bernardino Muslim terrorist also travelled to Saudi Arabia.

h. Between 2013 and 2014, the **FBI** interviewed Mateen multiple times while investigating his **links to Hezbollah and al-Qaeda**.

i. Mateen was **in contact with an American suicide bomber** in Syria, Moner Abu-Salha, who was formerly a member of Mateen's mosque and blew himself up during a military operation for al-Qaeda. The **FBI was aware** of Mateen's relationship with Salha.

j. Daniel Gilroy, a coworker with Mateen at the G4S security contractor, quit his job out of fear that Mateen was a real threat to that work environment. Mateen discussed "killing people" and "**killing all black people**," **and was prejudicially obsessed against Jews and women**. He also stated that **the Fort Hood "workplace violence" massacre was justified**.

k. In 2013, Mateen **threatened a Florida courthouse deputy** (after a trip to Saudi Arabia) that he could have al-Qaeda jihadists kill him and his family.

l. The FBI used informants to **try to entrap Mateen** in Islamic terrorist activities.

m. While working at G4S, Mateen was investigated for statements **declaring his loyalty to Islamist / jihadi organizations**. A background check turned up nothing, and Mateen was allowed to keep his firearms.

n. Mateen's **website history** included numerous visits to recruiters of international jihad, and **sites that supported ISIS, al-Qaeda, and Hezbollah**.

o. Mateen was a **religious** Muslim, who regularly prayed at the mosque.

p. Mateen was **reported to the FBI for praising radical al-Qaeda cleric Anwar al-Awlaki** by Mohammad Malik. Malik and Mateen attended the same mosque and knew each other for over ten years. The FBI ignored Malik.

q. Mateen's **Palestinian wife**, Noor Salman, helped him scout locations for a terrorist attack, including the Orlando nightclub and Disney World. **Disney reported Mateen's suspicious behavior to the FBI**, which did nothing. Authorities believe that Salman knew of the Orlando attack beforehand, and she did not inform the proper officials. Thus, she may be an accessory to mass murder. Coincidentally, on June 21, Obama's Department of Justice did not know the whereabouts of Noor Salman, despite the fact she was an alleged co-conspirator with this terrorist attack. The FBI let her slip away.

r. Five weeks before the Orlando attack, a Florida gun shop owner alerted federal authorities (**the FBI**) when Mateen generated suspicions after inquiring about **purchasing body armor**.

s. Mateen **posted on Facebook** just before his attack -
    i.   "The real Muslims will **never accept the filthy ways of the West**."
    ii. "In the next few days, you will see attacks from the Islamic State in the USA."
    iii. You kill innocent women and children by doing US airstrikes … Now taste the Islamic State vengence."

t. Three days before the Orlando attack, ISIS announced, "We will attack Florida."

u. During the massacre at the nightclub, Mateen called 911 and an Orlando cable news channel, and pledged his allegiance to ISIS. ISIS had recently encouraged its followers to "get prepared, be ready … to make it a month [Ramadan inspired jihad] of calamity everywhere for nonbelievers … in Europe and America."

v. Mateen was **shouting "Allahu Akbar" and reciting Muslim prayers during his murderous rampage**.

w. The first words spoken by Mateen when he called 911 were, "**Praise be to Allah**, and prayers as well as **peace be upon the prophet** *[Obama repeated this phrase during Cairo speech]* of Allah [in Arabic] … I did the shootings." *In the first edited transcript Obama released, he changed "Allah" to "G-d" multiple times, and thus attempted to divert attention away from Islam and the shooters religious devotion to carrying out Islamic jihad. After reading the original transcript, Obama lied and announced he did not know the etiology of the terrorist attack.*

x. Mateen identified himself as an "**Islamic soldier**" during the attacks.

y. Multiple witnesses inside the nightclub heard Mateen **speaking on the phone with a third party** who was not connected with 911 operators or the hostage negotiators. This would prove that Mateen was not "self-radicalized" and not a "lone wolf" – which are both descriptions that Obama repeatedly uses to describe radical Islamic terrorists striking American targets, and would represent Obama practicing taqiyya. Thus, Obama is protecting the higher network of ISIS or al-Qaeda handlers who have been directing these terrorist attacks. This scenario would parallel the Islamic terrorist attack in Mumbai, India where the assaulting terrorists were constantly in touch with their handlers in Pakistan.

z.   ISIS claimed responsibility for Mateen's terrorist attack hours after the assault.

aa.   The attack occurred **during Ramadan**, a holiday where Muslims are more prone to commit violence and advance jihad.

bb.   Senator Jeff Sessions attacked **Mateen's father**, **Seddique Mateen**, and remarked, "His father was clearly an **extremist**, a **Taliban** member, and, properly done, he wouldn't have been admitted." In 1997, Seddique Mateen was president of the Fort Pierce Florida chapter of the **American Muslim Alliance**, which has sponsored radical Islamic conferences, has defended convicted al-Qaeda affiliated terrorists, and has had a board member who was part of the Palestinian Islamic Jihad terrorist group. The AMA's political activism group included Muslim Brotherhood front groups such as CAIR (Council on American-Islamic Relations) and MPAC (Muslim Political Affairs Council). In 2000, the AMA sponsored a rally in Washington D.C. where speakers publicly pledged their allegiance to Hamas and Hezbollah. Mateen's father coincidentally has run for the Afghan presidency *[Ahmed's father ran for the presidency of Sudan and worked with CAIR as well – not a coincidence]*, frequently went to Capitol Hill and met with prominent congressmen, and participated in Afghan TV programming which was **sponsored by the CIA**. *There is much more to this story than is presently known to the public.* At the very least, Mateen was not a lone wolf based on his previous trips to Saudi Arabia and his father's possible CIA connections. The purpose of the attack, may have been to advance a hard-core gun control agenda before Obama left office. And Islamist organizations want strict gun control laws enacted so non-Muslims will not have the means to defend themselves when Islamic terrorism become more prominent in America as it is presently in the Middle East. It may not be a coincidence when Obama described a scenario that was nearly identical to the Orlando massacre when on June 1 at a PBS town hall meeting in Elkhart, Indiana, Obama stated, "I just came from a meeting today in the Situation Room in which I got people who we know have been on ISIL web sites, living here in the United States, U.S. citizens, and we're allowed to put them on the no-fly list when it comes to airlines, but because of the National Rifle Association, I cannot prohibit those people from buying a gun. This is somebody who is a known ISIL sympathizer. And if he wants to walk in to a gun store or a gun show right now and buy as much — as many weapons and ammo as he can, nothing's prohibiting him from doing that, even though the FBI knows who that person is."

cc.   Obama is aware of a hadith that sanctions the killing of homosexuals, where Mohammed states, "If you find anyone doing as Lot's people did, kill the one who does it, and the one to whom it is done." (Abu Daawud 38:4447)

Al-Qaeda and the Taliban

"He [Mohammed] declared undistinguishing and exterminating war, as a part of his religion, against all the rest of mankind … The precept of the Koran is, perpetual war against all who deny that Mahomet is the prophet of G-d. The vanquished may purchase their lives, by the payment of tribute; the victorious may be appeased by a false and delusive promise of peace; and the faithful follower of the prophet may submit to the imperious necessities of defeat: but the command to propagate the Moslem creed by the sword is always obligatory, when it can be made effective. **The commands of the prophet may be performed alike**, **by fraud** *[taqiyya]*, **or by force**." *President John Quincy Adams*

1. "Al-Qaeda is on the run." And "decimated." *Obama*
    a. Jake Sullivan, a State Department policy advisor, sent an email **to Hillary Clinton** on February 12, 2012, stating, "**AQ is on our side in Syria** … Things have basically **turned out as expected**."
    b. "When asked if the terrorists were on the run, we couldn't respond with any answer but 'no.' When asked if the terrorists were defeated, we had to say 'no.' Anyone who answers 'yes' to either of those questions either doesn't know what they are talking about, they are misinformed, or they are flat-out lying." *Retired Lt. General Flynn, former head of the DIA.*
    c. "Al-Qaeda affiliates have proven resilient and are positioned to make gains in 2016." *James Clapper, Director of National Intelligence, Worldwide Threat Assessment of the US Intelligence Committee, Senate Select Committee on Intelligence, February 9, 2016.*
    d. **Al-Qaeda has expanded into** "drug trafficking affiliated with Mexican drug cartels, kidnapping for ransom, smuggling of arms, wildlife, coal, oil, gas, timber, precious metals, and people … This has enabled them not only to become independent but also richer and more powerful." *2015 Global Terrorism Index report.*

2. Bergdahl "**served with honor and distinction** … assurances relating to the movement, the activities, the monitoring of **those detainees [five Taliban and al-Qaeda commanders]** give us confidence that they cannot and, in all likelihood, **will not pose a significant risk to the United States**. And that it is in our national interests that this transfer had been made." *Susan Rice, CNN interview, June 2014.* In December 2015, the military decided to pursue a general court martial against Bergdahl on charges of desertion. Obama celebrated Bergdahl's release with his parents at the White House, while the pro-Taliban father recited Islamic prayers in Arabic. With a proven 30% recidivism rate for released Gitmo prisoners returning to fight American and allied forces, at least two of these commanders will be directing war efforts against American troops, leading to increased American casualties. Obama will have American blood on his hands for this transaction. In March 2016, the Pentagon admitted that Americans have died secondary to Obama's Guantanamo release policy.

   a. "At the heart of this whole situation, there's still the decision to trade five Taliban de- tainees for a deserter, when there were in fact other options on the table. We're aware of those options and frankly, the White House made a big mistake," *Representative Duncan Hunter, Republican.*

   b. "We have a federal statute which makes it a felony to provide material assistance to any terrorist organization … It could be money, maps, professional services, any asset what- soever, (including) human assets." *Judge Andrew Napolitano, Fox News analyst, 2015.* The Bergdahl release alone should be grounds for impeachment since the release of the five Taliban and al-Qaeda commanders proved that Obama was aiding and abetting enemy forces during times of war, and was done before a cessation of hostilities was announced. Obama also purposely misrepresented the actions of Bergdahl, since Obama had access to information before Rice's statement that Bergdahl actively deserted his post.

3. "**We've targeted al-Qaeda's affiliate in Yemen**, and recently eliminated the top commander of its affiliate in Somalia … Now, it will take time *[stalling]* to eradicate a cancer like ISIL … This counterterrorism campaign will be waged through a steady, relentless effort to take out ISIL wherever they exist … **This strategy of taking out terrorists who threaten us, while supporting partners on the front lines, is one that we have successfully pursued in Yemen and Somalia for years**." *Obama, formal address discussing strategy against ISIS and rebels in Yemen, September 10, 2014.* Obama feigned ineffective support for the Yemen government allied with the United States at this time, which eventually succumbed to the Iranian-backed rebels.

   a. This administration has "mitigated the threat" terrorists in Yemen "have posed to the U.S. and the West," while simultaneously, "our personnel had to leave Yemen because the situation there has become so dangerous." *John Earnest, White House Press spokesman, refused to accept that U.S. policy in Yemen was a failure, March 25, 2015. This was Obama's position after Yemen's president fled when Iranian-backed rebels defeated government forces. John Earnest is taking talking points lessons from Bagdad Bob.*

b. "Al-Qaeda Captures Major Airport, Oil Terminal in South Yemen," *April 15, 2015, Ahmed Al Haj; SANAA, Yemen (AP)* – "Al-Qaida seized control of a major airport, a sea port and an oil terminal in southern Yemen on Thursday, consolidating its hold on the country's largest province amid wider chaos pitting Shiite rebels (backed by Iran) against forces loyal to the exiled president and a Saudi-led air campaign."

4. The Fort Hood massacre perpetrated by Major Hasan was referred to "**workplace violence**." *Taqiyya.* Obama removes Islam's role from a jihadi war against infidels, and is protecting radical Islam. Obama also called assaults against Islamic terrorists as "**overseas contingency operations**," and referred to Islamic terrorist attacks as "**man - caused disasters**."

5. "I am absolutely persuaded as are my top intelligence and military advisors that Guantanamo is used as a recruitment tool for organizations like ISIS and if we want to fight them then we can't give them these kinds of excuses. *[It is Obama who is actively rebuilding the leadership of al-Qaeda and the Taliban with his release policy.]* Keep in mind that between myself and the Bush administration hundreds of people have been released, and the recidivism rate … we assume there that out of four to five to six hundred people that get released a handful of them are going to be embittered *[Obama empathizes with al-Qaeda terrorists]* and still engaging in anti-U.S. activities and trying to link up potentially with their old organizations … The bottom line is that the strategic gains we make by closing Guantanamo will outweigh, you know, those **low-level individuals** *[Obama is **downplaying** the importance of the released al-Qaeda and Taliban operatives and commanders. Obama released senior al-Qaeda and Taliban leadership with the Bergdahl exchange which has helped the Taliban position themselves to take over Afghanistan at the end of the Obama presidency.]* who, you know, have been released so far." *Obama, Yahoo.com interview, December 13, 2015.*

a. "Barack Obama is releasing dangerous terrorists against the recommendations of military and intelligence professionals, he's doing so at a time when the threat level from radical Islamists is elevated, and he is **lying** about it. He is lying about how many jihadists he has released and lying about their backgrounds, all part of his effort to empty the detention facility at Guantánamo Bay." *Stephen Hayes, "Lying About Gitmo," Weekly Standard, December 28, 2015.*

b. "It doesn't match up at all. I think what we saw from the president there was sort of **aggressive**, **breath-taking dishonesty**. The president may not know how many Guantanamo detainees have been released but we do. 653. Of which, 196 (30.0%) are either confirmed or suspected recidivists. That is not a handful. That is about 40 handfuls. That's far more than the president is suggesting. *[taqiyya]* Beyond that, the president said the United States has released only low-level individuals. Again, unequivocally false. We have senior aides to Osama bin Laden that have been back. Senior Taliban officials including the Taliban 5 … Ibrahim Qosi was a senior aide to Osama bin Laden and now has a senior position in AQAP." *Stephen Hayes, The Weekly Standard, December 14, 2015.* Hayes is commenting on Obama's Gitmo release policy, after an Islamic terrorist released by Obama became an al-Qaeda leader in Yemen and AQAP. Qosi was assessed by the Joint Task Force on Guantanamo written by military and intelligence professionals (obtained via *Wikileaks*) as, "Detainee is an admitted al-Qaeda operative and one of Usama bin Laden's (UBL) most trusted associates and veteran bodyguard … Following a 1994 assassination attempt against UBL, UBL chose detainee to be one of approximately ten individuals assigned to his protection detail … Detainee has been very forthright regarding his commitment to UBL and al-Qaeda … Detainee is assessed to be a HIGH risk, as he is likely to pose a threat to the US, its interests, and allies." Qosi was released by Obama to Sudan in 2012, and later targeted the Saudi royal family for death. Obama is a Shiite and the Saudis are Sunnis.

6. "If you doubt America's commitment – or mine – to see that justice is done, ask Osama bin Laden. Ask the leader of al-Qaeda in Yemen, who was taken out last year, *[Yemen is a failed state as is Syria, Iraq and Libya – all anticipated outcomes of Obama's Middle East policies. Obama brags about killing one enemy in the whole country.]*… When you come after Americans, we go after you. *[Not American Jews or non-Jews who are killed by Hamas and PA-incited Palestinians in Israel, Jerusalem, and the West Bank. Not al-Qaeda operatives attacking Benghazi. Not the Taliban, Obama's "peace partners," who have killed and maimed thousands of Americans in Afghanistan. Not the many Gitmo detainees, whom Obama released.]* It may take time, but we have long memories, and our reach has no limit." *Obama, State of the Union Speech, January 13, 2016.* If Obama was so intent of killing bin Laden, why did Obama release one of bin Laden's bodyguards, Muhammad al Shamrani, just days before his address? Obama released al Shamrani despite knowing this al-Qaeda leader promised Gitmo guards that "When I get out of here, I will go to Iraq and Afghanistan and kill as many Americans as I can. Then I will come here and kill more Americans … I love Osama bin Laden." During the same period, Obama also released another al-Qaeda operative, Fayez al Kandari, who killed a U.S. Marine and whose military intelligence file described him as a "committed member of al-Qaeda who served as advisor and confidant to" bin Laden.[233] Obama also released another bodyguard of Osama bin Laden who became an al-Qaeda leader in Yemen.

   a. Obama views the killing of isolated *[inconsequential]* replaceable leaders as a major victory with which to fuel the public relations campaign to prove he is fighting earnestly against the Islamic terrorists, while in fact he is leaving their armies intact with minimal damage to their ability to initiate and advance armed conflicts. As Obama has left the

Taliban in Afghanistan poised to take over the country soon after he leaves the presidency, Obama publicly basked in a false sense of victory when he stated after a drone killed Taliban leader Mullah Mansour in May 2016, "It is my responsibility as commander in chief not to stand by, but to make sure that we send a clear signal to the Taliban and other that we're going to protect our people." Obama's rules of engagement, his disarming of American soldiers on American bases in Afghanistan while Taliban infiltrators murder allied forces there, his public identification of SEAL Team 6 as the killers of Bin Laden, which led to their murder, his purge of the most capable and experience military leaders in the U.S. armed forces, and the spike of allied deaths and casualties under his command speak otherwise of his concern for American troops and their allies.

7. "Al-Qaeda's cause is not Islam. It's a gross distortion of Islam." *Obama, White House, August 13, 2012*. Taqiyya. Obama is protecting violent jihad and al-Qaeda by disassociating Islam from terrorism.

8. "As we know, these men belonged to **al-Qaeda – a group of extremists who have distorted and defiled Islam, one of the world's great religions**, to justify the slaughter of innocents." *Obama, West Point Speech, December 1, 2009*. Taqiyya and proselytizing.

9. "**We must also engage, however, in the more difficult task of understanding the sources of such madness**. The essence of this tragedy, it seems to me, derives from a fundamental absence of empathy on the part of the attackers: an inability to imagine, or connect with, the humanity and suffering of others. Such a failure of empathy, such numbness to the pain of a child or the desperation of a parent, **is not** innate; nor, history tells us, is it **unique to a particular culture, religion, or ethnicity.** *[false moral equivalence]* It may find expression in a particular brand of violence, and may be channeled by particular demagogues or fanatics. *[Obama is removing Islam, the religion, as a root cause of Islamic terrorism.]* **Most often, though, it grows out of a climate of poverty and ignorance, helplessness and despair.**" *Obama editorial as an Illinois state senator, Hyde Park Herald, Chicago, September 19, 2001.* Obama's defense of Islam is part of his political make up early in his political career. He is expressing empathy for the Muslim terrorists who murdered over 3000 Americans on 9-11. He feels a stronger connection with the Muslim foreign terrorists than he does with America, since he does not immediately empathize with America's loss and tragedy. He is also lying, committing taqiyya, about the source of the motivation of the terrorists by focusing on false underlying economic conditions, when the real reason lies with the Quran inspired jihad, which has been present in Islam since its inception. Many studies have proven that the economic condition and background of the terrorists are unrelated to their actions. Many terrorists are from upper class families and have professional careers, for example, within al-Qaeda, bin Laden was a multi-millionaire, and his deputy was a physician. Obama also applies moral

equivalence between the al-Qaeda 9-11 attacks and extremists of other religions or political affiliations, and thus disassociates Islam from violence.

a. "But **we cannot win this war by killing them**. We cannot kill our way out of this war … We need in the medium to longer-term to go after the root causes that leads people to join these groups, whether it's a **lack of opportunity for jobs … We can help them build their economies so they can have job opportunities for these people …**" *State Department Spokeswoman Marie Harf reiterates Obama's point of view on MSNBC's Hardball with Chris Matthews, February 17, 2015, when discussing Obama's strategy regarding ISIL.*

b. "As to the relationship between Muslims and infidels, this is summarized by the Most High's Word: 'We renounce you. Enmity and hate shall forever reign between us—till you believe in Allah alone' [reference to Quran 60:4]. *Osama bin Laden. Economic grievances are moot when evaluating the root causes of the Muslims' hatred of the West.*

c. "In a recent article (*Dabiq, 2016*) titled "Why We Hate You & Why We Fight You," the Islamic State gives six reasons.   Reason number one says it all: '**We hate you, <u>first and foremost</u>, because you are disbelievers**; you reject the oneness of Allah – whether you realize it or not – by making partners for Him in worship, you blaspheme against Him, claiming that He has a son [Christ] … Furthermore, just as your disbelief is the primary reason we hate you, your disbelief is the primary reason we fight you, as **we have been commanded to fight the disbelievers** until they submit to the authority of Islam either by becoming Muslims, or by paying jizyah – for those afforded this option ["People of the Book"] – and living in humiliation under the rule of the Muslim [per Quran 9:29].' [234] … It is only in reasons five and six that ISIS finally mentions "grievances" against Western foreign policies – only to quickly explain: 'The fact is, even if you were to stop bombing us, imprisoning us, torturing us, vilifying us, and usurping our lands, we would continue to hate you because our primary reason for hating you will not cease to exist until you embrace Islam. Even if you were to pay jizyah and live under the authority of Islam in humiliation, we would continue to hate you."[235] *(Raymond Ibrahim, FrontPage Magazine, August 2016)*

d. The seven ISIS terrorists who killed twenty individuals at a restaurant in Dhaka, Bangladesh in early July 2016, all came from wealthy families and had university educations. Islam, not poverty, motivated these men to commit these terrorist acts. These terrorists slaughtered all their hostages who could not recite the Quran, as did ISIS terrorists in the Philippines in May 2017.

Islam

"Oh, East is East, and West is West, and never the twain shall meet,
Till Earth and Sky stand presently at G-d's great Judgment Seat;"
Rudyard Kipling (1865 – 1936), The Ballad of East and West

So why does Obama lie? There are many theories. First, his dysfunctional childhood with his mother's multiple marriages and homes, and eventually settling with his grandparents in Hawaii may have contributed to his propensity to lie as a coping mechanism which helped him get along and ingratiate himself to others. As his left-wing ideology took root in his thinking, lying may have become a legitimate strategy to advance legislation or political philosophy aligned with his beliefs which was not accepted by the majority of voters. The left viewed all the healthcare lies as "noble lies" necessary to pass Obamacare. The end justified the means. Lenin, the consummate left-wing ideologue, stated, "A lie told often enough becomes the truth." Obama travelled the country promoting his healthcare law and stated *ad infinitum*, "If you like your doctor, you can keep your doctor." Was Obama using Lenin's strategy in order to advance his political agenda?

Second, with Obama's strong proclivities towards Islam and his use of the presidency to advance Islamic interests in the West, and a jihadi agenda in the Middle East, taqiyya may be the driving force behind the continual bombardment of lies emanating from the White House. Basically, **taqiyya is the strategy where Muslims lie to non-Muslims in order to advance Islamic interests and jihad.**
Taqiyya is supported in various Islamic religious texts:

- Quran (9:3) – "Allah and His Messenger are free from liability to the idolaters."
- Quran (2:225) – "Allah will not call you to account for thoughtlessness in your oaths, but for the intention in your hearts."
- Quran (66:2) – "Allah has already ordained for you, (O men), the dissolution of your oaths."
- Quran (3:54) – "And they (the disbelievers) schemed, and Allah schemed (against them): and Allah is the best of schemers."

- <u>Bukhari (52:269)</u> – "The Prophet said, 'War is deceit.'"
- <u>Bukhari (49:857)</u> – "He who makes peace between the people by inventing good information or saying good things, is not a liar."
- <u>Reliance of the Traveler (p. 746, 8.2)</u> – "Speaking is a means to achieve objectives. If a praiseworthy aim is attainable through both telling the truth and lying, it is unlawful to accomplish through lying because there is no need for it. **When it is possible to achieve such an aim by lying … it is permissible to lie if attaining the goal is permissible** (i.e., when the purpose of lying is to circumvent someone who is preventing one from doing something permissible), **and obligatory to lie if the goal is obligatory** *[i.e., for Islam to dominate over infidels and to reestablish the Islamic caliphate]*."

Obama could be practicing taqiyya on many levels. Taqiyya allows Obama to hide his true Muslim faith, so he can be more effective in the political world of the West, especially in the United States. If Obama ran for a higher political office as a Muslim, it is doubtful that he would have won the election for the Illinois Senate seat or the presidency, especially after 9-11. If Obama could not win these offices, he could not make the fundamental transformations necessary in the United States or Europe so that Islam and jihad could thrive in the West. But there are real clues to Obama's true beliefs and intentions. Obama rejected his Christian name and identified himself with a Muslim name. He misspoke during George Stephanopoulos's interview, and he attacked Christianity and the Crusades while addressing the violence and terrorism perpetrated by ISIS. He supported the Muslim Brotherhood takeover of Egypt and has been very anti-Israel. Even Sisi, the president of Egypt, needed to forge a stronger unofficial relationship with Israel to protect himself and his nation from the savagery and barbarism of radical Islam and the Muslim Brotherhood. With Sisi wanting to reform Islam, imprisoning leaders of the Muslim Brotherhood, and working with Israel to combat ISIS in the Sinai and Hamas in Gaza, Obama politically and militarily gave Egypt the cold shoulder. These are the actions of a radical Muslim. In an interview with Bret Baier of *Fox News*, Sisi remarked that Obama's withholding of aid to Egypt and the suspension of military arm sales to Egypt **had given a "negative indication to the public opinion that the United States is not standing by the Egyptians."** Hamas, ISIS, the Muslim Brotherhood, and al-Qaeda are working to weaken and disrupt the present Egyptian government, and so is Obama.

Obama practices taqiyya by projecting Islam as a religion of peace, and completely disassociating it from the violence and terror that is a daily occurrence in the news, whether it is in the West or the Middle East. When Obama professed to the press that he did not have a strategy to defeat ISIS, he was practicing taqiyya since the real reason he doesn't have a strategy is that he wants to protect them and allow an Islamic caliphate to be established in the Middle East. When Obama said al-Qaeda was on the run, he was downplaying their strength and lying to the "infidel" American public so Americans would keep their guard down and not demand increased military or political action. When Obama was campaigning in 2008, he stated, "We must not negotiate with a terrorist group intent on Israel's destruction … We should only sit down with Hamas if they renounce terrorism, recognize Israel's right to exist, and abide by past agreements." Obama lied overtly to Israel, American Jewish voters, and the whole country. This is taqiyya, since if Obama had said he would support Hamas in their struggle against Israel knowing their charter called for the genocidal killing of all Jews worldwide, he would not have won the election for the presidency.

Obama's misleading political positions allowed him to secure 78% of the Jewish vote in the 2008 presidential election. Six years later, Hamas would merge with the Palestinian Authority without renouncing their genocidal objectives, and Obama supported their proposed takeover of half of Jerusalem and tried to force Israel to return to the 1967 borders, as dictated in Obama's two-state solution. Before a pro-Israeli audience at the 2008 American Israel Public Affairs Committee (AIPAC) Conference, Obama stated, "Jerusalem will remain the capital of Israel and it must remain undivided." This is again taqiyya, since years later Obama advocated giving East Jerusalem to Hamas and the PA / PLO, which was proven with Obama's support of UNSC Resolution 2334. Without the scrutiny of another presidential election in Obama's future, his true positions emerged in these volatile political negotiations. With Iran backing Hamas, and with over 50% of the Palestinians preferring Hamas to the PA, Obama attempted to give the West Bank and East Jerusalem to Hamas, Iran, and the IRGC. Thus, Obama aligned himself with countries and terrorist groups seeking Jewish genocide, which would be compatible with Obama's radical Muslim beliefs.

Obama admitted in 2007 his support for Israel was campaign rhetoric. Ali Abunimah commented on the opinion editorial page of *The Electronic **Intifada*** on March 4, 2007 stating, "The last time I spoke to Obama was in the winter of 2004 at a gathering in Chicago's Hyde Park neighborhood. He was in the midst of a primary campaign to secure the Democratic nomination for the United States Senate seat he now occupies. But at that time polls showed him trailing … As he came in from the cold and took off his coat, I went up to greet him. He responded warmly, and volunteered, '**Hey, I'm sorry I haven't said more about Palestine right now, but we are in a tough primary race. I'm hoping when things calm down I can be more up front**.' He referred to my activism, including columns I was contributing to *The Chicago Tribune* critical of Israeli and U.S. policy, 'Keep up the good work!' Abunimah made these comments after listening to Obama give a very pro-Israeli speech at an AIPAC conference. Abunimah continues, "If disappointing, given his historically close relations to Palestinian-Americans, **Obama's about-face is not surprising. He is merely doing what he thinks is necessary to get elected and he will continue doing it as long as it keeps him in power**." Abunimah has been a vice president and a member of the board of directors of the American Arab Action Network, which received funding from the Woods Fund while Obama and Ayers were on its board of directors. Abunimah had previously met Obama at the home of Rashid Khalidi during a political fundraiser.

Obama could view his whole political life as the ultimate taqiyya, the ultimate treachery, which would mirror in many capacities and at many levels the life of Na'im ibn Mas'ud and his interaction with Mohammed during the Battle of Trench. In *Taqiyya About Taqiyya, (www.raymondibrahim. com, April 12, 2014),* Raymond Ibrahim recounts, "This Muslim notion that 'war is deceit' goes back to the Battle of the Trench (year 627), which pitted Muhammad and his followers against several non-Muslim tribes known as Al-Ahzab. One of the members of Ahzab, Na'im ibn Mas'ud, went to the Muslim camp and converted to Islam. When Muhammad discovered that the Ahzab were unaware of his conversion *[as with CIA director Brennan or Obama's true religious affinities?],* and thus defection, he told Mas'ud to return and try to get the Ahzab forces to abandon the siege. It was then that Muhammad memorably declared, 'For war is deceit.' Mas'ud returned to the Ahzab without their knowing that he had switched sides and intentionally began to give his former kin and allies bad advice. He also went to great lengths to instigate quarrels between the various tribes until, thoroughly distrusting each other, they disbanded, lifting their siege." *(Mukaram, At-Taqiyya fi 'l-Islam, pp. 32-3).*

Could Obama be like Na'im ibn Mas'ud, convincing America and the West to abandon its confrontation and friction with the Muslim world without their knowing he was a Muslim? Would he intentionally give America bad advice and create quarrels among various domestic factions and foreign alliances to weaken America and foment political instability in the face of future radical Islamic challenges? Is this one of the major reasons why Obama attacked Christianity while addressing ISIS terrorism at a national prayer breakfast, belittled America repeatedly on the world stage, has publicly criticized many of America's long-term traditional allies, and promoted racial sectarian conflicts domestically? Even after Obama left the presidency, he may have sabotaged U.S. – German relations. Days before Chancellor Merkel met with President Trump regarding the Paris Climate Change treaty, Obama flew to Germany and held private meetings with the German leadership, an unprecedented and seditious action for a former U.S. president. Days after Trump left, Merkel declared, "The times in which Germany could fully rely on others is over." After meeting with Obama, Merkel distanced herself from the United States and Great Britain as allies, a major change in the post - WWII security structure of the West. Obama's input may have led to the start of the disintegration of the American – British – German alliance, whose relationship has kept the peace in Europe for over 70 years. Another leading German politician, social democrat Martin Schulz, attacked Trump by stating he was "the destroyer of all Western values." Of course, these Germans are in favor of massive Muslim immigration into Germany and the European continent while appeasing anti-West Sharia based Islamic values, to which Trump stands opposed. Obama is sewing dissension between the United States and its allies in order to advance the Muslim conquest of Europe via hijrah or immigration jihad. Is Obama mimicking Mohammed's strategy? Is history repeating itself?

The merger of the left and Islam has allowed Obama to speak his lies without the scrutiny of the mostly liberal mainstream media. Obama knew the media would not expose his dishonest and unethical presentations, and coupled with the short-term memory of the American public and Obama's status as a political rock star, Obama could push his untruths to the limit. Obama knew his major goals were to obtain the presidency, win the second term so that his political revolution could continue, and advance Islam and jihad at any opportunity. Obama's lies were taqiyya, and the left provided the political cover. When Obama forced birth control in Obamacare upon Catholic institutions, his real agenda was for the Christian community to have less children. As Obama advanced immigration reform, he sought to bring foreign jihadists into America, whether they crossed the Mexican border without the hassle of having the immigration laws enforced, or brought in huge numbers of Muslim (not Christian) refugees who are at high risk for supporting and initiating jihad in America. But, Obama was mostly concerned about increasing the percentage of Muslims in America, so their political power increases and the drive to institute Sharia law would be empowered. The Democrats see immigration reform as a means to enlarge the voting block for their political party so that they can more easily win elections and move the country to a one super party majority rule. It is a win-win situation for both Obama and the Democrats.

Since most of these new immigrants will be voting for Democrats, as most will be dependent on the government for entitlements, the Democrats will achieve their goal of a one-party system that will dominate all elections on local, state, and federal levels. As a Muslim, Obama wants a one-party Democratic system since the Democrats are more pro-Islam and anti-Israel, and more supportive of instituting blasphemy and Sharia laws in the West. It is a *quid pro quo* from Obama's view point, with the left-wing Democrats turning a blind eye toward the advance of Islam, the loss of individual liberties, and the proliferation of violence associated with jihad. This awkward symbiotic relationship can be applied to most major political issues where Obama falsified arguments to advance his interests. Besides misleading the American public with his reasons for supporting all avenues of immigration into America (or Europe), whenever Obama addresses a major policy topic or gives a significant presentation, lies and misleading statements are usually present.

1. "If you actually took the number of Muslim Americans, we'd be **one of the largest Muslim countries** in the world." *Obama, French TV station Canal Plus interview, early June 2009.* Obama is projecting his future vision of America with a French interviewer, while falsifying American history. Obama is exaggerating (taqiyya) the state of Islam in the America to a foreign audience, especially foreign Muslims, so they will become confident that jihad can succeed in America.

    a. "The Muslim American community remains relatively small – several million people in this country. And as a result, most Americans don't necessarily know – or at least don't know that they know – a Muslim personally." *Obama, Remarks by the President at the Islamic Society of Baltimore, February 3, 2016.* Obama is downplaying the role of

Muslims in America to the domestic American audience, so that America will drop its guard as Islam become more empowered in North America.

2. "These rituals remind us of the principles that we hold in common, and **Islam's role in advancing justice, progress, tolerance, and the dignity of all human beings**." *Obama, 2009 Presidential Statement on Ramadan.*

   a. Hadiths of Mohammad from Sunan Abu Dawud concerning wife-beating: "When one of you inflicts a beating, he should avoid beating the face … A man will not be asked as to why he beat his wife … Do not beat your wife as you beat your slave-girl."

   b. "After the warning and separation, comes the hitting – hitting that does not make her ugly. The Prophet [Mohammad] said [Hadith source]: 'Do not hit the face and do not make her ugly.' In other words, not hitting that will bring the police, and break her hand and cause bleeding, or hitting that makes the face ugly. No. As it is said [Hadith source] 'If not for this (fear of retaliation), I would give you painful blows." *Mufti of Gaza Hassan Al Laham, Palwatch.org, Official PA TV, February 8, 2016.*

   c. "Hating Jews is so part of Islam, so important to Islam, because if you don't hate Jews, if Jews are human beings, then Mohammed is an assassin … That is why killing Jews and hating Jews is such an important part of Islam *[Obama never mentioned this part of Islam]* … It strikes at the heart of their prophet, whether he is credible or not … To the average Muslim, routinely cursing Jews in mosques feels normal and even holy! *[especially at a mosque or madrassa in Indonesia for young children]* … Without Jew-hatred, Islam would self-destruct."[236] *Nonie Darwish, Muslim Egyptian-American human rights activist.*

      i. "Hating the Jews is a great honor for me and it makes me walk with my head high because they are worthy of hatred. They are not decent people. Any man of honor should hate the Jews." *Jordanian Member of Parliament Khalil Attieh, 2014, commenting on a Palestinian attack at Har Nof Synagogue in Jerusalem, where multiple rabbis were viciously murdered in an ax attack.*

   d. "And when We desire to destroy a city, We command its men who live at ease, and they commit ungodliness therein, then the Word is realized against it, and We destroy it utterly." *Quran (17:16)*

   e. "A significant section of the Muslim community danced when the attacks took place." *Interior Minister of Belgium Jam Jambon commented on the reaction of the Muslim community after ISIS terrorists committed a massacre at the international airport in Brussels in the spring of 2016. Interview with the Flemish newspaper De Standaard.*

   f. "The Mahdi will arrive soon, and if there are people or nations that oppose the imam and fight him, when captured, they will be subject to the laws regarding slaves and slave girls. If someone buys five or ten of these slave girls and keeps them in his home, and then, say, he has friends over, and he doesn't give his guest a slave girl with whom he had sex … He can keep the surplus girls as reserve – the defective ones – they don't have to be defective. He can allow his guest to have sex with the slave girl … And when it's over, he goes back home, he has no problem (telling his wife he was with his friend)." *Iraqi Ayatollah Abdul Karim al-Haeri, Director of the Karbala Hawza Shiite (pro-Iran) seminary. April 7, 2016.* It is not just ISIS that encourages and **legitimizes sex slavery**, but also the **senior Shiite ayatollahs backed by <u>Iran</u>**. This religious instruction would not be found in a Christian seminary or in a yeshiva. Mainstream Islamic leaders are also demeaning women and encouraging adultery, which is a violation of the Ten Commandments. Obama, who is pro-Shiite and pro-Iran, is purposely misleading the West with his praise of Islam while celebrating Ramadan.

g. "Khaled Al-Saqaby: Assalaam Alaykum. Allah's blessing upon you. **Welcome to our show, which will deal with wife beating**. … The beating should not be performed with a rod such as this one. Nor should it be with a headband, which some husbands use [to beat their wives], or with a sharp object, which, I'm sad to say, some husbands use. It should be done with something like the sewak tooth-cleaning twig – Ibn Abbas said that she should be beaten with a sewak, like this one, or with a handkerchief, because the goal is merely to make the wife feel that she was wrong in the way she treated her husband." *Khaled Al-Saqaby, a Saudi Arabian family therapist, teaches the art of wife beating on a popular Saudi national TV station. (source – MEMRI, February 24, 2016)*

h. The Council of Islamic Ideology in Pakistan supported a bill to be passed by their legislative body that allows husbands to "lightly" beat their wives under various circumstances, including talking to strangers and not wearing a hijab.

i. "The fact that in Mohammedan law (Sharia law) every woman must belong to some man as his absolute property, either as a child, a wife, or a concubine, must delay the final extinction of slavery until the faith of Islam has ceased to be a great power among men." *Winston Churchill, The River War, 1889.*

j. In May 2017, Mundhir Abdallah, a prominent imam in Copenhagen, preached in Arabic [so the locals won't understand] that the Islamic caliphate is coming and that "Judgment Day will not come until the Muslims fight the Jews and kill them." During the same week, an imam in Toronto preached at his mosque that the Muslims will eventually kill all the Jews. Is there a coordinated international effort to stir up anti-Semitism and promote attacks against Jewish communities in the Ummah?

k. "In some districts in major cities, I'd advise people not to identify themselves as Jews … Experience has shown that openly wearing a kippa or a necklace with the Star of David is enough to attract verbal or physical threats [from Muslim immigrants in Germany] … There is a legitimate concern when there are numerous people [Muslims from the Middle

East and Africa] who have grown up with Israel and anti-Jewish slogans. Whoever has been indoctrinated for a lifetime does not throw it off at the German border … The whole of society needs to take the problem of Muslim anti-Semitism very seriously." *Josef Schuster, president of the Central Council of Jews in Germany, interview with Bild am Sonntag, July 22, 2017.*

3. "In private encounters with other world leaders, Obama has argued that there will be no comprehensive solution to Islamist terrorism until Islam reconciles itself to modernity and undergoes some of the reforms that have changed Christianity." *The Obama Doctrine, Jeffrey Goldberg, The Atlantic, April 2016.* Obama lied to other world leaders in order to put them at ease regarding his false commitment to combat radical Islam. Obama never mentioned these ideas during his 2009 speech in Cairo, during any of his National Prayer Breakfast speeches, or during his 2016 presentation to the Islamic Society of Baltimore, which was affiliated with the Muslim Brotherhood, a very violent Islamist organization – so Obama may just be lying in order to protect his legacy.

4. "I've always been a Christian … The only connection I've had to Islam is that my grandfather on my father's side came from that country [Kenya]. But I've never practiced Islam." *Obama, December 2007, early taqiyya (strategic Islamic lying or misrepresentation)*

5. "Obama Has Never Been a Muslim, And Is a Committed Christian." *Obama Campaign Website, November 2007, early taqiyya*

   a. "Obama is a Muslim. With the information presented in this book *(Unexpected Treason)*, an objective reviewer could easily deduce Obama is a radical Muslim. Having a conservative Muslim as a leader of a country could advance many of the principles we cherish in America: free speech, capitalism, a nonviolent exchange of ideas, a clear delineation of good and evil, and a recognition of America's special and cherished role as a leader of the West and the free world. Unfortunately, a radical Muslim will continually side with America's enemies, will try to advance and embed Sharia law in the American ethos, and will do his best to destroy the two major enemies of fundamentalist Islam – America and Israel. Obama sided with the radical Muslim Brotherhood in Egypt, with a stated goal to destroy the United States, over General Sisi, who is a moderate Muslim and wants to reform Islam. Obama supported the radical Islamist Iranian regime with sanctions relief and a pathway to nuclear empowerment while refusing to support moderate Iranian student protesters in 2009. Obama is partners with CAIR, which is allied with Hamas and is identified as a terrorist organization by foreign governments, and has placed many Muslim Brotherhood sympathizers in sensitive government positions relating to defense, national security and intelligence. Obama empathizes with the "legitimate" grievances of ISIS terrorists, Hezbollah fighters, and al-Qaeda operatives who committed the 9-11 atrocities. Obama's words, actions and policies define his proclivities and support of radical Islam – which reinforces Obama's identity as a radical Muslim. Every one of Obama's major policy decisions weakens and/or harms America, whether he is increasing the budget deficit through various policies, gutting the defense establishment, advancing the interests of America's adversaries, strengthening the radical Islamic forces throughout the world, implementing "catch and release" policies with radical Muslim terrorists, releasing thousands of criminal illegal aliens throughout America by executive orders, or flooding America with poorly vetted Muslim immigrants from Middle Eastern nations supportive of jihad and Shari law. With respect to Israel, his major goals revolve around creating a peace agreement wherein a terror state is created in the heart of the Holy Land, creating or transferring radical Islamic armies on all of Israel's borders, or just humiliating Israeli leadership whenever he gets the opportunity. Most, if not all, of Obama's policies eventually help strengthen and expand radical Islamic forces and weaken or destroy those countries that do not support a caliphate or the Muslim Brotherhood. With Obama as president for eight years, the war against Islamic terrorism has shifted from the Middle East to Paris, San Bernardino, Chattanooga, Orlando, Brussels and Nice, which is an intentional result of Obama's pro-Islamist, pro-jihad rhetoric and policies."[237] *(Unexpected Treason, James McCormack, 2016)*

b.   "Obama was born a Muslim since Islam is passed paternally, and his father was a Muslim. Obama's whole family on his father's side is Muslim. Obama has a Muslim grandfather and grandmother, the latter of whom recently made the Hajj pilgrimage to Saudi Arabia at the age of 93. Obama's stepfather from Indonesia, with whom he lived for many years, was a Muslim. All of Obama's siblings, including sister and half-brothers are Muslims. Maya, Obama's Muslim sister, told Jodi Kantor of *The New York Times*, "My whole family was Muslim," and that includes her brother Barack. Obama's brother, Abongo "Roy" Obama is a militant Muslim. The Obama Foundation in Africa, which is named for Barack Obama, is aligned with Hamas and jihad. Obama said of Roy in *Dreams*, "The person who made me proudest of all was Roy," who has stated that the Black man must "liberate himself from the poisoning influences of European culture." Obama's paternal family originated from Sudan, an Arab Muslim country, before they migrated to Kenya. Romy Amir, one of Obama's classmates in Indonesia remembered, "Barry was previously quite religious in Islam," and "all the relatives of Barry's father were very devout Muslims." Obama's family formally registered him twice as a Muslim when he enrolled in two different elementary schools in Indonesia.[238] Emirsyah Satar, who was one of Obama's classmates and is now CEO of Garuda Indonesia, said of Obama, "He was often in the prayer room … He was quite religious in Islam, but only after marrying Michelle, he changed his religion. *[for political expediency]*" Tine Hahiyary, one of Obama's teachers and principals in Indonesia "remembered that he had studied 'mengaji' [recitation of the Quran in Arabic]." Mengaji studies are only undertaken by fundamentally religious Muslim families, and not by moderate or secular Muslim families.[239] Obama proudly recited the Muslim call to prayer with a perfect Arabic accent in a *New York Times* interview with Nicholas Kristof. According to many Islamic scholars, just reciting the call to prayer makes one a Muslim. Thus, Obama may be fluent or near fluent in Arabic and may be able to recite much of the Quran in Arabic from memory, which he has hidden from the American public. Arabic is a difficult language, and Obama would have to recite the prayers regularly to repeat them perfectly in an interview. Obama is a Muslim, and the world, especially the Muslim world, knows it. Obama never had a formally documented baptism. Where are the photos, the documents, or the witnesses to this event? Obama has admitted at least twice that he is a Muslim. Once with George Stephanopoulos, Obama acknowledged, during a 2008 campaign interview, "**my Muslim faith**." Lack of sleep and a difficult challenging campaign let the truth out for a split second. During his National Prayer Day Breakfast speech in 2015, Obama stated, "And so, as people of faith, we are summoned to push back against those who try to distort **our religion** -- any religion -- for their own nihilistic ends." Here Obama is complaining about people who try to project the violence of ISIS on the Islamic world as a whole. Obama stated his religion as "our religion," and not "their" religion. Reverend Wright and his church welcomed Muslims as members, and maintained strong ties with the Nation of Islam. Obama has admitted that Reverend Wright "dabbled" in Islam, and that Wright was his "spiritual mentor" for 20 years. Reverend Wright told Ed Klein that he "made it comfortable" for Obama to be a member of his church without having to renounce his Muslim faith.[240]"[241]

c.   "Obama changed his name from a Christian name of Barry Soetero to an Islamic name of Barack Hussein Obama after visiting Pakistan during a college vacation. Interestingly, Obama failed to mention his trip to Pakistan in his autobiography, as it is a trip he has tried to keep out of the public eye. This name change occurred after visiting countries specializing in jihad. In *The Audacity of Hope*, Obama declared his allegiance to Islam when he stated, "when the political winds shift in an ugly direction … I stand with the Muslims." After making a pro-Muslim Brotherhood speech in Cairo and an apologetic anti-American speech in Turkey, Obama bowed at the feet of the King of Saudi Arabia, the protector of Mecca, for all the world to see. With the rise of ISIS and the expansion of al-Qaeda since Obama became president, and with his predilection to advance and empower the Muslim Brotherhood, one can easily conclude that he is a radical Muslim."[242]

d.   "The sad truth is that the whole world knows Obama is a Muslim, with the exception of the American public, especially the liberal American public. Even the foreign minister of Egypt was told in confidence by Obama in 2009 that he was a Muslim. At a State

Department function, Obama confidently displayed the one finger affirmation of the Islamic faith in front of all the African delegates, which is also known as the Muslim gang sign. Obama was confirming his allegiance to Mohammed and Allah, and to the Muslim world, a world that is continually in a state of jihad against the West, with the ultimate goal of creating a worldwide Islamic caliphate. Unfortunately for America and the West, Obama gave the same sign that the ISIS terrorists give when they are victorious in the battlefield or when they are beheading infidels. Many influential and prominent Middle Easterners believe that Obama is a Shiite Muslim, a conclusion bolstered by Obama's support of the Iranian nuclear deal which kept Iran's nuclear infrastructure intact and gave the ayatollah's regime up to $150 billion in sanctions relief. Much of these funds would be directed toward strengthening Iran's military, an existential threat to neighboring Arab Sunni states. Individuals supporting this theory include Dhahi Khalfan Tamim, the head of general security for the emirate of Dubai, Taha al Lahibi, a former member of the Iraqi parliament, and Muhydin Lazikani, a well-respected Syrian writer. Hussein is the name of the Shiites' most worshiped and respected martyr, and is also Obama's middle name."[243]

6. "I said on many occasions that **President Obama tells me he's a Christian, I take him at his word**." Carly Fiorina, 2015, *on the presidential campaign trail. The odds favor the conclusion that Obama is lying again.*

    a. <u>**Phyllis Schlafly**</u>: "**Even the Reverend Jeremiah Wright, Obama's pastor of many years, now doubts that he is a believing Christian** (p. 5) ... Barack Obama has compiled a record of hostility to religion that is unmatched by any other president in American history. Author David Barton calls Obama '**America's most Biblically – hostile U.S. president**.' ... Speaking to reporter Edward Klein for his book, *The Amateur*, Wright acknowledged again that Obama's interest in his version of Christianity as political. Wright added that he had no idea if Obama is even a believing Christian, and that Obama's only religious knowledge upon meeting him derived from Islam ... Klein asked Wright: 'Did you convert Obama from Islam to Christianity?' Wright replied, 'That's hard to tell.' ...What does that say about the quality of the president's 'Christian' faith when the pastor who baptized him doesn't even know if he is a believing Christian? ... Church is still 'not their thing.' Only on rare occasions do the Obamas attend church services in Washington, D.C. ... **The great con continues**. (pp. 58-59)"[244] *Phyllis Schlafly, former advisor to President Reagan, president of the Eagle forum, and American's foremost conservative philosopher, calls Obama's profession of his Christianity – a "great con," in her best-selling book, No Higher Power, written in 2016 before she died. Schlafly continued, "For Obama, the growth of Christianity at home is more troubling than the spread of radical*

Islam abroad. His culture war with Christianity is of far more interest to him than are the battles of Afghanistan (p. 97) ... Obama's approach to Islam is one of tolerance and accommodation, even as he steps up his stiff-arming of Christians. Imagine if he treated Muslims as heavy-handedly as he treats pro-life Catholic doctors, nurses and pharmacists (p.98) ... Obama's boosterism for Islam could be termed Islamophilia ... In 2010, for example, NASA administrator Charles Bolden announced that the space program had adopted a groundbreaking new mission – to serve as a self-esteem project for global Islam (p. 99) ... Obama's **Islamophilia** extends well beyond NASA. It extends to his Justice Department, where Eric Holder initially planned to give a civilian jury trial to the Muslim planner of 9/11, and where he refuses to let his aides identify radical Islam as a terrorist motive. It extends to his National Security Council, where **John Brennan** endorses the concept of jihad as a harmless mode of self-improvement (p. 100) ... Obama is forever condemning Israel for this act or that act of 'brutality' even as he calls Islam a 'religion of peace. (p. 104)'"[245]

i.   "When I became the **NASA** administrator, [President Obama] charged me with three things ... One, he wanted me to help re-inspire children ... he wanted me to expand our international relationships; and third, and perhaps foremost, **he wanted me to find a way to reach out to the Muslim world and engage much more with dominantly Muslim nations** to help them feel good about their historic contribution to science, math, and engineering." *Charles Bolden, chief NASA administrator, October 2015 interview.* Obama turned the nation's space agency into an outreach program to the Muslim world. Obama was interested in transferring missile and space technology to the Muslim nations, most notably Iran and Pakistan, so the technology gap between the West and the Islamic world would close, and these countries could enhance their nuclear ballistic missile capabilities, and pose an increased threat to the United States.

ii. Background of **John Brennan**, Obama's former Homeland Security Advisor who was promoted to the Directorship of the CIA in 2013 and is suspected to be a clandestine Muslim convert.

   (1)   "In all my travels the city I have come to love most is al-Quds, Jerusalem, where three great faiths come together." *Only Muslims call Jerusalem, al-Quds.*

   (2)   "Nor do we describe our enemy as 'jihadists' or 'Islamists' because jihad is a holy struggle, a legitimate tenet of Islam, meaning to purify oneself or one's community, and there is nothing holy or legitimate or Islamic about murdering innocent men, women and children." *These lies advocated by Brennan originate for the Muslim Brotherhood and OIC playbook.*

(3) Has lauded "the goodness and beauty of Islam" publicly while describing Islam as "a faith of peace and tolerance."

(4) "A critical step toward improved U.S.-Iranian relations would be for **U.S. officials to cease public Iran-bashing**, a tactic that may have served short-term domestic political interests but that has heretofore been wholly counterproductive to U.S. strategic interests."

(5) Brennan was described as "instrumental in preventing …an operation … that would have killed or captured Osama bin Laden," in 1998 according to a former CIA official. *(source – www.discoverthenetworks.org)*

(6) In 2009, Brennan stated he was "pleased to see that a lot of **Hezbollah** individuals are in fact renouncing … terrorism and violence and are **trying to participate in the political process in a very legitimate fashion**."

b. **Obama**: "Let's not play games. What I was suggesting – you're absolutely right that John McCain has not talked about **my Muslim faith**. And you're absolutely right that that has not come." **Stephanopoulos**: "Christian faith?" **Obama**: "My Christian faith. Well, what I'm saying is that he (McCain) hasn't suggested that I'm a Muslim. And I think that his campaign's upper echelons have not, either. What I think is fair to say is that, coming out of the Republican camp, there have been efforts to suggest that perhaps I'm not who I say I am when it comes to my faith – something which I find deeply offensive, and that has been going on for a pretty long time." *Obama blows his cover after an exhausting campaign and a lack of sleep. This is the first time in history when a leading Western public figure has identified himself freely as a Muslim while being an "alleged" Christian. Interview with George Stephanopoulos, 2008.*

c. "And so, as people of faith, we are summoned to push back against those who try to distort **our religion** – any religion – for their own nihilistic ends." *National Prayer Breakfast Address, February 5, 2015. Obama admits for the second time he is a Muslim by saying "our religion" when talking about Islam, as "our" is the plural form of "my."*

d. "I think on the one hand, non-Muslims cannot stereotype. But I also think **the Muslim community** has to think about how <u>we</u> make sure that children are not being infected with this twisted notion that somehow they can kill innocent people and that is justified …" *Obama, G20 Summit closing news conference. November 16, 2015.* Obama subtly admits he is a Muslim by using the plural personal pronoun "we" after the phrase, "the Muslim community," while addressing the violence surrounding the ISIS attack in Paris where 130 civilians were murdered.

e. "So **I have known Islam** on three continents *[Obama has practiced Islam in Kenya, Indonesia and the United States.]* before coming to the region where it was **first revealed**." *Obama, Cairo University Speech, June 4, 2009.* Obama admits his Islamic faith by stating that he "knows" Islam. A non-Muslim would not use the term "first revealed." Only a person who believes in Islam and has studied many of its precepts would use the term "revealed."

f.   By **reciting the Islamic call to prayer** during a *New York Times* interview during his 2008 presidential campaign, Obama declared himself to be a practicing Muslim from a theological and spiritual perspective.

g.   "Many other Americans have **Muslims** in their families or have lived in a Muslim-majority country – I know, because **I am one of them**." *Obama, Turkish Parliament speech, 2009, where he basically states that he is one of those Muslims in families. This is a subliminal message to the Muslim world that he is a Muslim.*

h.   "**The American President told me in confidence that he is a Muslim**." *Egyptian Foreign Minister Ahmed Aboul Gheit, Nile TV, 2009.*

i.   *The Daily Caller,* in the article *"Book Says University of Chicago Medical Center VP Bribed Jeremiah Wright," from April 14, 2012,* discusses an interview between author Ed Klein and Reverend Wright reporting that "**Klein also said Wright told him he 'made it comfortable' for Obama to accept Christianity <u>without having to renounce his 'Islamic background</u> …'**" When Klein asked Reverend Wright if he actually converted Obama to Christianity, Klein reflected on Wright's response and commented, "He said, I don't know about that, but I can tell you that **I made it easy for him to come to an understanding of who Jesus Christ is and <u>not feel that he was turning his back on his Islamic friends and his Islamic traditions</u>** and his understanding of Islam." Reverend Wright, the man who would have supervised the conversion, admitted that Obama did not formally convert to Christianity. There are no photos or accompanying supporting documents that prove Obama was baptized or converted to Christianity.

j.   "**The future must not belong to those who slander the prophet of Islam**." *Obama, UN General Assembly speech, September 25, 2012. Obama was rallying against blasphemy and still promoting the video as the cause of the Benghazi attack.*

k.   In a *YouTube* video entitled "We Found It? Barack Obama! My Mother was a Muslim?," **Obama admitted that his mother was a Muslim convert**. During a taped interview at the Cambridge public library when Obama was at Harvard Law School, Obama was describing his mother at 40 seconds into the video and stated, "My mother was a m … a white American." Obama started to say the word "Muslim," and then stopped, paused and described his mother as "a white American." Since his mother was born a Christian, she had to formally convert to Islam. The fact that she married two Muslim men and moved to a Muslim country, and identified Barack as a Muslim on official school forms, is consistent with the fact that she viewed herself as a Muslim. With all of Obama's parents (mother, father, step-father) being Muslims, and with all his immediate family members being Muslims, it is highly likely that Obama is a Muslim.

l.   Obama **permits Afghan commanders and officers to commit pediatric rape on U.S. bases** in Afghanistan in the presence of U.S. military personnel, and punishes those American servicemen who attempt to prevent those crimes. **If Obama was a Christian or was grounded in Western morals**, **he would not allow this behavior to occur** in territory controlled by America, especially on U.S. military bases.

m.   "It is just wonderful to be back in Oregon. And over the last 15 months we have travelled to every corner of the United States. **I now have been in 57 states**. I think one left to go. One left to go." *Obama campaigning in Oregon in 2008.* The Harvard Law School graduate is either not familiar with the basic structure of the United States government or he made a **Freudian slip**. There are only 50 states in the United States, but **there are 57 Islamic member states in the Organization of the Islamic Conference (OIC)**. The OIC advances Islamic interests across the globe, and has spearheaded the adoption of blasphemy laws around the world, wants to spread Sharia law worldwide, and create a worldwide Islamic caliphate. This accidental reference is evidence that Obama's heart and mind is with the OIC and a future caliphate.

n.   "And if, in fact, we defend the legal right of a person to insult another's religion, we're equally obligated to use our free speech to condemn such insults – and stand shoulder-to-shoulder with religious communities, particularly religious minorities who are the targets of such attacks. **Just because you have the right to say something doesn't mean the rest of us shouldn't question those who would insult others in the name of free speech**." *Obama, National Prayer Breakfast Address, February 5, 2015.* Here, Obama is arguing for blasphemy laws, and is questioning our First Amendment right to criticize and honestly evaluate the moral flaws in Islam. Hasn't Obama been insulting and mocking Republicans and Christians during his whole political career? Hypocrite?

o.   "There's wisdom in our founders writing in those documents that help found this nation the notion of freedom of religion, because they understood the need for humility. They also understood the need to uphold freedom of speech, that there was a connection between freedom of speech and freedom of religion. **For to infringe on one right under the pretext of protecting another is a betrayal of both**." *Obama, National Prayer Breakfast Address, February 5, 2015.* Obama is arguing for blasphemy laws, and is questioning our First Amendment right to criticize and honestly evaluate the moral flaws in Islam. Obama is also arguing for fundamental Islam in its present form to be accepted as true religion, which should be protected by the Constitution. Islam is using "religion" as a pretext to shield a totalitarian theocratic Islamo-fascist political system, that is incompatible with Western democracies.

p.   "**I will stand with the Muslims** should the political winds shift in an ugly direction." *The Audacity of Hope. One of Obama's few moments of candor.*

q.   "The **sweetest sound I know is the Muslim call to prayer … one of the prettiest sounds on Earth at sunset**." *Obama Interview with Nicholas Christoff, The New York Times, March 6, 2007.* What about Christmas carols and church bells? Obama is declaring a special affinity for Islam here.

r.   "If there's an Arab-American family that's being rounded up by John Ashcroft (attorney general) without the benefit of due process, that threatens my civil liberties."[246] *Obama 2004 interview with Cathleen Falsani.* Even in 2004, Obama is exaggerating threats against Muslim Americans and is accusing the Republican administration of breaking the law by using the term "without the benefit of due process." Obama did not show the same concern for supporters of the Second Amendment when he supported the "no-fly, no-buy" policy, which prohibited all individuals who were placed on a government no-fly list from buying any firearms, even if they were placed on that list erroneously or secondary to political expediency, which denied them due process.

s.   "Likewise, **it is important for Western countries to avoid impeding Muslim citizens from practicing religion <u>as they see fit</u> – for instance, by dictating what clothes a Muslim woman should wear** *[or engaging in jihad]*. We cannot disguise hostility towards any religion behind the pretense of liberalism." *Obama, Cairo University speech, June 4, 2009.* Obama is supporting fundamental religious Islam, which is the basis for violent jihad. Why doesn't Obama use this platform to support the rights of Muslim women not to wear the hijab, niqab or burka in Saudi Arabia, Iran, or Afghanistan?

t.   "**I consider it part of my responsibility as president of the United States to fight against negative stereotypes of Islam wherever they appear**." *Obama, Cairo University speech, June 4, 2009.* Here, Obama is directly stating that he wants to defend Islam. Where is the defense of Christianity?

u.   "So let me say this as clearly as I can: **The United States is not, and will never be, at war with Islam**." *Obama, Turkish Parliament speech, April 6, 2009. Thus, Obama will never attack Iran, and all his threats of possible military action during the many years of difficult nuclear negotiations were lies.*

   i.   "We either live under the light of Islam or we die with dignity … **brace yourself for a <u>long war</u> against the world's infidels and their agents**." *Osama bin Laden, June 3, 2009.*

   ii. "If we put a nationwide infrastructure in place and marshaled our resources, **we'd take over this country** [the United States] **in a very short time … What a great victory it will be for Islam to have this country** in the fold and ranks of the Muslims." *Imam Zaid Shakir, co-founder of Zaytuna College, Berkeley, California and regular CAIR advisor and speaker. Obama has repeatedly partnered with CAIR during his presidency.*

iii. Imam Siraj Wahhaj, the director of the Muslim Alliance of North America stated, "In time, **this so-called democracy will crumble**, and there will be nothing. And **the only thing that will remain will be Islam**."

v. "There are elections in America now. Along came a **citizen of Kenyan African origins**, <u>a Muslim</u>, who had studied in an Islamic school in Indonesia. His name is Obama. **All the people in the Arab and Islamic world and in Africa applauded this man**. They welcomed him and prayed for him and for his success, and they may have even been **involved in legitimate contribution campaigns** to enable him to win the American presidency."[247] *Gaddafi quote.* Gaddafi supported Obama, before Obama decided to eliminate Gaddafi so the caliphate could spread through North Africa. This quote demonstrates Gaddafi's insight into **illegal foreign contributions** to Obama's 2008 campaign. Gaddafi realized too late, that Obama's election sealed his fate.

w. Obama stated that **Hamas and Hezbollah have "legitimate claims**." In an interview with David Brooks, on *The New York Times* Opinion page, Obama addressed the issues of US foreign policy with respect to Hamas and Hezbollah, and stated that America should have a foreign policy that, "looks at the root causes of problems and dangers … They're going down a blind alley with violence that weakens **their legitimate claims** *[destroying and occupying Israel]*."[248] In 2015, Obama removed Hezbollah from a formal U.S. terror watch list, and gave them along with Hamas relatively unlimited funding with the JCPOA mandated sanctions relief for Iran. In March 2016, the Arab League with the backing of Saudi Arabia labelled Hezbollah a formal terrorist organization. The United Arab Emirates subsequently labelled Hezbollah a terrorist organization. Not Obama.

x. "In early 2005, *Newsweek* published allegations that U.S. guards and interrogators at the Guantanamo Bay detention center had goaded and abused prisoners by, among other things, **flushing a Koran down the toilet**. The White House insisted there was absolutely no truth to the story. Without hard documentation and in the wake of violent protests in Pakistan regarding the article, *Newsweek* was forced to publish a self-immolating retraction. Several months later, the Pentagon released a report indicating that **some U.S. personnel at Guantanamo had engaged in multiple instances of inappropriate activity – including instances in which U.S. female personnel pretended to smear menstrual blood on detainees during questioning, and at least one instance of a guard splashing a Koran and a prisoner with urine**. The *Fox News* crawl that afternoon: 'Pentagon finds no evidence of Koran being flushed down the toilet.'" *Obama, The Audacity of Hope.* Obama once again defended the Quran and criticized America, while advancing unsupported hearsay, which further incited Muslims worldwide against

America. Obama's hatred toward Gitmo and the U.S. military is in part rooted in Obama's perceived blasphemous abuses directed at Muslims and the Quran.

y. Obama wears a gold band ring on his left fourth finger that looks remarkably similar to an Arabic inscription that states, "There is no G-d but Allah." He wore this ring before his marriage to Michelle and has continued wearing it since their marriage.

z. "There have been times where **my faith has at times been questioned** by people who don't know me, or they've said that **I adhere to a different religion**, **as if that were somehow a bad thing**." *Obama, India Trip, January, 2015.* A radical Muslim president who supports Sharia law and radical Islamic extremists is a bad thing for America and the West.

  i. "When they become a majority in any country then **they have the religious obligation to govern that country** … If that's what the citizens of a nation want, well, then, they should just allow this to go on. But if that's not what they want, then they have to find a way to deal with it … I think the appropriate response is to be firm about the Christian origin of our own nation, and certainly in Europe, and the Christian foundations of the government, and to fortify those. We have to say no, our country is not free to become a Muslim state … In reality, **there is no place for other religions** *[with an Islamic state]*."[249] *Senior Roman Catholic Cardinal Raymond Burke, July 2016.*

aa. "And lest **we get on our high horse** and think this is unique to some other place, remember that during **the Crusades and the Inquisition, people committed terrible deeds in the name of Christ. In our home country, slavery and Jim Crow all too often was justified in the name of Christ**." *Obama, National Prayer Breakfast Address, February 5, 2015.* Has Obama ever commented on the terrible things done in the name of Mohammed, or the over 270 million people killed by jihad via Muslim communities and armies since the inception of Islam? Despite all the atrocities that ISIS is committing on a daily basis, Obama is attacking Christianity.

bb. "On Easter I do reflect on the fact that as a Christian I am supposed to love. **And, I have to say that sometimes when I listen to less than loving expressions by Christians, I get concerned**. But that's a topic for another day." *Obama, criticizing Christians on Easter Sunday, 2015. Obama's lecturing of Christians on Easter occurred immediately after Muslim terrorists slaughtered over 150 Christian students in Kenya.*

cc. "… **so full of yourself** and so confident that you are right and that G-d speaks only to us, and doesn't speak to others … that somehow we alone are in possession of the truth." *Obama criticizing Christians at National Prayer Breakfast, February 2015.*

dd. "Whatever we once were, **we are no longer a Christian nation**." *Obama's 2006 Speech on Faith and Politics, June 28, 2006* ee. "**We do not consider ourselves a Christian nation**." *Obama, speaking in Turkey, April 2009.* Obama, as a radical Muslim, is changing American history, and attempting to eliminate its Judeo-Christian heritage.

ff. **Obama's Bitter Clingers speech**: "You got into these small towns in Pennsylvania and, like a lot of small towns in the Midwest, the jobs have been gone now for 25 years and nothing's replaced them. And they fell through the Clinton Administration, and the Bush Administration, and each successive administration has said that somehow these communities are gonna regenerate and they have not. **And it's not surprising then they get bitter, they cling to guns** *[anti-Second Amendment]* **or religion** *[anti-Christian]* **or antipathy to people who aren't like them or anti-immigrant sentiment** *[Obama has always wanted to flood the United States with immigrants – his fundamental change]* **or anti-trade sentiment as a way to explain their frustrations**." *Obama, 2008 presidential campaign, San Francisco. A short burst of campaign rhetoric reveals much of Obama's political philosophy.*

gg. "This is something that I'm sure I'd have serious debates with my fellow Christians about. I think that the difficult thing about any religion, including Christianity, is that at some level there is a call to evangelize and **proselytize**. There's the belief, certainly in some quarters**, that people haven't embraced Jesus Christ as their personal savior that they're going to hell … I find it hard to believe that my G-d would consign four-fifths of the world to hell. I can't imagine that my G-d would allow some little Hindu kid in India who never interacts with <u>the Christian faith</u> to somehow burn for all eternity. <u>That's just not part of my religious makeup</u>**."[250] *(Falsani interview with Obama, 2004)* Obama launched this attack on Christianity just moments after he declared he would protect Arab-American families from John Ashcroft. Ironically, Obama criticizes Christians for proselytizing, while he has spent most of his presidency proselytizing for Islam. Obama's heart lies with Islam.

hh. "I've said this before, and I know this raises questions in the minds of some evangelicals. **I do not believe that my mother, who never formally embraced Christianity as far as I know** *[As a law student at Harvard, Obama admitted his mother was a Muslim.]* … **I do not believe she went to hell**." *Obama, Newsweek Magazine interview during the 2008 campaign.* Obama openly expresses his disdain for Christianity by the way he interprets the religion would treat his mother.

ii. "In our household, the Bible, the Quran, and the Bhagavad Gita sat on the shelf alongside books of Greek and Norse and African mythology." *Obama, The Audacity of Hope*

jj. "**On Easter or Christmas Day, <u>my mother might drag me to church</u>**, just as she dragged me to the Buddhist temple, the Chinese New Year celebration, the Shinto shrine, and ancient Hawaiian burial sites." *Obama, The Audacity of Hope.* Notice that

Obama doesn't say that he was dragged to the mosque in Indonesia. Saying that would be derogatory towards his true religion.

kk.   "As a citizen, and as president, **I believe that Muslims have the same right to practice their religion as everyone else in this country. And that includes the right to build a place of worship and a community center on private property in Lower Manhattan**, in accordance with local laws and ordinances. This is America. Our commitment to religious freedom must be unshakable." *Obama, Remarks by the President at Iftar Dinner, August 13, 2010.* **Obama supported the building of a Mega Mosque on Ground Zero in Lower Manhattan, on the grounds where Islamic terrorists murdered over 3,000 Americans on 9-11.** Obama is ignoring over 70% of Americans who were against the construction of a mosque over the crushed and burnt remains of dead Americans. Obama is also supporting the Islamic strategy of building mosques on the locations of their military conquests over their enemies. Obama knew that the mosque in that location would become the most important historical mosque in America, signifying a significant victory of Islam over the "infidels." Obama is constantly lecturing America to respect Islam, but do the Muslims or Obama respect the Americans who would be emotionally harmed when visualizing a mosque on the site of the 9-11 attack?

ll.   "Here in America, many people personally don't know someone who is Muslim. They mostly hear about Muslims in the news, and that can obviously lead to a **very distorted impression**." *Obama, 2015 White House Iftar Dinner, June 22, 2015.* Obama rallies against Islamophobia.

mm.   "We'll constantly reaffirm through words and deeds that **we will never be at war with Islam** … [ISIS] Ideologies are **not defeated with guns**, **they are defeated by better ideas**, a more attractive and more compelling vision … This **will not be quick**, *[Obama is stalling, giving ISIS time to build a caliphate.]* this is a **long-term campaign** *[Obama wants a long-term conflict between Islamic terrorists and the West, so the West's will to win will be drained and its resources will be depleted. Obama followed this strategy in Afghanistan, the longest war in American history. This strategy has been outlined in al-Qaeda's war with the West.]* … I think it is important for us to recognize **the threat of violent extremism is not restricted to any one community. Here in the United States**, we've all kinds of home grown terrorism. *[false moral equivalence]* And tragically, recent history reminds how even a single individual can inflict horrendous harm on Americans. **So our efforts to counter violent extremism must not target any one community** *[Obama is diverting attention away from Islam.]*, **because of the patriotic Muslim Americans who are partners in keeping our country safe** *[CAIR tells Muslims not to work with the FBI.]*… We also have to acknowledge that ISIL has been particularly effective at reaching out to and recruiting vulnerable people around the world including here in the United States and they are **targeting Muslim communities** around the world … If we try to do everything ourselves all across the Middle East *[i.e., U.S. ground troops will not be involved which guarantees the survival of the Islamic terrorists.]*, all across North Africa, we'll be playing 'Whack-a-mole' and there will be a whole lot of unintended consequences that ultimately will make us less secure. *[Obama is protecting ISIS.]" Obama, July 6, 2015, Department of Defense Press Conference.* Again, Obama is declaring there is no special relationship between Islam and ISIS, violence, and terrorism. Obama sees a moral equivalency between ISIS and crime in America. Obama states he will not defeat ISIS and its culture with military force, and the conflict between ISIS and the West will be a long-term event. Obama has no real plans and no intentions to defeat ISIS during his term.

    i. "If they bring a knife to the fight, **we bring a gun**." Obama may not want to fight ISIS with a guns, but he is always willing to wage a political war [with theoretical guns] against Republicans, conservatives and Christians. Despite threatening political opponents with images of weapons, Obama will not hesitate to oppose Republicans and conservatives on guns control issues.

  nn. After Obama's passionate seven single spaced page pro-Islam speech at the Islamic Society of Baltimore in February 2016, Rush Limbaugh raised an interesting question, which is – why did Obama choose to become a Christian after being a Muslim his whole life? Obama has never defended Christianity or America with such passion and devotion. Limbaugh reflected, "President Obama is routinely defending it, talking it up, promoting it … He talks about how awesome Islam is all the time, one of the most beautiful sounds he's ever heard is the morning call to prayer in an Islamic country … He says it's the most peaceful, most giving religion out there, that the mosque called a prayer one of the most beautiful sounds in the world. And, at the same time, he's out there, and look what he says about Christians. He says he is one. Look, he talks about 'em as bitter clingers and they hold on to their guns when they're nervous. **My question is**, **given all this**, **why did he choose to become a Christian**? I've always wondered that … He's such a defender and promoter of Islam, and, on the other hand, he and his party are constantly denigrating Christians. I don't care what the issue is, whether it's guns, whether it's gay marriage, any cultural or social issue, or the bitter clinger comments. **I've always wondered about this**." Limbaugh is questioning whether Obama is a Christian or a Muslim. Rush is being politically correct and won't state his true opinion.

  7. "Now let's make two things clear: **ISIL is *not* Islamic**. *No* religion condones the killing of innocents." *Obama, Statement by the President on ISIL, September 10, 2014.* Obama is protecting Islam from its association with terrorism, while giving ISIS time and space to build

and establish the caliphate. Obama is practicing taqiyya by pretending that jihad and basic Islamic doctrine is not the driving force behind this Islamic-based terrorism. Obama told two lies.

    a.   "We cannot dismiss their actions by saying that they 'do not represent Islam' when most of their actions originate in books from our past heritage." *Saudi journalist Muhammad Aal Al Sheikh, Al Jazirah Daily, Saudi Arabia, 2016.*

8.   "As a student of history, **I also know civilization's debt to Islam**. It was Islam – at places like **al-Azhar University** – that carried the light of learning through so many centuries, **paving the way for Europe's Renaissance and Enlightenment**." *Obama, Cairo University speech, June 4, 2009.* **Muslims reinvent and falsify history to advance Islam.** Obama knows that Islamic military losses and the following Muslim expulsions from the European continent helped usher in the Renaissance.

    a.   Sheikh Mahmoud Sha'aban, a lecturer at **al-Azhar University, issued a fatwa in February 2012, calling for the death of protesting members of the National Salvation Front**, **the political opposition to Morsi and the Muslim Brotherhood**. Islamic Jihad Mufti and Professor Osama Qassem of al-Azhar University, also called for the death of Morsi protesters.

    b.   In June 2015, Al-Azhar University distributed a publication that called Christianity a "failed religion," and continued the incitement of Muslims against Christians.

    c.   "Those learned in Islamic law [*al-fuqaha*] and the imams of the four schools of jurisprudence consider apostasy a crime and agree that the apostate must either renounce his apostasy or else be killed. *[There is no freedom of religion in Islamic societies.]*"[251] *Sheikh Ahmed al-Tayeb, PhD in Islamic philosophy at the Sorbonne - Paris, former Grand Imam of Egypt, president of Al-Azhar University.* Tayeb is recognized as a "moderate" Muslim and has met with the Pope. Tayeb also calls Islam a religion and a form of government that is opposed to basic Western human rights that are contradicted by Sharia law.

    d.   "Will you allow the infidels to contemplate in peace the ravages they have committed on Christian people? … Fly then to arms; let the holy rage animate you in the fight, and let the Christian world resound with these words of the Hebrew prophet: 'Cursed be he who does not stain his sword with blood!'" *St. Bernard of Clairvaux rallying Frenchmen to defend their country and fight Muslim invaders and armies descending upon the European continent in 1146 in Vezelay, Burgundy.*

9.   "For over a thousand years, **Al-Azhar has stood as a beacon of Islamic learning**." *Obama, Cairo University speech, June 4, 2009. Al-Azhar has issued many fatwas denying the basic civil rights of women and non-Muslims and condoning murder.*

    a.   "I can't [condemn the Islamic State as un-Islamic]. **The Islamic State is a byproduct of Al-Azhar's programs**. So can Al-Azhar denounce itself as un-Islamic? Al-Azhar says there must be a caliphate and that it is an obligation for the Muslim world [to establish it]. Al-Azhar teaches the law of apostasy and killing the apostate. Al-Azhar is hostile towards religious minorities, and teaches things like not building churches, etc. Al-Azhar upholds the institution of jizya [extracting tribute from religious minorities]. Al-Azhar teaches stoning people. So can Al-Azhar denounce itself as un-Islamic?"[252] *Sheikh Muhammad Abdullah Nasr, graduate and scholar of Islamic Law at Al-Azhar University, 2015.*

b.   "The problem is that Sheikh Tayeb *[Imam of Al-Azhar mosque, professor of Islamic philosophy]*, once voted "world's most influential Muslim," and Al-Azhar, the important madrassa he heads, are part of the problem, not the solution. Tayeb is a renowned master of exhibiting one face to fellow Muslims in Egypt – one that supports the death penalty for "apostates," calls for the totality of Sharia-rule, refuses to denounce ISIS of being un-Islamic, denounces all art as immoral, and rejects the very concept of reforming Islam – and another face to non-Muslims … Now Behery *[an Egyptian Muslim reformer]* says that, ever since President Sisi implored Al-Azhar to make reforms to how Islam is being taught in Egypt three years ago, the authoritative madrassa "has not reformed a single thing," only offered words. "If they were sincere about one thing, they would have protected hundreds, indeed thousands of lives from being killed in just Egypt alone, said al-Behery. By way of examples, the scholar of Islam pointed out that **Al-Azhar still uses books in its curriculum which teach things like "whoever kills an infidel, his blood is safeguarded, for the blood of an infidel and believer [Muslim] are not equal.**" Similarly, he pointed to how Sheikh Ahmed al-Tayeb claims that **ISIS members are not infidels**, only deluded Muslims; but those whom they kill – such as the bombed Christians – are infidels, the worst label in Islam's lexicon. Debating Behery was an Al-Azhar spokesman who naturally rejected the reformer's accusations against the Islamic madrassa, adding that the source of problems in Egypt is not the medieval institution, but rather "new" ideas that came to Egypt from 20th century "radicals" like Hasan al-Bana and Sayyid Qutb, founding leaders / ideologues of the Muslim Brotherhood. Behery's response … 'The man who kills himself [Islamic suicide bomber] today doesn't kill himself because of the words of Hasan al-Bana or Sayyid al-Qutb, or anyone else. He kills himself because of what the consensus of the ulema, and the four schools of jurisprudence, have all agreed to. Hasan al-Bana did not create these ideas [of jihad against infidels and apostates, destroying churches, etc.]; they've been around for many, many centuries…. I am talking about Islam [now] … Hassan al-Bana and Sayyid al-Qutb are not the source of the terror, rather they are followers of these books. Spare me with the term Qutbism.'"[253] *(Raymond Ibrahim, Front Page Magazine)*

10. "And throughout history, **Islam has demonstrated through words and deeds the possibilities of religious tolerance and racial equality.**" *Obama, Cairo University speech, June 4, 2009.* Obama lies again to give Islam moral legitimacy on the world stage. Where are the Jews and Christians in the Middle East and Islamic countries? Outside of Israel, the Jews have disappeared from the Middle East and the Christians are becoming extinct because of persecution and murder by Muslims. Israel is the only country in the Middle East where Christian populations are increasing and don't fear religious persecution. There is massive and increasing Jewish emigration from all European countries because of Islamic harassment, assaults and increasing Islamic anti-Semitism. Islam has participated in the major genocides of the 20th century – the Holocaust, Armenia, and now ISIS' near extermination of Christian communities in Syria and Iraq.

    a. "Every time an extremist Muslims commits a horrifying crime against humanity, some people come out and shriek that he has nothing to do with Islam *[Obama for example]*, while ignoring the fact that **views and ideologies do not exist as abstract entities, but rather take shape in the minds and behavior of those who believe in them in accordance with the surrounding culture** that defines the nature of their relations with the other. *[Islamic families, communities, imams, the Quran, and Sharia law create the theological and political environment where Muslims feel harassment of non-Muslims, jihad, and mass murder are appropriate responses.]* The culture of our Islamic societies in this generation, particularly Arab societies, produces a **violent Islam whose believers simply murder anyone who disagrees with them** under the pretext of being offended." *Al Tahrir Egyptian Daily editorial, Amr Hosny, July 2016, published after the Orlando, Florida massacre.* There are no "lone wolfs."

    b. "Is **terrorism** attributed to religion related to the religion itself? The answer is yes. … Religious interpretations [from the Quran] that can easily be understood *[mainstream Islamic thought]* to mean that **martyrdom** means a cheap suicide [inside] a café or club frequented by "infidels" are <u>**very common**</u> *[not just the radicals]* **<u>in our religious, educational, and mosque culture</u>**, and must be dealt with … What view [can] we develop regarding non-Muslims if every week we hear **thousands of preachers call on Allah to "not leave a trace of them"**? Every day, our sons read texts and books in schools that establish nothing but a patronizing and **disrespectful view regarding non-Muslims.**" *Palestinian author and academic Khaled Al Hroub, Al Hayat editorial published in London after the Nice truck ramming massacre in mid-July 2016.* Muslims, not just radical Muslim extremists, view non-Muslims, especially Jews, as second-class political beings worthy of harassment and violent jihad, which ultimately results in genocide as Muslims gain control of the political apparatus in any society.

c. "About sixty-one percent of the contents of the Koran are found to speak ill of the unbelievers or call for their violent conquest; at best only 2.6 percent of the verses of the Koran are noted to show goodwill toward humanity. About seventy-five percent of Muhammad's biography (Sira) consists of jihad waged on unbelievers." *Dr. Moorthy Muthuswamy, Free Thought Nation website.*

11. "**Islam has a proud tradition of tolerance**." *Obama. Cairo University speech, June 4, 2009.* Obama is practicing taqiyya.

a. "I am referring here to the religious clerics … It's inconceivable that the thinking that we hold most sacred should cause the entire ummah [Islamic world] to be a source of anxiety, danger, killing and destruction for the rest of the world … Is it possible that 1.6 billion people [Muslims] should want to kill the rest of the world's inhabitants – that is 7 billion – so that they themselves may live? Impossible!" *Egyptian President Abdel Fattah al-Sisi, Al-Azhar, January 1, 2015.* With these opposing and divergent viewpoints, is it any wonder that Obama tried to prevent Sisi from becoming president of Egypt. Obama wants to continue the deception of Islamic tolerance, so that the Islamic sphere of influence can expand throughout the world. Obama despises Sisi, and considers his controversial reforming viewpoints to be blasphemy.

b. **Over 270 million people have been killed** as a result of Islam's expansionary violent jihad since its conception, which is a **conservative estimate**. Islam routinely kills all apostates in its jurisdiction and Sharia law treats all non-Muslims as second-class citizens at best.

c. The grand mufti of Saudi Arabia, Ibn Baz, who died in 1999, issued a fatwa during his tenure entitled, "Duty to Hate Jews, Mushrikun (idolaters) and Other Infidels." The grand mufti is the highest religious position in Saudi Arabia.

d. "Those who wrap themselves in the trappings of religion to mask their deadly project … those who want to announce to us a G-d of death, a Moloch that would rejoice at the death of a man and promise paradise to those who kill while invoking him, these cannot expect humanity to yield to their delusion."[254] *French Cardinal Andre Vingt – Trois commenting on jihadists and those who support Sharia law after a teenage Muslim Syrian refugee decapitated an 86-year-old priest during mass in Normandy, France while shouting "Allahu Akbar," and then gave a sermon in Arabic before he was killed by police.*

e. "The command of "no compulsion in Islam" was a unique command that had doctrinal authority for only a little over two years. It was abrogated both by the Sunnah and the Koran. Its short lifetime was preceded and followed by commands that non-Muslims were to be given the option of converting to Islam, fighting to the death, or, at times, paying the Jizyah. **Muhammad** was indeed the militant prophet of a militant religion that **supported forced conversions to Islam**." *(Islam's Militant Prophet: Muhammad and Forced Conversions to Islam, Stephen M. Kirby, 2016)*

f. "**We will bring you forth in [one] gathering (Jews in Israel), so that it will be easier to slaughter and kill you.**" (**Quran, Sura 17:104**)" *Obama loves, supports and proselytizes for the Quran, which advocates for the genocide of all Jews in Israel.*

12. "I know, too, that **Islam has always been a part of America's story**." *Obama, Cairo University speech, June 4, 2009.* Obama lying and changing history. The oldest mosque in America is located in North Dakota and was built in 1929. The oldest Jewish synagogue in America was built in Newport, Rhode Island in 1763. America's first major early encounter with Islam was when Presidents Jefferson and Adams sought to end the attacks by the Muslim Barbary Coast pirates on America's merchant trading ships off the coast of Africa. The pirates were stealing American property and enslaving American sailors. Both Jefferson and Adams studied the Quran in order to better understand how to confront and defeat these jihadi warriors.

a. Female genital mutilation (FGM – surgical excision of the clitoris), a common practice by Muslims around the world has never been a major problem in America, until recently, which coincided with Obama's massive importation of Muslims into America. An FBI report from May 14, 2016 stated, "More than 500,000 women and girls across the country – most of them living in metropolitan areas – are at risk of undergoing female genital mutilation (FGM), a procedure that has long been practiced in many African and Middle Eastern countries as a cultural custom but has been illegal in the U.S. since 1996. A report showing the number of women at risk was published in January by the Centers for Disease Control and Prevention, and the figure was much higher than previously estimated." That same year, the CDC announced that the number of Muslim girls undergoing FGM or at risk in America has increased by a factor of three over the past few decades. If Islam has always been part of America's story, FGM would also have been. Young Muslim girls are getting mutilated and physically tortured by their parents and Islamic communities. All young Muslim girls need to be examined by their pediatricians for FGM. If FGM is present, the parents need to be charged with physical and sexual abuse and all their children should be removed from their family by CPS and placed in the custody of non-Muslim custodians for their protection. The parents should face the full force of the law with respective penalties and lengthy jail terms for these crimes, and should be listed publicly as sexual offenders. Or, the whole families can choose to leave the United States and live in an Islamic society that accepts FGM as part of Sharia law. Pediatricians who cover up these crimes should have their licenses revoked, and be charged criminally as an accessory to the physical mutilation of their patients whom they are supposed to protect.

b. "And whoever among you cannot [find] the means to marry free, believing women, then [he may marry] from those whom your right hands possess of believing slave girls." *Quran, Surat An Nisa, verse 24. The Quran allows Muslim men to have sex slaves, which is not quite part of the American story.*

c. "Today, Muslims have re-written their history books to claim that Muslims originally built the ancient Jewish Biblical sites, and the United Nations Educational, Scientific and Cultural Organization (UNESCO) has bowed to the wishes of Qatar and the Organization of Islamic Cooperation (OIC) -- a bloc of 56 Islamic nations plus "Palestine" -- to back up this fiction. UNESCO recently passed resolutions obscenely declaring ancient Jewish Biblical monuments -- such as Hebron's Cave of the Patriarchs, Rachel's Tomb in Bethlehem and Jerusalem's Temple Mount, home of the great ancient Jewish Temples -- Islamic sites. Which country will be next? This escalating subversion should be reason enough for all Western democratic countries permanently to part company with the United Nations … jihadists today are stating that they also have a claim over Italy, Greece, and Spain -- **and now America**. Obama … actually just solidified such claims for future Muslim history books about who actually built America."[255] *(Nonie Darwish, Gatestone Institute, November 2016) Obama purposely has embellished and falsified Islam's role in America's history so future jihadi wars against America will be more legitimate in the eyes of Islamic warriors and terrorists.*

13. "**America and Islam are not exclusive** and need not be in competition. Instead, **they overlap**, **and share common principles** of justice and progress, tolerance, and the dignity of all human beings." *Obama, Cairo University speech, June 4, 2009. Obama is advocating a false moral equivalence between Islam and the West, and is practicing taqiyya. A Pew Poll released in May 2017 showed that at least 3 out of 10 American Muslims believe that Islam is incompatible with democracy.*

a. "**Democracy runs counter to Islam on several issues** … In democracy, **legislation is the prerogative of the people**. It is the people who draw up the constitution, and they have the authority to amend it as well. **On this issue we differ**." *Syrian Islamic scholar Abd Al-Karim Bakkar, Al-Arabiya TV interview, March 6, 2009. According to a leading Middle Eastern Islamic scholar, Islam and Sharia law are incompatible with Western democracy. Allah's word, Muhammed's decrees, and the Quran are the law in Islamic societies – and not the legislative actions of men. All Islamic societies gravitate or evolve toward fascist dictatorships, i.e., Morsi and the Muslim Brotherhood, Hamas, Iran, and Turkey. Obama has strongly supported all these political factions. Obama is lying when he says America and Islam (not just radical Islam) share common principles.*

b. "I would not offer prayer behind anyone who would seek to justify democracy."[256] *Pakistani Muslim leader Sufi Muhammad, May 2009.*

c. "Democracy, freedom, and human rights have no place [in Islam]."[257] *Iranian Shia Taliban leader Mesbah Yazdi, September 2010.*

d. "Electing a president or another form of leadership or council members is prohibited in Islam as it has been introduced by the enemies of Moslems ... [The idea of popular elections] ... has been brought by the anti-Islam parties who have occupied Moslem land."[258] *Saudi Islamic scholar Sheikh Abdul Rahman bin Nassir Al Barrak, January 2013.*

e. "'To hell with democracy! Long live Islam!' One hundred percent of Muslims agree with that. To say anything else is apostasy from Islam. **These two competing political systems are antithetical to each other**. You can't be democratic and be a Muslim or a Muslim and be a democrat. A Jew can't be a Nazi and a Nazi can't be a Judeophile."[259] *Famous Tunisian author Salem Ben Ammar, August 2013.*

f. "We should, frankly, test every person here who is of a Muslim background, and **if they believe in Sharia, they should be deported**. **Sharia is incompatible with Western civilization**." *Former Speaker of the House Newt Gingrich, July 15, 2016.* Gingrich is analyzing how democracies should move forward after a Muslim migrant murdered over 80 individuals in Nice, France by ramming them with a massive truck on Bastille Day. Weeks earlier a Muslim terrorist killed 49 Americans in a nightclub in Orlando. All these Muslim terrorists seek the institution of Sharia law, the establishment of an Islamic caliphate, and the destruction of Western Judeo-Christian countries.

g. Muslim migrants in the Swedish town of Nybro, Smaland are posting stickers throughout their new home town stating, "Women who don't wear a headscarf are asking to be raped," and "No Democracy. We just want Islam."[260]

h. "Both Egyptians and the West sorely need to understand that Islamic law, sharia, does not permit anything other than an Islamic government under the rule of Islamic law. Consequently, only military force can stand against sharia tyranny. The Muslim Brotherhood [with respect to Egypt] had proven once again that the only way out of Islamic theocracies is through military dictatorships."[261] *Nonie Darwish, Gatestone Institute, November 2016.*

i. "The legal penalty is obligatorily imposed upon anyone who fornicates or commits sodomy ... If the offender is someone with the capacity to remain chaste, then he or she is stoned to death ... A pregnant woman is not stoned until she gives birth and the child can suffice with the milk of another." *Reliance of the Traveller (Umdat al-Salik), A Classic Manual of Islamic Sacred Law.*

j. "Men such as Sayyid Qutb, Yusuf al-Qaradawi, or Osama bin Laden . . . claim that their vision, based on Sharia law, is in all ways superior to the norms prevailing in the West." Ignored by far too many in the West is that "[i]n Saudi Arabia, a woman's testimony is usually not accepted in criminal cases and is worth half a man's testimony in civil cases."

Also, "[i]n Iran, married women cannot leave the country without their husband's permission. After a child is seven years old, custody of the child automatically goes to the father [.] A mother also loses custody of her young children if she remarries. In 2016, the chair of Pakistan's Council of Islamic Ideology, an important advisory body, sanctioned 'light' wife-beating."[262] *(Ayaan Hirsi Ali, anti-Islamist activist)*

k. "Darwish *[Nonie Darwish, activist, author of Wholly Different: Why I Chose Biblical Values over Islamic Values]*, as a trained journalist and speaker of Arabic, cites canonical Islamic sources to support her points. "**Islam and democracy are contradictory and absolutely incompatible**," she writes. These are not her words. She is quoting an imam … The West is inspired by the Judeo-Christian Bible … In contrast, the Muslim world is founded on and inspired by the Koran and the life and sayings of Mohammed. Allah is not loving and he is not a father … **Allah demands that humans not love him, but submit to him**, as slaves submit to their masters, and to sacrifice their lives for him … Western rights did not emerge ex nihilo. They are founded on Judeo-Christian religion and Ancient Greek civilization. The rights we in the West take for granted are not universal, but rather are specific to the West, and based on our unique history. When we give up our foundations, we give up our rights … don't you dare, she warns, replace the word "Judeo-Christian" with the politically correct neologism "Abrahamic," meant to elevate Islam to Judeo-Christian status as a co-foundation for Western civilization. She links the term "Abrahamic" to a **Muslim Brotherhood document instructing followers to "present Islam as a civilizational alternative" and "destroy the Western Civilization from within**." The West's capitulation to this agenda, she says, "is undermining the Biblical values of the West." As proof, she cites the Army's disciplining of a soldier who attempted to rescue a boy sex slave from an Afghan police commander, who kept the boy chained to his bed *[The rape of young boys is permitted in Islamic societies. Not in the West. Not with Judeo-Christian ethics. It is the basis of the rape epidemics perpetrated by Muslim migrants as they immigrate to the West. Obama knew of these rapes on U.S. military bases in Afghanistan and prosecuted the soldier who attempted to protect the boy. That alone is proof Obama is a radical Muslim.]* … **Sixty-four percent of the Koran, she maintains, is devoted to denigrating commentary about kafirs, or non-Muslims**. "Do unto others as you would have them do unto you" is totally alien to Islam, she says. "Islam has nothing to do with Abraham and Biblical values. In fact, it awards the highest esteem to Muslims who kill the children of Abraham, the Jews." … "Why is it that people in the West stand in line to wait for their turn while in the Muslim world people step on each other to get to be first? Why is it that in the West government leaders leave their office at the end of their term peacefully while in the Muslim world their term ends with either natural death or assassination?" Even in asking these questions, she writes, she was violating cultural expectations. "Asking questions and doubting is taboo in Islam." … Darwish argues that Allah encourages Muslims to hide sin, seeing public admission of sin to be a sign of weakness, while the West encourages individuals to acknowledge and come to terms with their own faults … The Koran is replete with references to "shame," "disgrace," "humiliation," and "losers." There is no comparable mention of "losers" in the Bible. **In the Koran, in addition to being labeled** "losers," **Christians and Jews are also called** "pigs," "apes," **and** "unclean." This emphasis on hiding sin fuels honor killing, and Turkey's refusal to acknowledge the Armenian Genocide, Darwish argues … In the West, Yusuf [a respected religious leader] says, the attitude is "don't harm anyone." In the Islamic worldview, he says, **there is a harm when forbidden behavior** "emerges into the public space." … Darwish cites many of the Koran verses and Hadith that call for jihad. **One hadith promises that killing a Jew or a Christian offers a Muslim a chance to be redeemed** from ever having to go to Hell. Darwish comments on the public relations attempt to redefine "jihad" as peaceful self-improvement. In Islamic texts, she says, **jihad plainly means** "war with non-Muslims to establish the religion.""[263]

l. "My central argument is that **political Islam implies a constitutional order fundamentally incompatible with the US Constitution** and with the 'constitution of liberty' that is **the foundation of the American way of life** … Let it be said explicitly: <u>the Islamists' program</u> is <u>fundamentally incompatible with the US Constitution</u>, **religious tolerance, the equality of men and women, the tolerance of different sexual orientations, the ban on cruel and unusual punishment and other fundamental human rights** … The term "dawa" refers to activities carried out by Islamists to win adherents and enlist them in a campaign to impose sharia law on all societies. Dawa is not the Islamic equivalent of religious proselytizing, although it is often disguised as such by blending humanitarian activities with subversive political activities … **The ultimate goal of dawa is to destroy the political institutions of a free society and replace them with strict sharia.** Islamists rely on both **violent and nonviolent means** to achieve their objectives … According to one estimate, **10-15 percent of the world**'s **Muslims are Islamists**. Out of well over 1.6 billion, or 23 percent of the globe's population, that implies more than **160 million individuals** … Based on survey data on attitudes toward sharia in Muslim countries, total support for Islamist activities in the world is likely significantly higher than that estimate." *Ayaan Hirsi Ali, representing the Hoover Institute, anti-Sharia activist, testifying before the Senate Homeland Security and Government Affairs Committee on June 14, 2017.*

m. "Islam is like a train. You get off once you've reached your destination." *Turkish President Erdogan.* Erdogan supported a national referendum in 2016 that passed and essentially made him a dictator in Turkey. Muslims use democracies as a temporary political vehicle whose final destination is generally an Islamic theocratic dictatorship. Prime examples include Egypt with President Morsi and the Muslim Brotherhood, Iran with the ayatollahs, and Turkey with Erdogan.

n. Imam Ammar Shahin at the **Islamic Center of Davis in California** led public prayers on July 20, 2017, during the Muslim riots on the Temple Mount and called for the annhilation of all Jews. He stated, "The Prophet Muhammad said: '**Judgment Day will not come until the Muslims <u>fight the Jews</u>**, and the Jews hide behind stones and trees, and the stones and the trees say: Oh Muslim, oh servant of Allah…' … it will say: Oh Muslim. Muslim. When Muslims come back… 'Come, there is someone behind me … Oh Allah, support the Al-Aqsa Mosque and the rest of the Muslim lands. Oh Allah, liberate the Al-Aqsa Mosque from the filth of the Jews. Oh Allah, destroy those who closed the Al-Aqsa Mosque. **Oh Allah, show us the black day that You inflict upon them**, and the wonders of Your ability. Oh Allah, **count them one by one and <u>annihilate them down to the very last one</u>**. <u>**Do not spare any of them**</u>." Muslims are now leading public prayers in America calling for the death of Jews. It appears that Islam may not be compatible with the values of America. Obama lied. After the Obama presidency, Muslims feel empowered to pray in public for genocide against the Jews. Obama's America is based on Sharia law from the Middle East, and not on the Constitution written by the founding fathers. Obama declared in Cairo in 2009, "it is important for Western countries to avoid impeding Muslim citizens from practicing religion **<u>as they see fit</u>**," and Obama would certainly support this imam's right to express his "religious views," although he may not "publicly" agree with the preacher.

14. **"Islam is not part of the problem in combating violent extremism, it is an important part of promoting peace**". *Obama, Cairo University speech, June 4, 2009.* Islam uses terrorism as a mechanism to cause non-Muslims to "submit" to Islam (which means submission) via forced conversions or through the payment of confiscatory jizya taxes and as the pathway to build the Islamic caliphate. This statement shows a lack of understanding or a deliberate lie on Obama's part. Specific evidence shows the opposite of Obama's statement to be the truth.

a. "I was told to fight all men until they say there is no G-d but Allah." *Mohammed*

b. The Institute for National Security Studies revealed that 450 out of 452 suicide terror attacks (>99%) committed in 2015 were done by Muslims.

c. "**Islam is an open-ended declaration of war against non-Muslims** … *[religious citations to back up these arguments]* … "Kill the unbelievers wherever you find them" (Koran 2:191), "Make war on the infidels living in your neighbourhood" (Koran 9:123), "When opportunity arises, kill the infidels wherever you catch them" (Koran 9:5), "Maim and crucify the infidels if they criticize Islam" (Koran 5:33), "Punish the unbelievers with garments of fire, hooked iron rods, boiling water; melt their skin and bellies" (Koran 22:19), and "Terrorize and behead those who believe in scriptures other than the Qur'an" (Koran 8:12)."[264] *Jesuit Father Henri Boulad, Islamic scholar of the Egyptian Greek Melkite rite, National Catholic Register interview. June 15, 2017.*

d. "On the pretext of openness, tolerance and Christian charity – the Catholic Church has fallen into **the trap of the liberal left ideology which is destroying the West** … It is high time to emerge from a shameful and embarrassed silence in the face of this Islamism that attacks the West and the rest of the world. A systematically conciliatory attitude is interpreted by the majority of Muslims as a sign of fear and weakness … By defending at all costs Islam and seeking to exonerate it from the horrors committed every day in its name, one ends up **betraying the truth**."[265] *Jesuit Father Henri Boulad letter to Pope Francis, August 2016.*

e. "We cannot fool ourselves. **There is an Islamic problem** … All of them (Hamas, Hezbollah, Boko Haram, the Islamic State …) are killing by the name of Allah. The Muslim people have a problem, and their problem is in their belief system … Humanity needs to stand against this danger … The truth is that we are afraid and we are trying not to provoke them more, we are trying not to create a religious war. But there has been a religious war whether you like it or not … **When the president of the free world stands and says 'Islam is a religion of peace,' he creates the climate, he provides the climate, the perfect climate to create more terrorism**." *Mosab Yousef, son of a Hamas founder and former Israeli spy, speaking at the Jerusalem Post annual conference May 2016.* Yousef implies that Obama is either practicing taqiyya or purposely creating conditions to give the Islamists an upper hand with their war against the West. Muslim terrorists know they have a partner in the White House.

f. "Islam is a belligerent religion. One should not be blind that many who commit terror find inspiration in Islam. That is why **there is a connection between the number of Muslims in a country and the general security risk**." *Martin Henriksen, the Danish People's Party immigration spokesman. July 2016 interview with the Associated Press.* Denmark is a nation of tolerance, so the Islamic threat to the freedoms and welfare of its citizens must be real for a major political party to be critical of the Muslims in its country.

g. "For these enemies, the implementation of Islamic law – shariah – as the governing law of the land is the objective. This is true not only for jihadi groups like al-Qaeda, but also for dawah organizations such as the Muslim Brotherhood and ummah entities like the Organization of Islamic Cooperation (OIC), a transnational body that makes reasonable claims to represent the ummah, or the entire Muslim world. The catastrophic failure of American strategy in the War on Terror is the refusal to contend with the convergence of these three forces *(jihadi, dawah, and ummah),* which ... interact to our great detriment. (p. 26)"[266] *Stephen Coughlin, Catastrophic Failure, 2015*

h. "About four decades have passed since **Sheikh ʿAbdullah bin Muhammad bin Humaid** **(1908-1981), ex-Chief Justice of Saudi Arabia,** published his lengthy, impassioned, essay on jihad. This essay, still available on the Internet, is the only one that Saudi religious scholars chose to include with the *Noble Quran* -- a modern, nine volume, English translation of the Quran, which includes ancient commentary. A cursory reading of Sheikh bin Humaid's essay should forever silence any fantasies regarding traditional Islam's peaceful disposition toward the non-Muslim world. As the Saudi publisher says in his prefatory note: 'But, as regards the reward and blessing, there is one deed which is very great in comparison to all the acts of worship and all the good deed [s] -- and that is Jihad! ... Never before such an article was seen, describing Jihad in its true colours -- so heart evoking and encouraging! ... We are publishing this article and recommend every Muslim not only to read it himself but to offer every other Muslim brother within his read.' To be clear, Sheikh bin Humaid defines "jihad" as "holy fighting in Allah's Cause." This is not, in other words, the "greater jihad," or "spiritual struggle," that some Muslim apologists cite, possibly to obfuscate the primary historical usage of the word. Jihad is war fought with "the heart," "the hand (weapons, etc.)," and "the tongue." ... **Bin Humaid views jihad as a perpetual war that is to be waged against the world until submission to Islam is secured**. The time for patience is over; the time for judgment has come. He cites the famous "verse of the sword": "Fight those who do not believe in Allah or in the Last Day and who do not consider unlawful what Allah and His Messenger have made unlawful and who do not adopt the religion of truth from those who were given the Scripture – [fight] until they give the jizyah willingly while they are humbled." (Quran 9:29, Sahih International). Bin Humaid tells us that Allah ordered the Muslims: "to discard (all) the obligations (covenants, etc.) *[taqiyya, ceasefires, peace treaties – Israel beware]* and commanded the Muslims to fight against all the Mushrikun as well as against the people of the Scriptures (Jews and Christians) if they do not embrace Islam, till they pay the Jizya (a tax levied on the non-Muslims who do not embrace Islam and are under the protection of an Islamic government) with willing submission and feel themselves subdued" ... The call to jihad requires the support of the entire Muslim Ummah or people. It involves **the transformation of a religious community into a military machine**. Sheikh bin Humaid states: "And you will not find any organization past or present, religious or non-religious ... (ordering) the whole nation to march forth and **mobilize all of them into active military service as a single row for Jihad in Allah's Cause** so as to make superior the Word of Allah ... as you will find **in the Islamic Religion** and its teachings."[267] *(Gatestone Institute International Policy Council, May 12, 2017)*

15. "**As the Holy Koran tells us**, 'Be conscious of G-d and speak always the truth.' That is what I will try to do – to speak the truth as best I can, humbled by the task before us, and firm in my belief that the interests we share as human beings are far more powerful than the forces that **drive us apart**." *Obama, Cairo University speech, June 4, 2009.* Does Obama speak the truth to non-Muslims, especially with the line "if you like your doctor, you can keep your doctor?" By calling the Israeli Prime Minister a chicken shit and a liar, is Obama speaking the truth and releasing forces that drive one of America's most dependable alliances apart? Under Obama's leadership, the Democratic party has drifted away from the embedded bipartisan support for Israel that has been part of American politics since its birth in 1948.

16. "For instance, in the United States, rules on charitable giving have made it harder for Muslims to fulfill their religious obligation. **That is why I am committed to working with American Muslims to ensure that they can fulfill zakat**." *Obama, Cairo University speech, June 4, 2009.* Zakat is used to support terrorist groups like Hamas and al-Qaeda in the Middle East. Obama knows that a significant percentage of these donations will be funding Islamic terrorist organizations.

   a. "In most cases, calls for donations were published on Internet sites and forums. In one counter-terrorism investigation, it was noted that supposed humanitarian aid activities were promoted via Facebook ... Monetary donations were requested via an associated PayPal account. **Examples of charity misuse have been evidenced in support of several terrorist entities**. Furthermore, some non-profit organizations are also suspected of serving as fronts for disseminating terrorist propaganda and financing the recruitment of young persons for the conflict in Syria."[268] *(Europol 2014 report).*

   b. "Many Palestinians in Gaza and the West Bank are bracing for the fallout as authorities prepare to lay out the case against Mohammed El Halabi, the chief executive of World Vision and one of the most prominent aid executives in the territory ... Mr. El Halabi, who has been detained since June, was officially charged Thursday at a court in Beersheba with organizing a **five-year-long fraud operation** that prosecutors say helped Islamist militant group Hamas build arms-smuggling tunnels, amass arms and other supplies, and stage terrorist attacks against Israelis ... some $7.2 million annually [**60% of all funds collected**], largely **from donors and governments** in Western countries including the U.S., England and Australia – were **transferred to** Hamas **to strengthen its terrorist arm**."[269] *(Asma Jawabreh and Jacob Wirtschafter, The Washington Times, August 2016)* A significant portion of charitable funds collected for the Palestinians is redirected for the purpose of killing Jews. Obama fully supports these charities because he knows the funds will be used to attack Israel.

17. "**The Holy Koran teaches** that **whoever kills an innocent, it is as if he has killed all mankind; and whoever saves a person**, it is as if he has saved all mankind. The enduring faith of over a billion people is so much bigger than the **narrow hatred of a few**." *Obama, Cairo University speech, June 4, 2009.* Infidels are not innocent, so their murder is not associated with this statement. Obama is downplaying and marginalizing Islam's history of intolerance and violence. All polls of Muslims show a significant percentage of them support violent jihad and the death penalty for blasphemy, even in the United States.

a.   "Most Muslim countries were conquered violently by force. Few are the countries conquered any other way. … Mecca was conquered by force. Iraq was conquered by force, and so were Iran, Turkey, Egypt, Syria, and the countries of north Africa. **Most Islamic countries were conquered by force**, **through fighting**. Some may claim that Islam was spread by the sword. That's true. **Islam was spread by the sword. So what! Allah's true religion should be spread by the sword, by force. If you cannot talk people into converting to Islam, they should be made to <u>convert by the sword</u>. Such is the command of Allah** … This is <u>**our duty**</u> according to the Sharia. This is the meaning of voluntary <u>**jihad**</u>. What does voluntary jihad mean? That the Islamic army marches on the lands of the infidels *[millions of Muslim migrants entering Europe presently, over four million Muslim are waiting for the opportunity to move to Europe],* and propose they convert to Islam. If they agree to become Muslims – fine. If they refuse, they are told that they should pay the jizya tax, if they are from the People of the Book [Jews and Christians]. If they refuse to pay the jizya, they should be fought. If they are not from the People of the Book [Hindus …], they don't even get a chance to pay the jizya – **either they convert to Islam or they are killed**. *[Europe's and America's future per Obama, Erdogan, the Muslim Brotherhood, the OIC, and the UN since all are promoting immigration jihad.]* There is nothing wrong with this. Let Islam be spread by the sword." *Iraqi Shiite Cleric Sabah Shabr, Al-Maaref TV, religious instruction based on the teachings of Ayatollah Sistani, Bahrain, October 13, 2015.* Obama is practicing taqiyya when he proclaims Islam is a religion of peace and he disassociates Islam from terrorism. A large percentage of Muslim migrants from Iraq, Syria, Pakistan and other Islamic societies believe in jihad as described above.

18. "There is also one rule that lies **at the heart of every religion – that we do unto others as we would have them do unto us**." *Obama, Cairo University speech, June 4, 2009.* Obama practices taqiyya by falsely projecting a core tenet of Judeo-Christian ethics upon Islam. Like the stoning of gays, the murder of apostates, and the murder of blasphemers are all backed by fatwas issued by Muslim imams. The <u>**Islamic**</u> Republic of Iran incessantly calls for the annihilation of Israel.

a. Islam sanctions the rape of young boys which is a major problem with the sexual attacks on male children in European refugee camps and in public baths in Germany, Austria and in Scandinavia, as well on U.S. military bases in Afghanistan, where Afghan officers take Afghan boys from the community to their private quarters for sexual perversion. Theological support for these barbaric uncivilized acts is found in the Quran which states, "And they will be given to drink a cup whose mixture is of ginger, a fountain within Paradise named Salsabeel. There will circulate among them **young boys** made eternal. When you see them, you would think them **scattered pearls**. And when you look there, you will see **pleasure and great dominion**." *Quran (76:17-20)*. Obama supports the Quran when he prosecuted American military personnel who intervened to prevent the rape of young boys by Afghan Muslim military officers on U.S. military bases.

b. In August 2016, a twenty-year-old Muslim refugee raped a 10-year-old boy while he slept in Australia, and claimed his innocence since his actions were "culturally acceptable" in his homeland, Myanmar.[270] Pediatric rape is an acceptable practice in Islam, and Obama wants America to respect these cultural differences, while the children of America and Europe will be preyed upon.

19. "In ancient times and in our times, **Muslim communities have been at the forefront of innovation and education**." *Obama, Cairo University speech, June 4, 2009.* What technological and educational innovations have originated from the Muslim world after the crusades besides suicide bombers and other creative ways to advance violent jihad? Where are the liberal-tolerant universities in the Middle East outside of Israel?

20. "Ramadan is a celebration of faith known for great diversity and **racial equality**." *Obama, Statement by the President on the Occasion of Ramadan, August 11, 2010.* The word for black in Arabic also means slave. Islamic society and Sharia law views non-Muslims as second-class citizens.

21. "We've seen those results in generations of Muslim immigrants, farmers and factory workers, helping to lay the railroads and build our cities, the Muslim innovators who helped build some of our highest skyscrapers and who helped unlock the secrets of our universe." *Obama, Remarks by the President at Iftar Dinner, July 25, 2013.* Why did Obama specifically draw attention to Muslims building the railroads and cities? Many more members of religions other than Islam contributed to the building of our nation.

22. "Here in America, **Islam has been woven into the fabric of our country since its founding**. Generations of Muslim immigrants came here and went to work as farmers and merchants and factory workers, helped to lay railroads and to build up America. *[recycled speech from 2013 Iftar Dinner at White House]* … It is also a story that every American must never forget, because it reminds us all that <u>**hatred and bigotry and prejudice have no place in our country**</u>. *[Then should Islam be allowed in America since anti-Semitism is a core component*

of the religion? ***Is Obama inadvertently laying the groundwork for Islam being banned in the United States?]*** It is not just counterproductive. It doesn't just aid terrorists. It's wrong. It's contrary to who we are." *Obama, Remarks by the President in Closing of the Summit on Countering Violent Extremism, February 18, 2015.* Obama recycled this speech when he gave prepared remarks before the Islamic Society of Baltimore in early 2016, which is affiliated with the Muslim Brotherhood.

23. "It's why we speak out against the deplorable anti-Semitism that has resurfaced in certain parts of the world. **It's why we continue to reject offensive stereotypes of Muslims – the vast majority of whom share our commitment to peace**." *Obama, State of the Union Address, 2015.* Obama is using the deceptive argument of moral equivalence. Islam, throughout its history, has been associated with violence. Comparing Islamophobia based on an objective evaluation of reality and anti-Semitism is ironic since prejudice against Jews is embedded in Islamic culture, Sharia law and the Quran. Most Muslim countries refuse to recognize Israel's right to exist, which is hard-core anti-Semitism, but Obama has no problem with these long-term political positions. Obama will not admit that the amount of anti-Semitism is Western countries is directly proportional to the relative percentage of its Islamic inhabitants.

24. "We will convey our deep appreciation for **the Islamic faith, which has done so much over the centuries to shape the world – <u>including in my own country</u>**. *[fake history parallels fake news]" Obama, Turkish Parliament speech, April 6, 2009.* Obama is proselytizing for Islam. Contrary to Obama's portrayal of Islam as a force for peace and coexistence, the following quotes from a 2016 *Breitbart* article[271] outlined decisive battles the West fought and won against Islamic armies. These victories safeguarded the freedoms and culture of the West, which would have been destroyed with Islamic victories, and later ushered in the Renaissance, a great period of cultural enlightenment which would have never occurred in a society dominated by Islam.

    a. "**In AD 732** a Muslim army of as many as 200,000 men was defeated by the Christian **Charles Martel at Tours**. If that battle had been lost, all Europe would have fallen to militant Islam."

    b. "**In 1565 the relief of the Siege of Malta**, by a Christian alliance, ensured that the Mediterranean did not fall into Muslim hands and so give them a toehold in southern Europe."

    c. "Following the **defeat of the Muslim Turks by the Knights of St John at Malta in 1565**, there came the **Battle of Lepanto on 7th October 1571** when a fleet of the Holy League, a coalition of Spain (including its territories of Naples, Sicily and Sardinia), the Republic of Venice, the Papacy, the Republic of Genoa, the Duchy of Savoy, the Knights Hospitaller and others, decisively defeated the main fleet of the Ottoman Empire."

d. "There was that other **11 September – 1683 when Christian armies under Jan Sobieski arrived at the gates of Vienna** and defeated the last substantial Muslim incursion: the last, that is, before the one which we face at present."

25. "The **Holy Koran** tells us, 'O mankind! We have created you male and a female; and we have made you into nations and tribes so that you may know one another.'" *Obama, Cairo University speech, June 4, 2009.* Does Obama use embellishing adjectives when referring to other religious texts like the Holy Bible or the sacred or G-d given Torah? Obama does not mention that the next verse in the Quran defines Islamic supremacism when it states, "Surely, the noblest among you in the sight of G-d is the most G-d fearing of you." (Quran 49:13)

26. "All of us have a responsibility to work for the day when the mothers of Israelis and Palestinians can see their children grow up without fear … **peace be upon them**, joined in prayer." *Obama, Cairo University speech, June 4, 2009.* Only a Muslim would state "peace be upon them," after reciting Mohammed's name.

27. "**My job to the Muslim world** is to communicate that the **Americans are not your enemy. We sometimes make mistakes. We have not been perfect**." *Obama, Al Arabiya interview, January 27, 2009.* Obama is critical of the United States before a Middle Eastern audience, and launches his worldwide "apology tour" where he incessantly criticizes America before foreign audiences.

28. "I think that for us to be successful in fighting this scourge, it's very important for us to align ourselves with the **99.9 percent of Muslims who are looking for the same thing we're looking for**: **order**, **peace**, **prosperity** … And so I don't quibble with labels." *Obama, CNN interview, February 2015.* It is estimated that 10% - 25% of all Syrian "refugees" support ISIS. Over 80% of Egyptian Muslims support the stoning of apostates to death, and over 50% support suicide bombings. A Pew Research Center (Pew) poll in 2014 showed that 25% of American Muslims support suicide bombers, and 85% of Muslims in the Netherlands support violent jihad against infidels. In a 2012 poll, over 20% of American Muslims supported the death penalty for blasphemy, and over 30% believe Sharia law should rule the United States. In a 2014 worldwide survey of Muslims, 32% favor the forced institution of Sharia law over non-Muslims. Obama is downplaying the Muslim threat to the United States and the West. Compare this statement to:

a. "Violence … occurs between Muslims, on the one hand, and Orthodox Serbs in the Balkans, Jews in Israel, Hindus in India, Buddhists in Burma and Catholics in the Philippines. **Islam has bloody borders**." *Samuel Huntington, "The Clash of Civilizations" Foreign Affairs, 1993.*

b. "You can't say that Islam is a religion of peace, because Islam does not mean peace. Islam means submission … There is a place for violence in Islam. There is a place for jihad in Islam." *Anjem Choudary, British Islamist and Muslim community leader.*

c. A Pew Research Center poll released in November 2015 demonstrated **there are be-**
    tween 63 and 287 million ISIS supporters in the Muslim world. In Pakistan, only
    28% of Muslims have an unfavorable view of ISIS. In Turkey, 8% of Muslims view
    ISIS favorably. Assuming there are 75 million Muslims in Turkey, according to 2014
    estimates, **there are six million ISIS supporters in Turkey alone**. At a Turkish soc-
    cer game in November 2015, the vast majority of Turkish Muslim citizens booed and
    shouted "Allahu Akbar" throughout a moment of silence for the victims of the ISIS Paris
    massacre. The same reactions were displayed by Muslim citizens at a sporting event in
    Azerbaijan that same month.

d. "It is hard to believe that President Obama believes what he says about Islam *[taqiyya]*,
    because the day Osama bin Laden was killed was a day of mourning all over the Muslim
    world. When Obama realized that, he had bin Laden's body buried at sea so the Muslim
    world could not erect a monument in Mecca for him ... **It defies logic that only 0.1%**
    percent of Muslims are causing all this never-ending worldwide havoc, **and un-**
    speakable mayhem, torture, burning and beheading of hundreds of thousands of
    people around the world. If they are only 0.1% of the Muslim population, how come
    the brutal Islamic legal system is unable to round the jihadists up and behead them in
    the infamous public squares of Saudi Arabia? How come moderate Muslims, the 99.9%,
    are unable to explain away their passivity with jihadists while those jihadists are brutal-
    izing, honor killing and terrorizing apostates? How many jihadists have been declared
    apostates by Saudi Arabia? How many were beheaded in the Saudi or Iranian public
    squares? **Why has the "moderate" largest Islamic university in the world, Al-Azhar,**
    never issued a fatwa of death against ISIS fighters and anyone who joins ISIS? ...
    Obama claims to have the support of a coalition of moderate Muslim governments to
    fight ISIS. But we see no Muslim armies moving to Syria to rid the world of the 0.1%
    Muslim jihadists in ISIS. In fact, the real reason why Muslim leaders are not waging
    war on ISIS, even though they are capable of doing so, is because at least half of the
    Muslim army will defect and join ISIS. **Those nice moderate Muslim armies do not**
    want to violate Sharia law and destroy the newly declared Caliphate, **which is at**
    the center of Islam's religious goals *[and Obama's]* ... **If jihadists and terrorists were**
    only 0.1%, we would not have the worldwide Islamic terrorism of today ... How
    come the 0.1% of radical Muslims is capable of causing millions of Muslim refugees ...
    Survey after survey keeps confirming our fears that **the majority of Muslims are for**
    killing apostates. A majority **supports Sharia** and **believes in jihad** as a main require-
    ment and obligation for Muslims. Muslim citizens keep electing Islamist groups such as
    Hamas and the Muslim Brotherhood to power. **The majority of the commandments**

of Islamic holy books command Muslims to kill, terrorize, humiliate and subjugate non-Muslims … I have yet to see fatwas of death against jihadists in the Arab media or from Muslim political and religious leaders. It is clear where the heart of those who call themselves moderate Muslims is. It is not against jihadists, but against those who speak against jihad."[272] *Nonie Darwish, Egyptian-American human rights activist, founder of Arabs for Israel.*

e. "Despite France's huge Muslim population of around five million, just a few hundred turned up in churches around France to show "solidarity" during mass following the brutal jihadist murder of a priest in Normandy."[273] *(Raheen Kassam, Breitbart, July 2016)*

29. "There is **no religion whose central tenet is hate**. *[taqiyya – Actually, there is.]* There is no G-d who condones taking the life of an innocent human being." *Obama, National Prayer Breakfast Speech, February 5, 2009.* The only innocent human being in the world is a fundamental religious Muslim who wants Sharia law. This is similar to saying that Islam wants world peace, which will only come about when the whole world is ruled by Sharia law and everyone is a fundamental Muslim. By comparing Obama's declarations to actual quotes from the Quran, it becomes evident that Obama is proselytizing for Islam and is purposely misrepresenting its true tenets, so it can strengthen its foothold in the United States.

a. "O Ye who believe! **Fight those of the disbelievers who are near you, and let them find harshness in you**, and know that Allah is with those who keep their duty unto him." *Quran (9:123).*

b. "**Those who reject (Truth), among the People of the Book and among the Polytheists, will be in Hell – Fire, to dwell therein** (for aye). For they are the worst creatures." *Quran (98:6).*

c. "O ye who believe! **Take not Jews and the Christians for friends**. They are friends one to another. He among you who taketh them for friends is one of them." *Quran (5:51).*

d. "Then, when the sacred months have passed, **slay the idolaters wherever ye find them, and take them captive, and besiege them**, and prepare for them each ambush." *Quran (9:5).*

e. "**Fight those who believe not in Allah** nor the Last Day, nor hold that forbidden which hath been forbidden by Allah and His Messenger, nor acknowledge the religion of Truth (even if they are) of the People of the Book, until they pay the Jizya with willing submission, and feel themselves subdued." *Quran (9:29).*

f. Sheikh Farrokh Sekalshfar was invited to speak on religious topics including homosexuality at the Husseini Islamic Center in Sanford, Florida in 2013 where he preached with the approval of the mosque, "**Death is the sentence**. We know there's nothing to be embarrassed about this, death is the sentence … We have to have that compassion for people, with **homosexuals**, it's the same, out of compassion, **let's get rid of them now**."

30. "At the same time, we have reaffirmed again and again that the United States is not and never will be at war with Islam. **Islam teaches peace**. Muslims the world over aspire to live with dignity and a sense of justice. And when it comes to America and Islam, there is no us and them, there is only us – because millions of Muslim Americans are part of the fabric of our country." *Obama, UN Address, September 24, 2014. Obama is always promoting Islam as a religion of peace, despite Islamic groups from around the world using terrorism to advance their political and religious ideologies to institute Sharia law.*

   a. Islamic terrorist groups based on teachings from the Quran: al-Qaeda (in Iraq, in the Islamic Maghreb, in the Arabian Peninsula …), ISIS / ISIL and their affiliates, Hamas, Hezbollah, Boko Haram, Taliban, the Muslim Brotherhood, Abdullah Azzam Shaheed Brigade, Abu Sayyaf, al Aqsa Martyrs' Brigade, al Badr, al Shabaab, al Umar Mujahideen, Army of Islam Caucasus Emirate, Egyptian Islamic Jihad, Izz ad Din al Qassam Brigades, Harkat ul Jihad al Islami, Harkat ul Majahideen, Hizbul Mujahideen, East Turkestan Islamic Movement, Islamic Jihad, Islamic Movement of Uzbekistan, Jamaat ul Mujahideen Bangladesh, Libyan Islamic Fighting Group, Moroccan Islamic Combatant Group, Palestinian Liberation Front, PLO, Popular Front for the Liberation of Palestine, Islamic Jihad in Palestine, Tehreek e Nafaz e Shariat e Mohammadi, Abu Nidal Organization, World Uygur Youth Movement, al Gama'a al Islamiyya, Ansar al Islam, Armed Islamic Group of Algeria, Egyptian Islamic Jihad, Holy Land Foundation for Relief and Development, and many more.

   b. "British Muslims have been urged to "stop pretending" violence and terrorism are completely alien to Islam. The call was made by Maajid Nawaz, a former leader of the UK branch of the hardline Islamist group Hizb ut-Tahrir (HuT). Mr. Nawaz, a broadcaster and author, was speaking on London's LBC radio in the wake of Saturday night's terrorist atrocity in the British capital, in which seven people were killed and more than 50 injured. In response to a caller questioning whether Islam had anything to do with acts of terrorist violence, he had this to say: "When the **prophet Mohammed said: 'I have been ordered to fight the people until they declare there is no G-d but G-d and Muhammad is his messenger**', That's clearly got something to do with violence doesn't it?" Maajid suggested."[274] *(Breitbart, June 6, 2017)*

   c. "A leaked report from the **Swedish police confirms** that there are **at least 23 Muslim-controlled "<u>No-Go Zones</u>"** and some **60 "vulnerable areas"** where non-muslim citizens of the country can no longer visit safely … the areas are plagued with **violence**, **sexual assaults** and **gun crimes**, and things have gotten so bad that <u>**police and emergency services personnel refuse to enter**</u>."[275] *(Zero Hedge / SHTFplan.com, June 23,*

2017) No-Go Zones are also prevalent in Great Britain and France. No-Go Zones are the natural result of an increasing Muslim population in and Muslim immigration to any non-Muslim society. Muslims populations purposely create these enclaves of civil disobedience in order to prevent the application of local laws so Sharia law can be applied by their religious authorities and Islamic gangs. These Muslim communities are committing treason and are preparing for civil war. The creation of Islamic No-Go Zones by Muslim communities should be reason enough to stop Muslim immigration to the West.

    i.   **In Great Britain, the Muslim no-go zones have a documented much higher percentage of acid attacks against non-Muslims**. "Newham is the London borough with the highest number of acid attacks. It also has the second highest percentage of Muslims in the UK. 398 acid attacks occurred in 5 years in the area named as "the most ethnically diverse district in England and Wales". 33% of Newham consists of non-UK passport holders … the place with the third highest number of acid attacks is Tower Hamlets. Tower Hamlets is a Muslim no-go zone. … 35% of the population is Muslim. Most of those are Bangladeshis with a healthy sprinkling of Somalis. There were 84 acid attacks in what has been dubbed "The Islamic Republic of Tower Hamlets" … The second highest acid attack location in London was Barking and Dagenham, a growing Muslim enclave … The native British population made up 80% of Barking in 2001. Now it's fallen to less than half. According to the 2011 census figures, "All religious groups have increased except for Christian and Jewish religions". … Fifth on the acid list is Redbridge where the native British population fell by 40,844 in a decade. The last census showed British and Irish natives fleeing Redbridge while Pakistanis and Bangladeshis stormed in. The Christian and Jewish population fell while the Muslim population rose 11%. So did the acid attacks …"[276] *("The Acid Attacks of London's Muslim No-Go Zones," Front Page Magazine, 2017)*

    d. "I will attack you, tear you apart and stab you. I will do what's never been done before for the sake of the Al Aqsa Mosque, so that **the Jews will know who I am – a Muslim**, an Arab, a Palestinian. **I will kill you**, <u>I swear by my religion</u>. … An enemy lies in wait for you in every alley. You will be killed, I guarantee. An axe, a knife, a gun or a rifle will kill you – yes, kill, not take you prisoner. <u>**I will cleanse my country of every Jew**</u>. I will strive for that with all my might." *Popular song broadcast in Hebrew on Hamas media. Summer 2017.*

31. "We know that **military force alone cannot solve this problem** [Islamic terrorism]. Nor can we simply take out terrorists who kill innocent civilians *[Obama does not want to kill Muslim terrorists while they wage war and terror against America.]* … Groups like al-Qaeda and ISIL promote a **twisted interpretation of religion that is rejected by the**

overwhelming majority of the world's Muslims. *[taqiyya]* The world must continue to **lift up the voices of Muslim clerics and scholars who teach the true peaceful nature of Islam**. *[Obama is proselytizing for Islam.]* … We can help Muslim entrepreneurs and youths work with the private sector to develop social media tools to counter extremist narratives on the internet … Efforts to counter violent extremism will only succeed if citizens can address **legitimate grievances** through the democratic process and express themselves through strong civil societies. *[Obama wants the radical Muslim terrorists – ISIS and al-Qaeda – to have a role in the governance in the societies they terrorize.]*"[277] *Obama, 2015.* Obama is insisting that America and the West address the "legitimate grievances" of ISIS terrorists. This is similar to what Obama wrote as an Illinois state senator after the 9-11 terrorist attacks, "we must engage … in the more difficult task of **understanding the source of such madness**." Obama also has stated that Hamas and Hezbollah have "legitimate claims" and is allied with their interests. This alone coupled with Obama's stated reluctance to kill Muslim terrorists who live to kill Americans proves that Obama is a radical Muslim.

32. "It **breaks my heart** every time you read about or hear about these kinds of incidents … What we know, is that **the number of people who die from gun-related incidents around this country dwarfs any deaths that happen through terrorism**." *Obama, responding to the shooting deaths of two CBS reporters on August 26, 2015.* Obama is downplaying Islamic terrorism and advancing gun control.

33. "Remember that **violent extremism is not unique to any one faith** *[Obama is advancing moral equivalency between Islamic terrorism and any extremists associated with other religions.]* … **No one should be profiled** or targeted simply **because of their faith** … [and] we have to commit ourselves to build diverse, tolerant, inclusive, societies that **reject anti-Muslim and anti-immigrant bigotry that creates the divisions**, **the fear**, **and the resentments upon which extremists can prey**." *Obama, UN speech at Leaders' Summit on Countering ISIL and Violent Extremism, September 29, 2015.*

34. "**They're just like our kids**, and they deserve love, and protection … and an education." *Obama White House Tweet, November 21, 2015.* Obama is making the case for admitting Syrian Muslim refugees to America by using widows, orphans, and children as political human shields. **ISIS has used many children to execute their prisoners of war or infidels in their jurisdictions**. The Palestinians also indoctrinate their youth from birth to kill Jews and destroy Israel. These children are not like our kids, and they would be prime candidates to commit future violence against Americans in the years to come. These Muslim children need to be resettled in Muslim countries, and Obama is making no effort to redirect the immigration of these migrants to Gulf state countries, Pakistan, Iran, or Indonesia, since his major concern is advancing immigration jihad.

a. Two Palestinian girls, aged 14 and 16, stabbed a Jewish man and a Palestinian man in Jerusalem on November 24, 2015. The young girls mistakenly identified the Palestinian man as a Jew.

b. In 2016, three Sudanese and Iraqi Muslim boys who were recent immigrants to Twin Falls, Idaho, with two boys acknowledged to be 7 and 10 years-old, "allegedly" sexually assaulted and raped a 5-year-old girl. According to an eye witness, the Muslim boys peed on the naked American girl and in her mouth after the assault. The Muslim rape epidemics of Europe and the Muslim sex grooming gangs of Great Britain, will now be coming to American communities as foreign Muslims who have been taught Sharia law and jihad from birth by their parents and their Islamic communities, attempt to assert their supremacism over American infidels. Within one week of the attack, Obama proved he sided with the migrant boys when a federal prosecutor that he appointed, threatened the Twin Falls community and its inhabitants with prosecution in support of the Muslim children "allegedly" committing the sexual assaults and molestations. United States Attorney Wendy Olson warned the local community, "**The spread of false information** or inflammatory or threatening statements about the perpetrators or the crime itself reduces public safety and **may violate federal law**. We have seen time and again that the spread of falsehoods about refugees divides our communities." This parallels Attorney General Lynch's threat to prosecute any Americans if they engaged in "anti-Muslim rhetoric" after Muslim terrorists murdered fourteen Americans at a Christmas party in San Bernardino, which is the institution of Sharia law in the United States. In 2015, Olson had criticized Idaho citizens who were against the transfer of Middle Eastern Muslim migrants to their small communities by equating their concerns with "extremist ideologies," which will allow the Obama administration to target political activists (via IRS tax audits or prosecution) against his policies. A few days later, Olsen again threatened local law abiding citizens who expressed concerns over this heinous crime by stating, "Certain threatening or harassing communications may violate federal law and will be investigated." Obama's appointees are more concerned with subjugating the local population than with protecting the safety of the community against certain Muslim migrants. Sounds like Sharia law.

c. The 2016 Arab Youth Survey, a poll which reflected the views of 200+ million Arab and Muslim youths in the Middle East and North Africa revealed that 22% (44 + million) of those polled were not concerned about ISIS, and 13% (26 + million) admitted they would support ISIS if they used less violence.[278]

d. In a poll released by the Jerusalem Media and Communications Center in mid-April 2016, over 50% of Palestinian youth in the West Bank support the stabbing attacks against Israeli citizens and over 78% of the youth in the Gaza strip support the stabbing attacks.

e. Muslim children who attended a Gaza annual children's festival in 2016 celebrated by pretending to kill Israeli troops, stabbing Israeli soldiers, and shooting them in their heads.

f. In 2015, 80% of sexually assaults in Swedish bathhouses are committed by foreigners and immigrant [Muslim] children.

g. Muslim children learn the Quran from a very young age, before they start their formal elementary education. Lessons include – Jews are descendants from apes and pigs, "Take not the Jews and the Christian for your friends," "Fight those who believe not in Allah," "Cast into the unbelievers' hearts terror," and "When you meet the unbelievers, smite their necks."

h. Twenty-three year-old Muslim Syrian immigrants were posing as young teenagers so they could gain entrance to Fredericton High School in New Brunswick, Canada, where they sexually harassed 14-year-old girls, bullied Jews, and threatened teachers, while refusing to learn English. These same scenarios will soon be happening across America.

i. ISIS "cubs," otherwise known as ISIS child soldiers, were shown executing Afghan soldiers in Afghanistan or Pakistan in June 2016. ISIS is allied with the Taliban, Obama's "moderate peace partners." ISIS "cubs" are also being trained as suicide bombers.

j. A Middle Eastern Muslim girl in a full burka, who was about 6-8 years-old, was chanting a pro-ISIS song while decapitating a toy doll with a knife. She was singing, "State of Islam, attack and defeat the religion of heresy … Instill terror, exterminate the leftover remnants (of the army), and slaughter… Allahu Akbar."[279]

k. In mid-August 2016, a child suicide bomber estimated between the ages of 12 and 14-year-old, murdered over two dozen people at a Turkish wedding.

l. In September 2016, according to *Die Welt*, the chief of police in Frankfurt warned that very young Muslim boys are being taught to support jihad and murder in Salafist schools in Germany, and referred to them as "hate children."

m. Forty percent of the Muslim migrants classified as children in Sweden are between the ages of twenty and thirty. Some of the unaccompanied minors who are seeking asylum in Sweden are between the ages of thirty and forty. The estimated 31,000 unaccompanied minors seeking asylum may be an inflated number since a large percentage of these individuals are adults.[280] Later in 2017, the percentage was increased from 40% to 75%.

35. **"Yours [Iran] is a great civilization, with a vibrant culture** that has so much to contribute to the world – in commerce, and in science and the arts." *Obama praised Iran after he approved over $150 billion in sanctions relief for Iran and also paid them a $1.7+ billion ransom for four American political prisoners. January 17, 2016.* Obama loves Iran and has never complimented America with this tone.

36. "How easily we learn to justify violence in the name of some higher cause. **Every great religion promises a pathway to love and peace and righteousness**, and yet no religion has been spared from <u>believers who</u> have claimed their faith as a <u>license to kill</u>. *[false moral equivalence]* Nations arise telling a story that binds people together in sacrifice and cooperation, allowing for remarkable feats. But those same stories have so often been used to oppress and dehumanize those *[attacks America]* who are different." *Obama, Hiroshima remarks, May 27, 2016.* Even in Japan while addressing WWII and the terrors of a nuclear war, Obama espouses a moral equivalency between Islam and all other religions, and thus shields Islam from criticism regarding its advancement of violent jihad. Unfortunately for the world, Islam's path to love, peace and righteousness is through the subjugation of all non-Muslims, especially Jews and Christians, which leads to their paying a severe confiscatory tax (jizya), forced conversion to Islam, or their torture and murder. This has been Islam's modus operandi since its inception. Islam views ultimate peace as a society with no Muslims remaining. That is why Sharia compliant societies always have a decreasing percentage of non-Muslims as part of their population as time progresses.

37. "…by working with **partners** around the world, including **Muslim communities**, to push back against **hateful ideologies that twist and distort Islam, a religion that teaches peace and justice and compassion**. *[taqiyya and proselytizing for Islam.]* We **will defeat these ideologies by offering a better vision of development and economic progress**. *[taqiyya – Obama views only economic factors, and not Islam as the motivating forces for the ISIS terrorists. Yet, in Bangladesh in early July 2016, Islamic terrorists massacred over twenty people, and all the assailants came from wealthy families. Obama is protecting ISIS by advancing economic assistance instead of effective military strategy to defeat the terrorists.]* So people, especially young people, have more hope and opportunity, and are less susceptible to extremism and violence in the first place. And **we will continue to promote political opportunity and democracy, so citizens have a say in their future**. *[taqiyya – Obama knows that democracy does not thrive in Islamic societies.]* And we will win this fight by staying true to our values. Values of pluralism *[The paradigm of multiculturalism is failing in the West.]*, and rule of law *[taqiyya – Obama supports BLM, ISIS, Erdogan (July 2016 coup), and the Muslim Brotherhood, who all have contempt for Western laws and civility.]*, and diversity, and freedoms — like the freedom of religion *[taqiyya – not for Jews and Christians in Islamic societies]*, freedom of speech *[taqiyya – Obama supports blasphemy laws.]* and assembly *[not with student protesters in Iran]*, the very freedoms that the people of Nice were celebrating last night on Bastille Day." *Obama, responding to the Nice truck massacre perpetrated by an ISIS terrorist. July 14, 2016.* Obama does not mention Islam as a motivating factor in the attack, but uses this solemn heart-breaking event as an opportunity to praise and promote Islam on the world stage.

38. *Landmark Remarks by the President at* **The Islamic Society of Baltimore***, February 3, 2016:* This mosque, like so many in our country, is an all-American story *[has been associated with the Muslim Brotherhood, Hamas and al-Qaeda in the past]* ... To the folks watching this today who haven't – think of your own church, or synagogue, or temple, and a mosque like this will be very familiar. *[Most churches and synagogues in America do not have links to the Muslim Brotherhood or al-Qaeda, and support the genocide of Jews in Israel.]* This is where families come to worship and express their love for G-d and each other. *[To teach the Quran is to spread anti-Semitism.]* There's a school where teachers open *[indoctrinate]* young minds ... With interfaith dialogue *[taqiyya]*, you build bridges of understanding *[only one way]* with other faith communities – Christians and Jews. *[Mutual respect is generally a one-way street with interfaith dialogue.]* There's a health clinic that serves the needy, regardless of their faith. *[Muslim charities don't build hospitals in America, like Catholic, Presbyterian, Episcopal, Christian or Jewish organizations, where their funds would be used to help non-Muslims.]* And members of this community are out in the broader community, working for social justice *[Promoting Sharia law. Any push back against Muslim supremacism and Sharia law is identified as Islamophobia and discrimination.]* and urban development *[building new mosques and Islamic centers, many of which are sponsored by foreign radical Islamic governments like Saudi Arabia and Wahhabism]* ... As one of your members said, "just look at the way we live ... we are true Americans." *[Muslims generally don't assimilate. According to a survey conducted by the Center of Security Policy in 2015, 51% of American Muslims believe they should have a choice to choose Sharia law over American law, only 39% believe they should be subject to the ruling of American courts, and nearly 20% of American Muslims believe that propagating violence – violent jihad – in the United States is a legitimate path in order to install Sharia law in America (2015 Center for Security Policy poll). According to a recent Pew poll, 60% of Muslims under age 30 admitted they felt greater loyalty to Islam than America. Sharia law is incompatible with the United States Constitution since it mandates that Jews and Christians are second-class citizens, homosexuals can be stoned, apostates and blasphemers can receive the death penalty, and women are subject to discrimination and viewed as property. Sharia law also sanctions statutory rape since Muslims can marry pre-pubescent girls, sometimes less than ten-years-old, like Mohammed. A prominent Danish imam, Oussama El Saadi, supported Muslim men marrying young Muslim girls among the migrants living in Denmark by stating "One should look at these cases from a different perspective. It is an extraordinary humanitarian situation, and I think you have to take care of these families. They're married, and even if the man is twice as old as they have built a family. We have to accept that it is a different culture, and we cannot destroy family life." In Norway, one of the Muslim migrants was married to an eleven-year-old girl. Polygamy, which is illegal in America, is condoned by Islam. Muslim men can legally strike or assault their wives under Sharia law.]* So the first thing I want to say is two words that Muslim Americans don't

hear often enough – and that is, thank you. *[Thank you for not helping law enforcement find and apprehend Islamic terrorists and sympathizers.]…* Thank you for lifting up the lives of your neighbors, and for helping keep us strong and united as one American family. *[Sheikh Abdelhadi Sweif, Imam of the Great Mosque of Brussels, with other Belgian imams refused to pray for any of the souls of the Christians who were killed in the ISIS Brussels bombing terrorist attack in March 2016. He stated that "This initiative was rejected by the council of imams [in Belgium], to hold a prayer for the souls of the victims of the Brussels attacks – on the grounds that this runs counter to the Islamic Sharia, and that such a prayer can be held only for the souls of Muslims." These Muslim mainstream religious leaders in Belgium are no different than the imams in the United States, all of whom are not interested in forming a long-term united society with non-Muslims. This is one insight into the many religious reasons why the majority of Muslims are not interesting in assimilation. The Belgian imams may be allied with ISIS.]* We are grateful for that … I know that in Muslim communities across our country, this is a time of concern and, frankly, a time of some fear … your entire community so often is targeted or blamed for the violent acts of the very few. *[Obama downplays the acceptance of violent jihad in the Muslim community. For Muslims to believe in the Quran and emulate the life of Mohammed, then they must support terrorism.]* The Muslim American community remains relatively small – several million people in this country. *[Obama always downplays threats to America. Years ago, Obama once said America was the largest Muslim country. Obama is accelerating Muslim immigration into America during his last year to increase its political power and to plant the seeds for jihad and the battle for the institution of Sharia law in America.]* … And as a result, many only hear about Muslims and Islam from the news after an act of terrorism, or in **distorted media portrayals** in TV or film, all of which gives this hugely distorted impression. *[Reporting the news accurately is viewed as being Islamophobic by Obama. Analyzing the Quran and criticizing Mohammed is blasphemy for Obama.]* And since 9-11, but more recently, since the attacks in Paris and San Bernardino, you've seen too often people conflating the horrific acts of terrorism with the beliefs of an entire faith. *[The genocide of ISIS and Islamic jihad is mostly based on the Quran and its commentaries. Killing infidels while shouting "Allahu Akbar" is part of Islamic jihad and Islamic terrorism. Beheadings are sanctioned in the Quran. Islam has "bloody borders." **Where are all the Christians and Jews in Islamic nations?** Why are the populations of non-Muslims as a percentage of the total population in any Islamic country always decreasing?]* And of course, recently, we've heard inexcusable political rhetoric against Muslim Americans that has no place in our country. *[Anti-Trump. Obama treats free speech as blasphemy, thus is supporting Sharia law. Muslim immigration bans that prevent ISIS terrorists from entering America and setting up terrorist attacks is only logical.]* No surprise, then, that threats and harassment of Muslim Americans have surged. *[Taqiyya. Hate crimes against Muslims is still only 25% of the number of documented hate crimes committed against Jews.]* Here at this

mosque, twice last year, threats were made against your children. Around the country, wom-
en wearing the hijab – just like Sabah – have been targeted. *[When does Obama fight for the
rights of Muslim women not to wear the hijab?]* We've seen children bullied. *[pediatric political
human shields]* We've seen mosques vandalized. *[mostly by Muslims]* … I just had a chance to
meet with some extraordinary Muslim Americans from across the country who are doing all
sorts of work. Some of them are doctors; some of them are community leaders; religious
leaders. *[50% of all educated Muslims worldwide support Sharia law.]* All of them were doing
extraordinary work not just in the Muslim community but in the American community
[Obama is always proselytizing for Islam.] … And you couldn't help but be inspired, hearing
about the extraordinary work that they're doing. But you also could not help but be heart-
broken to hear their worries and their anxieties. *[Why do these Muslims stay affiliated with
organizations that are front groups for the Muslim Brotherhood? Why do they support Sharia law?
Because they support the Muslim Brotherhood's long-term goal to destroy America from within.]*
Some of them are parents, and they talked about how their children were asking, are we going to be forced out of the country, or, are we going to be rounded up? Why do people treat
us like that? Conversations that you shouldn't have to have with children *[Children should
ask their parents: Why do you want to hurt and harass all non-Muslim? Why can't I criticize
Mohammed? Why did Mohammed marry a six-year-old girl? Where did all the Jews and
Christians go in the Middle East? Why are rapes epidemic throughout Europe and almost always
committed by Muslims against non-Muslims? Why did you cut off the genitals of my little sister?]*
– not in this country. *[Somali Muslims have been documented throwing stones at gays in
Minneapolis. America needs to have the conversation to determine whether these racists and ho-
mophobes should be allowed to live in the United States and whether these and other barbaric
atrocities should be protected by the Constitution. Obama should be stating: "Not in this country!"]* … We're one American family. *[The majority of Muslims in Canada are more loyal to
their religion and Sharia law than to their country. These statistics are likely to be repeated in the
United States. Increasingly Muslims insist on "Muslim only" swims in public pools and pork-free
cafeterias in public schools, thus disregarding the desires and rights of other Americans. The Quran
clearly instructs all Muslims not to take Jews or Christians as friends. Why should tax payer dollars
be used to fund Muslim foot baths or mosques in public places?]* … For more than a thousand
years, people have been drawn to Islam's message of peace. *[taqiyya – Islam has always had
"bloody borders." Over 270 million non-Muslims have been killed by Islamic jihad since the inception of Islam. Peace or hudnas (ten-year truces; The JCPOA, drafted by Obama, is a ten-year
hudna) only occur when Muslims are militarily or politically weak or lose a war, and then need
time to rebuild and strengthen. Otherwise there is no peace with non-Muslims unless they all
convert to Islam or are expelled or killed.]* And the very word itself, Islam, comes from salam –
peace. *[taqiyya – The direct translation of Islam is "to submit," and not peace. Islam is the verb*

form of the root "aslama" which means "to submit." Peace comes when Islam dominates over all non-Muslims, or when all non-Muslims are either forced to convert to Islam or killed.] ... And like so many faiths, Islam is rooted in a commitment to compassion and mercy and justice and charity. *[taqiyya x 4 – In May 2016, a Muslim mob comprised of about 300 armed men stripped, beat, and marched an elderly Christian woman through the streets of a southern Egyptian town when her son was suspected of having an affair with a Muslim woman, and then burned down the homes of seven Christian families. The local police took two hours to arrive at the scene and waited until the Muslim mob had dispersed. These events are not uncommon in most Muslim dominated societies. This mentality runs through most Muslim societies, especially within the immigrant communities that are building up the Muslim populations in Europe and America. Muslims were videotaped throwing stones and urine at Christians at the 2012 Arab International Festival in Dearborn, Michigan. The Islamic hatred and violence of the Middle East is coming to America.]* Whoever wants to enter paradise, the Prophet Muhammad taught, "let him treat people the way he would love to be treated." *[Obama is proselytizing for Islam. That is Judeo-Christian ethics, not Islamic ethics.]* For Christians like myself, I'm assuming that sounds familiar. *[taqiyya]* ... Here's another fact: Islam has always been part of America. *[Obama is altering history. Muslims have always altered history to support Islam. ISIS and the Taliban have destroyed many famous religious sites that proved other religions existed before Islam. Many Muslims deny the proven fact that Jewish temples existed on the Temple Mount before Mohammed was born, and deny Judaism's historical and religious connection with Jerusalem.]* Starting in colonial times, many of the slaves brought here from Africa were Muslim. *[Sold by Muslim African slave traders. Islam is the only culture in the world today that actively engages in slavery.]* ... Jefferson and John Adams had their own copies of the Koran. *[John Adams quote: "He [Mohammad] denies that laws were made for him, and claims everything by force of arms." John Quincy Adams quote: "The precept of the Quran is* **perpetual war** *against all who deny that Mahomet is the prophet of G-d." John Adam's edition of the Quran in his possession had a preface that stated, "This book is a long conference of G-d, the angels, and Mahomet, which that false prophet very grossly invented ... Thou wilt wonder that such* **absurdities** *have infected the best parts of the world, and will avouch that the knowledge of what is contained in this book, will render that law contemptible."[281] Jefferson and Adams had their own copies of the Quran so they could understand why the Muslim Barbary pirates were attacking the U.S. merchant ships off the coast of Africa and to understand the ambassador from Tripoli who told them in Europe "It was written in their Quran that all nations which had not acknowledged the Prophet were sinners, whom* **it was the right and duty of the faithful to plunder and enslave;** *and that every mussulman [Muslim] who was slain in this warfare was sure to go to Paradise."]* ... Generations of Muslim Americans helped to build our nation. They were part of the flow of immigrants who became farmers and merchants. *[An extremely small percentage, since almost all* *immigrants came from Christian Europe or the Far East.]* … Muslim Americans enrich our lives today in every way. *[Not when they wanted to build a mega mosque over the remains of over 3,000 Americans killed by al-Qaeda terrorists in New York City.]* … So Muslim Americans are some of the most resilient and patriotic Americans you'll ever meet. *[like the al-Qaeda and Hamas supporters in this mosque, and Major Hasan]* … And you can tell good stories while still representing the **reality of our communities**. *[polygamy, child marriages, honor killings, prejudice, anti-LGBT, support for Sharia law, vast majority anti-Israel, pro-PLO/pro-Hamas/pro-Hezbollah – all dedicated to destroying Israel, a significant minority support suicide bombings and death to blasphemers in America, female genital mutilation for their daughters, charitable donation that support terrorism, always advancing pro-Muslim agendas regardless if it is in America's interest]* …   Even as the overwhelming majority – and I repeat, the overwhelming majority – of the world's Muslims embrace Islam as a source of peace *[taqiyya: 15 – 30% of all Muslims worldwide support jihad and over 50% support the institution of Sharia law]*, it is undeniable that a small fraction of Muslims propagate a perverted interpretation of Islam. *[15-30% of all Muslims worldwide support ISIS, where are the fatwas against the terrorists?]* This is the truth. *[taqiyya – Obama lies again.]* Groups like al-Qaeda and ISIL, they're not the first extremists in history to misuse G-d's name. *[false moral equivalence]* We've seen it before, across faiths. *[Obama is linking Judaism and Christianity with ISIS atrocities and genocide.]* But right now *[taqiyya – always]*, there is an organized extremist element that draws selectively from Islamic texts *[throughout the Quran and its commentaries]*, twists them *[very common and accepted interpretations]* in an attempt to justify their killing and their terror. *[Islamic terrorism has been present since the times of Mohammed. It is supported by al-Azhar University, which Obama praised in his 2009 Cairo University speech and the religious leaders of Saudi Arabia and Iran. Obama is running cover for ISIS. ISIS was born and has grown during Obama's presidency. Christian genocide in the Middle East started and accelerated with Obama via ISIS. According to DIA documents, Obama was one of the original founders of ISIS.]* They combine it with false claims that America and the West are at war with Islam. *[But the majority of Muslims who support Sharia law are at war with the West since they want to replace Western democracies and republics with societies governed by Sharia law by any means including violent jihad.]* And this warped thinking that has found adherents around the world – including, as we saw, tragically, in Boston and Chattanooga and San Bernardino – is real. It's there. *[It's not there because Obama refuses to call it radical Islamic terrorism, thus he shields the Quran and Sharia law from criticism. Then, Obama labels any criticism of Mohammed and the Quran as Islamophobia and racism.]* And it creates tensions and pressure that disproportionately burden the overwhelming majority of law-abiding Muslim citizens. And the question then is, how do we move forward together? *[Consider: Reform Islam or ban it. Reform the Quran or ban it. Remove all hate speech from the Quran, since millions of Muslims around the* *world and in the United States take those passages literally. Make Sharia law illegal. Outlaw the Muslim Brotherhood and its front groups. Close down all mosques that support Sharia law, Islamic radicals, or any Muslim Brotherhood affiliated group. Deport all radical imams and their supporters. Ban the Burka. Deport all supporters of Sharia law from all Western democracies, which may be at least 50% of all Muslims. Deport all Muslim who support blasphemy laws and rally against free speech. Criminalize parents who force FGM upon their children, and charge them with sexual abuse and remove their children from their guardianship. No foreign funding of mosques, and those funds must be returned to their places of origin or given to the U.S. govern-ment. Arrest all people working with organizations (the Muslim Brotherhood) and their front groups that support terrorist groups, since we are at war with radical Islam. Enforce treason laws. Stop all Muslim immigration, since the majority of foreign Muslims support Sharia law. Any sup-porters of Sharia law should not be allowed to immigrate to Western democracies. No citizenship in the West for Muslims who believe in Mohammed or the Quran. Hungary, Myanmar and Samoa are actively trying to ban Islam. Gert Wilders, the leader of the most popular political party in the Netherlands, has proposed closing down all mosques and Muslim schools, banning the Quran, and halting Muslim immigration in his country. Non-Muslims are forbidden to become citizens in Saudi Arabia and Kuwait, so why not forbid Muslims from attaining citizenship in Western countries, which are targeted for destruction by the OIC and the Muslim Brotherhood. Muslims will vote for other Muslims who want to install Sharia law in Western democracies, so Western countries must consider not allowing Muslims to have citizenship or voting rights in their countries, in order to protect themselves from subversive Muslim politicians (like Obama) whose main goal is to embed Sharia law in free countries, which will eventually lead to the annihilation of their basic freedoms as defined by the Constitution or equivalent documents. Reverend Ma'auga Motu, the Secretary General of the Samoa Council of Churches observed, "We are not going too far (wanting to ban Islam) ... We are still wanting our own people to be prevented from this kind of influence, even though there are so many people who are good people but still there are some dangerous people among them who might come and threaten our peace."[282]* **Governments exist primarily to protect the peace of their countries.** *Muslims who believe in Sharia law and emulate the life of Mohammed eventually always threaten the peace wherever they go. As President John Quincy Adams rightly observed, the Quran advocates for "perpetual war" against the infidels and periods of peace are "delusive" and temporary. President Theodore Roosevelt observed that Islam drives out foreigners, while "plundering and slaying the local Christian." Saint Thomas Aquinas realized that "Muslims were brutal men ... ignorant of all divine teaching, through whose numbers Mohammad forced others to become his followers by the violence of his arms." Putting a break on Muslim influence in the West that protects civil liberties and the peace should be considered legitimate policies.]* How do we keep our country strong and united? *[If you believe in supporting any blasphemy laws, you should not be in the United States.]* How do we defend ourselves against organizations that are bent on killing innocents? *[The Quran states, "Say (O Muhammad):* **O ye who are Jews***! If ye claim that ye are favoured of Allah apart from (all) mankind,* **then long for death** *if ye are truthful." Quran (62:6), and "***When you meet the unbelievers, smite their necks.***" Quran (47:4), and* **The Jews** *"strive to do mischief on earth" [and will be punished]* "**they will be killed or crucified** *Quran (5:33), and "***Soon shall We cast terror into the hearts of the Unbelievers.***" Quran (3:151), and "***As for one who disbelieves, we will fight him forever in the Cause of Allah. Killing him is a small matter to us.***" Tabari IX:69. If Obama was true to his convictions, he would focus his wrath and disdain on Islam. Obama should ask – "How do we defend ourselves against Islam that is bent on killing innocents and propagating hate and civil strife?"]* And it can't be the work of any one faith alone. *[But Obama has emasculated the government's ability to identify and counteract Islamic terrorism creating a Catch 22 situation.]* It can't be just a burden on the Muslim community *[Muslim communities in Europe protected ISIS terrorists involved in the Paris and Brussels attacks. Obama protects the terrorists and the Islamists by telling the Muslim community they are not primarily responsible for creating the conditions in the mosques that radicalize individuals, and not reforming Islam. CAIR, Obama's partner, tells the Muslim community not to cooperate with the FBI.]* … I just want to suggest a few principles that I believe can guide us. We are all G-d's children. **We're all born equal** *[Then Obama should condemn and support outlawing Sharia law since it subjugates non-Muslims as second-class citizens.]* which, with inherent dignity … "O mankind," the Koran teaches, we have "made you peoples and tribes that you may know one another." *[The following sentence in this verse in the Quran affirms Islamic supremacism.]* … Second, as Americans, we have to stay true to our core values, and that includes freedom of religion for all faiths. *[Muslims attempt to impose Sharia law on all other faiths, which is not freedom of religion for non-Muslims. Islam is not a religion. It is a fascist, discriminatory, racist, genocidal political order directed to destroy its host countries. Even the president of Al-Azwar University said Islam is a political organization.]* … Part of what's happened in the Middle East and North Africa and other places where we see sectarian violence is religion being a tool for another agenda – for power, for control. *[That is Islam – to build an Islamic caliphate, for Islam to control the Middle East, North Africa, Europe and eventually the United States, which is part of Obama's political agenda.]* Freedom of religion helps prevent that *[taqiyya]*, both ways – protects religious faiths, protects the state from – or those who want to take over the state from using religious animosity as a tool for their own ends. *[As the political power of Islam increases in a society, the harassment and intimidation of all other religions increases, so their ability to resist Islamic domination decreases over time. Obama wants more freedom, rights, and power for the Muslim community so that in the long-term, all other religions will be subdued and eventually made extinct, and Sharia law will prevail. Look at the Middle East and especially Lebanon. Lebanon was a thriving Christian country until Islamic migration and* *influence led to the rise of Hezbollah, and a terror state was created with a rapidly declining Christian population. In the long-term, that is Obama's vision for America.]* ... But we have to respect the fact that we have freedom of religion. *[Any religion that advocates anti-Semitism, the inferiority of non-believers, and the establishment of a political body in opposition to the principles of the U.S. Constitution should not be permitted to advance its agenda in the United States.]*... And that civil activism *[to institute Sharia law]*, that civic participation that's the essence of our democracy, it is enhanced by freedom of religion. *[Obama wants Muslims to have the freedom to institute Sharia law.]* **Now, we have to acknowledge that there have been times where we have fallen short of our ideals**. *[Obama is criticizing America in a radical Islamic mosque that has supported al-Qaeda and Hamas. Hasn't the Muslim community fallen short of their "ideals" with so many terrorist attacks originating from their sphere of influence? Hasn't Obama fallen short of our "ideals" by walking away from the Benghazi attack and letting Ambassador Stevens and three other Americans get murdered, or supporting a Muslim Brotherhood takeover in Egypt?]* ... Anti-Semitism in this country has a sad and long history *[Islamic anti-Semitism is so much more severe than any anti-Semitism that has existed in America. Jews don't have to fear for their life, limb, family and property as they do in Muslim countries, yet Obama hypocritically does not mention that anti-Semitism is a core part of Islam.]*, ... And when any religious group is targeted, we all have a responsibility to speak up. *[Obama never mentioned that the San Bernardino Christmas party attack or Oregon massacre targeted Christians, or the ISIS Paris attack targeted Jews. Obama refused to label the atrocities in the Middle East against the Christians as genocide until Congress voted overwhelmingly in favor of genocide being the proper terminology.]* And we have to reject a politics that seeks to manipulate prejudice or bias, and targets people because of religion. *[Obama used anti-Semitism when lobbying for support of the JCPOA. Islam attacks Judaism relentlessly, so why isn't Obama critical of that bias?]* We've got to make sure that hate crimes are punished *[but not when imams or the Quran are the guiding influence]*, and that the civil rights of all Americans are upheld. *[But not hate crimes committed by Muslims or minority left-wing activists attacking Trump supporters.]* And just as faith leaders, including Muslims, must speak out when Christians are persecuted around the world – or when anti-Semitism is on the rise *[secondary to increasing Muslim populations in Europe, Obama is a hypocrite since he has hurt Israel more than any other leader in modern history since WWII.]* – because the fact is, is that there are Christians who are targeted now in the Middle East, despite having been there for centuries *[Just earlier in this speech, Obama said Islam has been promoting peace for over 1,000 years, but now Obama downplays the longevity of Christianity describing its existence in centuries instead of millennia, even though Christianity is older than Islam. This proves Obama favors Islam over Christianity.]*, and there are Jews who've lived in places like France *[Obama avoids mentioning that most Muslim countries don't recognize Israel's right to exist and yearn for the elimination of all Jews from the Middle*

East.] for centuries *[since the diaspora which is longer than the lifespan of Islam, actually mille-nia]* who now feel obliged to leave because they feel themselves under assault – sometimes by Muslims *[almost always by Muslims – There is a proven direct correlation between anti-Semitism and the increasing percentage of Muslims in a general population. As the Muslim population in Europe grows, the emigration of Jews from Europe accelerates upward. Obama downplays the Islamic source of violence against Jews that originates in the Quran].* We have to be consistent in condemning hateful rhetoric and violence against everyone. *[Not Obama – he refuses to associate Islam with violence and refuses to acknowledge "Islamic terrorism." Obama does not mention that in 2014, Jews were targets of hate crimes four times more often than Muslims in America. Obama needs to start with the Quran.]* And that includes against Muslims here in the United States of America. So none of us can be silent. *[Why not bring up Muslim anti-Semitism?]* … And the suggestion is somehow that if I would simply say, these are all Islamic terrorists *[Words matter and shed clarity on reality]*, then we would actually have solved the problem by now … Groups like ISIL are desperate for legitimacy. They try to portray themselves as religious leaders and holy warriors who speak for Islam. I refuse to give them legitimacy. *[Obama is protecting and advancing Islam by refusing to acknowledge its true and historical relationship with violence and terrorism. ISIS obtains its legitimacy from the Quran and its worldwide Islamic support, and not from Obama.]* We must never give them that legiti-macy. They're not defending Islam. *[When did Obama become a leading worldwide expert on Islam? What books or scholarly reports has he authored?]* … The vast majority of the people they kill are innocent Muslim men, women and children. *[taqiyya – protecting Islam]* And, by the way, the notion that America is at war with Islam ignores the fact that the world's religions are a part of who we are. *[No leading American politician has stated we are at war with Islam. But the Quran states "Whoever seeks a religion other than Islam will never have it accepted of him." (3:85) and "fight those who believe not … until they pay the jizya with willing submission and feel themselves subdued." (9:29)]* We can't be at war with any other religion because the world's religions are a part of the very fabric of the United States *[taqiyya]*, our national char-acter. *[America can be at war with people and organizations that want to destroy our republic and who support the Islamic terrorists and philosophies that aim to destroy America. Obama wants to mainstream jihad and the quest for Sharia law into the American community.]* And we can't suggest that Islam itself is at the root of the problem. *[Why not? Obama is protecting jihad and Islamic based terrorism.]* That betrays our values. *[One of Obama's hackneyed over-used phrases. Obama again is critical of America. American values are rooted in the honest evalu-ation of the root cause of Islamic terrorism, which can be traced directly to the imams, the Quran, jihad, and the implementation of Sharia law.]* … Here at this mosque, and across our country and around the world, Muslim leaders are roundly and repeatedly and consistently condemning terrorism. *[taqiyya]* ... And it was interesting, in the discussion I had before I came out, some people said, why is there always a burden on us? *[Why are these Muslims blind to the hate and violence generated by their society and their religious beliefs? Over 270 million non-Muslims have been killed in wars with Muslim societies since the inception of Islam. Why does Islam have "bloody borders." Why is anti-Semitism at the core of Islam? Why is there a mass exodus of Jews from Europe as the Muslim population in Europe grows? Why have all major religions had reformations, except for Islam? Where did all the Christians and Jews go in the Middle Eastern countries? Why shouldn't the burden be at the source of the problem?]* ... This is a struggle between the peace-loving, overwhelming majority of Muslims around the world *[taqiyya]* and a radical, **tiny** minority. *[Obama is again downplaying the terrorist threats to the West. Obama called Iran a "tiny" threat while campaigning in 2008. Whenever Obama uses the word "tiny,' he is aiming to harm America.]* ... These are the voices of Muslim clerics who teach that Islam prohibits terrorism, for the Koran says whoever kills an innocent, it is as if he has killed all mankind. *[The Quran passage to which Obama refers is actually a threat against Jews. "The real 5:32 verse is not a promise of peace, but an Islamic threat against Jews, who are dubbed the "people of Israel" in the Koran ... According to a website that offers multiple classical translations of each Koranic commandment, the 5:32 verse says: "For that cause We [Allah] decreed for the Children of Israel [Jews] that whosoever killeth a human being for other than manslaughter or corruption in the earth, it shall be as if he had killed all mankind, and who so saveth the life of one, it shall be as if he had saved the life of all mankind. Our messengers came unto them [the Jews] of old with clear proofs (of Allah's Sovereignty), but afterwards lo! many of them became prodigals [wanderers, or transgressors] in the earth."[283]]* These are the voices of Muslim scholars, some of whom join us today, who know Islam has a tradition of respect for other faiths *[taqiyya – The Quran identifies Jews as apes and pigs.]*; ... Now, that doesn't mean that Muslim Americans aren't free to criticize American – U.S. foreign policy. *[But Americans cannot criticize Islam or Mohammed since Obama considers that racism, Islamophobia, and blasphemy. Obama proves himself to be a hypocrite. Obama stated at the UN, "The future must not belong to those who slander [or criticize or question] the prophet of Islam." Most Muslims are anti-Israel, anti-Semitic, and pro-Sharia law, so Obama wants their voices heard.]* That's part of being an American. I promise you, as the president of the United States, I'm mindful that that is a healthy tradition that is alive and well in America. *[Then why can't Americans criticize Mohammad and Islam according to Obama?]* ... Like people of all religions, Muslims living their faith in a modern, pluralistic world are called upon to uphold human rights *[taqiyya – Obama is silent when Muslims execute or stone homosexuals in Iran or in ISIS controlled territory, or when Islamic preachers instruct their followers on the merits of wife beating. If Obama is true to his word, he should publicly condemn Sharia law.]* ... If we expect our own dignity to be respected, so must we respect the dignity of others. *[Obama did not treat Netanyahu, the Jewish Israeli Prime Minister, with dignity. The Muslim communities along with Muslim migrants have established over 900 "no-go" zones throughout Europe according to the Hungarian government. These Muslim communities attack or harass any non-Muslims who enter their territory, including firefighters and police. There is no respect for non-Muslim trespassers. These "no-go" zones will soon be spreading throughout America. Obama supports mass Muslim migration into Europe which has led to Muslim rape epidemics that don't respect the dignity of non-Muslim women. Obama incited black activists against police, which eventually violated the dignity and safety of all law enforcement officials.]* … There's no one single profile of terrorists. *[Not all Muslims are terrorists, but the majority of terrorists are Muslims. Ninety-nine percent of all suicide bombers in 2015 were Muslims.]* We can't securitize our entire relationship with Muslim Americans. *[Obama is providing cover for the Muslim Brotherhood and Islamists who want to replace the Constitution with Sharia law.]* We can't deal with you solely through the prism of law enforcement. *[Then the Muslims need to reform Islam and gut it from its anti-Semitism, its violence, Sharia law, childhood sexual perversions, anti-women and anti-gay doctrine, and Mohammed who committed statutory rape.]* We've got to build trust and mutual respect. *[Mutual respect is a two-way street, and that includes the freedom of speech. Obama and Muslims showed no respect to America when they wanted to build a mega-mosque on the remains of dead Americans who were killed by the Islamic terrorist attacks on the World Trade Center towers, or when they support blasphemy laws in direct opposition to the First Amendment of the Bill of Rights.]* … We are one American family. *[taqiyya]* We will rise and fall together. It won't always be easy. There will be times where our worst impulses are given voice. *[Obama is referring to halting Islamic immigration from jihadi countries. In September 2016, an Australian poll revealed that 49% of Australians support a ban on Muslim immigration with the major reasons being their association with terrorism, the belief that Muslim immigrants don't assimilate nor do they share Western values. Obama is blind to the crime, lawlessness, rape epidemics, and the infiltration of Islamic terrorists throughout Europe secondary to significant increase in Muslim refugees and migrants. Even Pope Francis stated in March 2016 to the L'Osservatore Roman, "Today we can talk about an Arab invasion. It is a social fact. … How many invasions has Europe experienced in the course of its history?" A popular Polish weekly news magazine ran a politically incorrect cover story called the "Islamic Rape of Europe," which identified the pan-European rape epidemics caused by the Muslim migrants and also discussed the suicide of Western civilization secondary to these policies. In Cologne Germany, there were over 1,000 crimes reported on New Year's Eve alone, with at least 126 reported crimes of gang rapes by Muslim migrants and over 600 sexual offences. Cologne was not alone. There were over 1,200 sexual assaults reported throughout Germany on that night, and over 2,000 young Muslim men were involved in these crimes, with over 50% of the perpetrators being recent Muslim immigrants. Throughout Europe on New Year's Eve in 2016, organized Muslim migrant rape gangs attacked European women in many major cities with minimal intervention from the authorities. The head of Europol, Rob Wainwright, estimated that about 3,000 to 5,000 ISIS terrorists have infiltrated Europe by February 2016 with the free flow of migrants from Syria and the Middle East. Obama is very critical of Americans who want to protect the United States from a violent and barbaric future that is clearly evident in many parts of Europe. Americans know that Obama's policies will bring the same fate to America that is now emerging in Europe. Obama views the need to protect America from terrorist infiltration and to keep our society safe for our children and grandchildren as our "worst impulses."].*

39. "We are fighting **terrorists** who claim to fight on behalf of Islam. But they **do not speak for over a billion Muslims around the world**, and they **do not speak for American Muslims**, including many who wear the uniform of the United States of America's military. If we stigmatize good, patriotic Muslims, that just feeds the terrorists' narrative. It fuels the same false grievances that they use to motivate people to kill. If we act like this is a war between the United States and Islam, we're not just going to lose more Americans to terrorist attacks, but we'll also lose sight of the very principles we claim to defend. So let <u>my final words to you as your Commander-in-Chief</u> … **The United States of America is not a country that imposes religious tests** as a price for freedom. We're a country that was founded so that **people could practice their faiths as they choose**. *[Let Muslims promote Sharia law.]* The United States of America is not a place where some citizens have to withstand greater scrutiny, or carry a special ID card, or prove that **they're not an enemy from within** *[Obama supports the Muslim Brotherhood that has pledged to destroy America from "within"]* … We're a nation that believes freedom can never be taken for granted and that each of us has a responsibility to sustain it. The universal right to speak your mind and to protest against authority, to live in a society that's open and free, that can criticize a President without retribution *[not true – if you criticize Obama, you are quickly called a racist or a propagator of fake news]* -- a country where you're judged by the content of your character rather than **what you look like** *[Obama promoted "white privilege" training]*, **or how you worship** *[Obama blocked Christian Middle Eastern refugees from entering the United States.]*, **or what your last name is**, **or where your family came from** – that's what separates us from tyrants and terrorists." *Obama, Remarks by the President on the Administration's Approach to Counterterrorism, MacDill Air Force Base, Tampa, Florida, December 6, 2016.* Obama devoted a significant part of his speech concerning U.S. national security concerns to protecting and promoting Islam. Obama used his final words as president addressing the military establishment regarding critical U.S. national security concerns to demonstrate his support of massive Muslim immigration,

or immigration jihad to the United States. By bringing huge numbers of Middle Eastern Muslims to America, the majority who support Sharia law, Obama is laying the foundation for the domestic Muslim community to build a political system that is incompatible with the Constitution of the United States and will eventually confront and threaten to destroy the freedoms non-Muslims have enjoyed in the West for centuries, so that Western societies can be eventually converted to Sharia compliant pro-Muslim societies. Obama's final words addressing U.S. national security matters support immigration jihad, which is one of Mohammed's major pathways to convert non-Muslim societies to Islam, is al-Qaeda's number one strategy to fight and destroy Western democratic nations, and is ISIS's major strategy to destroy Europe. With these final words as president supporting a major strategy of radical Islam, Obama demonstrates where his true loyalties lie. If American Muslims believe in Sharia law, odds are they support the terrorists.

CHAPTER 13

Israel

"Obama views lies as legitimate political tools. He uses lies strategically to accomplish through mendacity what he could never achieve through honest means."
Caroline Glick, October 2013, former editor of the Jerusalem Post and advisor to Benjamin Netanyahu.

1. "There should not be a shred of doubt by now: **When the chips are down**, <u>**I have Israel's back**</u>." *Obama, 2012, AIPAC conference.* Obviously, a lie, considering all he has done to not support Israel. Obama has also stated, "This administration has **done more for the security of the state of Israel** than any previous administration." Taqiyya.

   a. Proof this is a lie: UNSC Resolution 2334. Obama opens the door for BDS sanctions and declares East Jerusalem and the Western Wall are occupied Palestinian territory, thus he is giving the heart of Israel to the PLO, Hamas, and the IRGC.

   b. "Obama views **lies as legitimate political tools**. He uses lies strategically to accomplish through mendacity what he could never achieve through honest means … The mendacity at the heart of Obama's political playbook is something that Israel needs to understand if it is to survive his presidency without major damage to its strategic viability … *[Obama supports the Palestinian position.]* The Palestinian document claims not only all of Judea and Sumaria, and eastern, northern, and southern Jerusalem. It demands the northern Negev, the Hula Valley, Latrun and the Elah Valley. And it demands them all free of Jewish presence. They demand that Israel relinquish its rights under international law to Judea, Samaria and Jerusalem by agreeing that they are 'occupied.' They demand full control over the airspace over Judea, Samaria, Gaza and Jerusalem, and over the waters off the Gaza coast … They demand control over all the underground aquifers, and over the electromagnetic spectrum. Moreover, the Palestinians are demanding that Israel allow 5 million foreign-born Arabs the right to freely immigrate to its remaining territory. They refuse to accept Israel's right to exist [as a Jewish state] … Abbas and his cronies don't want peace. They want to destroy Israel … Obama's national security advisors summoned American Jewish leaders to the White House to demand that they stop speaking in favor of intensified [Iranian] sanctions. Also this week, US Secretary of State John Kerry took a swipe at PM Benjamin Netanyahu for daring to question the administration's total commitment to negotiating with Iran. Kerry indignantly insisted, 'We will not succumb to fear tactics' against holding talks with Iran. The same day that Kerry decried Israel for supposedly sowing fear unnecessarily about the status of Iran's nuclear weapons program, Olli Heinonen, the former deputy head of the IAEA, said that the Iranians may have already passed the breakout phase and have the capacity to build an atomic weapon within two weeks … By using the term (strategic interests) in the context of the freeing of murderers, Netanyahu and Ya'alon made clear that the US has blackmailed Israel into keeping up concessions to the PLO … And just as Obama has blamed Israel for Palestinian intransigence and radicalism for the past five-and-a-half years, so he will blame Israel for the failure of the current talks … Obama will tip Iran off to an impending Israeli strike on its nuclear facilities … Government officials have whispered periodically that Obama is threatening to curtail weapons sales to Israel. Such a move could quickly paralyze the air force … Obama's weakening of the US alliance with Israel – and with Saudi Arabia and Egypt – is well known." *Caroline Glick, previous editor of the Jerusalem Post and advisor to Benjamin Netanyahu, commenting on Obama's strategy regarding Iran and Israel. "Obamacare Victims and Israel." Caroline Glick's website. October 31, 2013.*

c.   "Israel is now considered not an ally, not even a neutral, but apparently a hostile state worthy of more presidential invective than is Iran … The Middle East over the next decade may see three or four additional new nuclear powers."[284] *Professor Victor Hanson, Stanford University, Hoover Institution, "**Is Obamism Correctible?**" The National Review, September 15, 2015.*

d.   "It is so naive that he would trust the Iranians … By doing so, he will take the Israelis and march them to the door of the oven." *Former Arkansas governor Mike Huckabee, 2016 presidential campaign.* If you are the president of the United States and are sponsoring an agreement which paves the way for a theocratic Iran to obtain nuclear weapons, while the religious leaders of Iran announce that their divine mission is to destroy Israel, and you reach out and appease these men while giving them incredible funding, downplaying their threats, and promising to help defend Iran if Israel were to attack Iran either militarily or with a cyberattack as guaranteed in the JCPOA, then you are aligned against Israel.

e.   "I think **no one has ever opened the door to more harm of Jewish people** in the history of the world than Mr. Kerry and Mr. Obama. And there is some kind of **deep-seated physiological drama** *[Obama is a radical Muslim]* being played out here for them to hurt Israel this much." *Former Nixon speech writer, economist, and political commentator, Ben Stein*

f. "After Obama's election victory in 2008, Hamas instigated a war with Israel (Operation Cast Lead) in December by firing countless rockets and mortars at civilian targets. In November 2012, Hamas repeated their strategy of attacking Israel with the assurance that Obama would be president for the next four years. On November 11, 2008, Hamas launched over 80 rockets at Israeli targets. **Hamas became more aggressive knowing that either they had a sympathetic Muslim president residing in the Oval office, or Obama gave his tacit approval for Hamas to harass Israel.** Immediately after Obama's victory in 2012, Syria also commenced shelling the Golan Heights, marking the first time since 1973 that Syria had attacked Israel. Rockets originating from the Sinai under Muslim Brotherhood control hit southern Israel as well. One of the major reasons behind Obama's and Erdogan's desire for regime change in Syria is that the Assads have maintained a truce and peaceful border with Israel for almost 40 years, which is unacceptable to radical Muslims and Islamists. **Creating an actively hostile northern and southern border with Israel is one of Obama's major goals with his support of ISIS, al-Qaeda, other Syrian "moderate" rebels and later with Iran's increasing military role in Syria and Iraq.** Rockets are now being launched at Israel from the north, west, and south. On day five of hostilities in 2012, Obama protected Hamas by telling Israel to delay any ground campaign against Gaza targets and by backing a ceasefire between Israel and Hamas before Israel could launch a ground invasion of Gaza, and before they could respond to a bus bombing in Tel Aviv that injured 24 civilians. It was also reported that Obama told Israel that with any ground invasion that defeated Hamas, Abbas and the Palestinian Authority would assume control of Gaza and a unified Palestinian state would be declared. Obama's sponsored ceasefire also prevented Israel from retaliating to missile attacks on Tel Aviv and Jerusalem." *(Unexpected Treason, 2016)*

    i. In September 2009, Obama **called upon Israel to investigate itself for war crimes** during its defensive war with Hamas in 2008. Michael Posner, U.S. Assistant Secretary of State affirmed, "We encourage Israel to utilize appropriate domestic (judicial) review and meaningful accountability mechanisms to investigate and follow-up on credible allegations ... If undertaken properly and fairly, these reviews can serve as important confidence-building measures that will support the larger essential objective which is a shared quest for justice and lasting peace."

g. "In March 2009, Obama reversed a Bush administration policy and joined the United Nations Human Right Council, despite its anti-Israel agenda. Secretary of State Clinton proclaimed, "Human rights are an essential element of American global foreign policy."

Even *The Washington Post* noticed that it 'has devoted excessive attention to alleged abuses by Israel and too little to abuses in [other] places.'" *(Unexpected Treason, 2016)*

h. In March 2010, during Vice President Biden's visit to Israel, in response to Israel's announcement of the approval of 1600 housing units for construction in Jerusalem, **Secretary of State Hillary Clinton** called Netanyahu "to make clear the United States considered the announcement a **deeply negative signal about Israel's approach** to the bilateral relationship and **counter to the spirit of the vice president's trip** … this action had **undermined trust and confidence in the peace process and in America's interests**," according to State Department spokesman Crowley. Obama advisor David Axelrod commented on NBC that "This was an affront, it was an insult, but most importantly, it undermined this very fragile effort to bring peace to that region … For this announcement to come at that time was very, very destructive." All this negativity was generated because Israel publicly announced the building of previously approved apartment buildings in their capital city. Ambassador Michael Oren commented that, due to the contentious Jerusalem building project announcement, "**Israel's ties with the United States are in their worst crisis since 1975 … a crisis of historic proportions**." Oren also referred to a phone call between Netanyahu and Secretary of State Clinton. Clinton was instructed by Obama to demand Israel release a large number of Palestinian prisoners, stop all West Bank and Jerusalem settlement activities, allow a significant number of Palestinians the "right of return" to formal Israel with an agreement, lift the blockade on Gaza, and immediately resolve the status of Jerusalem. **Clinton concluded** the phone call with "**If you refuse these demands … the United States government will conclude that we no longer share the same interests**." Clinton also called Ambassador Oren to the State Department, where he was severely chastised. At the same time, the Palestinians were honoring terrorist Dalal Mughrabi by dedicating a town square named in her honor, despite her role in murdering 37 Israelis, including 10 children, 32 years previously. In March, Secretary of State Clinton addressed AIPAC stating "I underscored the longstanding American policy that does not accept the legitimacy of continued settlements. As Israel's friend, it is our responsibility to give credit when it is due and to tell the truth when it is needed." This is in contrast to Clinton's statement in 2008 where she stated during her presidential campaign "the United States will never pressure Israel to make unilateral concessions."

i. Between 2010 and 2012, **Secretary of State Clinton** was receptive to an initiative having international billionaires help fund a future Palestinian state through donations. Clinton also supported fomenting a Palestinian revolt during this period where she hoped increased Palestinian violence against the Israelis would force Israel to make major concessions in future peace talks with the PA. This plan was outlined by former U.S. ambassador to Israel, **Thomas Pickering** on December 18, 2011. Pickering wanted third parties and foreign NGOs to assist the Palestinians with their resistance so that the State Department could distance itself from these anti-Israel actions. Pickering also requested that his ideas remain private, because if Israel discovered this policy, relationships between the United States and Israel would be significantly harmed and Obama's input in the Middle East peace process would be compromised. Clinton also had **other anti-Israel advisors** who may have had significant input into shaping America's hostile relationship with Israel during her tenure as secretary of state or who reinforced Clinton's own prejudice against Israel. Rabbi Shmuley Boteach surmised in *The Jerusalem Post*, "In the entire forced dump of Clinton's emails, you will be hard pressed to find a single one sympathetic toward the Jewish state from any of the people she relied on. The negative, poisonous approach to Israel throughout this email expose shows the atmosphere that she had established around herself. These emails seem to demonstrate that a huge segment of her close advisors and confidantes were attacking Israel, condemning Prime Minister Benjamin Netanyahu, and strategizing how to force Israel to withdraw from Judea and Samaria at all costs."[285] With Hillary Clinton's documented associations, it is not unreasonable to say that she supports Islamists, radical Muslims and their agenda, and thus would be expected to back anti-Israel policies.

i.   **Huma Abedin** is part of Clinton's inner circle, one of her few close advisors, and later became co-chairman of her 2016 presidential campaign. Abedin had previously **worked for an al-Qaeda financier and her parents were affiliated with the Muslim Brotherhood**. As a student, Abedin was active in the Muslim Student Association, a Muslim Brotherhood front group. As secretary of state, Clinton supported the Muslim Brotherhood's rise to power in Egypt and Morsi's quest for the Egyptian presidency, which would replace America's long-term ally Hosni Mubarak. Morsi had Clinton's full support despite his anti-Semitic history. Clinton politically supported and gave significant military aid to the man who freely stated his disgust and revulsion of Jews and proclaimed multiple times his desire to destroy Israel. Abedin probably had significant influence into guiding Clinton to support Morsi and the Muslim Brotherhood. Interestingly, Abedin's mother worked with Morsi's wife at the Guidance Bureau of the Muslim Sisterhood. With Abedin's mother working directly with individuals married to the leadership of the Muslim Brotherhood, it is surprising that Abedin received the security clearance that allowed her to work at a high level in the State Department. It is not a coincidence that Clinton kept most of her email correspondences with Abedin on her private email server, which shielded the Clinton Foundation and the Clinton Global Initiative functions from public scrutiny, and may have revealed embarrassing contacts between Clinton and the Muslim Brotherhood.

(1)   In 2009, Abedin corresponded by email to Doug Band, an aide to former President Bill Clinton, and recommended that the former president not address the annual AIPAC conference. Abedin wrote, "U really want to consider sending him **into that crowd**? [Band: Go or no go?] … **No go to AIPAC**." Abedin demonstrated open hostility to Jews and Israel by referring to them as "that crowd." Abedin is Hillary Clinton's chief advisor.

ii.   Clinton chose Virginia Senator **Tim Kaine** as her vice-presidential running mate in July 2016. Kaine joined other members of Congress who boycotted Netanyahu's speech arguing against the JCPOA in March 2016. Kaine is a **major supporter of J Street** and the J Street PAC has given Kaine's senate campaign over $200,000. Kaine **has significant connections with the Muslim Brotherhood**. In 2007, as Virginia governor, Kaine apponted **Esam Omeish**, a former president of the Muslim American Society, which is a Muslim Brotherhood front group, to the Virginia Commission on Immigration. Omeish was also on the board of directors of the Islamic Society of North America for two years. Omeish was a vice president at his mosque, the Dar al Hijrah Islamic Center, which has been known for its radical associations and had two of the perpetrators of the 9-11 hijackings frequently attend its functions. In 2000, Omeish recommended Anwar al-Awlaki as his mosque's imam and stated that al Awlaki "has no inclination or active involvement in any events or circumstance that have to do with terrorism."[286] Al Awlaki was later found to be an al-Qaeda leader who was the spiritual mentor of Major Hasan, the man who committed the "workplace violence" Fort Hood massacre. Omeish has praised Ahmed Yassin, a Hamas spiritual leader and has proclaimed that jihad is necessary for the Palestinians in their war against Israel. Omeish also worked with Yousef al Qaradawi, the Muslim Brotherhood spiritual leader, on the board of Islamic American University. In 2011, Kaine gave a speech at the New Dominion PAC, honoring **Jamal Barzinji**, who was labelled by the Global Muslim Brotherhood Watch as a "founding father of the U.S. Muslim Brotherhood." Barzinji has been investigated by the FBI for possible ties to Muslim Brotherhood front groups seeking to initiate an Islamic revolution in America. This PAC has donated over $43,000 to Kaine's campaigns for governor and over $250,000 to the Virginia Democratic Party.

iii.   **Secretary of State Hillary Clinton chose Hassan Nemazee, <u>an Iranian lobbyist</u>, as her 2008 presidential <u>national campaign finance chairman</u>**. Nemazee advocated for normalizing relations with Iran.

iv.   Clinton also labelled as "interesting reading" an editorial by **Max Blumenthal**, the anti-Semitic son of one of her chief advisors, Sidney Blumenthal. Blumenthal had published an anti-Israel conspiracy theory article in *Al Akhbar*, a Hezbollah-affiliated publication. Max Blumenthal also stated that the Palestinians "want to recover their dignity, and one way they can find it is through the *al-Qassam* Brigades or another armed faction," and he also praised Hamas terrorist attacks against Israel.[287] Clinton also agreed with Max Blumenthal's critical analysis of Israel's boarding of the *Mavi Marmara* and sided with Turkey and Hamas. After Elie Wiesel died, Blumenthal tweeted, "Elie Wiesel went from a victim of war crimes to a supporter of those who commit them. He did more harm than good and should not be honored." Wiesel was a Holocaust survivor and Pulitzer Prize winner. The Blumenthal and Clinton families have been close for over twenty years and Max is in Clinton's circle of influence. Clinton has even emailed Max's father and stated, "**Your Max is a mitzvah**." A major requirement to be Obama's secretary of state was to be anti-Israel or at least have advisors who are anti-Semitic and who ally themselves with the terrorists.

v.   **Sidney Blumenthal**, the father of Max Blumenthal and a chief advisor to Hillary Clinton, wrote an email to Clinton recommending a more "open" and pro-Hamas, anti-Israel United States policy after the *Mavi Marmara* flotilla interception. He stated, "Someone in authority needs to read the riot act to the Israelis ... The clean faced Michael Oren has been ubiquitous on US TV with the bald faced lie that Hamas is unelected ... The US should not be in the business of reinforcing Israeli propaganda on the incident ... Another aid ship is due to arrive in Gaza tomorrow, June 2. How it is handled by the Israelis will be another occasion for international outrage even without an armed attack and casualties. Intercepting it will intensify any reaction ... The ship should be allowed to land. It should be met by the UN – and the UN, not the Israelis, should be in charge of cataloging and distributing its aid ... Perhaps **US approaches to Hamas**, **of course short of recognition**, **should be more open**."

vi.   Clinton responded positively to the Director of Policy Planning **Anne Marie Slaughter**'s email that said, "Suppose we launched a 'Pledge for Palestine' campaign ... Such a campaign among billionaires / multi-millionaires around the world would reflect a strong vote of confidence in the building of a Palestinian state ... There would be a certain shaming effect re Israelis who would be building settlements in the face of a pledge for peace." Clinton responded "I am very interested. Pls flesh out. Thx."

vii.   Hillary Clinton has had close ties to **Abdurahman Alamoudi**, who is currently in prison for his role in an assassination plot against Saudi Crown Prince Abdullah. "Alamoudi organized White House events during the Bill Clinton administration.

Under Hillary's supervision, **he held official positions: Alamoudi was strategically placed at the White House, the Pentagon, and the State Department** … Later, he was identified by the Treasury Department as an Al-Qaeda fundraiser who had operated inside the United States … Hillary Clinton and Abdurahman Alamoudi were no mere acquaintances. According to an affidavit filed in court by Georgetown professor John Esposito, **Alamoudi was asked by Hillary Clinton to arrange the first White House Ramadan Iftar dinner in 1996** [and its guest list] … Under the Clinton administration, Alamoudi was tasked with founding and developing the Defense Department's first-ever Muslim chaplain program. **Alamoudi himself handpicked the Pentagon's Muslim chaplain corps** … one of those chaplain trainers was al-Qaeda cleric Anwar al-Awlaki … after Alamoudi's 2003 arrest a federal agent testified in an affidavit about a recording of Alamoudi complaining to an audience that the 1998 al-Qaeda bombings of the U.S. embassies in Kenya and Tanzania **did not kill enough Americans.** Years before he was helping Hillary Clinton arrange official dinners at the White House, Alamoudi had already been known to the FBI for al-Qaeda fundraising … After the 1993 bombing of the World Trade Center, the speechwriter for the "Blind Sheikh" Omar Abdel Rahman told the FBI that **Alamoudi had been funneling $5,000 payments from Osama bin Laden to Rahman** … **Alamoudi's donation to Hillary Clinton's 2000 U.S. Senate campaign** became an issue in October 2000. Then, **Alamoudi was caught on video speaking in Lafayette Park across from the White House publicly announcing his support for Hamas and Hezbollah**." [288] *(Patrick Poole, PJ Media, 2016)* Besides working with Huma Abedin, Hillary Clinton has had other direct ties to al-Qaeda and Islamic activists who support the destruction of Israel. With all of the above anti-Israel associates and despite her political rhetoric supporting Israel while she has been campaigning for political office, Hillary Clinton most likely supports many aspects of radical Muslim doctrine.

viii. Although he is not a formal advisor to Hillary Clinton, **Khizir Khan** gave a significant speech to the Democratic National Convention, right before Hillary Clinton delivered her nomination acceptance speech before the nation. Khan was given prime time exposure since he gave his speech about an hour before Clinton appeared on the stage to accept the nomination, thus his presence needed to be approved personally by her. Unfortunately for America, the Democrats neglected to mention that Khan is **probably a member of the Muslim Brotherhood** and would likely support the imposition of Sharia law in the United States and be anti-Israel.

(1)   Khan argued for Sharia law in an academic paper he wrote in 1983 while living in Saudi Arabia, entitled *Juristic Classification of Islamic Law*, in which he

stated, "The invariable and basic rules of Islamic law are only those prescribed in the Shari'ah … [the Quran] is the absolute authority from which springs the very conception of legality and every legal obligation … **All other juridical works** *[including the U.S. Constitution and corresponding federal, state, and local laws]* … **must always be subordinated** to the Shari'ah."

(2)   Unknown to the American public, years earlier while living in Saudi Arabia, Khan, had **publicly supported and praised a leader in the Muslim Brotherhood**, who was the grandson of Hassan al Banna, the founder of the Muslim Brotherhood. Shoebat.com exposed the details of Khan's background and revealed, "The Muslim who attacked Donald Trump, Khizr Muazzam Khan, is a Muslim Brotherhood agent, working to bring Muslims into the United States … Khan is a promoter of Islamic Sharia Law in the U.S. He was a co-founder of the *Journal of Contemporary Issues in Muslim Law (Islamic Sharia).* Khan's fascination with Islamic Sharia stems from his life in Saudi Arabia."

ix.   Although not a known formal advisor to Hillary Clinton's 2016 presidential campaign, **Seddique Mateen**, the father of the ISIS supporting, Muslim extremist who murdered fifty young Americans at an Orlando, Florida nightclub, was invited either by Clinton's campaign staff or Democratic party operatives to sit **directly behind Clinton on stage** while she was making a campaign speech in Kissimmee, Florida. With Mateen given such a prominent position behind Clinton, it is highly likely that either Clinton or Abedin requested or gave their personal approval for his presence at her campaign rally. Even after his presence was public knowledge, Hillary Clinton would not make a public statement disavowing his support. Mateen is a supporter of the Taliban and Sharia law.

x.   **Gilbert Chagoury**, a Nigerian billionaire has pledged over $1 billion and donated millions of dollars to the Clinton Foundation, has been denied entry to the United States and has been on the U.S. no-fly list secondary to his ties with Islamic terrorism and Hezbollah. Chagoury has had easy access to former President Clinton and his wife while she was secretary of state. His input may have contributed to Clinton's anti-Israel positions, Clinton's policy to transfer arms from Benghazi to al-Qaeda and ISIS terrorists, and Clinton's decision to withhold declaring Boko Haram a terrorist organization.

xi.   In 2016, the Clinton Foundation honored a Palestinian teacher, Hanan an-Hroub, whose husband was convicted of being an accomplice to a bombing in Israel that killed six Israelis. He subsequently served ten years imprisoned in Israel. While honoring an-Hroub on their website, the Clinton Foundation ignored her connection to Palestinian terrorism.

xii. Clinton supports Black Lives Matter, who have declared in their political platform in 2016 that Israel is committing **genocide** against the Palestinians.

xiii. Before delivering her acceptance speech for president at the 2016 DNC, Representative Hank Johnson, a Clinton super delegate and advisor, called the Jews of Jerusalem, "termites." Clinton did not reprimand him.

xiv. As First Lady and a representative of the United States, Hillary Clinton embraced and kissed the wife of Yasser Arafat in 1990, immediately after she declared that the Israelis were using poisonous gas to kill Palestinian women and children.

j. Liz Cheney, wife of the former vice president, criticized Obama's reaction to the Gaza *Mavi Marmara* flotilla incident by stating for Keep America Safe, "Yesterday, President Obama said the Israeli action to stop the flotilla bound for the Gaza Strip was 'tragic.' What is truly tragic is that **President Obama is perpetuating Israel's enemies' version of events**. The Israeli government has imposed a blockade around Gaza because Hamas remains committed to Israel's destruction, refusing to recognize Israel's right to exist and using territory under their control to launch attacks against Israeli civilians. The Israeli blockade of Gaza, to prevent the rearming of Hamas, is in full compliance with international law. Had the Turkish flotilla truly been interested in providing humanitarian aid to Gaza, they would have accepted the Israeli offer to off-load their supplies peacefully at the Israeli port of Haifa for transport into Gaza. **President Obama is <u>contributing to the isolation of Israel</u>, and sending a clear signal to the Turkish-Syrian-Iranian axis that their methods for ostracizing Israel will succeed, and will be met by no resistance from America** … Either the United States stands with the people of Israel in the war against radical Islamic terrorism or we are providing encouragement to Israel's enemies – and our own. Keep America Safe calls on President Obama to **reverse his present course and support the state of Israel** immediately and unequivocally." Obama did not comment on the attacks upon the Israeli soldiers who boarded the flotilla aid ship. Obama refused to veto a Turkish UN resolution condemning Israel. Obama also supported the lifting of the Gaza blockade, giving Iran an opportunity to ship an unlimited supply of weapons to Hamas. Panetta demanded that Israel "restore good relations with Egypt and Turkey." Former Obama Defense Secretary Gates described Israel as "**an ungrateful ally harming American interests**." Cheney later stated that "**there is no other president who has done more to delegitimize and undermine the State of Israel than Obama.**" Obama's antagonistic relationship with Israel has been mimicked by Turkey. **Obama has reversed U.S. policy that had generally rewarded those countries with favorable relations with Israel and penalized those countries actively seeking to harm Israel**. Turkey and Iran have both been supported by Obama; he has also harmed Egypt and Jordan, which signed peace treaties with Israel.

k. Obama **supports J Street**, which is basically a far-left, anti-Israel lobbying group funded by George Soros, that subverts the American Jewish community's support for Israel. Obama's close relationship with J Street was clearly defined by White House Chief of Staff McDonough, in his keynote speech to their annual conference in 2015, when he said, "I started out with President Obama as part of his national security team, but as his Chief of Staff – and with **appreciation for all the work J Street has done as our partner** … **J Street is an organization that**, **in the best tradition of the American Jewish community**, shares a set of values about the type of country that we are – a democracy where all of our people can access opportunity." Various J Street anti-Israel positions include supporting the JCPOA (The Ploughshares Fund / Soros gave J Street $576,500 – one third of their 2014 budget – to support Obama's position against Israeli security interests.), supporting the defeat of pro-Israeli senators, demanding that Israel lift the blockade on Hamas (Egypt also has a blockade on Hamas), supporting the division of Jerusalem, which will be under the jurisdiction of the PA and Hamas (opposed by Elie Wiesel and the vast majority of Israelis), supporting the Goldstone report (which inaccurately and prejudicially concluded that Israel committed war crimes by defending itself against Hamas' rocket barrage against Israeli civilian targets) by arranging meetings between Congress and Judge Goldstone, and by opposing the funding of the Iron Dome anti-missile system through support of representatives who voted against it. Jeremi Ben-Ami, the president of J Street, defended and endorsed Keith Ellison, a former member of the Nation of Islam and a politician who is affiliated with and a backer of front groups for the Muslim Brotherhood in America, for chairman of the Democratic National Committee. In an editorial entitled "Stop Smearing Keith Ellison," Ben-Ami commented in *The Washington Post*, "Let's be clear: Like all of us, Ellison has made mistakes for which he has apologized … I personally have talked at length with Ellison about Israel and the Middle East. I've traveled with him to the region, where we met Israeli and Palestinian officials, activists and civilians. I - and all those who've taken the time to get to know him - have **always found him to be deeply thoughtful and well-informed** … it is absolutely clear that **Ellison is qualified for the position** … campaigns such as the one directed at [against] Ellison shamefully misdirect ire toward people who agree with the Jewish community's values of tolerance and respect. Recent polling makes clear that **Ellison represents the policy views of the significant majority of Democrats and of Jewish Americans**. Leaders with similar views and values are going to be the future of the Democratic Party, of our country and of the American Jewish community. It is time for those who disagree to **halt the personal attacks** and smears … **Campaigns grounded in name-calling** and character assassination aimed at silencing dissent are **unacceptable** and need to stop."[289] J Street cannot call itself pro-Israel while it allies itself with a supporter of the Muslim Brotherhood and the Nation of Islam.

i. "The group claims it is pro-Israel, but it is fundamentally divisive and philosophically **more in tune with the Arab lobby than the pro-Israel lobby**. This was most recently apparent when J Street decided to support President Obama's catastrophic nuclear deal with Iran despite the opposition of both the Netanyahu government, the opposition Labor Party, and, according to the polls, approximately 80 percent of both the Israeli and American population … There is a fundamental distinction between the consensus of the pro-Israel community and those who claim to represent Israel's best interests. The former do not substitute their judgement for that of Israeli citizens who must live with the consequences of policy decisions, and who must fight and sometimes die for their country. Even more critically, J Street chooses to ignore Middle East history and all of the complex factors - religion, geography, history, politics, psychology – that make the conflict in the region so enduring and reduce the problem to Israel's presence in the West Bank. It is particularly ironic that J Street emerged after the disengagement from Gaza, which should have put to rest once and for all the myth that occupation and / or settlements are the reasons that the Middle East is not Eden … According to blogger, Lenny Ben-David, **the group's political action committee took money from 'pro-Saudi activists, Arab-American leaders, Muslim activists, State Department Arabists, a Palestinian billionaire, and even a Turkish American who helped produce the anti-American and anti-Semitic film Valley of the Wolves.'** These do not appear to be the silent majority of pro-Israel Jews J Street claims to represent."[290] *(Shmuley Boteach, Times of Israel, 2016)*

l. "Failure of the talks will increase Israel's isolation in the world … The alternative to getting back to the talks is a **potential of chaos**. I mean, **does Israel want a third intifada?** … I believe that if we do not resolve the issues between Palestinians and Israelis; if we do not find a way to find peace, there will be an **increasing isolation** of Israel. There will be an **increasing campaign of de-legitimization** of Israel that's taking place on an international basis. That if we do not resolve the question of the settlements and who lives where and how and what rights they have; if we don't end the presence of Israeli soldiers perpetually within the West Bank, then there will be an increasing feeling that if we cannot get peace with a leadership that is committed to nonviolence, **you may wind up with leadership that is committed to violence.**" *Secretary of State Kerry is threatening Israel with a third violent revolt by the Palestinians in November 2013.* In the fall of 2015, the Palestinians initiated the "knife" intifada, probably with the Obama administration's approval. He is also threatening Israel with international isolation, possible sanctions, and de-legitimization if they don't follow Obama's plans for the Middle East. Obama has legitimized Palestinian violence and has given the EU his approval to initiate an economic war against Israel.

m. In February 2014, Kerry repeated some of his threats in Munich when he said, "You see, for Israel there's an **increasing de-legitimization campaign** that has been building up. People are very sensitive to it. There are **talk of boycotts and other kinds of things** [sanctions, BDS]. Are we all going to be better with all of that?" Obama and Kerry are again threatening Israel with boycotts and sanctions in addition to Arab violence and de-legitimization. **Kerry is laying the groundwork for a BDS campaign**.

n. While testifying before Congress in March 2014, **Kerry admits he feels it would be a mistake to insist the Palestinians recognize Israel as a Jewish state**. He said, "I think it's a mistake for some people to be raising it again and again as the critical decider of their attitude toward the possibility of a state, and peace, and we've obviously made that clear." **Obama omitted calling Israel a Jewish state when describing the peace process endpoints** by saying, "two states, side by side, in peace and security – a state that allows for the dignity and sovereignty of the Palestinian people and a state that allows Israelis to feel secure and at peace with their neighbors." For Obama, it is not critical that Israel remains a Jewish state.

o. In April 2014, despite the formation of a Palestinian unity government with Hamas and on the eve of Holocaust Remembrance Day, Kerry compares Israel to an apartheid state in remarks to the Trilateral Commission where he stated, "A two-state solution will be clearly underscored as the only real alternative. Because **a unitary state winds up either being an apartheid state** with second-class citizens, or it ends up being a state that destroys the capacity of Israel to be a Jewish state." It is ironic (or a double standard) that Kerry does not use the apartheid term to describe any Arab or Muslim country, where all infidels are viewed as second-class citizens, or in Saudi Arabia, where non-Muslims drive in isolated lanes in certain parts of the country.

p. By July 2014, Hamas had initiated incessant missile launches at Tel Aviv and Israeli civilian targets. A formal limited war between Israel and Hamas was underway. An analysis of Obama's input and reaction to the war demonstrated his allegiance was with the Palestinians. Obama continued support for the Palestinians and their vision of a two-state solution despite their departure from bilateral negotiations as promised by the Oslo Accord, their formation of a unity government with a terrorist group and their complicity in the recent murder of three Israeli teenagers. As war waged, Obama said, "Israel has a right to defend itself from rocket attacks that terrorize the Israeli people. There is no country on Earth that can be expected to live under a daily barrage of rockets." Nevertheless, Obama sought to reign in Israel's response, as the following observations show:

i.   As Israel planned to protect its country and civilians from continued rocket barrages (Operation Protective Edge) **Obama called on Israel to show restraint** as hundreds of missiles were fired at their cities, and not to harm Palestinian civilians. State Department spokesperson Edgar Vasquez stated, "We are concerned about the safety and security of civilians on both sides … and **urge the protection of civilians**." Obama knows that Hamas uses women and children as human shields and launched their rockets from mosques, schools, hospitals and apartment complexes, so Obama is laying the groundwork for others to criticize and delegitimize Israel when they launch counterattacks against the terrorists.

ii. While Hamas is raining a constant barrage of rockets down on Tel Aviv and middle and southern Israel, **Obama published an editorial in *Haaretz* on July 8, 2014, praising Abbas, who is a full political partner with Hamas**. While the PA unity government started a war with Israel and targeted mostly Israeli civilians, Obama says of Abbas, "And, **in President Abbas, Israel has a counterpart committed to a two-state solution and security cooperation with Israel** [*Abbas wants Israeli troops removed from the West Bank and East Jerusalem.*]… **a commitment to non-violence** [*taqiyya*], **adherence to past agreements** [*taqiyya – not the Oslo Accords*], and the **recognition of Israel** [*not as a Jewish state*]… All parties must exercise restraint and work together to maintain stability on the ground." In his letter to the Israelis, Obama praised Abbas, ignored Netanyahu and urged Israel to restrain itself as the Palestinians fire hundreds of rockets throughout Israel.

(1) "**We bless every drop of blood that has been spilled for Jerusalem, which is clean and pure blood, blood spilled for Allah**, Allah willing. Every Martyr (Shahid) will reach Paradise, and everyone wounded will be rewarded by Allah. The Al-Aqsa [Mosque] is ours, **the Church of the Holy Sepulchre is ours** [Islamic supremacism over Christians and Jews], and **they** [the Jews] **have no right to defile them with their filthy feet**. We will not allow them to, and we will do everything in our power to protect Jerusalem." PA President Abbas, September 16, 2015. How could anyone with such deep hatred for Jews make a sustainable long-lasting sincere peace treaty with the State of Israel?

(2) In October 2014, Abbas incited Palestinians to murder Jews who enter the Temple Mount, the formal site of the first and second Jewish temples. **Abbas** stated "**We must prevent them** [the Jews / settlers] **from entering** [the Temple Mount] **in any way … They have no right to enter and desecrate it. We must confront them and defend our holy sites**." Abbas's calls to attack the Jews were rebroadcast 19 times on PA television stations. Subsequently, there were two terrorist attacks on Jews leading to murder and the attempted

murdered of an Israeli rabbi. Neither Obama nor Kerry condemned Abbas's incitement, and only demanded more concessions from Israel, including Jewish ethnic cleansing from East Jerusalem and denying Jews the right to build on Jewish property in Arab neighborhoods in East Jerusalem.

(3)   "Two days after the bus bombing in Jerusalem (April 16, 2016), Palestinian President Mahmoud Abbas' Fatah movement posted_a chilling video on its Facebook page calling on young Palestinians to become martyrs by carrying out stabbing attacks against Israelis. The 9-minute video, titled 'Martyrdom-seeking unites us,' features a staged car-ramming and stabbing attack. Three young Palestinians are seen planning and carrying out the attack. They kill two Israeli soldiers by ramming their car into one of them and stabbing the other."[291]

(4)   "Allah, punish Your enemies, the enemies of religion, count their numbers and **kill them to the last one**, and bring them a black day. Allah, punish the wicked Jews." *Official Palestinian Authority TV religious leader, Palestinian Media Watch, April 22, 2016.* The PA publicly preaches genocide against the Jews. There is no comment from the Obama administration. Days earlier, Biden spoke at the annual J Street gala and condemned Netanyahu for failing to compromise and make geographical and political concessions to people who publicly state their desire to kill Jews and destroy Israel.

(5)   "The call to prayer will be heard from on top of the White House and from the red palace of the Kremlin in Moscow … Oh Allah, blow up their capital cities and their planes, pulverize their ships, and kill their soldiers. Oh Allah, we ask You to subjugate them and burn them." *Sheikh Muhammad Ayed, Al Asqa Mosque sermon, Jerusalem, MEMRI, September 2016. Ayed is a Palestinian religious leader and an Abbas ally, who is preaching the Islamic takeover of America.*

(6)   "These Israeli's have no belief, no principles. They are an advanced instrument of evil. I believe that Allah, will gather them so we can kill them." *Abbas Zaki, Member of Fatah Central Committee, Official PA TV – controlled by Abbas, March 12, 2014.* Official Palestinian Authority (i.e. – Abbas) view on Jews in Israel.

(7)   "Here are the Zionists, who have gathered from all around. They occupy and usurp Jerusalem and its environs, and so the promise of Allah is realized: "**We will bring you forth in [one] gathering, so that it will be easier to slaughter and kill you. (Quran, Sura 17:104)**" *Muhammad Sala Abu Rajab, Hamas religious authority, Al-Aqsa TV, Hamas controlled TV station, August 22, 2014.* Official Hamas political view upon Jews in Israel. Abbas is allied with Hamas.

(8) Abbas "is **the most anti-Semitic leader in the world** … But with regard to the Israeli-Palestinian issue, I am not optimistic. Abu Mazen [Abbas' second name] doesn't begin to meet the most basic requirements to be a partner for peace … In Washington, he spoke about peace and educating for peace. But the basic messages of the Palestinian educational system is that Israel must disappear from the map sooner or later. Jews are terrible people that must be gotten rid of and terrorists are heroes … On top of that Abu Mazen does not control Gaza [or its terrorist infrastructure] … What is the point of coming to an agreement with him, if he does not have a mandate, not in Gaza and not in Judea and Samaria." *Israeli Energy Minister Yuval Steinitz, The Jerusalem Post Annual Conference, New York City, May 2017.*

(9) "**Israel's greatest enemy is the Fatah movement** [Abbas' political party]. Some of you didn't even pray before 1989." Jibril Rajoub, member of the central committee of Fatah, television interview on al-Quds network, early May 2017. Rajoub is criticizing and mocking Hamas for not being tough enough with Israel.

(10) "The Palestinian Authority [under Abbas' leadership] has paid out some NIS 4 billion – or $1.12 billion – over the past four years to terrorists and their families, a former director general of the Ministry of Strategic Affairs and ex-head of the army's intelligence and research division told a top Knesset panel on Monday. Setting out the figures, Brig.-Gen (res.) Yossi Kuperwasser told the Foreign Affairs and Defense Committee that the longer the period for which a Palestinian security prisoner is jailed, "the higher the salary… Anyone who has sat in prison for more than 30 years gets NIS 12,000 ($3,360) per month," said Kuperwasser, according to the (Hebrew) NRG website. "When they're released, they get a grant and are promised a job at the Palestinian Authority. They get a military rank that's determined according to the number of years they've served in jail." Kuperwasser also told the committee that PA claims that the payments to terrorists' families are social welfare benefits to the needy are false."[292] *(The Times of Israel, May 29, 2017)*

(11) "Even if I will have to leave my position, I will not compromise on the salary (*rawatib*) of a Martyr (*Shahid*) or a prisoner, as I am the president of the entire Palestinian people, including the prisoners, the Martyrs, the injured, the expelled, and the uprooted." *Abbas quote, Official Fatah Facebook entry, July 2, 2017.* Leaders in the American Jewish community responded, "We are appalled by widespread media reports that **President Abbas** and other officials of the Palestinian Authority have recently made statements in Palestinian

social and other media **reaffirming their commitment to continue payments exceeding $300 million annually to reward terrorists and their families for attacking and killing Israelis.**" *Conference of Presidents of Major American Jewish Organizations Chairman Stephen M. Greenberg and Executive Vice Chairman and CEO Malcolm Hoenlein.*

(12) "A recent in-depth study in Israel calculates that all terror incentives and rewards paid by the Palestinian Authority over the **past four years** total a mind-numbing **one billion dollars** ... The salaries increase on a sliding scale. **The more carnage inflicted, the longer the prisoner sentence, the higher the salary** ... senior PA officials – including <u>President Mahmoud Abbas himself</u> – scrutinized the details of terrorist carnage before <u>approving monthly salaries</u> ... On November 1, 2016, just a week before the American election, former Israel intelligence officer Yossi Kuperwasser put all the numbers together for the Jerusalem Center for Public Affairs. He documented that the salaries, plus "martyr" payments to families, plus regular terror bonuses, including other related expenditures, had increased to **$300 million per year**. In the nearly four years since the original 2013 disclosures, the PA had spent a stunning one billion dollars on terror. In 2016, nearly **<u>30 percent of all foreign money received was diverted to the cause of terror</u>**."[293] *(Front Page Magazine, July 14, 2017)*

(13) Through his official Fatah party in mid-July 2017, Abbas announced, "the **campaign for Jerusalem** has effectively begun and **<u>will not stop until a Palestinian victory</u>** and the release of the holy sites from Israel occupations," and called for Palestinians to "take acts for the protection of al-Aqsa and their **struggle against the Israeli plans**, while <u>**sacrificing souls and blood**</u>." Abbas effectively declared war against Israel and official launched another intifada. Abbas's actions were in response to Israel screening Muslims going to prayers on the Temple Mount with metal detectors after Palestinian terrorists used the al-Aqsa mosque grounds as a safe haven through which they smuggled automatic weapons on the Temple Mount which were used to kill two Israeli security guards, and another 19-year-old Palestinian terrorist stabbed to death three family members celebrating Shabbat at the Halamish settlement. Massive riots in Jerusalem and the West Bank immediately followed Abbas's incitement.

iii. When Netanyahu declined Obama's offer to mediate a ceasefire on July 11, 2014, Philip Gordon, **Obama's special envoy to the Middle East, criticized Netanyahu** by saying, "How will we prevent other states from supporting Palestinian efforts in international bodies if Israel is not seen as committed to peace?" Israel elected to continue their military campaign, which targeted Hamas' military and tunnel infrastructure and their vast arsenal of over 10,000 rockets aimed at Israel, which Obama tried to protect. Contrary to Obama's position, Egyptian officials praised Israeli actions against Hamas, since Hamas was allied with the Egyptian Muslim Brotherhood and was involved in terrorist attacks against Egyptian targets.

iv.   As Israel prepared to launch a ground invasion of Gaza, Obama telephoned Netanyahu and told him "the United States and our friends and allies are **deeply concerned about the risks of further escalation and the loss of more innocent life … we have serious concerns about the rising number of Palestinian civilian deaths** and the loss of Israeli lives, and that is why it now has to be our focus and the focus of the international community to bring about a ceasefire that ends the fighting and that can **stop the deaths of innocent civilians**." In other words, Obama is telling Israel not to fight back and to not cause any casualties. **Obama is allowing Hamas to use human shields to protect their military targets and rocket launchers, which is a war crime.**

v.   John Kerry was overheard commenting on Israeli military operations against Hamas – "**It's a hell of a pinpoint operation**, it's a hell of a pinpoint operation."

vi.   On July 21, 2014, Obama announced that he is sending $47 million in "humanitarian" aid to Hamas in Gaza.

vii. On July 22, 2014, under the direction of Obama, **the FAA banned all flights to and from Ben Gurion airport after a Hamas missile landed near the airport**. By banning these flights, Obama attempted to **paralyze the Israeli economy** in response to continued Israeli military action against Hamas. Senator Cruz commented, "The facts suggest that **President Obama has just used a federal regulatory agency to launch an economic boycott on Israel**, in order to try to force our ally to comply with his foreign-policy demands." Hamas officials declared, "The success of Hamas in closing Israeli airspace is a great victory for the resistance, and is the crown of Israel's failure." **Obama directed U.S. agencies to implement policies that were the primary military goals of Hamas.** As Obama took these actions against Israel, Israel was on the ground in Gaza identifying and destroying a maze of tunnels that have been built by Hamas to infiltrate Israel and that would have been used for terror attacks. The tunnels were to be used to deploy Palestinian terrorists into Israel and were dug under Israeli schools as a means to kill schoolchildren with bomb attacks. They were also in place to facilitate kidnappings. **Obama is pushing for a ceasefire not only to preserve Hamas' rocket arsenal, but to protect Hamas' tunnel infrastructure**. It is ironic that Obama suspended all flights to Israel, yet he did not shut down air traffic to Ukraine or Russia when a passenger flight was shot down in a war zone over Ukraine with a surface-to-air missile. Nor did Obama suspend flights to countries confronted with the highly contagious Ebola epidemic, when Ebola cases were appearing in the continental United States.

viii. *The Wall Street Journal* reported Obama **halted a shipment of air-to-ground "Hellfire" missiles to Israel during the 2014 Gaza war** as a means to pressure Israel to accept Qatar and Turkey as mediators in their conflict with Hamas.

ix. As the war continued and casualties mounted on both sides, **Obama**, on July 27, demanded a ceasefire "that both allows Palestinians in Gaza to lead normal lives and **addresses Gaza's long-term development and economic needs**, while strengthening the Palestinian Authority ..." On the same day, Kerry demanded a ceasefire before Israel had located and destroyed all of Hamas's tunnels, which could be used to launch future invasions into formal Israel. **Kerry's ceasefire proposal, which was probably authored by Hamas, Turkey and Qatar, demanded Israel stop all military operations against Hamas's rockets and tunnels, lift the Gaza blockade and open Gaza's border with Egypt.** There was no mention of creating a demilitarized Gaza. Obama would have allowed Hamas to keep its arsenal and military infrastructure intact, and the lifting of the blockade would have allowed Hamas to rearm via shipments from Hezbollah and Iran. The proposal was immediately rejected by Israel. Even the left-wing newspaper *Haaretz* commented with an editorial by Barak Ravid that the ceasefire "might as well have been penned by Khaled Mashaal [Hamas leader]. It was everything Hamas could have hoped for. What Kerry's draft spells for the internal Palestinian political arena is even direr: It crowns Hamas and issues Palestinian President Mahmoud Abbas with a death warrant." One day later Kerry flew to Paris to meet with Turkish and Qatari diplomats (Israeli, Egyptian and Palestinian officials were not present) to modify the ceasefire proposal. Both Qatar and Turkey are strong supporters of Hamas. Qatar's government has significant input from the Muslim Brotherhood, and Hamas is a formal branch of the Muslim Brotherhood. Qatar is also a major financier to ISIS. Obama turned to Qatar and Turkey after Israel accepted an Egyptian ceasefire that proposed Hamas's demilitarization. **Obama worked exclusively with Israel's enemies to secure a ceasefire, attempted to shut down the Israeli economy by banning flights to Ben Gurion airport**, and **sought to preserve Hamas' military infrastructure. It appears Obama has abandoned Israel and is allying himself with Hamas and the Muslim Brotherhood.** Obama also ignored the heinous dimensions of Hamas's use of human shields as part of their overall strategy to delegitimize Israel on the world stage. Isi Leibler commented in the *Jerusalem Post* on July 27, 2014, "most of the civilian casualties in Gaza were incurred because Hamas had ordered women and children to ignore Israeli early warnings to evacuate, obliging them to act as human shields at rocket launching sites and command posts. Schools, hospitals, mosques, and UNRWA headquarters were used to stockpile armaments and launch missiles. By this behavior, Hamas is responsible for every civilian casualty, and is unquestionably guilty of war crimes."

x. On July 28, Obama **backed the UN Security Council with its call for an "immediate and unconditional" ceasefire**, knowing that a significant part of the Hamas tunnel infrastructure remained in place. Kerry stated one day earlier, "I understand that Israel can't have a cease-fire in which they are not able to - that somehow the tunnels are never going to be dealt with. The tunnels have to be dealt with. We understand that … By the same token, **the Palestinians can't have a ceasefire in which they think the status quo is going to stay and they're not going to have the ability to be able to begin to live and breathe more freely and move within the crossings and begin to have goods and services that come in from outside**." Kerry is supporting the lifting of the blockade against Hamas, which will result in their rearming and acquiring advanced missiles that will be able to strike any target within Israel. **Kerry** is using the Palestinians' war against Israel to advance their negotiating position and **affirming there is no downside for the Palestinians' initiation of violence**.

xi. Obama increased his pressure on Israel by **calling Netanyahu on July 28 and demanding an unconditional, immediate and <u>unilateral</u> humanitarian ceasefire, the opening of Gaza's border with Egypt and the ending of Israel's blockade of Gaza**. A formal transcript of the call was released from reliable Israeli sources backed by a senior-level U.S. official. Its content revealed Obama's true allegiances. Obama, acting as a proxy for Hamas, **did not insist on a bilateral ceasefire**. ("I demand that Israel agree to a unilateral ceasefire and stop all offensive actions – especially air strikes.") He said Hamas would answer "quiet for quiet." Again, Obama is pushing Netanyahu to allow Gaza to have open borders. Obama does not want Hamas defeated and deplored Palestinian civilian casualties resulting from the use of human shields. Obama insisted Qatar and Turkey, both allies of ISIS and Hamas, be intermediaries in any future negotiations, and told Netanyahu "Israel is not in a position to choose the mediator." Netanyahu countered the formal American position in an interview with Candy Crowley by pointing out, "Obviously, we hope we can get a sustainable quiet as soon as possible. I think the only path to do that is by adopting the Egyptian initiative … We **need demilitarization**. *[But Obama wants Hamas rearmed with open borders and no maritime blockade]* … People said to us, enable concrete and cement to go into Gaza so they can rebuild, build schools, build hospitals *[taqiyya]* and so on. They took all that cement and built this vast tunnel network penetrating into Israel, so they can come out under our towns, our cities, our schools and explode our children. *[Obama wanted an immediate ceasefire and all building supplies would be available to Hamas engineers]* ... Remember, Hamas is firing at our cities, at our people, firing from these areas, from these homes, schools, mosques, hospitals ... **You don't want to give the terrorists immunity because they use civilians as a human shield**." Obama is protecting the best interests of the terrorists.

xii. Obama **cancelled the Israeli U.S. tourist visa program at the U.S. embassy in Tel Aviv after Israelis shelled Palestinian rocket and mortar launching positions adjacent to a UN school that resulted in 15 deaths**. The Palestinians have been hiding rockets in UN facilities throughout Gaza. It was thought that this harsh response by Obama was, in part, retaliation for Israel's leak of the transcript of the most recent phone conversations between Obama and Netanyahu. The White House called the shelling incident "**total unacceptable and totally indefensible** ... [Israel] can and should do more to protect the lives of innocent civilians." A Pentagon spokesperson said, "Civilians casualties in Gaza have been too high, and it's become clear that the Israelis have to do more to live up to their very high and public standards for protecting civilian lives." It is a shame that Obama blames Israel for the deaths of civilians who are forced to become human shields, so that their deaths can advance the propaganda war against Israel, instead of castigating Hamas. Obama is only reinforcing Hamas's barbaric behavior since Hamas knows Obama will attack Israel with each civilian casualty. **Obama is denying Israel the ability to protect its citizens, which is one of the major functions of a sovereign state**.

xiii. **Conclusion 1** – With Obama's strong support of Hamas during this military engagement, **Obama has solidified world opinion that he is allied with the Muslim Brotherhood**, an organization universally recognized as an Islamic terrorist group. This view of Obama is reinforced with his "New Beginnings" speech in Cairo, where he invited the Muslim Brotherhood as guests over the objections of Mubarak, and his subsequent support of the Muslim Brotherhood after Mubarak was forced from office. Another sign that Obama supports the Muslim Brotherhood is that he supported an Egyptian-sponsored ceasefire between Hamas and Israel in 2012 when the Muslim Brotherhood was in power and Obama wanted to enhance Morsi's role in the Middle East. Contrast this to his jettison of a similar Egyptian-sponsored ceasefire in 2014, specifically sponsored by Sisi, who was seeking to reform Islam. Obama then turned to Qatar and Turkey for an agreement. Both countries have

close ties with the Muslim Brotherhood, promote radical Islam, and are more blatantly anti-Semitic.

xiv. **Conclusion 2 - Events surrounding the 2014 Israel-Hamas war may have put
the two-state solution permanently out of reach as a viable political alternative**. **First**, when thc PA **formed a unity government with Hamas**, this alliance
**guaranteed an independent Palestinian state in the West Bank would be ruled
by Iran**, since the majority of Palestinians in the West Bank support Hamas and
Hamas is an Iranian proxy. **Second**, when **Obama suspended all U.S. flights to
Israel for two days**, he demonstrated that **one shell or rocket landing near Ben
Gurion airport could paralyze Israel** with the cessation of all air traffic coming into the country. **Thus, Obama made it impossible for Israel to cede territory capable of striking Ben Gurion airport via short range rockets from the
Palestinians**, who could easily shell the airport indiscriminately and paralyze the
country at their whim. This territory is in the heart of the West Bank. **Third**, as
the **Palestinian society celebrated the kidnapping and murder of three Israeli
teenagers**, all Jewish Israelis realized the ultimate goal of the Palestinians is the
death of all Jews in Israel and the destruction of the State of Israel. The **land for
peace policy failed** in Gaza and southern Lebanon, and it will fail in the West Bank
and East Jerusalem. **Fourth**, **with Hamas in control of the West Bank, Israel
should expect the same military political scenario** as in Gaza. Palestinian forces
in the West Bank would have advanced rockets and arms supplied by Iran, as well
as hundreds if not thousands of tunnels penetrating much of Israel's eastern border
with the West Bank. With indefensible boundaries and a well-trained Palestinian
army with advanced munitions on its eastern border, which would undoubtedly
be reinforced with troops from the IRGC, Israel would have to expect major military fronts on the east, west and north in all future wars. With central Israel only
nine miles wide, Israel would easily be split in two during a future major war, and
the State of Israel as it exists today could not survive. **Fifth, Israel does not trust
Obama** *(or maybe any Democrat since House minority leader Pelosi said, "Hamas is a
humanitarian organization")* **to create a peace agreement that will protect their
security interests, thus no solution to the Israeli Palestinian quagmire could
be finalized during Obama's tenure**. This is based on Obama's support of the
unity government with Hamas, Obama's reticence during the 18-day search for the
three Israeli teenagers who were kidnapped and murdered, Obama's demand that
Israel institute a unilateral ceasefire before all the tunnels were destroyed while lifting the Gaza blockade, and Obama's removal of Egypt from the ceasefire talks and
replacing them with Qatar and Turkey, who are staunch enemies of Israel. All these

episodes prove Obama's heart lies with the radical Muslims. Israel knows it, and the world knows it. Given the obvious conclusion that Obama treats Israel more harshly than any enemy of the United States, demands concessions from Israel and never from the Palestinians and ignores genocidal incitement from Iran, the Palestinian Authority, Hamas and the Muslim Brotherhood, **Obama could never be trusted to be an honest broker**. American security guarantees are worthless under an Obama administration, which was proven by Obama's withdrawal of support for Mubarak, a long-time U.S. ally, in favor of the Muslim Brotherhood, and Obama's disregard of Gulf state concerns over Iran's future nuclear program. And with the passage of the JCPOA and Iran's huge funding potential for their terrorist proxies on Israel's border, Israel cannot withdraw to less secure borders. Obama's strong support for Hamas (and Iran) and an untenable political solution may have been the major factors that prevented the Palestinians from having their own state with East Jerusalem as its capital. If Obama and his associates had been honest brokers, the chances for a durable peace in the Middle East would have been much higher.

q. The OneVoice Movement, which helped fund the Israeli Victory 15 campaign, received $350,000 in State Department grants. The V15 campaign, which was guided by Obama operatives, is an organization seeking to replace Netanyahu with a more compliant liberal Israeli leader, who will advance Obama's agenda in Israel. **Obama directly interfered in Israeli elections and embedded his leading 2012 Obama reelection campaign operatives to increase liberal and Arab voter turnout as a track to defeat Netanyahu**. Obama put his community-organizing skills to work unifying the Arab vote as a solidified political block directly opposing Netanyahu. Ultimately, millions of dollars were sent from State Department-related organizations to advisors, consultants, and political groups dedicated to defeating Netanyahu. Jeremy Bird, Obama's 2012 national campaign director, was sent to Israel to supervise efforts to aid V15. Obama's operatives introduced slogans such as "Anyone but Bibi," and "Hope" and "Change" (not "Hope and Change"). On voting day, Obama's operatives arranged transportation of Arabs to the voting booths and there was a significant increase in voting fraud. Elections were held in March 2015, and Netanyahu won reelection as prime minister. Obama actively interfered in Israel's domestic national elections.

r. In March 2015, Obama instructed the **U.S. Ambassador to the UN Human Rights Council to remain silent and not defend Israel during their prejudicial evaluation of Israeli actions** with respect to the Palestinians.

s. In *The Washington Post* on September 15, 2015, David Ignatius published an interview with Ben Rhodes, Obama's deputy national security advisor. Both men praised Obama's victory over Netanyahu in manipulating and ratifying the JCPOA through Congress and viewed the deal as Obama's greatest foreign policy achievement. Ignatius commented "A weak president Obama may be. **But a paradox of his presidency is that he has been at his toughest in fighting for the Iran nuclear deal against Netanyahu**, the leader of one of America's closest allies." Obama has been at his best not fighting for American interests or American security or a more stable Middle East, but fighting *against* Netanyahu, prime minister of a Jewish state in favor of the Iranian state. Since Netanyahu's major goal was preventing Iran from developing a nuclear arms arsenal and decreasing Iran's negative influence in the Middle East, Obama was at his best in fighting for a nuclear Iran and a more dangerous and chaotic Middle East. Obama was at his best and achieved his greatest victory when fighting Israel and validating an agreement opposed by the overwhelming majority of the American public, a bipartisan majority in Congress and all long-term U.S. Middle East allies. Obama has proven himself to be America's first anti-American president. The victory also belongs to Iran since it achieved all its negotiating goals and will have an arsenal of nuclear weapons in the foreseeable future.

t.   "As secretary of defense, he tells me, one of his most important jobs was keeping Prime Minister Benjamin Netanyahu of Israel and his defense minister, Ehud Barak, from launching a pre-emptive attack on Iran's nuclear facilities. 'They were both interested in the answer to the question, 'Is the president serious?' Panetta recalls. 'And you know my view, talking with the president, was: If brought to the point where we had evidence that they're developing an atomic weapon, I think the president is serious that he is not going to allow that to happen.' Panetta stops. 'But would you make that same assessment now?' I ask him. '**Would I make that same assessment now**?' he [Panetta] asks. '**Probably not**.'"[294] *(David Samuels, Panetta interview, The New York Times Magazine, May 2016)* **Obama's former secretary of defense admits the Obama administration's major foreign policy objective was to protect Iran's nuclear infrastructure from an Israeli attack**, and that Obama never had any intention to bomb Iranian nuclear facilities under any condition. His promises that "all options were on the table" were a lie designed to fool the Israelis into believing that Obama would not let Iran develop nuclear weapons, and to mislead the American public that Obama was protecting American interests. **Leon Panetta was hoodwinked** by Barack Obama on the most important foreign policy and national security issue of his presidency.

u.   Obama responded to the June 8, 2016 murder of four Israelis by Palestinians posing as Orthodox Jews at a popular Tel Aviv marketplace by telling Israel to keep a low profile and do nothing except to express their outrage verbally at the murders. Dan Toner, the State Department spokesman, remarked, "We understand the Israeli government's desire to protect its citizens after this kind of terrorist attack … We would just hope that any measures that Israel takes would be designed to **not escalate tensions any further**, but we certainly **respect their desire to express outrage**." How can Israel effectively respond without escalating tensions? Obama wants to paralyze Israel in the face of Palestinian terrorism.

v. By guiding and supporting the passage of UNSC Resolution 2334, Obama and the world community have designated the Western Wall and the Jewish Quarter of the old city as "illegal Jewish settlements," and "occupied Palestinian territory."

    i. "The American Jewish Congress urges immediate congressional hearings following the **change of U.S. policy that resulted in the United Nations Security Council (UNSC) resolution** on December 23, 2016. There are serious questions that need to be asked of the Obama administration following UN Security Council Resolution 2334, with the **US refusing to veto a <u>one-sided anti-Israel biased</u> resolution that puts Israel in international legal jeopardy and takes the position that <u>the Jewish holy sites in Jerusalem</u>, including the <u>Western Wall are no longer a part of Israel</u>**. We urge the US Congress to investigate the actions taken by the Obama administration leading up to the vote. Such a seismic shift in America Foreign Policy in the transition period, must be fully reviewed and accounted for, specifically, Samantha Power and Ben Rhodes should explain the process which led to their actions, particularly in light of questions being raised. Further, **there are worrying reports circulating of additional harmful resolutions at the UNSC** *[Obama wants to unilaterally recognize a formal Palestinian state with its boundaries determined by Obama, the PLO, Hamas and the UNSC, with its capital in East Jerusalem]*, and so we strongly believe that the American people deserve to be aware of the Obama Administration's intentions and **their change in policy towards the State of Israel**." *American Jewish Congress statement after the passage of UNSC Resolution 2334.* Obama waited until after the presidential elections at the very end of his second term to launch this diplomatic and economic war against Israel, because he did not want to hurt the Democratic Party during the last election cycle of his presidency. Obama's true hatred against Jews and Israel finally revealed itself to the American Jewish community, the American public, and the world. The reason Obama wanted to transfer control of most of the Jewish and Christian holy sites to radical Islamic terrorist organizations and their supporters (the PLO, Hamas, al-Qaeda, the Muslim Brotherhood, Iran, the IRGC, and eventually ISIS) is because Obama is a radical Muslim, who is dedicated to jihad, and establishing Jerusalem as the capital of a Middle East Islamic caliphate.

w. Obama always calls ISIS – "ISIL," because Obama includes the word "Levant" in the formal title, since **Levant includes Israel** as part of the Islamic state, and Obama wants

Jerusalem at the capital of the Islamic caliphate. "That Obama uses ISIL in discussing the terrorists is extremely telling and chilling. To those of us who keep our fingers on the pulse of Middle Eastern geopolitics, the distinctions separating ISIS and ISIL are by no means meager. It's readily apparent that Obama considers both Israel and its prime minister, Benjamin Netanyahu, thorns in each of his sides. Since 2009, his atrociously dismissive treatment of Netanyahu has been highly embarrassing, shocking, and outrageous, especially to those of us who cherish our relationship with the Jewish state … Despite some disagreements between the U.S. and the Jewish state, no previous president has shown such a hideous and blatant disregard for Israel's head of state as has Obama. Nor has any previous president ever considered (to our knowledge) or suggested in a way bordering on insistence that Israel relinquish the land it now controls by contracting to its pre-1967 borders. Obama wants just that. Why? For Israel, a return to those boundaries would be suicidal, shrinking the country to a width of a very svelte nine miles and making it essentially indefensible … Taken together, all of this gets us closer to understanding why Obama refuses to call Islamic terrorists what they are. His use of ISIL could be a strong indication that he supports re-establishing Muslim rule and sharia law throughout the Levant, and **good riddance to Israel**."[295] *("Why Does Obama call ISIS 'ISIL,'" American Thinker, 2015)* After Donald Trump became president, the Pentagon officially renamed the Islamic State, "ISIS," from "ISIL," which was used by the Obama administration.

x. With just hours remaining in his presidency, during the morning of Donald Trump's inauguration as president, Obama **released $221 million in aid to the Palestinian Authority**, that was previously frozen by Congress after the PA unilaterally went to various world organizations to obtain recognition as an independent state without obtaining a peace agreement with Israel. Although the aid was to be used for humanitarian purposes, the funds would also be used to finance families whose members committed terrorist acts against Israelis and were subsequently killed, or to those Palestinians who were jailed for committing terrorist acts against Israel. Thus, Obama was funding terrorism against the Jews. As *The New York Post* noted, "And Team Obama didn't make the case, nor even announce the move openly. Instead, they chose to move surreptitiously, saving official notification for a time when members of Congress would be preoccupied with the inauguration. No, the funding hardly endangers Israel, though we have doubts how much of this "humanitarian" aid will actually go for humanitarian purposes. But **the real intention here was less to aid the Palestinians and more to stick it to Netanyahu. What a tawdry final move**."[296] Obama first major contact with a foreign leader as president on his inauguration day in 2009, was to call President Abbas, and Obama finished his presidency on inauguration day eight years later by releasing over 200 million dollars to the PLO as his final act. Obama is allied with the Palestinian Islamic terrorists.

y. Israel's former Foreign Ministry director general Dore Gore revealed in an interview with *Makor Rishon* on January 20, 2017, that Susan Rice, Obama's national security adviser stated that, "**Even if Israel and the Palestinians reach an accord, it's possible that the US will oppose it.**"[297] This statement revealed that Obama was more interested in harming Israel than in supporting a peace agreement that was supported by the Palestinian leadership. Obama wanted to make sure that Israel would have to give up enough land to make it overly vulnerable in any future conflicts between the Palestinians and the Israelis. Thus, Obama was not interested in peace, but in Israel's demise.

2. "America's strong bonds with Israel are well known. This bond is *[used to be]* unbreakable. It is based upon cultural and historical ties, **and the recognition that the aspiration for a Jewish homeland is rooted in a tragic history that cannot be denied**." *Obama, Cairo University speech, June 4, 2009.* Obama is stating that the Jews' yearning for a Jewish homeland is based on the Holocaust and European anti-Semitism, and not on an historical or religious connection to the land of Israel which has existed for over 3000 years. This is the same argument that the Arabs use to say that they are suffering with Jews living in the Middle East as a result of European persecution, and that the Jews should leave the Middle East and go back home to Europe. Obama is also supporting the tenets of the Palestinian Nakba or "catastrophe," where Israeli-Arabs state that Israel was founded by stealing Arab land, which is a method to delegitimize Israel as a nation. Obama reveals his ingrained anti-Semitism and Arabic-Sudanese background, by supporting a fabricated Islamic, Arabic interpretation of Jewish history.

3. "And **there's not a smidgen of evidence** [**that I am anti-Semitic**], other than the fact that there have been times where I've disagreed with a particular Israeli government's position on a particular issue." *Obama **denied he is anti-Semitic** in a Forward Magazine interview with Jane Eisner, which was published on August 31, 2015.* Obama used the word "smidgeon" when he denied there was any corruption at the IRS, which was later proved false when it was revealed that the IRS was targeting conservatives, Tea Party activists and Obama's political opponents with audits and denials of tax-exempt non-profit status.

a. Obama's acceptance and even possible embrace of anti-Semitism may have been a major factor leading to the breakup of his relationship with Sheila Miyoshi Jager in their 20s. According to David Greenberg in *Politico*, "Jager also told Garrow that the scene, in *Dreams*, that precipitated their breakup – a bitter row about race after they saw a play by an African-American playwright – misrepresented the issues that actually divided them. In Jager's telling, the searing fight took place after they saw an exhibit at Chicago's Spertus Institute about the 1961 Adolf Eichmann trial, a very different context. Where

Dreams portrayed the lovers' rift as at bottom a function of racial difference, Jager, while acknowledging the racial component of their strains, insisted she was mainly upset that day that Obama, in her recollection, was less than unequivocal in condemning "black racism"; it was at a moment when the **overt anti-Semitism of Steve Cokely**, a black mayoral aide in Chicago, had become a *cause célèbre* in local politics. To Jager, what doomed their future together was Obama's incorrigible "realism," his perpetual **readiness to accept and work within given realities**."[298] Jager may have realized that day, that Obama agreed with Cokely and his anti-Semitism, and maybe she couldn't marry an anti-Semite. Even *The New York Times* reported, "Mr. Cokely charged that Jews are involved in an international conspiracy to control the world and that ''the AIDS epidemic is a result of doctors, especially Jewish ones, who inject AIDS into blacks.'' He has attacked … the late Mayor Washington for having Jewish advisers … Mr. Cokely has asserted that the crucifix is a ''symbol of white supremacy'' … Mr. Cokely accepted a job with the Rev. Louis Farrakhan, leader of the Nation of Islam, who remarked that Mr. Cokely had offended Jewish leaders only ''because the truth hurts.''"[299] Obama later supported Black Liberation Theology and the Nation of Islam, which were also embraced by Cokely.

b.   "Obama has many close friends and political associates who are anti-Semitic, which indicates that Obama agrees with much of their political thought, including their anti-Israel and anti-Semitic sentiments. As an African-American, would Obama praise and keep in his company individuals who were openly anti-Black with their statements or innuendo? If Obama really was concerned about Jews and Israel, would he befriend so many people who despised Israel and aligned themselves with Palestinians and other radical Muslims? People in general do not **continually** socialize with individuals who have negative or racist opinions against various minorities, especially those minorities with whom one may have a genuine affinity. Ironically, Obama has expressed his special relationship with Jews and Judaism on many occasions, where he has spoken Hebrew, Yiddish, and verbalized various positive Jewish colloquialisms in front of Jewish audiences. Is this taqiyya or politics? If Obama truly had a special relationship with the Jewish world, he would not have surrounded himself during his life with so many people who despise Israel and are anti-Semitic. One or two crossed paths may be acceptable for an ambitious politician, but too many of Obama's past and present associates have prejudicial pasts." *(Unexpected Treason)*

•   Obama's half-brother, **Malik Obama**, who is head of the Obama foundation, supports the Muslim conquest of Jerusalem.

•   **Dr. Khalid al Mansour**, a Muslim convert and advisor to the Saudi royal family, helped Obama gain admittance to Harvard Law School, and may have helped pay for his educational expenses. Monsour is pro-Palestinian and views Israel as a racist state.

- Obama supported **Odinga** in his quest for the Kenyan presidency, and Odinga favored Sharia law, in which Jews would be second-class citizens.

- Obama launched his political campaign for Illinois state office from the home of **Bill Ayers**, who advocated stopping all United States aid to Israel, and viewed Israel as a racist country.

- **Obama's spiritual mentor**, **Reverend Wright**, supported the Palestinians in the Israeli-Palestinian conflict. Reverend Wright maintained a very close friendship with Louis Farrakhan, head of the Nation of Islam, who called Hitler a 'great man' and described Judaism as a 'gutter' religion. In 2007, Wright praised **Farrakhan** in his church magazine while honoring him with Obama at an annual gala by commenting "Minister Farrakhan will be remembered as one of the 20th and 21st century giants of the African American religious experience. **His integrity and honesty have secured him a place in history** as one of the nation's most powerful critics … a religious leader who is sincere about his faith and his purpose." Wright had Hamas advisors author anti-Israel editorials in his church newsletter, and expressed anti-Semitic views in his sermons and writings. For over twenty years, Obama listened to Reverend Wright's anti-Israel, pro-Palestinian remarks, and mostly likely said "Amen" at the end of every sermon while increasing his donations. Wright's quotes include:
  - "We bombed Hiroshima, we bombed Nagasaki and we nuked far more than the thousands in New York and the Pentagon and we never batted an eye … **We have supported state terrorism against the Palestinians** and Black South Africans and now we are indignant because the stuff we have done overseas is now brought right back into our own front yards. Americans' chickens are coming home to roost." *2001*. Reverend Wright places the interests of the Palestinians ahead of the interests of Black South Africans by listing them first.
  - "The Israelis have illegally occupied Palestinian territories for almost 40 years now. It took a **divestment campaign** *[Obama may eventually support the BDS campaign against Israel]* to wake the business community up concerning the South Africa issue. Divestment has now hit the table again as a strategy to wake the business community up and to wake Americans up concerning the **injustice and the racism under which the Palestinians have lived because of Zionism**." *2005*.
  - "Part of the fight going on now in terms of the religious arguments and tension and polarization and hatred among the fundamentalists especially in each of the

major world religions has to do with the political, especially as it pertains to the **political decision made in 1948 to solve a European problem of European Jews by putting them in somebody else's country.**" *2008.* This sentiment parallels remarks and anti-Israel concepts advanced in Obama's 2009 Cairo University speech, where Obama defined Israel's links to the Holy Land as a consequence of the Holocaust.

- Obama was honored at a dinner with **Louis Farrakhan**, head of the Nation of Islam, who called Judaism a gutter religion, and labelled Hitler as a "great man." Obama employed National of Islam members in his senate office, and always had positive remarks for Nation of Islam members in his two books. Obama's wife regularly socialized with Farrakhan's wife and helped maintain social links between their two families.

- **Rashid Khalidi**, a former member of the PLO and close associate of Yasir Arafat, was good friends with Obama while Obama lived in Chicago.

- **Malcolm X**, one of Obama's role models, felt that Israel needed to withdraw from the 1949 Armistice Line, and thus was truly in favor of the dissolution of the State of Israel.

- **Al Sharpton**, who visited the White House over 50 times during Obama's presidency, incited a mob riot with anti-Semitic slurs that led to the murder of an innocent Jewish bystander early in his activist career. Sharpton has the distinction of leading the first American pogrom that killed Jews.

- **Samantha Powers**, a close friend of Obama and currently the U.S. Ambassador to the UN, had proposed assembling an international force to invade Israel and liberate the West Bank from Israeli control, which would result in the establishment of a Palestinian state.

- **Robert Malley**, before joining the Obama administration, worked with former PLO officials and advocated that the United States should hold official talks with Hamas, a designated terrorist organization, before Obama became president. In March 2015, Obama named **Robert Malley as the director of the National Security Council's Middle East desk**. Malley had previously blamed Israel for the collapse of the 2000 Camp David peace talks, in contrast to formal American and Israeli viewpoints. Malley met with Hamas officials as Obama's representative while Obama was campaigning for the presidency in 2008. At that time, Hamas was designated by the State Department as a formal terrorist group.

- **Former Senator Chuck Hagel**, **who was appointed by Obama as a Defense Secretary**, was one of the rare senators who almost never supported AIPAC pro-Israel letters and opposed additional sanctions on Iran. Hagel publicly complained in 2006 that the "Jewish lobby intimidates a lot of people up here."

- **Recip Erdogan**, the prime minister and president of Turkey and one of Obama's best friends during his presidency, equated Judaism with Nazism, and called Zionism a crime against humanity. Erdogan supports Hamas and ISIS. Not unexpectedly, Obama and Erdogan despise Benjamin Netanyahu, the Prime Minister of Israel. In May 2017, Erdogan stated, "Each day that Jerusalem [all of Jerusalem, not just East Jerusalem] is under occupation is an insult to us [all Muslims] … What's the difference between the present acts of the Israeli administration and the racist and discriminatory politics that were practiced against black people in the past in America – and up until a short time ago in South Africa? … [we need to work with the Palestinian Authority] to protect Jerusalem against attempts of Judaization." Erdogan wants the Muslims [namely himself] and a future Islamic caliphate to control all of Jerusalem, and is against Jews building and having children in Jerusalem.

- Obama supported **Morsi and the Muslim Brotherhood** with their violent campaign to win the presidency of Egypt after Mubarak resigned from that post. Morsi advocated a Muslim invasion of Jerusalem and called Jews "the descendants of apes and pigs." With respect to Israel, Morsi has said "The Zionists have no right to the land of Palestine … What they took before 1947-48 constitutes plundering, and what they are doing now is a continuation of this plundering. By no means do we recognize their Green Line. The land of Palestine belongs to the Palestinians, not to the Zionists." Morsi wants Israel annihilated, and Obama backs him politically with billions of dollars in military and financial aid. While Morsi was president of Egypt and the Muslim Brotherhood was in power, Obama advocated giving this terrorist regime over $1 billion in military aid including supplying them with advanced American weaponry, which would eventually be used against Israel.

- Obama has appointed dozens of **Muslim Brotherhood operatives** throughout many departments in the U.S. government. One of the spiritual leaders of the Muslim Brotherhood, Qaradawi, stated, "The only thing that I hope for is that **as my life approaches its end, Allah will give me an opportunity to go to the land of Jihad and resistance, even if in a wheelchair. I will shoot Allah's enemies, the Jews,** and they will throw a bomb at me, and thus, I will seal my life with martyrdom. Praise be to Allah." Obama used Qaradawi to help mediate negotiations between the Taliban and the United States. Obama invited one of Qaradawi's aides to the White House.

- Obama **secured his legacy with a deal that paved Iran's path to nuclear weapons**, and empowered the number one state sponsor of terrorism in the world with over $150 billion, which will be used to fund the jihad against Israel with the aim of destroying the Jewish state and killing all the Jews.

- Obama wanted President Abbas of the Palestinian Authority to control the West Bank and East Jerusalem. **Abbas is a Holocaust denier and entered into a unity agreement with Hamas, a branch of the Muslim Brotherhood, which wants to kill all the Jews in the world and replace Israel with an Islamic Palestinian state**. Hamas leader Meshaal has recently stated in 2012, "Palestine is ours from the river to the sea and from the south to the north. There will be no concession on an inch of the land … We will never recognize the legitimacy of the Israeli occupation and therefore there is no legitimacy for Israel, no matter how long it will take." Abbas wrote his PhD dissertation questioning whether the Holocaust occurred by stating in his thesis, "It seems that the interest of the Zionist movement, however, is to inflate this figure [Holocaust deaths] so that their gains will be greater. This led them to emphasize this figure [six million] in order to gain the solidarity of international public opinion with Zionism. Many scholars have debated the figure of six million and reached stunning conclusions – fixing the number of Jewish victims at only a few hundred thousand … The Zionist movement led a broad campaign of incitement against the Jews living under Nazi rule to arouse the government's hatred of them, to fuel vengeance against them and to expand the mass extermination." When addressing the issue of NATO troops in a future Palestinian state, Abbas commented in 2010, "I will not agree that there will be Jews among NATO forces and I will not allow even one Israeli to live amongst us on the Palestinian soil." Abbas was the first world leader who Obama called immediately after his inauguration as president in January 2009. How can a man whose political ideology is so based in hatred be expected to live in peace with a Jewish state? Knowing all of the above, Obama still embraced Abbas as a moderate.

c. "In **Obama's Cairo speech entitled "A New Beginning"** to the Muslim world in June 2009, Obama established a **moral equivalence between the Holocaust and the sufferings of the Palestinians** under "occupation" at the hands of the Israelis. Obama called the Palestinian situation "**intolerable**" but does not make an equivalent statement toward Islamic anti-Semitism. Obama also **compared the Israeli treatment of Palestinians with the treatment of Blacks in America during the age of segregation**. This comparison is illegitimate since African-Americans leaders during the Civil Rights era never instituted suicide bombers, and never publicly preached for the death of all White Americans and the destruction of America. Obama stated the Jewish quest for a homeland is "rooted in a tragic history," thus **blaming the Holocaust for the establishment of the State of Israel**. This is the argument put forth by radical Muslims who state that the Arabs in the Middle East should not be burdened with the Jewish population in Israel since the Europeans perpetuated the Holocaust. Obama delegitimized the existence of the State of Israel. Obama does not mention that there has been a continual thriving Jewish population in Israel for over three thousand years. Incidentally, **the date of Obama's speech in Cairo coincided with exact date that Mohammed started a war with the Christian world by attacking the Byzantine expeditionary force in 629 AD**. Obama paid strict attention to every detail of his Cairo speech, including the date of delivery, which was not a coincidence. Radical Muslims take anniversary dates very seriously. Obama views this date, June 4, 2009, as the start of a transformational battle against the Christian Western world by Islam, which would be spearheaded and directed by his standing and influence as president of the United States. Obama's insistence that the Muslim Brotherhood attend his speech was a signal to Islamic radicals that he would support their agenda throughout the Middle East during his presidency. Any impression that his speech would promote peace was taqiyya." *(Unexpected Treason)*

d. Obama declared that he wanted to **put daylight between the United States and Israel** as one of his first major foreign policy objectives as president in 2009.

e. "'A two-state solution will be clearly underscored as the only real alternative. Because a unitary state winds up either being **an apartheid state** or … a state that destroys the capacity of Israel to be a Jewish state. Once you put that frame in your mind … which is the bottom line, you understand how imperative it is to get to the two-state solution.' Secretary of State Kerry. Kerry makes an anti-Semitic statement against Israel by subtly referring to it as an 'apartheid state,' despite knowing that all Arabs within the State of Israel have equal political and economic rights as Jews. An Arab girl has won the Miss Israel pageant, and the judge who sentenced former Israeli President Katsav to seven years in prison for rape is an Arab. Not quite apartheid." *(Unexpected Treason)*

f. "In the spring of 2009, Obama **strongly pressured Israel to stop the planned demolition of illegally built Palestinian homes on Jewish-owned land in East Jerusalem** adjacent to the Temple Mount. Obama was reportedly in favor of ejecting all Jews from the West Bank, making that territory *Judenrein*, or free from all Jews, like in most Arab countries. Abbas reiterated Obama's position after attending meetings with him. Obama also demanded that the **Jews stop building homes anywhere in East Jerusalem and the West Bank**, reversing United States' policy that allowed for "natural growth" in existing Jewish communities. Former national security advisor to President Bush, Elliott Abrams (senior fellow for Middle Eastern Studies at the Council on Foreign Relations, National Security Council – Middle East Affairs 2001 – 2009), stated in *The Wall Street*

Journal ("Hillary is Wrong About the Settlements," June 26, 2009), "for reasons that re-main unclear, the Obama administration has decided to abandon the understandings about settlements reached by the previous administration with the Israeli government. We may be abandoning the deal now, but we cannot rewrite history and make believe it did not exist." In 2004, President Bush assured Israel that they were entitled to secure borders [not 1967 - Auschwitz borders] with no right of return for displaced Palestinian refugees in a future peace agreement with the Palestinians. State Department spokes-man Ian Kelly stated, with regard to the settlement freeze, "We're talking about all settlement activity, yes in the area across the [Green] line [or pre-1967 armistice line]." Obama is implying that Jews living in the disputed territories, including Jerusalem, should not have children or be allowed to grow their families. Israeli Interior Minister Eli Yishai stated, "The American demand to freeze construction means expulsion for young people living in large locales … **The concessions they're demanding of us are a security impediment we cannot withstand**." Obama's policies parallel those of previ-ous radical Islamic leaders who demanded Jewish expulsions from any lands viewed as Islamic territory, which is contrary to Obama's general support of civil rights. Obama is contradicting his own advice he gave at a recent G20 meeting where he stated that the United States should "forge partnerships as **opposed to simply dictating solutions**." He also told al-Arabiya that under his leadership, America will "start by listening, be-cause all too often the United States starts by dictating." Applying a double standard is anti-Semitic. In a June 2009 poll sponsored by the Jerusalem Post, only 6% of Israeli Jews saw Obama as pro-Israel. With Obama taking more extreme positions against Israel than the Palestinian Authority, Obama's policies allowed Abbas to withdraw from ne-gotiations with Israel and wait to see the result of Obama's overbearing pressure tactics. The Palestinians had never demanded a complete Israeli settlement freeze like Obama did." *(Unexpected Treason)*

g. During Prime Minister Netanyahu's visit with Obama in Washington in November 2009, **Obama demonstrated obvious hostility towards Netanyahu**. Obama would not publicly announce Netanyahu's visit on his calendar beforehand. Netanyahu was brought to the White House at night in an unmarked van, and was not greeted out front during the day, as is typical for foreign leaders visiting the White House. Obama refused to have his picture taken with Netanyahu. At the end of the meeting, Netanyahu was ushered out of the White House alone, exiting through a side door. Subsequently, Netanyahu approved a 10-month settlement freeze in the West Bank. Obama also de-manded that Israel release over 1,000 Palestinian terrorist prisoners from Israeli jails. In March 2010, when Netanyahu was visiting the White House, Obama would not allow any photographs to be taken with him and Netanyahu, nor would he allow reporters to witness the two leaders shaking hands when meeting. In the evening, Obama left Netanyahu in the White House for a private dinner, which was called by one Israeli newspaper "a hazing in stages." Obama attempted to humiliate Netanyahu multiple times in response to Israel's not implementing a freeze on all construction in East Jerusalem and the West Bank and the poorly timed Israeli housing announcement. Obama treated the Israeli prime minister as a diplomatic pariah.

h. In September 2012, **President Obama refused to meet with Prime Minister Netanyahu** in Washington or in New York at a UN General Assembly Meeting. Tensions between the two leaders were escalating over disagreements on how to deal with the Iranian nuclear program. Netanyahu was lobbying for harsher sanctions against Iran and wanted Obama to define a "red line" for unacceptable Iranian nuclear enrichment activity. In a response to Obama, Netanyahu stated, "Those in the international community who refuse to put red lines before Iran don't have a moral right to place a red light before Israel." Clinton responded, "We're not setting deadlines." **Obama then called Netanyahu's concerns "noise"** by stating in an interview with *60 Minutes* on September 23, 2012, "When it comes to our national security decisions, any pressure that I feel is simply to do what's right for the American people. **And I am going to block out any noise** that's out there." Although Obama was not able to meet with the Israeli prime minister in New York City at the UN, he was able to tape a guest appearance on *The David Letterman Show* that day. Obama proved that he did not follow his own advice when he told graduates of Notre Dame in 2011 "In this world of competing claims about what is right and what is true, have confidence in the values with which you've been raised and educated. **Be unafraid to speak your mind when those values** *[but not Israel]* **are at stake. Hold firm to your faith and allow it to guide you on your journey.**" Obama is holding Israel and its leaders to a double standard. That is anti-Semitism.

i. **Obama orchestrated a boycott of Israeli Prime Minister Netanyahu's UN General Assembly speech on October 1, 2015**, when Secretary of State John Kerry and UN Ambassador Samantha Powers refused to attend the event. Junior diplomats of the U.S. delegation refused to applaud the prime minister at any time during his speech. This is Obama's second boycott of Netanyahu and reflects the hatred Obama feels toward the Jewish state and its leader. Obama's first boycott of a Netanyahu speech occurred when the Israeli prime minister argued against the JCPOA before a special joint session of Congress. Obama has never boycotted a speech by Putin, who invaded Ukraine and Crimea, nor any speech by the Iranian leaders who preach for a second Holocaust almost on a daily basis.

j. In June 2014, soon after Obama gave his political and financial support to the PA-Hamas unity government, **Hamas operatives kidnapped and murdered three Israeli**

teenagers (one being a U.S. citizen) while hitchhiking in the West Bank. Obama made no comment and seemed indifferent to the fact that the Palestinian unity government he supported was a partner to this murder. Obama remained silent to the plight of the kidnapped teenagers for almost three weeks until their bodies were found. And when Obama did speak, **he did not differentiate between the Israeli victims and the Palestinians who celebrated the atrocity,** by stating "From the outset, I have offered our full support to Israel and the Palestinian Authority to find the perpetrators of this crime and bring them to justice, and I encourage Israel and the Palestinian Authority to continue working together in that effort. I also **urge all parties to refrain from steps that could further destabilize the situation." Obama's amoral indifference to dead Jewish teenagers reflects that his heart is with the Palestinian terrorists.** Obama did not even threaten or chastise Hamas as a partner in the unity government for the murder of an American citizen. Obama asked the PA to help bring the terrorists to justice, but the PA partners with Hamas, the terrorist group that committed the murders. That the Palestinian society as whole openly rejoiced and celebrated these murders demonstrated their support for the goals of the Hamas and Palestinian charters that call for the annihilation of Israel. This event alone proves that Obama's two-state solution would only be a stepping stone for the Palestinians and the Muslims to further their war against the Jews from a more advantageous position. Obama's false moral equivalence may be based in anti-Semitism.

k. In mid-November 2014, **two Palestinian terrorists armed with axes and pistols viciously murdered and mutilated five Orthodox Jews, including four rabbis, three of whom were American citizens, during morning prayers.** Obama responded saying that "**too many Palestinians have died**" and that "the majority of Palestinians" want peace. **Obama resorted to moral equivalence** by stating, "Tragically, this is not the first loss of life that we have seen in recent months ... Too many Israelis have died, and too many Palestinians have died. And at this difficult time, I think it's important for both Palestinians and Israelis to try to work together to lower tensions and to reject violence." Bret Stephens of *The Wall Street Journal* called Obama's utterances "moral blindness." The Palestinians even celebrated the murder of these righteous individuals, as they had when three Israeli teenagers were kidnapped and murdered earlier in the year, and when the Fogel family was murdered and beheaded as they slept.

l. After the incitement against Jews by the Palestinian political and religious leaders in early October 2015, Palestinians initiated a rampage of indiscriminate stabbings and attempted murder against Jewish Israelis. Obama probably gave his approval to this new wave of Islamic terror against the Jews when he and senior U.S. diplomatic representatives boycotted Netanyahu's speech on October 1 and treated Israel like a pariah, an isolated and despised nation. Abbas declared at the UN that the Palestinians would no long abide by the Oslo Accords. Just days earlier, Fatah terrorists murdered an Israeli rabbi and his wife in front of their four children. Mohmoud Al-Aloul, a senior member of the Fatah Central Committee admitted, "The Al-Aqsa Martyrs' Brigades, the military wing of the Palestinian National Liberation Movement Fatah, accepted responsibility for the Itamar operation carried out against settlers, leading to their deaths." Other officials from Fatah and Hamas praised the attack. On September 16-19, 2015, Abbas declared, "The Al-Aqsa [Mosque] is ours ... and **they have no right to defile it with their filthy feet**. We will not allow them to, and **we will do everything in our power to protect Jerusalem ... We bless every drop of blood that has been spilled for Jerusalem, which is clean and pure blood, blood spilled for Allah, Allah willing**. Every Martyr (*Shahid*) will reach Paradise, and everyone wounded will be rewarded by Allah ... We have to prevent them, in any way whatsoever, from entering the Sanctuary. This is our Sanctuary, our Al-Aqsa and our Church [of the Holy Sepulchre]. **They have no right to enter it. They have no right to defile it. We must prevent them**. Let us stand before them with chests bared to protect our holy places." (September 17-19, 2015; Abbas' speech was repeated 19 times.) A leading Muslim cleric in Gaza implored the Palestinians in the West Bank, saying, "This is the grace of Allah. We recall what He did to them in Khaybar. ... You have come of your own volition to be slaughtered on our land ... **Stab**! Oh young men of the West Bank: Attack in a group of three, four, or five. **Attack them in groups. Cut them into body parts.**" **Abbas gave his approval to the murders by stating "We bless you. We welcome every drop of blood spilled in Jerusalem.**" A Muslim driver plowed into a group of Israelis in Tel Aviv, killing many, and then jumped from the car and hacked at the survivors with a meat cleaver, imitating an "educational" video produced by the Palestinian leadership. In one day, four Muslim terror attacks killed three Israelis and wounded scores of other civilians. After young teenagers attacked multiple people and stabbed a 13-year-old boy, the PA hailed one of the young assailants, a 15-year-old boy who was shot dead by the Israelis in self-defense, as a hero and a martyr. **Obama accused Israel of committing terrorism and using excessive force** with the State Department spokesman John Kirby saying, "**Certainly individuals on both sides of this divide have proven capable of and are guilty of acts of terror** ... We're always concerned about **credible reports of excessive use of force against civilians**, and we routinely raise our concerns about that." Obama does not want Jews defending themselves from Muslim terrorist attacks, since he views Jews as second-class citizens whose rights of self-defense are secondary to a Muslim's right to kill them. **Kirby also lied to the press when he blamed Israel for changing the status quo at al Aqsa mosque** by stating, "Certainly, the status quo has not been observed, which has led to a lot of the violence." Ignoring the Palestinian incitement from Abbas and other religious leaders, **Kerry blamed the attacks on Israel** and the settlements by stating, **"There's been a massive increase in settlements over the course of the last years ... Now you have this violence** because there's a frustration that is growing, and a frustration among Israelis who don't see any movement." Throughout this whole ordeal, which is the equivalent of the third intifada, Obama has remained relatively silent regarding Palestinian incitement and their glorification of murdering Jews. On October 16, 2015 **Obama** held a press conference and **declared a moral equivalence between the Palestinians and the Israelis while criticizing relatively non-existent Israeli rhetoric**, which are statements of self-defense, by saying, "We condemn in the strongest possible terms violence directed against innocent people *[Palestinians who knife Israelis and ram them with their car and then are subsequently shot are not innocent victims.]* ... We also believe that's important for **both Prime Minister Netanyahu and Israeli elected officials and President Abbas and other people in positions of power to try to tamp down rhetoric that may feed violence or anger** or misunderstanding and try to get all people in Israel and the West Bank to recognize **this kind of <u>random violence</u> is not going to result in anything."** Obama also downplayed Palestinian attacks, aimed at killing and terrorizing Jews for religious reasons by calling them "random violence." As in Paris, Oregon, Iraq and Libya, Obama won't admit that the Palestinians or Muslims are specifically targeting Jews or Christians. He is protecting and denying the formal jihadi motivations of the Muslim assailants.

i. On November 7, 2015, Vice President Biden doubled down on the administration being an advocate for the moral equivalence between the Palestinian incitement and Israel's identification of the root cause of many of the issues contributing to the recent wave of Palestinian attacks that have led to the murder of over 20 Israelis. Biden stated, "**both sides need to demonstrate restraint and avoid incitement**." Biden is admonishing Israel for the deaths of Palestinians who were shot while attempting to murder Jews via knife attacks and car rammings. Biden also chastised Israel over statements from an Israeli media czar appointee who called Obama anti-Semitic. Biden stated, "there is no excuse, there should be no tolerance for any member or employee of the Israeli administration referring to the president of the United States in derogatory terms. Period. Period. Period. Period." What about Obama's official calling Netanyahu "chickenshit" or Obama's rude behavior directed at Netanyahu at early White House meetings?

m. In mid-October 2015, the State Department released an official tweet condemning the Palestinian attacks on Israeli Jews as "tragic and outrageous," and Obama had the tweet deleted within minutes of its initial appearance.

n.   Within a few days of the anniversary of Kristallnacht, the German pogrom that ush-
     ered in the Holocaust, and the departure of Prime Minister Netanyahu to Israel after
     high-level meetings in Washington, **Obama approved the EU's special labelling of
     Jewish products** originating from East Jerusalem, the Golan and the West Bank, which
     will probably be the first steps leading to an economic boycott of the Jewish state. Mark
     Toner, a spokesperson for the State Department said, "If Israel continues to expand settle-
     ment activity, it shouldn't come as a surprise to – if some in the international community
     pursue steps to limit commercial relations with the settlements … we do not believe that
     labelling the origin of products is equivalent to a boycott. And as you know, we do not
     consider settlements to be part of Israel." Israel is the only state targeted by the EU for
     product labelling and possible boycotts where there are territorial disputes between vari-
     ous political parties. Netanyahu commented, "The labelling of products of the Jewish
     state by the European Union brings back dark memories. Europe should be ashamed of
     itself. It took an immoral decision. Of the hundreds of territorial conflicts around the
     world, it chose to single out Israel and Israel alone, while it's fighting with its back against
     the wall against the wave of terror. The European Union is not going to hurt the Israeli
     economy. It's strong enough to weather this, but it's the Palestinian workers in Israeli en-
     terprises in Judea and Samaria that will be hurt. This will not advance peace." The Nazis
     also forced the Jews to label all their products before the outbreak of WWII, so that the
     German public could boycott Jewish goods and services. Obama is moving slowly to-
     ward a BDS position in early November 2015. **Obama is also supporting political and
     economic attacks on the Israeli tourist industry**, since now it will be illegal in Europe
     to state that the Western Wall or the Dome of the Rock are Israeli attractions.

     i.   The Czech Republic outright rejected the EU's and Obama's support of this preju-
          dicial anti-Israel labelling policy. A Czech official stated that they must "reject the
          efforts to discriminate against the only democracy in the Middle East … if Israel
          fell, Europe would finally fall as well." A Czech MP told the EU foreign relations
          chief Frederica Mogherini, "You wouldn't dare [coerce] Russia to label products
          from Crimea or China to label Tibetan products, or Turkey to label products from
          the Turkish Republic of Northern Cyprus. You dare to do this to Israel and I am
          ashamed of this policy." Greece and Hungary also rejected the EU labelling policy.
          Applying a double standard is anti-Semitism.

o.   UNSC Resolution 2334

p.   On January 18, 2016, the Obama administration showed an insensitivity, if not a bla-
     tant disregard for Jewish lives when **Obama's ambassador to Israel criticized the
     Jewish state while Israel was burying a mother of six who had been murdered by a
     Palestinian terrorist**, in her home, in front of her children, and while another pregnant

Israeli was stabbed by a Palestinian. U.S. Ambassador Shapiro stated, "Too many attacks on Palestinians lack a vigorous investigation or response by Israeli authorities; too much vigilantism goes unchecked; and at times there seem to be two standards of adherence to the rule of law: one for Israelis and another for Palestinians." Shapiro raised "honest questions about Israel's long-term intentions."

q.   "Dr. Ben Carson, an educated African-American ex-chairman of the Department of Neurosurgery at Johns Hopkins Medical School and who was a Republican presidential candidate in 2016, confirmed his belief that Obama was anti-Semitic by stating, "**I think anything is anti-Semitic that is against the survival of a state** that is surrounded by enemies, and by people who want to destroy them. And to sort of ignore that, and to act like everything is normal there, and that these people are paranoid, I think that's anti-Semitic." Carson is an objective observer, being Christian and African-American. Empowering a terrorist state financially and militarily, whose main goal is to destroy Israel, and kill Jews is anti-Semitism. Obama is aware of this daily genocidal rhetoric and Iran's support of organizations that want to kill all the Jews worldwide. Either Iran's intentions are immaterial to him or Obama may quietly agree with the ayatollahs. The latter may be true since Obama not only produced an agreement allowing Iran to go nuclear, but he inserted clauses in the JCPOA for the United States to help Iran defend itself against various Israeli attacks, cyber or otherwise. Obama has allied the United States with Iran against Israel, which reflects the actions of an American leader supporting Iran's political philosophy and that of a Shiite Muslim who is helping the mullahs achieve their worldwide objectives. There was no need to insert a clause in the JCPOA that guaranteed America's assistance to help Iran defend its militarized nuclear facilities, but Obama insisted that supporting Iran against Israel should be part of the deal." *(Unexpected Treason, Chapter 9 – Israel and anti-Semitism, James McCormak, 2016)*

r.   "Obama's disregard for Jewish lives became apparent to the world when he commented in February 2015 on the murder of four Jewish adults at a Paris kosher deli at the hands of an ISIS-trained radical Muslim who asked his victims their religion before he shot the Jews dead. Obama reflected on the event and commented, "It is entirely legitimate for the American people to be deeply concerned when you've got a bunch of violent, vicious zealots who behead people or randomly shoot a bunch of folks in a deli in Paris." There are four major points that deserve scrutiny and reveal Obama's true feelings. First, and most importantly, Obama dehumanized the Jewish victims by calling them simply a "bunch of folks" and would not recognize they were murdered explicitly because they were Jewish. Second, he would not recognize that the crime occurred in a kosher deli, where the perpetrator knew he could target Jews; he called the crime scene simply a "deli in Paris." Third, he refused to identify the assailants as Muslims and ignored that they were motivated by their religious obligation as Muslims to kill Jews by calling the killers "violent, vicious zealots." And fourth, he is denying the victims were singled out for their Jewish religion by using the phrase "randomly shot." There is nothing random about selecting a kosher deli where one knows Jews will congregate, and then asking for the religion of your hostages and subsequently killing the one identified as Jews. All these observations from this one incident support the obvious conclusion that Obama is an anti-Semite … Obama refused to attend the Paris rally that mobilized world leaders to condemn the attacks on the Jews at the deli and the murder of the *Charlie Hebdo* staff. This again shows Obama stands with the radical Muslims since he would not participate in an event condemning the punishment of blasphemy. Obama stands with radical Islam and would not mourn for those who perished for expressing their political beliefs opposing Sharia law and fighting for their right to criticize Islam. Retired Admiral James Lyons commented on Obama's reaction to events in Paris in early 2015 by reflecting at the National Press Club, "The transformation of America has been in full swing ever since 2008. President Obama's no-show in Paris was an embarrassment for all Americans. But it also was a signal to the Islamic jihadists. It is one of many signals he sent over the years while he's in office." Lyons all but admitted that Obama was allied with the radical Muslims, and all radical Muslims are anti-Semitic." *(Unexpected Treason)*

s. On November 19, 2015, Palestinian terrorists murdered five Jews in Israel and the West Bank, including an 18-year-old American citizen. Obama expressed no outrage at the terrorist act, nor did he make any statement that he would not tolerate the killing of American citizens. Americans were also murdered in terrorist attacks in Paris and Mali, and **Obama said nothing regarding the death of American citizens** he is supposed to protect. As opposed to remaining silent with the death of an American Jew as a result of Palestinian terrorism, the State Department labelled the beating of an Arab-American, who participated in violent Palestinian protests (throwing stones and covering his face with a kaffiyeh) against the Israeli government and suffered only a black eye and a swollen lip, by Israeli police an "outrage." The State Department finally acknowledged the Jewish victim a little less than one week after his murder, but only after multiple complaints were voiced to the Obama administration. Obama waited over one week to express his condolences to the Jewish family and did not send any White House representatives to his funeral.

t. "Obama **allowed anti-Semitism to enter into the debate over the JCPOA**. "Obama's political allies called Democratic Senator Schumer of New York a traitor for not supporting Obama and the JCPOA. When Senator Schumer called Obama to tell him of his decision to oppose the JCPOA before he made a public announcement, the White House prematurely leaked the information to MoveOn.org, which commented, "Our country doesn't need another Joe Lieberman [emphasizing the Jewish background of Lieberman, or "another Jew who supports Israel and not the Democratic leadership"] in the Senate." Reza Marashi who was representing the National Iranian American Institute stated, "shame on Chuck Schumer for putting Israel's interests ahead of America's interests." *The Daily Kos* published a cartoon questioning Senator Schumer's loyalty. The New York Post editorialized, "Anti-Semitism is all over the drive to make Chuck Schumer shut up about his opposition to the Iran nuke deal." Anti-Semitism was present in other facets of the debate. Thomas Friedman editorialized in *The New York Times* that congressional resistance "comes … from a growing tendency by many American lawmakers to do whatever the 'Israel lobby' asks them to do in order to garner Jewish votes and campaign donations." Democratic Jewish Senator Feinstein of California remarked in the Senate that we cannot "let Israel determine when and where the United States goes to war." In January 2015, President Obama warned Senate Democrats in Baltimore that additional sanctions could lead to war, and those favoring increasing sanctions were acting on the behalf of political [Jewish] "donors." *Tablet Magazine* commented in an editorial "Crossing a Line to Sell a Deal," on August 7, 2015, "What we increasingly can't stomach … is the use of Jew-baiting and other blatant and retrograde forms of racial and ethnic prejudice as tools to sell a political deal, or to smear those who oppose it. Accusing Senator Schumer of loyalty to a foreign government is bigotry, pure and simple. Accusing senators and congressmen whose misgivings about the Iran deal are shared by a majority of the U.S. electorate of being agents of a foreign power, or of selling their votes to shadowy lobbyists, or of acting contrary to the best interests of the United States, is the kind of naked appeal to bigotry and prejudice that would be familiar in the politics of the pre-Civil Rights Era South. This use of anti-Jewish incitement as a political tool is a sickening new development in American political discourse, and we have heard too much of it lately – some coming, ominously, from our own White House and its representatives … Murmuring about 'money' and 'lobbying' and 'foreign interests' who seek to drag America into war is a direct attempt to play the dual-loyalty card. It's the kind of dark, nasty stuff we might expect to hear at a white power rally, not from the president of the United States – and it's gotten so blatant that even many of us who are generally sympathetic to the administration, and even this deal, have been shaken by it.'" *(Unexpected Treason)*

u.   "In August 2015, during the heat of the debate on the JCPOA, Obama again relied on anti-Semitic innuendo to advance his war on opponents of the Iranian deal during a conference call with liberal activists. Obama stated critics were opposed to any deal with Iran, were warmongers who were "responsible for getting into the Iraq war," *[Bill Kristol - Weekly Standard publisher - Jewish]* and accused opponents of being "well financed lobbyists" *[AIPAC - Jewish]*, "big check writers to political campaigns" and "billionaires"

[Sheldon Adelson - Jewish] associated with super-PACs. In contrast, Obama had no problem with J Street spending millions of dollars for ads supporting the agreement, or other liberal Jews in favor of the agreement. In an interview with Fareed Zakaria of *CNN*, Obama called Israel's vocal opposition to Iran's future acquisition of nuclear weapons and Netanyahu's protesting the increased risk of a second Holocaust "unprecedented" interference in American affairs, and then added, "I don't recall a similar example." Yet Obama quickly forgot his "unprecedented" interference with the Israeli elections when he tried to organize an electoral defeat for Netanyahu, or when he travelled to Great Britain to lobby against support for Great Britain leaving the European Union. John Kerry declared the administration would **put the blame on Israel if the deal was rejected by the Congress**, even though the overwhelming majority of congressmen allied against the deal were not Jewish, and the American public did not support the agreement by a ratio of almost 2 to 1. Obama even admitted that he was using anti-Semitic tactics in a meeting with Jewish leaders by stating, "It's my birthday and I'm going to be blunt … If **you guys** *[not exactly a term of endearment]* would back down, **I would back down from some of the things I'm doing** *[anti-Semitic rhetoric]*." Obama concluded with "You'd think **they'd** *[the Jews]* would be nicer to me on my birthday." Obama is telling the Jewish leadership of America that they don't have the right to express their political thoughts or advance collective Jewish interests if they are opposed to Obama's policies, or they will face anti-Semitic verbal assaults along with political, economic (IRS audits), and quite possibly physical harassment. With Obama having attended an Islamic religious school for many years and with his embrace of Islamic tenets, Obama may be treating the Jews as second-class citizens or *dhimmis*, as is done throughout the Islamic world. The basic concerns of the American Jewish leadership focus on the best policy to prevent Iran from developing nuclear weapons and using them against Israel, in order to avoid a second Holocaust. In contrast, Obama responded with threats and prejudice. His actions and words do not reflect the civility he promised at the Tucson memorial services associated with the shooting of Representative Gabby Giffords in 2011, when he stated "to listen to each other more carefully, to sharpen our instincts for empathy … usher in more civility in our public discourse." It appears that Obama does not live up to the lofty ethical standards he established in his eloquent speeches. Would Obama treat the collective concerns of other minorities with such rhetoric and disdain? African Americans, Hispanics, Muslims, Occupy Wall Street activists? Highly doubtful. Applying a double standard is anti-Semitism." *(Unexpected Treason)*

v.   "Despite knowing that Islam has bloody borders, that there are basically no indigenous Jews in Islamic countries, and that the Christian populations in Islamic countries are shrinking exponentially, Obama states "Islam has a proud tradition of tolerance." Obama

opposed General Sisi's coup against the Muslim Brotherhood in Egypt, and even opposed Sisi when he called for an Islamic revolution where violence against non-Muslims
should be purged from Islam. Despite the strong backing of ISIS and al-Qaeda among
the Muslims worldwide, as demonstrated in multiple international polls, Obama states,
"Islam is not part of the problem in combating violent extremism, it is an important
part of promoting peace." Despite the many fatwas that have been issued by clerics at
Al-Azhar in Egypt against infidels and apostates, which have led to their harassment
and death, Obama declared, "For over a thousand years, Al-Azhar has stood as a beacon
of Islamic learning." At the UN, Obama defended Islam and attacked people critical
of Islamic violence and Islamic incitement to violence in the Quran by declaring to
the world, "The future must not belong to those who slander the prophet of Islam."
Whenever Obama quotes from or makes a reference to the Quran, he calls it the "Holy"
Quran and refers to Mohammed as "the Prophet Mohammed," but does not refer to
the Torah or the Christian Bible as "the Holy Torah" or "the Holy Bible." Nor does he
refer to Abraham as "the Prophet Abraham" or embellish the name of Jesus Christ, who
he supposedly accepts as his Savior. Obama punishes those critical of Islam, (meaning
those who commit blasphemy), as reflected by his arrest of the man who made the video
on which Obama blamed the Benghazi attack, and the multiple apologies for an alleged
Quran desecration to the Afghan nation by multiple senior Obama administration and
military officials, and his failure to attend the Paris rally that defended the freedom
of expression of the cartoonists who satirized Islam as a form of political expression.
Most recently, Obama has been supporting massive Muslim immigration into Europe
and the United States. With these known affinities, it is very likely, if not certain, that
Obama backs the anti-Semitic statements in the Quran and its associated supporting
religious texts. Obama has never recognized anti-Semitism as a component of Islam and
the Quran, just as he has never recognized violence and incitement against infidels as a
real component of the Islamic world. These texts are part of the religious indoctrination
Obama received while studying at the madrassa in Indonesia for many years, and are
well known to him. As a student in Indonesia, Obama was noted to be quite religious
by his friends. The following quotes are dispersed throughout the Quran and the other
religious associated texts, and so it is highly unlikely that Obama is unaware of the
anti-Semitic tenets and genocidal inclinations forming the core belief structure of Islam.
Obama has never criticized anti-Semitism or anti-Christian behavior by Muslims, or any
of the official or accepted harassment of non-Muslims in any Islamic community. It is
highly probable that Obama agrees with the following religious statements and **would
consider it blasphemy to criticize or disagree with such tenets**[300] **that help form the**

core of Islam." *(Unexpected Treason)* Obama is enamored with the Quran and Islamic religious doctrine. Obama is an anti-Semite.

- **"Strongest among men in enmity to the believers** wilt thou **find the Jews**." Quran (5:82).
- "Say (O Muhammad): **O ye who are Jews**! If ye claim that ye are favoured of Allah apart from (all) mankind, **then long for death** if ye are truthful." Quran (62:6)
- **"The last hour would not come unless the Muslims will fight against the Jews** and the Muslims would kill them until the Jews would hide themselves behind a stone or a tree and **a stone or a tree would say**: **Muslim, or** the servant **of Allah, there is a Jew behind me; come and kill him**; but the tree Gharqad would not say, for it is the tree of the Jews." *Sahih Muslim Book 041, Hadith Number 6985.* This passage is found in the Hamas Charter.
- **Khaybar war chant**: "Khaybar, Khaybar, **O Jews**, the army of Muhammad will **return**." *Chanted on the Turkish boat Mavi Marmara, which attempted to break the Gaza blockade early in Obama's presidency.* This chant commemorates Mohammed's victory over the Jews in Saudi Arabia, which resulted in their extermination in that country. This is also chanted at Muslim anti-Israel protests around the world.
- "And when judgment day arrives, **Allah will give every Muslim a Jew or a Christian to kill**." Mohammed says in the *"Mishkat Al Masabih,"* Vol. 2. No. 555.
- "Those whom Allah has cursed and put far away from His mercy and with whom he is angry-turning some of them into **monkeys and into pigs** by transmogrification - and who worshipped false gods. **These are the Jews**." Quran (5:60). The Quran is the direct source of Muslims demeaning Jews worldwide by calling them the descendants of "apes and pigs."
- **"Curses were pronounced on those among the Children of Israel** who rejected Faith, by the tongue of David and of Jesus the son of Mary: because they disobeyed and persisted in excesses." Quran (5:78).
- "O ye who believe! **Take not the Jews and the Christians for your friends** and protectors: They are but friends and protectors to each other. And he amongst you that turns to them (for friendship) is of them." Quran (5:51).
- **"Let not the believers Take for friends or helpers Unbelievers** rather than believers: if any do that, in nothing will there be help from Allah." Quran (3:28).
- **"Fight those who believe not in Allah** nor the Last Day, nor hold that forbidden which hath been forbidden by Allah and His Messenger, nor acknowledge the religion of Truth, (even if they are) of the People of the Book, **until they pay the Jizya with willing submission, and feel themselves subdued**." Quran (9:29).

- "Surah 9 is a command to disavow all treaties with polytheists and to subjugate Jews and Christians (9.29) so that Islam may 'prevail over all religions' (9.33). It is fair to wonder whether any non-Muslims in the world are immune from being attacked, subdued or assimilated under this command. Muslims must fight, according to this final chapter of the Quran, and if they do not, then their faith is called into question and they are counted among the hypocrites (9.44-45)."[301] Treaties between Israel and radical Muslim organizations such as Hamas or the Palestinian Authority are generally worthless in the long run.

- "**When you meet the unbelievers, smite their necks**, then, when you have made wide slaughter among them, tie fast the bonds; then set them free, either by grace or ransom, till the war lays down its loads." Quran (47:4).

- "When thy Lord was revealing to the angels, ´I am with you; so confirm the believers. I shall cast into the unbelievers' hearts terror; so smite above the necks, and smite every finger of them!" Quran (8:12).

- "In the name of God, the Merciful, the Compassionate; Praise belongs to G-d, the Lord of all Being; the All-Merciful, the All-Compassionate, the Master of the Day of Doom. Thee only we serve; to Thee alone we pray for succor. **Guide us in the straight path**, The path of those whom Thou hast blessed, **not of those against whom Thou art wrathful** [Jews], nor of those who are astray." *Quran, first chapter, repeated five times per day by Muslims.* Obama recited this prayer with a perfect Arabic accent in a *New York Times* interview with Nicholas Kristof, thus he is quite familiar with the anti-Semitic overtones in Islam. Obama himself may repeat this prayer five times per day as well.

- "Allah hath heard the taunt of those who say: 'Truly, Allah is indigent and we are rich!' We shall certainly record their word and (their act) of slaying the prophets in defiance of right, and We shall say: '**Taste ye the penalty of the Scorching Fire**!'" Quran (3:181).

- "The People of the Book know well that that is the truth from their Lord. Nor is Allah unmindful of what they do." Quran (2:143-144).

- **The Jews** "strive to do mischief on earth" [and will be punished] "**they will be killed or crucified**, or have their hands and feet on alternate sides cut off, or will be **expelled out of the land**. That is a degradation for them in this world." Quran (5:33).

- "**And because of their breaking their covenant, we have cursed them** and made hard their hearts. They change words from their context and forget a part of that whereof they were admonished. **Thou wilt not cease to discover treachery from all** save a few of them." Quran (5:13).

- "O Messenger! let not those grieve thee, who race each other into unbelief: (whether it be) among those who say 'We believe' with their lips but whose hearts have no faith; or it be among the Jews … **For them there is disgrace in this world**, and in the Hereafter a heavy punishment." Quran (5:41).

- "There is a party of them **who distort the Scripture with their tongues** [Jews], that ye may think that what they say is from the Scripture, when it is not from the Scripture. And they say: It is from Allah, when it is not from Allah; and they speak a lie concerning Allah knowingly." Quran (3:78).

- "But because of their breach of their covenant, **We cursed them, and made their hearts grow hard**; they change the words from their (right) places and forget a good part of the message that was sent them, nor wilt thou cease to find them - barring a few - ever bent on (new) deceits." Quran (5:13).

- "And when there comes to them a Book from Allah … they refuse to believe in it but **the curse of Allah is on those without Faith**." Quran (2:89).

- "**And prepare against them what force you can** and horses tied at the frontier, to frighten thereby the enemy of Allah and your enemy and others besides them, whom you do not know (but) Allah knows them; and **whatever thing you will spend in Allah's way, it will be paid back to you fully** and you shall not be dealt with unjustly." Quran (8:60).

- "**Fighting is prescribed for you**, and ye dislike it. But it is possible that ye dislike a thing which is good for you, and that ye love a thing which is bad for you. But Allah knoweth, and ye know not." Quran (2:216).

- "**Whoso fighteth** in the way of Allah, be he slain or be he victorious, on him **We shall bestow a vast reward**." Quran (4:74)

- "**As to those who reject faith, I will punish them with terrible agony in this world** and in the Hereafter, nor will they have anyone to help." Quran (3:56).

- "**Soon shall We cast terror into the hearts of the Unbelievers**." Quran (3:151).

- "We are disassociated from you and from whatever you worship other than Allah. We have rejected you, and there has arisen, between us and you, **enmity and hatred forever until you believe in Allah alone**." Al-Mumtahanah 4 [i.e., Quran (60:4)].

- "**When you meet your enemies** who are polytheists [or non-Muslims], invite them to **three courses of action**. If they respond to any one of these, you also accept it and withhold yourself from doing them any harm. **Invite them to (accept) Islam**; if they respond to you, accept it from them and desist from fighting against them

... **If they** refuse to accept Islam, **demand from them the Jizya**. If they agree to pay, accept it from them and hold off your hands. If they refuse to pay the tax, seek Allah's help and **fight them** [**kill them**]." Mohammed quote, Sahih Muslim, Book 019, Number 4294.

- "If anyone desires a religion other than Islam (submission to Allah), never will it be accepted of him." Quran (3:85).
- "**Fight and slay the Pagans** (**idolaters**) wherever ye find them, and seize them, beleaguer them, and lie in wait for them in every stratagem (of war)." Quran (9:5).
- "I was ordered to **fight all men until they say 'there is no god but Allah.'**" *Mohammad's farewell address, 632.*
- "the **most vile of created beings**." Quran (98:6), reference to non-Muslims.
- "Those who disbelieve our revelations. **We shall expose them to fire. As often as their skins are consumed**. We shall exchange them for fresh skins that **they may taste the torment**." Quran (4:56).
- "Muhammad is the apostle of Allah. Those who follow him are merciful to one another, but **ruthless to the unbelievers**." Quran (48:29).
- "O Prophet! **Strive hard against the unbelievers** and the hypocrites and be un-yielding to them; and **their abode is hell, and evil is the destination**." Quran (9:73).
- "O you who believe! **Fight those of the unbelievers who are near to you and let them find in you hardness**." Quran (9:123).
- Abu Hurayra reported that the Prophet said, "Do not give the **People of the Book** the greeting first. **Force them to the narrowest part of the road**." Al-Bukhari, Al-Adab al-Mufrad, 1103.
- "Verily, those who disbelieve from among the people of the Scripture and Al-Mushrikun **will abide in the Fire of Hell**. They are **the worst of creatures**." Quran (98:6).
- "And **kill them [unbelievers, infidels] wherever you find them**, and turn them out from where they have turned you out. And Al-Fitnah [disbelief or unrest] is worse than killing … And **fight them until there is no more Fitnah** [disbelief and worshipping of others along with Allah] and worship is for Allah alone. But if they cease, let there be no transgression except against Az-Zalimun (the polytheists, wrong-doers)" Quran (2:191 - 193). Translation from the Noble Quran.
- "**Fight them until all opposition ends** and all submit to Allah." Quran (8:39).
- "I will fight them until they are like us." Muslim (31:5917).
- "Then **fight in the cause of Allah**, and know that Allah Heareth and knoweth all things." Quran (2:244).

- "**Arabs** [*Obama's paternal family is from Sudan, an Arab country – Obama has Arabic lineage.*] **are the most noble people in lineage**, **the most prominent**, and the best in deeds [*source of misguided Muslim supremacism*]. We were the first to respond to the call of the Prophet. We are Allah's helpers and the viziers of His Messenger. We fight people until they believe in Allah. He who believes in Allah and His Messenger has protected his life and possessions from us. **As for one who disbelieves, we will fight him forever in the Cause of Allah. Killing him is a small matter to us**." Tabari IX:69.
- The morning after the murder of Ashraf, the Prophet declared, "**Kill any Jew who falls under your power**." Tabari 7:97.
- "The Messenger of Allah said: **I have been commanded to fight against people till they testify that there is no G-d but Allah**, that Muhammad is the messenger of Allah." Muslim (1:33).
- "**Killing Unbelievers** is a **small matter** to us." Tabari (9:69). Muhammad quote.

4. "I don't think any country would find it acceptable to have missiles raining down on the heads of their citizens … The first job of any nation state is to protect its citizens … if somebody was sending rockets into my house where my two daughters sleep at night, **I'm going to do everything in my power to stop that. And I would expect Israelis to do the same thing**."[302] *Obama, December, 2008, before assuming the presidency.* Obama supported Hamas in the ceasefire negotiations with Israel in 2014 after they fired thousands of missiles at Israeli civilian targets and depleted their inventory of rockets and missiles.

5. Obama always intended to allow Iran to become a nuclear power, but in 2009, he tried to **mislead Israel into believing that if they supported a two-state solution with East Jerusalem as the capital of the Palestinian state, then Iran would not become a nuclear power**. Hillary Clinton told the House of Representatives Appropriations Committee in April 2009, that Arab countries "believe that Israel's willingness to re-enter into discussions with the PA strengthens them in being able to deal with Iran." An Obama official stated, "The order is first a Palestinian state, and then Iran." *Wikileaks* revelations demonstrated that the Gulf state countries with Egypt and Jordan backed policies that would prevent Iran from becoming a nuclear power and did not link them with Israel's negotiations with the Palestinians. Saudi King Abdullah beseeched Obama to "cut off the head of the [Iranian] snake." Arab leaders were more concerned with weakening Iran than supporting the Palestinians. **Obama lied** to the Israelis.

6. "Polls of Israelis and **Palestinians** show there is still strong **support for the two-state solution**." *Secretary of State Kerry, December 2016.* "A two-state solution … **the vast majority of** Israelis and **Palestinians, they think that it is the right way to go**." *Vice President Biden,*

December 2014. "Consistently over the last decade, **polling on both sides reveals majority support for the two-state solution**." *Martin Indyk, Obama appointed special envoy for Israeli - Palestinian negotiations, May 2014*. "Let me be clear: The United States strongly supports the goal of two states, Israel and Palestine, living side by side in peace and security. **That is a goal shared by Palestinians**, Israelis, and people of goodwill around the world." *Obama, April 2009*. "There are certain aspirations that we all share – to get an education, to provide for our families, to practice our faith freely, **to live in peace** and security." *John Brennan, CIA Director in the Obama administration*. Morton Klein, President of the Zionist Organization of America, published an editorial refuting the belief that the Palestinians seek peace with the two – state solution. "However, the idea that Palestinians prioritize peace, statehood and prosperity flies in the face of reality. Consistent polling of Palestinians tells a diametrically opposite story. For example, a June 2016 joint poll conducted by the Israel Democracy Institute and the Palestinian Center for Policy and Survey Research (PSR) found that **58% of West Bank Palestinians oppose a Palestinian state involving mutual recognition between Israel and the envisaged Palestinian state** and an end of claims. For another, the June 2015 Palestine Center for Public Opinion poll found that, for the near term (the next five years), **49% of Palestinians support** "**reclaiming all of historic Palestine from the river to the sea**," while only 22% favored "a two-state solution" as the "main Palestinian national goal." Indeed, Daniel Polisar of Jerusalem's Shalem College, in a recent examination of literally hundreds of Palestinian surveys, established that majorities of **Palestinians reject Palestinian statehood alongside Israel <u>by an average of more than 3 to 1</u>** … In the past month, official Palestinian Authority (PA) TV <u>joined</u> the family of a jailed Palestinian terrorist, As'ad Zo'rob, who murdered an Israeli who had given him a ride, lauding him as a "heroic prisoner" and a source of "pride for …. all of Palestine." … Fatah Central Committee member and Commissioner of Treasury and Economy, Muhammad Shtayyeh, publicly reaffirmed that Fatah, Mahmoud Abbas' party, which controls the PA, "does not recognize Israel. The topic of recognition of Israel has not been raised in any of Fatah's conferences." The PA, after all, is a regime that names schools, streets, sports teams and youth camps in honor of suicide bombers, pay stipends to jailed terrorists and pensions to the families of dead ones. It also routinely denies that Jews have any connection with Jerusalem or the land."[303]

7. US ambassador to the UN Susan Rice stated in 2011, when the U.S. vetoed a UN resolution condemning Israeli settlements that this "should not be misunderstood to mean we support settlement activity … Unfortunately, **this draft resolution risks hardening the positions of both sides and could encourage the parties to stay out of negotiations**." Less than one month before Obama left office, he instructed his UN ambassador to support a UN resolution which referred to East Jerusalem and the Western Wall as occupied territory which belonged to the Palestinians. Obama misled the Israelis and the American public in 2011,

pretending to support Israel, since if he allowed this resolution to pass, he would probably have been a one-term president. Obama waited and staged his attack against the Jewish state until weeks before he left his presidency, since there would be no political repercussions for him at this time.

8. "The United States' long-standing position - that Israeli settlement activity in territories occupied in 1967 undermines Israel's security, harms the viability of a negotiated two-state outcome, and erodes prospects for peace and stability in the region. **Today, the Security Council** *[with Obama's support and agreement]* **reaffirmed its established consensus that settlements have no legal validity**." *U.S. Ambassador Samantha Power to the UN, Explanation of Vote at the Adoption of UNSC Resolution 2334 on the Situation in the Middle East, December 23, 2016.*

    a. **The Balfour Declaration** (1917): "His Majesty's government view with favour the **establishment in Palestine of a national home for the Jewish people**, and will use their best endeavours to facilitate the achievement of this object, it being clearly understood that nothing shall be done which may prejudice the civil and religious rights of existing non-Jewish communities in Palestine, or the rights and political status enjoyed by Jews in any other country." *Arthur James Balfour, British Secretary of State for Foreign Affairs*

        i.   Originally, the Jewish national home included vast territories east of the Jordan River, but by the early 1920s, this territory which eventually became Trans-Jordan, was assigned to the Arab Hashemites. Thus, this early partition could be considered the first two-state solution, where the Arabs obtained almost 80% of the territory originally assigned to the Jews. The Jewish national home lost all territories east of the Jordan River.

        ii. "The [Balfour] Declaration was endorsed at the time by several of the Allied Governments; it was reaffirmed by the Conference of the Principal Allied Powers at San Remo in 1920; it was subsequently endorsed by unanimous resolutions of both Houses of the Congress of the United States; it was embodied in the Mandate for Palestine approved by the League of Nations in 1922; it was declared, in a formal statement of policy issued by the Colonial Secretary in the same year, 'not to be susceptible of change.' "[304]

        iii. In 1920, the Mandate for Palestine assigned all the territories west of the Jordan River and in what was to become Trans-Jordan, as land belonging to the Jewish national homeland. **By the time the Mandate for Palestine was finalized in 1922, the Jewish Homeland was legally assigned all the territory west of the Jordan River**, which presently includes pre-1967 Israel, the West Bank, and the Golan Heights.

iv. In 1923, **the British and the French transferred the Golan Heights**, which was originally part of the Jewish national home, **to French-occupied Syria**. The Jewish national home lost the Golan Heights.

b. "When it is asked what is meant by **the development of the Jewish National Home in Palestine**, it may be answered that it is not the imposition of a Jewish nationality upon the inhabitants of Palestine as a whole, but **the further development of the existing Jewish community**, with the assistance of Jews in other parts of the world, in order that it may become a centre in which the Jewish people as a whole may take, on grounds of religion and race, an interest and a pride. But in order that this community should have the best prospect of free development and provide a full opportunity for the Jewish people to display its capacities, **it is essential that it should know that <u>it is in Palestine as of right</u> and not on sufferance**." *Winston Churchill, British Secretary of State for the Colonies, June 1922.* In 1919, President Woodrow Wilson "agreed than in Palestine shall be laid the foundation of a **Jewish Commonwealth**." On June 30, 1922, the U.S. Congress passed a resolution supporting Palestine as the "national home for the Jewish people," and further stated, "That the United States of America favors the establishment in Palestine of a **national home for the Jewish people**." In September 1922, President Harding signed a congressional resolution supporting the creation of a Jewish National Home in Palestine.

c. <u>**The Palestine Mandate**</u> (1922): <u>**The Council of the League of Nations: Preamble:**</u> Whereas the Principal Allied Powers have agreed, for the purpose of giving effect to the provisions of **Article 22** of the Covenant of the League of Nations, [Article 22: To those colonies and territories which as a consequence of the late war have ceased to be under the sovereignty of the States which formerly governed them and which are **inhabited by peoples not yet able to stand by themselves** under the strenuous conditions of the modern world, there should be applied the principle that the **well-being and development of such peoples form a sacred trust of civilization** and that securities for the performance of this trust should be embodied in this Covenant … Certain communities formerly belonging to the Turkish Empire have reached a stage of development where their existence as independent nations can be provisionally recognized subject to the rendering of administrative advice and assistance by a Mandatory until such time as they are able to stand alone. The wishes of these communities must be a principal consideration in the selection of the Mandatory] to entrust to a Mandatory selected by the said Powers **the administration of the territory of Palestine**, which **formerly belonged to the Turkish Empire**, within such boundaries as may be fixed by them; and Whereas the Principal Allied Powers have also agreed that the Mandatory should be responsible for putting into effect the declaration originally made on November 2nd, 1917, by the Government of His Britannic Majesty, and adopted by the said Powers, in favor of <u>**the establishment**</u>

in Palestine of a national home for the Jewish people, it being clearly understood that nothing should be done which might prejudice the civil and religious rights of existing non-Jewish communities in Palestine, or the rights and political status enjoyed by Jews in any other country; and **Whereas recognition has thereby been given to the historical connection of the Jewish people with Palestine and to the grounds for <u>reconstituting their national home in that country</u>**; and … **Article 2**: The Mandatory shall be responsible for placing the country under such political, administrative and economic conditions as **will secure the establishment of the Jewish national home**, as laid down in the preamble, and the development of self-governing institutions, and also for **safeguarding the civil and religious rights of all the inhabitants of Palestine**, irrespective of race and religion. **Article 4**: **An appropriate Jewish agency shall be recognized as a public body for the purpose of advising and co-operating with the Administration of Palestine** in such economic, social and other matters as may affect the establishment of the Jewish national home and the interests of the Jewish population in Palestine, and, subject always to the control of the Administration to assist and **take part in the development of the country**. The Zionist organization, so long as its organization and constitution are in the opinion of the Mandatory appropriate, shall be recognized as such agency. It shall take steps in consultation with His Britannic Majesty's Government to secure the co-operation of all Jews who are willing to **assist in the establishment of the Jewish national home**. **Article 5**: The Mandatory shall be responsible for seeing that **no Palestine territory shall be ceded or leased to, or in any way placed under the control of the Government of any foreign Power**. **Article 6**: The Administration of Palestine, while ensuring that the rights and position of other sections of the population are not prejudiced, **<u>shall facilitate Jewish immigration</u> under suitable conditions and shall encourage, in co-operation with the Jewish agency** referred to in Article 4, **<u>close settlement by Jews on the land</u>, including State lands and waste lands not required for public purposes** … **Article 7**: The Administration of Palestine shall be responsible for enacting a nationality law. There shall be included in this law provisions framed so as to facilitate the **acquisition of Palestinian citizenship by Jews** who take up their permanent residence in Palestine … **Article 9**: The Mandatory shall be responsible for seeing that the judicial system established in Palestine shall assure to foreigners, as well as to natives, a complete guarantee of their rights. **Respect for the personal status of the various peoples and communities and for their religious interests shall be fully guaranteed**. In particular, the control and administration of Wakfs shall be exercised in accordance with religious law and the dispositions of the founders … July 24, 1922."

i.   The Mandate for Palestine was a legally binding document that assigned all of modern Israel, the Golan Heights, the West Bank, and East Jerusalem as the legal basis for the Jewish National Homeland. All fifty-one nations of the League of Nations, supported this declaration. Since this document is still legally binding, any attempt to prevent Jews from settling in the West Bank or East Jerusalem is illegal. The Mandate for Palestine has never been legally repealed, rescinded, or replaced with an overriding internationally recognized legal document or agreement. The Arabs were given four other mandates in Lebanon, Syria, Iraq and Trans-Jordan.

ii. The Mandate recognizes the historic connection of the Jewish people with the all of Palestine including the West Bank, encourages Jewish immigration and "close settlement" of Jews to Palestine, and makes illegal "any foreign power" control of Palestine. Since Jews have lived in the West Bank and East Jerusalem for thousands of years, the Mandate recognizes Jewish rights in these territories, and includes the right of settlement and maintaining a community. Thus, the Mandate legalizes Jewish settlement in the West Bank and East Jerusalem, which contradicts Obama's legal position on Israeli settlements, and proves UNSC 2334 has no legal standing. The Palestinian Authority can be viewed as a foreign power in the context of Palestine since it has strong alliances with al-Qaeda, the Muslim Brotherhood and Iran, and because a large percentage of the Palestinian Muslim population has immigrated to Israel and the West Bank since the conception of the Mandate for Palestine, and can be viewed as a foreign entity with respect to the original population of the region and the fact that these territories were assigned for the establishment of a Jewish homeland.

iii. "The Mandate for Palestine, an historical League of Nations document, laid down the Jewish legal right to settle anywhere in western Palestine, a 10,000-square-miles area between the Jordan River and the Mediterranean Sea. The legally binding document was conferred on April 24, 1920 at the **San Remo Conference**, and its terms outlined in the **Treaty of Sèvres** on August 10, 1920. The Mandate's terms were **finalized and unanimously approved on July 24, 1922, by the Council of the League of Nations**, which was comprised at that time of 51 countries, and became operational on September 29, 1923. The "Mandate for Palestine" was not a naive vision briefly embraced by the international community in blissful unawareness of Arab opposition to the very notion of Jewish historical rights in Palestine. The Mandate weathered the test of time: On April 18, 1946, when the League of Nations was dissolved and its assets and duties transferred to the United Nations, the international community, in essence, reaffirmed the validity of this international accord and reconfirmed that the terms for a Jewish National Home were the will of the international community, a "sacred trust" – despite the fact that by then it was patently clear that the Arabs opposed a Jewish National Home, no matter what the form." *(Mandate for Palestine, The Legal Aspects of Jewish Rights, Eli E. Hertz, www.mythsandfacts.org)*

    iv.   The Mandate for Palestine did not grant any political rights or guarantees of statehood to Arabs within the 1922 boundaries that established the Jewish National Home.

d. **Chapter 12**, **Article 80 of the UN Charter** recognized and perpetuated the legal validity of the Mandate of Palestine established by the League of Nations in 1922. This included the rights of Jews to settle in territory between the Jordan River and the Mediterranean Sea.

e. In 1947, the **UN attempted to partition the Jewish national home with UN General Assembly Resolution 181**, which was non-binding between the Jews and the Arabs. Since the Arabs never accepted the borders of this partition, formerly voted against the plan, and immediately declared war with the establishment of the Jewish State in 1948, the partition boundaries were not legally binding, since they were never accepted by surrounding Arab countries. The Arab Muslims never recognized the right of a Jewish state to exist. The Arabs never tried to establish their own state or a Palestinian state within the boundaries established by the 1947 partition when they controlled the majority of that territory between 1947 and 1967, thus proving that establishing an Arab state in the West Bank and East Jerusalem was not a priority. The Jewish national home lost the West Bank and East Jerusalem.

f. The **1949 "Green Line" or armistice demarcation lines** were ceasefire lines and were never recognized as legally binding permanent definitive borders. Each party was still entitled to pursue its claims, and the legal parameters of the Mandate of Palestine was still in effect.

g. UN Resolution 242 supported the Mandate since it allowed Israel to keep territory guaranteed to it by the Mandate in order to maintain "secure borders."

h. This puts quite a different spin on Israeli behavior from that which Kerry presents. For him, it is Israel that keeps trying to deny the "Palestinians" everything, whereas it is those same "Palestinians" under Abbas as under Arafat, who have turned down Israeli offers, and most important, continue to refuse even to recognize Israel as a Jewish state. The list of Arab refusals starts with the Partition Plan of 1947, then the refusal to make the armistice lines of 1949 into permanent borders as offered by Israel, then the further refusal, for 12 years after the Six-Day War, by all the Arab states to recognize, or to negotiate, or to make peace with Israel (the Three No's of Khartoum) until Sadat made his separate peace.

i. Other facts supporting Israel's legal rights to Israel, the West Bank, and East Jerusalem:

i.   Kerry ignored Article 80 of the UN Charter and the Mandate of Palestine, since he knew these internationally legally binding documents supported Israel's right to at least maintain settlements in the West Bank.

ii.   There has never been an independent sovereign Arab / Muslim nation in Palestine.

iii. There has never been an Arab Muslim Palestinian state in Palestine.

iv.   The Palestinian people were invented in the 1960s as a political counterweight to Zionism and a Jewish state. The Palestinians are primarily Muslim Arabs from Jordan, Egypt, and Saudi Arabia, who immigrated to the Jewish national home in order to obtain work from the Jewish community or to commit jihad against the Jews.

v.   Jerusalem has never been an Arab or Muslim capitol.

vi.   Jerusalem is never mentioned in the Quran.

vii. The 1947 UN partition of Palestine was divided between Jews and Arabs, and not between Jews and Palestinians.

viii. The Arabs made no attempt to establish a Palestinian state in the West Bank or Gaza between 1947 and 1967, when these respective territories were under the control of Jordan and Egypt. The "Palestinians" made no attempts during these two decades to assert their independence.

ix.   Israel won the 1967 war, which was a defensive war, thus is legally entitled to keep the territories relinquished by Jordan.

x.   After the 1967 Six-Day War, Israel offered the West Bank to Jordan in exchange for a permanent peace agreement, and the Arab League responded with three nos: no peace, no negotiations, no recognition.

xi.   With relatively non-stop terrorist attacks against the Jewish state from all surrounding Arab neighbors, even before Israel controlled the West Bank, Israel has the right to determine its own security requirements, and should not be forced to accept the dictates of third parties, whether they originate from France, the UN, Russia, or the European Union – all of whom have a strong history of anti-Semitism.

xii. Why do the Arab or Palestinian claims to territory in the West Bank or East Jerusalem supersede Israeli claims, especially with the Mandate for Palestine still legally binding and promising a Jewish national home in territories where Jews have a "strong historical" connection to the land.

xiii. With surrounding Arab and Muslim forces, including IRGC and Hezbollah forces to the north, and Palestinian terrorist organizations to the east, Israel has a national and moral obligation to maintain control of territory that provides for an advantageous defense of the Jewish state, especially around Jerusalem, which is a declared target of conquest by Iran, Turkey, ISIS, al-Qaeda, Hezbollah, Hamas, the

Palestinian Authority and the Muslim Brotherhood. President George Bush recognized these threats and promised Israel has the right to maintain "secure and defensible" borders.

xiv. The Palestinians have rejected at least two formal offers by Israel for them to establish a Palestinian state. Arafat rejected an Israeli offer by Prime Minister Barak in 2000 at Camp David to establish a formal Palestinian state, and Abbas rejected an offer from Prime Minister Ohlmert in 2007. These Palestinian rejections of Israeli peace offers prove the Palestinians are only interested in continuing their wars and terrorism, and not recognizing the existence of a Jewish state, rather than living in peace in the region.

xv. The Palestinians and the Arabs have rejected four formal offers by Israel to transfer the West Bank to their control in exchange for peace: Resolution 181 in 1947, post the 1967 War, Arafat at Camp David in 2000, and Abbas with Ohlmert in 2007. These rejections are based on the Muslims complete belief that Jews have no rights to live in the Middle East, and that a Jewish national home promised by the Balfour Declaration and the Mandate for Palestine is an illegitimate aspiration. The Palestinians have always refused to recognize the existence the Jewish state, which is in line with their charter, and negates the precepts of the Mandate for Palestine, which sought to establish a Jewish national home. With all these Muslim rejections of peace offers coupled with the failure of land for peace agreements that occurred in Gaza and southern Lebanon, why should Israel even consider offering the Palestinians any more territory in exchange for future broken promises?

9. In early December 2016, John Kerry lied to the international Jewish community that he would veto "a **biased**, **unfair** resolution calculated **to delegitimize Israel**." Days before the UNSC passed resolution 2334 on December 23, 2016, UN Secretary-General Ban Ki-Moon admitted, "Decades of political maneuverings have created **a disproportionate volume of resolutions, reports and conferences criticizing Israel** … In many cases, rather than helping the Palestinian cause, this reality has hampered the ability of the UN to fulfill its role effectively." Although Ban Ki-Moon acknowledged the UN's obvious bias against Israel, he still supported the UN resolution.

a. The 1920 San Remo Resolution allowed Jews to legally settle on territory west of the Jordan River. With the facts that there has never been a Palestinian state in the West Bank, Israel wrestled East Jerusalem and the West Bank from Jordan in 1967 during a defensive war, and Jews have lived in East Jerusalem and the West Bank for over 3000 years, the West Bank and East Jerusalem are not occupied territories. In 1988, Jordan renounced all claims to these disputed territories, thus any claim that Israel advances on East Jerusalem or the

West Bank is just as a valid as any Palestinian claim to the territory, and probably more so. Yet the text of the resolution is blatantly biased against Israel and states that Israel's settlements have "no legal validity and constitutes a flagrant violation under international law." The Committee for Accuracy for Middle East Reporting in America stated, "Article 49 of the Fourth Geneva Conventions, which is relied upon by those who claim the settlements are illegal, does not apply in the case of the West Bank. This is because the West Bank was never under self-rule by a nation that was a party to the Convention, and therefore there is no "partial or total occupation of the territory of a High Contracting Party," as Article 2 of the Convention specifies. Moreover, even if it did apply, by its plain terms, it applies only to forcible transfers and not to voluntary movement. Therefore, it can't prohibit Jews from choosing to move to areas of great historical and religious significance to them."[305]

b.   The resolution never specifically mentioned Palestinian anti-Israel incitement, and focused on Israel occupation, proves the resolution was biased.

c.   The Palestinian Hamas Charter, which calls for the annihilation of Israel, and the death of all Jews around the world, was never mentioned in resolution 2334.

d.   The resolution which calls for Palestinian control over half of Israel's capital, the Jewish quarter in the old city, and the Jew's holiest site, the Western Wall, proves the resolution was biased.

e.   The resolution, which declares that any construction in East Jerusalem, Israel's capital, is illegal, proves it is biased.

f.   Since the resolution declares that "natural growth" is illegal in East Jerusalem, Obama supports a resolution that states Jews cannot have children in its capital and proves that Obama, Kerry and the resolution are biased against the Jews.

g.   The UN resolution calls for Israel to "refrain from provocative actions," yet the UN wants to force Israel to accepted indefensible boundaries for its state while giving Hamas, Iran, and al-Qaeda a base of operations with which it can attempt to destroy Israel from a more strategic geopolitical platform, is a very provocative anti-Semitic action.

h.   By supporting a UNSC resolution that requested all states to "distinguish, in their relevant dealings, between the territory of the State of Israel and the territories occupied since 1967," Obama sanctioned and approved an international BDS (boycott, divestment, sanctions) campaign against the state of Israel since almost 800,000 Israelis live and work in the West Bank and East Jerusalem. By supporting the passage of this resolution, Obama launched an economic war designed to delegitimize the Jewish state.

10. After UNSC Resolution 2334 passed with Obama's approval, a senior Israeli official stated, "President **Obama and Secretary Kerry are behind this shameful move** against Israel at the UN … the **US administration secretly cooked up with the Palestinians an extreme anti-Israeli resolution behind Israel's back** which would be a tailwind for terror and

boycotts and effectively make the Western Wall occupied Palestinian territory … This is an **abandonment of Israel** which breaks decades of US policy of protecting Israel at the UN … All the signs show that this was **a [diplomatic] hit by Obama** against Netanyahu and the settlements." The Obama administration via deputy national security advisor Ben Rhodes immediately denied Israel's accusations when he stated, "**We did not draft this resolution**; we did not introduce this resolution. **We made this decision when it came up for a vote**." Another senior U.S. official close to Obama stated, "Contrary to some claims, the administration **was <u>not involved in formulating the resolution</u> nor have we promoted it**."

a. About one month before the resolution was passed by the UNSC, New Zealand's foreign minister, **Murray McCully revealed that he had a comprehensive meeting with Secretary of State Kerry in New Zealand on November 13th**, and commented, "It is a conversation we are engaged in **deeply** and we've spent some time talking to Secretary Kerry about where the US might go on this … It is something that is **still in play** … I think there are some very important decisions that the Obama administration is going to have to make in its lame-duck period on this issue." New Zealand, which held a non-permanent rotating seat on the UNSC, was a co-sponsor of Resolution 2334, and worked with Kerry and the Obama administration on the exact wording of the resolution, and the strategy with which to move it forward to a vote at the UNSC. The Obama administration played a central role in allowing the resolution to be approved by the UNSC, and thus lied with its denial of involvement with its formulation and passage.

b. **Vice President Biden called the president of Ukraine** and convinced him / forced him to vote in favor of UNSC Resolution 2334.

c. "An Egyptian paper published what it claims are the transcripts of meetings between top US and Palestinian officials that, if true, would corroborate Israeli accusations that the Obama administration was behind last week's UN Security Council resolution condemning Israeli settlements … **In a meeting in early December with top Palestinian negotiator Saeb Erekat, US Secretary of State John Kerry told the Palestinians that the US was prepared to cooperate** with the Palestinians at the Security Council, Israel's Channel 1 TV said, quoting the Egyptian *Al-Youm Al-Sabea* newspaper. Also present **at the meeting were US National Security Advisor Susan Rice**, and Majed Faraj, director of the Palestinian Authority's General Intelligence Service. Kerry is quoted as saying that he could present his ideas for a final status solution if the Palestinians pledge they will support the proposed framework. The US officials advised the Palestinians to travel to Riyadh to present the plan to Saudi leaders."[306] Days after the passage of UNSC Resolution 2334, Israel's ambassador to the United States announced that Israel had secured definitive evidence that Obama, Kerry and Rice orchestrated the passage of

UNSC Resolution 2334. As Obama negotiated with Iran behind Israel's back when formulating the JCPOA, Obama also negotiated and worked with the Palestinians without Israel's knowledge or input leading the acceptance of UNSC Resolution 2334.

d.   "First of all, that [Obama] didn't have a hand in this. The resolution shows up and they decide to abstain is ridiculous. Does anybody think that Venezuela and New Zealand spent nights slaving over the wording of this resolution? They were the ones who introduced it. Of course not. **This was a US operation all the way**." *Syndicated columnist Charles Krauthammer, Fox News Channel's Special Report, December 26, 2016.*

e.   "**We have it on absolute incontestable evidence that <u>the United States organized, advanced and brought this resolution to the United Nations Security Council</u>**. We will share that information with the incoming administration; some of it is sensitive, it's all true; you saw some of it in the protocol released in the Egyptian paper – there's plenty more, that's just the tip of the iceberg." *Israeli Prime Minister Netanyahu, December 28, 2016.*

f.   During an interview with Israeli journalists, US ambassador to Israel Dan Shapiro revealed that **Obama made the decision to support a UNSC resolution** supporting the Palestinians and declaring that all Israel settlements outside the pre-1967 boundaries were illegal, **during the summer of 2016**. Thus, Obama was working for five months supervising the drafting of the resolution (although it was introduced by other countries), and organizing the support to ensure it would pass the UNSC.

g.   "One veteran foreign policy insider and former government official who requested anonymity in order to speak freely described **senior Obama administration officials as "<u>lying sacks of shit</u>" who routinely feed the press disinformation**. A senior congressional aide who is working on a package of repercussions aimed at the U.N. told the *Free Beacon* the administration is scrambling to provide excuses in response to the breakdown in its own narrative regarding the resolution. "The administration got caught red handed, and now they're talking out of both sides of their mouth," said the source, who was not authorized to speak on record. "First they claimed the resolution was simply not objectionable. Now they say it will actually help advance peace. These denials only look more ridiculous with each passing day as new **evidence surfaces that the White House was behind this anti-Israel resolution**."[307]

h.   ""Anyone with an ounce of common sense knows how the real world works and the United Nations Security Council works. Senegal and Malaysia, some of the countries that sponsored the resolution, don't call the shots there. If Barack Obama and John Kerry and Samantha Power hadn't been speaking for months about the prospect of this resolution and had not been creating a climate inside the security council to let it come forward without firmly saying we will veto any one-sided anti-Israel resolution, no country would have brought that resolution forward. **It only could have been brought forward and passed with explicit United States coordination with other members of the security council**." *Senator Tom Cotton, Fox News Sunday, January 1, 2017.*

i.   "In a lengthy speech last Wednesday to lay out his "vision for Middle East peace," US Secretary of State John Kerry engaged in customary moral turpitude. First, **he lied about the role the United States played in advancing UN Resolution 2334**, which was adopted by the international body's Security Council a week ago Friday. Then he defended his administration's decision to abstain in the vote, rather than veto it, by claiming that the move was "in accordance with American values." He even raised his voice when declaring that the US under **President Barack Obama has never permitted the delegitimization of, or boycotts against, Israel – both of which the resolution enables and promotes (another lie)**. Just ask the Palestinians, who not only lauded it in general but stated outright that it paved the way not only for divestment and sanctions, but for lawsuits at the International Criminal Court at The Hague. And they're right."[308] *(Ruthie Blum, Jerusalem Post op-ed, January 1, 2017)*

11. When Secretary of State John Kerry gave his speech regarding the future of the two-state solution on December 28, 2016, he emphatically repeated, "**We reject the notion that somehow the US was the driving force behind this UN resolution** … The United States did not draft or originate this resolution. Nor did we put it forward *[Obama had other countries introduce his resolution.]* … It was possible that if the resolution were to be balanced, and it were to include references to incitement and to terrorism, *[There was no mention of Palestinian terrorism or the Hamas Charter dedicated to killing all Jews worldwide, or Abbas's stated desire to remove all Jews from the territory under his control, or his refusal to recognize Israel as a Jewish state.]* that it was possible that the United States would then not block it. **If it was balanced and fair**." Obama and Kerry worded the resolution so the PLO, Hamas and their allies including Iran, would control the holiest Jewish and Christian sites in Jerusalem. Most of Kerry's speech and the UN resolution dealt with Israeli settlements, and ignored Palestinian terrorism, incitement and their refusal to recognize Israel as a Jewish state. On December 28, 2016, Ben Rhodes again stated, "What I can tell you with certainty is that we did not draft this resolution, and we did not put this resolution forward." Rhodes is disingenuous and deceptive with his arguments, since he knows that Obama supervised the wording of the resolution, organized its presentation, and colluded with the Palestinians and other enemies of Israel to ensure its passage. After Netanyahu accused Obama of playing games and charades, Rhodes announced that the United States would veto any further anti-Israel resolutions at the UNSC. The major reason that Obama decided to cease his attacks on the Jewish homeland was because he was informed that Russia would veto any further anti-Israel resolutions in the UNSC.

a. "Now, I must express my deep disappointment with the speech today of John Kerry. **A speech that was almost as unbalanced as the anti-Israel resolution passed at the UN last week**. In a speech about peace between Palestinians and Israelis, Secretary **Kerry played lip service to the unremitting campaign of terrorism that has been waged by the Palestinians against the Jewish state for nearly a century**. What he did was to spend most of his speech blaming Israel for the lack of peace by passionately condemning a policy enabling Jews to live in their historic homeland and in their internal capitol Jerusalem. **Hundreds of suicide bombings**, **tens of thousands of rockets**, **millions of Israelis in bomb shelters are not throwaway lines in a speech**. They're the reality that the people of Israel had to endure because of mistaken policies." *Israeli PM Netanyahu responding to Kerry's two-state solution speech on December 28, 2016.*

12. "And I am convinced that there is no short cut to the end of a conflict that has endured for decades. Peace is hard work. <u>**Peace will not come through statements and resolutions at the United Nations**</u> – if it were that easy, it would have been accomplished by now. Ultimately, it is the Israelis and the Palestinians who must live side by side. Ultimately, it is the Israelis and the Palestinians – not us – who must reach agreement on the issues that divide them: on borders and on security, on refugees and Jerusalem. **Ultimately, peace depends upon compromise** among people who must live together long after our speeches are over, long after our [UN] votes [at the Security Council] have been tallied." *Obama, Remarks to the UN General Assembly, September 21, 2011.* Five years later, just weeks before Obama would no longer be president, Obama supported the passage of UNSC Resolution 2334, which declared the West Bank, East Jerusalem, the Jewish Quarter of the old city of Jerusalem, and the Western Wall, were illegally occupied Palestinian territory. The Palestinians have initiated no compromises during the Obama presidency, since Obama has been pressuring, coercing, and threatening Israel throughout his presidency in order to establish a Palestinian terror state supported by Iran in the heart of Israel. Obama unilaterally gave half of Jerusalem to the Palestinians without any input from the Israelis, and completely bypassed all negotiations, so the Palestinians could legally claim all their negotiating demands.

    a. "We are very concerned about trends on the ground and we do have a sense of urgency about the two-state solution. **We will consider all of our options** for advancing our shared objectives of lasting peace between Israelis and Palestinians, but I'm not going to comment on a draft Security Council Resolution." *John Kirby, State Department spokesman, April 14, 2016.* Obama is considering dictating a solution against Israeli interests.

13. Obama tells lie after lie to the attendees of the **2012 annual AIPAC conference**, in order to garner Jewish support for his 2012 presidential campaign. All these lies must be analyzed in relationship to Obama's role in creating, supporting, and lobbying to ensure the passage of UNSC Resolution 2334, which insisted that the Western Wall and the Jewish Quarter

of Jerusalem were occupied Palestinian territories, which Obama wanted transferred to the control of the PLO and Hamas. Obama also insisted that Jews could not have children in East Jerusalem or the West Bank, since the resolution declared the "natural growth" of Jewish communities in these locations was illegal. Obama's UNSC Resolution 2334 also laid the groundwork for an international BDS campaign against Israel. The following are isolated quotes from **Obama's March 2012 speech to AIPAC**.

a.   "Rosy, you've been **a dear friend of mine** for a long time and a tireless advocate for the **unbreakable bonds** between Israel and the United States … You carry with you an extraordinary legacy of more than six decades of friendship between the United States and Israel …"

    i.   In 2012, **the White House Press secretary refused to identify which city the Obama administration identifies as the capital of Israel** – Tel Aviv or Jerusalem. During this time, Republican presidential candidate Romney identified Jerusalem as Israel's capital and stated he would move the U.S. Embassy from Tel Aviv to Jerusalem.

    ii.   "As I told John Kerry on Thursday, friends don't take friends to the [UN] Security Council." *Israeli Prime Minister commenting on Obama and Kerry supporting UN Resolution 2334 that condemns Israel for all West Bank and East Jerusalem "settlements," and declaring that the Western Wall and the Jewish Quarter in Jerusalem are "illegally occupied Palestinian territory."*

    iii.   "By claiming this speech is a framework for peace in the Middle East, **President Obama and John Kerry are playing the Jewish community for fools** … Their recent actions at the United Nations did nothing more than allow President Obama to take a parting shot at Israel and Prime Minister Netanyahu, while at the same time creating new roadblocks to peace. True peace in the region cannot be achieved by isolating Israel in the international community, but rather can only be achieved through direct negotiations between the Israelis and Palestinians." *Republican Jewish Coalition Executive Director Matt Brooks commenting on Kerry's speech and Obama's action regarding UNSC Resolution 2334.*

    iv.   "President Obama **has very negative views on the state of Israel** … He thinks they're the obstruction in the peace process in the Middle East, not the Palestinians or some of the more radical Arab states. In many respects, what he did in this resolution by the Security Council just before Christmas was **try to define the boundaries of the state of Israel**. It's a **rejection of 50 years of bipartisan American foreign policy** that says that the parties in the dispute themselves have to work this out." *Former U.S. ambassador to the UN John Bolton, during a radio interview on New York AM 970, January 1, 2017.*

v. "The way this administration is behaving in its last days of power is like a person who has to leave an apartment because the lease is up, and before they leave they are going to break every window, pull the plumbing out of the walls, and punch holes in the ceiling … Last year the UN took one resolution on Russia, one on Syria, one on North Korea, and one regarding Iran … They had 20 regarding Israel. Anyone – and I don't care how much they hate Israel – anyone with even a tinge of objectivity cannot possibly believe that Israel deserved 20 spankings, and Russia, Iran, North Korea and Syria deserved only one each. I mean, no one in his or her right mind can say that the UN has become anything but a farce, rather than a force." *Former Arkansas Governor and Republican presidential candidate Mike Huckabee, January 2, 2016 interview with The Jerusalem Post.* Huckabee called UNSC Resolution 2334 and Kerry's subsequent speech at the State Department as a "**cowardly betrayal**" of Israel.

vi. Obama **did not visit Israel during his first presidential term**, despite giving a landmark speech in Cairo and later addressing the Turkish parliament. Obama's decision to not visit Israel after his Cairo speech signaled to the Muslim world that he viewed Israel's concerns and priorities as secondary matters.

vii. In 2015, **Michael Oren**, Israel's former ambassador to the United States, published a book, *Ally: My Journey Across the American - Israeli Divide*, in which he stated, "**It turns out that, as bad as things looked between the Obamans and the Israelis from the outside, it was even worse on the inside**." For example:

(1) Obama threatened Netanyahu at their first meeting in 2009 when Obama demanded a complete settlement freeze and said, "Not a single brick … **I know how to deal with people who oppose me**."

(2) Secretary of State **Clinton refused to meet with Ambassador Oren** earlier in Obama's first presidential term.

(3) Oren and Israeli leaders were especially appalled at Obama's linkage of Israel's legitimacy to the Holocaust in his 2009 Cairo speech.

(4) When the Palestinians considered seeking unilateral UN recognition for a future state that may have forced the American government to stop funding the PA, Tom Nides, a State Department official, told Oren "You don't want the f—king UN to collapse because of your f—king conflict with the Palestinians, and you don't want the f—king Palestinian Authority to fall apart either."

(5) UN Ambassador Susan Rice threatened Israel when she told Ambassador Oren "Israel must freeze all settlement activity … otherwise the United States will not be able to protect Israel from Palestinian actions at the UN."

(6) Obama supported the anti-Semitic, anti-Israel, pro-Muslim Brotherhood, and pro-ISIS Turkish Prime Minister Erdogan with Israeli leaders at the White

House, saying, "He's not living in the 16ᵗʰ century *[this is debatable with Erdogan's false flag coup]* … **We could do much worse than having a bunch of Erdogans in the Middle East**."

(a) Obama lied when he was praising Erdogan at the White House with the Israelis. In mid-April 2017, Erdogan ordered the aerial bombings or Kurdish positions in Iraq and Syria, and refused to suspend its operations after the Trump administration requested a halt. Erdogan, as a member of NATO, bombed allies of the United States and NATO. During Obama's presidency, Erdogan also attacked Kurdish positions multiple times and put U.S. troops who were embedded with the Kurds at significant risk.

(b) Former Israeli Defense Minister Moshe Ya'alon described Erdogan by stating, "Erdogan aspires for there to be a Muslim Brotherhood hegemony in the Middle East and is working toward an Islamic Europe." Both of these insights were major foreign policy goals of President Obama.

(c) "Today, three different streams of Islamic extremism aspire to global hegemony, said Ya'alon, who announced he will compete for the Israel premiership in the next elections. "Iranian Shiite Islam, the Sunni Islamic caliphate and the Muslim Brotherhood, led by Erdogan." The Turkish president for years allowed jihadists from across the world to come to Syria and Iraq and return to their countries as skilled fighters, the former minister charged … "Erdogan is acting like a leader of the Muslim Brotherhood and he wants to Islamicize Europe," Ya'alon said. "So when the Europeans demanded he stop this stream [of refugees], what did he ask them? To allow Turks to go to Europe without visas. And what did he tell Turks living in Europe three weeks ago? To increase their birth rates! That's the Islamization of Europe.""[309] *(Times of Israel, June 6, 2017)*

(7) Obama told Oren that America would support Israel in any future war by stating "If war comes, we're with you, [only] because that's what the American people want." *[But it's not what I want.]*

b. "Yes, **we are bound to Israel** because of the **interests that we share** – in security for our communities, prosperity for our people, the new frontiers of science that can light the world. But ultimately it is our common ideals that provide the true foundation for our relationship."

i. Speaker of the House Paul Ryan commented on Obama's support of UNSC Resolution 2334 that after Obama, the new administration would need to "**reverse the damage** done by this administration, and **rebuild our alliance with Israel**."

Ryan also said that Kerry "after allowing this anti-Israel resolution to pass the UN, **has no credibility** to speak on Israeli-Palestinian peace."

c. "That is why **America's commitment to Israel has endured under Democratic and Republican presidents**, and congressional leaders of both parties. In the United States, **our support for Israel is bipartisan**, and that is how it should stay…"

    i. "These acts are **shameful**. They are designed to secure a legacy, and indeed they have: **history will record and the world will fully understand Obama and Kerry as relentless enemies of Israel**." *Senator Ted Cruz of Texas* commenting on the UNSC resolution and the role Obama and Kerry played in its passage.

    ii. "And what was Samantha Power *[and Obama]*, the great anti-genocide campaigner doing while Aleppo and its residents were being reduced to rubble? **Why**, **scheming against Israel**, **of course**! Samantha Power should have resigned over Syria long ago. She decided instead to embrace the hypocrisy of having written a Pulitzer-prize winning book condemning previous American administrations who were bystanders to genocide while becoming one herself. That was bad enough. What we know now is far worse. Aleppo was ignored as she focused instead on the condemning the Jewish state. Earth to Samantha: 500,000 Arabs died in Syria. Do you really think the problem in the Middle East is Jews building extra bedrooms in communities in Beit-El? You couldn't pass even one United Nations Security Council Resolution condemning Russia, Syria, and Iran for the slaughter in Syria. But you passed this motion condemning peace-loving Jews who live in the ancient Biblical lands of Judea and Samaria? … adopting a policy of humiliating silence as Iran threatened genocide against Israel and actual genocides were carried out in parts of Africa and the Middle East."[310] *(Rabbi Shmuley Boteach, The Jerusalem Post, December 26, 2016)* Obama is prejudiced against Israel and the Jews.

    iii. In December 2012, at the Saban Forum, Secretary of State Clinton harshly criticized Israel by stating, "So, look, I'm not making excuses for the missed opportunities of the Israelis, or the **lack of generosity**, **the lack of empathy** that I think goes hand-in-hand with the suspicion. So, yes, **there is more that the Israelis need to do to really demonstrate that they do understand the pain of an oppressed people** in their minds, and they want to figure out, within the bounds of security and a Jewish democratic state, what can be accomplished." Clinton made this statement against the backdrop of Hamas targeting missiles at civilian Israel communities.

d. "But as you examine my commitment, you don't just have to count on my words. You can look at my deeds. Because over the last three years, as president of the United States,

I have kept my commitments to the state of Israel. At every crucial juncture – at every fork in the road – we have been there for Israel. Every single time."

i. "This fits the pattern of the Obama administration. **Punishing American allies** and **accommodating American enemies**." *Stephen Hayes, editor of The Weekly Standard, Fox News, December 26, 2016. Discussions regarding the passage of UNSC Resolution 2334.*

ii. "**We are <u>outraged</u>** over the U.S. failure to veto this biased and unconstructive UNSC resolution on Israel … This resolution will do little to renew peace efforts between Israel and the Palestinians. It will only **encourage further Palestinian intransigence** vis-à-vis direct negotiations with Israel in favor of unilateral, one-sided initiatives … The Obama administration repeatedly stated that a solution to the conflict cannot be imposed on the parties but must be achieved directly by the parties themselves … It is **deeply troubling** that this **biased** [one-sided] **resolution** appears to be the **final word of the [Obama] administration** on this issue." *Left-wing pro-Obama Anti-Defamation League CEO Joel Greenblatt.*

iii. "Sometimes, we need to be reminded from above that we can count on no one but our Father who art in heaven … **Even America … forsook us last week at the UN**."[311] *Chief Sephardic Rabbi of Israel Yitzhak Yosef discussing Obama's support for UNSC Resolution 2334.*

iv. "Kerry's speech [and the passing of UNSC 2334] was very disturbing for so many reasons … It is disturbing that this is the point to which US foreign policy has fallen. It's sad, tragic and dangerous. **We don't need this relationship. We don't need this America**." *Michael Oren, former Israeli ambassador to the United States expressed his misgivings of the Obama administration during a Times of Israel interview.*

v. "The resolution, passed during the week that Aleppo was conquered by President Assad in the midst of brutal torture and massacres of thousands of innocent civilians, **highlights the duplicity and hypocrisy of the United Nations, a body dominated by anti-Israel and rogue states**, with democracies groveling in an effort to appease the dominant Muslim nations. It will serve as an instrument for Israel's adversaries **to further promote boycott, divestment and sanctions, and the International Criminal Court will be encouraged to define Israel as a criminal state**. It officially **nullifies the disastrous Oslo Accords, negates Security Council Resolution 242** and **repudiates the concept of defensible borders**. It paves the way **for criminalizing all settlers**, including those in the major blocs that will always remain part of Israel, and **even Jews resident in Jewish neighborhoods of east Jerusalem**. It actually defines the **Old City of Jerusalem and** the Kotel (Western Wall) as occupied Palestinian territory. In this context, the Palestinians will demand that any negotiations accept these bizarre territorial definitions as opening benchmarks – a status that no Israeli government would ever contemplate accepting. The UN resolution has effectively negated the concept of direct negotiations, thus ensuring that a peaceful solution to the conflict is more remote than ever."[312] *(Isi Leibler, The Jerusalem Post, December 29, 2016)*

e.   "Four years ago, I stood before you and said that, "**Israel's security is sacrosanct. It is non-negotiable**." That belief has guided my actions as president. The fact is my administration's commitment to Israel's security has been unprecedented …"

   i.   Obama has always insisted Israel use the pre-1967 boundaries, which are indefensible suicide borders, as a basis for future negotiations. This was reaffirmed in UNSC Resolution 2334, which stated that the UN "**will not recognize any changes to the 4 June 1967 lines**, **including with regard to Jerusalem**, other than those agreed by the parties through negotiations." Obama did not consult with Israel on the resolution before voting to secure its passage.

   ii.   "While Secretary Kerry mentioned Gaza in his speech, he [and Obama] seems to have forgotten the history of the settlements in Gaza, where the Israeli government forced settlers to withdraw from all settlements and the Palestinians responded by sending rockets from Gaza into Israel." *Democratic Senator Schumer critically analyzing Kerry's December 28, 2016 speech and Obama's policies.*

   iii.   "**The resolution** *[UNSC Res. 2334 crafted by Obama]* **essentially calls for Israel's physical and spiritual destruction** with its demand for a return to the indefensible 1967 borders, and its claim that the heart and soul of the Jewish people, its eternal spiritual (and physical) capital, its holiest city, doesn't belong to Israel. This is a complete abandonment of justice. The America in which I grew up stood for the value of the fabled president George Washington's "I cannot tell a lie" story. So how can that same country allow for the passage of a resolution that identifies **Judea and Samaria as "Palestinian territory?" This is an outright lie!** *[another Obama lie.]* **This land was occupied illegally by the Jordanians until the Six Day War in 1967**. The Jordanians have since rescinded their claim to this land, leaving it as "**disputed territory**" until it is resolved via negotiations."[313] *(Dov Lipman, The Jerusalem Post, December 29, 2016)*

f.   "And make no mistake: **We will do what it takes to preserve Israel's qualitative military edge** – because Israel must always have the ability to defend itself, by itself, against any threat … And just as we've been there with our security assistance, we've been there through our diplomacy …" But when Obama gave an extensive interview to Jeffrey Goldberg in the April 2016 issue of *The Atlantic* entitled "The Obama Doctrine," he reversed his earlier position when Goldberg stated, "According to Leon Panetta, he has questioned why the U.S. should maintain Israel's so-called qualitative military edge, which grants it access to more sophisticated weapons systems than America's Arab allies receive."[314]

i.   "In 2009, Obama actively sought to diminish Israel's defensive capabilities and its abilities to attack Iran by denying Israel refueling tankers for combat aircraft in-flight, the ability to install advanced electronics in F-35s, and the ability to purchase Apache helicopters and F-22 stealth aircraft fighter jets. Obama would not let Israel have access to first-hand data from American advanced radar stations in the Negev. In 2012, Obama denied the sale of V-22 Osprey aircraft and Massive Ordnance Penetrator 30,000 pound bunker-busting bombs to Israel." *(Unexpected Treason)*

ii.   In 2010, Obama **diverted a shipment of smart bunker buster munitions** destined to Israel, sending them instead to Diego Garcia.

iii. In June 2010, an Obama official leaked details of a secret agreement between Israel and Saudi Arabia that would allow Israeli jets to use Saudi airspace to attack Iranian nuclear facilities. This arrangement died after the leak.

iv.   In August 2010, **Obama cut, by $50 million, funding to Israel's Arrow 3 anti-ballistic missile (ABM) program**. The Arrow 3 ABM program is Israel's main defense against Iranian ballistic missiles. Earlier, **the Pentagon refused Israel's request to install its own electronic systems on the advanced F-35 jets**, which would optimize the aircraft if they were to be used in a strike against Iranian nuclear sites.

v.   In 2011, **Defense Secretary Leon Panetta** criticized Israel for its "**increasing isolation**" in the world community, and scolded Israel to "**Just get to the damn table.**" Later in the year, Panetta publicly **exposed Israel's potential plans to attack Iran between April and June**. It appears that Obama is more concerned about preventing Israel from striking Iran than preventing Iran from developing nuclear weapons.

vi.   Between 2011 and 2012, **Obama significantly increased intelligence activities against Israel**, out of fear that Israel might conduct an airstrike against Iranian nuclear installations. **Obama refused to inform Netanyahu of secret negotiations between Iran and the United States** starting in 2011, which led to increasing distrust between the Israel and the United States. The CIA actively sought to recruit junior Israeli officers as U.S. agents, who would reveal information of Israel's anti-Iran strategies, thus treating Israel as an enemy.

vii. In 2012, Obama **leaked classified information about Israeli plans to use airbases in Azerbaijan to attack Iran**. Obama is protecting Iran's domestic nuclear program, as well as their nuclear militarization program.

viii. In 2012, Obama sent an additional aircraft carrier group to the Middle East, out of fear Israel would attack Iran, and may have considered to use U.S. forces against Israeli planes and military positions.

ix. In 2012, Chairman of the Joint Chiefs of Staff Dempsey referred to any Israeli attack on Iran as a crime when he stated, "I don't want to be complicit if they choose to do it."

x. In September 2012, Obama **forced Israel to cancel a planned attack on Iranian nuclear facilities**.

xi. In June 2013, Obama **released the specifications of a secret Arrow 3 ballistic missile defense system to be built in Israel, south of Jerusalem**. The public information would jeopardize the viability of this critical Israeli defense project. The project was initiated to counter future Iranian ballistic missiles that might be armed with nuclear warheads.

xii. American intelligence analysts or defense department officials **leaked details of an IAF strike on a Syrian site housing Russian surface-to-sea missiles** being transferred to Hezbollah in July 2013.

xiii. In late 2013, the Obama administration **pressured Israel to release 104 terrorists** from their jails as a prerequisite for the Palestinian Authority to continue peace negotiations. The Palestinians made no reciprocal concessions.

xiv. In March 2014, **Obama slashed American funding for a joint missile defense program with Israel** by two-thirds ($200 million).

xv. Obama approved the sale of **$11 billion of weapons to Qatar**, a supporter of Hamas (on Israel's western border) and ISIS (on Israel's northern border).

xvi. At the end of October 2014, Secretary of State Kerry, Vice President Biden, and National Security Advisor Susan Rice refused to meet with Israel's Defense Minister Ya'alon while he was visiting Washington, D.C.

xvii. In late February 2015, Obama **declassified a Defense Department report documenting Israel's nuclear program**, which broke the United States' promise to Israel to remain quiet regarding Israel's nuclear capacities. The released report showed photographs of Israel's clandestine nuclear sites.

xviii. In March 2015, Kuwaiti newspaper *Al-Jarida* reported that **Obama threatened to shoot down a planned Israeli IAF strike against Iranian nuclear facilities in 2014**. The Israeli leadership presented the plan to Kerry before the strike and Obama responded with the threat to shoot down the Israel aircraft before they reached Iranian airspace.

xix. In March 2015, Obama **refused to renew an emergency oil supply pact with Israel that would guarantee Israel's supply of oil in the event of war**, other embargo or trade interruption.

xx.　According the *The Wall Street Journal*, Obama used the NSA to spy on Israel, congressmen and American citizens (pro-Israeli lobbying groups) in order to counter political strategy that would be used to argue against implementing the JCPOA.[315] Israel was Obama's number one espionage target during his administration. Earlier in his presidency, Obama wanted to know if Netanyahu was going to strike Iranian nuclear facilities and if Israel discovered Obama's secret negotiations with Iran, which reportedly started in 2011. Obama is treating Israel and pro-Israel congressmen as the enemy and using the NSA to advance and protect the interests of Iran.

xxi.　In late October 2015, U.S. government officials confirmed to *The Wall Street Journal* that Israel assassinated numerous Iranian nuclear scientists.

xxii.　"I mean, Hezbollah has 70,000 – 80,000 rockets. What do they need that for?" *Secretary of State Kerry, Davos Summit, January 23, 2016.* Kerry and Obama are completely ignorant of and oblivious to Israel's security needs and of Hezbollah's and Iran's desire to destroy Israel. Or are they downplaying Hezbollah's arsenal since they have over 100,000 – 150,000 rockets and missiles aimed at Israel?

xxiii.　In January 2016, Israel revealed that the **United States' and Great Britain's intelligence services had cracked Israeli encrypted communication systems between fighter jets**, **drones and their command structures and allowed them to compromise Israel's advanced drone technologies**. Obama used these intelligence gains in order to monitor Israel's plans regarding attacking Iranian nuclear installations. Obama may have transferred Israeli drone technology to the Iranians, which may have been used by Hezbollah. A senior Israeli official stated, "It means that they have forcibly stripped us, and no less important, that probably none of our encrypted systems are safe from them. This is the worst leak in the history of Israeli intelligence." It is unlikely that Obama focuses more intelligence resources on any other country.

xxiv.　In early 2016, **Obama cut funding for American anti-missile defense in 2017 by 10%**, **but slashed funding for a parallel Israeli anti-missile defense program by 60%** (Arrow program for anti-ballistic missiles from Iran and David's Sling program for mid-range missiles from Hezbollah), and decreased funding for the Iron Dome (short range missiles from Gaza) anti-missile defense system by 25%. Obama's funding cuts for Israel's anti-missile defense systems follows the passage of the JCPOA which gave Iran up to $150 billion in sanctions relief, much of which will be used to bolster and modernize their offensive missile capabilities directed at Israel from Iran and their proxies in Gaza and Lebanon.

xxv.　In June 2016, the Obama administration **opposed** the House of Representatives' desire to increase **funding for Israeli missile defense systems** by $455 million in the 2017 fiscal year budget. "The administration told lawmakers that it 'opposes the addition of $455 million' in additional funding for Israeli missile defense projects in the fiscal year 2017 budget, which is working its way through Congress, according to a letter from the White House. Israel requested $601 million in U.S. funding for missile defense programs that are jointly shared with the United States and help defend both countries. However, the Obama administration said it would only provide the Jewish state with $146 million … Senator Mark Kirk said, 'Israel faces growing missile threats, especially after the flawed nuclear deal gave Iran's terror-sponsoring regime over $100 billion in sanctions relief and as Iran has accelerated testing of ballistic missiles capable of striking Israel.' A senior congressional aide reflected, 'The White House claims it's the most pro-Israel administration in history, yet it's objecting to a $455 million increase to meet requirements for Israel's missile cooperation with the United States while, at the same time, complaining we need to do more for Iran's terror-sponsoring regime because the nuclear deal's $100 billion in total sanctions relief isn't enough … **This doesn't add up**.'"[316] Obama's behavior "adds up" and makes perfect sense when one considers that he is working with Iran to destroy Israel. Obama funded Iran's ballistic missile program with sanctions relief and by reviving their economy, while he slashed Israel's funding for its missile defense systems.

xxvi. A multi-year American-Israeli defense / security assistance package promoted by Obama will dramatically increase Israel's dependence on the U.S. government, most notably the executive branch. "The agreement bars Israel from asking that Congress augment the assistance that Obama has offered and bars Congress from acting. So if a future administration chooses to breach the agreement, or to suspend it, or if conditions change and Israel requires other assistance, Congress would be barred from stepping into the breach … the deal that Obama is now trying to coerce Netanyahu to sign will require Jerusalem to give up the 25 percent of the military assistance it is now allowed to spend at home. Oren noted that such a concession will cost thousands of Israelis their jobs [and greatly weaken Israel's home based military industries]."[317] *(Caroline Glick, Jerusalem Post, June 2016)*

xxvii. In late 2016, Iran announced they will be introducing nuclear powered ships and air craft carriers to their navy. The Iranian military projects will be funded in part by Obama's sanctions relief initiatives, and his transfer of billions of dollars of cash and gold to the Iranian government as part of the implementation of the JCPOA.

xxviii. As Russia increased their presence in Syria, they introduce advanced surface to air missiles, which could shoot down Israeli jets flying over northern Israel. Obama created the vacuum in the Syria that allowed Russia and Iran to insert their forces and advanced defense technologies into Syria, adjacent to Israel's northern border.

g.   "**When <u>one-sided resolutions</u>** are brought up at the Human Rights Council, **we oppose them** ..."

   i.   Australian prime minister Malcolm Turnbull condemned the resolution [UNSC Resolution 2334] in a speech to the Central Synagogue in Sydney on Friday, according to *Australian Jewish News*. He described the resolution as "**deeply unsettling** for our community" and "**one-sided**" and vowed that "Australia stands with Israel. We support Israel, the only democracy in the Middle East ... We support a peaceful resolution of the disputes between Israel and the Palestinians ... we support a two-state solution just as the government of Israel does." He added that the peace process "... is not assisted by **<u>one-sided resolutions</u> made at the councils of the United Nations** *[initiated by Obama]* **or anywhere else**, and that is why Australia has not, and does not, support one-sided resolutions," and he emphasized that "above all, we stand shoulder to shoulder with Israel in the fight against terrorists."[318] (*Jerusalem Post*, December 30, 2016)

h.   "When there are efforts to boycott or divest from Israel, we will stand against them."

   i.   Obama laid the groundwork for the legalization of the BDS economic war against Israel, by ensuring Resolution 2334 would be approved by the UNSC, which stated in paragraph 5, "Calls upon all States, bearing in mind paragraph 1 of this resolution, **to distinguish, in their relevant dealings, between the territory of the State of Israel and the territories occupied since 1967.**"

i.   "And whenever an effort is made to **delegitimize** the state of Israel, my administration has opposed them."

   i.   "The Obama administration's decision to abstain from today's UN Security Council vote is disgraceful ... The adopted resolution is **anti-Israel** and anti-peace. Congress and the incoming administration will stand with our friends and allies, and **oppose all efforts to delegitimize Israel**." *Rep Peter Roskam (R., IL)* acknowledging that Obama's support for UNSC Resolution 2334 attempts to delegitimize Israel, and make them more vulnerable to a BDS campaign and legal action at the International Criminal Court.

   ii.   "While we appreciate Secretary Kerry's concern about policies and dynamics that may jeopardize the path to a two-state solution, we are deeply disappointed by elements of his speech and cannot separate it from the US abstention at the UN Security Council ... Despite Secretary Kerry's explanation, the US abstention has the potential to **set in motion many initiatives that <u>delegitimize</u> and demonize Israel**, rather than advancing the peace process ... **disconnected from [the] reality** that there are two parties involved in this process … the international community [and Obama and Kerry] is **dictating terms to Israel with the demands of the Palestinians.**" *Anti-Defamation League (ADL) CEO Jonathan Greenblatt, December 2016. Greenblatt is far left-wing liberal and has been extremely supportive of Obama during his presidency.* Obama's crafting and support of UNSC Resolution 2334 was based on his desire to delegitimize Israel weeks before he left the presidency, allowed the PLO and Hamas to dictate the final terms of the peace agreement with Israel, and supported radical Muslim control over half of Jerusalem which will advance their war against Israel and the Jews.

   iii. "The secretary's [Kerry's] speech [at the State Department and Obama's approval of UNSC Resolution 2334], which followed the UN resolution, **I found quite troubling** because of the **attacks on Israel** and in many ways <u>**undermining**</u> the **government of Israel itself** <u>**in terms of its own legitimacy**</u> and the talks." *Rex Tillerson, Donald Trump's Secretary of State nominee, Senate Foreign Relations Committee confirmation hearing, January 11, 2017.*

j. "So, there should not be a shred of doubt by now – <u>**when the chips are down, I have Israel's back**</u>. Which is why, if during this political season, you hear some questions regarding my administration's support for Israel, remember that it's not backed up by the facts."

   i. "**What he did was so nasty**, he pulled a bait and switch. He said to the American public this is all about the settlements deep in the West Bank. And yet, he allowed his representative to the UN to abstain – which is really a vote for – a resolution that says the **Jews can't pray at the Western Wall, Jewish students can't go to Hebrew University … Jews can't live in the Jewish Quarter [of Jerusalem] where they have lived for thousands of years**. And he's going to say, 'Whoops, I didn't mean that! Well, read the resolution! You're a lawyer, you went to Harvard law School … He was trying to get even … He called me into the Oval Office before the inauguration -- he said he wanted my support, and **he told me he would always have Israel's back … I didn't realize what he meant: That he would have Israel's back so he could stab them in the back, and** <u>**he just stabbed them in the back**</u>." *Democratic Harvard Law School Professor Alan Dershowitz on Fox and Friends, December 26, 2016.* Dershowitz is commenting on Obama's betrayal of Israel and his attempting to force the PLO, Hamas, and Iran, all radical Islamists, to gain control of the Western Wall and the Jewish Quarter in Jerusalem.

   ii. "**UN Security Council resolution 2334 systematically removes Israel's sovereignty over East Jerusalem, which contains both Judaism's and Christianity's' holy sites**. Therefore Sec. Kerry's remarks today, including the condemnation of the

UNESCO resolutions *[certifying the Western Wall is part of al Aqsa mosque and is an Islamic holy site]* over the summer are inconsistence with his support for UNSC 2334, because the operative language of the resolution <u>**severs Israel's sovereignty over East Jerusalem**</u> *[including the Western Wall and the Jewish Quarter].* The American Jewish Congress supports Prime Minister Netanyahu's assertion that the conflict has always been rooted in the refusal of the Palestinians to recognize the Jewish State. UNSC 2334 dangerously changes the status quo for a path to peace that has existed for many decades, which **radically alters American policy and potentially empowers the Palestinians to never have to negotiate and recognize the Jewish State** of Israel." *American Jewish Congress Statement on Sec. Kerry's and PM Netanyahu's Remarks, December 28, 2016.*

iii. "Abstaining from the UN Security Council Resolution that condemned all Israeli settlements, including East Jerusalem, as having "no legal validity," deemed the Western Wall as Palestine proper, backtracked on UN Security Council Resolution 242 by redrawing Israel's border back to the pre-1967 armistice line and reneging on the entire "land for peace" principle, is **a bitter betrayal**. This is not the way to treat a friend and ally …**His toughest hand was always reserved for Israel**, which became the repository for his anti-colonialist impulses. In his mind, Israeli settlements were the reasons for Palestinian suffering, which this UN Security Council Resolution now codifies as a "major obstacle" to peace. Civilian casualties during the Gaza War were always due to Israel's lack of restraint. Palestinian rockets, terror tunnels, human shields, and knife stabbings – not so much. Indeed, when this UN Security Council Resolution addresses terrorism and incitement, it never specifies which side is responsible for the violence. Its one-sided condemnation would make someone unfamiliar with the true practitioners of the trade to believe that terrorism was Israel's fault, too. **Surely there are those who will continue to credit President Obama with having Israel's back. But will they now finally acknowledge that <u>Israel's back now has a knife in it?</u>** … By abstaining on a Security Council charade that he could have easily vetoed – something he did eight years ago, with a similar anti-settlement measure – **he sided with the forces of darkness and converted the war on terror into a celebration**. Possessing the power to veto an injustice, and choosing instead to abstain, President Obama became **a willing accomplice and bystander to Israel's isolation**. Worse still, <u>**he may have colluded with, and emboldened the Palestinians to stay away from the negotiating table, bide their time while launching more rockets and stabbing more Israelis**</u>. *[Obama may have committed war crimes by encouraging the Palestinians to kill Israelis instead of attempting to negotiate a fair peace agreement.]* After all, why wouldn't the Palestinians now feel that "diplomacy" – Obama-style – is their fast track to statehood with Jerusalem as a Hanukkah gift given to the altogether wrong people."[319] *(Thane Rosenbaum, Times of Israel)*

k. "And remember that **the U.S. - Israel relationship is simply too important to be distorted by partisan politics**. America's national security is too important. Israel's security is too important … And I've made it clear that there will be no lasting peace unless Israel's security concerns are met …" Obama made Israel a partisan issue where the Democratic Party has morphed into the pro-Palestinian, pro-Islam party. The placement of Keith Ellison, congressman and former member of the National of Islam, as deputy chairman of the DNC in 2017 will help cement the differences on Middle East issues between the Democratic and Republican parties.

   i. Nancy Pelosi, the **Democratic Minority Leader** in the House, **supported UNSC Resolution 2334**, which called the Jewish holy sites in East Jerusalem "occupied Palestinian territory," and **praised Obama and Kerry after the UNSC vote** by stating they have "worked tirelessly to try to bring Israeli and Palestinian leaders to the table for direct and constructive talks." The Democrats are now official the anti-Israel political party in America, especially with the strong partisan support for Keith Ellison, a former member of the Nation of Islam and supporter of the Muslim Brotherhood, running for DNC chairman in 2016 – 2017.

   ii. "As predicted, on the eve of his retirement President Barack **Obama betrayed Israel**. The former long-standing congregant of the paranoid anti-Semitic pastor Rev. Jeremy Wright who has a penchant for supporting to the Muslim Brotherhood, <u>**broke with 40 years of US bipartisan policy of protecting the Jewish state**</u> from the wolves at the United Nations. His action as a lame duck president was a last-ditch effort aimed at undermining his successor's intended policies, carried out with the understanding that it is virtually impossible to rescind a Security Council resolution. At the end of his eight years in office he **exhibited an unprecedented abuse of power**, knowing that in his last month he would be unaccountable, despite the fact that his vindictive initiative was totally opposed by Congress, the American people and by many members of his own party."[320] *(Isi Leibler, The Jerusalem Post)*

   iii. Seventy-six Democrats voted against House Resolution 11 on January 5, 2017, which objected to UNSC Resolution 2334, and stated that the resolution "undermines the prospects for Israelis and Palestinians resuming productive, direct negotiations" and needs to be "repealed or fundamentally altered." Speaker of House Paul Ryan commented on the floor of the House of Representatives, "**Our government [Obama] abandoned our ally Israel when she needed us the most** … It is time to repair the damage done by this misguided hit job at the UN." Matt Brooks, RJC Executive

Director responded to his House vote by stating, "Five years ago, Democrats on the floor of their convention booed a pro-Israel resolution, and yesterday 76 Democrats in the House voted against another pro-Israel resolution. **Today's Democrat Party is no longer a home for pro-Israel voters**."

iv. "Obama is the titular head of the Democratic Party. At the Democratic National Convention in 2012, a motion was made to declare that Jerusalem, not West Jerusalem, was the capital of Israel. The convention chairman took a yea or nay vote on the motion, and initially the nays, which were accompanied with belligerent yelling and dissension, seemed to be in the overwhelming majority. The chairman took several votes before it was declared passed by the leadership, despite the loud booing that was heard around the world. This event reflected an anti-Israel sentiment by the Democratic delegates to the convention. The increased number of Muslim delegates on the floor may have contributed to the increased resistance to a pro-Israel platform. The Democrats also removed from their 2012 political platform America's commitment to sustain Israel's military advantage with respect to their Middle East neighbors." *(Unexpected Treason)*

v. "In February 2015, a Gallop poll indicated that less than half of all Democrats (48%) sympathized more with the Israelis than with the Palestinians. A similar Pew Poll showed only 44% of Democratic respondents expressed support for Israel over the Palestinians." *(Unexpected Treason)*

vi. "Senator Bernie Sanders garnered much political support during his 2016 presidential campaign and was blatantly anti-Israel. Sanders accused Israel on the national stage of killing over 10,000 Palestinian civilians during the 2014 Israeli-Hamas war, when the total Palestinian death count was actually much less – about 2000, where 44% were conservatively estimated to be enemy combatants. Sanders also accused Israel of responding disproportionately to the thousands of missiles that Hamas launched at civilian targets inside Israel, thus telling Israel that it had limited rights of self-defense. Sanders chose Simone Zimmerman as his campaign Jewish outreach coordinator, knowing that she supported Boycott, Divestment, and Sanctions (BDS) against Israel, and opposed Israel's 2014 military campaign against Hamas despite the missile attacks, which she felt was valid secondary to Israel's "occupation." Unfortunately for her argument, Israel does not occupy Gaza. She also described Netanyahu on Facebook as "arrogant, deceptive, cynical, manipulative asshole." Eventually, Sanders suspended her from the campaign secondary to the political fallout. Daniel Sieradski, who directed Jews for Bernie, blamed Israel for Hamas' terrorist attacks and defended Hamas by stating they "just want to make life better for their people." Sanders' New York State campaign director was Robert

Becker, who also defended Hamas during the 2014 war and listed his name in Arabic on his Twitter account. Becker also actively supported the Muslim Brotherhood in its bid to control Egypt while overthrowing Mubarak. Becker was convicted by an Egyptian court for seeking to cause unrest and illegally funding Egyptian political operations after Sisi became president." *(Unexpected Treason)*

(1)   "Sanders appointed three blatant anti-Semites (James Zogby, Keith Ellison, Cornel West) to the Democratic Platform Committee for the 2016 convention, and their acceptance by the Democratic Party leaders portends an ominous future for Jews and Israel with respect upcoming Democratic Party policies. First, James Zogby has worked with the Arab-American Institute and the American-Arab Anti-Discrimination Committee. He has supported Hezbollah and has called them "armed resistance." Zogby has also described Israelis as "Nazis" and stated that Israel is committing a holocaust against the PLO and the Palestinians. Zogby is also an Obama political appointee. At the Democratic National Convention, Zogby stated, "I had no idea the [platform] fight would be over 'occupation' and 'settlements … We can't do it because Sheldon Adelson will come out against us."[321] Zogby, a leading Democrat, wants the Democratic platform to refer to Israel's presence in its capital and the West Bank as "occupation" and "settlements," and is mocking Adelson because he is Jewish." *(Unexpected Treason)*

(2)   "Second, Congressman Ellison has been documented to be a former member of and spokesman for the Nation of Islam, and has ties with the Muslim Brotherhood. Ellison also has been a strong supporter of CAIR, ISNA, MAS, and MPAC – all Muslim Brotherhood front groups, along with most Palestinian causes. Ellison has compared Israel to South Africa's apartheid regime, and favors empowering Hamas at the expense of Israel's security needs. In 1990, Ellison sponsored Stokely Carmichael to speak at his law school, who gave a speech discussing, "Zionism: Imperialism, White Supremacy or Both." Michelle Obama also idolized Carmichael as a young adult. In 1995, Ellison defended Louis Farrakhan against charges of anti-Semitism in a Minneapolis periodical and claimed he was a role model for the African-American population. Ellison defended Joanne Jackson of the Minnesota Initiative Against Racism in 1997 after she was quoted to say, "Jews are the most racist white people I know." During the same speech, Ellison also defended Farrakhan by stating, "He is not a racist. He is also not an anti-Semite. Minister Farrakhan is a tireless public servant of Black people." Ellison has spoken at numerous CAIR events knowing that CAIR was an unindicted co-conspirator in the

Holy Land Hamas terrorist group funding case, that CAIR has refused to denounce Hamas or Hezbollah as terrorist groups, and it has been designated a terrorist group by the United Arab Emirates. In 2008, Ellison went on a hajj to Mecca, which was funded by the Muslim American Society, a group affiliated with the Muslim Brotherhood. The leader of the MAS, Esam Omeish, supported Palestinian jihad against Israel, which has led to the death of many Israeli civilians. Ellison has praised Omeish publicly by stating, "I just want to again thank Dr. Omeish, and let brother Esam know that he is my beloved brother and I love you and you are the best and your family is so beautiful and again, you know, you put it out there." In 2010, Ellison made an anti-Israel statement at one of his congressional fundraisers when he said, "The message I want to send to you by donating to this campaign … is positioning me and positioning Muslims in general to help steer the ship of state in America…. **The United States foreign policy in the Middle East is governed by what is good or bad through a country of seven million people [Israel]**. A region of 350 million all turns on a country of seven million. **Does that make sense**? Is that logic? Right?" Ellison pressured his Jewish constituents when he told them, "Do you stand with the President on stopping settlements in East Jerusalem, because that is the policy of my president and I want to know if you're with the President. Are you with the President?" And, "Why are we sending $2.8 billion a year over there when they won't even honor our request to stop building in East Jerusalem? Where is the future Palestinian state going to be if it's colonized before it even gets up off the ground?" Ellison wants U.S. aid to focus on Muslim countries so America will move away from its special relationship with Israel when he said, "We should be building the bilateral business relationships between the United States and the Muslim world … Morocco, we gotta build it up. Saudi Arabia, we gotta build it up. The Gulf countries, we gotta build them. Pakistan, we gotta build them … We need to have so much goods and services going back and forth between this country and the Muslim world that if we say we need this right here, then everyone is saying, OK. Understand my point? You've got to be strategic … These business relationships can be leveraged to say that we need a new deal politically." In mid-2016, Ellison tweeted a photo of a poster displayed in Hebron (the West Bank) that accused Israel of apartheid and racism." (*Unexpected Treason*)

(3)   "In early 2017, Vincent Tolliver was expelled as a candidate for the DNC chairmanship after he criticized Islam and Keith Ellison, when he stated, "His being a Muslim (Ellison) is precisely why DNC voters should not vote for him.

Muslims discriminate against gays. Islamic law is clear on the subject, and being gay is a direct violation of it. In some Muslim countries, being gay is a crime punishable by death." Even though Tolliver told the truth about Islam, he was ostracized the Democratic Party when Donna Brazile, the interim DNC chairman, commented "Mr. Tolliver's **disgusting comments** attacking the religion of a fellow candidate fall far short of that standard. Accordingly, Mr. Tolliver is no longer a candidate for DNC Chair."[322] The Democratic Party is embracing Sharia law and discouraging free speech by forbidding any criticism, however valid, of Islam. This seismic anti-Constitutional shift of Democratic Party values could not have occurred without Obama's influence." *(Unexpected Treason)*

(4)   "Third, Cornel West, a Princeton professor, signed a letter in 2007 to the Black community stating, "It is time for our people to once again demand that the silence be broken on the injustices faced by the Palestinian people resulting from the Israeli occupation … the Israeli government … emulated South Africa's treatment of its Black majority in its own treatment of the Palestinian people." West is a close associate of Louis Farrakhan, and served on the advisory board for the Nation of Islam's Million Man March in Washington. In 2012, West worked with Reverend Wright and other Islamists to support a demonstration against Israel with the "Global March to Jerusalem." West signed a letter supporting Palestinian political positions and their propaganda, which stated, "We, the Advisory Board of the Global March to Jerusalem, are alarmed and deeply troubled by the continuing repression of Palestinians in Jerusalem and by the deliberate and systematic attempts to expel and reduce the Christian and Muslim Palestinian population of the city as part of the policy called 'Judaisation,' which is being applied to every part of historic Palestine." West's position against the 'Judaisation' of Jerusalem parallels the political positions of Erdogan, Abbas, Hamas, and the Muslim Brotherhood. With Huma Abedin as one of her chief advisors, Hillary Clinton is not going to protest the input of these pro-Muslim Brotherhood, Islamist, anti-Semitic, anti-Israel Democratic Party policy makers. Barack Obama has been a trail blazer for allowing anti-Semitism and anti-Israeli politicians to advance through the ranks of the Democratic Party." *(Unexpected Treason)*

vii. "At the 2016 Democratic National Convention, delegates were waving the Palestinian flag on the convention floor on the first night, with no U.S. flags nearby. On the same day, Democratic Representative and Clinton super-delegate Hank Johnson called Jews living in the West Bank or East Jerusalem, the capital of Israel, "termites," which is reminiscent of Nazi propaganda. Johnson is supported by J Street. Black Lives Matter, which is fully supported by Obama and had strategy sessions with Obama at the White House and later issued an anti-Semitic platform at the DNC stating, "Israel is an apartheid state with over 50 laws on the books that sanction discrimination against the Palestinian people ... Israeli soldiers also regularly arrest and detain Palestinians as young as 4 years old." BLM also claimed that Israel was committing "genocide ... against the Palestinian people" with U.S. assistance and advocated cutting off all military aid to Israel. Even liberal Democrat Alan Dershowitz commented, "Until and unless Black Lives Matter removes this blood libel from its platform and renounces it, no decent person – black, white, or of any other racial or ethnic background – should have anything to do with it."[323] During the primary season, leaked emails showed the Democratic National Committee openly debated whether to use Sanders' Jewish identity against him. An internal email from Brad Marshall, the CFO of the Democratic National Committee stated, "It might make no difference, but for KY and WVA can we get someone to ask his belief. Does he believe in a G-d? He had skated on saying he has a Jewish heritage ... this could make several points difference with my peeps." Amy Lacey, a chief executive with the DNC answered, "Amen." Although Sanders was pro-Palestinian and appointed multiple anti-Semitic politicians to the Democratic platform committee, the DNC leadership still considered pursuing an anti-Semitic attack on him. A May 2016 Pew Poll found that only 33% of liberal Democrats supported Israel over the Palestinians. The majority of Democrats under Obama's political leadership supported the Palestinians, even when the Palestinian Authority formed a unity government with Hamas, an organization that has called for the extermination of all Jews worldwide, not just in Israel. With Obama as the leader of the Democratic Party, anti-Semitic rhetoric and policies are sadly finding a home in the party of Roosevelt and Kennedy." *(Unexpected Treason)*

viii. "In contrast, 83% of Republicans supported the Israelis over the Palestinians in a Gallop poll. Thus, there is at least a 35 - 40% difference in support for Israel when Democrats are compared with Republicans. Another poll of active Democrats taken by Frank Luntz in July 2015 revealed that 47% of Democrats believed Israel was a racist country (as opposed to 13% of Republicans), and that only 18% of Democrats would support a pro-Israel politician (as opposed to 76% of Republicans). By continually criticizing and harassing Israel in the public arena, Obama has made Israel a highly-charged partisan issue during his presidency. By continually advancing Palestinian rights and ignoring their support for the murder of Jews, whether by dismemberment or by suicide bombings, and downplaying the Palestinians' desire to destroy the Jewish state, Obama has painted Israel as a racist society, and that image has been accepted by the left-wing of the Democratic Party." *(Unexpected Treason)*

ix. "The partisan approach to Israeli issues was reflected in the congressional support for the JCPOA, where no Republican senators announced they would vote in favor of the Iranian nuclear agreement as with Obamacare. The bill's only support came from the Democratic Party, despite 90% of all Israelis being against the approval of the JCPOA. **In a rare display of anti-Israel sentiment, President Obama, Vice President Biden, and the Democratic Black Congressional Caucus boycotted Israel's Prime Minister Netanyahu's speech before a joint session of Congress, where he outlined his sincere fears and opposition to the pending agreement.** It is doubtful that these national leaders and congressmen would have boycotted any other head of state speaking before a special session of Congress. Liberal Democrats also hurled anti-Semitic slurs at Senator Schumer when he announced his opposition to Obama and his support for Israel with this vote. It seems that as the Democratic Party shifts to the left and embraces Obama's vision for America and the world, it is also heading into an anti-Israel and an anti-Semitic direction." *(Unexpected Treason)*

l. "We have continued to insist that any Palestinian partner **must recognize Israel's right to exist**, and **reject violence**, and **adhere to existing agreements**." *Obama ignored the Palestinians' abrogation of the Oslo Accords, the Palestinian knife intifada, and their refusal to recognize Israel as a Jewish state.*

i. In a violation of the Oslo accords **in April 2014, the Palestinians signed applications for joining 15 treaties, conventions and international organizations, commencing a unilateral bid for statehood** after Israel failed to release Palestinian prisoners and initiate a complete settlement freeze. Earlier in Obama's presidency, Israel instituted a nine-month settlement freeze and released large numbers of terrorists as a sign of good faith, with no reciprocal concessions or good will demonstrated by the Palestinians. The signing of the documents coincided with Kerry's visit, which caused the American diplomat great embarrassment. This move by Abbas was a blatant demonstration of contempt for the Americans, Israelis and the peace process, since the Palestinians had always agreed that their future statehood would be linked to a peace treaty with Israel. Yet, unlike the harsh response Obama gave Israel when they announced housing starts during Vice President Biden's 2010 visit to Israel, Obama expressed mild concern and did not blame any one party for an action that sabotaged all the diplomatic efforts of the U.S. government for decades. Obama's muted reaction demonstrated he was fully allied with the Palestinian cause. **Abbas demonstrated bad faith and abrogated the 1993 Oslo Accord (Article V),** which stated "It was understood that several issues were postponed to permanent status negotiations, including: Jerusalem, refugees, settlements, security arrangements, borders, relations and co-operation with other neighbors, and other issues of common interest. **The outcome of these permanent status negotiations should not be prejudiced or pre-empted by the parties**." Obama did not threaten to withhold American funding for the Palestinians, as is required by law in response to their unilateral actions initiating the establishment of a Palestinian state. The Palestinians were also demanding the release of Israeli Arab citizens from Israeli prisons, which was a request outside their area of jurisdiction. Other **Palestinian demands preceding the renewal of talks** included lifting the Gaza blockade, freeing Marwan Barghouti – a popular Palestinian leader imprisoned for his orchestration of suicide bombings, freeing an additional 1,200 Palestinian prisoners, 15,000 reunion permits for Palestinians, a complete halt to all settlement activity, PA sovereignty in Area C, a cessation of IDF operations throughout the territories controlled by the Palestinians, reopening the Gaza border crossings, an Israeli acceptance of the pre-1967 borders for a future Palestinian state and establishing East Jerusalem as its capital. If Israel accepted these preconditions for further talks, there would be no need for additional negotiations. The left-wing Finance Minister Yair Lapid commented, "the list of PA demands … appeared more like a tool to ruin the negotiations." Even with all these demands, Abbas still refused to recognize Israel as a Jewish state. Abbas' demand for such unobtainable preconditions stemmed from his belief that Obama would support these tactics. **Kerry blamed Israel and backed the Palestinian position**, despite its unreasonable demands when he stated, "A day went by. Day two went by. Day three went by. And then in the afternoon, when they were about to maybe get there, 700 settlement units were announced in Jerusalem and, **poof, that was sort of the moment**." Kerry ignored that the Palestinians refused to negotiate unless a significant number of their negotiating endpoints were met beforehand. The 700 homes were in the heart of a 40-year-old Jewish suburb in East Jerusalem, long recognized by all parties as remaining under Israeli control with any future settlement. Kerry expected Israel to stop building in Jerusalem, the capital of Israel, while the Palestinians boycotted all discussions. Obama and Kerry demonstrated again that they were proxies for the Palestinian negotiators. An official in Netanyahu's office stated, "Secretary Kerry knows that it was the Palestinians who said 'no' to continued direct talks with Israel in November; who said 'no' to his proposed framework for final-status talks; who said 'no' to even discussing recognition of Israel as the nation-state of the Jewish people; who said 'no' to a meeting with Kerry himself; and who said 'no' to an extension of the talks … Therefore, the Palestinian claim that building in Jerusalem, Israel's capital, was a violation of the understandings is contrary to the facts. Both the American negotiating team and the Palestinians know full well that Israel made no such commitment."

m. "**And that is why my administration has consistently rejected any efforts to short-cut negotiations or impose an agreement on the parties** …"

i. "This will make peace much more difficult to achieve because the Palestinians will now say 'we can get a state through the UN, we can get a state through the BDS movement,' because this will encourage that. 'We can get a state through the International Criminal Court … we don't have to negotiate, we don't have to make painful compromises.' He will go down in history, President Obama, as one of the worst foreign-policy presidents ever." *Dershowitz, Fox and Friends, December 26, 2016.*

ii. "**It is tragic** that the administration chose to **mar its legacy** of support for the Jewish State and set back the prospects for Israeli-Palestinian peace …. The administration's decision **undermined a core principle of American foreign policy** that has been embraced by Democratic and Republican Administrations for decades: that the only route to a solution to the Israeli-Palestinian conflict is through direct negotiations between the parties." *The Jewish Federation of North America commenting on Obama support of UNSC Resolution 2334.*

iii. "I am extremely disappointed by this action and today's vote. **Blaming Israel** for the continuation of the conflict is not only **wrong and unjust**; it will also do nothing to move the parties closer to a peaceful and lasting solution. This resolution **ignores the culpability of Palestinian leaders** and groups for engaging in violent acts, inciting violence against civilians, and **delegitimizing Jews' ancient and historic connection to the land**. Furthermore, the United States' abstention risks lending legitimacy to efforts by Palestinians to impose their own solution through international fora and trough unjustified boycotts or divestment campaigns. Only direct, bilateral negotiations can bring an end to this conflict. Neither the international community **nor the United States can impose one**. I join in expressing my very significant disagreement with the Administration's decision to abstain." *House Minority Whip Steny Hoyer of Maryland, the number two Democrat in the House, voicing criticism of Obama's support of UNSC Resolution 2334.*

n. "As Rosy noted, last year, I stood before you and pledged that, "**the United States will stand up against efforts to single Israel out at the United Nations**." As you know, that pledge has been kept …"

i. "Secretary Kerry's vision for peace, must be examined in the context of what he has achieved in office. His policy decisions in the Middle East: ISIS, Iran and Russia's takeover of Syria have all been at the least questionable and at the worst wrong. Based on his record, we have no faith in his Middle East policy decisions. Therefore, we don't believe that he is right with the polices that he laid out today on the Israeli-Palestinian conflict. Nonetheless, **despite the horrific scenes of over 250,000 innocent people massacred**, **including women and children in Syria, <u>the Obama Administration has used its remaining time to single out Israel</u>**." *Jack Rosen, President of the American Jewish Congress, Remarks concerning Kerry's speech on the Middle East after Obama organized the passage of UNSC Resolution 2334. December 29, 2016.*

o. "Last September, I stood before the United Nations General Assembly and reaffirmed that any lasting peace must acknowledge the fundamental legitimacy of Israel and its security concerns**. I said that America's commitment to Israel's security is unshakeable**, our friendship with Israel is enduring … the United States will insist upon Israel's security and legitimacy …"

    i. "We cannot continue to let Israel be treated with such total disdain and disrespect. **They used to have a great friend in the US, but not anymore**. The beginning of the end was the horrible Iran deal, and now this (UN Resolution 2334). *President Elect Donald Trump, December 28, 2016.*

    ii. Kerry and Obama "decided to cater to the demands of freedom's enemies and devote and entire speech to disparaging a country that is one of our closest allies." *Florida Senator Marco Rubio.*

p. "No Israeli government can tolerate a nuclear weapon in the hands of a regime that denies the Holocaust, threatens to wipe Israel off the map and sponsors terrorist groups committed to Israel's destruction." *Obama*

q. "And so, **I understand the profound historical obligation that weighs on the shoulders of Bibi Netanyahu** and Ehud Barak, and all of Israel's leaders …"

    i. Obama called Netanyahu "**<u>chicken-shit</u>**" during his second term.

    ii. In an interview with Jeffrey Goldberg in *The Atlantic* from January 2013, Obama lobs criticisms at Netanyahu by stating, "**<u>Israel doesn't know what its own best interests are</u>** … [Goldberg paraphrasing Obama:] **If Israel, a small state in an inhospitable region, becomes more of a pariah, one that <u>alienates even the affections of the U.S.</u>, its last steadfast friend** *[or me]* – **<u>it won't survive</u>**."[324] Obama also calls Netanyahu a "**political coward**" because he refuses to put Israel in a suicidal geopolitical positon with respect to the Palestinians. Obama threatens Israel's survival if the Jews don't do as he says.

r. "That is where we are today – because of our work. Iran is isolated, its leadership divided and under pressure. And by the way, the Arab Spring has only increased these trends, as

the hypocrisy of the Iranian regime is exposed, and its ally – the Assad regime – is crumbling …"

s.   "I have said that when it comes to preventing Iran from obtaining a nuclear weapon, **I will take no options off the table**, and I mean what I say. That includes all elements of American power: A political effort aimed at isolating Iran; a diplomatic effort to sustain our coalition and ensure that the Iranian program is monitored; an economic effort that imposes crippling sanctions; and, yes, **a military effort to be prepared for any contingency.**"

t.   "Iran's leaders should understand that **I do not have a policy of containment**; I have a **policy to <u>prevent Iran from obtaining a nuclear weapon</u>** …" At the end of the terms of the JCPOA, Iran will be able to legally build and stockpile nuclear weapons. Obama allowed Iran to enrich weapons-grade uranium during the terms of the JCPOA.

u.   "And as we do, rest assured that the Iranian government will know our resolve, and that our coordination with Israel will continue …"

v.   "**<u>But I'm also mindful of the proverb, "A man is judged by his deeds, not his words." So, if you want to know where my heart lies, look no further than what I have done</u>**." Since Obama supported UNSC Resolution 2334, which declared that the Western Wall and the Jewish Quarter in East Jerusalem are "occupied Palestinian territory," and also decried the "natural growth" of Jewish communities in East Jerusalem [or Jews having babies in their capital], Obama's heart lies with the Palestinian terrorists, the PLO, and Hamas, all of whom are allied with Iran, al-Qaeda and ISIS.

14.   "We are **not endorsing a resolution** that seeks to impose a resolution to the conflict, it deals with incitement and violence on the Palestinian side *[the genocidal Hamas Charter is not mentioned, there is no specific wording the directly refers to Palestinians violence or incitement]* … **deals [only] with obstacles to peace** *[Obama views Jews living and praying at Jewish holy sites an obstacle to peace.]* … when we see the facts on the ground, again, **deep into the West Bank, beyond the separation barrier**, we feel compelled to speak out against those actions." *During an Israeli Channel 2 news interview, Ben Rhodes, Obama's deputy national security advisor, lies to the Israelis and the American public, implying the UNSC resolution only deals with settlements deep in the West Bank.*

a.   "Condemning all measures aimed at altering the demographic composition, character and status of the **Palestinian Territory occupied since 1967, including East Jerusalem** *[Western Wall, Jewish Quarter – not just deep settlements in the West Bank]*… in violation of international humanitarian law and relevant resolutions … a freeze by Israel of all settlement activity, **including "natural growth,"** *[Jews cannot have children in their capitol – the eastern half of Jerusalem or in the Jewish Quarter of the old city]* and the **dismantlement of all settlement outposts erected since March 2001 … the** establishment by Israel of settlements in the Palestinian territory <u>occupied since 1967, including East Jerusalem</u>, has no legal validity and constitutes a flagrant violation under international law ... Israel immediately and completely cease all settlement activities in the occupied Palestinian territory, **including East Jerusalem** ... it **will not recognize any changes to the 4 June 1967 lines, <u>including with re-gard to Jerusalem</u>**. ..." *UNSC Resolution 2334, devised and passed under the guidance of Obama.*

b. "Ben Rhodes, on the occasion of the US abstention, characterized the resolution as be-ing one with respect to settlements ... **This resolution really runs contrary to UN Security Council resolutions 242 and 338,** *[i.e. – Rhodes is lying]* which set the frame-work and parameters – from the point of view of the Security Council – [for] what the basis for conflict resolution in the Middle East is." *Irwin Cotler, a former Canadian justice minister, attorney-general and parliament member while speaking at Yad Veshem's International School for Holocaust Studies.*[325]

c. "Resolution 2334 harms Israel in two ways. **First, it effectively abrogates Resolution 242 from 1967 which formed the basis of Israeli policy-making for the past 49 years. Second, 2334 gives a strategic boost to the international campaign to boycott the Jewish state.** Resolution 242 anchored the cease-fire between Israel and its neigh-bors at the end of the Six Day War. It stipulated that in exchange for Arab recognition of Israel's right to exist in secure and defensible borders, Israel would cede some of the territories it took control over during the war. **Resolution 242 assumed that Israel has a right to hold these areas and that an Israeli decision to cede some of them to its neighbors in exchange for peace** would constitute a major concession. Resolution 242 is deliberately phrased to ensure that Israel would not be expected to cede all of the lands it took control over in the Six Day War. The resolution speaks of "territories," rather than "the territories" or "all the territories" that Israel took control over during the war. Resolution 2334 rejects 242's founding assumptions. **Resolution 2334 asserts that Israel has no right to any of the lands it took control over during the war.** From the Western Wall to Shiloh, from Hebron to Ariel, 2334 says all Israeli presence in the areas beyond the 1949 armistice lines is crime. **Given that Israel has no right to hold terri-tory under 2334, it naturally follows that the Palestinians have no incentive to give Israel peace.** So they won't. **The peace process, like the two-state solution, ended last Friday night** to the raucous applause of all Security Council members. As for the boycott campaign, contrary to what has been widely argued, 2334 does not strengthen the boycott of "settlements." It gives a strategic boost to the boycott of Israel as a whole. It calls on states "to distinguish in their relevant dealings, between the territory of the State of Israel and the territories occupied since 1967." Since no Israeli firm makes that distinction, **all Israeli economic activity is now threatened with boycott.**"[326] *(Caroline Glick, The Jerusalem Post, December 2016)*

15. Five days after the UNSC passed Resolution 2334, **Secretary of State John Kerry** spoke at the State Department, defending the Obama administration's support of the resolution. There were many lies throughout Kerry's presentation, including -

    a. "Throughout his Administration, President **Obama has been deeply committed to Israel and its security,** and that commitment has guided his pursuit of peace in the Middle East." Obama withheld Hellfire missiles from Israel during their 2014 war with Hamas, and rejected Israel's request that Egypt be a mediator for a ceasefire. Obama forced Israel to accept Turkey and Qatar to be the mediators, both of whom were very pro-Hamas. Obama insisted on a unilateral ceasefire before Israel could dismantle all of Hamas' terror tunnels crossing into Egypt, so that Hamas could maintain offensive capabilities to launch surprise terror attacks into Israel. A two-state solution that allows for the return of Palestinian refugees will easily allow ISIS, al-Qaeda and IRGC terrorists and militias to enter the West Bank disguised as refugees, as ISIS fighters have penetrated Europe posing as destitute Middle Eastern refugees.

    b. "The two-state solution is **the only way to achieve a just and lasting peace** between Israelis and Palestinians." The two-state solution as proposed by Kerry would allow the Palestinians to establish a terror state in the heart of Israel where Israel would only be nine miles wide. Any Arab military forces emerging from this territory would be able to quickly divide Israel in half in any future conflict. Mortar fire originating from the high grounds in the western edge of the West Bank would easily shut down Ben Gurion airport and terrorize much of the civilian population of Tel Aviv, as the rockets from Gaza have done. Obama had the FAA halt all U.S. flights to Ben Gurion during the 2014 Hamas war when only when mortar landed in the vicinity of the airport, proving Israel could not allow the Palestinians to control those territories in the future. As Obama attempted to paralyze Israel's supply lines and links to the outside world, a future Palestinian state could easily target Ben Gurion airport and achieve the same effect. Hamas has had multiple political partnerships with the PA and in early 2017, floated the idea of forming a Palestinian federation between Gaza and the West Bank. With all polls indicating Hamas is much more popular than the PA in the West Bank, the creation of a Palestinian state in the West Bank would ensure Hamas would dominate its political apparatus, and an anti-Semitic genocidal terror state would be formed with Obama's and Kerry's blessing in the heart of Israel. This terror state would also control the Jewish and Christian holy sites in East Jerusalem. This set of circumstances established by Obama and UNSC Resolution 2334 would probably lead to the destruction of Israel, which is Obama's ultimate goal, since Obama is a radical

Muslim. The borders proposed by Obama, Kerry and the UNSC have repeatedly been called Auschwitz borders.

c.　"The two-state solution is the only way to achieve a just and lasting peace between Israelis and Palestinians. It is the only way to ensure Israel's future as a Jewish and democratic state, living in peace and security with its neighbors. It is the only way to ensure a future of freedom and **dignity for the <u>Palestinian people</u>**."

　　i.　"No Arab leaders or diplomats or intellectuals mentioned the "Palestinian people" until 1967, when the need for such became apparent. As Zuheir Mohsen, leader of the Palestinian Arab terror group As Saiqa, famously told a journalist in 1977: '**The Palestinian people does not exist. The creation of a Palestinian state is only a means for continuing our struggle against the state of Israel for our Arab unity**. In reality today there is no difference between Jordanians, Palestinians, Syrians and Lebanese. Only for political and tactical reasons do we speak today about the existence of a Palestinian people, since Arab national interests demand that **we posit the existence of a distinct** "**Palestinian people**" **to oppose Zionism**. Yes, the existence of a separate Palestinian identity exists only **for tactical reasons**, Jordan, which is a sovereign state with defined borders, cannot raise claims to Haifa and Jaffa, while **as a Palestinian**, **I can undoubtedly demand Haifa, Jaffa, Beer-Sheva and Jerusalem**. However, the moment we reclaim our right to all of Palestine, we will not wait even a minute to unite Palestine and Jordan.'"[327] *(Hugh Fitzgerald, Jihad Watch, January 2017)*

d.　"We could not, in **good conscience**, stand in the way of a resolution at the United Nations that makes clear that both sides must act now to **preserve the possibility of peace**." This resolution will only bring war, since by declaring that the Western Wall and the Jewish Quarter in East Jerusalem are "occupied Palestinian territory," Israel will be less likely to relinquish any territory to the Palestinians and the Palestinians will now feel legally entitled to control all the Jewish holy sites in Jerusalem. Palestinian terrorism will increase and the Israelis will respond more forcefully. If Obama acted with a "good conscience," he would have refused to support the language establishing the Western Wall as Palestinian territory, especially when there has never been a Palestinian state, and the Palestinians have never relinquished terrorism as a core strategy when fighting the Jews.

e.　"Friends need to tell each other the **hard truths**, and friendships require **mutual respect**." Mutual respect must cut both ways. This resolution does not respect Israel as a Jewish state, since it gives the Western Wall to the Palestinians, and does not respect Israel's security needs, while its fails to establish any consequences for the continuation of Palestinian terror attacks. Israel needs to tell Obama and Kerry the hard truth – that they are anti-Semites and support Islamic terrorism.

f.   "This friend [Obama, Kerry, America] that **has blocked countless efforts to delegiti-mize Israel**." Obama and the United States officially delegitimized all Jews living in East Jerusalem – over half of Israel's capital, the Jewish Quarter, and the West Bank by declaring their presence in these contested territories is officially illegal. By attempting to downplay and negate Israel's ties to Jerusalem and declaring that the holiest Jewish sites in Jerusalem are "occupied Palestinian territory," Obama and Kerry have delegitimized the Jewish State of Israel and have basically denied Israel's historical connection to the land of Israel. Later during this same speech, Kerry stated, "And when Israel celebrates its 70th anniversary in 2018, the Palestinians will mark a very different anniversary: 70 years since what they call the Nakba, or catastrophe." **Kerry applied a moral equiva-lence to the creation of Israel**, **and the Palestinians' desire to destroy the Jewish state**, **since they refer to its creation as a catastrophe**. Thus, Kerry has delegitimized the existence of Israel from another perspective.

g.   "In fact, this Administration has been Israel's greatest friend and supporter, with an absolutely **unwavering commitment to advancing Israel's security** and **protecting its legitimacy**."

h.   "Time and again we have demonstrated that we have Israel's back. We have strongly **op-posed boycotts**, **divestment campaigns**, **and sanctions** targeting Israel in international fora, whenever and wherever its legitimacy was attacked." Obama and Resolution 2334 paves the way for BDS attacks and economic war against Israel, by formally recom-mending governments around the world take to "**distinguish in their relevant deal-ings**, between the territory of the State of Israel and the territories occupied since 1967." (paragraph 5)

i.   "They can choose to live together in one state, or they can separate into two states. But here is a fundamental reality: if the choice is one state, **Israel can either be Jewish or democratic – it cannot be both – and it won't ever really be at peace**." Neither a one or two-state solution will bring peace, since the Palestinians are dedicated to replacing all of Israel with a Palestinian state and eventually ethnically cleansing the Jews from Israel. This endpoint is clearly defined in the Hamas Charter and in the curriculum taught throughout the Palestinian educational system. As long as there are religious Muslims believing in the Quran, Islam will always be propagating a genocidal war against the Jews and Israel. Regarding democracy, why should Israel give Palestinians who want to destroy Israel, the right to vote, so that their representatives will be a fifth column in any Israeli political system.

j.   "Let me say it again: There is **absolutely no justification for terrorism**, and there never will be." Resolution 2334 justified terrorism since the UNSC and Obama gave Hamas and the PA all of their negotiating demands, including large section of the Jewish homeland and its holy sites, without renouncing or diminishing their terror attacks or incitement. By declaring the Western Wall and the Jewish Quarter are illegally occupied Palestinian territory, Obama and Kerry have legitimized Palestinian terrorism against the Jewish state ad perpetuum, since the world community has recognized that the Palestinians are fighting a legal and moral battle against perceived and declared Jewish "occupiers."

k. "Far too often, **the Palestinians have pursued efforts to delegitimize Israel** in international fora. **We have strongly opposed these initiatives**, **including the recent wholly unbalanced and inflammatory UNESCO resolution** regarding Jerusalem." The UNESCO resolution declared that the Western Wall was part of the al Aqsa mosque. By defining the Western Wall as illegally occupied Palestinian (Arab, Muslim) territory, Obama and the United States are supporting the previous UNESCO resolution attempting to transfer control of this Jewish holy site from an Israeli to a Palestinian guardianship.

l. "We have made **clear our strong opposition to Palestinian efforts against Israel at the ICC** (International Criminal Court), which only sets back the prospects for peace." Obama and Kerry have significantly strengthened the Palestinian argument against Israel at the ICC and other legal forums by stating in paragraph 1 of UNSC Resolution 2334, "the establishment by Israel of settlements in the Palestinian territory occupied since 1967, including East Jerusalem, **has no legal validity and constitutes a flagrant violation under international law**." After this resolution passed, the Palestinian leadership immediately announced their intentions to continue their diplomatic warfare at the ICC, which would be used to convict Israel of war crimes based on their support of settlements in contested territories.

m. "The Israeli prime minister publicly supports a two-state solution, but his current coalition is the **most right-wing in Israeli history**, with an agenda **driven by the most extreme elements**." Kerry states that only the most extreme elements in Israel's society want to maintain control of major Jewish settlements in the West Bank, and want to maintain control of their entire capital, the Western Wall and the Jewish Quarter, as well as the Christian holy sites. Jews who want to safeguard Israel's security in a way that is not in line with Obama's or Kerry's vision are extremist. The Israelis have seen the unprecedented chaos that the Obama administration has wrought upon Syria, Iraq, and Libya, and do not want this American administration to force their vision of Israel's future upon Jerusalem and the West Bank, when the same results are highly likely. A common tactic of the left is to lie and label your political opponents as racists and extremists, even when they are your most stable and trusted ally in the Middle East. Of course, Kerry did not label Hamas or the PLO as extremists – only Israel's leadership – because Kerry and

Obama most likely agree with the Palestinians' ultimate goals. Ironically, **Obama and Kerry are <u>the most far left-wing anti-Semitic administration</u>** in American history.

n.   "If Israel goes down the one state path, it will never have true peace with the rest of the Arab world, and I can say that with certainty." Maybe, maybe not. Israel already has formal relations with Egypt and Jordan, and an unofficial alliance with Saudi Arabia and other Gulf states. With Iran's increasing hegemony in the Middle East, the Sunni majority states may formally ally with Israel in order to strengthen their positions against Iran.

o.   "We could not in good conscience turn a blind eye to Palestinian actions that fan hatred and violence." What have been the threatened consequences of continued Palestinian violence and terrorism? They have never been threatened with the loss of land or the removal of support for a Palestinian state. UNSC Resolution 2334 rewards the Palestinians with a state and Jerusalem, even though they still incite and enact terrorism directed against Israelis and Jews. The world has turned a blind eye to this evil.

p.   "The Obama Administration has **always defended Israel against any** effort at the UN and any international fora or **biased and one-sided resolutions** that seek to undermine its legitimacy or security, and **that has not changed. It didn't change with this vote**." Everything changed with this vote. Obama invalidated Resolution 242, which recognized Israel's right to keep some of the territory it won in a defensive war against Jordan in 1967. Resolution 242 was the basis of the land for peace strategy. It defined Israel as an illegal occupying power in its own capital. It instantaneously created over 600,000 Jewish refugees who are now living in East Jerusalem and the West Bank. It gave the Palestinians ownership of the holiest Jewish and Christian religious sites in East Jerusalem. It made illegal the natural growth of Jewish communities in the Jewish Quarter of the old city, or it is illegal for Jews to have children in territories contested by the Palestinians. It destroyed any chance of implementing a two-state solution, and made peace between the Israelis and the Palestinians an increasing impossibility, especially when the Palestinians were not pushed to compromise. The UNSC and Obama backed Abbas, when he stated in 2010, "I cannot allow even one concession to Israel." By allowing UNSC Resolution 2334 to pass, Obama proved that he is allied with radical Islamic terrorists, since he is supporting Hamas and the PLO to control half of Israel's capital and control access to the holiest religious sites in Christianity and Judaism. As Ron Dermer, Israel's ambassador to the United States concurred during a *CNN* interview, "Israel's enemies are celebrating this resolution. That tells you all you need to know."

q.   "So, we reject the criticism that this vote abandons Israel."

r.   "In fact, this resolution simply reaffirms statements made by the Security Council on the legality of settlements over several decades. **<u>It does not break new ground</u>** … **We**

fully respect Israel's profound historic and religious ties to the city and to its holy sites. We've never questioned that." **UNSC Resolution 2334**: "Condemning all measures aimed at altering the demographic composition *[Jews are not allowed to move to the eastern half of their capital or have children in Jewish communities that have existed there for over 3000 years]*, character and status of the Palestinian Territory occupied since 1967, including East Jerusalem … the establishment by Israel of settlements in the Palestinian territory occupied since 1967, **including East Jerusalem**, has **no legal validity** and constitutes a **flagrant violation under international law** … Israel immediately and completely cease all settlement activities in the occupied Palestinian territory, including East Jerusalem … will not recognize any changes to the 4 June 1967 lines, including with regard to Jerusalem … to distinguish, in their relevant dealings, between the territory of the State of Israel and the territories occupied since 1967 *[supports the BDS campaign]* …"

i.   "The United States has historically backed Israel's view that **UN Security Council Resolution 242**, adopted on November 22, 1967, does not require a full withdrawal to the 1949 Armistice Lines (the 1967 borders). Moreover, in addition to that interpretation, both Democratic and Republican administrations have argued that Israel was entitled to "defensible borders." In other words, the American backing of defensible borders has been bipartisan, right up to its latest rendition that was provided by President George W. Bush in April 2004. And it was rooted in America's long-standing support for the security of Israel that went well beyond the various legal interpretations of UN resolutions … It is important to recall that UN Security Council Resolution 242 of November 22, 1967, was a joint product of both the British ambassador to the UN, Lord Caradon, and the U.S. ambassador to the UN, Arthur Goldberg. This was especially true of the withdrawal clause in the resolution which called on Israeli armed forces to withdraw "from territories" and not "from all the territories" or "from the territories" as the Soviet Union had demanded. The exclusion of the definite article "the" from the withdrawal clause was not decided by a low-level legal drafting team or even at the ambassadorial level. And it was not just a matter for petty legalists. Rather, President Lyndon Baines Johnson himself decided that it was important to stick to this phraseology, despite the pressure from the Soviet premier, Alexei Kosygin, who had sought to incorporate stricter additional language requiring a full Israel withdrawal.[1] The meaning of UN Security Council Resolution 242 was absolutely clear to those who were involved in this drafting process. Thus, Joseph P. Sisco, who would serve as the U.S. Assistant Secretary of State for Near Eastern and South Asian Affairs, commented on Resolution 242 during a *Meet the Press* interview some years later: "I was engaged in the negotiation for months of that resolution. That resolution did not say 'total withdrawal.'"[2] This U.S. position had been fully coordinated with the British at the time. Indeed, George Brown, who had served as British foreign secretary in 1967 during Prime Minister Harold Wilson's Labour government, summarized Resolution 242 as follows: "The proposal said, 'Israel will withdraw from territories that were occupied,' not 'from the territories,' which means Israel will not withdraw from all the territories."[3] … President Johnson's insistence on protecting the territorial flexibility of Resolution 242 could be traced to his statements made on June 19, 1967, in the immediate wake of the Six-Day War. In fact, Johnson declared that "an immediate return to the situation as it was on June 4," before the outbreak of hostilities, was "not a prescription for peace, but for renewed hostilities." He stated that the old "truce lines" had been "fragile and violated." What was needed, in Johnson's view, were "recognized boundaries" that would provide "security against terror, destruction and war."[328] *(Hugh Fitzgerald, Jihad Watch)*

ii.   "'Where the prior holder of territory had seized that territory unlawfully, the state which subsequently takes that territory in the lawful exercise of self-defense has, against that prior holder, better title.' *(Stephen W. Schwebel, the Executive Director of the American Society of International Law, who would become the Legal Advisor of the U.S. Department of State and later serve on the International Court of Justice in The Hague, American Journal of International Law (64\344,1970))* In the international legal community there was an acute awareness that Jordan, the West Bank's previous occupant prior to 1967, had illegally invaded the West Bank in 1948, while Israel captured the territory in a war of self-defense."[329]

iii.   "Already in 1973, in subsequently disclosed private conversations with **Kissinger**, in referring to the 1967 lines, **Nixon** explicitly admitted: 'you and I both know they [the Israelis] can't go back to the other borders.'"[330]

iv.   "President Ford provided Prime Minister Rabin with a letter on the future of the Golan Heights that stated: 'The U.S. has not developed a final position on the borders. Should it do so it will give great weight to Israel's position that any peace agreement with Syria must be predicated on Israel remaining on the Golan Heights.'"[331]

v.   "It was the administration of **President Ronald Reagan** that most forcefully articulated Israel's right to defensible borders, just after President Carter appeared to give only lukewarm support for the U.S.-Israeli understandings of the Ford-Kissinger era. Reagan himself stated in his September 1, 1982, address that became known as the "Reagan Plan": 'In the pre-1967 borders, Israel was barely ten miles wide at its narrowest point. The bulk of Israel's population lived within artillery range of hostile armies. I am not about to ask Israel to live that way again.' Reagan came up with a flexible formula for Israeli withdrawal: 'The extent to which Israel should be asked to give up territory will be heavily affected by the extent of the peace and normalization.'"[332]

vi. **"Secretary of State George Shultz** was even more explicit about what this meant during a September 1988 address: 'Israel will never negotiate from or return to the 1967 borders.' ... Shultz was saying that the West Bank should be divided between Israel and the Jordanians according to different functions of government, and not in terms of drawing new internal borders. In an address to the Council on Foreign Relations in February 1988, he asserted: 'the meaning of sovereignty, the meaning of territory, is changing, and what any national government can control, or what any unit that thinks it has sovereignty or jurisdiction over a certain area can control, is shifting gears.'"[333]

vii. "We simply do not support the description of the territories occupied by Israel in the 1967 war as 'occupied Palestinian territory." *U.S. Secretary of State Madeline Albright, March 1994.*

viii. "U.S. support for defensible borders had clearly become bipartisan and continued into the 1990s, even as the Palestinians replaced Jordan as the primary Arab claimant to the West Bank. At the time of the completion of the 1997 Hebron Protocol, **Secretary of State Warren Christopher** wrote a letter of assurances to Prime Minister Benjamin Netanyahu. In the Christopher letter, the **Clinton administration** basically stated that it was not going to second-guess Israel about its security needs: 'a hallmark of U.S. policy remains our commitment to work cooperatively to seek to meet the security needs that Israel identifies' (emphasis added). This meant that Israel would be the final arbiter of its defense needs. Christopher then added: 'Finally, I would like to reiterate our position that Israel is entitled to secure and defensible borders (emphasis added), which should be directly negotiated and agreed with its neighbors.'"[334]

ix. "First, the United States remains committed to my vision and to its implementation as described in the roadmap. The United States will do its utmost to **prevent any attempt by anyone to impose any other plan**. Under the roadmap, **Palestinians must undertake an immediate cessation of** armed activity and **all acts of violence against Israelis anywhere**, and all official Palestinian institutions **must end incitement** against Israel ... Second, there will be no security for Israelis or Palestinians until they and all states, in the region and beyond, join together to fight terrorism and **dismantle terrorist organizations**. The United States reiterates its steadfast commitment to Israel's security, including **secure, defensible borders, and to preserve and strengthen Israel's capability to deter and defend itself**, by itself, against any threat or possible combination of threats … The United States is strongly **committed to Israel's security and well-being as a Jewish state** … As part of a final peace settlement, **Israel must have secure and recognized borders**, which should emerge from negotiations between the parties **in accordance with UNSC Resolutions 242 and 338**. In light of new realities on the ground, including already existing **major Israeli populations centers**, **it is unrealistic to expect that the outcome of final status negotiations will be a full and complete return to the armistice lines of 1949**, and all previous efforts to negotiate a two-state solution have reached the same conclusion. It is realistic to expect that **any final status agreement will only be achieved on the basis of mutually agreed changes that reflect these realities**." *President George W. Bush, Letter From President Bush to Prime Minister Sharon, April 14, 2004.* Obama and Kerry completely discarded most of President Bush's 2004 promises made to Israel. "Less than a year later, on March 27, 2005, Secretary of State Condoleezza Rice explained on Israel Radio that "Israeli population centers" referred to "the large settlement blocs" in the West Bank."[335]

s.   "We also strongly reject the notion that somehow the United States was the driving force behind this resolution." Proven false.

t.   "We made clear to others, including those on the Security Council, that it was possible that if the resolution were to be balanced and it were to include references to incitement and to terrorism *[there is no specific mention of Palestinian terrorism or the genocide directed against the Jews in the Quran or the Hamas Charter]*, that it was possible the United States would then not block it, that – **if it was balanced and fair**." There are no consequences in the resolution to the Palestinians for their continued incitement and terrorism. The UNSC blames Jews building homes in their historic homeland as the major impediment to peace while ignoring Islam's war against the Jews, which has been implemented in various capacities since the birth of Islam, and is now manifest in the Palestinians' quest to eliminate the Jewish state.

u.   "We also made crystal clear that **the President of the United States would not make a final decision about our own position until we saw the final text**." Obama made the decision to bring this resolution before the UNSC during the summer of 2016, thus he already decided to support the resolution almost half a year before the vote. In reality, Obama decided to support this resolution in 2009 when he became president, and declared in Cairo that Israel was born as a result of the atrocities of WWII and decided to put daylight between the United States government and the Israeli leadership. Obama waited until the end of his presidency to support the transfer of East Jerusalem and all its non-Islamic holy sites to the PA and Hamas out of political expediency.

v. "And we all understand that Israel faces very serious threats in a very tough neighborhood. Israelis are rightfully concerned about making sure that there is not a new terrorist haven right next door to them, often referencing what's happened with Gaza, and we understand that and we believe there are ways to meet those needs of security … **We have called for the Palestinians to do everything in their power to stop violence and incitement**, including publicly and consistently condemning acts of terrorism and stopping the glorification of violence." But what and where are the consequences to the Palestinians if they continue with the terrorism? If the Palestinians continue their incitement and terrorism, will they lose the option of obtaining an independent state of their own? No. Thus, Kerry is lying and only paying lip service to the Israelis and ignoring the threats to Israel's security.

w. "And much progress can be made in advance of negotiations that can lay the foundation for negotiations, **as contemplated by the Oslo process**." The Oslo process is dead, since the Palestinians violated the parameters of the Oslo accord by bypassing negotiations with Israel as they sought to unilaterally establish a Palestinian state through the United Nations and other world bodies.

x. "The only effective response to the waves of anti-Semitic horrors sweeping across Europe was to create a state in the historic home of the Jewish people, where their ties to the land **went back centuries**." 3500 years, not a few hundred years. Kerry is downplaying the extent of the Jews' historical ties to the land of Israel.

y. "It has been more than 20 years since Israel and the PLO signed their first agreement – the Oslo Accords – and **the PLO formally recognized Israel**." The PLO have not recognized Israel, because they don't recognize it as a Jewish state.

z. "There is also broad recognition of Israel's need to ensure that the **borders are secure and defensible** … Everyone understands that no Israeli Government can ever accept an agreement that does not satisfy its security needs or that risk creating an enduring security threat like Gaza transferred to the West Bank." Obama's borders are "Auschwitz borders." Hamas controls Gaza, which became a terror state, and Hamas will control an independent West Bank, which will follow in Gaza's path should the Palestinians be granted an independent state as defined by Obama or UNSC Resolution 2334.

16. "**I don't think it caused a major rupture in relations** between the United States and Israel. If you're saying that [Israeli] Prime Minister Netanyahu got fired up, he's been fired up repeatedly during the course of my presidency … **We have defended them consistently in every imaginable way**. *[Not at the UNSC or during the 2014 Gaza war with Hamas or*

when Obama ordered senior American UN officials to boycott Netanyahu's speech before the UN General Assembly in 2015.] But I also believe that both for our national interests and Israel's national interests that allowing an ongoing conflict between Israelis and Palestinians that could get worse and worse over time is a problem." *Obama, discussing UNSC Resolution 2334 during a "60 Minutes" interview with Steve Croft on December 15, 2016.* After the vote, senior Israeli government officials complained that Obama "abandoned" Israel. Obama allowed the UNSC to pass a resolution that declared the Western Wall, the Jewish quarter in the Old City of Jerusalem, and all Jewish communities in East Jerusalem and the West Bank were occupied Palestinian territory, or territory belonging to the PLO and Hamas, both organizations that are committed to destroying Israel as demonstrated by their charters, policies and rhetoric. Not only did Obama give the heart of Israel to the Palestinians, he gave Israel indefensible boundaries which countered the guarantees of UNSC Resolution 242 and countless prior American presidents and secretaries of state. The Palestinians would be able to not only easily shell Tel Aviv from their West Bank positions, they would also be able to shut down Ben Gurion airport with similar missile attacks. Obama also gave the PLO and Hamas de facto control of the holiest Christian sites in Jerusalem, thus betraying his "professed" Christian religion. As Obama prepared to leave the presidency, he attempted to position radical Islamic jihadists and their allies into advantageous geographical locations that would be used to advance the destruction of Israel and the genocide of Jews in the Middle East, thus implementing part II of the Final Solution.

17. "All we are trying to do is speak as a good, solid best friend of Israel and **we have done more for this government**, **more for Israel** than any other administration … **We speak out of a caring and concern for Israel**." *Kerry, CNN interview, January 16, 2017.* Obama and Kerry stabbed Israel in the back when they plotted to give the Wailing Wall, and all the Jewish communities in East Jerusalem to the PLO and Hamas and their allies – all Islamic jihadi terrorist organizations, committed to destroy Israel and the Jewish holy sites. Neither Obama or Kerry insisted that the PLO, Fatah, or Hamas change their charters or constitutions which all call for the destruction of Israel, so these U.S. leaders acquiesced in the Palestinians' goal of ridding the Middle East of its largest Jewish presence.

18. "**America will align our policies with those who pursue peace**, and say in public what we say in private to Israelis and Palestinians and Arabs." *Obama, Cairo University speech, June 4, 2009. Taqiyya.* Obama has always supported Hamas, despite its genocidal charter calling for the murder of all Jews worldwide. Obama is also threatening Israel saying that if you do not pursue a "peace" that is in line with his vision, then American policies will not support you.

    a. A leading Palestinian threatened the West if they failed to force Israel to accept a political settlement on Palestinian terms. He stated on Palestinian Authority's *Awdha TV* on

February 1, 2016, "Do we have to hijack your planes and destroy your airports again to make you care about our cause? Are you waiting for us to cut off your oil supply? You always wait for things to reach a boiling point and explode, causing you harm, before you intervene to end the crimes and violations." *Nabil Shaath, former foreign minister of the Palestinian Authority, Fatah Central Committee member.* Shaath made these threats after the Palestinian "knife intifada" killed over 30 Israeli and Jewish individuals in Israel and the West Bank.

b. *The Associated Press* suppressed videos that showed **thousands of Palestinians in the West Bank publicly celebrating al-Qaeda's attacks** on New York and Washington on September 11, 2001. Obama is allied with a society that supports al-Qaeda, and later they demonstrated the **strongest support for ISIS among Arabs** in the Middle East. There is a significant alliance between Hamas and ISIS, where Hamas gives ISIS terrorists a safe haven in Gaza and supports ISIS operations in the Sinai.

c. After a group of Palestinians disguised as Orthodox Jews murdered four Israelis and wounded nine others in a massive shooting attack at a popular outdoor market in Tel Aviv, on June 8, 2016, Palestinians in Gaza [firework displays], the West Bank [handing out sweets and candy], and Turkey were publicly celebrating the success of the terrorist attack against the Jews. The Muslims in the Middle East have started the celebration of Ramadan by killing Jews. The Palestinians have also held public celebrations after 9-11 and the Boston Marathon bombing.

d. Obama allowed the Palestinian Authority to pay stipends to the terrorists who murdered Israelis with U.S. aid.

19. "**Palestinians <u>must</u> abandon violence**. Resistance through violence and killing is wrong and does not succeed. **For centuries, Black people in America suffered the lash of the whip as slaves and the humiliation of segregation. But it was not violence that won full and equal rights**. It was a peaceful and determined insistence upon the ideals at the center of America's founding … **It's a story with a simple truth: that violence is a dead end. It is a sign of neither courage nor power to shoot rockets at sleeping children, or to blow up old women on a bus**. That is not how moral authority is claimed; that is how it is surrendered." *Obama, Cairo University Speech, June 4, 2009.* Taqiyya. Obama is comparing the plight of the Palestinians with the African-American struggle for equal rights in America, despite the violence, anti-Semitism and genocidal intentions embedded in their struggle for a Palestinian state. African-Americans, unlike the Palestinians, were not blowing up civilian buses or decapitating children in their homes after killing their parents. Although shooting rockets at civilian targets and killing all Jews is at the core of Hamas' strategy, Obama still supports their quest for an independent state in the heart of Israel. Obama did not repeat this belief (Palestinians must abandon violence) during the third intifada, when Palestinians were

indiscriminately knifing Israelis and ramming them with cars six years after Obama's initial proclamation. Even though the Palestinians have never abandoned violence or incitement against the Jews, Obama still wants to give them half of Jerusalem, a judenrein West Bank, and many Jewish holy sites. Therefore, Obama lied when he used the word "must."

20. "**Nobody** is suffering more than the Palestinian people."[336] *Obama. 2008 presidential campaign trail.* Nobody? The Palestinians have the highest literacy rate in the Muslim world.

21. "On the other hand, it is also undeniable that **the Palestinian people** – **Muslims and Christians** *[There are very few Christians left in Palestinian controlled territories secondary to discrimination, harassment and murder.]* – **have suffered in pursuit of a homeland**. For more than sixty years they have endured the pain of dislocation. Many wait in refugee camps in the West Bank, Gaza *[Obama lies since why should there be camps in their home country]*, and neighboring lands for a life of peace and security they have never been able to lead. **They endure the daily humiliations – large and small – that come with occupation**. So let there be no doubt: **the situation for the Palestinian people is intolerable. America will not turn our backs on the legitimate Palestinian aspiration for dignity, opportunity, and a state of their own**." *Obama, Cairo University speech, June 4, 2009.* Obama states quite clearly he will use the presidency to advance Palestinian interests over Israeli interests. The Palestinians have the highest standard of living and the highest literacy rates of all Muslims in the Middle East. Obama never directly addresses the ingrained Palestinian incitement to kill and attack Jews, or their desire to destroy Israel, the major impediment to securing their full autonomy. Presently, the Christian population in the territories controlled by the Palestinians has shrunk to 1.3%, because of the harassment, persecution, and the murder of Christians. Muslims inflict daily humiliations on the Christians living in the West Bank and Gaza. In 1949, when Israel was declared an independent country, the Christian population of Bethlehem was 85%. Now, due to oppression by Muslims, it is less than 12%. When does Obama, as a supposedly Christian president, use his bully pulpit to castigate any Muslim nation for their discriminatory practices against their minority citizens? Why not transfer Syrian Christian refugees to Bethlehem, and let them establish their own local police force? When have the Christian Palestinians ever advocated for a Christian Palestinian homeland? With almost no Christians remaining in Gaza, it is doubtful that Christians in the West Bank will have a brighter future if another Palestinian state is created in the heart of Israel.

   a. "**The Palestinian people does not exist**. The creation of a Palestinian state is only a means for continuing our struggle against the state of Israel." *PLO executive committee member Zahir Muhsein.* In fact, the Palestinians already have two states, Gaza and Jordan. A sovereign political entity in the West Bank and East Jerusalem would give them three states, and thus any future negotiated settlement between Israel and the Palestinians would be known as the "four-state solution."

b. "U.S. President Franklin Delano Roosevelt noted that "Arab immigration into Palestine since 1921 has vastly exceeded the total Jewish immigration during this whole period." Winston Churchill made the identical observation: "Despite the fact that they were never persecuted, masses of Arabs poured into the country and multiplied until the Arab population grew more than what all of world Jewry could add to the Jewish population." ... In March 2012 Hamas's Interior Minister in Gaza, Fathi Hamad, pleaded for pan-Arab help against the IDF "so that we can continue the jihad ... Praise Allah, we all have Arab roots and every Palestinian in Gaza and all over Palestine can prove their Arab roots, whether they be in Saudi Arabia and Yemen, or anywhere else. We have blood ties." Hamad elaborated by personal example: "half my family is Egyptian ... There are over 30 clans in the Gaza Strip with the surname Al-Masri [Egyptian] ... Half of all Palestinians are Egyptians, and the other half are Saudi. Who are the Palestinians? We have many families called Al-Masri whose roots are Egyptian ... We are Egyptians." ... [former Arab Israeli Knesset member Bishara admitted that the Palestinian national movement narrative was a fraud since the Palestinians and surrounding Arab societies felt] "obligated to nationalize the history of Arab-speaking peoples and to make it into a national history that goes back from before the time of Islam all the way to contemporary times ... Acting out of a need to compete with Zionism, the Palestinian national movement has anchored its origins to those of the Canaanites [in order to] achieve its own, unique starting-off point in the past that precedes that of the Hebrew tribes, which Zionism claims as its natural ancestors."[337] (*Sarah Honig, The Jerusalem Post, May 2015).* There was never a Palestinian people, a Palestinian nation, a Palestinian culture, or a Palestinian society. The vast majority of Muslims in Israel and the West Bank who call themselves Palestinians are actually Arab migrants who came to Israel to take advantage of the economic opportunities made available by Israel's Jewish inhabitants or just to pursue jihad against the Jews living in Palestine.

c. "I don't think there is a Palestinian nation at all. I think there is an **Arab nation**. I always thought so ... I think it's a colonialist invention – a Palestinian nation. When were there any Palestinians?" *Azmi Bishara, founder of Israel's Balad party which represents the interests of Arab Israeli citizens, Israel's Channel 2, 1996*

d. "Where ARE all those Palestinians, the proclaimed one million of them who lived in Israel before they were 'displaced'? Nowhere. Nowhere, because they never existed. And where are all the mosques for those "1 million Palestinians"? With Muslims comes mosques. There can be no Muslim population without a large proportion of mosques. If they had been 1 million at the turn of the Century, or even in 1920 after they began immigrating to fight the British, with their rapid population growth Palestine would consist of over 40 million people today and not 4 million. That alone proves the Palestinian jihad lies.

Their population is small because they are new invaders and occupiers who arrived late with an aim to commit jihad. They never lost land that was never theirs to begin with! … Felix Bonfils (1831 – 1885) was a French photographer and writer who was active in the Middle East. Four years after his arrival he reported 15,000 prints of Egypt, Palestine, Syria and Greece … He travelled the region several times and we hear of no mass population of Palestinians … His pictures did not manage to capture any photographs of a single so-called 'Palestinian' who are supposed to have lost land to Jewish occupation … Because the "Palestinian" people as we know them today never existed … Palestinians are a fake creation ordered and constructed by the Grand Mufti Haj Mohammed Effendi Amin el Husseini [1889 – 1974]. They … originate from mass immigration from Egypt and Saudi Arabia with the purpose to commit jihad. The Egyptian fighters ended up in Gaza and the Saudi fighters ended up in the West Bank, according to their rout of entry. This has been well documented by British government reports from the British Mandate and from Transjordan. It also fits the video clips and rants by Hamas leaders."[338] *(The Palestine-Israeli Conflict, 2013) None of the historical photos showed mosques, which would be present with any significant indigenous Muslim population.*

e.   The Palestinian flag before 1948 had a star of David in the center.

22.   "That is why the security of the Jewish people in Israel is so important – because it can never be taken for granted. But make no mistake: those who adhere to the ideology of rejecting Israel's right to exist might as well reject the earth beneath them and the sky above, because **Israel is not going anywhere**." *Obama addressing Israeli students during his 2013 trip to Israel.*

a.   **An intelligence report**, "**Preparing for a Post-Israel Middle East**," commissioned by the Obama U.S. Intelligence Community in 2012, argues that Israel is a significant threat to American national security interests since its policies interfere with American relationships with the Arab and Muslim world, as well as the whole international community. Is Obama laying the groundwork for a world without Israel?

23.   In an interview with Jeffrey Goldberg in *The Atlantic* from January 2013, Obama lobs criticisms at Netanyahu by stating, "<u>**Israel doesn't know what its own best interests are**</u> … [Goldberg paraphrasing Obama:] **If Israel, a small state in an inhospitable region, becomes more of a pariah, one that alienates even the affections of the U.S., its last steadfast friend** [or me] – **it won't survive**."[339] Obama also calls Netanyahu a "**political coward**" because he refuses to put Israel in a suicidal geopolitical position with respect to the Palestinians.

24.   Obama **compares the plight of African-Americans during the civil rights era with the Palestinians' desire to ultimately destroy Israel and kill the Jews**. Obama stated in Ramallah during his 2013 trip to Israel, "Whenever I meet these young people, whether

they're Palestinian or Israeli, I'm reminded of my own daughters, and I know what hopes and aspirations I have for them … because there was a time when my daughters could not expect to have the same opportunities in their own country as somebody else's daughters." Obama ignores the incitement, daily genocidal rhetoric and indoctrination to hate all Jews advanced by the Palestinian government and society, as well as the anti-Semitism embedded in the Quran. Obama is legitimizing Palestinian hatred and genocide, and insists Israel create conditions on the ground in the name of peace that will give the Palestinians the upper hand as they initiate the next phase of their war to destroy Israel.

25. During a speech in Israel in 2013, **Obama stated**, "Of course, Israel cannot be expected to negotiate with anyone who is dedicated to its destruction. **But while I know you have had differences with the Palestinian Authority, I believe that you do have a true partner in President Abbas** *[taqiyya – Obama, in the tradition of Malcolm X, is trying to hoodwink Israel.]* and Prime Minister Fayyad." One year later, **Abbas formed a unity government with Hamas** and supported their missile barrage on civilian Israeli targets.

   a. In 2015, Abbas publicly **incited the Palestinians to kill Jews** on the Temple Mount, and later stated "[**the Jews] have no right to defile them** [places on or near the Temple Mount] **with their filthy feet.**"

   b. In 2015, Abbas wrote a letter to the family of a slain terrorist who tried to kill an activist rabbi in Jerusalem. He **praised the terrorist** and said "With anger, we have received the news of the vicious assassination crime committed by the terrorists of the Israeli occupation army against [your] son Mu'taz Ibrahim Khalil Hijazi, **who will go to heaven as a martyr.**"

   c. "No Jew, civilian or otherwise, would be permitted to live in the future Palestinian state." *Abbas, Cairo, July 2013.*

   d. In June 2016, Abbas addressed the European Union Parliament and promoted anti-Semitic blood libel that was reminiscent of hate speech from the Nazis and those political forces that initiated pogroms against Jewish communities in Europe and the Middle East throughout history. Abbas declared, "**We are against incitement** *[taqiyya]*… [but] … Certain **rabbis in Israel** have said very clearly to their government that **our water should be poisoned in order to have Palestinians killed**. That is provocation and we are against this sort of call for violence. Is this not clear incitement, to the mass murder of the Palestinian people? *[taqiyya from Obama's moderate peace partner].*" The European Union Parliament gave Abbas a standing ovation with prolonged applause. Obama has always supported the European Union and their political agenda, especially with their input in the Middle East. Obama never refuted Abbas' original comments. Although Abbas retracted his remarks two days after his speech, within a week of his blood libel, a Palestinian teenager broke into the home of an American-Israeli family and stabbed to death a 13-year-old girl, Hallel Ariel, in her bed in Kiryat Arba. The young girl was an American citizen. The same day, another Palestinian stabbed two Israelis in Netanya, one being critically injured. Danny Dannon, Israel's ambassador to the United Nations responded, "There is a direct line between Mahmoud Abbas' **words of incitement** in the European Parliament to the ghastly murder of Hallel Ariel." Immediately after the murder, the Palestinian authority, headed by Abbas, declared the Palestinian teen was a "martyr" or "shahid," which is viewed as the highest honor achievable in Islam. The killer's family is now eligible for a monthly stipend from the PA for killing the young Jewish girl. The killer's mother heaped praises upon her son saying, "My son is a hero. He made me proud. My son died a Martyr defending Jerusalem … Allah willing, all of them will follow his path, all of the youth of Palestine. Allah be praised." The Palestinian leadership and society openly support the killing of Jewish children and civilians. Abbas refused to take calls from world leaders, who asked him to condemn this atrocity. Even though Ariel was an American citizen, Obama remained silent on the murder, which is exactly the opposite of his immediate condemnation of events surrounding the deaths of Michael Brown and Freddie Gray. When a Palestinian Muslim murders a young American Jewish girl, Obama remains silent. But when an African-American thug is killed by a police officer, who fired in self-defense in order to save his life, Obama immediately lashes out against the police and American society. It is time to cast aside political correctness and admit that Obama is anti-Semitic and a racist.

e.   In late June 2016, Sultan Abu al-Einein, an **advisor to Abbas** and a member of the Fatah Central Committee, stated during an interview with *Donia al-Watan News*, "**Wherever you find an Israeli, slit his throat**." Days later, a Palestinian teenager stabbed to death a 13-year-old girl in her bed after he broke into her home.

f.   While campaigning for reelection **in 2016, Abbas boasted that Fatah had killed over 11,000 Israelis as a reason to vote for him**.

g.   In 2016, Abbas wrote a message to the parents of a Palestinian who attempted to run over an Israeli soldier, and praised her saying, "we see in her a martyr who watered the pure earth of Palestine with her blood."

h.   In January 2017, for days after a Palestinian drove a truck through a group of Israeli soldiers, killing four – Abbas maintained his silence and would not condemn the attacker. David Keyes, spokesman for Prime Minister Netanyahu, declared Abbas' silence was "**outrageous**." *The [liberal] Jerusalem Post* commented in an editorial, "Jerusalem Attack Exposes **Israel's False Peace Partner**," – "The failure by **Palestinian President Mahmoud Abbas** to condemn the attack by Monday night – more than 36 hours since it took place – is part of a culture of hate, violence and intransigence. A "peace partner" does not remain silent when innocent 20-year-olds are deliberately run down by a truck on a sunny Sunday afternoon in Jerusalem. A real peace partner speaks up, shouts and condemns. But maybe that is the difference between Israel and the PA. Following the rare few instances of Jewish terrorism – like the Duma arson attack in 2015 that killed three members of the Dawabshe family – every single Israeli politician from across the spectrum condemned it in the harshest of terms. Our 'peace partners' apparently don't know how."[340]

i. Abbas has **never distanced himself from the PLO Charter or the Fatah Constitution**, which do not recognize Israel as Jewish state, and advocates armed struggle until Israel is annihilated. The Palestinians' goal is to establish an Arab Muslim state in all the land delineated in the Mandate for Palestine, since Article 2 of the **PLO Charter** states, "Palestine, with the boundaries it had during the British Mandate, is an indivisible unit." Other Palestinian guiding documents only advocate jihad such as –

   i. **PLO Charter Article 9**: **Armed struggle is the only way** to liberate Palestine. Thus, it is the overall strategy, not merely a tactical phase. The Palestinian Arab people assert their absolute determination and firm resolution to continue their armed struggle and to **work for an armed popular revolution** for the liberation of their country and their return to it. They also assert their right to normal life in Palestine and to exercise their right to self-determination and sovereignty over it.

   ii. **PLO Charter Article 19**: **The partition of Palestine in 1947 and the establishment of the state of Israel are entirely illegal**, regardless of the passage of time, because they were contrary to the will of the Palestinian people and to their natural right in their homeland, and inconsistent with the principles embodied in the Charter of the United Nations, particularly the right to self-determination.

   iii. **PLO Charter Article 20**: **The Balfour Declaration, the Mandate for Palestine, and everything that has been based upon them, are deemed null and void.** Claims of historical or religious ties of Jews with Palestine are incompatible with the facts of history and the true conception of what constitutes statehood. **Judaism, being a religion, is not an independent nationality**. Nor do Jews constitute a single nation with an identity of its own; they are citizens of the states to which they belong."

   iv. **Fatah Constitution, Article 12**: **Complete liberation of Palestine**, and **obliteration** of Zionist economic, political, military, and cultural existence.

   v. **Fatah Constitution, Article 13**: Establishing an independent state with complete sovereignty on all Palestinian lands, and Jerusalem is its capital city … armed revolution is a decisive factor in the liberation fight and in **uprooting the Zionist existence**, and **this struggle will not cease unless the Zionist state is demolished** and Palestine is completely liberated.

vi. **Hamas Charter, core philosophy of Palestinian Authority Hamas Unity government**: Israel will rise and remain erect until Islam eliminates it as it had eliminated its predecessors ... For our struggle against the Jews is wide ranging and grave ... until the enemies are defeated and Allah's victory prevails ... The Day of Judgment will not come about until Muslims fight the Jews (killing the Jews), when the Jew will hide behind stones and trees. The stones and trees will say O Muslims ... there is a Jew behind me, come and kill him ... Israel, by virtue of its being Jewish and of having a Jewish population, defies Islam and the Muslims ... There is no solution to the Palestinian problem except by Jihad. The initiatives, proposals and international conferences are but a waste of time, an exercise in futility.

j. "If Iran produces a nuclear bomb – and I pray to Allah that Iran will produce 1,000 nuclear bombs, ... it will be used to defend, at the very least, the Islamic Republic and its principles *[and to destroy Israel]." Salah al-Zawawi, PLO envoy to Iran, interview with Lebanese TV station Al-Manar, which is associated with Hezbollah, February 20, 2017.*

k. "Our right to armed struggle is indisputable ... we want to liberate our homeland. After we liberate our homeland, we will have no problem with living in a democratic state in which Jews, Muslims and Christians **live in a <u>Palestinian Arab</u> democratic state**. [no state for the Jews] ... You are occupied. **<u>Your land was stolen</u>**. Your rights were taken. Therefore, **<u>I've never seen any problem with carrying out the armed struggle while diplomatic and political activity supporting your cause is being carried out</u>**." *Nabil Shaath, Fatah Commissioner of International Relations, **previous Palestinian foreign minister**, Fatah's Awdah TV interview, January 2017.* A very senior Palestinian official admits that the Palestinian's goal is to eliminate the Jewish state with continued armed struggle and terrorism. Negotiations and diplomatic agreements are only interim temporary solutions with the end goal of destroying Israel. By advancing Abbas as a true diplomatic partner, Obama is using the Palestinians and peace negotiations as a stepping stone to eliminating Israel from the Muslim-controlled Middle East.

l. In 2017, Abbas lied to President Trump during his visit to the White House in order to obtain American support for his position regarding future peace talks with Israel. As Obama utilized taqiyya to promote a false image of Abbas, Abbas then uses taqiyya to obtain as much land as possible from the Israelis before he continues the Palestinians' armed struggle to eradicate the State of Israel. As Noah Beck noted in *Front Page Magazine* in May 2017, "PA President Mahmoud Abbas met with President Donald Trump last week to discuss the peace process. He blatantly lied throughout his public remarks. Speaking before Abbas, Trump said that "there cannot be lasting peace unless the Palestinian leaders speak in a unified voice against incitement to ... violence and hate ... All children of God must be taught to value and respect human life, and condemn all of those who target the innocent." Abbas then made statements that seemed intended to allay Trump's fears: "I affirm to you that we are raising our youth, our children, our grandchildren on a culture of peace," Abbas said. "And we are endeavoring to bring about security, freedom and peace for our children to live like the other children in the world, along with the Israeli children in peace, freedom and security." Apparently anticipating that Abbas would promote such falsehoods to Trump and the American public, Israeli Prime Minister Benjamin Netanyahu shared a video on his Facebook page exposing the extent of Abbas' lies. The video montage shows several examples of Palestinian incitement to violence – including by Abbas himself – and the indoctrination of children to hate and attack Jews. "Our strategic choice is to bring about peace based on the vision of the two-state," Abbas declared alongside Trump. "A Palestinian state with its capital of East Jerusalem that lives in peace and stability with the state of Israel based on the borders of 1967." But Netanyahu's video shows **Palestinian children being taught that** "**Palestine is an Arab land from the river to the sea**," effectively brainwashing them to reject the territorial compromise required by the two-state solution Abbas claims to accept. That anti-peace, anti-Israel message extends far beyond the classroom. "**Every grain of soil in Palestine is ours ... Haifa, and Jaffa, and Acre**," (all cities in Israel), Najeh Bakirat, a religious leader and the head of the Waqf's Al-Aqsa Academy of Heritage and Antiquities said last June. "**Therefore it is forbidden to relinquish a single grain of its soil**," Bakirat continued, in his remarks titled "Palestine in the Quran," which were broadcast on official PA TV. While the Fatah-affiliated PA likes to present itself as more moderate than Hamas, its rejection of Israel is essentially the same. "**The Fatah Movement never demanded that Hamas recognize Israel**," said Fatah Central Committee member and Commissioner of Treasury and Economy Muhammad Shtayyeh, on official Palestinian Authority TV last March. "To this moment, Fatah does not recognize Israel. **The topic of recognition of Israel** [as a Jewish state] **has not been raised in any of Fatah's con-ferences**." ... Trump "raised concerns about the **payments to Palestinian prisoners in Israeli jails who have committed acts of terror**," said White House Press Secretary Sean Spicer. But a senior PA official rejected the idea as "insane," claiming that PA payments to imprisoned terrorists are like salaries paid to IDF soldiers *[taqiyya]* ... A few weeks before the Trump-Abbas meeting, the Palestinian Information Center called **Tel-Aviv a** "**settlement**" in a tweet, implying that **even Israel's commercial capital** – considered well within Israel proper by international consensus – **should be part of a future Palestine**. Josh Block, head of The Israel Project, uncovered the tweet, which was released on Holocaust Remembrance Day. The Palestinian Information Center tweet referred to the "**so-called Holocaust**." ... Hamas' actions confirm that nothing has changed about the group's bloodthirsty, fanatical, and cynical nature. Last month, the

group used a girl with cancer to smuggle explosives into Israel for a future terror attack."[341] And there are multiple videos on YouTube and Facebook where Palestinian children as young as six-years-old express their desire to kill Jews when they grow up. The
Palestinians and its leadership are not interested in a true peace with the Jews, and have
not deviated from their long-term desire to pursue an armed struggle to destroy Israel as
a Jewish state and replace her with a radical Palestinian Islamic state. Any withdrawal
by Israel from East Jerusalem or the West Bank will result in a chaotic and pro-radical
Islamic political and geographical debacle, as Israel's withdrawal from Gaza and southern Lebanon led to the creation of active Islamic terrorist enclaves upon Israel's borders.
The peace process advanced by the PLO or Hamas is a rouse perpetuated to gain control
of East Jerusalem and to establish a better geo-strategic position from which they can
continue their armed struggles against all the Jews in Israel.

m. Multiple Palestinian political factions planned on implementing "A Day of Rage" during
President Trump's visit to Israel in May 2017, which is being used as a launching pad for
the new president's search for a path to peace between Israel and the Palestinians. These
protests could not be implemented with the approval of President Abbas.

n. "It is an Islamic endowment (the Western Wall – the holiest Jewish religious site in East
Jerusalem) that absolutely cannot belong to non-Muslims. It is our property and endowment. It is impossible to concede one millimeter of it."[342] *Mahmoud Habash, religious
affairs advisor to President Abbas, June 2017.*

26. In June 2015, David Axelrod revealed in an interview that Obama has said "You know, **I
am the closest thing to a Jew that has ever sat in this office** *[but not necessarily a friend of
Israel]*." Axelrod was a financial supporter of the New Israel Fund from 1991 through 2002,
which has endorsed an economic boycott of Israel. Martin Indyk, who was Obama's U.S.
Special Envoy for the Israeli Palestinian Negotiations from 2013-2014, has been a board
member of the New Israel Fund.

a. "Obama's disregard for Jewish lives became apparent to the world when he commented
in February 2015 on the murder of four Jewish adults at a Paris kosher deli at the hands
of an ISIS-trained radical Muslim who asked his victims their religion before he shot the
Jews dead. Obama reflected on the event and commented, "It is entirely legitimate for
the American people to be deeply concerned when you've got a bunch of violent, vicious
zealots who behead people or randomly shoot a bunch of folks in a deli in Paris." There
are four major points that deserve scrutiny and reveal Obama's true feelings. First, and
most importantly, Obama dehumanized the Jewish victims by calling them simply a
"bunch of folks" and would not recognize they were murdered explicitly because they
were Jewish. Second, he would not recognize that the crime occurred in a kosher deli,
where the perpetrator knew he could target Jews; he called the crime scene simply a "deli

in Paris." Third, he refused to identify the assailants as Muslims and ignored that they were motivated by their religious obligation as Muslims to kill Jews by calling the killers "violent, vicious zealots." And fourth, he is denying the victims were singled out for their Jewish religion by using the phrase "randomly shot." There is nothing random about selecting a kosher deli where one knows Jews will congregate, and then asking for the religion of your hostages and subsequently killing the one identified as Jews. All these observations from this one incident support the obvious conclusion that Obama is an anti-Semite." *(Unexpected Treason)*

27. Obama **lied to Israeli leadership and to friends of Israel in Congress when he promised to compensate Israel with increased military aid that would be used to counter the increased threats against Israel caused by the JCPOA and sanctions relief,** which would give Iran, Hamas, and Hezbollah access to more sophisticated weaponry and more funding for their respective military organizations. During the JCPOA negotiations, Obama wrote a letter to Democratic Representative Nadler of New York, stating, "Our support for Israel is … an important element in deterring Iran from ever seeking a nuclear weapon … Throughout my time in office I have consistently viewed Israel's security as sacrosanct … My administration has pursued an unprecedented level of military, intelligence, and security cooperation with Israel." These assurances won over many Congressional votes that would support the JCPOA despite Israel's vociferous objections. In early 2016, Obama denied an Israeli request for an additional $1.9 billion in military aid. Obama then told Israel to decrease its request to $900 million, which was subsequently refused. Obama offered the F-35 Joint Strike fighter, and refused additional F-15s to the Israeli military. The F-35's controls must be updated by internet after every mission from computers based in the United States, or they may not be operational. Thus, Israel's F-35 could be grounded with internet problems or from computer sabotage originating from American military or intelligence officials. Obama would not allow Israel to operate the F-35s independently of the American computer network.

28. *Obama's remarks on International Holocaust Remembrance Day, Israeli Embassy, Washington D.C., January 27, 2016*: "Too often, especially in times of change, especially in times of anxiety and uncertainty, we are too willing to give into a base desire to find someone else – someone different – to blame for our struggles. *[Obama is referring to the resistance to Islamic immigration in the West, and not to Israel's troubles.]* … Here, tonight, we must confront the reality that around the world, anti-Semitism is on the rise. *[Mostly secondary to Obama's pro-Islamist policies.]* We cannot deny it. When we see some Jews leaving major European cities – where their families have lived for generations – because they no longer feel safe … when we see all that and more, we must not be silent. *[Yet Obama supports the continued mass Islamic immigration to the West, which is directly responsible for this unacceptable rise in anti-Semitism. Obama ignores the repeated calls of the Iranian leadership to annihilate Israel,*

and has attributed this incitement to mere rhetoric. Kerry and Obama have admitted that funds from sanctions relief will be used by Iranian proxy forces surrounding Israel to eventually attempt to destroy Israel, knowing that an increased number of Israelis would be killed in the future because of his actions.] … **We are all Jews … As president**, **I've made sure that the United States is leading the global fight against anti-Semitism**. *[Obama downplayed the killing of Jews at a Paris deli by calling them a "bunch of folks," refused to attend the following protest rally after the Charlie Hebdo murders, and launched anti-Semitic attacks directed at Jewish opponents of the JCPOA. The United Nations, which is a Muslim majority organization, incessantly attacks Israel whether Secretary General Ban blames Israeli policies for the Palestinian terrorism in Israel or the vast majority of passed resolutions passed by the UN have targeted Israel. Obama ignores the anti-Semitic indoctrination embedded in Palestinian society, and wants the Palestinians to control half of Jerusalem, including many Jewish holy sites, and demands no concessions from them during peace negotiations. Obama's left-wing constituency is leading the BDS campaign on university campuses, which is anti-Semitic since they only target the Jewish state. The Democratic party has becoming more anti-Israel and pro-Palestinian during Obama's stewardship as president.]* … **It means taking a stand against bigotry in all its forms** *[Obama does not stand against Islamic / Quranic bigotry – Jews are apes and pigs, stoning of gays, death penalty for apostates and blasphemers]*, **and rejecting our darkest impulses** *[Obama supports Black Lives Matter, which has promoted killing police officers.]* … **as the only value in our communities and in our politics."**

a. During Obama's last year as president, anti-Semitic attacks on Jews increased 45% on American college campuses. These events were mostly propagated by members of the far-left and Islamists, two of Obama's major political constituencies. Obama said nothing of this disturbing trend at any time during his presidency, despite his generalized public proclamations deploring anti-Semitism.

29. In a speech to the UN General Assembly in September 2009, Obama announced **"America does not accept the legitimacy of continued Israeli settlements** [including Jewish neighborhoods in East Jerusalem] … **The United States does Israel no favors when we fail to couple an unwavering commitment to its security with an insistence that Israel respect the legitimate claims and rights of the Palestinians."** Obama is forecasting "tough love" for Israel during his presidency. Former U.S. Ambassador to the UN John Bolton stated, **"This is the most radical anti-Israel speech I can recall any president making."** Obama also demanded that the Palestinians obtain **"a viable Palestinian state with <u>contiguous</u> territory that ends the occupation that began in 1967** [indefensible Auschwitz borders]." Obama wants Gaza connected to the West Bank, which would divide Israel through its center. Obama wants Jerusalem divided with East Jerusalem free from Jews. All these divisions weaken Israel. This is in contrast to Obama's statement at an AIPAC conference in 2008: "[**Jerusalem**] **will**

remain the capital of Israel, and <u>it must remain undivided.</u>" *[taqiyya]* Obama became the first American president to declare the land captured by Israel in 1967 by a defensive war was "occupied territory."

a. "One does not have to be a military expert to easily identify the critical defects of the armistice lines that existed until June 4, 1967. A considerable part of these lines is without any topographical security value; and, of no less importance, the lines fail to provide Israel with the essential minimum of strategic depth." *Former IDF General and acting Israel Prime Minister Yigal Allon, 1976.*

b. After Obama delivered his address at the funeral of Shimon Peres, the White House issued a transcript of the speech in a document which labelled Jerusalem as part of Israel. Hours later, the White House reissued an amended transcript which crossed out Israel following Jerusalem, which appeared as: "Jerusalem, ~~Israel~~." The ceremony occurred at Mount Herzl, which is located in western Jerusalem and has always been part of the state of Israel since its inception. Eastern Jerusalem may be contested, but western Jerusalem has never been questioned as being separate from Israel. Obama does not recognize any part of Jerusalem as a sovereign section of Israeli territory. Obama lied when he told AIPAC in 2008, "Jerusalem will remain the capital **of Israel**, and it must remain undivided."

Final Moments as President

"I hold the maxim no less applicable to public than to private affairs, that honesty
is the best policy." *George Washington, Farewell Address, September 17, 1796*

1. "There is only one person who is truly qualified to be president of the United States, and that
    is our friend Hillary Clinton … That is what Barack and I think about every day, as we try
    to **guide and protect our girls** through the challenges of this unusual life in the spotlight.
    How we urge them to ignore those who question their father's citizenship or faith. How we
    insist that this hateful language they hear form public figures on TV does not represent the
    true spirit of this country. How we explain that when someone is cruel or acts like a bully you
    don't stoop to their level. No, <u>**our moto is**</u>: <u>**when they go low, we go high**</u>." *Michelle Obama,
    Democratic National Convention speech, August 25, 2016.* Hillary Clinton repeated this motto
    regularly on the 2016 presidential campaign trail.
    a. After Trump responded to pro-Sharia, Democratic National Convention speaker Khazir
        Khan, Obama responded at a press conference with the leader of Singapore on August 2,
        2016, "Yes, I think the Republican nominee is **unfit to serve as President**. I said so last
        week, and he keeps on proving it. The notion that he would attack a Gold Star family
        that had made such extraordinary sacrifices on behalf of our country, the fact that **he
        doesn't appear to have basic knowledge** around critical issues in Europe, in the Middle
        East, in Asia, means that he's **woefully unprepared to do this job**."
    b. Obama lambasted Donald Trump one day before the presidential election in November
        2016, saying, "It's bad enough being arrogant. It's worse being **arrogant and not know-
        ing anything**."
    c. Michelle Obama refused to take a picture with Melania Trump and their respective
        husbands, when they first visited the White House on November 10, 2016, and ignored
        a long standing White House / American tradition.
    d. Hillary Clinton refused to make a concession speech to Donald Trump the night she lost
        the presidential election, and waited until the following late morning to make a formal

statement. The vast majority of Clinton's campaign rhetoric was negative, with which she attacked Trump's demeanor, character, and capabilities.

e. Both Obamas embraced Black Lives Matter, which organized violent rallies during Obama's last years as president, and whose supporters openly advocated killing police officers. BLM also accused Israel of committing genocide against the Palestinians in their official DNC political platform.

f. For days after Trump's election victory, supporters of Obama and Clinton organized violent riots in cities throughout the United States. There were instances of Trump voters being assaulted, and protesters marched outside Trump Tower in New York City parading signs including, "Rape Melania (Trump's wife)" and "Not My President." Neither Obama nor Clinton made a public statement telling the protestors to go home and accept the election results. This was in sharp contrast to Obama declaring after his 2008 election victory, "We won. Elections have consequences. Get over it." While Obama was meeting with Donald Trump immediately after the election, the president told the president-elect, "**It's really important to try to send some signals of unity**," even though Obama and Clinton supporters and agitators of the left-wing of the Democratic Party were the cause of most of the turmoil. Just one week later while giving a joint press conference with Angela Merkel of Germany on November 17, 2016, Obama hypocritically encouraged the violent left-wing protests against a Trump presidency by stating, "I've been the subject of protests during the course of my eight years ... So I would not advise people would feel strongly or are concerned about some of the issues that have been raised during the course of the campaign, **I wouldn't advise them to be silent**." Obama took the low road by instigating and encouraging violent protests against the will of the American people and a legitimate Trump election victory. Just days after Obama encouraged his supporters to continue their protests, many of which were violent, police officers were ambushed and shot in San Antonio (murdered), Sanibel Florida, Gladstone Missouri, and St. Louis (shot twice in the face). Earlier in the year, a similar scenario occurred when police officers were killed in Dallas and Baton Rouge after Obama made public statements decrying police racism.

g. "**<u>Now we're feeling what not having hope feels like</u>**. Hope is necessary ... What else do you have if you don't have hope ... Barack has been that for the nation in ways that people will come to appreciate. **Having a grown-up in the White House** who can say to you in times of crisis and turmoil – hey it's going to be okay." Michelle Obama criticized Donald Trump's presidential election victory during an interview with Oprah Winfrey in mid-December 2016, and appears to be a sore loser. Michelle Obama implies that Trump is not a grown-up and is immature and unfit for the presidency, which are unprecedented, unnecessary and derogatory remarks from the First Lady. Maybe, the loss of hope by the American electorate was secondary to her husband's policies at home and abroad, along with his inclination to increase divisions among America's various ethnic and economic groups. This statement contrasted sharply with her positive outlook and her anti-American sentiments which she expressed when her husband won a major primary vote in 2008, when she stated, "**For the first time in my adult life I am proud of my country** because it feels like **hope is finally making a comeback**." Michelle Obama is slightly delusional believing that hope rises and falls only with the political fortunes of her husband's career. Michelle is ignoring the crushed hopes and dreams of Christians and non-Muslims in territories controlled by ISIS as Islamic State fighters perpetrated genocide against them with minimal resistance from Obama. The African-American community dreams of a better economic environment were a reality when the first Black president was elected, but severe disappointment set in eight years later, when Black unemployment and poverty kept increasing and continued to surpass that of the rest of the nation. Obama mocked the hope of millions of Americans when he promised lower healthcare costs, as Obamacare ushered in the era of unaffordable high insurance premiums couples with astronomical deductibles that negated the purpose of buying insurance. The hopes that the United States would become a post-racial society with the election of Obama were dashed with the most divisive politics instituted by any president since the start of the Civil War. Michelle Obama is blind to the reality that Trump's victory was a complete rejection and repudiation of her husband's radical domestic and foreign policies.

h. During his last press conference in 2016, when asked if Clinton lost because of Russian hacking of the DNC and Podesta's emails, Obama responded, "**I don't think she was treated fairly during the election**." Days before this press conference, Obama had his press secretary, Josh Earnest, announce that Trump may have known and approved of Putin's alleged intervention (which has not been proven nor has intelligence been released to support this accusation) during the 2016 presidential election. Earnest stated, "There's ample evidence that was known long before the election and in most cases long before October about the Trump campaign and Russia – everything from the Republican nominee himself calling on Russia to hack his opponent *[an Obama lie that was never proved]* … It might be an indication that he was obviously aware and concluded, based on whatever facts or sources he had available to him, that Russia was involved and their involvement was having a negative impact on his opponent's campaign *[lie]* … [**and Trump**] **was encouraging them to keep doing it**." Obama was agitating his political base and hoping to persuade Republican Electoral College delegates to switch their votes to Clinton or just not voting for Trump before the formal Electoral College vote days later. Obama was delegitimizing Trumps presidential victory, and encouraging Trump's political opposition to block his path to the presidency. Obama was subtly advocating that Democrats should attempt to steal the presidential election by having Republican delegates vote for Clinton in the Electoral College vote despite a majority of their state's voters clearly choosing Trump as their candidate for president.

    i.   Although Obama and his surrogates may be alleging that Trump colluded with Russia during the 2016 election, there is glaring proof that **President Obama colluded in Russia in 2012** before the presidential election, when he privately told the Russian president on an open mike, "On all these issues, but particularly missile defense, this, this can be solved but it's important for him to give me space ... This is my last election. After my election, I have more flexibility." Obama was preparing to sacrifice American security interests regarding missile defense and other issues, and told the Russians they would have to wait until after the election since Obama knew his concessions would not be acceptable to the American public and could cost him the election.

i.   Obama politicized the CIA and intelligence agencies by having them write and advance intelligence reports that allegedly proved that Russian hacking of the DNC's and Podesta's emails helped secure Donald Trump's presidential victory. Catherine Herridge, of *Fox News*, reported on January 6, 2017, the day that the intelligence services presented their reports to President-elect Trump, that the report was "nothing but Obama's attempt to undermine the Trump administration." John McAfee, a world recognized leader in cyber security called the allegation that the hacks were performed by Russia, "utter nonsense" and "ignorant and naïve."

j.   On January 15, 2017, Obama refused to label Trump as a "legitimate" president. In an interview with *CNN's* "State of the Union," Obama's White House Chief of Staff Denis McDonough, stated when asked if Obama thought that Trump was legitimate, "The president has made very clear that he believes that he is the "freely elected" president. He will be inaugurated on Friday."

k.   Michelle Obama tweeted her support of Representative Lewis's calling President-elect Trump an "illegitimate" president.

l.   Biden attacked Trump during his Davos Summit speech on January 18, 2016, saying, "Popular movements on both the left and the right have demonstrated a **dangerous** willingness to revert to political **small–mindedness** – to the same **nationalist, protectionist, and isolationist agendas** that led the world to consume itself in war during in the last century. As we have seen time and again throughout history, **demagogues and autocrats** have emerged – seeking to capitalize on people's insecurities. In this case, using **Islamophobic, anti-Semitic**, or **xenophobic rhetoric** to stoke fear, sow division, and advance their own narrow agendas. This is a politics **at odds with our values** and with the vision that built – and sustains – the liberal international order. The impulse to hunker down, shut the gates, **build walls**, and exit at this moment is **precisely the wrong answer**." By mentioning "building walls," Biden proves he is directing these insulting comments at Trump. If Obama and Biden were so concerned about anti-Semitism, why did he agree with UNSC Resolution 2334, which effectively gave the holiest Jewish sites in Jerusalem to the PLO and Hamas, both which are dedicated to destroying the Jewish state and killing Jews? The resolution also paved the way for economic warfare against Israel via the BDS movement, and criminalized Jews living in Jewish communities in Jerusalem and the West Bank, where Jews have been living for thousands of years. This resolution was at odds with American values, yet was supported by Biden. Allowing Iran to obtain nuclear weapons in the near future while their leadership promised to destroy the United States and Israel, is opposed to the values and security interests of America, yet Biden supported the JCPOA. Letting Europe getting overrun by Muslim migrants and compromising Western civilization was embraced by Biden and Obama.

m. During Trump's first State of the Union speech in February 2017, the Democrats in Congress **refused to stand** when Trump proclaimed he would put America's interests first, he would create millions of high paying jobs for Americans, and **when he honored the widow of Navy SEAL Ryan Owens**, who was killed in Yemen during a raid on an al-Qaeda stronghold.

n. In response to the revelation that National Security Advisor Susan Rice unmasked civilians working for Donald Trump in intelligence intercepts, which were then used to advance Obama's agenda, former UN Ambassador John Bolton stated during a *Fox Business News* interview with Lou Dobbs, "This is stunning news. And you can't, even somebody as senior as the National Security Advisor, can't just decide they'd like to unmask names to find out whose name is involved in a particular intercept… If she said that even somebody as senior as her but her real motivation was political she was committing a kind of **fraud on the intelligence gathering system** and if she participated in that kind of fraud to help the political misuse of that intelligence **she's got serious legal problems here**." The unmasking and subsequent intelligence leak is a **violation of the espionage act**, and is a **felony** with a possible **five-year jail sentence** according the Representative Nunes, chairman of the House Intelligence committee.

o. **Former Vice President Biden repeatedly attacked President Trump** while speaking at Cornell's 2017 commencement by stating, "I thought we had passed the days when it was acceptable for political leaders at local and national levels to **bestow legitimacy on hate speech** and fringe ideologies … There are a lot of folks out there who are both afraid and susceptible to this kind of **negative appeal** … The immigrant, the minority, the transgender, **anyone not like me became a scapegoat** … **Just build a wall**, keep

Muslims from coming into the United States." Obama and his wife, Valerie Jarett, many of Obama's former aides, and now Biden attack the president on the national and international stage, breaking almost all historical precedents set by former administrations.

2. "If people, whether they are conservative or liberal, left or right, are **unwilling to compromise** and engage in the democratic process, and are taking absolutist views and demonizing opponents, then democracy will break down." *Obama. Joint Press Conference with Chancellor Merkel of Germany, German Chancellory, Berlin. November 17, 2016.* Obama had disingenuously supported political compromise as a necessary strategy just days earlier when he stated at the Stavros Niarchos Foundation Cultural Center in Athens, Greece, "**Democracy**, **like all human institutions**, **is imperfect**. It can be slow; it can be frustrating; it can be hard; it can be messy. Politicians tend to be unpopular in democracies, regardless of party, because, by definition, democracies require that you don't get a hundred percent of what you want. **It requires compromise**." Obama misrepresented his ability to compromise, since his intransigence led to significant Republican victories in 2012, 2014, and 2016.

   a. "**Elections have consequences**, and at the end of the day, I won." Obama, January 2009 speaking to House Minority Whip Eric Cantor on the third day of his presidency.

   b. Obama's stimulus package in early 2009 garnered zero GOP votes, since the bill was written by Democrats behind closed doors without any Republican input.

   c. Using procedural gimmicks and special deals, Obama forced Obamacare through Congress without any Republican votes or support.

   d. In 2012, like with many other high level executive appointments, Obama bypassed the Senate by installing Richard Cordray as head of the Consumer Financial Protection Agency without an up or down vote. Obama claimed to use his powers of "recess" appointments, but the Senate was still in session. Later, the United States Court of Appeals for the District of Columbia nullified three of his other "recess" appointments to the National Labor Relations Board and called them unconstitutional. Chief Judge David Sentelle stated for the majority, that Obama "would demolish the checks and balances inherent in the advice and consent requirement, giving the president free rein to appoint his desired nominees at any time he pleases … even when the Senate is in session and he is merely displeased with its inaction. This cannot be the law."

   e. In his 2013 State of the Union Address, Obama threatened Congress regarding his climate change initiatives, "**If Congress won't act soon to protect future generations**, **I will**. I will direct my cabinet to come up with executive actions we can take."

   f. Obama bypassed Congress with his green / climate change agenda by instituting regulations and signing executive orders. After getting re-elected in 2012, Obama threatened Congress by stating, "**I've got a pen and I've got a phone** … and I can use that pen to sign executive orders and take executive actions and administrative actions."

g.   Obama bypassed the Senate treaty ratification requirements with the JCPOA, by treating it as an executive agreement and not a treaty.

h.   Obama attempted to coerce Israel into unfavorable diplomatic two-state solution agreements by taking positions that were harsher than those of the Palestinian Authority while interacting with Netanyahu.

i.   The JCPOA and UNSC Resolution 2334 were adopted without any significant Israeli input.

3.   "If people, whether they are conservative or liberal, left or right, are unwilling to compromise and engage in the democratic process, and are taking absolutist views and **demonizing opponents**, then democracy will break down." *Obama. Joint Press Conference with Merkel of Germany in November 2016.*

a.   Obama attacked Trump by saying he is "unfit to serve as president" and "doesn't appear to have basic knowledge."

b.   Obama called Republicans against the JCPOA - "warmongers." He also associated the Republican opposition to radical Iranian politicians who support terrorism by stating, "It's those hard-liners chanting 'Death to America' who have been most opposed to the deal … They're making common cause with the Republican caucus."

c.   Obama called Netanyahu a liar with the French president and later called him "chicken shit."

d.   Obama called the founding fathers, evangelical Christians and orthodox Jews – "radical extremists" on par with al-Qaeda in defense documents.

e.   During the 2012 presidential campaign, Mitt Romney, the Republican nominee criticized Obama by stating, "This idea of criticizing and attacking success, of **demonizing those in all walks of life who have been successful**, is something that is so foreign to us that we can't understand." Obama had earlier mocked successful Americans by complaining, "**you didn't build that**."

4.   "As I've said before the concern I have has less to do with any particular misinformation or propaganda that's being put out by any particular party and **a greater concern about the general information from all kinds of sources, both domestic, foreign, on social media**, that make it very difficult for voters to figure out what's true and what's not… In general, **if we have elections that aren't focused on issues and are <u>full of fake news and false information</u> and distractions** then the issue is going to be… what are we doing to ourselves from the inside." *Obama, press conference at the APEC conference in Lima, Peru, November 17, 2016.* Obama hypocritically attacked alternative sources of information originating from outside the major networks which regularly support the Democrats, by stating they disseminate "**fake news**," when **his whole presidency has been inundated on a daily basis with lies and taqiyya, as outlined in this book**. Obama should start his review with news reports

from the mainstream media that showed Clinton was leading Trump by 12 percentage points less than two weeks before the election, Trump planned on opening internment camps, Hillary Clinton was healthy with no major medical problems during the 2016 campaign, and Trump had no path to winning 270 Electoral College votes which was needed to win the presidency, which was all misinformation originating from the Democratic Party and the Clinton campaign. Other examples of pro-Obama / Clinton fake news included: shovel ready jobs with the stimulus, hands up don't shoot rallies (Black Lives Matter / Michael Brown), police are generally racist, 50% of all Trump voters are deplorable and racists, CNN gave Democratic primary debate questions to Hillary Clinton in advance, Clinton never received or sent classified documents from her server, an internet video caused the Benghazi attack, unemployment numbers, economic statistics, Obama would not confirm a terrorist connection with the San Bernardino attacks, the Fort Hood attack by Major Hasan was workplace violence, Bergdahl served with honor and distinction, al-Qaeda was on the run, ISIS is contained and is JV, Middle East immigrants are fully vetted, destitute Muslim child refugees are generally male adults seeking jihad and rape (as proven in Sweden), the Muslim Brotherhood has evolved as a peaceful moderate stable Egyptian political party, Syrian rebels are moderate (they are actually al-Qaeda), Rouhani and his Islamic Iranian government are moderates, Abbas is a credible peace partner for Israel, anytime anywhere Iranian nuclear facility inspections, Islam is a religion of peace, you can keep your doctor and your premiums will go down with Obamacare, Obama did not pay a ransom for four American hostages held by Iran, global warming morphing to climate change, Russia / fake news / American racism / misogyny / Comey / Wikileaks caused Clinton to lose the presidency, and many more. Obama, along with his Deputy National Security Advisor Ben Rhodes, created an "echo chamber" among partisan analysts and the news media, which propagated misleading details concerning the JCPOA, so that the Iranian nuclear agreement would obtain the support of Congress. The "echo chamber" was a prime example of fake news originating from the Obama administration and was funded by George Soros. Clinton later echoed Obama's sentiments when she stated after her election loss, "The **epidemic of malicious fake news and false propaganda** that flooded social media over the past year – it's now clear that so-called fake news can have real world consequences … This isn't about politics or bipartisanship. Lives are at risk." Ironically, both Obama and Clinton, leaders of a "liberal" Democratic Party, are rallying against free speech and the first amendment, when the free exchange of ideas leads to their electoral defeats.

5. Mark Knoller, the *CBS* White House correspondent, tweeted on January 4, 2017, that "Earnest says **Pres Obama wants to afford his successor the same customs and courtesies he received from Pres GW Bush – <u>staying on the sidelines</u>**." Ten days after Obama left the presidency, the former president jumped into the political fray via his personal spokesperson who

stated, "President Obama is heartened by the level of engagement taking place in communities around the country. In his final official speech as President, he spoke about the important role of citizens and how all Americans have a responsibility to be the guardians of our democracy – not just during an election but every day. **Citizens exercising their Constitutional right to assemble, organize and have their voices heard** by their elected officials is exactly what we expect to see when American values are at stake." Obama is encouraging his supporters to actively protest against Trump's new temporary immigration restrictions.

a. Obama **met with German Chancellor Merkel just days before Trump held meetings with her regarding climate change and the NATO alliance** in May 2017. After meeting Trump, and probably with Obama's guidance, Merkel started distancing herself from Germany's post-WWII alliance with the United States and Great Britain. About two weeks later, Germany announced they would begin withdrawing troops from Turkey's Incirlik air force base, along NATO's southern flank. The cover story for Germany's withdrawal from NATO's southern flank wass Turkey's refusal to allow German lawmakers to visit their troops at the base. Even after Obama left the presidency, his input is leading to the partial dissolution, or at least weakening, of NATO.

b. "It was **steady, principled American leadership** on the world stage that made that achievement (Paris Climate Agreement) possible. It was **bold American ambition** that encouraged dozens of other nations to set their sights higher as well … even in the **absence of American leadership**; even as this Administration joins a small handful of nations that **reject the future**; I'm confident …" *Ex-President Obama praises himself and shamefully attacks President Trump after Trump withdraws the United States from the Paris Climate Agreement. Obama's press release hours after Trump's decision.* Obama, against all American historical precedent as a former president, is now leading the opposition against a sitting U.S. president. June 1, 2017. One week later, Valerie Jarrett reiterated Obama's sentiments when she stated, "I think it signals to the world that **the United States is not serious about protecting our planet** … And what it means is the rest of the world will move forward without us and the United States has always been that **beacon of hope**, the leader, the world leader, that's why we're called **the world leader** and we're basically abdicating that role."

c. "When the top 1% amass a bigger and bigger and bigger share of wealth and income, the concern among many in our countries is that the game is fixed against them, *[Obama's economic policies for eight years created this scenario – it's partially his fault]* that their governments are serving the interests just of the powerful *[Obama's crony capitalism - Solyndra]* … that's a recipe for more cynicism and more polarization, **less trust in our institutions and less trust in each other**, and it's part of **what leads people to turn to populist alternatives** *[Obama doesn't realize that his policies led to the election of Donald*

Trump. Obama is out of touch with political reality.] that may not actually deliver but are tempting … If we begin to question the very real gains *[Lies. Obama's true legacy - economic stagnation, shrinking middle class, racial polarization, record food stamps, record poverty, the rise of ISIS, chaos throughout the Middle East, destabilizing uncontrolled Muslim immigration to the West, the weakening of the major U.S. alliances, rise of anti-Semitism, the rise of Islamic terrorism throughout the West, Christian genocides in Iraq and Syria, record scandals]* that have been made over the last several decades, and **we violate our principles** *[Obama criticizes America in a foreign country for electing Trump. People who vote for Trump violated their principles defined by Obama? Obama attacks all Trump supporters. This parallels Clinton's statement – "To just be grossly generalistic, you can put half of Trump supporters into what I call the basket of deplorables. Right? Racist, sexist, homophobic, xenophobic, Islamophobic, you name it."]* because of fear and uncertainty, then we can't expect the progress *[Obama brought chaos and fear of the future]* that is just now taking hold in many places *[not in the Middle East or Europe and not in middle America. Obama lies and misrepresents reality.]* around the world to continue. And instead we are going to be inviting in those who argue **democracy doesn't work**, that **restrictions on the press** are necessary, *[Obama basically calls Trump a fascist, while he ruled by executive orders and bragged about governing with a phone and a pen.]* and that **intolerance and tribalism** *[Obama criticizing America again.]* and **organizing ourselves along ethnic lines** *[Obama supported BLM and the Muslim Brotherhood. Obama chose Al Sharpton as his racial ambassador. Obama argues against his own policies.]* are the answers to today's challenges … We're going to have to find a way to **push back against propaganda** *[Obama is one of the originators of fake news – Benghazi video, JCPOA echo chambers, Russian / Trump collusion]* and cultivate independent journalism *[The mainstream media supported Obama 95%.]* and listen to those with whom we disagree *[Obama bypassed the Republican with Obamacare and bypassed the Senate with the JCPOA and the Paris Climate agreement* …even with the temporary **absence of American leadership** *[Criticizes Trump.]* … extreme nationalism and xenophobia *[Love and support for your home country is a sin for Obama]* the **politics of "us-versus-them"** *[Obama political legacy: war on women, war on the elderly, war on minorities, BLM, war against Islamophobia, war on immigrants, advanced concept of 'white privilege', you're a racist if you oppose Obama's political agenda, unisex bathrooms for children]* … In times of disruption we may **go backward** instead of forward *[Obama criticizes Trump in a foreign country. The apology tour continues.]* … We're going to have to **replace fear with hope** *[Again, Obama criticizes the sitting U.S. president.]* **Obama**. **Montreal speech** *as a private citizen. June 7, 2017.* Obama repeatedly criticizes America, President Trump, and his supporters. A classic Obama speech, which proves Obama as a hypocrite and a liar.

d. On June 22, 2017, Obama attacked the healthcare bill being crafted in the U.S. Senate by declaring, "It's **a massive transfer of wealth** from the middle class and poor families to the richest people in America … this bill **will do you harm** … small tweaks … cannot change the **fundamental meanness at the core** of this legislation." The fundamental meanness was Obama lying to the public promising that healthcare premiums would decrease and then having premiums and deductibles skyrocket.

e. Just days after South Korean President Moon Jae-in met with President Trump in Washington, **Obama flew to Seoul and held <u>private meetings with the South Korean president.</u>** The *Korea Herald* reported on July 3, 2017 that, "President Moon Jae-in renewed his resolve to pursue sanctions and dialogue to tackle North Korea's nuclear program during a meeting with former U.S. President Barack Obama on Monday … During the 40-minute talk, Moon shared the results of his recent summit with his incumbent U.S. counterpart Donald Trump, asking for Obama's advice on ways to advance the relationship." ("*Moon Meets Obama, Says Last Chance for NK Talks*," *Korea Herald*) While in Korea, Obama attacked Trump by saying a "**temporary absence of American leadership**" led to the rejection of the Paris climate agreement, and promoted progressive globalism and a new international order while attacking American patriotism by stating, "**I deeply believe in the <u>liberal international order</u>**; order **based not just on** military power or **<u>national affiliations … is the only choice</u>**." It is unbelievable that Obama met with the South Korean president and was briefed by him and other South Korean officials on their talks with President Trump. This is the second time within a few months that Obama flew to meet with world leaders within days of their holding discussions with President Trump. Obama did the same in Germany with Chancellor Merkel just months earlier. With Obama keeping his embedded loyalists in the federal government and with him maintaining contact and discussion with world leaders as they meet with President Trump, it appears that Obama is **trying to maintain a shadow presidency**, an event unprecedented in American history. Obama may have broken the law by violating the Logan Act, which prohibits private citizens negotiating with foreign governments against United States interests.

6. Obama put forth many misleading statements during his **last press conference** on January 18, 2017.

a. Obama discussing the role of the press: "You're not supposed to be sycophants, you're supposed to be skeptics. You're supposed to ask me tough questions. You're not supposed to be complimentary, but **you're supposed to cast a critical eye on folks who hold enormous power and make sure that we are accountable to the people who sent us here**. <u>And you have done that.</u> And you've done it, for the most part, in ways that I could appreciate for fairness even if I didn't always agree with your conclusions. And having you in this building has made this place work better. **It keeps us honest**." The vast majority of the mainstream media basically recited the talking points of the Obama administration and the DNC, and actively supported the candidacy of Hillary Clinton. Chris Matthews, at *MSNBC*, stated after the 2008 presidential election, "My job is to make the Obama presidency a success." Over 90% of reporters in the mainstream media are liberals. The press generally did not question the almost daily bombardment of lies coming from Obama for over eight years, as documented in this book. The press did not keep Obama honest. Where were the investigative reports questioning the role of the video in the Benghazi attacks, or the lies surrounding the passage of Obamacare where Obama promised premiums would decrease and the electorate could keep their policies and preferred doctors? They covered his trail and watched his back, so their liberal agenda would gain the maximum support among the general public.

b.   "This is a job of such magnitude that you can't do it by yourself. **You are enormously reliant on a team**. Your Cabinet, your senior White House staff, all the way to fairly junior folks in their 20s and 30s, but who are executing on significant responsibilities." Obama ignored almost all his senior advisors when he did not sign a status of forces agreement with Iraq and withdrew almost all U.S. forces from Iraq, leaving a geopolitical vacuum that would be filled by ISIS and Iran. During the night of the Benghazi attack, Obama disappeared for the evening, so he would not be confronted by the input and options presented to him by his military and intelligence advisors. Obama's lack of action led to the death of Ambassador Stevens and three other Americans. Obama created secret side deals with the JCPOA, where most of his advisors were not aware of the details, including Secretary of State Kerry, who testified before Congress that he did not know the details or existence of various side deals. Valerie Jarrett was his major confidante, and her opinions and guidance overruled almost all other input channels to Obama at the executive level.

i.   "But the 'Trump doesn't respect the intel community's argument *[From the outset, Trump doubted both the argument that Russia hacked the Democratic National Committee and that the release of damaging emails was designed to give him an advantage over his rival.]* raises another issue. Why doesn't Obama get the same criticism for rejecting his national security and intelligence team's advice on Iraq? As a candidate, Obama called the Iraq War "dumb." He vowed to withdraw the troops and reposition them in Afghanistan – the good war. As President, this is exactly what he did. But he did so against the unanimous advice of the major national security voices in his administration. Then-Secretary of State Hillary Clinton urged him to keep a stay-behind force. So did his secretary of Defense, the head of the CIA, the Joint Chiefs of Staff, the United States ambassador to Iraq and his national security adviser. Army Gen. Ray Odierno, former member of the Joint Chiefs of Staff, said shortly after his retirement that had there been a stabilizing force in Iraq, ISIS could've been dealt with: 'I go back to the work we did in 2007 (through) 2010, and we got into a place that was really good. Violence was low, the economy was growing, politics looked like it was heading in the right direction. ... We thought we had it going exactly in the right direction, but now we watch it fall apart. It's frustrating that it's falling apart. ... I think, maybe, if we had stayed a little bit more engaged, I think maybe it might have prevented it.' Think about it. Obama, with barely two years of experience in the Senate, and no foreign-policy experience, rejected the unanimous advice of his mission security team. He pulled completely out of Iraq, a decision that aided and abetted the rise of ISIS. Trump gets hammered for ignoring the unanimous opinion of the intelligence community; Obama makes one of the most consequential decisions by completely ignoring their advice. And, as usual, Obama gets a pass."[343] *(Larry Elder, FrontPage Magazine, January 2017)* Obama withdrew American forces against the advice of all his senior advisors since, as a radical Muslim, he already had plans to create a geopolitical vacuum in Iraq, so that ISIS could expand its reach and pave the way for the creation of an Islamic caliphate. According to DIA documents, Obama was one of the founders of ISIS. Thus, Obama's policies were geared toward protecting and enabling ISIS, which would be the progenitor of the Islamic caliphate.

c.   "So, I hope that people pay a lot of attention to making sure that everybody has a chance to vote. Make it easier, not harder. **This whole notion of election – of <u>voting fraud</u>, this is something that has constantly been disproved**. **This is <u>fake news</u>** – the notion that there are a whole bunch of people out there who are going out there and are not eligible to vote and want to vote." Just days before the presidential election, **Obama encouraged illegal aliens to vote**. Obama implemented open borders in part because illegal aliens almost always vote for Democrats, and is why Obama wanted to make it easy for any alleged citizens to vote without proper identification. The largest sanctuary cities vote predominantly for Democrats. Studies showed that in Detroit, Michigan, 37% of the precincts recorded more votes than the number of legal voters in those districts. Voter fraud is probably prevalent in all major cities, which usually vote for Democrats.

i.   "Well, I tell you what, **it helps in Ohio that we got Democrats in charge of the machines**. But look, I come from Chicago, so, so I want to be honest. It's not as if it's just Republicans who have monkeyed around with elections in the past. Sometimes Democrats have, too. **<u>Whenever people are in power they're, you know, they have this tendency to try to, you know, tilt things in their direction</u>**. That's why we've got to have a I believe a **voting rights division in the Justice Department** that is non-partisan, and is serious about **investigating cases of vote fraud**." *Obama, 2008 campaign trail, responding to the question, "I would just like to know what you can say to reassure us that this election will not be rigged or stolen?"* Obama admitted there was significant voting fraud before he became president, and wanted to have a permanent division in the Justice Department to pursue legitimate areas of fraud. When Obama acknowledges voter fraud and wants and investigation, the press stays quiet, yet when Trump discusses voting fraud, the press goes on the attack, and calls him a liar. Obama admitted there is voter fraud, worked with ACORN which promoted voter fraud, and then encouraged illegal aliens to vote. Obama knows that he and the Democrats are dependent on voter fraud in order to win close elections, thus he and the Democrats will push back against any initiative by Trump to investigate the topic.

ii. "Somewhere **between 38,000 and almost 2.8 million non-citizens voted in the 2008 elections**, according to a study published in Electoral Studies journal in 2014 ... Old Dominion University professors Jesse Richman and David Earnest, the study's co-authors, concluded that 'some non-citizens participate in U.S. elections, and that this participation has been large enough to change meaningful election outcomes including Electoral College votes, and Congressional elections ... Non-citizen votes likely gave Senate Democrats the pivotal 60th vote needed to overcome filibusters in order to pass health care reform and other Obama administration priorities in the 111th Congress,' they continue."[344] *(The Daily Caller, January 2017)*

iii. "**No single group in American history ever outdid <u>ACORN</u> in terms of voter registration fraud**. At least 52 individuals who worked for ACORN or its affiliates, or who were connected to ACORN, have been convicted of voter registration fraud. ACORN itself was convicted in Nevada last year of the crime of "compensation." Under the leadership of ACORN official Amy Adele Busefink, who was also convicted of the same crime, ACORN paid voter registration canvassers cash bonuses for exceeding their quotas. This is illegal because it gives people an incentive to commit fraud by adding Mickey Mouse and Mary Poppins to the voter rolls. Under Busefink's leadership, ACORN and its affiliate Project Vote generated an impressive 1.1 million voter registration packages across America in 2008. The problem was that election officials invalidated 400,000 -- that's 36 percent -- of the registrations filed. It is highly unlikely that typographic and other innocent errors alone generated so much bogus paperwork. And this is only one activist group's fraudulent activities in one election. It is irresponsible for law enforcement officials to view those 400,000 registrations as mere mistakes. All 400,000 bogus registrations should be presumed to constitute individual attempts at fraudulent voting that got caught early."[345]   Obama has had many connections with ACORN, thus Obama may have been directly involved in promoting voter fraud activities before he became president. In the 1990s, Obama conducted leadership training sessions for ACORN. Obama helped arrange grants from the Woods Fund, where he served on the board of directors with Bill Ayers, totaling about $190,000, to the Chicago branch of ACORN from 2000 – 2002. The Obama campaign paid over $800,000 in 2008 to Citizens Services, Inc. (CSI), which is a subsidiary of ACORN, for "get out the vote" projects. Obama represented ACORN as an attorney in Chicago. While campaigning in 2008, Obama stated, "I've been fighting alongside ACORN on issues you care about my entire life. Even before I was an elected official, when I ran the Project Vote voter registration drive in Illinois, ACORN was smack dab in the middle of it." Yet, Obama lied on www.barackobama.com in the 'Fight the Smears' section, where his campaign stated in 2008, "Barack was never an ACORN community organizer … ACORN never hired Obama as a trainer, organizer or any other type of employee."[346] *(James McCormack, Eighteen Insights)*

iv.   "A Tunica, Mississippi jury sent Mississippi NAACP official Lessadolla Sowers to prison for five years in 2011. She was convicted **of voting 10 times using the names of other people**, some of whom were **dead**. Colorado Secretary of State Scott Gessler (R) unveiled a study last year showing that almost **5,000 illegal aliens cast votes** in the U.S. Senate election in that state in 2010. A conservative watchdog group, Minnesota Majority, claims that **felons' illegally cast votes** may have put Al Franken (D) over the top in the bitterly contested Minnesota Senate race. The group reported that at least 1,099 felons voted in that 2008 election, which is far larger than Franken's final, official, post-recount margin of victory over then-incumbent Sen. Norm Coleman (R). In Milwaukee, Wisconsin, a police department report found that in the 2004 election, as many as **5,300 more ballots were cast than voters who showed up at polling stations to vote** … But why do we have all this voter fraud? The answer is the National Voting Rights Act of 1993, also known as the Motor Voter law. As John Fund writes at pages 27-8 of *Stealing Elections*: "Perhaps no piece of legislation in the last generation better captures the 'incentivizing' of fraud... than the 1993 National Voter Registration Act[.] ... **Examiners were under orders not to ask anyone for identification or proof of citizenship**. States also had to permit **mail-in voter registrations**, which allowed anyone to register without any personal contact with a registrar or election official. Finally, **states were limited in pruning 'dead wood' - people who had died, moved or been convicted of crimes - from their rolls**. ... Since its implementation, Motor Voter has worked in one sense: it has fueled an explosion of **phantom voters**." And who pushed Motor

Voter? Marxists Richard Cloward and Frances Fox Piven *[Obama's associates with the New Party and Bill Ayers' SDS early connections and Columbia professors]* were instrumental in the passage of the law by Congress … 'Between 1994 and 1998, nearly 26 million names were added to the voter rolls nationwide, almost a 20 percent increase,' according to Fund. Motor Voter has 'been **registering illegal aliens**, since anyone who receives a government benefit [including welfare] may also register to vote with no questions asked.'"[347]

v. "A study by political scientist Jesse Richman from Old Dominion University in Virginia found that **6.4 percent of the 20 million noncitizens who reside in the United States voted in November's presidential election**. He then extrapolated these results into support for each presidential candidate, estimating that Clinton would have received 81 percent support from noncitizens, therefore receiving an extra 834,000 votes. The number of 834,000 is significant enough to have tipped some of the closest races in Clinton's favor, including New Hampshire, Nevada, and Maine, all of which Clinton won by margins of under 3 percent."[348]

vi. "A new report by the **Pew Center** on the States finds that more than **1.8 million dead people are currently registered to vote**. And **24 million registrations are either invalid or inaccurate**."[349] *(NPR, 2012)*

vii. "I've actually having worked before on a campaign in New Hampshire and I can tell you, this issue of bussing voters into New Hampshire is widely known by anyone who has worked in New Hampshire politics. It's very real, it's very serious…voter fraud is a serious problem in this country. You have millions of people who are registered in 2 states, people who are dead are registered to vote. 14% of non-citizens according to academic research at a minimum that are registered to vote which is an astounding statistic!" *Stephen Miller, Senior advisor to President Trump, February 12, 2017, ABC News interview with George Stephanopoulos.*

viii. In 2016, DHS computers attempted to hack into the Georgia electoral network ten times and initiated over 14,000 scans of the Indiana electoral systems without the approval of either state. Did Obama direct Jeh Johnson, the head of Homeland Security, to attempt to access various state electoral voting networks?

ix. Jane Kleeb, the Nebraska Democratic Party Chairperson, admitted that they have created **refugee welcome baskets** which contains a letter from the Nebraska Democratic Party and **voter registration forms**. *March 2017.*

x. There is significant **voting fraud in Detroit**, which was revealed during Jill Stein's recount after the 2016 presidential election. According to *The Detroit News*, "One-third of precincts in Wayne County could be disqualified from an unprecedented statewide recount of presidential election results because of problems with ballots …

officials couldn't reconcile vote totals for 610 of 1,680 precincts during a county-wide canvass of vote results late last month. Most of those are in heavily Democratic Detroit, where the number of ballots in precinct poll books did not match those of voting machine printout reports in 59 percent of precincts, 392 of 662."[350]

xi.   According to the *Washington Free Beacon*, **there are at least 7.2 million voter registrations that have appeared in two states simultaneously**. "The new voter data was gathered from the Kansas-run interstate voter registration crosscheck program, which is used to identify 'possible duplicate registrations among states.' The program began in December 2005 and conducted its first crosscheck in 2006. It is administered by the office of Kansas Secretary of State Kris Kobach, who was tapped recently to help lead President Trump's voter fraud commission. The newest data is from crosschecks of voter registrations across 28 states that participate in the program. At least 7.2 million registrations appeared in two states at once, according to the data."[351]

xii.   The Public Interest Legal Foundation revealed in a 2016 voting report based on 133 **Virginia** voting jurisdictions that, "Virginia election officials quietly removed 5,556 voters for non-citizenship between 2011 and May 2017; 1,852 of those removed as noncitizens cast ballots; A total of 7,474 illegal ballots were cast from the pool of removed noncitizens."[352] The report was entitled, "**One Third of Noncitizens Found Voted Illegally**."

xiii.   "A research group in New Jersey has taken a fresh look at postelection polling data and concluded that the number of noncitizens voting illegally in U.S. elections is likely far greater than previous estimates. **As many as 5.7 million noncitizens may have voted in the 2008 election**, which put Barack Obama in the White House. The research organization **Just Facts**, a widely cited, independent think tank led by self-described conservatives and libertarians, revealed its number-crunching in a report on national immigration … Mr. Agresti's analysis of the same polling data (Old Dominion University) settled on much higher numbers. He estimated that as many as 7.9 million noncitizens were illegally registered that year and 594,000 to 5.7 million voted … He **cites government audits that show large numbers of noncitizens use false IDs and Social Security numbers** in order to function in the U.S., which could include voting."[353] *(Washington Times, June 19, 2017)*

xiv.   An audit conducted by Rhode Island's Secretary of State Nellie Gorbea found that **19% of the state's official voter rolls are non-state residents** in 2017.

xv.   Fearing Trump's future investigations into voter fraud which is supported by Colorado's Secretary of State Wayne Williams, over 3,400 Colorado voters de-registered by July 2017.

xvi. "In the United States, **there are over 3.5 million more people registered to vote than there are living adult citizens**. Such staggering inaccuracy is an engraved invitation to vote fraud. The Election Integrity Project of *Judicial Watch*, a Washington-based legal-watchdog group, analyzed data from the U.S. Census Bureau's 2011 - 2015 American Community Survey and last month's statistics from the federal Election Assistance Commission. The latter included figures from 38 states. According to Judicial Watch, 11 states gave the EAC insufficient or questionable information."[355] *(Dallas News, August 11, 2017)*

7. "Because that, after all, is why we serve. **Not to score points or take credit**, but to make people's lives better." *Obama's Presidential Farewell speech, Chicago, January 10, 2017.* During Obama's same farewell speech, **he referred to himself 75 times**.

   a. **Obama declared himself to be the** "**founder of the Tea Party**," since he "invigorated the grassroots in the Republican Party as well as the Democratic Party," during an interview with George Stephanopoulos on *ABC's News* "This Week," on January 8, 2017. Not surprisingly, Obama did not take credit for the decimation of the Democratic Party during his two terms as president.

8. "I committed to President-elect Trump that **my administration would <u>ensure the smoothest possible transition</u>**, just as President Bush did for me." *Obama's Presidential Farewell speech, January 10, 2017.* Trump had to tweet at one point, "Doing my best to disregard the many inflammatory President O statements and roadblocks. Thought it was going to be a smooth transition – NOT!"

   a. Obama encouraged U.S. troops at MacDill Air Force Base in Tampa, Florida on December 6, 2016, to question and disobey their future commander in chief, Donald Trump. By stating, "each of us has … the universal right to **speak your minds** and to **protest against authority**; to live in a society that's open and free; that can **criticize our president without retribution**," Obama is **encouraging sedition and rebellion within the military of the United States**, which would not have been tolerated during his administration.

   b. Obama politicized the intelligence reports that focused on Russian interference in the 2016 presidential election via hacking into the DNC and John Podesta's emails, which inferred that Trump was possibly allied with Russia, and that **Trump's electoral victory was** "**illegitimate**." Obama was never interested in Russian hacking or any other American adversary that hacked into government or private enterprise computers until the Democrats lost the presidency to Trump. Liberals followed Obama's lead as Juan Williams on *Fox News Network's*, "The Five," stated, "It's really up to Donald Trump to prove he's legitimate." Senior Democratic representative **John Lewis** stated on "Meet the Press," – "**I don't see the president-elect as a legitimate president** … I think there was a conspiracy on the part of the Russians, and others, that helped him get elected." Democratic California **Senator Feinstein** agreed with Lewis and said, "I understand why John Lewis feels the way he does." Obama and the liberal Democrats are all attempting to delegitimize the new president, and are having a very difficult time relinquishing their hold on power at the executive branch level. Russian Foreign Ministry spokeswoman, Maria Zakharova commented, "If 'Russian hackers' hacked anything in America, there were two things: Obama's brain … Obama and his illiterate foreign policy team have dealt a crushing blow to America's prestige and leadership … [Obama and his foreign policy team are] a bunch of geopolitical losers, enraged and shortsighted … [Obama still has a few days left] to destroy the world."[354] Obama is doing his best to destroy America's future relationship with Russia, since there might be a chance there will be an alliance between Russia and the United States with the new Trump administration to destroy ISIS.

i.   Michelle Obama supported Lewis' derogatory comments on Trump one day after Lewis's "Meet the Press" interview by tweeting, "Thinking of Dr. King (MLK Day) and **great leaders like @repjohnlewis** who carry on his legacy. **May their example be <u>our call to action</u>**." Michelle Obama is also declaring Trump illegitimate, and is rallying the liberal base to reject Trump as a legitimate - legal president, which may lead to violent riots. **Michelle would not have sent out this tweet without the approval of her husband. Michelle goes low** and demonstrates her contempt of the will of the American people, unless her husband or other left-wing radicals are in power. It parallels her comment during the 2008 presidential primaries when she stated after Barack Obama had a primary victory, "For the first time in my adult life, I am proud of my country." Barack, Michelle and all the Democrats are ignoring Hillary's high negatives and lack of trust by the electorate, her strategic flaw focusing her campaign on the East and West coasts while ignoring middle America, Wisconsin, and the working class, the death of four Americans in Benghazi during her watch, and her disregard for U.S. national security protocols by conducting government business on her private unprotected server.

c.   **Obama's outgoing CIA director, John Brennan, warned and threatened Trump** during a *Fox News Sunday* interview just days before the inauguration, after Trump criticized aspects of the U.S. intelligence operations. Brennan told Trump, "**I don't think he has a full understanding of Russian capabilities** and the actions they are taking on the world … I think Mr. Trump has to understand that absolving Russia of various actions it has taken in the past number of years is a road that he need to be very, very careful about moving down … Spontaneity is not something that protects national security interests … [Trump needs] … **<u>to watch what he says</u>**." Veteran liberal journalist Bob Woodward commented, "I think what is under reported here is Trump's point of view on it. You laid it out when those **former CIA people said these things about Trump, that he was a recruited agent of the Russians, and a useful fool**, they started this in Trump's mind … I've lived in this world for 45 years where you get things and people make allegations, **that is a garbage document** … It never should have been presented as part of an intelligence briefing."[355] Obama used the U.S. intelligence agencies to delegitimize Trump as president before the inauguration and to complicate his relationships with the Russian government. Trump responded that Brennan himself may have leaked the intelligence dossier which floated the possibility of an illicit Trump – Russian relationship. Days later, chief of staff Priebus stated on *Fox News* Sunday, "I think that John Brennan has a lot of things that he should answer for in regards to these leaked documents. I find the whole thing despicable, I think that it's unprofessional … I don't know what's in his head." Brennan had the motive to discredit Trump since as Obama's national security advisor and head of the CIA, he helped dismantle U.S. counterintelligence defense strategies by implementing Muslim Brotherhood talking points that labelled jihad as a benign theological pursuit and that Islam had no relationship with violence or terrorism. Brennan, who called Jerusalem, al-Quds, was thought to be a Muslim convert and helped Obama empower the Muslim Brotherhood and the radical jihadi Iranian regime during his eight-year tenure. Even days after Trump became president, Brennan, who was immediately removed from his position as CIA director, unprofessionally attacked Trump, who visited the CIA during his first full day as president, by saying Trump "should be ashamed of himself" and that Brennan was "**deeply saddened and angered** at Donald Trump's **despicable display** of self-aggrandizement in front of CIA's Memorial Wall of Agency heroes." As CIA director and as a private citizen, Brennan repeatedly attempted to discredit Trump in front of the American intelligence and defense communities, since Brennan's and Obama's pro-Muslim and pro-jihad agenda was going to be reversed.

i.   "Although Russians may have aspired to influence the November election, the real election meddlers were Democrats in the Obama administration who conspired with foreign intelligence agencies against Donald Trump's campaign, new media reports suggest. The key player, we are learning, is the already infamous John O. Brennan but FBI Director James Comey also played a role. From January 2009 to March 2013, Brennan was Assistant to the President for Homeland Security and Counterterrorism, and then Director of the Central Intelligence Agency from March 2013 until Obama's last day as president. George Neumayr explains at the *American Spectator* how pro-Islam, pro-Communist Brennan appears to have masterminded the operation. "Seeking to retain his position as CIA director under Hillary, Brennan teamed up with British spies and Estonian spies to cripple

Trump's candidacy. He used their phony intelligence as a pretext for a multi-agency investigation into Trump, which led the FBI to probe a computer server connected to Trump Tower and gave cover to [then-National Security Advisor] Susan Rice, among other Hillary supporters, to spy on Trump and his people." Drawing from a news article in the *Guardian* (UK), Neumayr adds: "Brennan got his anti-Trump tips primarily from British spies but also Estonian spies and others. The story confirms that the seed of the espionage into Trump was planted by Estonia. The BBC's Paul Wood reported last year that the intelligence agency of an unnamed Baltic State had tipped Brennan off in April 2016 to a conversation purporting to show that the Kremlin was funneling cash into the Trump campaign." Estonians were indeed tense after Trump's seeming ambivalence about NATO on the campaign trail and the prospect that as president he might leave that former Soviet province at the mercy of Russian President Vladimir Putin. British spy agencies, too, were rife with Trump-haters. The *Guardian* reports that Robert Hannigan, then-head of the British foreign surveillance service, Government Communications Headquarters (GCHQ), "passed material" to Brennan in summer 2016 … Brennan was the CIA's station chief in Riyadh, Saudi Arabia. "I saw how our Saudi partners fulfilled their duty as custodians of the two holy mosques of Mecca and Medina," he said. "I marveled at the majesty of the Hajj and the devotion of those who fulfilled their duty as Muslims by making that privilege – that pilgrimage." … Brennan admitted he supported the Kremlin-funded Communist Party USA at the height of the Cold War, even voting for CPUSA presidential candidate Gus Hall in 1976. That fact alone should have instantly and permanently disqualified Brennan from all national security-related government posts."[356] Obama, Brennan and Rice did all they could to sabotage and undermine the Trump presidency. The fact that General Michael Flynn was fired as Trump's National Security Advisor, that Trump allowed thousands of Syrian refugees to enter the United States early in his presidency thus violating a campaign promise, and that Trump agreed to transfer thousands of stranded Syrian refugees from Australia to the United States shows that Obama's sabotage of and infiltration into the Trump administration has been somewhat effective. Trump made a conscious decision not to purge his administration of many Obama holdovers from intelligence and defense, who have political agendas that are in direct opposition to the political platform advanced by Trump which cemented his 2016 election victory. Trump's reversal of a campaign promise to immediately move the U.S. embassy in Israel from Tel Aviv to Jerusalem and to bomb assets of the secular Assad regime also showed significant Obaman influence over Trump's Middle East foreign policy.

d. As Obama led Democratic boycotts of Israeli Prime Minister Netanyahu's speech before a joint session of Congress in early 2015 and his follow up speech at the UN, Obama privately encouraged **Democrats to boycott Trump's inauguration**. During the week before Trumps inauguration, over 60 Democrats announced they would not attend the event out of protest.

e. The Democrats are forgoing the traditional one-hundred day honeymoon that a new president has with the opposing political party in Congress.

f. In response to the President-elect's tweets, Vice President Biden criticized Trump during a *PBS NewsHour* interview saying, "**Grow up**, **Donald**. **Grow up**. Time to be an adult. You're president. You've got to do something. Show us what you have." Biden continued to criticize Trump by stating, "I think it's danger – for a president not to have confidence in, not to be prepared to listen to the myriad of intelligence agencies from defense intelligence, to the CIA, et cetera, **is absolutely mindless**. It's just mindless."

g. On December 23, 2016, Obama **supported UNSC Resolution 2334**, which **significantly altered U.S. Middle East foreign policy** by declaring the Palestinians' were legally entitled to most of the holiest Jewish and Christian sites in East Jerusalem and the Jewish quarter in the old city of Jerusalem, and that the pre-1967 Israeli borders were the starting point for any peace negotiations. Obama's actions pushed a negotiated peace in the Middle East further away from reality.

h. Obama attempted to **sabotage Trump's and America's relationship with Israel** at the end of his presidency by warning Israeli intelligence officials that Trump's close ties to Russia could compromise Israeli agents and operations, since Russia is an ally with Iran. According to *YNetNews*, "Israeli intelligence officials fear that top-secret information that has been exposed to the United States will be leaked to Russia – and from Russia to its close ally, Iran … The Americans implied that their Israeli colleagues should "be careful" as of January 20, Trump's inauguration date, when transferring intelligence information to the White House and to the National Security Council (NSC), which is subject to the president. According to the Israelis who were present in the meeting, the Americans recommended that until it is made clear that Trump is not inappropriately connected to Russia and is not being extorted – Israel should avoid revealing sensitive sources to administration officials for fear the information would reach the Iranians."[357]

i. Obama **increased tensions between Russia and the United States** by increasing sanctions and expelling a large number of Russian diplomats, in response to their hacking of the DNC and Podesta's emails. Obama also moved American troops and tanks along the Russian border, which increased the risk of an armed confrontation between Russia and the NATO alliance. Russia reinforced anti-aircraft missiles around Moscow, while Obama moved U.S. forces into Poland. One of the major reasons Obama implemented sanctions against Russia at the end of his presidency, was to lay a trap for Trump and senior members of his administration, where any contact with Russian officials and a possible discussion of easing the sanctions could be presented as anti-American and a potential case for treason and / or impeachment, in light of the unproven allegations that Trump officials colluded with the Russians in the 2016 presidential election. **The Russian sanctions were instituted to entrap Trump** and protect his legacy, Obamacare, Iran, and Islamic interests.

j. After Obama instituted significant sanctions against Russia, he gave many U.S. intelligence agencies new powers where they could easily access the communications of all senior members of the Trump administration and ultimately sabotage them by having the transcripts more readily available to embedded Obama allies throughout the intelligence community, who could eventually leak the classified information to the press. According *to The New York Times*, "In its final days, the Obama administration has expanded the power of the National Security Agency to share globally intercepted personal communications with the government's 16 other intelligence agencies before applying privacy protections. **The new rules significantly relax longstanding limits on what the N.S.A. may do with the information gathered by its most powerful surveillance operations**, which are largely unregulated by American wiretapping laws. These include collecting satellite transmissions, phone calls and emails that cross network switches abroad, and messages between people abroad that cross domestic network switches. **The change means that far more officials will be searching through raw data**. Essentially, the government is reducing the risk that the N.S.A. will fail to recognize that a piece of information would be valuable to another agency, but **increasing the risk that officials will see private information about innocent people**."[358]

i. "There was a sea-change here at the NSA with an order that came from president Obama 17 days before he left office where he allowed the NSA who used to control the data, it now goes to 16 other agencies and that just festered this whole leaking situation, and that happened on the way out, as the president was leaving the office. Why did the Obama administration wait until it had 17 days left in their administration to put this order in place if they thought it was so important. They had 8 years, they didn't do it, number one. Number two, it changed the exiting rule which was an executive order dating back to Ronald Reagan, that has been in place until 17 days before the Obama administration was going to end, that said the NSA gets the raw data, and they determine dissemination. Instead, this change that the president put in place, signed off by the way by James Clapper on December 15, 2016, signed off by Loretta Lynch the Attorney General January 3, 2017, they decide that now 16 agencies can get the raw data and what that does is almost creates a shadow government. You have all these people who are not agreeing with President Trump's position, so it just festers more leaks. If they had a justification for this, wonderful, why didn't they do it 8 years ago, 4 years ago, 3 years ago. Yet they wait until 17 days left." *Jay Sekulow, Civil Rights and First Amendment Expert Lawyer, Hannity interview on Fox, February 17, 2017.* Obama changed the laws so it would be nearly impossible to find the source of the leaks, and would allow Obama's allies scattered among all 17 agencies, access to classified Trump administration documents and conversations, which now are readily available to the liberal mainstream media. Obama controls the intelligence agencies through his embeds, and uses their positions and this new directive to undermine and eventually impeach Trump, so he can protect the JCPOA, Iran, the flow of unvetted Muslim immigrants into America, and the bulk of his legacy. Unfortunately, **Obama's actions are seditious** and should be considered illegal, since he is using an unauthorized relationship with the intelligence community as a private citizen to actively undermine and destroy the president.

    ii. "In summary: the Obama administration **sought, and eventually obtained, authorization to eavesdrop on the Trump campaign**; continued monitoring the Trump team even when no evidence of wrongdoing was found; **then relaxed the NSA rules to allow evidence to be shared widely within the government**, virtually ensuring that the information, including the conversations of private citizens, would be leaked to the media. Levin called the effort a "**silent coup**" by the Obama administration and demanded that it be investigated."[359]

k. With less than two weeks into the Trump presidency in early February 2017, **Rosa Brooks**, a former Obama Pentagon counselor and advisor to the State Department, advocated in *Foreign Policy* magazine, that **instituting a military coup or invoking the 25th Amendment** of the Constitution, which would declare Trump mentally unfit to be president, as the **quickest way to end the Trump presidency**. Obama most likely gave Brooks his approval for advancing these divisive topics. After Trump became president, Brooks was hired by the New America Foundation, a liberal think-tank funded by George Soros.

l. "In what's shaping up to be a highly unusual post-presidency, **Obama** isn't just staying behind in Washington. **He's working behind the scenes to set up what will effectively be a shadow government** to not only protect his threatened legacy, but **to sabotage the incoming administration and its popular "America First" agenda**. He's doing it through a network of leftist nonprofits led by **Organizing for Action**. Normally you'd expect an organization set up to support a politician and his agenda to close up shop after that candidate leaves office, but not Obama's OFA. Rather, it's gearing up for battle, with a growing war chest and more than 250 offices across the country. Since Donald Trump's election, this little-known but well-funded protesting arm has beefed up staff and ramped up recruitment of young liberal activists, declaring on its website, "We're not backing down." Determined to salvage Obama's legacy," it's drawing battle lines on immigration, ObamaCare, race relations and climate change. **Obama is intimately involved in OFA operations** and even tweets from the group's account. In fact, he gave marching orders to OFA foot soldiers following Trump's upset victory."[360] *(Paul Sperry, The New York Post, February 2017)* Ed Klein commented on *Fox and Friends* in December 2016, during the Obama – Trump transition period, "For the past 100 years every president who is outgoing has packed up his stuff gone home and not criticized his successor. This is not what the Obamas are planning to do. They rented an eight-bedroom mansion in the section of Washington near Joe Lockhart, Bill Clinton's last press secretary. In that house there's enough room for Valerie Jarrett and Michelle and the kids. A place for ten cars to park. They are **setting up what they are calling a shadow government** …They are staying there because **despite what the president said in his press conference (Obama lied), he's in a sense of outrage over this incoming Trump Administration, which he thinks is going to wipe out his legacy.** So, he's setting up this kind of almost insurgency, picking people in foreign affairs, labor, abortion, union matters and setting them up to start appearing on television, making speeches and doing op-ed pieces for next four years, **you're going to see not only a Trump Administration but you're going to see a shadow government opposing the Trump**." Obama lied when he told the public he was staying in Washington so Sasha could finish high school there. The real reason for his remaining in D.C. is to run the opposition and interference against the Trump presidency, which started during the transition period. Obama will be controlling an army of over 30,000 agitators via OFA, who will be participating in demonstrations, some of which have already turned violent. The funding of OFA will primarily come from Obama's political networks and those of George Soros.

i.   "Pulitzer Prize-winning journalist Michael Goodwin asserts the 'Trump Derangement Syndrome,' is no temporarily insane reaction, but rather "a calculated plan to wreck the presidency, whatever the cost to the country." The beginnings of this "rolling coup" happened in broad daylight in the taking down of Lieutenant General Michael Flynn as Director of National Security by residual players within the Obama intelligence community -- including the CIA and the NSA. Political correctness remains so dominant in language and culture in the U.S., that no one dares utter the word "sedition." Unbeknownst to most Americans, Barack Obama is the first ex-president in 228 years of U.S. history to structure and lead a political organization, a shadow government, for the explicit purpose of sabotaging his successor -- duly elected President Donald Trump. The primary vehicle of this campaign is Organizing for Action (OFA), legally founded in January 2013 by First Lady Michelle Obama and her husband's 2012 campaign manager Jim Messina, with input from David Axelrod."[361]

ii. "**Barack Obama is turning his new home** in the posh Kalorama section of the nation's capital – just two miles away from the White House – **into the nerve center of the mounting insurgency against his successor**, **President Donald J. Trump**. Obama's goal, according to a close family friend, is **to oust Trump from the presidency either by forcing his resignation or through his impeachment**. And Obama is being aided in his political crusade by his longtime consigliere, Valerie Jarrett, who has moved into the 8,200-square-foot, $5.3-million Kalorama mansion with the former president and Michelle Obama, long time best friends."[362] Obama is leading the political insurgency and an American president in order to protect his legacy, to strengthen the far-left political wing of the Democratic party, and to protect radical Islamic interests worldwide, including hijrah into the United States.

iii. "There is indication that Obama has **set up a secret operation in a war room** just about 2 miles from the White House, where Michelle has her offices and so do **many of the former aides to Obama**. And they meet there and have **a twice daily conference call** … Every morning. And they develop talking points for the media … on how to undermine and sabotage Trump … And all the key players on on that conference call … Lately its been devoted and dedicated trying to defeat Trump's healthcare reform … The cast of characters will be very familiar *(Kathleen Sebelius, former secretary of HHS; Andrew Slavitt, former head of center for Medicare and Medicaid; Jeanne Lambrew, chief White House architect of Obama's healthcare law still working with OMB and the Congressional budget office, former Obama Deputy Director of the White House Office of Health Reform; Leslie Dash, runs war room and former top Obama official; Valerie Jarrrett)* … So much for smooth presidential transitions. Now, of course, that's the overt part of the resistance. The **covert part of the resistance** are these moles buried deep in the Trump administration who are **leaking to sabotage Trump** … These leaks are leaks by government officials often of national secuurity data designed to destroy the president … What Obama did. He embedded his employees deep within the bowels of these agencies by moving them into civil services positions and away from appointed jobs … and now is there forever … A big part of this conspiracy by the Democrats is to slow walk and place obstacles in the way of the confirmation of the Trump appointees by demanding roll call votes, demanding hearings, and placing all sorts of procedural obstacles there… and they won't be able to get rid of the leakers that are embedded in the administration … The media picks up on the leaks … and refuses to name who the leakers are … And that conspiracy directed really by this operations room, … **this war room**, is **how they are trying to topple Donald Trump**." *Dick Morris, former President Clinton advisor and political consultant, YouTube broadcast, July 2017. Obama is not only trying to sabotage Trump's healthcare agenda, but also most aspects of his domestic and foreign policy agendas.*

m. During the first few weeks of Trump's presidency, **confidential calls** between Trump and the leaders of Mexico and Australia, and conversations between National Security Advisor Michael Flynn and the Russian ambassador to the United States **have been probably leaked to the public via <u>Obama moles in the White House, the FBI, the NSA and other intelligence agencies</u>**, including the CIA. The conversation between Flynn and the Russian ambassador led to the resignation of the new national security advisor. A significant number of CIA operatives and divisional directors are probably still reporting to former CIA director John Brennan and Obama, and bypassing the new CIA director Mike Pompeo. Obama is leading a shadow government of federal employees who are loyal to him and are taking orders from Obama and / or are initiating intelligence actions that are purposely undermining President Trump and his new administration, especially those individuals who are dedicated to destroying Obama's legacy and targeting radical Islam or Iran as a threat to the West. Obama, with his embedded allies in the federal government, targeted Flynn for political destruction since Flynn was very anti-Islam and anti-Iran. Flynn has stated that Islam is an "ideology based on a religion," *[blasphemy]* that "radical Islamists [are attempting to build] an Islamic state right here at home … a totalitarian state under the dictates of the most rigid version of Sharia" *[Obama is protecting the expansion of the Islamic caliphate in the United States]*, radical Islam is a grave lethal threat to the United States, and that there is "no doubt that they [radical Muslims] are dead set on taking us over and drinking our blood." He has also said, "I am certain, I am deadly certain that we cannot win this war unless we are free to call our enemy by name: Radical Islamicists." Flynn also wanted to expose al-Qaeda's close relationship with Iran and was going to possibly reveal additional secret side deals that could put the JCPOA in jeopardy and solidify the argument that Obama committed treason against the United States, by producing and enacting the Iranian nuclear deal. By stating that the "**Obama administration knowingly decided to support al-Qaeda and the Muslim Brotherhood in Syria**, **and directly enabled the rise of the Islamic State**," Flynn was a real threat to Obama, his agenda, and his legacy. Thus, purging Flynn from the national security apparatus was a high priority for Obama and his associates. Obama's ultimate goal is to impeach Trump or force him to resign.

i. *The Wall Street Journal* reported that U.S. intelligence officials are withholding intelligence from President Trump, while simultaneously illegally leaking classified information to the press. It was reported, "**Officials have decided not to show Mr. Trump the sources and methods that the intelligence agencies use to collect information, the current and former officials said**. Those sources and methods could include, for instance, the means that an agency uses to spy on a foreign government … It wasn't clear Wednesday how many times officials have held back information from Mr. Trump."[363] These intelligence officials are loyal to Obama, and not the new president.

ii. Judge Jeamine Pirro stated on "Fox and Friends" on February 17, 2017, "There are people in the intelligence community who are so livid about what Donald Trump is saying about them, that they will retaliate. And what you have seen is what they did. They were in a position to do it, and they leaked it. This, by the way, they don't play around … **these are Obama people** **who were leftovers**. And what Donald Trump needs to do is move into the bureaucracies and find out who the leakers are because a lot of these people are very much embedded into the system."

n. "Several intelligence insiders have come forward over the past few days to describe a 'shadow government' of Obama holdovers leaking information to derail the Trump presidency, with **National Security Advisor Mike Flynn's resignation** their first great success. There are even allegations that **former President Barack Obama himself is actively involved, citing his establishment of a command center in Washington and continuing involvement with activist organizations**. Retired Lt. Colonel Tony Schaffer, formerly a CIA-trained defense intelligence officer, said in a *Fox Business News* appearance on Wednesday: 'I put this right at the feet of John Brennan, and Jim Clapper, and I would even go so far as to say **the White House was directly involved before they left**.' He also mentioned Ben Rhodes. The *Washington Free Beacon* quoted 'multiple sources in and out of the White House' on Tuesday to describe a '**secret, months-long campaign by former Obama administration confidantes to handicap President Donald Trump's national security apparatus and preserve the nuclear deal with Iran**.'"[364]

o. "This story is not about **Jeff Sessions**. This story is not about illegal talks between Trump and his campaign people and the Russians. **This story is about Barack Obama and the Democrat Party attempting to sabotage the Trump presidency and do everything they can to either render it meaningless and ineffective or to get him impeached or force him to resign**." Rush Limbaugh discussing attempts by the Democrats to get Attorney General Sessions to resign based on discussions he had with Russian diplomats before Trump was inaugurated, even though Sessions adamantly denied he had no contacts with any Russians discussing any aspects of the Trump presidential campaign. *February 2017.* Another fake news story.

  i. "The hook on which the *Post* attempts to hang Sessions is that he did not disclose the meetings to the Senate when he was asked about "possible contacts between members of President Trump's campaign and representatives of Moscow." Sessions's spokesperson at the Department of Justice, Sarah Isgur Flores, says his answer in January was truthful because he was asked about "the Trump campaign – not about meetings he took as a senator and a member of the Armed Services Committee."[365] *(Breitbart, Fake News and Senator Sessions)* The transcripts of Sessions interchange with Senator Franken is as follows (via C-SPAN): **Franken:** "CNN just published a story alleging that the intelligence community provided documents to the president-elect last week, that included **information that "Russian operatives claim to have compromising personal and financial information about Mr. Trump."** These documents also allegedly say "there was a **continuing exchange of information during the campaign between Trump surrogates and intermediaries for the Russian government.**" Again, I'm telling you this as it's coming out, so you know. But if it's true, it's obviously extremely serious, and if there is any evidence that anyone affiliated with the Trump campaign communicated with the Russian government in the course of this campaign, what will you do? **Sessions:** Senator Franken, **I'm not aware of any of those activities.** I have been called a surrogate at a time or two in that campaign and **I did not have communications with the Russians** [regarding the above activities you mentioned and directed the question at], and I'm unable to comment on it."

 ii. "In the **Obama administration's** last days, some White House officials scrambled to spread information about Russian efforts to undermine the presidential election – and about possible contacts between associates of President-elect Donald J. Trump and Russians – across the government. Former American officials say they had **two aims:** to ensure that such meddling isn't duplicated in future American or European elections, and **to leave a clear trail of intelligence for government investigators.**" *(The New York Times, March 1, 2017)*[366]

p. On March 4, 2017, President Trump revealed through a series of tweets, that **Obama most likely authorized the U.S. national intelligence agencies to spy on Trump Towers and the Trump campaign**, by obtaining an unsubstantiated FISA warrant. The Obama administration's initial request to obtain a **FISA warrant** was refused by the FISA court in June 2016. Obama finally obtained the warrant just weeks before the presidential election in October, in order to troll for an "October surprise" that could blow up the Trump campaign and secure a Clinton presidential victory. When the "October surprise" did not materialize, Obama and his staff used the information to sabotage the Trump transition and his presidency. The monitoring of Trump officials continued throughout the transition period after the November election, and possibly after the inauguration.

    i.   "**Susan Rice**, who served as the National Security Adviser under President Obama, has been identified as **the official who requested unmasking** of incoming Trump officials, *Cernovich Media* exclusively reported. The White House Counsel's office identified Rice as the person responsible for the unmasking after examining Rice's document log requests. The reports Rice requested to see are kept under tightly-controlled conditions. Each person must log her name before being granted access to them. "Unmasking" is the process of identifying individuals whose communications were caught in the dragnet of intelligence gathering. While conducting investigations into terrorism and other related crimes, intelligence analysts incidentally capture conversations about parties not subject to the search warrant. The identities of individuals who are not under investigation are kept confidential, for legal and moral reasons. Under President Obama, the unmasking rules were changed." The only other Obama officials who can "unmask" civilians in intelligence reports were Attorney General Lynch, CIA Director Brennan, and the Director of National Intelligence Clapper.

q.   "I think that **the Obama administration has done everything that it can possibly do**, and that's probably been verified somewhat by *The New York Times*, to make sure that enough people have seen some of the meetings and some of the connections *[regarding unsubstantiated Russian collusion with the election]*, so that they have something to go on when the investigations are really underway." *Congresswoman Maxine Waters, Democrat, March 2017.*

r.   On March 15, 2017, Obama took an unexpected trip to Hawaii two days before **Judge Derrick Watson**, who was **a classmate of Obama's at Harvard law school**, **issued an order to freeze Trump's second executive order** that temporarily suspended immigration from six terror-prone Muslim majority countries in the Middle East. The judge issued his 43-page ruling only two hours after the case was formally filed with the court. Thus, Judge Watson, was given his formal written response by third parties, which mostly likely originated from Obama or lawyers working under his guidance. A major plaintiff in this case is Imam Ismail Elshikh, who is the leader of the largest mosque in Hawaii, which is owned by the North American Islamic Trust, which is affiliated with the Muslim Brotherhood. Thus, Obama probably partnered with the Muslim Brotherhood to overturn Trump's executive orders by having the plaintiff affiliated with the Muslim Brotherhood file a lawsuit in the court of a classmate and fellow liberal, who declared Trump's executive order unconstitutional, and was given the brief, by third parties, possibly Obama, which formally outlined his opinion. **Obama and the Muslim Brotherhood are controlling immigration policy**, even during Trump's presidency.

s.   The **Secret Service removed detection sensors** in one section of the fence surrounding the White House grounds **at the end of Obama's second term**, and failed to replace them. In March 2017, Jonathan Tran scaled the fence and was able to reach the back door of the president's residence before being apprehended. Tran was on the White House grounds for over 17 minutes undetected.

t.   "Outside of the White House, meanwhile, a team of former Obama administration officials is working to subvert Trump's agenda. Former Obama administration officials such as Ben Rhodes, the architect of Obama's pro-Iran press operation, and Colin Kahl, a senior national security adviser to former Vice President Joe Biden, have engaged in public efforts to "purge" the current White House of officials they disagree with. Earlier this month, Kahl admitted on Twitter that he is seeking to provoke the firings of Trump's handpicked team "in the West Wing," including senior advisers Steve Bannon, Stephen Miller, and Sebastian Gorka, and NSC leaders Michael Anton and KT McFarland. As part of this effort, Kahl, Rhodes, and others have leaked damaging stories about these officials to allies in the media *[creating an echo chamber that successfully allowed the Iranian nuclear deal to be enacted]*. The latest target, Gorka, has been falsely accused of being a Nazi sympathizer and an Islamophobe. The campaign against Flynn unfolded in a similar manner and sources who spoke to the *Free Beacon* about the matter speculated that these leaks will continue."[367]

u.   An Obama loyalist still working for Trump at the White House **removed the phrase "radical Islamic terrorism" from an executive order** about to be signed by the president, and replaced that phrase with Obama's politically correct terminology related to nonspecific violent extremism.

v.   Obama may have ordered Rice to focus U.S. intelligence operations on "incidentally" collected Trump and associates conversations so that Rice's unmasking of political opponents could eventually undermine and destroy a future Trump presidency, which was a threat to Obama's legacy. As Frank Gaffney, president of the *Center for Security Policy* noted, "I think that there's unquestionably a political warfare operation being run by their former boss, Barack Obama. And I think there's a lot of evidence that they're still lashed up with him and therefore I think it's a safe assumption that they are probably performing opposition research, if you wish to call it that, for Organizing for Action … and their purpose for it is pretty clear – destroying the Trump presidency."[368]

w. "As Adam Kredo from *The Washington Free Beacon* has documented, in its last months, **the Obama administration ensured that the National Security Council's budget would be depleted**, **in order to deny the Trump administration the ability to hire new staffers**. It hired political appointees into the civil service and then burrowed them in the National Security Council and other key government departments, to undermine and discredit the Trump administration from within. For instance, in its waning days, the State Department extended Yael Lempert's tenure at the National Security Council for two years. Lempert is a foreign service officer notorious for her rabid opposition to Israel. In another example, last July, Obama moved Sahar Nowrouzzadeh from his National Security Council, where Nowrouzzadeh served as Iran director, to the State Department, where he is now in charge of policy planning on Iran and the Persian Gulf."[369]

x. "Well, **you have a politicization of the agencies**. *[Over 60% of employees who work at the National Security Council have been appointed by the Obama administration, which is why there are so many leaks.[370] Obama loyalists have pledged their allegiance to Obama and not the new president, and they are working to destroy the Trump presidency.]* That is **resulting in leaks from anonymous unknown people and the intention is to take down a president**. This is very dangerous to America. It is a threat to our republic. It constitutes a clear and present danger to our way of life. What is the motive of these people? *[They are Obama loyalists, who take their orders from Obama. Obama is protecting his political legacy and the ability of Muslims to continue jihad and hijrah in the Europe and the United States.]* Who's putting these leaks out? Why isn't somebody coming forward to make that charge and put their name and their reputation behind it instead of attacking through the media and not substantiating their position?" *Former Democratic Representative Dennis Kucinich on Hannity of Fox News, May 16, 2017. Kucinich is one of the few Democrats who is a neutral objective observer of some of the problems surrounding the Trump presidency.*

y. "On Friday's broadcast of the *Fox News Channel's* "Special Report," columnist **Charles Krauthammer** argued *the New York Times'* report about President Trump's conversations with Russian officials about FBI Director James Comey's firing *[obtained via White House leaks]* shows that **there's "a loyalty problem inside the White House**."[371] *(Breitbart, May 19, 2017)* Obama holdovers in the executive branch are loyal to Obama and not to Trump, and are working with Obama to bring down the Trump presidency.

z. In May 2017, during Trump's first major foreign tour while the new president was making stops in continental Europe (the Vatican and NATO headquarters), **Obama delivered anti-Trump remarks in Germany** while supporting Chancellor Merkel in her re-election bid by saying, "We can't isolate ourselves. **We can't hide behind a wall**." Obama is also hypocritically interfering in Germany's domestic elections by actively campaigning in support of Merkel. After meeting with Obama *[Why is Obama interfering with the making of American foreign policy and subverting the new president?],* and then Trump, Merkel put distance between the German alliance with the United States and Great Britain. **Obama also made anti-Trump statements in Canada, Indonesia, and South Korea over the next few months**.

aa.   A Senate Homeland Security and Governmental Affairs Committee report released in July 2017 revealed that the Trump administration has had up to **7x more national security leaks** during its first 126 days than previous administrations. The report acknowledged that "Since President Trump assumed office, our nation has faced an unprecedented wave of potentially damaging leaks of information." The sources of these leaks are Obama loyalists, who are attempting to destroy the Trump presidency and are doing the bidding of former President Obama.

bb.   "What we have is a **coordinated attack** between elements of the press, elements in the bureaucracy and then sitting – during the transition – **and now former Obama officials** *[embedded Obama loyalists working for Obama]* **weaving this vast Trump-Putin conspiracy theory**, which doesn't hold up under scrutiny … We knew the Russians were involved in all kinds of nefarious actions and **we did nothing until December 29th [2016] just before the Trump inauguration** … One of the psychological benefits to the Democrats of this Russian collusion nonsense is that it has **completely white-washed the appeasement of the Russians by Obama**." *Michael Doran, former senior director of the national Security Council with President George W. Bush, Hudson Institute conference, July 6, 2017.* A former NSC official admits that Obama's allies are actively working to undermine President Trump.

cc.   "[An] unrelenting witch hunt … has been unleashed by Imperial Washington against the legitimately elected President of the United States, Donald J. Trump. **This campaign of lies, leaks and Russophobia is the handiwork of <u>Obama</u>'s top national security advisors**, who blatantly misused Washington's surveillance apparatus to discredit Trump and **to effectively nullify America's democratic process** … **The enabling culprits are Obama's last CIA director, <u>John Brennan</u>**, his national security advisor **Susan Rice** and UN Ambassador **Samantha Power**. There is now mounting evidence that it was they who illegally "unmasked" NSA intercepts from Trump Tower; they who confected the Russian meddling narrative from behind the protective moat of classified intelligence; and they who orchestrated a systematic campaign of leaks and phony intelligence reports during the presidential transition – all designed to delegitimize Trump before he even took the oath of office … **<u>CIA Director John Brennan</u>** gained access to a sensitive intelligence report from a foreign intelligence service. This service claimed to have technically penetrated the inner circle of Russian leadership to the extent that it could give voice to the words of Russian President Vladimir Putin as he articulated Russia's objectives regarding the 2016 U.S. Presidential election – to defeat Hillary Clinton and help elect Donald Trump, her Republican opponent. This intelligence was briefed to President Barack Obama … The explosive nature of this intelligence report, both in terms of its sourcing and content, served to drive the investigation of Russian meddling in the American electoral process by the U.S. intelligence community. The problem, however, was that it wasn't the U.S. intelligence community, per se, undertaking this investigation, but rather (according to the *Washington Post*) **a task force composed of "several dozen analysts from the CIA, NSA and FBI,"** <u>**handpicked by the CIA direc-tor and set up at the CIA Headquarters**</u> who "functioned as a sealed compartment, its work hidden from the rest of the intelligence community. The result was a closed circle of analysts who operated in complete isolation from the rest of the U.S. intelli-gence community. The premise of their work – that Vladimir Putin personally directed Russian meddling in the U.S. Presidential election to tip the balance in favor of Donald Trump – **was never questioned** in any meaningful fashion, despite its **sourcing to a single intelligence report from a foreign service**." *(David Stockman, former Reagan Office of Management and Budget (OMB) director, David Stockman's Contra Corner, July 22, 2017)* Obama orchestrated these attacks against America's democratic process and the Constitution, and its new president. Obama and Brennan most likely planted the story from the foreign source and used it to initiate anti-Trump policies originating from the their tightly controlled pro-Obama intelligence operatives whose only goal was to de-stroy Donald Trump. This same group probably spied on the Supreme Court, members of Congress, and other prominent Americans on behalf of Obama.

dd. Days after David Stockman published the above article and identified John Brennan as Obama's major point man who would lead the campaign to destroy Trump, Brennan counter attacked and stated in public that if Trump fired special counselor Robert Mueller, then the Congress should impeach President Trump or the U.S. government should stage a coup against the sitting president. In an interview with Wolf Blitzer and James Clapper at the Aspen Security Forum, Brennan *[voted for communists before join-ing the CIA, ? converted to Islam while working in Saudi Arabia, blocked an American raid to kill Osama bin Laden, praised jihad as a legitimate tenet of Islam]* stated, "I would like to think that we all, all Americans want to get this behind us because it is hurting us. I like to think that Mr. Trump and other people in the White House would like to get this behind us. The best way to do that is to have as much transparency as possible. If there is nothing to hide there then they should cooperate fully in an accelerated fashion with the special counsel and others. But I think time after time after time one only comes away with the impression that there is a resistance to having more information come out, and that just feeds suspicions. And I do think -- I'm hoping that this is going to, you know, be addressed sooner rather than later in terms of what is there. If there's nothing there, let's move on. But this is where the work of Robert Mueller is critical to our future as a country because, you know, in some respects we're a government and a nation in crisis right … They don't come any better … **And if he's any fired by Mr. Trump or attempted to be fired by Mr. Trump, I hope I really hope that our members of Congress, elected representatives are going to stand up and say enough is enough** and stop making apologies and excuses for things that are happening that really flout I think our system of laws and government. *[Blitzer: When you say enough is enough what will -- if he's fired and he's the President of the United States, he could tell Rosenstein to fire him if he wants, but if he's fired what would you want Congress to do?]* … **First of all, I think it's the obligation of some executive branch officials to refuse to carry out some of these orders that again are inconsistent with what this country is all about**. But I would just hope that this is not going to be a partisan issue that Republicans, Democrats are going to see that the future of this country is at stake, and there needs to be some things done for the good of the future." If Trump fires Mueller, then Obama is calling for a coup against the president via his former CIA director, who has probably maintained his partial control over the intelligence establishment. Any evidence that Mueller discovers will probably be planted by Obama and Brennan, and if Trump fights back, then an ex-CIA director is advocating for the overthrow of the president with the approval of Obama. Both Obama and Brennan, who are [most likely] undercover Muslims, need to halt Trump's agenda, which is a hindrance to the plans of the OIC and the Muslim Brotherhood to take over the West and maintain control over Washington, which was put into motion during the Obama administration. Brennan, as a private citizen, is probably violating federal laws by publicly supporting a coup and possiblly using his previous contacts in the government to undermine President Trump.

ee. Former Ambassador to the UN, Samantha Power, may have had a major role in unmasking Trump allies and his presidential transition team while working within Obama admnistration in order to undermine the new Trump presidency. Representative Devin Nunes, Chairman of the House Permanent Select Committee on Intelligence wrote a letter to Daniel Coats, Director of National Intelligence, complaining of leaks from the government that were undermining the Trump administration. Nunes stated on July 27, 2017, "We have found evidence that current and **former government officials had easy access to U.S. person information** and that it is possible that they used this information **to achieve partisan political purposes**, including the selective, **anonymous leaking** of such information … The committee has learned that **one official (Samantha Power**), whose position had **no apparent intelligence related function**, made **hundreds of unmasking requests** during the final year of the Obama administration." According to *The Washington Free Beacon*, "Power's role in this unmasking effort is believed to be particularly questionable given her position as the U.N. ambassador, a post that does not typically require such sensitive unmasking activities, according to former U.S. officials and other sources familiar with the matter."[372] Power abused her political position and used classified intelligence to attempt to destroy President Trump, which is sedition and possibly treason, since her actions also undermined the security of the United States and its allies. Obama, as president and her boss, most likely directed her actions.

ff. "Former Obama White House National Security Adviser **Ben Rhodes** is now an emerging as **a person of interest in the House Intelligence Committee's unmasking investigation**, according to a letter sent Tuesday by the committee to the National Security Agency (NSA). This adds Rhodes to the **growing list of top Obama government officials** who may have improperly unmasked Americans in communications intercepted overseas by the NSA, *Circa* has confirmed."[373] *(Circa, August 1, 2017)*

9. "I've lived long enough to know that **race relations are better than they were ten**, **or twenty**, **or thirty years ago**." *Obama's Presidential Farewell speech, January 10, 2017*. All major national polls have indicated that race relations were at a nadir at the end of Obama's presidency. Just one week earlier, four African-American young adults, inspired by Black Lives Matter, a group Obama has mentored, abducted a handicapped white man and tortured him live on Facebook while shouting racist and anti-Trump profanities. Black activists in Congress inspired by Obama's confrontational community organizing strategies, posted a picture on the Capitol grounds depicting policemen as pigs confronting and pointing guns at black protesters. The Black Congressional Caucus argued for the right to hang a divisive and hateful piece of art in the halls of Congress.

a. Keith Ellison, a radical Muslim congressman supported by Obama, attacked Donald Trump one week before he was sworn in as president, saying that his victory "brought **white supremacism back to the White House**."

b. In November 2016, after the presidential election, Symone Sanders, the former national press secretary to Democratic presidential candidate Senator Bernie Sanders and a senior *CNN* political analyst stated on *CNN Newsroom* in response to the possibility of Howard Dean leading the DNC, "**We don't need white people leading the Democratic Party** right now."

c. *Liberal CNN commentator, Lamont Hill*, proved himself to be a racist, when he denigrated Steve Harvey and other black entertainers, when Hill commented at the time of Trump's inauguration, "It was a bunch of **mediocre Negroes being dragged in front of TV** as a photo-op for Donald Trump's exploitative campaign against black people."

    d.   "Black lives matter, and it makes me sad that we're even having that conversation, and that tells me that **white leaders in our party have failed**. We have to accept that there is **prejudice that exists within our own party**, and we have to able to have that conversation. We cannot sweep that under the rug … **My job is to shut other white people down** when they want to interrupt. My job is to shut other white people down when they want to say, oh, no, I'm not prejudiced. I'm a Democrat. I'm accepting. My job is to make sure that they get that they have privilege … [we need to teach people] **to shut their mouths if they're white**." *Idaho Democratic Party Executive Director Sally Boynton Brown, DNC chairperson candidate, DNC debate, January 23, 2017.*

    e.   On February 2, 2017, Nancy Pelosi, the Democratic minority leader in the House, called Steve Bannon, a "**white supremacist**" after he was named as a permanent member of the National Security Council.

    f.   Senator Warren of Massachusetts attributed Trump's election victory in part to "**an ugly stew of racism**" on *MSNBC* with Rachel Maddow in April 2017. Warren, a leading presidential contender for the Democratic Party in 2020 calls almost half of the voting American public – racists.

10. "Democracy does require a basic sense of solidarity – the idea that for all our outward differences, we are all in this together; **that we rise and fall as one**." *Obama's Presidential Farewell speech, January 10, 2017.* Obama stoked racial tensions throughout his presidency, which was demonstrated when he repeatedly blamed police for being racist, and viewed American society as subsets of race, religion, and economic achievement. Even in his farewell speech, he focused on the racial differences between Americans by using terms such as "white guys" and "brown kids."

11. "The ability of Republican leaders to rile up their base, helped along by folks like Rush Limbaugh and some commentators on *Fox News*, I think created an environment in which Republican voters would punish Republicans for cooperating with me." *Obama interview with Lester Holt on Dateline, January 13, 2017.* Obama falsely blamed Rush Limbaugh and Sean Hannity for much of the resistance to his domestic and international agenda. In reality, many of the Republican politicians in Washington, and the American electorate in November 2016 rejected Obama's far left-wing, anti-American, pro-Islam, pro-Iran, pro-jihadi, anti-capitalist, and anti-Semitic agendas. Obama wrongly implies that objective criticism from the media hindered his ability to be an effective president.

12. "Last night, I congratulated Donald Trump and offered to work with him on behalf of our country. I hope that he will be a successful president for all Americans … Donald Trump is going to be our president. We owe him an open mind and a chance to lead." *Hillary Clinton's November 8th concession speech acknowledging Trump won the election, the morning after the*

votes were tabulated. "Because to say you won't respect the results of the election, that is a direct threat to our democracy. The peaceful transfer of power is one of things that makes America, America. It is not a joke. Some people [Donald Trump] are sore losers." *Hillary Clinton rally days before the 2016 presidential election.* On November 26, 2016, 18 days after the presidential election, Clinton joined forces with the Green Party's Jill Stein seeking recounts in Wisconsin, Michigan, and Pennsylvania, thus is attempting to overturn the presidential election she has already formerly conceded. Obama also admitted that Trump won the election fairly in an interview in *The New York Times* on November 24. Yet the recount initiative could not have attained the political and financial support of Democratic Party supporters without Obama's acquiescence. The Democrats only targeted states where Trump had a narrow but significant margin of victory, thus proving they were only motivated to overturn an overtly fair election without any concrete evidence of foul play or fraud.

13. "I think that he's [Obama] genuinely concerned about – he's somebody who was involved in public service because **he wanted to see the country succeed**, and he certainly viewed the White House and the federal government as an institution that could be used to advance the interest of the American public. **There's a sense of a lot of action and movement in Washington, DC, but not a lot of movement forward. And I think that's a source of some concern, not just for the former president of the United States**, but for Americans of both parties all across the country." *Josh Earnest, former Obama White House press secretary, MSNBC interview, March 31, 2017.* Obama is most concerned about preventing Trump from advancing his agenda via his embedded moles in the White House staff, intelligence agencies and throughout the federal government, about protecting his progressive legacy, about bringing down Trump via fake news, his media allies, the Democratic leadership, and well-placed RINOs, about keeping the narrative that the Trump campaign colluded with the Russians alive, and about preventing his indictment secondary to his role related to illegally surveilling the Trump campaign before and after the 2016 presidential election.

Obama Loves America?

"I know my country has **not perfected itself**. At times, **we've struggled** to keep the promise of liberty and equality for all of our people. We've made **our share of mistakes**, and there are times when our actions around the world have **not lived up to our best intentions ... But I also know, how much I love America**."
Obama, 2008 campaign speech in Berlin. Lies or Taqiyya?

"**I love this country**, and so do you, and so does John McCain." *Obama, 2008, DNC speech.*

DOES OBAMA LOVE America? He professed his love for America multiple times at the end of the 2008 presidential campaign when he met significant political resistance for explaining why his patriotism should not be questioned for not wearing an American flag pin, and when he refused to put his hand over his heart while the national anthem played while campaigning. Yet during his presidency, he rarely expressed his love for America, and continually criticized the United States before domestic and foreign audiences. Even during his final speech in Chicago as president and during his final weekly address, Obama did not profess his love for the country that gave him so many opportunities and privileges. Throughout the many stages of his life, Obama continually associated himself with people who despised the United States. As an adolescent, he grew up under the tutelage of Frank Marshall Davis, a member of the communist party, who was an activist seeking to foment revolution in America. In college, Obama picked his friends carefully, and associated with Marxists, revolution-aries, and radical Muslims. For over twenty years, Obama attended the church of Reverend Wright, who gave sermons such as "G-d Damn America," without Obama blinking an eye or questioning his support. He embraced the church's underlying theological doctrine, black liberation theology, which was based on anti-white politics. Obama launched his political career from the home of Bill Ayers, former head of the Weather Underground, a domestic terrorist organization that killed Americans. Obama also served on the board of the Woods Organization with Ayers, and invited him to the White House on numerous occasions. Obama appeared with Louis Farrakhan, the leader of the

Nation of Islam, on the front cover of *Trumpet Magazine*, always talked positively about the Nation of Islam, and had no problem with Farrakhan's anti-Semitism or his wish to destroy America at the hands of Muslims until these issues were brought up in the 2008 presidential campaign. Michelle Obama was in Farrakhan's wife's social circle. Frank Marshall Davis, Bill Ayers, Saul Alinsky, Che Guevara, Malcolm X, Louis Farrakhan, and Reverend Wright all preached anti-American revolution, and were all people Obama admired. And with Obama's continual support for Islam and Sharia law, which is at odds to constitutionally protected Western freedoms, and his refusal to criticize prejudicial, anti-Semitic, anti-Christian, anti-gay, anti-women rights, and pro-pedophilia tenants in Islam, one can easily question Obama's allegiance to the American pro-Western constitutional republic. Thus, it is a legitimate debatable topic to question whether Obama loves America. Many of his statements as president, support the politicly incorrect answer to this question.

1. In 2015, Michael Oren, the former Israeli Ambassador to the United States, published a book, *Ally: My Journey Across the American - Israeli Divide*. Oren commented on Obama's book, *Dreams from My Father*, realizing **Obama said "nothing good about America."** He also deduced, "**More alarming for me still were Obama's attitudes towards America**. Vainly, I scoured ***Dreams from My Father*** for some expression of reverence, even respect, for the country its author would someday lead. Instead, **the book criticizes Americans for their capitalism and consumer culture**, **for despoiling their environment and maintaining antiquated power structures**. Traveling abroad, they exhibited "**ignorance and arrogance**" – the very shortcomings the president's critics assigned to him."

2. "**We are five days away from <u>fundamentally</u> transforming the United States of America**." *Barack Obama, October 30, 2008*. Does one fundamentally change something they love and respect? Obama's transformation takes America away from capitalism, individual freedom, superpower status, and Judeo-Christian ethics toward socialism. communism, Islam, and appeasement. Other transformational events include massive illegal immigration across our southern border, massive Muslim immigration from the Middle East into Europe and eventually into the United States, creating a dominant one-party system supported by these immigration trends, disregarding the Constitution, empowering the federal government to be responsive to Islamic political and religious needs that will lead to the implementation of Sharia law, emasculating America as a superpower, destroying the alliance between Israel and America, laying the groundwork for Iran to become a regional if not a worldwide superpower, and devastating America's military so she can no longer project its power to protect Western interests around the world.

3. "But, **the Supreme Court never ventured into the issues of redistribution of wealth, and of more basic issues such as political and economic justice in society**. To that extent, as radical as I think people try to characterize the Warren Court, it wasn't that radical. **It didn't**

break free from the <u>essential constraints</u> that were placed by the Founding Fathers <u>in the Constitution</u>, at least as it's been interpreted, and the Warren Court interpreted in the same way, that generally **the Constitution is a <u>charter of negative liberties</u>**. Says what the states can't do to you. Says what the federal government can't do to you, but **doesn't say what the federal government or state government must do on your behalf** *[Obama is advocating socialism.]*... And that hasn't shifted and one of the, I think, tragedies of the civil rights movement was because the civil rights movement became so court-focused I think **there was a tendency to lose track of the political and community organizing and activities on the ground** *[BLM protests, ACORN, Occupy Wall Street, social media input via alliances with Google – Facebook – Twitter]* **that are able to put together the actual coalition of powers through which you bring about redistributive change** [socialism / communism]. In some ways, we still suffer from that." *Obama during a 2001 radio interview where he advanced heavy criticism upon the U.S. Constitution.* Contrast Obama's values with those of Abraham Lincoln, who stated, "You cannot help men permanently by doing what they could and should do for themselves. You cannot help the wage earner by pulling down the wage payer. You cannot keep out of trouble by spending more than you earn. You cannot bring about prosperity by discouraging thrift. You cannot strengthen the weak by weakening the strong. You cannot further the brotherhood of man by encouraging class hatred. You cannot build character and courage, by taking away man's initiative and independence." *(Abraham Lincoln, February 21, 1859)*

4. "**I cannot swallow whole the view of Lincoln as the Great Emancipator** ... Scholars tell us too that Lincoln wasn't immune from political considerations and that his temperament could be indecisive and morose. But it is precisely those imperfections – and the **painful self-awareness of those failings** etched in **every crease of his face** and reflected in those **haunted eyes** – that make him so compelling ... this man could **overcome depression, self-doubt, and the constraints of biography** and not only act decisively but retain his humanity. Like a figure from the Old Testament, **he wandered the earth**, **making mistakes**, loving his family but **causing them pain, despairing** over the course of events, trying to divine G-d's will. He **did not know** how things would turn out, but he did his best."[374] *Obama, Time Magazine Essay, June 26, 2005.* Obama is critical of Abraham Lincoln, one of the most revered presidents in our nation's history, and his role in helping to abolish slavery. It is possible that Obama was very critical of Lincoln in part because he strenuously voiced his opposition to socialism, as stated above. Obama launched an attack against Lincoln calling him depressed and haunted with self-doubts, a wanderer with failings, who caused his family pain and made mistakes. Has he ever spoken this way about Islam, Mohammed or anything related to Islam?

a. Obama **skipped the 150ᵗʰ anniversary of Lincoln's Gettysburg address**. Lincoln's speech should have been important for Obama since it was focused on advancing the concept that all men are created equal, and that the abolition of slavery was a legitimate consequence of the Civil War and the creation of the Declaration of Independence. The Gettysburg address was among the greatest speeches ever given by a president in American history, and possibly one of the greatest speeches given in the history of man. With Lincoln being associated with the freeing of African American slaves, Obama should have made an effort to honor Lincoln, but with his documented negative remarks and criticisms of Lincoln and his avoidance of this important ceremony, Obama revealed his dislike and disdain for Lincoln. Lincoln being an American and a Christian may have contributed to Obama's negative insights.

5. "When Democrats … insist we live in the worst of political times, that a creeping fascism is closing its grip … I may mention … the **Alien and Sedition Acts under John Adams or one hundred years of lynching**." *Obama disparages a founding father, and associates him with fascism, racism, and the killing of Blacks in The Audacity of Hope.*

6. "To give everyone one big refund on their government, divvy it up by individual portions, in the form of tax breaks, hand it out, and encourage everyone to use their share to go buy their own health care, their own retirement plan, their own child care, their own education, and so on. … **In Washington … they call this the Ownership Society. But in our past, there has been another term for it, Social Darwinism, every man or woman for him or herself. It's a tempting idea, because it doesn't require much thought or ingenuity**. … But there is a problem. **It** [capitalism] **won't work**." *Senator Obama, 2005 Knox College commencement address.* Obama is critical of capitalism, American society, and rewarding individual achievement, and is laying the political foundation for his socialist / communist visions and the politics of envy or class warfare.

7. "Let's stop sending mixed messages. Let's work together and set immigration fees at a level that are fair and consistent with our commitment to being an open, democratic, and **egalitarian** *[socialist / communist]* **society**." *Obama Senate speech, March 7, 2007.* Obama is always advocating for increased immigration into America. Compare with:

a. "The problem with socialism is that you eventually run out of other people's money." *Margaret Thatcher, former prime minster of Great Britain.* Obama doubled the federal deficit during his presidency.

b. "I am for doing good to the poor, but I differ in opinion of the means. I think the best way of doing good to the poor, is not making them easy in poverty, but leading or driving them out of it … In short, you offered a premium for the encouragement of idleness, and you should not now wonder that it has had its effect in the increase of poverty."

Benjamin Franklin. Franklin easily predicted Obama's economic policies would increase poverty and dependence on the federal government.

c.   "**Socialism** is the … **younger brother of despotism** which it wants to inherit. Socialism wants to have the fullness of state force which before only existed in despotism … However, it goes further than anything in the past because it **aims at the formal destruction of the individual** … who … can be used to improve communities by an expedient organ of government." *Friedrich Nietzsche*

d.   "Socialism is a **philosophy of failure**, the creed of ignorance, and **gospel of envy**, its inherent virtue is the **equal sharing of misery**." *Winston Churchill*. Churchill's view on socialism could have contributed to Obama removing his statue from the Oval Office on the first day of his presidency.

e.   "Socialism needs to pull down wealth … destroy private interests … kill enterprise … assails the preeminence of the individual … exalts the rule … attacks capitalism." *Winston Churchill*

f.   "Socialism … must have a dictatorship. It will not work without it." *Moa Zedong, China*

8.   "Hey, Obama has just nationalized nothing more and nothing less than General Motors. Comrade Obama! Fidel [Castro], careful or we are going to end up to his [Obama's] right." *Hugo Chavez, 2009*

9.   "Re-electing Obama is not sufficient to bring economic recovery or even relief to our people. Only a different class configuration in political power can do necessary minimum reforms to give us a chance. **But <u>re-electing Obama is absolutely essential</u>**. Now is not the time for hand washing the complexities and tactics away – or failing to triage the most critical questions from those that are less critical. **We cannot win everything at once**!" *John Case, author of numerous* **<u>Communist Party USA</u>** *publications.*

10. "The point is, though, that … and it's not just charity, it's not just that I want to help the middle class and working people who are trying to get in the middle class … it's that when we actually make sure that everybody's got a shot – when young people can all go to college, when everybody's got decent health care, when everybody's got a little more money at the end of the month. John McCain and Sarah Palin, they call this socialistic. … **You know I don't know when, when they decided they wanted to make a virtue out of selfishness**." *Obama criticizing the capitalistic system.*

11. "They get **bitter**, **<u>cling to guns or religion</u>** or antipathy to people who aren't like them or **anti-immigrant sentiment** or anti-trade sentiment as a way **to explain their frustrations**." *Obama's negative view of small town middle Americans, Christianity, and the 2nd Amendment, also known as* **the 'bitter clingers' speech**. For Islam to dominate in the West, Obama needs to disarm the population so they cannot fight back effectively against Muslim terrorist attacks and insurrections, and create a more secular society with less knowledge of the scriptures,

so people drift away from a life guided by Judeo-Christian ethics. **This one statement outlines Obama's political philosophy regarding empowering Islam in America – import Muslims, disarm the American public so jihad can flourish, and attack Christianity.**

12. In a speech in San Antonio on the night of the Texas primary in 2008, Obama declared that America is "**substituting bluster and <u>bullying</u> for direct diplomacy.**" **The words Obama uses to describe America are very similar to those used by Castro, Chavez, Ortega, and the Hamas leadership.**

    a. When speaking before the UN Generally Assembly on September 23, 2008, President Ahmadinejad of Iran spoke of the United States by saying, "A few **<u>bullying</u>** powers have sought to put hurdles in the way of the peaceful nuclear activities of the Iranian nation by exerting political and economic pressures against Iran."[375] *Obama and Ahmadinejad are both attacking the United States with the same political arguments. Does Obama share the same political philosophy as the president of Iran? Obama supported the JCPOA that ensured Iran's status as a regional, if not world, superpower.*

13. *In New Hampshire during an August 27, 2007 town hall meeting, Obama stated,* "We've got to get the job done there and that requires us to have enough troops so that we're not just **air-raiding villages and killing civilians.**" Obama is very critical of U.S. military policy, and he is on the verge of calling the U.S. military war criminals. When Muslim fighters use women and children as human shields, a large share of Western strategy and tactics become ineffective, making it more difficult to defeat the enemy. Obama is validating the Islamic human shield strategy. Obama's anti-war sentiments and his desire to protect the Muslim terrorists paved the way for his pro-Islamist rules of engagement.

14. "I am running for president … (struggling and grasping for words with no teleprompter) … **America is no longer uh would it could be, what it once was.** And I say to myself, I don't want that future for my children." *Obama 2008 campaign statement.*

15. "Just to take a, sort of a realist perspective … there's a lot of change going on outside of the Court, um, that, that judges essentially have to take judicial notice of. I mean you've got World War II, you've got uh, uh, uh, the **doctrines of Nazism**, that, that we are fighting against, that start **looking uncomfortably similar to what we have going on, back here at home.**" *Obama comparing the U.S. to Nazi Germany, 2001.* Ironically, Obama supports the Muslim Brotherhood, which was allied with the Nazis during World War II and actively participated in the Holocaust. **Obama is a socialist** and the Nazi party is short for "National **Socialist** German's Worker's Party." Obama wants Israel to adopt suicidal border and supports Hamas and the PA, who have repeatedly declared their genocidal intentions against Israel and the Jews. Obama is closer to Nazi doctrine than he realizes.

16. "Everybody's watching what's going on in Beijing right now with the Olympics. Think about the amount of money that China has spent on infrastructure. **Their ports, their train**

systems, their airports are all vastly superior to us now." *Obama is critical of America, but is complimentary to China, a communist regime and host of the 2008 Summer Olympic Games.* Obama had eight years to improve the U.S. infrastructure, which did not happen.

17. Obama **refused to put his hand over his heart during the National Anthem** and formally violated the U.S. Code. *Iowa, 2008 presidential campaign.*

18. "You know, the truth is that right after 9-11, I had a pin … Shortly after 9-11, particularly because as we're talking about the Iraq War, that became a substitute for I think true patriotism, which is speaking out on issues that are of importance to our national security, **I decided <u>I won't wear that pin on my chest</u> … Instead … I'm going to try to tell the American people what I believe will make this country great, and hopefully that will be a testimony to my patriotism**." *Obama's response to not wearing an American flag pin, October 2007.*

19. Obama took the American flag off the tail of his campaign plane, and replaced it with his "O" logo. *Obama's 2008 Campaign.*

20. In 2012, no American flags are on the Obama campaign bus.

21. During the first two days of the 2016 Democratic National Convention, there were no American flags on the floor of the convention or on the podium.

22. "The system isn't working when 12 million people live in hiding, and hundreds of thousands are crossing our borders illegally each year. When companies hire undocumented immigrants instead of legal citizens because they want to avoid paying overtime or to avoid unionization or exploiting those workers. **When communities are terrorized by ICE immigration raids. When nursing mothers are torn from their babies. When children come home from school to find their parents missing**. When people are detained without access to legal counsel." *Obama's remarks at the National Council of La Raza Convention in 2008.* Obama is critical of U.S. agents who are legally and humanely enforcing the laws of the United States and describes them as terrorists. Obama is using pediatric human shields (even babies torn from nursing mothers is a bit dramatic) to protect his political talking points.

23. "**We must engage … in the more difficult task of understanding the source of such madness**. The essence of this tragedy … **derives from a fundamental absence of empathy** on the part of the attackers… Most often, though, it **grows out of a climate of poverty and ignorance, helplessness and despair** … We will have to make sure, despite our rage, that **any U.S. military action takes into account the lives of innocent civilians** *[Obama allows the terrorists to use human shields to protect themselves.]* **abroad**." *State Senator Barack Obama, D – Hyde Park, Hyde Park Herald, **September 19, 2001**.* Obama empathizes with the terrorists immediately after 9-11. Nothing has changed when in February 2015, Obama believes jobs programs and improving the standard of living of Muslims in the Middle East is a major component of the fight against ISIS' religious jihad war and genocide against the West and

infidels. Obama is advocating helping to fund the terrorist infrastructure in the Middle East, by proposing job programs for the terrorists. Obama also proposed massive aid programs to help support the overwhelming Muslim immigration into Europe. Through multiple policies, Obama always advocates to fund jihad.

24. "Thank you to the citizens of Berlin and to the people of Germany … I come to Berlin as so many of my countrymen have come before. Tonight, I speak to you not as a candidate for president, but as a citizen – a proud citizen of the United States, and **a fellow citizen of the world**." *Obama, "A World That Stands as One," Speech during German Tour, Berlin, July 24, 2008.* Obama has **four possible citizenships** – the United States, Kenya (dual citizenship with his father), Indonesia (Obama was registered at his Indonesian school as an Indonesian citizen and there is no proof he legally changed his citizenship to the United States when he moved to Hawaii), and the World. Can he be loyal to all four while promoting the best interests of the United States of America as president?

25. At UCLA in early 2008, Michelle Obama gave a speech and stated, "I'm interested in organizations, not movements … because movements dissipate but organizations don't … more and more people will begin to feel their story is somehow part of this larger story of how **we're going to reshape America in a way that is less <u>mean-spirited</u> and more generous** [more socialistic and more redistributive]." *Michelle Obama is discussing organizations like ACORN, which has been implicated in voter registration fraud that benefitted Obama.*

26. "**For the first time in my adult life**, I have been proud of my country." A reinterpretation of the same statement would read: "Up until this point in time, I have never been proud of my country." *Michelle Obama during the 2008 campaign. She was not proud of defeating the Nazis in WWII, not proud of landing men on the moon, and not proud of the Emancipation Proclamation.*

27. "**My faith in the American people was vindicated and what you started here in Iowa swept the nation**." *Obama's statement on the last weekend before the presidential election paralleling his wife's troubling insights, 2008. Americans aren't racist as long as they vote for Obama.*

28. In an interview with Lauren Collins in *The New Yorker Magazine*, **Michelle Obama called America "just downright mean," and "guided by fear."** "Obama begins with a broad assessment of life in America in 2008, and life is not good: we're a divided country, we're a country that is "**just downright mean**," we are "**guided by fear**," we're a **nation of cynics, sloths, and complacents**."[376]

29. "In 2008, we are still a nation that is too **divided**. We live in **isolation**, and because of that isolation we **fear** one another. … We are too isolated. And we are still a nation that is still too **cynical**. We look at it as 'them' and 'they' as opposed to us. We don't engage because we are still **too cynical** … Because Barack Obama is the only person in this race who understands that … Our **souls are broken** in this nation … **Change will always be hard**." *Michelle*

Obama's UCLA speech, February 15, 2008. Michelle is using many negative descriptive terms when describing America and her people.

30. Obama was listed as a **member of the socialist New Party** when running for an Illinois State Senate seat in 1996. The New Party was **established by the Democratic Socialists of America**, which had communists as its leaders, as well as Noam Chomsky and Frances Fox Piven, one of the originators of the Cloward-Piven strategy. Members of Committees of Correspondence, which was previously associated with the Communist Party USA, also helped form the New Party. Minutes from the January 11, 1996 Chicago chapter New Party meeting stated, "He [Barack Obama] signed the New Party 'Candidate Contract' and requested an endorsement from the New Party. He also **joined the New Party.**" While Obama ran for president is 2008, he lied by denying he was a member in the New Party, even when confronted with evidence that the New Party publication in the spring of 1996 confirmed, "New Party members won three other primaries this Spring in Chicago: Barack Obama (State Senate) …" After the election Obama proclaimed, "These victories prove that small 'd' democracies can work."[377] That last sentence questions Obama's commitment to democracy as a political process.

31. "I chose my friends carefully … The more politically active black students. **The foreign students**. The Chicanos. **The Marxist professors** and structural feminists," *Obama discussing his relationships at Occidental College in Dreams from My Father.*

32. "If nationalism could create a strong and effective insularity, deliver on its promise of self-respect, then <u>the hurt it might cause</u> … or **the inner turmoil it caused people like me**, **would be <u>of little consequence</u>**." *Obama, Dreams from My Father.* Obama is stating the ends justify the means. If Obama can use a weak economy, an economic crisis, or the advancement of Obamacare to consolidate the power of the federal government and diminish individual freedoms, then the pain he causes to the average American would be inconsequential to him. The pain would be in part reflected by much higher deductibles and premiums for health insurance paid by the average worker, and a significant decrease in the median earned income for the American middle class during Obama's presidency.

After Obama became president, his basic impressions of America and its history did not change.

1. "We are a nation of **Christians and Muslims**, Jews and Hindus, and nonbelievers … And because we have tasted the bitter swill of **civil war and segregation** and emerged from **that dark chapter** stronger and more united, we cannot help but **believe that the old hatreds shall someday pass**; that the lines of tribe shall soon dissolve; that as the world grows smaller, our common humanity shall reveal itself; and that America must play its role in

ushering in a new era of peace. **To the Muslim world**, **we seek a new way forward**, based on mutual interest and mutual respect." *Obama's 2009 Inauguration Speech*. Obama is criticizing America during his first inauguration speech by stating the old racial hatreds are still significantly present in the fabric of American society, despite his election to the presidency, then immediately portrays the Muslim community in a positive manner. Obama subtly reveals where his loyalties lie. Obama views Muslims as only second to Christians as a political factor in America's domestic balance of power, and has pushed aside the Jews. This speech would reveal the format of many of Obama's future speeches, which is attack and criticize America, followed by promoting and praising Islam.

2. "My job to the Muslim world is to communicate that the Americans are not your enemy. **We sometimes make mistakes. We have not been perfect**." *Obama with Al-Arabiya interview, January 27, 2009*. Obama's first foreign press interview as president foretells his support of Muslim interests worldwide and his critical view of America.

3. "In recent years, we've allowed our alliance to drift. I know that there have been honest disagreements over policy, but we also know that there's something more that has crept into our relationship. **In America, there's a failure to appreciate Europe's leading role in the world**. Instead of celebrating your dynamic union and seeking to partner with you to meet common challenges, **there have been times where America has shown arrogance and been dismissive, even derisive**." *Obama, Strasbourg Town Hall, Strasbourg, France, April 3, 2009*.

4. "The United States is still working through some of our own **darker periods in our history**. Facing the Washington Monument that I spoke of is a memorial of Abraham Lincoln, the man who freed those who were enslaved even after Washington led our Revolution. Our country still struggles with the **legacies of slavery and segregation, the past treatment of Native Americans. Human endeavor is by its nature imperfect**. [American] **History is often tragic, but unresolved, it can be a heavy weight**." *Turkish Parliament speech, April 6, 2009. Part of Obama's Worldwide Apology Tour*. Obama always has a dark view of American history while he ignores the imperfections, flaws and conflicts in almost all other societies and cultures.

5. "That's why, in the United States, we recently ordered the prison at Guantanamo Bay closed. **That's why we prohibited – without exception or equivocation – the use of torture. All of us have to change. And sometimes change is hard**." *Turkish Parliament speech, April 6, 2009. Part of Obama's worldwide tour apologizing for America*. Obama is stirring hatred for America in the Islamic world by advancing the concept that America routinely tortures Muslims at Guantanamo Bay, and that the practice will be very hard to change since it is ingrained in our methodology. Obama can be viewed as inciting Muslims against America.

Waterboarding was used very infrequently, and only to prevent future terrorist attacks and save American lives.

6. "While the United States has done much to promote peace and prosperity in the hemisphere, **we have at times been disengaged**, and at times **we sought to dictate our terms**. But I pledge to you that we seek an equal partnership … I am very grateful that President Ortega – I'm grateful that President Ortega did not blame me for things that happened when I was three months old. Too often, an opportunity to build a fresh partnership of the Americas has been undermined by **stale debates**. And we've heard all these arguments before, these debates that would have us make a false choice between rigid, state-run economies or unbridled and **unregulated capitalism** … I think it's important to recognize, **given historic suspicions, that the United States' policy should not be interference in other countries** … The United States will be **willing to acknowledge past errors where those errors have been made**." *Obama speech at the Summit of the America, Trinidad and Tobago, April 17, 2009.* Obama criticizes American capitalism and past foreign policies.

7. "**More recently, tension has been fed by colonialism that denied rights and opportunities to many Muslims, and a Cold War in which Muslim-majority countries were too often treated as proxies without regard to their own aspirations**. Moreover, the sweeping change brought by modernity and globalization led many Muslims to view the **West as hostile to the traditions of Islam**." *Obama, Cairo University speech, June 4, 2009.* Obama travels the world and criticizes America. Obama views America's (and the West's) colonialism as subjugating Muslims and the third world in a very negative way. In the last sentence, even Obama acknowledged that modern Western society may be incompatible with Islam, but Obama sides with Islam. The traditions of Islam include the subjugation of non-Muslims, treating women as property, child marriages, pedophilia, the killing of apostates, homosexuals, blasphemers and infidels, carrying out jihad, and the quest to dominate all other non-Muslim societies.

8. "9-11 was an enormous trauma to our country. The fear and anger that it provoked was understandable, but in some cases, it led us **to act contrary to our traditions and our ideals**." *Obama, Cairo University speech, June 4, 2009.* Obama is criticizing America reacting to massive terrorist attacks against New York City, Washington D.C, the Pentagon, and Pennsylvania. Obama wants to handcuff America's response to defend herself.

9. "I took office at a time when many around the world had come to view America with skepticism and distrust. Part of this was due to misperceptions and misinformation about my country. Part of this was due to opposition to specific policies, and a belief that on certain critical issues, **America has acted unilaterally, without regard for the interests of others. This has fed an almost reflexive anti-Americanism, which too often has served as an excuse for our collective inaction**." *Obama, UN General Assembly speech, September 23, 2009.*

10. "**I am a student of history** so I tend to actually be familiar with many of these episodes that have been mentioned. **I am the first one to acknowledge that America's application to concern around human rights has not always been consistent**. And, I'm certainly mindful that **there are dark chapters in our own history** in which we have not always observed the principles and ideals upon which the country was founded … **America never makes a claim about being perfect**, we do make a claim about being open to change." *Obama criticizing the United States at the Summit of the Americas in Panama City, agreeing with South and Central American communists and dictators. April 11, 2015.* Obama shook the hand of Raul Castro at the same conference, and started normalizing relationships with communist Cuba without reciprocal gestures from Cuba. During this period Obama was reaching out to Cuba and Iran, while treating Israel and Republicans as the enemy.

11. "The way I think about it is, this is a great, great country that **had gotten a little soft and we didn't have that same competitive edge that we needed over the last couple of decades. We need to get back on track**." *Obama, Orlando WESH-TV interview, September 30, 2011.*

12. Obama calls Americans "a little bit lazy." "But **we've been a little bit lazy**, I think, over the last couple of decades. We've kind of taken for granted – well, people will want to come here and we aren't out there hungry, selling America and trying to attract new business into America." *Obama, CEO Summit at the APEC meeting, November 13, 2011.*

13. "I believe in American exceptionalism just as **I suspect that the Brits believe in British exceptionalism and the Greeks believe in Greek exceptionalism**." *Obama, Strasbourg Town Hall, France, April 3, 2009. Obama's Worldwide Apology Tour.* Obama does not believe in American exceptionalism. In 2013, Obama cancelled the Mars Rover landing exploration, and all other planetary missions. Is Obama's policy to prevent American exceptionalism?

14. "We can't just lock up low-level [drug] dealer without asking why this boy, barely out of childhood, felt he had no other options … Yes, you've worked hard, **but you've also been lucky**. *[You're lucky not to be a drug dealer.]* That's a pet peeve of mine: **People who have been successful and don't realize they've been lucky**. That G-d may have blessed them; **it was <u>nothing you did</u>. So don't have an attitude**." *Obama, 2016 commencement address at Howard University*, an historically black university. First, Obama does not believe in American exceptionalism if high achievers are just lucky. As Obama **insults the mostly African-American graduates**, he **placates drug dealers**. This remark parallels Obama's 2012 campaign statement where he belittled entrepreneurs when he stated "You didn't build that," as he mocked the achievements of hard-working Americans.

15. "Our moral authority is derived from the fact that generations of our citizens have fought and bled to uphold these values in our nations and others. And that's why **we can never sacrifice them for expedience's sake**. That's why I've ordered the closing of the detention center in Guantanamo Bay. That's why I can stand here today and say **without equivocation**

or exception that the United States of America does not and will not torture. In dealing with terrorism, **we can't lose sight of our values** and who we are. That's why I closed Guantanamo. That's why I made very clear that we will not engage in certain interrogation practices. I don't believe that there is a contradiction between our security and our values. **And when you start sacrificing your values**, **when you lose yourself**, **then over the long-term that will make you less secure**." *Obama, Strasbourg Town Hall, France, April 3, 2009.* Obama is protecting the Muslim terrorists, and has turned Guantanamo Bay, a prisoner of war camp, into a sociological rehabilitation facility with excellent healthcare services (better than the Veterans Administration), great meals, job rehabilitation programs, and high-end athletic facilities.

16. "I know that promises of **partnership have gone unfulfilled** in the past, and that **trust has to be earned** over time. While the United States has done much to promote peace and prosperity in the hemisphere, **we have at times been disengaged**, and at times we **sought to dictate our terms**." *Obama, Summit of the Americas, Opening Ceremony, April 17, 2009.*

17. "Too often, the United States **has not pursued and sustained engagement with our neighbors**. We have been **too easily distracted** by other priorities, and **have failed to see that our own progress is tied directly to progress throughout the Americas**." *Obama, "Choosing a Better Future in the Americas," Miami Herald op-ed, April 16, 2009.*

18. "I would like to think that **with my election** and the early decisions that we've made, that you're **starting to see some restoration of America's standing** in the world … it is very important for us to be able to forge partnerships **as opposed to simply dictating solutions.** Just to try to crystallize the example, there's been a lot of comparison here about Bretton Woods. 'Oh, well, last time you saw the entire international architecture being remade.' **Well**, **if there's just** <u>Roosevelt and Churchill</u> **sitting in a room with a brandy, that's an easier negotiation.** But that's not the world we live in, and **it shouldn't be** the world that we live in." *Obama, G20 Summit of World Leaders, News conference, London, April 2, 2009.*

19. "Unfortunately, faced with an uncertain threat, **our government made a series of hasty decisions**. I believe that many of these decisions were motivated by a sincere desire to protect the American people. But I also believe that all too often our government **made decisions based on fear rather than foresight**; that all too often our government **trimmed facts and evidence to fit ideological predispositions**. Instead of strategically applying our power and our principles, too often **we set those principles aside** as luxuries that we could no longer afford. And during **this season of fear**, too many of us – Democrats and Republicans, politicians, journalists, and citizens – **fell silent**. In other words, **we went off course** … It was an assessment that … **called for a new approach – one that rejected torture and one that recognized the imperative of closing the prison at Guantanamo Bay**." *Obama, National Archives speech, Washington D.C., May 21, 2009.*

20. "There is also no question that **Guantanamo set back the moral authority** that is America's strongest currency in the world … our government was defending positions that **undermined the rule of law**. In fact, part of the rationale for establishing Guantanamo in the first place was **the misplaced notion that a prison there would be beyond the law** – a proposition that the Supreme Court soundly rejected. Meanwhile, instead of serving as a tool to counter terrorism, **Guantanamo became a symbol that helped al-Qaeda recruit terrorists to its cause**. Indeed, the existence of Guantanamo likely created more terrorists around the world than it ever detained." *Obama, National Archives speech, Washington D.C., May 21, 2009.* Obama gives excuses so that he can set the Muslim terrorists free, whether they are al-Qaeda or Taliban operatives or commanders. Obama's main goal is to strengthen jihadi military forces.

21. "I realize that America's critics will be quick to point out that at times **we too have failed to live up to our ideals**; that America has **plenty of problems** within its own borders. This is true. In a summer marked by instability in the Middle East and Eastern Europe, **I know the world also took notice of the small American city of Ferguson**, **Missouri – where a young man was killed**, and a community was divided." *Obama speech to the UN General Assembly, September 24, 2014.* Obama does not mention that the young man assaulted a store clerk, assaulted a police officer, grabbed for his gun, and then charged him with the intent to harm or kill the officer before he was shot in self-defense. Obama defended a street thug at the UN, who acted contrary to values of decent civilized people everywhere.

22. "So **don't be discouraged by what's happened** in the last few weeks. Don't be discouraged that we have to acknowledge potentially **we've made some mistakes**. That's how we learn. But the fact that **we are willing to acknowledge them** and then move forward, that is precisely why … you should be proud to be members of the CIA." *Obama, Addressing CIA employees at CIA headquarters regarding released information on enhanced interrogation techniques. April 20, 2009.*

23. "I was very clear in the immediate **aftermath of 9-11 we did some things that were wrong** … We did a whole lot of things that were right, but we tortured some folks. **We did some things that were contrary to our values.**" *Obama commenting on the Senate Intelligence Committee Report concerning the CIA and 9-11. August 1, 2014.*

24. "I think what we've also seen is that **the legacy of discrimination – slavery, Jim Crow –** has meant that some of the institutional barriers for success for a lot of groups **still exist**. African-American poverty in this country is still significantly higher than other groups [and has increased with my administration]." *Obama, Binghamton University, August 23, 2013.*

25. "The prime minister is the first to acknowledge that Malaysia has still got some work to do on these issues, just like **the United States**, **by the way**, **has some work to do**." Obama with the Malaysian prime minster in 2014 discussing human rights, civil liberties, and American deficiencies.

26. "**This bill was written in a tortured way to make sure CBO did not score the mandate as taxes**. If [the Congressional Budget Office] scored the mandate as taxes, the bill dies. … if you had a law which said that healthy people are going to pay in … and sick people get money *[redistribution of wealth]* – it would not have passed … **Lack of transparency is a huge political advantage**. And basically, **call it the stupidity of the American voter**, or whatever, but basically that was really, really critical for the thing to pass. And it's the second-best argument. Look, I wish Mark was right that we could make it all transparent, but I'd rather have this law than not. *[same strategic theory with Obama's JCPOA presentation]" Jonathan Gruber, professor at MIT, chief architect and advisor to the president on Obamacare.* Gruber helped create the strategy to get Obamacare passed, as well as gave significant input into creating the law, which was over 2000 pages. These strategies were discussed with and approved by President Obama. Gruber visited the White House at least 21 times during Obama's presidency. Obama showed contempt for the American voter with all his lies and his lack of transparency with the political process.

    a. "The way to make government accountable is to make it transparent so that the American people can know exactly what decisions are being made, how they're being made, and whether their interests are being well served … I will also hold myself, as president to **a new standard of openness** … **Transparency and the rule of law** *[not with illegal immigration]* **will be the touchstones of this presidency**." *Obama, Remarks at the Swearing-In Ceremony, January 21, 2009. Obama delivered big lies during his first hour as president.*

27. "We hold these truths to be self-evident, that all men are created equal, endowed *[by their Creator]* with certain inalienable rights: life, liberty and the pursuit of happiness." *Obama drops the word Creator when quoting the Declaration of Independence. September 2010.* Obama is uncomfortable with references to Christianity and Judaism in America's founding documents.

28. The Arizona State Immigration Law was included by the Obama administration in a detailed report to the UN of human rights abuses, **linking Arizona with North Korea**, **Libya**, **Cuba**, **and the Taliban**. Obama is using the UN human rights committees to help implement and support his domestic immigration agenda.

29. Obama is blocking America from becoming energy independent by vetoing the Keystone Pipeline Bill in 2015, and earlier delayed and blocked offshore oil and gas drilling permits in the lower forty-eight states and Alaska. Even former President Clinton called these actions "ridiculous." But Obama wanted to give aid to Brazil so they can develop their offshore oil reserves, and sell their oil products to the United States.

30. Michelle Obama invited Lonnie Rashid Lynn "Common" to read her **poetry at the White House**. Lynn's poetry has included references to **shooting police**, and the burning of

ex-President George Bush. *[The Obamas are inciting Black activists to kill police before the rise of Black Lives Matter.]* A sample of Lynn's poetry, "Dem boy wanna talk… [indistinguishable] Whatcha gon do if ya got one gun? I sing a song for the hero unsung with faces on the mural of the revolution. No looking back cos' in back is what's done. Tell the preacher, G-d got more than one son. Tell the law, my Uzi weighs a ton. I walk like a warrior, from them I won't run. On the streets, they try to beat us like a drum." Common posted on Twitter in 2011, "Flyer says FREE MUMIA on my freezer." Mumia Abu-Jamal is a Muslim Black Panther who murdered Daniel Faulkner, a Philadelphia police officer, in 1981.

31. In November 2011, President Obama told Australian teenagers that American teenagers have "**fallen behind**" with respect to their education.

32. On November 20, 2015, Obama criticized America in Malaysia to young Asian leaders when **he warned them to avoid multiple "pitfalls" in the American economic and political system** like income inequality and racial politics. Ironically, income inequality has been greater under the Obama administration than any recent president in modern history.

33. Obama complained about taking pictures with soldiers on a visit to Baghdad.

34. "There are a lot of wealthy, successful Americans who agree with me, because they want to give something back. **They know they didn't – look**, **if you've been successful**, **you didn't get there on your own. You didn't get there on your own**. I'm always struck by people who think, well, it must be because I was just so smart. There are a lot of smart people out there. It must be because I worked harder than everybody else. Let me tell you something – there are a whole bunch of hardworking people out there. … **If you've got a business – <u>you didn't build that</u>. Somebody else made that happen**. The Internet didn't get invented on its own. Government research created the Internet so that all the companies could make money off the Internet." *Obama Campaign speech, Roanoke, Virginia, July 13, 2012.*

35. Obama is outsourcing launching American astronauts into space via the Russian space program, while decimating NASA.

36. "And we also recognize that **most of the guns used to commit violence here in Mexico come from the United States**." *Obama, Mexican speech, May, 2013.* Obama is criticizing America abroad like with previous apology tours and is trying to use the Fast and Furious program to advance gun control in the United States by giving arms to Mexican drug cartels.

37. Obama **cancelled Fleet Week** in 2013, on Memorial Day weekend secondary to budgetary constraints.

38. "**In U.S. history, there are many examples of extremist ideologies and movements**. The colonists who sought to free themselves from British rule and the Confederate states who sought to secede from the Northern states are just two examples." *Department of Defense*

training documents present the Founding Fathers of America as extremists and label conservative organizations as hate groups.

39. Obama **puts his shoes on his desk in the Oval Office** in 2013 while taking phone calls. *Obama shows no respect for the office of the presidency.*

40. When Major General Harold Greene was assassinated in Afghanistan, the first American General to die in combat since Vietnam, Obama made no comment or statement, nor did he attend his funeral.

41. Obama tells Ferguson activists to **stay the course** at a White House meeting, and their associates later destroyed many businesses while **rioting and looting**.

42. "**Whether we like it or not**, we remain a **dominant military superpower**." *Obama's Freudian slip at the Nuclear Security Summit in 2010.* Obama's subconsciousness reveals that he does not want America to be a dominant nuclear or military power. That is why he is slashing the American nuclear arsenal and paving the way for Iran to become a major nuclear power with ICBMs capable of reaching the United States. Most Americans like the security of living in a strong nation that is considered a superpower. Not Obama. He wants America to be subservient to Islam, and decimating America's military is part of his strategy.

    a. "I've spent my entire adult life with the United States as a superpower, and one that had no compunction about spending what it took to sustain that position. It didn't have to look over its shoulder because our economy was so strong. This is a different time … To tell you the truth, that's one of the many reasons it's time for me to retire, because frankly **I can't imagine being part of a nation**, **part of a government … that's being forced to dramatically scale back our engagement with the rest of the world**." *Outgoing Secretary of Defense Robert Gates makes a candid accurate assessment in June 2011 that Obama is downgrading U.S. military capabilities that will result in America no longer being able to maintain its superpower status.*

43. "I say this as the president of a country that not very long ago **made it hard for somebody who looked like me to vote much less be president** of the United States." *Obama, Remarks to the Turkish Parliament, April 6, 2009.* Obama criticizes America as racist.

44. "**This is something that is deeply rooted in our society, it's deeply rooted in our history** … **When you're dealing with something as deeply rooted as racism or bias** … you've got to have vigilance but you have to recognize that it's going to take some time, and you just have to be steady so you don't give up when we don't get all the way there." *Obama on BET discussing Ferguson issues.* Obama never discusses 'deeply rooted' anti-Semitism in Islamic societies.

45. "Even today, South Asian Americans, **especially those who are Muslim**, Hindu and Sikh, are **targets of suspicion and violence**." **Obama, May 1, 2014**. *Obama is lying about prejudice against Muslims in America, despite a decreasing frequency of hate crimes against them.*

46. "Generations of Asian Americans, Native Hawaiians and Pacific Islanders have helped make this country what it is today. Yet they have also faced **a long history of injustice – from the overthrow of the Kingdom of Hawaii** and its **devastating impact** on the history, language and culture of Native Hawaiians; to opportunity-limiting laws like **the Chinese Exclusion Act of 1882 and the Immigration Act of 1924; to the internment of Japanese Americans** during World War II." *Obama, May 1, 2014.*

47. During the partial government shutdown with the sequester in 2013, Obama prohibited American veterans from visiting the open-air mall in Washington D.C., which housed the World War II Memorial, yet allowed a rally for illegal aliens promoting amnesty in the mall.

48. Since Obama despises Islamophobes and blasphemers, here are great Americans, other historical figures, and leaders of the West that Obama surely hates. All these insights by outstanding American leaders (and others) surely contribute significantly to the animosity Obama feels toward America (and Europe):

   a. "He [Mohammed] declared undistinguishing and exterminating war, as a part of **his religion, against all the rest of mankind ... The precept of the Koran is, <u>perpetual war</u>** against all who deny that Mahomet is the prophet of G-d. The vanquished may purchase their lives, by the payment of tribute; the victorious may be appeased by a false and delusive promise of peace; and the faithful follower of the prophet may submit to the imperious necessities of defeat: **but the command to propagate the Moslem creed by the sword is always obligatory** [*Islam is not a religion of peace*]**, when it can be made effective**. The commands of the prophet may be performed alike, by fraud, or by force." *President John Quincy Adams.*

   b. "[Mohammed] poisoned the sources of human felicity at the fountain, by degrading the condition of the female sex, and the allowance of polygamy; and **he declared <u>undistinguishing and exterminating war, as a part of his religion, against all the rest of mankind</u>**. THE ESSENCE OF HIS DOCTRINE WAS VIOLENCE AND LUST: TO EXALT THE BRUTAL OVER THE SPIRITUAL PART OF HUMAN NATURE." *President John Quincy Adams. Adams put the last sentence in capital letters in order to emphasize his conclusion.*

   c. "This book is a long conference of G-d, the angels, and **Mahomet**, which that <u>**false prophet**</u> very grossly invented ... Thou wilt wonder that such **absurdities** have infected the best part of the world, and wilt avouch, that the knowledge of what is contained in this book, will **render that law contemptible**." *President John Adams.*

   d. "The ambassador answered us that ... was founded on the Laws of the Prophet, that it was written in their Koran, that **all nations who should not have answered their authority were sinners**, that it was **their right and duty to make war upon them**

wherever they could be found, and to **make slaves of all they could take as prisoners**, and that every Mussulman who should be slain in battle was sure to go to Paradise." *President Thomas Jefferson.*

e.   "The real strength of the Nationalist movement in Egypt ... lay not with these Levantines of the café but with the mass of **practically unchanged bigoted Moslems** to whom the movement meant **driving out the foreigner, plundering and <u>slaying the local Christian</u>** *[Islam has not changed over 100 years.]*, **and a return to all the violence and corruption which festered under the old-style Moslem rule (Sharia law)**, whether Asiatic or African." *Former President Theodore Roosevelt, reflections after visiting Cairo in a letter to Sir George Trevelyan, 1911.*

f.   "That is a simple rule, and easy to remember. When I, a thoughtful and unblessed Presbyterian, examine the Koran, I know that beyond any question **every Mohammedan is insane**; not in all things, but **in religious matters**." *Mark Twain.*

g.   "To me it seems certain that the **fatalistic teachings of Muhammad** and the utter **degradation of women** is the outstanding cause for the arrested development of the Arab. **He is exactly as he was around the year 700, while we have kept on developing.**" *General George Patton.*

h.   "The Koran does not permit Mohammedans to drink. **Their natural instinct do not permit them to be moral.** They say the Sultan has 800 wives. This almost amounts to bigamy." *Mark Twain, "The Innocents Abroad," Chapter XXXIV.*

i.   "In regard to religion, mutual toleration in the different professions thereof is what all good and candid minds in all ages have ever practiced, and, both by precept and example, inculcated on mankind. And it is now generally agreed among Christians that this spirit of toleration, in the fullest extent consistent with the being of civil society, is the chief characteristical mark of the Church. Insomuch that Mr. Locke has asserted and proved, beyond the possibility of contradiction on any solid ground, that **such toleration ought to be extended to all whose doctrines are not subversive of society. <u>The only sects which he thinks ought to be, and which by all wise laws are excluded from such toleration, are those who teach doctrines subversive of the civil government under which they live</u>**." *Samuel Adams, Founding Father, Governor of Massachusetts, cousin of President John Adams, 1772, "The Rights of the Colonists."* The founding fathers may have wanted to exclude Islam from toleration, since they knew that a Muslim's adherence and devotion to Sharia law supersedes obedience to civil laws in the West, and in America – the U.S. Constitution. Islam means submission, which directs Muslims to treat all non-Muslims as second-class citizens, since they regard all other religions as inferior and worthy only of debasement. As the Muslim population grows in a non-Muslim society, their level of civil disobedience increases, which always results in civil insurrection and civil war, and ultimately the harassment and extermination of non-Muslims. This process may take centuries or a millennium, but one must question why there are no Jews and Christians in so many Islamic nations, and why their populations as a percentage of the total population of an Islamic community is always decreasing, both on a local level and on a national level. When Muslims control the political apparatus of society, the laws are based on the Quran, which favors Muslims and subjugates non-Muslims to harsher more threatened lives. This proves there is no freedom of religion in those regions. Non-Muslims in a pure Islamic society have three options – convert to Islam, pay an over-bearing harsh tax or jizya, or die. Muslims are ultimately only devoted to Mohammed and the Quran. Civil peaceful societies are seen as a temporary political environment that should be used to advance Sharia law and their supremacist ideology. Sharia law is not compatible with the Constitution of the United States. There is no separation of church and state in Islam since the state is based on Islamic theology and Sharia law. There is no freedom of speech, because people who criticize Mohammad or Islam can be jailed, flogged, and executed. Gays are executed routinely under Sharia law. Muslim men are allowed to legally beat their wives. People who convert from Islam to other religions are jailed, beaten, and executed. Women do not have equal rights. Female genital mutilation is a common procedure in Islamic societies and should be formally banned in the West. Honor killings are common and condoned by Muslim families throughout the world. Popular elections aren't tolerated in Muslim societies, where non-Muslims can be elected to significant positions of power. Saudi Islamic scholar Sheikh al-Barrak said that elections "have been brought by the anti-Islam parties who have occupied Muslim land." Islam has been associated with four major genocides in the modern era – Muslims were allied the Nazis and helped plan the Holocaust. Turkish Muslims killed over one million Christian Armenians, Muslims have been indiscriminately killing Christians in Africa in Darfur, Nigeria, and via Boko Haram. ISIS has been committing genocide in Syria and Iraq against many non-Muslim societies. Throughout Europe when Muslim protestors support Sharia law, they also promote dismantling Western democracies. Sharia law and fundamental Islam are incompatible with the Constitution and free societies. Bending over back-wards to protect the rights and freedoms of people who want to destroy your society and eliminate your freedoms is guaranteeing a hostile and life-threatening society for your children and grandchildren. **A 2010 report entitled "Sharia – The Threat to America" produced by the Center for Security Analysis concluded that Sharia law was a "totalitarian" political system incompatible with Western democracies and the U.S. Constitution**. Wherever Muslims go, conflict follows. **<u>Society has a right</u>**

to allow its citizens to live in peace and prevent the creation of circumstances that will lead to groups of citizens actively seeking the harassment and destruction of other groups with different religions and mindsets. Any support of an Islamic caliphate in a non-Muslim country is an act of subversion and should not be tolerated. Thus, a religious Muslim who follows the Quran views subversion of their civil non –Islamic government as a directive and a goal of their life's endeavors.

j. "[Mohammad] seduced the people by promises of carnal pleasure to which the concupiscence of the flesh goads us. His teaching also contained precepts that were in conformity with his promises, and he gave free rein to carnal pleasure *[he sanctioned raping non-Muslims and the acquisition of sex slaves]* … In all this, as is not unexpected, he was obeyed by carnal men … As for proofs of the truth of his doctrine, he brought forward only such as could be grasped by the natural ability of anyone with a very modest wisdom. Indeed, the truths that he taught he mingled with many fables and with doctrines of the greatest falsity … No wise men, men trained in things divine and human, believed in him from the beginning … [**Muslims**] **were brutal men and desert wanderers, utterly ignorant of all divine teaching, through whose numbers Mohammad forced others to become his followers by the violence of his arms** … Mohammad said that he was sent in the power of his arms, which are signs not lacking even to robbers and tyrants … [Mohammad] **perverts almost all the testimonies of the Old and New Testaments** by making them into fabrications of his own, as can be seen by anyone who examines his law." *Saint Thomas Aquinas, 13ᵗʰ century esteemed scholar, Catholic priest, theologian and philosopher.* Aquinas combined Aristotelian philosophy with Catholic theology. According to Obama, the future must not belong to educated and esteemed people like St. Thomas Aquinas, whom he views as a blasphemer and a bigot for criticizing Mohammad. Maybe all these insightful political and religious leaders of the West are right and Obama is wrong.

k. "Arabs have never invented anything except Islam." *Louis Bertrand (1866 – 1941), French novelist and historian.*

l. "Quran … **an accursed book** … So long as there is this book there will be no peace in the world." *William Goldstone (1809 – 1898), served four separate times as British prime minister.*

m. "The **Islamic conquest of India** is probably the bloodiest story in history. It is a discouraging tale, for its evident moral is that civilization is a precious good, whose delicate complex of order and freedom, culture and peace, can at any moment be overthrown by **barbarians invading from without** or **multiplying from within**." *William Durant (1885 – 1981), American writer, philosopher and historian.*

n. "If the peoples of Europe in the seventh and eight centuries, and on up to and including the seventeenth century, had not possessed a military equally with, and gradually a growing superiority *[why Obama has slashed defense spending and has transferred resources and technology over to Iran]* over the Mohammedans who invaded Europe, Europe would at this moment be Mohammedan and the Christian religion would be extinct … **Wherever the Mohammedans have had complete sway**, **wherever the Christians have been unable to resist them by the sword**, **Christianity has ultimately disappeared** … There are "social values" today in Europe, America and Australia only because during those thousand years, the Christians of Europe possessed the warlike power to do what the Christians of Asia and Africa had failed to do – that is, to beat back the Moslem invader." *Theodore Roosevelt, 26ᵗʰ president of the United States.* According to Roosevelt, the Western Judeo-Christian heritage of Europe and America will only survive if Islam is defeated militarily and subsequently made illegal, which did not happen in the aftermath of WWII, when Islam was allied with the Nazis. Roosevelt feared the day when a radical Muslim who embraced Islam and Sharia law would be president of the United States.

o. In 1942, R.G. Collingwood described Islam in *The New Leviathan* as "**a barbarism**."

p. "That erection of a temporal monarch under the pretence of a spiritual authority, which was not possible in Christendom but by the extinction or entrancement of the spirit of Christianity, this was effected in full by **Mahomet**, to the establishment of **the most extensive and complete despotism that ever warred against civilisation and the interests of humanity**." *Samuel Coleridge, On the Constitution of Church and State, 1930.*

49. "Racism, we are not cured of it. **And it's not just a matter of it not being polite to say n*gger in public.** That's not the measure of whether racism still exists or not. It's not just a matter of overt discrimination. **Societies don't**, **overnight**, **completely erase everything that happened 200 to 300 years prior** … **[slavery] casts a long shadow and that's still part of our DNA that's passed on**." *Obama calls America a racist nation after the Charleston church murders, during an interview with Mike Maron in June 2015, while using the N word and disrespecting the office of the president.* At the 2016 White House Correspondents' Dinner Obama enjoyed and celebrated being called "my N*igga" by the African-American host of the event during the closing remarks. The following day Obama said he had "appreciated the sentiment" of the description.

50. "For centuries, **Black people in America suffered the lash of the whip** of slaves, and the humiliation of segregation." *Obama, Cairo University speech, June 2009.*

51. "For too long we have been blind to the ways that **past injustices continue to shape the present**, perhaps we see that now … **racial bias can infect us** even when we don't realize it … **subtle impulse to call Johnny back** for a job interview **but not Jamal** … [Americans

are] avoiding uncomfortable truths about the **prejudice that still infects our society.**" *Obama continues to call America racist during his stay in Charleston, June, 2015.* **If Obama is so insistent on separating violence and terrorism from Islam**, **why is he so insistent on linking America with racism**? **This alone proves that Obama's allegiance is with Islam and jihad**, **and not with America and freedom**. Why is Obama advancing Muslim interests during the condolence period for the murder of African-American Christian worshippers? Why can't Obama give Americans the benefit of the doubt, like he constantly does with Islam and Islamic terrorists? Obama criticized America as racist against Muslims by using Jamal, an Arabic name, as a reference.

52. "The president holds the opinion of the United Nations in higher esteem than the American people." *Senator John Thune, Chairman of the Senate Republican Conference, commenting after Obama wants the UN to approve the Iranian nuclear agreement before Congress. The UN is a Muslim majority organization. July 2015.*

53. "Now when I ran for president eight years ago as a candidate who opposed the decision to go to war in Iraq, I said that America didn't just have to end that war, **we had to end the mindset that got us there in the first place**. It was a mindset characterized by a **preference for military action over diplomacy. A mindset that put a premium on unilateral U.S. action over the painstaking work of building international consensus. A mindset that exaggerated threats beyond what the intelligence supported**. *[Obama altered ISIS intelligence assessments to protect the Islamic terrorists.]* **Leaders did not level with the American people** *[Obama calls former U.S. presidents – liars]* about the cost of war. Insisting we could easily **impose our will on a part of the world with a profoundly different culture and history**. And, of course, **those calling for war labeled themselves strong and decisive**." *Obama, Washington D.C. speech where he lobbies for congressional approval of the Iranian nuclear agreement. August 5, 2015.* Obama sounds like a radical foreigner who despises America and its history. These are the words of a foreign leader residing in Tehran, Havana, and Venezuela, and not a president who loves his country and wants to fight for freedom and the ideals that made America great. Part of Obama's fundamental transformation of America includes changing the mindset of Americans so they prefer appeasing and supporting the totalitarian dictators of the world without the benefit of a strong military. With Obama's obvious disdain for the U.S. military and its ability to project our strength around the world to protect American interests and our allies, it is clear that Obama's multi-year effort to emasculate, decimate and paralyze American military forces was a pre-planned hidden goal with Obama's "hope and change" campaign. With this speech, Obama repeatedly lied to the American people when he stated that "all options were on the table" with respect to the Iranian nuclear negotiations, since he never intended to use any military options against Iran under any circumstances. Obama continues to view Americans as bullies when he states we

impose our will on other cultures. Ironically, Obama called many, if not most of our former presidents, liars, with respect to his statements regarding exaggerated threats and not leveling with the American people, when he himself has told more lies than any leading politician in American history.

54. "The fact that this took place in a black church obviously also **raises questions about a dark part of our history**. This is not the first time that black churches have been attacked. And we know that **hatred across races** and pose a particular threat to our democracy and our ideals." *Obama, Statement by the President on the Shooting in Charleston, South Carolina, June 18, 2015.* Why hasn't Obama used the last sentence in this statement when remarking about the radical Islamic terrorism and murders in Fort Hood, Boston, Chattanooga, San Bernardino, or Orlando?

55. Obama refers to the **murder of Ambassador Stevens and three other Americans** in Benghazi as a "**bump in the road**" during a *60 Minutes* interview. In late 2015, Obama calls the murder of 130 civilians in Paris by ISIS terrorists – a "**setback**." Obama called the jihadi murder of four marines in Chattanooga, a "heartbreaking **circumstance**."

56. "And as a report that came out just this week reminded us, there are a lot of African-Americans not just me who have that same kind of story of being pulled over or frisked or something and the data shows that this is not an aberration … It doesn't mean each case is a problem. It means that when you aggregate the cases and you look at it, you have to say **there's some racial bias in the system. Now, problems of racial justice or injustice have been running themes throughout this country's history in every institution, in every institution**." *Obama speaking before the International Association of Chiefs of Police's annual conference. October 27, 2015.* Obama's incitement against law enforcement officials definitely contributed to the doubling of the number of officers killed while on duty in 2016.

57. Obama is not interested in implementing the will of the American people, and focuses on advancing radical and Islamic causes. The vast majority of Americans have been against most of Obama's major political initiatives including – Obamacare, increasing massive budget deficits, implementing the JCPOA, supporting Hamas and the PA while ostracizing Israel, reestablishing diplomatic relations with Cuba, closing the Guantanamo Bay detention center, trading Bergdahl for five Taliban and al-Qaeda commanders, accelerating the Syrian Muslim refugee resettlement program in America, building a mega-mosques at the site of al-Qaeda's attack upon the World Trade Center towers, forcing American children to share bathrooms in all public schools with members of the opposite sex with his promotion of a transgender agenda, relinquishing control of the internet to powers outside the United States, and having an open southern U.S. border. A 2015 A.T. Kearney poll reported by *Bloomberg Businessweek* found that out of 2590 Americans, 61% agreed with "continued immigration into the country jeopardizes the United States."

58. In mid-November 2015, in the aftermath of ISIS's terrorist attacks on Parisian civilians, **Obama attacked and mocked Republicans and other Americans who supported pausing and reevaluating U.S. immigration procedures more passionately than any remarks he has directed at ISIS** or other Islamic terrorist groups. Patriotic American who want to protect their communities are not "shameful," but presidents who denigrate their domestic political opponents while advancing the interests of enemy forces **in front of foreign audiences** are "shameful." What is more disheartening and demonstrates that Obama views these Americans as his true enemies is that he castigated his American opponents in the back drop of France declaring war on ISIS and in multiple foreign countries. Instead of focusing on instituting the best policies that would protect American citizens, Obama's prime objective is to import as many Muslim refugees / migrants, many of whom will be enemy Islamic combatants, into the United States. In Manilla Obama stated, "But apparently, **they're scared of <u>widows and orphans</u> coming into the United States of America as part of our tradition of compassion. First, they were worried about the press being too tough on them during debates. Now they're worried about <u>three-year-old orphans</u>. That doesn't sound very tough to me**." Obama also stated, "And when I hear folks say that, well, maybe we should just admit Christians but not the Muslims, when I hear political leaders suggesting that there would be a religious test … **that's shameful, that's not American**." Obama is the one who is discriminating and racist with the selection of immigrants from the Middle East since less than 2-3% of the immigrants accepted by the Obama administration are Christians. Obama also has partnered with the UN and the OIC to help select the Syrian Muslim immigrants who will gain entry into the United States, thus guaranteeing these individuals will be loyal to the Quran and Sharia law over the Constitution and the Bill of Rights. In 2016, Obama wanted to maximize Muslim migration to the West, and on New Year's Eve, an estimated one thousand organized Muslim migrants committed mass orchestrated sexual assaults including many rapes against German women and launched fireworks into celebratory crowds in Cologne. These criminals were not "widows and orphans." Sexual assaults by Muslim migrants were reported against Western women in every major German city and throughout most major European and Scandinavian cities on the same night. Muslims in France and Scandinavia torched up to two thousand cars during New Year's Eve "celebrations." America and Europe are getting a clear look at Obama's vision of "hope and change." The Slovak Prime Minister Robert Fico commented upon the Muslim migrants / invaders, "We don't want what happened in Germany to happen here. … the migrants cannot be integrated, it's simply impossible," and supported plans to halt all Muslim immigration into his country.

    a.   "Following the discovery of a terrorist cell in Texas allegedly operated by an Iraqi who entered the United States as a refugee, *The Washington Free Beacon* has learned of an additional forty-one individuals who have been implicated in terrorist plots in the United States since 2014, bringing the total number of terrorists discovered since that time to 113, according to information provided by Congressional sources. Since August, however, the Obama administration has stonewalled Congressional efforts *[Obama is protecting the terrorist cells]* to obtain more detailed immigration histories of these individuals, prompting frustration on Capitol Hill and accusations that the administration is covering up ..."[378]

b.   The suicide bomber that killed ten German tourists in Istanbul in January 2016 was a Syrian refugee who had declared his allegiance to ISIS.

c.   An Obama sponsored Iraqi refugee was arrested by federal agents in Texas for planning to bomb multiple Houston malls with the guidance of ISIS in early 2016.

d.   A teenage Muslim Syrian immigrant beheaded an elderly French priest during mass in Normandy, France in July 2016.

e.   Two Muslim migrants who were residing in Sweden lied about their ages so they could gain access to housing for unaccompanied minors in 2016. They subsequently raped a twelve-year-old boy. The assailants were estimated to be 19 and 44-years-old, which was supported by Facebook data and dental records.

f.   Two Iranian Muslim migrants who were both adults and with one perpetrator who was at least 21-years-old, lied about their ages so they could gain access to a children's school in Dusseldorf, Germany, where they forced a twelve-year-old girl to commit sex acts with them.

g.   A police report originating from Sweden indicated that 80% of sexual molestations in Swedish bathhouses in 2015 were perpetrated by asylum seeking foreign [Muslim] boys. The report stated these sexual assaults at the bathhouses and other public places "have created a sense of helplessness and girls affected have felt deeply offended and scared to go out."[379]

h.   "ISIL has large cadre of western fighters who could potentially serve as operatives for attacks in the West. The group is probably exploring a variety of means for infiltrating operatives into the West, including in refugee flows, smuggling routes and legitimate methods of travel." *CIA Director John Brennan, Congressional testimony, June 16, 2016.* Immediately after Brennan's statement, Austria arrested three Islamic terrorists who were disguised as migrants at one of their refugee centers. These jihadis had previously worked with al-Qaeda affiliates, ISIS, and an Iranian backed militia.

i.   **"The European Union's counter terrorism agency has identified fake passports destined for alleged members of the Islamic State** group in Greek refugee camps, an Italian newspaper has claimed. According to the daily, *La Stampa*, officials from Europol conducted an investigation into the trafficking of fake documents for Islamic State in Iraq and the Levant (ISIL) in four countries – Iraq, Syria, Greece and Austria … there were concerns about how potential terrorists from Syria and Iraq may have avoided government controls in Greece by hiding among refugees and using false Syrian passports to make their way to Austria and other parts of Europe."[380] *(Josephine McKenna, Telegraph, August 2016)*

j.   In mid-2017, a study showed that 75% of Muslim children refugees entering Sweden were actually over 18 years-old.

59. Obama chastised the vast majority of Americans two days before Thanksgiving Day 2015 for not welcoming Syrian Muslim refugees, many whom are ISIS supporters or terrorists, by stating, "There have been **times in our history in moments of fear when we have failed to uphold our highest ideals**, and **it has been to our lasting regret**." The only regret Obama has is not transferring more high-risk radical Muslims throughout the United States under the protection and umbrella of America's refugee policies. In 2016, Obama planned on accelerating the Syrian Muslim migration into the United States by instituting "alternative legal pathways" which included student visas, medical transfers, academic scholarships, extended family reunifications, work authorizations, and private sponsorships. Obama is speeding up the processing of applications to various programs where government approval can be achieved in three months instead of the standard ten years. Thus, Obama can bypass the legal limits set by Congress regarding formal "refugee" admissions, and can have relatively unlimited Muslim migration into America during his last year as president.[381] By June 2016 Obama had established a "resettlement surge center" which was routinely admitting over 100 Muslim Syrian refugees on a daily basis, with a peak daily total of 225 refugees. Over 1000 Syrian refugees were admitted to the United States during the previous month. At this rate, it would be impossible to adequately vet all the applicants. Assuming 1-2% of these refugees are hard-core ISIS supporters, Obama is transferring a minimum of one to two ISIS terrorists into America on a daily basis, with many more individuals being sympathetic to ISIS and al-Qaeda, since the vast majority of these Muslims are Sunnis.

a.   "They'll never admit that **there is a direct link between opening their nation's borders to people from chaotic war-torn nations, and horrific terrorist attacks**. They're constantly reassuring their citizens that they have nothing to worry about from refugees who come from terror prone regions, and to suggest otherwise is racist and Islamophobic. *[Obama's strategy]* In fact, rather than admitting that the **refugee community is riddled with terrorist sympathizers**, and that this is a problem that needs to be addressed, the globalist try to normalize terrorism. In Sweden, the government tries to rehabilitate and reintegrate ISIS fighters who have returned to their country. They give them free "housing, employment, education and financial support" rather than throwing them in jail. And in the UK, **London mayor Sadiq Kahn has tried to convince everyone that terror attacks are "part and parcel of living in a big city."** … The nations that have become the hottest destinations for refugees, are also the nations with the most terrorist attacks. France, Germany, Sweden, and the UK are brimming with terror incidents. Meanwhile, countries that didn't take in so many refugees, like Poland, Slovakia, and the Baltic states, have very few terrorist attacks or none at all … a few days before **<u>FBI director James Comey</u>** was ousted by Trump, he stood before a Senate committee and admitted **<u>that 15% of his agency's terror related investigations involved refugees.</u>** That's a shocking number when you consider that the US admitted 85,000 refugees last year, and the percentage of the population that would consider themselves to be refugees is probably less than 1%."[382] *(Mac Slavo, SHTFplan.com, May 10, 2017)*

60. "**The United States of America** *[Obama]* **not only recognizes our role in creating this problem** *[global warming which evolved to climate change]*, we embrace our responsibility to do something about it." *Obama, Remarks by President Obama at the First Session of COP21, Paris, France, Climate Change Conference, November 30, 2015.* Obama criticizes the United States before the world at the Paris Climate Change Conference.

61. "This is part of American leadership by the way. And this is part of the debate of what we have to have in the United States more frequently. For some reason, too often in Washington, **American leadership is defined by whether or not we're sending troops somewhere.**" *Obama, Climate Change Conference, Paris, France, November 30, 2015.* Obama calls America a nation of warmongers on the world stage. Obama initiates military conflicts or arms proxies that wage destructive wars, but only when he has the chance to expand the realm of radical Islam and remove powers that might be resistant to the creation of an Islamic caliphate. He supported the war in Libya to remove Gaddafi, when Gaddafi's only crime was fighting al-Qaeda rebels in his own country. Obama backed NATOs involvement in Libya and armed al-Qaeda rebels there as well. Obama has been attempting to remove Assad from power in Syria by arming radical Muslim extremists there who are supported by Turkey. Obama supported the takeover of Egypt by the Muslim Brotherhood, whose initial declared goals were the abrogation of the peace treaty with Israel and the conquest of Jerusalem. Obama's main foreign policy accomplishment during his presidency was the JCPOA, which guaranteed Iran would have nuclear ballistic missiles in the future and Obama provided unlimited funding for radical Islamic terrorist groups via $150 billion in sanctions relief for the Islamic theocracy in Iran. Since Obama became president, there has been uninterrupted war and chaos throughout the Middle East. In reality, Obama is the warmonger, but only for jihad and radical Islamic causes.

62. "It is the responsibility of all Americans – of every faith – to reject discrimination. It is our responsibility to reject religious tests on who we admit into this country. It's our responsibility to reject proposals that Muslim Americans should somehow be treated differently. Because when we travel down that road, we lose. That kind of divisiveness, that **betrayal of our values** …" *Obama, Oval Office Address to Americans regarding the San Bernardino Christmas party massacre. December 6, 2015.* Obama calls those political opponents who want to implement policies that want to protect America from radical Muslims and their supporters – bigots. Obama still insists on importing terrorism into America, by continually supporting the right of Muslim Syrian refugees to be settled in America, despite inadequate vetting measures.

    a.   Obama has a religious test for refugees seeking to enter the United States from the Middle East and they must be Muslims. In May 2016, Obama admitted 1037 Syrian refugees into America, and 1035 were Muslims. Only 2, or less than 0.2% where Christians. Obama is accelerating immigration jihad into the United States during his last year as president. In May 2016, the number of Muslim Syrian refugees Obama admitted compared to the previous month increased by 130%.

63. "We would do a disservice to those warriors of justice, Tubman and Douglas, and Lincoln and King, were we to deny that the scars of **our nation's original sin are still with us today.**" *Obama, speech commemorating the 150ᵗʰ anniversary of the end of slavery. December 9, 2015.*

64. Obama did not visit the sight of the mass murder of Americans by ISIS inspired Muslim terrorists in San Bernardino nor did he visit with any of the families affected by this tragedy until two weeks after the attack, while going on vacation. Obama did not send White House representatives to any of their funerals. In comparison, Obama attended the funerals and delivered the eulogy for the murdered victims of the Charleston Black church attack. Obama also sent representatives to the funerals of Michal Brown and Freddie Gray, who both were inspirations for the Black Lives Matter protests.

65. In early 2016, Obama planned on allowing over 100,000 foreign workers with college degrees to obtain work permits so that they can enter the American workforce. Obama is making jobs for recent American college graduate more difficult to obtain by diluting the workforce with foreigners who will accept less money for equivalent work since they have a minimal student loan debt burden and Obama is exempting them from the huge expenses of Obamacare requirements. Obama is helping to create a permanently unemployed U.S. labor constituency since there are over 94 million workers who have given up looking for jobs and are no longer counted in the unemployment statistics. **Obama is attacking the American white collar workers**, **just as illegal immigration across the southern border has attacked American blue collar workers**.

66. In mid-February 2016, Obama **refused to attend Supreme Court Justice Scalia's funeral** in Washington, D.C. Days before the funeral Obama announced that he would be visiting the Castro brothers in Cuba, the next step after he re-established diplomatic relations with Cuba in 2015. Earlier in February, Obama gave a landmark pro-Islam speech at a Baltimore mosque that had connections to al-Qaeda, the Muslim Brotherhood, and Hamas, refused to bomb ISIS positions in Libya, and reneged on a promise to give Israel significant increased military aid which was needed to compensate for the strengthening of Iran with the JCPOA. Presidential candidate Donald Trump commented, "I wonder if President Obama would have attended the funeral of Justice Scalia if it were held in a mosque?" Regarding Cuba, Obama re-established relations with the communist nation and instituted moves to improve its economy, after it was revealed that Hezbollah had established a formal base of operations in Cuba that would be used to support terrorist operations in South and Central America, and eventually in United States. Since Iran is the major funder of Hezbollah, Obama is strengthening Iran's terrorist capabilities in the Americas and giving Iran a proxy base of operations that can be used against American interests while fortifying radical Islamic interests in the Western hemisphere. Obama made Castro's Cuba more financially secure, thus stabilizing Iran's presence on America's border.

67. In early March, Obama decided to **skip Nancy Reagan's funeral**. Instead of paying his respects to the former first lady and her husband, President Reagan, Obama decided to attend the South by Southwest music tech and film festival in Austin, Texas. Other funerals that Obama skipped included Supreme Court Justice Antonin Scalia (conservative, funeral in DC with minimal potential travelling), Margaret Thatcher (conservative, former British prime minister, compatriot of Winston Churchill who committed blasphemy), Major General Harold Greene (high ranking officer killed by a Taliban infiltrator), Chris Kyle (record breaking American sniper, but he targeted Muslims in the Middle East), and Israeli General and Prime Minister Ariel Sharon (Jewish general who defeated many Arab armies). Obama did attend Nelson Mandela's funeral in South Africa where he publicly flirted by taking selfies with Denmark's attractive prime minister in front of his wife. In comparison to Obama's snubbing of very prominent conservative and Jewish funerals, Obama stood at full attention his chin up while taking photos in front of a huge portrait of Che Guevara while visiting Cuba.

68. Obama expounded upon many criticism of the United States and its allies in "The Obama Doctrine," which was published in the April 2016 issue of *The Atlantic*. Obama's responses were a compilation of many interviews with Jeffrey Goldberg. "The Obama Doctrine" can be condensed to – insult as many of the leaders and American long-term allies in the West as possible, empower Iran and Islamic terrorist groups, have America form alliances with our

enemies while alienating our friends and allies, and diminish America's role as a superpower and the guardian of the Judeo-Christian world. Supporting excerpts include:

a. "Obama also shared with McDonough a long-standing resentment: He was **tired of watching Washington unthinkingly drift toward war in Muslim countries**."[383] With this attitude, Obama would never have attacked Iran over their nuclear progam, and all his related threats of 'not taking any options off the table' were lies. Obama views America as anti-Muslim while deciding whether to launch an attack against Syria in 2013. Obama may have finally decided not to bomb Syria in 2013 because Syria has been an ally to Iran, and Obama wanted to keep Iran's hegemonic alliances intact in the Middle East.

b. "There's a playbook in Washington that presidents are supposed to follow. It's a playbook that comes out of the foreign-policy establishment. And the playbook prescribes responses to different events, and these responses tend to be militarized." *Obama is critical of the U.S. foreign policy establishment and their support to defend U.S. interests and those of our allies, when recollecting his decision not to bomb Syria.*

c. "A widely-held sentiment inside the White House is that many of the most prominent foreign-policy think tanks in Washington are doing the bidding of their Arab and pro-Israel funders." *vs. policy inputs from al-Qaeda, the Muslim Brotherhood, the PLO, Hezbollah or Iran – the remaining Middle East political powers?* Obama questions why these opposing entities aren't represented more in U.S. foreign policy decisions. Maybe because they are enemies of the United States? Maybe Obama is satisfied with his policy advisory inputs from Ayers, Khalidi, Jarrett, Rhodes, and Farrakhan instead of pro-American think tanks?

d. ""Free riders aggravate me," he told me. Recently, Obama warned that Great Britain would no longer be able to claim a "special relationship" with the United States if it did not commit to spending at least 2 percent of its GDP on defense *[or did not approve membership in the European Union].* "You have to pay your fair share," Obama told David Cameron, who subsequently met the 2 percent threshold." *Obama is critical of Cameron and Great Britain, and is threatening to destroy a 200+ year alliance.* As a radical Muslim, a major goal for Obama is to destroy U.S. alliances which will result in diminishing its superpower status.

e. "We have history in Iran, we have history in Indonesia and Central America. So, we have to be mindful of our history when we start talking about intervening, and understand the source of other **people's suspicions**." *Obama has been against traditional U.S. foreign policy and is not emotionally or politically affected by Iran's seizing the U.S. embassy or holding its occupants hostage for over one year.* Obama is critical of America's historic battles against the worldwide expansion of communism backed by Russia and China. What does Obama do to mitigate the suspicions many American have that Obama is actively hurting American interests and supporting pro-Islamist military and political interests around the world?

f. "He has also been eager to question some of the long-standing assumptions undergirding traditional U.S. foreign-policy thinking … **To a remarkable degree, he is willing to question why America's enemies are its enemies, or why some of its friends are its friends**." *Obama discarded Egypt, Saudi Arabia, and Israel for Iran.* Not because of academic issues. Obama's loyalties lie with Iran and Islamists and one of the main the purposes of the Obama presidency was to advance Iranian military and economic interests. **To a remarkable degree, the American people must be willing to ask the question – "Did Obama commit treason and betray his country?"**

g. "And on the sidelines of a NATO summit in Wales in 2014, Obama pulled aside King Abdullah II of Jordan. Obama said he had heard that Abdullah had complained to friends in the U.S. Congress about his leadership, and told the king that if he had complaints, he should raise them directly. The king denied that he had spoken ill of him." *Obama alienated another U.S. ally, King Abdullah of Jordan, a Sunni Muslim and an antagonist to Iran and the Muslim Brotherhood.*

h. ""At that point, you've got Europe and a number of Gulf countries who despise Gaddafi, or are concerned on a humanitarian basis, who are calling for action. But what has been a habit over the last several decades in these circumstances is people pushing us to act but then showing an unwillingness to put any skin in the game." "Free riders?," I interjected. "Free riders," he [Obama] said." *Obama insults Saudi Arabia along with the rest of the GCC, as well as our European allies.* Saudi Arabian leaders were livid and refused to meet Obama at the airport as a sign of their displeasure with these comments when he arrived in Saudi Arabia for a GCC summit in April 2016.

i. ""Aren't the Saudis your friends?" Turnbull asked. Obama smiled. "It's complicated," he said." *Obama again insults another major U.S. ally.* Obama complimented Qatar many times and they were later implicated with Iran in supporting radical Islamic terrorism and attempting to undermine the Saudi monarchy. The threats were so grave that Saudi Arabia had to institute a naval blockade against Qatar. Some of the demands issued by Saudi Arabia concerning Qatar included, "Qatar must reduce diplomatic representation with **Iran** (*Obama is a major supporter of Iran with the JCPOA*), Qatar must immoderately shut down the **Turkish military base** that is being established (*Obama's closest ally and friend among world leaders has been Recip Erdogan of Turkey who is aligned with ISIS, al-Qaeda and Qatar*), Qatar must announce severance of ties with terrorist ideological & sectarian orgs (**MB, ISIS, AQ, HTS, Hezbollah**), Qatar must cease any funding activities to extremist and terrorist individuals, must hand over all designated terrorists, Qatar must shut down **Al Jazeera** (*partnered with former Democratic Vice President Al*

Gore and paid him up to $70 million for a failing cable network) and all affiliated channels.”[384] Obama has been allied with the forces that planned on overthrowing Saudi Arabia – including Turkey, Iran, ISIS, and other terrorist groups. Obama filled his administration with **Muslim Brotherhood** sympathizers. Obama was one of the founders of **ISIS**. Obama was allied with **al-Qaeda** in Libya, Egypt, and Syria. Obama protected the **Houthis** with calls for cease fires whenever the Saudi inflicted significant losses to those rebels. Obama took **Hezbollah** off U.S. terrorist watch lists and called their grievances legitimate. It appears one of Obama’s major goals as president was not only destroy Israel, but to overthrow Saudi Arabia and give Mecca to Iran and its allied Islamic terrorist organizations. Obama lied with his statement. This political situation was not complicated. Obama set out to eliminate the Saudi monarchy, as the Russian revolution eliminated the Romanoffs.

j. ““When I go back and I ask myself what went wrong,” Obama said, “there’s room for criticism, because **I had more faith in the Europeans**, given Libya’s proximity, being invested in the follow-up,” he said. He noted that Nicolas Sarkozy, the French president, lost his job the following year. And he said that British Prime Minister David Cameron soon stopped paying attention.” *Obama blames the British and the French for the failure of his Libyan policy.* Obama is critical of more U.S. allies, and puts the blame anywhere but upon himself. Truman’s motto, “The buck stops here,” does not apply to Obama. For Obama, the Libyan intervention was a success since ISIS now controls an increasing part of the country and Libya is a springboard for massive Muslim immigration into Europe.

k. “But he [Obama] went on to say that **the Saudis need to “share” the Middle East with their Iranian foes**. “The competition between the Saudis and the Iranians – which has helped to feed proxy wars and chaos in Syria and Iraq and Yemen – requires us to say to our friends as well as to the Iranians that they need to find an effective way to share the neighborhood and institute some sort of cold peace.” *Obama is advancing Iranian interests and hegemony in the Middle East at the expense of Saudi Arabia and the GCC.* This should be expected of an agent of Iran.

l. “I believe that we have to avoid being simplistic. I think we have to build resilience and make sure that our political debates are grounded in reality.” *Obama’s responds to a reporter asking “Why can’t we take out these bastards [ISIS]?” Obama is protecting ISIS by saying – killing their leadership and their ranks is simplistic and not based in reality.*

m. “When I saw Chávez, I shook his hand and he handed me a Marxist critique of the U.S. - Latin America relationship,” Obama recalled. “And I had to sit there and listen to Ortega” – Daniel Ortega, the radical leftist president of Nicaragua – “make an hour-long rant against the United States." *Obama listened attentively to Ortega's entire speech and said nothing to defend the United States, its traditions or history.* If Obama was so concerned about being polite, he could have politely excused himself. Years later, Obama went out of his way to proudly take photos in front of a large Che Guevara portrait while visiting Cuba.

n.   "As I recall, because apparently nobody in this town does. Putin went into Georgia on Bush's watch, right smack dab in the middle of us having over 100,000 troops deployed in Iraq." *Obama is critical of Bush 43.*

o.   "But let's examine the Nixon theory," he [Obama] said. "So we dropped more ordnance on Cambodia and Laos than on Europe in World War II, and yet, ultimately, Nixon withdrew, Kissinger went to Paris, and all we left behind was chaos, slaughter, and authoritarian governments that finally, over time, have emerged from that hell." *Obama is critical of Nixon and Kissinger.*

p.   "If you think about, let's say, the Iran hostage crisis, there is a narrative that has been promoted today by some of the Republican candidates that the day Reagan was elected, because he looked tough, the Iranians decided, 'We better turn over these hostages,'" he said. "In fact what had happened was that there was a long negotiation with the Iranians and because they so disliked Carter – even though the negotiations had been completed – they held those hostages until the day Reagan got elected. **Reagan's posture, his rhetoric, etc., had nothing to do with their release. When you think of the military actions that Reagan took, you have Grenada – which is hard to argue helped our ability to shape world events** … You have the Iran-Contra affair, in which we supported right-wing paramilitaries and did nothing to enhance our image in Central America, and it wasn't successful at all." *Obama downplays Reagan's role with the release of the Iranian hostages in early 1981, and provides a cover story for the ayatollahs so it appears they did not release the American hostages out of fear of U.S. military action.* Even with events from 35 years ago surrounding Iranian terrorism and lawlessness, Obama is critical of the U.S and empathetic with Iran. Obama is also critical of Reagan's other foreign policy endeavors.

69. "President Castro has also **addressed what he views as shortcomings** in the United States around basic needs for people in **poverty and inequality and race relations** and **we welcome that constructive dialogue** as well. … Because we believe that when we share our deepest beliefs and ideas with an attitude of mutual respect *[Obama always wants mutual respect for Muslim fundamentalists, Sharia law, communists and radicals – but not for Republicans, conservatives, U.S. allies and Israel.]* that we can both learn and make the lives of our people better … **I actually welcome President Castro commenting on some of the areas where**

he feels <u>we're falling short</u> because I think we should not be immune or afraid of criticism or discussion as well … In his view, making sure that everyone is getting a decent education or healthcare. Has basic security in old age. Those things are human rights as well. **<u>I personally would not disagree with him</u>**." *Obama with Raul Castro on March 21, 2016.* Obama agrees with Castro's public criticism of America, and again belittles America in front of a foreign audience. Obama also allows Castro to equate a moral equivalence between depriving human rights and the potential torture of political prisoners in Cuba and advancing universal healthcare in the United States. As Obama has advocated for the civil and human rights for Islamic terrorists around the globe and in Palestine, he ignores the plight of the political prisoners in Cuban jails. Other criticisms Obama leveled at America during this trip include:

a. "**The United States** when it reflects on what happened here [in Cuba] **has to examine its own policies as well and its own past**. Democracies have to have the courage to acknowledge when **we don't live up to the ideals that we stand for**. We've been **slow to speak out on human rights** and that was the case here."

b. "Separation of powers and decentralization. This makes it hard sometimes for America to change as rapidly as we need to – to respond to changed circumstances or problems."

c. "**We have more work to do to promote equality in our own country to reduce discrimination based on race** in our own country."

d. "Cuba like the **United States was built in part by slaves**. Like the United States, the Cuban people can trace their heritage to both slaves and slave owners."

e. "We do have too much money in American politics. We do have challenges with **racial bias in our communities**, **in our criminal justice system**, **in our society**, **the legacy of slavery and segregation**. In 1959, the year my father moved to America, it was illegal for him to marry my mother who was white in many American states … When I first started school, we were still struggling to desegregate schools across the American south … Not because American democracy is perfect. But precisely because we're not … It isn't always pretty the process of democracy. You can see that in the election *[bashing Trump]* going on back home." *It is unbecoming of a president of the United States to criticize his own country incessantly in a foreign country while establishing new relations with a totalitarian communist dictatorship, and with the Castros in Cuba nonetheless.*

70. "Here's my message to the Cuban government and the Cuban people … The **ideals that are the starting point for every revolution**, **America's revolution**, **Cuba's revolution**, **the liberation movements** around the world …" *Obama speaking to the Cuban people in March 2016.* Obama expresses a false equivalency between the American revolution which established capitalism, freedom, the Bill of Rights, the Constitution, a free press, and the foundation for the richest most productive country in the history of man – and the Cuban revolution, which established a communist totalitarian state with a long history of political

prisoners, crushing political dissent, politically motivated assassinations, murder, alliances with Russia and Iran, and extreme poverty. Obama called the Cuban revolution a liberation movement even though it established a one-man dictatorship that impoverished Cuba for generations. These words revealed Obama's preference for the communism as a model government, and his disregard for America and capitalism.

71. "I figured you might want to hear from the president of the United States what I think the United States is going to do [if the British public votes in favor of the Brexit from the European Union. A new trade agreement with Great Britain] is not going to happen anytime soon … Our focus is in negotiating with a big block of the European Union to get a trade agreement done, and **UK is going to be in the back of the queue**. I'm not coming here to fix any votes … **I'm offering my opinion**." *Obama at a press conference with British Prime Minister Cameron in London on April 22, 2016.* Obama is threatening Great Britain economically if they decide to leave the European Union by not backing a future trade agreement with an independent national British entity outside of the EU. With this threat, Obama proves he does not feel there is a special relationship between the United States and Great Britain which has been present for generations. Tory Justice Minister Dominic Raab commented "You can't say on the one hand that the relationship is essential and always will be, then say that if you don't take my advice you'll be at the back of the queue for a free trade deal. I don't think the British people will be blackmailed by anyone." While visiting the United States in August 2016, Nigel Farage, leader of the Brexit movement commented, "we were visited by one, Barack Obama. And he talked down to us. He treated us as if we were nothing." Obama publicly castigated America's closest European ally as he did one month earlier when he blamed Cameron for the bad outcome of the allies' military intervention in Libya. Obama had just left Saudi Arabia where a confidante of the Saudi Royal family declared the special relationship between Saudi Arabia and America did not exist with Obama as president. **One by one**, **including Israel**, **Obama is alienating America's closest allies and embracing her enemies – namely Iran**, **the Muslim Brotherhood and Cuba**. [Poor diplomacy, bad manners, dislike of America's traditional friends and allies, or treason?] Obama is in favor of the European Union remaining intact since the EU supports the mass migration of Muslim migrants and refugees to all the European countries which enables immigration jihad and empowers Islam's quest to eventually dominate Western Europe. The EU provides less border restrictions which facilitates mass Muslim migration throughout Europe. Obama also proved himself to be a hypocrite since he lambasted Israeli Prime Minister Netanyahu when he came to the United States to rally against the JCPOA, yet Obama had no problem lobbying the British public to vote against a British exit from the European Union.

    a.   A possible reason that Obama criticizes and alienates America's traditional allies is that he wants those countries, including Britain, France and Saudi Arabia, to walk away from the historical use of the U.S. dollar as the world's reserve currency as established by the Bretton Woods agreement after World War II, and support the Chinese and Russian efforts to establish a new economic order based on a new reserve currency which would be dominated by Russia and China. This transfer of economic clout away from the United States would quickly devastate U.S. equity prices, U.S. real estate values, and cause a relative collapse of the U.S. economy, all events that would be supported by Obama.

72. "Obama's **particular <u>revulsion</u> against a certain kind of [American] global power politics** is a product, Rhodes suggests, of his having been raised in Southeast Asia."[385] *Ben Rhodes interview, Obama top aide, policy analyst and speechwriter. (David Samuels, The New York Times Magazine, May 2016)* In other words, Obama's particular revulsion of America being the leader of the free world, the protector of Judeo-Christian ethics, and a superpower is secondary to his having been raised and educated in an Indonesian Islamic madrassa, and growing up as a fundamental Muslim overseas. Rhodes has been at Obama's side since 2007, and knows Obama's soul since he also said, "I don't know anymore where I begin and Obama ends."

   a. "In other words, the emotion driving the administration's foreign policy is contempt – contempt for allies, colleagues, and the generations of American policymakers who built the post-WWII order, ensuring relative global stability, and peace and prosperity at home."[386] *(Lee Smith, The Weekly Standard, May 2016)* The author is commenting on Obama's foreign policy after evaluating the Rhodes interview in *The New York Times Magazine* and the Obama interview ("The Obama Doctrine") in *The Atlantic*, all published in 2016.

73. "He [Obama and Rhodes] had also developed a healthy contempt for the American foreign policy establishment … who now whine incessantly about **the collapse of the American security order in Europe and the Middle East.**"[387] *(David Samuels, The New York Times Magazine, May 2016) The collapse of the American security order around the globe was always a major goal of Obama, since as a radical Muslim, he pursued policies where Islamic jihad could thrive.*

74. "When you hear someone **longing for the** "**good old days**," take it with a grain of salt. … But I guess it's part of human nature, especially in times of change and uncertainty, to want to look backwards and long for some **imaginary past** when everything worked, and the economy hummed, and all politicians were wise, and every kid was well-mannered, and America pretty much did whatever it wanted around the world. *[Obama called America a bully and is mocking good-natured Americans who have strong work ethics.]*… **The** "**good old days**" **weren't that great** … Set aside life in the '50s, when women and **people of color were systematically excluded** from big chunks of American life. Since I graduated, in

1983 – which isn't that long ago." *Obama, Commencement Address, Rutgers State University of New Jersey, May 15, 2016.*

75. "To some degree **this is not fair**, I think it's important to note. Because if you think about **Western industrial development** before we knew anything about climate change, they used enormous amounts of carbon energy … It's not entirely fair then to say then to countries that are developing now [China and India], you have to stop because of climate change." *Obama, Vietnam presidential visit, May 25, 2016.* Obama criticizes the Western industrial revolution and capitalism with respect to climate change.

76. "Nations are sovereign, and no matter how large or small a nation may be, its sovereignty should be respected, and it territory should not be violated. **Big nations should not <u>bully</u> smaller ones**. *[Obama calls America a bully (again) with respect to its historical relationship with Vietnam and then continues to denigrate America during his historic trip to Vietnam.]* … **No nation is perfect**. Two centuries on, the United States is still striving to live up to our founding ideals. We still deal with <u>**our shortcomings**</u> – **too much money in our politics**, and rising **economic inequality**, <u>**racial bias**</u> in our criminal justice system, **women still not being paid as much as men** doing the same job. We still have **problems**. And we're not immune from criticism, I promise you. I hear it every day. But that scrutiny, that open debate, **confronting <u>our imperfections</u>** …" *Obama, Remarks by President Obama in Address to the People of Vietnam, National Convention Center, Hanoi, Vietnam, May 24, 2016.* Obama cannot give a major speech to foreigners without criticizing and belittling America. While criticizing America, Obama praised the "shared ideals" between America and Ho Chi Minh, Vietnam's historic communist leader who murdered over one million Vietnamese citizens and routinely executed property owners so he could purge his society of capitalists and free markets. Obama demonstrated a total <u>**ignorance**</u> of the differences between free market societies and brutal totalitarian communist dictatorships, but then Obama has reestablished relationships with the communist totalitarian regime in Cuba and has empowered an extremist Islamic Iranian theocratic dictatorship with an advanced nuclear program and over $150 billion in sanctions relief. Obama's heart does not lie with the West, but with third world dictatorships and radical Islamic theocracies.

77. "They're *[European and world leaders]* **rattled by him** *[Trump]* and for good reason. Because a lot of the proposals that he's made display either <u>**ignorance of world affairs**</u> or a cavalier attitude or an interest in getting tweets and headlines instead of actually thinking through what is required to keep America safe." *Obama, G7 press conference in Japan, May 26, 2016.* Obama criticizes a fellow American and a possible future president in front of the whole world in a foreign country and calls him ignorant, which is a first for any standing president. Obama demonstrates complete ignorance for proper presidential etiquette. A few of the countries rattled by Obama are Great Britain, Israel, Syria, Egypt, Libya, Jordan, Iraq, Saudi

Arabia, Yemen, South Korea, Poland, and the Czech Republic. Obama pretends his policies keep America and the world safe when crime and rapes have soared in Europe secondary to his support of massive Muslim immigration there, his policies caused a huge spike in the number of American casualties in Afghanistan, and he is an advisor and mentor for Black Lives Matters, a radical organization dedicated to instituting violence with their protests and supports individuals who openly advocate for the murder of law enforcement officials. Obama's soundbites do not match the reality of his actions and policies. The real reason the G7 leadership is rattled by Trump is that they are mostly socialists and globalists, and are not interested in individual rights guaranteed to American citizens by the U.S. Constitution or the sanctity of national borders. As Obama, these leaders ignore the desire and aspirations of the vast majority of the citizens within their jurisdictions.

78. "Seventy-one years ago on a bright cloudless morning, death fell from the sky and the world was changed … A flash of light and a wall of fire destroyed a city, and demonstrated that mankind possessed the means to destroy itself … Let all the souls here rest in peace, for **we shall not repeat the evil**. We come to ponder the terrible force unleashed in the not so distant past." *Obama, Hiroshima remarks, May 27, 2016.* Obama called Harry Truman's decision to drop an atomic bomb which ended the war with Japan and saved millions of lives who would have died secondary to a U.S. land invasion of Japan, evil. This is the first time in U.S. history that a sitting president has called the policy of one of his predecessors, evil.

    a. "The victims of the bombings deserve the world's sympathy, as do victims of the war on both sides of the fighting. Nevertheless, this should not change the consensus on the anti-fascist side about the necessity and justification for the use of atomic weapons against militarist Japan." *China Daily editorial whose viewpoints reflect the Chinese government in Bejing. May 27, 2016.*

79. "The world war that reached its brutal end in Hiroshima and Nagasaki was fought among **the wealthiest and most powerful of nations**. *[Obama makes no distinction between the motivations or the morals of the Japanese Imperial Army and the opposing American forces. Obama conveniently neglected to consider the Nanjing massacre, the Bataan death march, the forced sex slavery by the Japanese of indigenous women of captured territory, the murder of American pilots, and the bombing of hospital ships.]* … And yet **the war grew out of the same base instinct for domination or conquest** that had caused conflicts among the simplest tribes, an old pattern amplified by new capabilities and without new constraints." *Obama, Hiroshima remarks, May 27, 2016.* Obama views America's involvement in WWII, with respect to Japan and Germany, as a mechanism for domination and conquest, which in reality was a war based on self-defense. Obama made no mention that both Japan and Germany had initiated WWII by their actions. Obama asserts similar blame for wars in the Middle East upon Israel, when in reality each regional conflict started by Arab aggression or Israel's need to act in self-defense.

Either way, Obama sees America and Israel, both liberal democracies, as guilty parties although they are consistently fighting against despotic totalitarian regimes.

    a. "He listed, in this speech several causes of war. One of them that he did not list was self-defense, which was why we were in WWII to begin with. I think when you look at what he said overall, it's a criticism of the United States." *Former Ambassador to the UN John Bolton, Breitbart News Daily Interview with Stephen Bannon on SiriusXM, May 27, 2016*

80. "Nations arise telling a story that binds people together in sacrifice and cooperation, allowing for remarkable feats. But those same stories have so often been used to **oppress and dehumanize those who are different**." *Obama, Hiroshima remarks, May 27, 2016. While discussing WWII in general terms, Obama calls America an "oppressor" and racist.*

81. "My own nation's story began with simple words: All men are created equal and endowed by our creator with certain unalienable rights including life, liberty and the pursuit of happiness. **Realizing that ideal has never been easy, even within our own borders, even among our own citizens**." *Obama, Hiroshima remarks, May 27, 2016.* Obama is critical of America again. Obama concluded the paragraph with "The irreducible worth of every person, the insistence that every life is precious, the radical and necessary notion that we are part of a single human family – that is the story that we all must tell." Why doesn't Obama attack Sharia law as an obvious violator of these philosophical principles, while he only focuses on America? Islam means submission, so how can Islam view every life as precious and with equivalent worth, when Sharia law subjects non-Muslims to a second-class inferior status in all Muslim societies? Obama does not attack Sharia law, because as a Muslim, he believes in Sharia law and will not commit blasphemy.

82. "What a precious thing that is. It is worth protecting, and then **extending to <u>every child</u>. That is a future we can choose**, a future in which Hiroshima and Nagasaki are known not as the dawn of atomic warfare but as the <u>start of our own moral awakening</u>." *Obama, Hiroshima remarks, May 27, 2016.* Obama calls Truman as a president without morals, and may even consider America as an amoral society. **Obama uses a child as a human shield which protects his argument from criticism** while he attacks a respected and beloved American president and America. Obama may have preferred that the United States should have invaded Japan, since millions of people would have died, all of them being infidels. Or maybe Obama is just a coward, who would have done nothing after the Japanese bombed Pearl Harbor. Truman made the moral decision that saved millions of American and Japanese lives. In this one speech, Obama has called America evil, a society looking for domination and conquest, an oppressor, racist, and amoral. All these remarks were dispersed throughout the speech, and not just in one section. Obama's hatred of America has permeated his whole speech, just as it has permeated all his policies – foreign and domestic – as president. Obama

is the last person to be giving lectures on morality. He lied about Obamacare in order to pass the legislation, he misrepresented the JCPOA so Iran would become a nuclear power, and he altered intelligence assessments about ISIS so he would have the fraudulent rationale not to bomb them. He went to sleep and refused to rescue Americans trapped in an eight-hour al-Qaeda assault on the Benghazi compound which resulted in the murder and rape of Ambassador Stevens. He lied about his love and concern for America during two presidential campaigns so that Iranian and Islamic interests could be advanced over American interests as Obama exercised the powers of the American presidency.

a. "That bomb caused the Japanese to surrender, and it stopped the war. **I don't care what the crybabies say now**, because they didn't have to make the decision." and "I knew what I was doing when I stopped the war that would have killed a half a million youngsters on both sides if those bombs had not been dropped. I have no regrets and, under the same circumstances, I would do it again." *President Truman's comments on his decision to drop the bomb, which can be used as a retort to Obama.*

b. "The Allies were preparing for "Operation Downfall" – the code name for the invasion of the Japanese mainland. Experts predicted it would be ten times bloodier than Iwo Jima. Casualty estimates ran into the millions – for both sides. Lest we forget, Imperial Japan was a ruthless warrior culture whose war crimes rivaled the Nazis. Surrender was not in their cultural vocabulary. At Iwo Jima, the Japanese fought to the death – literally committing suicide – rather than surrender. My dad would have been part of that massive invasion force. G-d only knows if he would have made it out alive … In fact, G-d only knows how many Japanese are alive today because instead of firebombing all of their cities and turning them into moonscapes like we did Tokyo, we targeted two … President Truman knew this. He made the moral calculus … **Barack Obama's speech at Hiroshima today was another attempt to strip away America's moral authority**. But this time it was even worse. **He spat in the face of our fathers and grandfathers**. He dishonored our Greatest Generation by suggesting they're no better than the butchers who committed the massacre of Nanjing, the rape of the Comfort Women, and the Bataan Death March … But if my dad were alive to hear Obama's speech today, I think he would allow me this one exception (swearing) on his behalf: President Obama, respectfully, go to hell." *(source – "**Harry Truman Saved My Life, But Barack Obama Doesn't Approve**," Rebecca Mansour, Breitbart, May 27, 2016)*

c. "Presidents should adhere to our values and the Constitution, and not **treat America's enemies as morally equivalent to us** … His penchant for apologizing is central to his legacy … He knows the foreign audiences will get his meaning. It is, in fact, Obama's subtlety that makes **his effort to reduce America's influence** in the world so dangerous … Then there's his penchant for bowing to foreign leaders. He has bowed to the king of

Saudi Arabia. He bowed to the emperor of Japan on a previous visit. He has bowed to China's leader, Xi Jinping. [And to Russian President Putin.] For those who may wonder, the diplomatic protocol on bowing is clear: Heads of state don't bow to other heads of state, monarchs or otherwise. Period. And Americans don't bow to anyone … **Obama's narcissism**, his zeal for photo opportunities with him at the center, whether in Havana or Hiroshima, **too often overcomes lesser concerns - like the best interests of the country**. He puts his vanity before our nation's pride."[388] *Former Ambassador John Bolton, May 2016.*

    d.   "Obama closed the apology tour today in Hiroshima *[an eight-year tour]*. … And the president speaking as president, representing the United States, I thought it was embarrassing utopianism and **the implicit apology dishonored our nation**. It's not something he should have done." *Charles Krauthammer, Fox News analyst with Bret Baier, May 27, 2016.*

83. "We have been hearing this story for decades. Tales about welfare queens, talkin' about takers, talkin' about the 47%. It's the story that is broadcast every day … On some cable news stations, on right-wing radio. It's pumped into cars and bars and **VFW halls** all across America and right here in Elkhart [Indiana]. And if you're hearin' that story all the time, you start believin' it! It's no wonder people think big government is the problem." *Obama criticizes veterans and views them as close minded with points of view tainted by Fox News and talk radio. The VFW is the largest veterans' organization in the United States. June 2, 2016.* The VFW National Commander John A. Biedrzyck Jr responded to Obama's "denigration" of veterans by stating, "I don't know how many VFW Posts the president has ever visited, but our near 1.7 million members are a direct reflection of America … We don't have confused politics, we don't need left or rightwing media filters telling us how to think or vote, and **we don't need any president of the United States lecturing us about how we are individually [affected] by the economy**."

    a.   "As president, I consider it my obligation to help make sure that, even though less than 1 percent of Americans wear the uniform, that 100 percent of Americans honor your sacrifices and your service." *Obama, addressing the July 2015 VFW convention. Another Obama lie, especially when you consider his disregard for the VA healthcare system.*

84. "Maybe your family has been in this city for generations, or maybe like my family, they came to this country centuries ago in chains. And graduates, it's the story that I witness every single day when I wake up in **a house [White House] that was built by slaves**, and I watch my daughters, two beautiful black young women head off to school … **I think it's fair to say that our Founding Fathers never could've imagined this day [laughing]** …" *Michelle Obama mocking the founding fathers and calling them racists and criticizing the heritage of the White House at the City College of New York commencement speech, June 2016.*

85. "It makes Muslim Americans feel like their government is betraying them. *[Americans feel betrayed by Obama who wants to disarm them with gun control against future attacks by Muslim terrorists he is importing from the Middle East.]* **It betrays the very values America stands for**. *[Maintaining the safety of American communities from Islamic jihad and trying to prevent future Islamic terrorist attacks against American communities is an American value which is envied around the world by non-Muslims.]* **We've gone through moments in our history before when we <u>acted out of fear</u>, and we came to <u>regret</u> it. We've seen our government <u>mistreat</u> our fellow citizens. And it has been a <u>shameful</u> part of our history**. *[When Obama's passions flow – he lashes out at America.]* This is a country founded on basic freedoms – including freedom of religion. *[First, Islam is not a religion. It is a fascist violent political doctrine and is not guaranteed a protected sanctuary in America where it might thrive. Obama uses the First Amendment of the U.S. Constitution which establishes freedom of religion to protect Islam and Sharia law, although it is incompatible with the U.S. Constitution and seeks its destruction. Second, free societies that are guided by constitutional rights, equal protection under the law, due process, and the equality of all men and women, don't have to commit political suicide by protecting Sharia law, which opposes many of the rights and freedoms established in the U.S. and Western legal systems. Third, since Sharia law mandates jihad, which eventually instructs Muslims to make war against their host societies, Islam should not receive the same constitutional protections of people who aren't subversive in free societies and plot to establish a discriminatory, totalitarian and genocidal Islamic caliphate. The endpoint of Islam is always genocide because eventually, there are never any Jews, Christians, or other non-Muslims in societies dominated by Islam.]* We don't have religious tests here. *[taqiyya - Obama is the one with the religious test, since he only admits Muslims as refugees, even though the Christians in Syria and Iraq are the individuals targeted for genocide, sex slavery, and harassment.]* Our founders, our Constitution, our Bill of Rights, are clear about that. And if we ever abandon those values, we would not only make it a lot easier to radicalize people here and around the world, but we would have betrayed the very things we are trying to protect: the pluralism and the openness, our rule of law, our civil liberties. The very things that make this country great, the very things that make us exceptional. *[Obama is taking advantage of the Constitution and the openness of American society by importing Muslims from different cultures who will not assimilate in American society and support Sharia law, which is not compatible with the Constitution.]* And then the terrorists would have won. And we cannot let that happen. *[Obama has already let that happen. There were over 300% more jihadi / terrorism plots by Muslim-Americans in 2015 than were recorded in 2011 or 2012. At the time of the attack, ISIS is still generating $2 - $4 million per day with oil sales and other illegal activities and control territory with over 6 million inhabitants. ISIS has successfully infiltrated Europe and the United States. Obama has removed the mention of Islam and jihad from all intelligence and law enforcement agencies making it*

much more difficult to track and arrest potential Islamic terrorists. According to Congressional Research Services, ISIS has over 43 affiliate organizations operating in 19 countries. Factors that have facilitated ISIS' growth include strong foreign fighter recruitment abilities and poor coopera-tion between Western and Middle Eastern intelligence and counterterrorism agencies. Obama's policies have contributed to the rise of ISIS and the increasing threat of Islamic terrorism.] **I will not let that happen.** *[Obama will not stop Muslim immigration jihad from high risk areas in the Middle East under any circumstances, even when he knows a small percentage of these refugees will be clandestine ISIS terrorists. Obama, the radical Muslim, proves he stands with his fellow Muslims over the security interests of the United States and the will of the majority of U.S. citi-zens, even when the Muslim refugees actively support or are sympathetic with ISIS and Islamic terrorism.]" Obama passionately defends Muslims, argues against a temporary halt to Muslim im-migration proposed by Trump, and criticizes America after a radical religious Muslim-American who is allied with ISIS, who hates America, and shouted "Allahu Akbar" while he murdered 49 defenseless American citizens in Orlando and altered the political environment during the 2016 presidential campaign. June 14, 2016*

86. "When people can start their own businesses it helps people and families succeed … It offers a positive path for young people seeking to make something of themselves and can empower people who **previously have been locked out of the existing social order**, **women**, **minori-ties**, **others** who aren't part of the **old-boys network**." *Obama, 2016 Global Entrepreneurship Summit, June 24, 2016*

87. "The abolition movement was contentious. The effort for women to get the right to vote was contentious and messy. There were times when activists might have engaged in rhetoric that was overheated and occasionally counterproductive. But the point was to raise issues so that **we**, **as a society**, **could grapple with it**. *[anti-police incitement, Dallas murders?]* The same was true with the Civil Rights Movement, the union movement, the environmental move-ment, the anti-war movement during Vietnam. **And I think what you're seeing now is part of that longstanding tradition** … whenever those of us who are concerned about fairness in the criminal justice system attack police officers, you are doing a disservice to the cause *[Obama downplays the attack on police by calling the murder of police officers an attack and is very callous when discussing the five murders, by saying that those deaths caused by activists do a disservice to the political cause.]* … I don't think that you can hold well-meaning activists who are doing the right thing and peacefully protesting responsible for everything that is uttered at a protest site *[Obama defends the hateful rhetoric at Black Lives Matter protests, and says that when BLM leaders and activists call for the death of policemen, the BLM organization is not responsible for all the rhetoric it advances.]." Obama, Press conference with President Mariano Rajoy of Spain, Madrid, Spain, July 11, 2016.* Obama is defending Black Lives Matter after a participant of the protest murdered five Dallas police officers. Obama is commenting on

the Black Lives Matter's anti-police rhetoric and their incitement advocating the killing of police officers, anti-White rhetoric, BLM's violent protests, and the fact that the murderer of five Dallas police officers originated from the Black Lives Matter protests. Although BLM is a racist anti-American hate group that has morphed into a terrorist group, Obama has compared them with Martin Luther King and the women's right to vote. Obama is elevating the BLM protestors and thugs, and the New Black Panthers to political entities on a par with great American civil rights and social movement leaders. Obama is using a false moral equivalence. Obama always sides with the terrorists, whether they are in the Middle East, or are home-grown in America, pretending to be a civil rights movement. Obama is giving the hateful rhetoric of the BLM, which directly led to the shooting and murder of five Dallas police officers – political legitimacy. A BLM organizer, Melina Abdullah, stated, "The black community is and has been under the assault, under, kind of the **occupation** of police who are operating as an **occupying** force." Some BLM supporters are making an indirect anti-Semitic comparison of the police to Jews and Israel by using the phrase, 'occupation' and relating it to the West Bank. The BLM leadership later released a political platform that stated Israel was committing genocide in the Middle East.

88. "And if police organizations and departments **acknowledge that there's a problem** and there's an issue, then that too, is going to contribute to real solutions. And as I said yesterday, that is what's going to ultimately **help make the job of being a cop a lot safer**." *Obama. Press conference with Spain's President Mariano Rajoy, July 11, 2016.* Obama tell cops to admit they are racists after five Dallas police officers were murdered. Obama wants the police organizations to admit their guilt so it will be easier for him to place their organizations under federal control, which he views as a "real solution." Obama is also blackmailing all the officers in the United States with the threat of death by telling them if they admit their guilt, it will "make the job of being a cop a lot safer." If police don't admit their guilt, then the killings will continue. Since Obama has had multiple strategy sessions with BLM leaders and activists at the White House, **Obama admitted that he has the power to stop the violence against the police**, **which proves he can be viewed as an accessory to crimes committed by BLM activists**, leaders, and supporters.

89. Days after giving the above comments in Europe, Obama flew to Dallas to speak at the memorial services for the five slain police officers on July 12, 2016. Obama was **preoccupied with race**, and again inappropriately criticized America as a racist country on this most solemn occasion. Obama stated, "In the aftermath of the shooting, we've seen Mayor Rawlings and Chief Brown, **a white man and a black man with different backgrounds**, working not just to restore order and support a shaken city … We also know that **centuries of racial discrimination, of slavery, and subjugation, and Jim Crow; they didn't simply vanish with**

the law against segregation. They didn't necessarily stop when a Dr. King speech, or when the civil rights act or voting rights act were signed … But we know, but America, we know that **bias remains** … we have all seen this **bigotry in our own lives** at some point. We've heard it at times in our own homes. If we're honest, perhaps we've heard **prejudice in our own heads** and felt it in our own hearts. … Although most of us do our best to guard against it and teach our children better, **none of us is entirely innocent**. *[Obama views America as a racist society, and is one of the root causes of his dislike of his own country. After eight years as president, Obama has not developed an affinity for his homeland, yet only praises the virtues of Islam where Blacks are viewed as inferior, women sex slaves are common, and non-Muslims, apostates, blasphemers and gays are routinely murdered. Why? Because Obama is a radical Muslim.]* No institution is entirely immune, and that includes **our police** departments … And so when African-Americans from all walks of life, from different communities across the country, voice a growing despair over what they perceive to be unequal treatment … **we cannot simply turn away and dismiss those in peaceful** *[lies – most BLM protests are not peaceful]* **protest as troublemakers or paranoid** *[BLM – Obama is supporting the racist violent protests of Black radicals supported by the New Black Panthers and radical Islamic jihadi groups.]* … So that if you're black, you're more likely to be pulled over or searched or arrested; more likely to get longer sentences; more likely to get the death penalty for the same crime … With an open heart, **police departments** will acknowledge that just like the rest of us, **they're not perfect**. That **insisting we do better to root out racial bias** is not an attack on cops, but an effort to live up to our highest ideals." *Obama called the cops racists as they mourn for their friends and comrades.* Obama used this attack, which should be considered an act of war against our law enforcement agencies, as an opportunity to attack America as a racist society, to tell the police they have racist inclinations, to support BLM protests, and to hint at gun control. Ironically, Obama proved his racism by allowing almost only Muslims into America as immigrants, while leaving Christians in Syria and Iraq at the mercy of the radical jihadists. His abysmal treatment of Israel and his blind eye to the blatant anti-Semitism in the Muslim community worldwide proves his racism and anti-Semitism. The fact that Obama will never criticize Blacks for their statistical higher rates of intra-community crime and the extremely high percentage single parent black families, and will never criticize Sharia law or the violent jihad that has accompanied almost every Muslim community for 1700 years, yet heaps endless disdain on American society proves Obama is a racist. The fact that Obama supports Islam alone prove Obama is a racist, knowing the discrimination that exists in Islamic societies against Jews, Christians, apostates, gays, and anyone who criticizes Mohammed or Islam.

90. "As of right now, <u>**we don't know the motive of the killer**</u>. *[Because the victim is a police officer or a Christian. If the victim were a Muslim or a radical black activist, Obama would*

immediately declare the motive would be racism. The killer, Gavin Eugene Long, was a __member of the Nation of Islam and a Muslim convert__, who recently made racist videos on YouTube. Gavin also promoted black liberation ideology, which formed the theological background of Obama's religious practice at the Trinity Church of Christ while in Chicago, and admired Huey P. Newton and Malcolm X, just like Obama. Obama is shielding the Nation of Islam.] We don't know whether the killer set out to target police officers or whether he gunned them down as he responded to a call ... **We don't need inflammatory rhetoric**. *[For Obama, discussing the merits of the case and the motivations of the killer is racism and incitement. But it is Obama that continually calls the police and America racists, which is rhetoric that lays the groundwork for this revolutionary violence.]* We don't need careless accusations thrown around to score political points or to advance an agenda. *[Only Obama gets to use a bully pulpit.]"* Obama's comments *after a radical black activist murders three policemen in Baton Rouge, Louisiana, July 17, 2016.* Obama is protecting the black activist, who is probably at the very least sympathetic to Black Lives Matter, as is Obama, from accusations he was incited to kill police officers. Obama repeated his feigned ignorance of the motivations of the killer when he issued his official "Statement by the President," which said, "We may not yet know the motives for this attack."

91. "We're going to have to do more work together in thinking about **how we can build confidence that after police officers have used force**, **particularly deadly force**, **that there is confidence in how the investigation takes place** and justice is done ... The **roots of the problems** we have saw this week date back not just decades, **date back centuries**. *[Obama clearly states that America has always been a racist country.]* There are cultural issues, and there are **issues of race in this country**, and poverty, and a whole range of problems, that will not be solved overnight." *Obama's response to the murder of three police officers in Baton Rouge. July 17, 2016.* After the murder of the police officers, Obama doesn't castigate the murderer and his ideology or motivations, but criticizes police officers' use of deadly force and places doubt on the ability of the police officers to investigate themselves, which paves the way for Obama to institute regulations to control all state and local police officers throughout the country. These political moves, will place all national, state, and local law enforcement officials under the control of whomever Obama appoints as the overseer of these agencies, which will probably be a black radical who will institute guidelines that will protect all radical activists who break the law, or a radical Islamist, who will use the opportunity to advance Muslim supremacism and the tenets of Sharia law throughout the country by further handcuffing law enforcement's ability to investigate and identify Islamic terrorist threats. Either way, Sharia law will become more institutionalized. Obama has incited the black community with his speeches, and has worked with Black Lives Matter to foment riots and chaos, so that Obama will have the ammunition and events that he can use to advance his agenda to take control of all law enforcement officials in the United States via federal government regulations. States

and local governments will lose their rights, and Obama will have, in effect, propagated a coup with all law enforcement officials becoming subservient to the federal government (not their local or regional communities), which takes its orders from President Obama. The killing of the Dallas and Baton Rouge officers (as well as any other episode where a police officer shoots an African-American citizen or other minority) are being used by Obama as false flag events to assert political control over all law enforcement in the country. If Obama can accomplish this directive, then he will, in effect, be an authoritarian dictator in America, since all local and state police must answer to him, and most federal agencies have been militarized with loyalty only to the executive branch, i.e., Obama. Obama has decimated the U.S. military throughout his presidency in order to negate America's presence as a superpower, but also to make U.S. forces unable to protect American citizens and the Constitution from an unauthorized and unconstitutional power grab by the executive branch, i.e., Obama, for whatever reason. The Second Amendment and armed free citizens are the last major obstacles that could potentially interfere with Obama's (or other radical / far left-wing / Muslim president) plans to have the ability to assert unconstitutional authority over the United States, which is why he incessantly advances a gun control agenda at every available opportunity. Coincidentally, Obama was moving forward with his attacks upon police officers and his attempts to centralize authoritative power over law enforcement officials, at the same time that Erdogan instituted a major coup in Turkey, which transitioned the country from a democracy to an Islamo-fascist state, which was supported by Obama.

a. Proof of Obama's strategy to take control of all local, state and regional law enforcement officials was revealed in a document leaked from George Soros' Open Society Foundation organization. A meeting titled, "Police Reform: How to Take Advantage of the Crisis of the Moment and Drive Long-Term Institutional Change in Police-Community Practice," recommended the administration take advantage of the unrest generated by the killings of African-American individuals during confrontations with police. A document from a board meeting stated, "We are gaining a better understanding of these efforts in order to determine **how best USP (Open Society Foundation U.S. Programs) can use this moment to create a <u>national</u>** [police or law enforcement] **movement**." First, Obama is following one of his major strategy tenets of his administration, which is, "never let a crisis go to waste." Second, Obama was following Che Guevara's advice when Guevara declared, "The revolution is not an apple that falls when it is ripe. **You have to make it fall**." Obama held many meetings with BLM leaders and activists at the White House, where Obama directed them to maintain the violent protests so that the police would possibly kill or harm Black protestors, which would lead to Obama's insistence in a sensational national address that changes needed to be implemented in order to address the "obvious" abuses against Obama's allies. George Soros helped pay the salaries of the protestors and the infrastructure of BLM, which kept the violent protests moving forward. Soros placed his operatives on potential committees that would be in charge of instituting the reforms that would eventually give Obama or his Democratic successor dictatorial control over all police officers in the United States. As Obama incited the radicals by calling America and police racists, even while eulogizing for dead police officers in Dallas, more police were assassinated in Baton Rouge by Obama's allies from the Nation of Islam, which forced Obama to retreat from his aggressive stance. As a radical Muslim, Obama was attempting to concentrate all law enforcement powers in his office, as radical Muslims have done in Iran, Turkey, or wherever they gain power, either by elections or grabbing the reins of government by force. Obama attempted to institute a coup in America, with George Soros paving the way. Obama and Soros were informed allies in the movement to transform the presidency into an authoritarian dictatorship. Soros has financed other revolutionary activities such as the Muslim mass migration into Europe, advocating for open borders, backing instability in Ukraine, and an attempt to unseat Netanyahu and install a liberal Israeli leader whom he and Obama could control, all with Obama's blessings – so why not in America?

92. Obama refused to illuminate the White House at night in a blue light after the murder of police officers in Dallas and Baton Rouge, which would have demonstrated Obama's support for police officers who have been recently attack by black radicals.

93. "Americans across the country are feeling a sense of helplessness, of uncertainty and of fear. **These feelings are understandable and they are justified** … We must take a hard look at the ease with which wrongdoers can get their hands on deadly weapons and the frequency with which they use them." *Attorney General Lynch empathizes with the killer of three police officers in Baton Rouge, Louisiana, and then pushes for gun control.* She totally ignored the fact that the assailant was a member of the Nation of Islam, and that he was motivated by the hateful rhetoric and incitement originating from Obama, Farrakhan, and Black Lives Matter leaders. Obama and his cabinet sided with the anarchists and Muslim terrorists.

94. During the first night of speeches at the **2016 Democratic National Convention** in Philadelphia, there were **no American flags** on the floor of the convention or on the podium, but there were delegates waving Palestinian (radical Islamic support) and Russian (communist support) flags during Michelle Obama's speech. Obama, as head of the Democratic Party, and his aides had significant anti-American and anti-freedom influence in determining the political layout of the convention grounds.

95. Obama views NATO as a hindrance, a threat, a problem, rather than an ally. Retired Air Force General Phillip Breedlove, who was a supreme allied commander of NATO, described Obama's view of NATO as a "warmonger," and in an email to Colin Powell, stated, "I do not see this WH really 'engaged' by working with Europe / NATO. Frankly I think we are

a 'worry', … i.e., a threat to get the nation drug into a conflict."[389] Obama views NATO as a real threat to peace, while he embraces Iran, the Muslim Brotherhood, and Cuba. Obama is opposed to the alliance, with America at its core, that keeps the peace and security in Europe and the West.

96. While in Laos, on September 7, 2016, Obama called Americans racists before young Asians, when he complained, "When the economy is not doing well, and so people feel stressed … Typically, when people feel stressed, **they** (Americans) **turn on others who don't look like them** … When suddenly things are harder, people start saying, 'Ah, you know what, this is the fault of the Chinese,' or 'This is the fault of Jews,' or 'This is the fault of the Houthi,' or whatever."[390] Obama used the third person plural word, "they" when describing Americans, thus Obama subtly did not include himself in his generic description of his fellow citizens. **The president of the United States may not view himself as an American**. *Obama, Remarks by President Obama at YSEALI Town Hall, Luang Prabang, Laos, September 7, 2016.*

97. Obama also called Americans "lazy," during the same Laos presentation. Obama stated, "Usually when you see the environment destroyed, it's not because it's necessary for development … It's usually because **we're being lazy** and we're **not being as creative** as we could be … If you're in the United States, sometimes you can feel **lazy** and think we're so big **we don't have to really know anything about other people**."[391]

98. "Think about the U.S. relationship with Laos. For nine years, there was a secret war in which the United States was **dropping bombs on this country** … I'll be honest, everywhere we go, including here at ASEAN, sometimes people say, "Ah, why are the Americans talking about these issues? This is none of their business; they shouldn't be **meddling in other people's business**. And also, **America is not perfect**. Look, it still has **racial discrimination**. It still has its own problems. It should worry about its own problems." **And I agree with that** … And look, the United States is still learning how to do this, and we've been at it a long time. But **we used to have terrible pollution everywhere** … I would say that the areas where we still fall short are – there are **still too many children in poverty** in the United States who still aren't getting enough to eat … And we still have a lot of children in a country so wealthy that on a day-to-day basis are **not getting the kinds of educational opportunities** that they deserve … Often times they are **poor African American or Latino who are still held back historically by discrimination**. And sometimes it's harder to get the society as a whole to invest in these kids …Because we're such a big country, we haven't always had to know about other parts of the world … As many of you know, **the way that Native Americans were treated was tragic**." *Obama, Remarks by President Obama at YSEALI Town Hall, Luang Prabang, Laos, September 7, 2016.*

99. "We didn't think through all the implications of what we did when you see the dropping of cluster bombs … trying to figure out how that was going to be effective … a lot of those

consequences were not ones that served out interests … The United States has a moral obligation to help Laos heal … **The United States dropped more bombs on Laos than Germany and Japan** during World War II … The United States dropped more than two million tons of bombs here on Laos … You can see some of these displays showing everything that landed on relatively simple homes like this … As one Laotian said, 'The bombs fell like rain, villages and entire valleys were obliterated, the ancient plain of Jars was devastated, countless civilians were killed.' … By some estimates, more bombs per capita were dropped on Laos than on any other country in the world." *Collection of Obama quotes during his 2016 Laos trip.*

100. "We're a nation that was founded on the belief of the **dignity** of every human being. Sometimes we **struggle to stay true to that belief.**" *Obama, 2016 Laos trip.*

101. "There's a reason why we haven't had a woman president – that **we as a society still grapple with what it means to see powerful women** … And it still troubles us in a lot of ways, unfairly, and that expresses itself in all sorts of ways." *Obama, September 18, 2016.* Obama calls Americans sexist at a New York fundraiser when discussing why Clinton is not doing better in the polls heading into the November 2016 election.

102. During Obama's final address to the UN General Assembly on September 20, 2016, Obama criticized his home country before the world many times and promoted Islam.

    a. "And as these real problems have been neglected, alternative visions of the world have pressed forward both in the wealthiest countries and in the poorest: Religious fundamentalism; **the politics of ethnicity, or tribe, or sect**; <u>aggressive nationalism</u> *[people who support America first over globalism lack humanity and compassion]*; **a** <u>**crude popu-**</u> <u>**lism**</u> *[Trump supporters are crude]* – sometimes from the far left, but **more often from the far right** – which seeks to restore what they believe was a better, simpler age **free of outside contamination** *[Trump supporters and conservatives are racists].* We cannot dismiss these visions. They are powerful. They reflect dissatisfaction **among too many of our citizens**. *[Obama is criticizing and mocking the majority of American citizens before the world.]* I do not believe those visions can deliver security or prosperity over the long term, but I do believe that **these visions** <u>**fail to recognize**</u>**, at a very basic level,** <u>**our**</u> <u>**common humanity**</u>."

    b. "Moreover, I believe that the **acceleration of travel** and technology and telecommunications – together with a global economy that depends on a global supply chain – makes it self-defeating ultimately for those who seek to reverse this progress. **Today, a nation ringed by walls would only imprison itself.**" *Obama is campaigning against Trump's wall. Obama believes in borderless societies which will accelerate Islamic immigration and eventually cause the collapse of the West via economic, jihadi and sociological pressures.*

c. "In developing countries, labor organizations have often been suppressed, and the **growth of the middle class has been held back by <u>corruption</u>** *[Obama's Solyndra, shovel ready jobs, and the Obamacare website for example?]* **and underinvestment**." *Obama mistakenly blames capitalism for corruption, when the weakening of the middle class is secondary to Obama's policies with respect to immigration suppressing wages, Obamacare's real expenses, and over taxation and regulation creating an economic environment that hurts the middle class and impedes the creation and growth of new businesses.*

d. "A world in which one percent of humanity controls as much wealth as the other 99 percent will never be stable." *Obama attacks capitalism yet the gap between the rich and the poor widened during Obama's two terms as president. Obama wants to transfer more wealth from the West to the third world, despite the increasing economic pressures and debt load in the developed world.*

e. "It does not require succumbing to a <u>**soulless**</u> **capitalism** that benefits only the few, but rather recognizes that economies are more successful when we close the gap between rich and poor, and growth is broadly based." *Obama attacks capitalism.*

f. "The United States worked with many nations **to curb the excesses of capitalism**."

g. "In countries held together by **borders drawn by colonial powers**, with ethnic enclaves and tribal divisions, politics and elections can sometimes appear to be a zero-sum game." *Obama attacks [the West] the Sykes Picot Agreement that was formulated by France and Great Britain after the defeat of the Ottoman empire at the end of WWI. Obama sides with Erdogan and Turkey, and ISIS, who wanted to change the post WWI boundaries of the Middle East.*

h. "Our nation began with a **promise of freedom** that **applied only to the few**." *Obama views America's early years as racist.*

i. "Yes, in America, **there is too much money in politics**; **too much entrenched partisanship**; too little participation by citizens, in part because of a patchwork of **laws that makes it harder to vote**."

j. "Too often, in capitals, decision-makers have forgotten that democracy needs to be driven by civic engagement from the bottom up, not governance by experts from the top down." *Obama lied to the world since he governed with executive orders and executive regulations instead of working with Congress to achieve a bipartisan consensus.*

k. "And in Europe and the **United States**, you see people wrestle with concerns about immigration and changing demographics, and suggesting that **somehow people who look different are corrupting the character of our countries**." *Obama attacks Americans and Westerners as racist, while ignoring that terrorism and prejudice only increase as the Muslim population of any society increases. Obama ignores Islamic supremacism along* with the brutality and genocidal inclinations of Sharia law. Why should any country import a culture that introduces hatred, cultural conflict, and the need to destroy the freedoms in the West in order to advance Sharia law. Why should the West have to deal with female genital mutilation, honor killings, the murder of homosexuals and apostates, increased terrorism, and the rabid anti-Semitism in order to foster an atmosphere of mutual respect. A large percentage of the Muslim population is anti-Semitic. Common sense and uncontestable observations prove this point. Muslims were allied with the Nazis during WWII and there are basically no Jews remaining in Muslim majority countries. And as the Muslims stream into Europe, hate crimes against the Jews increase as their population throughout Europe decreases. These arguments are in part supported by the Jerusalem Post article entitled, "Half of Muslim Youth in Austria Hold Anti-Semitic Views," published on June 19, 2017.

l.   "We see liberal societies express opposition when women choose to cover themselves." *Obama supports Islamists and the rights of Muslim women to hide their faces in public in the West with burkas or niqabs, but never lobbies for Muslim women not to wear these garments in societies dominated by Sharia law. The West, by definition is a free and open society, and if Muslim women feel the need to hide their faces while interacting with the public, then they should be living in Sharia compliant societies and not in the West.*

m.   "In too many places **perversions of a great faith** were tolerated." *Obama proselytizes for Islam and again fraudulently disassociates terrorism and violent jihad from Islam.*

n.   "Surely, we can rally our nations to solidarity while recognizing equal treatment for all communities -- whether it's a ... or a racial minority right here in the United States." *Obama calls Americans racists again.*

o.   "As President of the United States, I know that for most of human history, power has not been unipolar. The end of the Cold War may have led too many to forget this truth." *Obama belittles America as a superpower.*

p.   "I believe America has ... made **our share of mistakes** over these last 25 years ... When **we've made mistakes, we've tried to acknowledge them**."

q.   "And we can only realize the promise of this institution's founding – to replace the ravages of war with cooperation – if powerful **nations like my own accept constraints**." *Obama agrees with the downsizing of U.S. influence, i.e., negating America's role as a superpower was always an objective for Obama. Obama wants to transfer this power to Muslim nations, the OIC, the Muslim Brotherhood, Iran, China, and Russia.*

r.   "Sometimes I'm criticized in my own country for professing **a belief in international norms** and multilateral institutions. But I am convinced that in the long run, giving up some freedom of action – not giving up our ability to protect ourselves or pursue our core interests, but **binding ourselves to international rules** over the long term -- enhances our security." *Obama wants to surrender a significant portion of the sovereignty of the United States to global organizations like the United Nations and the OIC, both of which are Muslim majority organizations. Examples include advancing blasphemy laws, combating Islamophobia, climate change, the JCPOA, Obama's internet give-a-way, and gun control.*

s.   "And we should all understand that, ultimately, our world will be more secure if we are prepared to help those in need and the nations who are carrying the largest burden with respect to accommodating these refugees." *Obama wants more Muslim migrants in the West in order to advance hijrah.*

t.   "Big countries for most of history have **pushed smaller ones around**." *Obama calls America a bully.*

103.   "On Oct. 1, President Obama inexplicably gave away American stewardship of one of the greatest technological advancements in the history of the world. The Internet was created in the U.S. ... As a medium for communication and commerce and a product and forum for our First Amendment right of free speech ... **the president gave away the control of the future of the Internet to an international body with no promise of protection for free speech** ... No one can explain why the president *[Obama is enforcing Sharia law so that bloggers and any free individuals will be unable to criticize Islam and Mohammed]...*[was] so **obsessed with transferring control of the Internet to a global body**. We passed legislation to block the transfer, held hearings, wrote letters and pushed national media to take notice; but in the end, he still gave it away. The **damage to free speech** will not be felt for a few years, but there is no question that the Internet, as we know, is changing. Now, **China, Russia and Iran [North Korea and Saudi Arabia] have the same voice on its future** as the United States of America."[392] *Senator James Lankford, The Washington Examiner, October 2016.* Obama transferred control of the internet to an international UN body so that Islamic countries would eventually control its content so blasphemy could not occur and Sharia law would be enforced. Obama wants third world dictatorships and communist countries to dominate the internet instead of the United States because Obama's overriding goals as president were to hurt America, dismantle American constitutional freedoms including freedom of speech, and to empower governments and cultures hostile to America.

104.   While in Greece during his final European trip, Obama subtly criticized the majority of Americans and the results of the November 2016 presidential election leading to Trump's victory by stating, "Faced with this new reality where cultures clash, it's inevitable that some will **seek a comfort in nationalism or tribe or ethnicity or sect** ... American democracy is bigger than any one person [Donald Trump]." Obama is belittling the decision-making process of the average American, who has been substantially hurt on an economic level *[Obama doubled the national debt over eight years while over 95 million American adults were without a*

job] while watching America's decline on the world stage. By dismissing nationalism, Obama demonstrated his true loyalties lie with a globalist agenda and permanently open borders, which facilitates the mass migration and colonization of Europe and the United States as advocated by Franz Fanon, leading to increased worldwide Islamic influence.

105. After Trump's 2016 election victory, Obama agreed with Chancellor Merkel of Germany during his final European tour as president when she advocated placing restrictions on free speech in order to curb her political opposition when she commented, "this wave of populism that seems to engulf us, well, look at -- **and it seems, in your words, to come from the United States**. Look at the European Parliament. There are a lot of people who are looking for simplistic solutions, who are sort of preaching policies of -- well, very unfriendly policies (nationalism, not globalism) … **And to take up where the President left off**, digitization is, in a way, a disruptive force, a disruptive technological force that brings about deep-seated change, transformation of a society … Very often it led to enormous transformational processes within individual societies, and **it took a while until societies learned how to find the right kind of policies to contain this and to manage and steer this**."³⁹³ Obama transferred control of the internet to a UN international body in order to restrict political speech so progressive lies could not be challenged, to advance taqiyya so Islam can be promoted, and to prevent criticism / blasphemy against Islam and Mohammed. When Merkel complained that populism originating from America was threatening her political world, Obama did not defend America's right to freely chose its political future.

106. During his final press conference on December 16, 2016, Obama derided the Electoral College by saying, "The Electoral College is a **vestige**, it's a carryover from an earlier vision of how our federal government was going to work that put a lot of premium on states … that sometimes are **going to disadvantage Democrats**." Without the Electoral College, a few major cities would determine the outcome of national elections, and politicians running for president would generally focus their efforts in the largest cities in America. Thus, individuals in rural areas and in states without the largest urban centers would be disenfranchised from the federal government, and would have minimal incentives to stay in the union, which could lead to the dissolution of the United States. Determining the presidential elections on the popular vote would be empowering illegal aliens, since they tend to reside in large urban areas, where the Democratic Party adjust voting regulations where non-citizens could easily vote and negate the electoral wishes of citizens outside large urban areas. Obama's policies which maintain open borders, encourage illegals to vote, and attempt to abolish the Electoral College would all but guarantee Democratic control of the presidency in perpetuum. Obama does not like the Electoral College since it hinders his quest to maintain absolute power over the federal government. If abolishing the Electoral College is coupled with removing the two term limits for the president, Obama

or a popular Democratic national candidate could become a relative dictator in America, with guaranteed electoral victories for life.

107. "You know, my general theory is that, if I was clear in my own mind about who I was, comfortable in my own skin, and had clarity about the way in which **race continues to be this powerful factor in so many elements of our lives** … But that **it is not the only factor in so many aspects of our lives, that <u>we have, by no means overcome the legacies of slavery and Jim Crow and colonialism and racism</u>**, but that the progress we've made has been real and extraordinary, if I'm communicating my genuine belief that **<u>those who are not subject to racism can sometimes have blind spots</u> or lack of appreciation of what it feels to be on the receiving end of that**, but that doesn't mean that they're not open to learning and caring about equality and justice and that I can win them over because there is goodness in the majority of people." *Obama interview with Daily Show host Trevor Noah on December 13, 2016.* Obama is critical of mainstream America and sees most Americans as racists. He seems to have forgotten that he won two presidential elections. Obama's views have not changed since he was in college or worked in Chicago as a community organizer.

   a. As revealed in *Rising Star: The Making of Barack Obama*, a 2017 biography, Obama decided to terminate a relationship with a white girl friend whom he asked to marry, secondary to her race. This has been confirmed by multiple first-hand sources. Obama was overheard saying to his girlfriend, "The lines are very clearly drawn … If I am going out with a white woman, I have no standing here [with the black voting community]." Obama dumped his girlfriend because she was white and he valued his political future inside the black community ahead of his loved ones. Obama is a racist. The countless years and speeches where Obama repeatedly called the majority of Americans racists, were merely a psychological projection of his views on the white community.

108. Even during **Obama's Farewell Address**, delivered in Chicago on January 10, 2017, Obama was critical of America.

   a. "So, that's what we mean when we say America is exceptional – **not that our nation has been flawless from the start** … After my election, **there was <u>talk of a post-racial America</u>**. And such a vision, however well-intended, **was <u>never realistic</u>. <u>Race remains a potent and often divisive force in our society</u>**." Obama admitted that with his eight years as president, he was not able to improve racial relations, and refused to acknowledge his policies and rhetoric greatly contributed to the exacerbated racial tensions which appeared in numerous polls and was the topic of many editorials. Obama was often referred to as the "Divider in Chief." Even during his last minutes of his presidency, he is calling traditional Americans – racists.

   b. "If every economic issue is framed as a struggle between a hardworking **white middle class** and an **undeserving minority**, then **workers of all shades** are going to be left fighting for scraps while the wealthy withdraw further into their private enclaves. (Applause.) If we're unwilling to invest in the **children of immigrants**, just because **they don't look like us**, we will diminish the prospects of our own children -- because those **brown kids** will represent a larger and larger share of America's workforce … For **blacks and other minority groups**, it means tying our own very real struggles for justice to the challenges that a lot of people in this country face -- not only the **refugee**, or the **immigrant**, or the **rural poor**, or the **transgender** American, but also **the middle-aged white guy** … <u>**For white Americans, it means acknowledging that the effects of slavery and Jim Crow didn't suddenly vanish in the '60s**</u> - that **when minority groups voice discontent, they're not just engaging in reverse racism or practicing political correctness**. When they wage peaceful protest, **they're not demanding special treatment** but the equal treatment that our Founders promised." Even at the end of his presidency, Obama views America as pockets of race and religion, and native Americans vs. immigrants and refugees. His policies and rhetoric generally favored minorities, refugees and immigrants at the expense of the traditional American middle class and Christianity. Even in his last major speech, he was critical of his perceived racism that he views is prevalent throughout America, and focused his efforts as president upon improving the economic and political circumstances of minorities, refugees, and immigrants at the expense of all other American citizens, on a domestic and international level.

c. "Our Constitution is a remarkable, beautiful gift. But **it's really just a piece of parchment**. It **has no power on its own**." At the end of his speech, Obama showed his disdain for the Constitution, just as he criticized the Electoral College weeks earlier by calling it a "vestige" of an earlier time, or just as he has continually criticized America as being racist and a bully throughout his political career. Ironically, Obama did reintroduce and inferred the concept of America being a bully in his speech when he stated, "Rivals like Russia or China cannot match our influence around the world – unless we give up what we stand for – and turn ourselves into just another big country that bullies smaller neighbors." Obama would never call the Quran just a piece of paper, and it demonstrated where Obama's true loyalties lie. In reality, the Constitution is just words, words that have inspired billions of people to cherish freedom and self-governance; words that have changed the course of human history and solidified the leadership and superiority of Western civilization as the vehicle spearheading the positive development of humanity. Obama seems to have contradicted one his most memorable speeches, which he coincidentally plagiarized from former Massachusetts governor Patrick Deval – "Don't tell me words don't matter. I have a dream. Just words. **We hold these truths to be self-evident and that all men are created equal**. **Just words**. We have nothing to fear but fear itself. Just words. Just speeches." In reality, Obama again misled America with this speech, feigning love for the Constitution and America, since as he leaves the presidency, he views America's most sacred document as not even words, but "just a piece of parchment" to be molded, adjusted, or possibly – eventually abolished – at his will.

109. Obama is critical of the First Amendment and America's cherished freedom of speech, when he attacked his political opponents in the media during a "60 Minutes" interview days before the end of his presidency, by saying in response to presidential candidates winning primaries despite high negative ratings, "It indicates that there is a lot of cynicism out there. It indicates that the **corrosive nature** of everything **from talk radio _(Hannity and Fox News)_ to fake news _(Breitbart)_** to negative advertising has made people lack confidence in a lot of our existing institutions."

110. During Obama's final press conference on January 18, 2017, with less the 48 hours remaining in his presidency, Obama continued to attack America, stating, "And it is important for **the United States** to stand up for the basic principle that big countries **don't go around and invade and bully smaller countries** … And this is a good example of the vital role that America has to continue to play around the world in **preserving basic norms and values** … **The United States has not always been perfect in this regard**. There are times where we, by necessity, are dealing with **allies or friends or partners who**, **themselves**, **are not meeting the standards** that we would like to see met when it comes to international rules and norms." When talking about his daughters, Obama stated, "But both of them have grown up in an environment where I think they could not help but be patriotic, to love **this country** deeply, **to see that it's flawed**." Describing the United States as "flawed" is Obama's final reflection as president.

111. Instead of **celebrating July 4ᵗʰ** in the United States in 2017, Obama spent his first July 4ᵗʰ weekend as a private citizen in Indonesia, the largest Muslim country in the world and where he spent many years as a Muslim Indonesian citizen, **criticizing Trump and the United States** while praising the Indonesian political system. Obama declared, "In Paris, we came together around the most ambitious agreement in history about climate change, an agreement that **even with the temporary absence of American leadership**, can still give our children a fighting chance." Obama also lamented the increased patriotism in America and rallied against the travel ban by arguing, "The world is at a crossroads … We start seeing a rise in sectarian politics, we start seeing a rise in **an aggressive kind of nationalism _[Obama is upset with the surge of American patriotism on the July 4ᵗʰ holiday_** with the Trump presidency]_, we start seeing both in developed and developing countries an increased resentment

about minority groups and the **bad treatment of people who don't look like us** *[Obama argues against the travel ban which was supported by the Supreme Court and **<u>calls Americans racists</u>**]* or **practice the same faith as us**. *[Obama decries Islamophobia, despite the record number of Islamic terror attacks worldwide during Ramadan in 2017, which had just ended.]*"

Addendum - Benghazi Revisited

THERE ARE MULTIPLE consequential unanswered questions regarding the Benghazi tragedy. Why was there no attempt at a rescue while Americans were under siege at the American consulate for over 7-8 hours? Why was a stand down order issued by the president, the only man in America who could tell the Pentagon not to intervene militarily in this prolonged conflict? What were President Obama and Secretary of State Clinton doing for the seven and half hours between their initial notification of the attack at Benghazi and the cessation of hostilities at the compound? According to Defense Secretary Panetta in testimony before the Senate, Obama never contacted him after their initial prescheduled meeting, nor did Panetta have any contact with White House or national security personnel. No strategy was discussed with the executive branch, nor did anyone in the executive branch ask for or discuss military options for intervening in the battle. Obama remained completely detached, uninvolved, and unavailable during most of this period. In fact, no one spoke with or saw Obama until the next morning – his exact whereabouts being unknown for the entire evening. He disappeared. And why did Obama and his subordinates lie repeatedly about the video being the major instigating factor in this tragedy?

There are many reasons why Obama blamed the video for almost two weeks even though he knew that narrative was false. Obama was very concerned that failing to protect the consulate against a repeat al Qaeda attack on 9-11 could be the event that would destroy his chances to winning a second term as president. Both Obama and Clinton stonewalled all attempts to release specifics surrounding the events leading up to the attack. Survivors of the attack were not allowed to testify before Congress, and their identities remained shrouded in secrecy so that other third parties could not contact them. Congressional committees could not even obtain their names. If the fact that Clinton had denied requests to increase security at the Benghazi consulate became public before the election, in light of recent attacks at the International Red Cross and the British consulate, the administration could have been accused of a serious lapse of good judgment. One of the major planks of the 2012 Obama presidential campaign was that al Qaeda was on the run, and the truth would have exposed Obama to charges that he was lying to the public on the dead bodies of four Americans, in order to win an election. Both Obama and Clinton may have wanted to shield the existence of a gun running operation from Benghazi to Syria through Turkey, and stonewalling could have kept this enterprise buried at least until the election results were finalized. Organizing an arms transfer to potential al Qaeda and ISIS forces without the knowledge of Congress would have created a major political crisis before the election and may have generated a shadow of impeachment overhanging the Obama administration. Other grounds for impeachment emanating from the Benghazi issues could include lying about the video, walking away from his responsibility as Commander in Chief by letting four Americans die without even considering a rescue operation, giving the stand down order, and being unreachable after his initial contact with Panetta for the following seven hours of the conflict. Dereliction of duty and abetting the enemy are serious charges for a president of the United States. Obama's blaming of the video gave him a path to advance blasphemy laws in the United States, by arresting and imprisoning the producer, and by allowing Obama to continually criticize and scorn any criticism of Mohammed and Islam on multiple talk shows and before the UN.

Besides lying and blaming the video, why would Obama not attempt to fight back against the terrorists and refuse to attempt a rescue the cornered Americans trapped in the Benghazi consulate? And why would Obama disappear for the remainder of the evening? The following scenario is part conjecture, part thinking out of the box, and a possible scenario based on available facts.

The attack on the Benghazi consulate was a pre-planned orchestrated attempt to kidnap the United States Ambassador to Libya, Christopher Stevens. A Defense Intelligence Agency report issued on September 12, 2012, stated that the attacks may have been organized by the "Brigades of the Captive Omar Abdul Rahman." Rahman is also known as the blind sheik, and is currently in prison for life after being convicted of conspiracy for planning and supporting the 1993 World Trade Center bombing. Rahman was the spiritual leader of Jamma Islamyya, an extremist fundamental Islamic group that was an ally of al Qaeda, and a U.S. designated terror group. Rahman was an inspiration for al Qaeda's future terrorist attacks, including their repeat attacks on the World Trade Center in 2001. President Morsi of Egypt, who was actively supported by and in frequent communication with Obama, announced during his campaign and after he was elected, that a major goal of his presidency was to obtain Rahman's freedom.

Besides Obama being in regular contact with Morsi, there are other links between the White House and the associates of Rahman. In June 2012, the Obama administration, breaking federal law, gave Hani Nour Eldin, a member of the known Egyptian Islamic terrorist group, Gamaa Islamiya, a visa to not only enter the United States, but also to meet with National Security Council representatives inside the White House. Eldin was previously arrested in Egypt on terrorism charges in 1993, and was later imprisoned by Mubarak. Eldin used this time at the White House to advocate for the release of the blind sheik to senior Obama advisors. Al Qaeda had also been seeking ways to free Rahman, and the links between al Qaeda and Morsi have been previously documented.

Representative Michelle Bachmann also detailed Eldin's visit to the White House in her letter to Representative Keith Ellison on July 13, 2012, which documented the infiltration of the

Muslim Brotherhood in the U.S. government. Yusuf Qaradawi, the spiritual leader of the Muslim Brotherhood, had also been advocating for Rahman's release. Rashid Hassain, who was member of Obama's National Security Council, had met with aides of Qaradawi, and Hussain may have been petitioned to lobby for Rahman's release at the White House. And with Obama's proclivity to supporting the Muslim Brotherhood and radical Islamists, it is very probable that Obama was looking for a legitimate political scenario where he could release Rahman without any major political repercussions. The kidnapping of Stevens and his exchange for Rahman, could provide Obama with that opportunity. The Muslim Brotherhood and al Qaeda would not have undertaken such a dangerous mission unless they had assurances from the White House that Obama had agreed to the exchange beforehand. Thus, Obama, at the very least, gave his approval for the attack and the subsequent exchange, which may have led to the paucity of security surrounding the Benghazi consulate and Stevens. For the kidnapping to be successful, the security surrounding the ambassador had to be minimalized. Obama has shown a proclivity to release captured Islamic terrorists and Gitmo detainees throughout his presidency, so why wouldn't he want to continue this policy with respect to Rahman with a possible hostage exchange?

Obama has a history of releasing Islamic radicals and terrorists using various strategies, policies, and ploys. Obama instituted a catch and release program when dealing with the Taliban in Afghanistan and Islamic terrorists in Iraq. Obama masterminded the trade of five Taliban commanders and al Qaeda leaders at Guantanamo for an American Muslim deserter who colluded with the Taliban and committed treason. Obama forced Israel to release a large number of Palestinians with blood on their hands from Israeli prisons as a pre-condition for the Palestinian Authority to continue negotiations with the Israelis. For years, Obama has been releasing or transferring Gitmo prisoners, many of whom have returned to the jihadi war against America and the West. Trying to create circumstances that would lead to the release of the blind sheik, a radical Islamic extremist spiritual leader who is an ally of the Muslim Brotherhood and his good friend Morsi, would be a realist policy expectation for Obama. If al Qaeda did capture the ambassador alive, a potential trade for Rahman could have also included a significant ransom, which could have helped fund that terrorist organization, just as the Iranian nuclear agreement and subsequent hostage exchange immediately enriched the Iranian government, the leading state sponsor of terrorism in the world, by over $150 billion with sanctions relief and with over $1.7 billion for the four American hostages.

Obama had three major meetings during the late afternoon, when the attacks on the Benghazi commenced. The State Department notified the White House and the Pentagon at 4:05 PM EST of the assault. Immediately after the attacks commenced, Hillary Clinton contacted the president to inform him of the events that were escalating out of control in Benghazi. Obama probably already knew the attack would occur that afternoon, and being contacted by Clinton would only confirm the plan was moving forward. During this discussion, Obama stalled and probably said he needed more time and more information to make any decisions about a possible military and rescue operation to save the American officials. The al Qaeda operatives on the ground in Benghazi had probably planned for a quick abduction and withdrawal, so Obama was hoping events would terminate expeditiously. Al Qaeda also set in motion an attack on the U.S. embassy in Cairo, which would be a diversionary operation and would distract world attention away from their Benghazi operation, and their main target, Ambassador Stevens.

Their mission would be facilitated by a lack of security surrounding Stevens and the consulate. Previously, State Department officials denied Stevens request for increased security and a sixteen man Special Forces team was removed from a security detail in Benghazi in the months leading to the attack, making Stevens much more vulnerable. Obama also told Clinton to blame the attacks on the video and describe the commotion as a spontaneous Libyan riot in response to that video. Obama wasn't going to intervene militarily early in the attack since the goal was to capture Ambassador Stevens, and intervening American forces would upset that strategy. Obama set up Ambassador Stevens for the kidnapping. Obama probably gave assurances to the Benghazi personnel at the beginning of the attack that the safe house and the private security forces would be able to repel the assault and protect the consulate personnel. Unfortunately for Ambassador Stevens and his staff, the attacking forces already knew the location of the safe house, and the hired security fled the scene at the start of the conflict. Clinton probably agreed immediately with Obama since she was involved in an illegal gun running operation out of Benghazi which supplied al Qaeda forces in Syria with advanced weapons looted from Gaddafi's arsenal, and if the compound was overtaken by U.S. Special Forces, they could obtain evidence that could destroy her political career, or at least initiate congressional investigations.

Obama's next major meeting, which was already on the formal schedule at 5 PM, was with Secretary of Defense Panetta and Vice President Biden at the White House. All three men were aware of the attack, which had been going on for over one hour. They all had access to live video, audio and satellite input of the events. Obama was aware of the pleas for help from Ambassador Stevens and the other consulate officials. Generals in Washington and overseas within striking distance to Libya were requesting authorization to launch a counter raid and rescue operation. General Ham had forces under his command ready to respond. Special Forces were only a few hours away and a C-110 training over Croatia was only just three hours away. Fighter jets could have reached the scene in less time.

Panetta forwarded this information to the president. Panetta asked Obama if he wanted to intervene militarily at the consulate. Units were ready to be activated. Obama said no. There would be no military operation. Special Forces in Tripoli were denied permission to accompany a relief flight to Benghazi early in the fight. Combat aircraft in Italy only two hours away were forbidden to intervene. Other specialty groups that were formed for intervening in crisis situations were told to stay put. Obama, as the president of the United States and the only man who could initiate a rescue operation, issued his stand down order, and sentenced many Americans to their deaths. Obama told Panetta, the safe house would be adequate and that by the time forces arrived at the scene and violated any numerous international protocols, the perpetrators would be long gone. It would be interesting to know if Panetta resisted this decision and tried to persuade Obama to follow the advice of his generals, or took Obama's initial words without a fight. Only Obama, Biden and Panetta know the answer to that question. Panetta departed and had no further contact with Obama or his staff that evening, and four Americans died. After that meeting, Obama disappeared and was not seen again by his staff until the following day.

Obama met with one other official that evening, and this meeting or meetings were not on the official schedule. Obama knew that his presidency was in jeopardy. American lives were on the line, and he had just broken a major American military tradition by abandoning the ambassador and his staff that were under attack. He needed advice from a source that was reliable and that he could trust, someone who would not be detailing these events in their memoirs after the Obama presidency was history. Someone who was involved in every major and minor decision at the White House. That person was his consigliore, Valerie Jarrett.

Jarrett maintained a full-time presence in the White House. She had open access to all meetings, and had Obama's full confidence. Like Obama, she was probably aware of the plans to kidnap the ambassador, and would probably be staying close to Obama during the afternoon and evening on that fateful September day. The initial strategy was not to intervene so that the al Qaeda operatives on the ground would be able to accomplish their mission without interference. As the Arab Spring riots were pre-planned with Obama's input, so was the attack on Benghazi.

Fortunately, there were two former Navy SEALs, Tyrone Woods and Glen Doherty, who initially fought the invading group, killing over 60 enemy combatants before they were killed. During the fight, Ambassador Stevens and Sean Smith, a foreign service officer were also killed. Stevens was locked in a building and beyond the reach of the terrorists, so they set the building on fire and Stevens succumbed to smoke inhalation. When the terrorists did eventually capture Stevens, in the frenzy of the moment he was raped. When the Islamic terrorists on the ground in Benghazi called their superiors and informed them that Stevens was under their control, but was in critical condition or might be dead, their commanders started to panic. They knew that the Americans, even Obama, would not trade the blind sheik for a dead ambassador. At this point, the overseers of the operation, possibly in Cairo, informed their Washington contact, or possibly Obama, who told them to take Ambassador Stevens directly to the closest hospital. Obama was hoping Stevens was still alive, if even on life support, so that a hostage exchange could be expeditiously arranged. But the hostage trade was in disarray. Ambassador Stevens was dead along with three other Americans. The medical staff at the Benghazi hospital were unable to resuscitate Stevens, and he was declared dead. Obama and Jarrett had to devise a strategy to ward off and stonewall the upcoming investigations, and prevent the discovery of this very damaging information.

The major clue in this whole scenario that proves that the attack on the consulate was a pre-planned kidnapping operation, was that the al Qaeda operatives took Stevens directly to the hospital. This behavior is just not in their modus operandi. When has al Qaeda ever taken a target of their terror attacks to a hospital? Never. If their goal was to attack the consulate and kill the ambassador, they would have celebrated their victory upon obtaining Stevens' dead body, and would have informed their commanders and left the compound. It is unimaginable that al Qaeda would ever take a victim of their terrorist attacks to a hospital. They would want to kill as many infidels and wreak as much destruction as possible. When has Boko Haram, ISIS, the Muslim Brotherhood, Hamas or Hezbollah ever been concerned about the welfare of their victims? Yet, someone of very high authority, demanded that Stevens be immediately taken the hospital in order to salvage the main goal of the operation, which was exchanging a living ambassador for the blind sheikh. Specialists at the hospital confirmed Stevens was dead and beyond any attempt of a successful resuscitation, the commanders of the operation were informed, their Washington contacts were notified, and new plans were set into motion.

Obama and Jarrett discussed the situation and implemented basic strategies to cover up this disaster. Obama and his administration would continue pushing the video as the root cause of the Benghazi maelstrom. A time tested basic Islamic diversionary strategy would come into play which is to blame blasphemy, Islamophobia, or the Jews. But since Obama is not the leader of an Islamic republic (not yet), blaming the Jews was not a realistic option. Blasphemy and Islamophobia would be the diversion. The powers that be could then harass critics of Islam, and advance the fight against Islamophobia. Obama and Clinton made their promises and the producer of the video was quickly arrested in the middle of the night on inconsequential parole violations. The video excuse was proven a hoax since the Obama administration chose between two different videos on which to blame the attack. Obama continued this charade for almost two weeks, and ultimately made multiple references to these faux causes in his United Nations speech in late September.

The next decision was relatively easy to make. There would be no military intervention in Benghazi at any time or under any circumstances. All military units within striking range never received any orders to proceed to Benghazi. Obama already gave the initial stand down orders during his earlier meetings with Panetta or Clinton, and there was no need to repeat them. The terrorists on the ground were then told to destroy as much of their targets as possible and given a relatively open time frame, since they were informed there would be no American counterstrike. This information came directly from the White House. It is probably the main reason why the attack lasted 7 ½ to 8 hours. There were multiple reasons to not intervene militarily. Obama wanted as many witnesses to the event dead, so that any future investigations would have limited input. Surviving witnesses were not allowed to testify before Congress, and their names were not revealed. They were also forced to sign non-disclosure agreements. Obama wanted to maximize the destruction of evidence at the consulate, so the terrorists were given free rein to wreak as much havoc and kill as many people as time allowed while being uncontested for as long as possible. The evidence would pertain to the transfer of Libyan arms to Syria through Turkey, and any role the ambassador and his staff played in this operation. If participants in these clandestine activities perished, it would only decrease the risk of these impeachable felonies coming to public light, thus shielding Obama's presidency and his reelection bid, and Clinton's future political career. This scenario was supported by the fact the FBI was not allowed to investigate the physical crime scene in Benghazi until up to three weeks after the attack, and no participants in the raid were arrested or apprehended by U.S. authorities or our allies for years after the attack. Obama did not want U.S. Special Forces to capture any al Qaeda operatives in the counterattack, who may have revealed information under questioning that could have implicated the Obama administration, or identified contacts between Benghazi, Cairo and Washington D.C.

It is highly likely that Morsi was involved in the planning and approval of the operation. Morsi had a documented alliance with al Qaeda, and the attack on the consulate may have been part of a continuing relationship where al Qaeda operatives fomented violence in Egypt supporting the Muslim Brotherhood during the tumultuous period that led to Morsi's rise to power as president of Egypt. If any key operatives were captured in Benghazi, Morsi's role, along with the Muslim Brotherhood's role in the kidnapping may have been revealed. With Obama's close relationship to Morsi and with Obama's government having multiple political appointees and administrators who were affiliated with the Muslim Brotherhood or who had expressed sympathies toward many of its numerous affiliated organizations, even Morsi's documented involvement alone may have led to the fall of Obama. Obama may have been impeached without even a proven role in the attempted kidnapping. There may have been a purge of the Muslim Brotherhood affiliated individuals in the administration, the Muslim Brotherhood and its affiliates may have been declared illegal entities in the United States, aid to Egypt would have been terminated, and the question of war against Egypt would have to be evaluated by the U.S. Congress. What were the alternatives if the president of a major country was involved in the kidnapping attempt and murder of a U.S. ambassador? The Muslim Brotherhood has been involved in deleterious acts of violence and terrorism since its inception, and why not now? Why is it difficult to believe that Morsi was just following through on a campaign pledge to free Rahman that was central to his candidacy? And of course, Obama was not going to send in infidel forces to kill Islamic terrorists who were working to free the blind sheik and protect Obama's political future. Thus, Obama's decision not to intervene in Benghazi was not as difficult as it would be for a president who had a love for the country, and a sense of obligation and duty to protect the lives of the consulate officials.

The next decision was not as easy. Obama and Jarrett knew that as the attack progressed at the consulate, military and intelligence officials would be more vocal in demanding some sort of intervention. If Obama was present in the situation room or had further meetings with Panetta or other national security officials, the pressure to send some type of rescue mission and/or reinforcements would only increase. As president of the United States, it was Obama's duty and obligation to stay on top of the situation, and watch out for the welfare of the consulate officials, yet direct intervention could destroy him and his presidency. Obama chose to disappear and be unreachable. There would be no more meetings and no more orders. With Obama unavailable, the decision-making process was paralyzed, the al Qaeda operatives destroyed much of the compound, no terrorist prisoners were taken, the plan to exchange Rahman for a kidnapped ambassador remained covert, and Obama won the reelection campaign in November. Obama was able to stonewall inquiries concerning the video, the lack of intervention, and his disappearance that evening with his legal skills and a compliant press. Although Obama was teetering on the edge of impeachment, he escaped the implications of one of the worst moments of presidential decision making in the history of the republic, and an act of treason that would have been unthinkable for a standing president to commit before a radical Muslim was elected in 2008.

2017 Predictions

1. Michael Richard Pence will be the next President of the United States. (In early 2016, the author correctly predicted that Trump would win the 2016 presidential election.)
2. The United States will move the U.S. Embassy in Israel from Tel Aviv to Jerusalem during President Trump's first full term.
3. Jordan will lose its custodianship of the Temple Mount in Jerusalem during Trump's presidency. Israel will reassert its sovereignty over the heart of its capitol.
4. Secondary to a conflict in the Middle East, the price of oil will climb to over $150-200 per barrel before 2019.
5. Despite formulating the JCPOA which was against American national security interests and illegally spying on his political opposition, Obama will not get indicted.
6. Obama will continue to maintain significant influence over the United States national security and intelligence establishments since Trump did not thoroughly purge his administration of embedded Obama loyalists. Obama's influence and control over the national security establishment is exemplified by the appointment of General H.R. McMaster as Trump's national security advisor, after General Flynn, a Trump loyalist, was fired. McMaster's loyalty to Obama is demonstrated by his supporting the JCPOA, by his purging of loyal Trump pro-Israel anti-Iran anti-Islam National Security Council staff (Rich Higgins, Derek Harvey, Ezra Cohen-Watnick and others), protecting Obama holdovers who are leaking, recognizing Palestine as a country, calling Israel an occupier, tried to prevent Trump from visiting the Western Wall during his trip to Israel but was able to prevent Netanyahu from joining the president, has kept pro-Hamas pro-Muslim Brotherhood Robert Malley on the NSC staff, has kept Valerie Jarrett's and Ben Rhode's staff in place within the national security staff, worked for a Soros-funded pro-Obama think tank that lobbied for the JCPOA, being publically defended by CAIR which is affiliated with the Muslim Brotherhood, stated that former national security advisor Susan Rice did nothing wrong with her unmasking of Obama's political opponents, gave Rice unlimited unrestricted access to classified national security documents (which are probably being given to Obama) as a civilian, stated the term "radical Islamic terrorism" is unproductive, and stated that Islamic terrorists do not represent Islam. Trump has allowed Obama to maintain control over his national security staff and to

protect his legacy. It is apparent why Obama set up his post-presidential political command center just two miles from the White House, since for the first time in American history we may have two presidents running the country. Caroline Glick recognized this problem during a *Breitbart Sirius XM* interview on August 11, 2017 with Alex Marlow when she stated, "Whether it's Iran and countering Iranian influence and rising hegemony in Syria and in Iraq, Lebanon, Yemen, Bahrain, and, of course, Iran's nuclear weapons program, these are very, very key issues for the United States and for all of its allies in the Middle East.   And on all of these issues, in practice, we see that the policies that the National Security Adviser, H.R. McMaster, is pushing are at loggerheads with – completely contradict – the policies that President Trump ran on and continues to say that he wants. … This is President Obama's policy, was to try to get the United States to help Iran to take over Syria, without allowing the American people to know … This, we see, is a policy that President Trump continues to implement … It's a very, very troubling thing." With many of Obama's loyal employees still working throughout the federal government and special counsel Mueller filling his investigative staff with Obama and Clinton supporters, Trump will have much trouble moving his agenda forward and runs the real risk he may not finish his first term.

7. Saudi Arabia will face increasing internal dissent and domestic terrorism, which will originate from Iran. Saudi Arabia's war with the Iranian backed Houthi rebels will expand. Saudi Arabia will also face increasing risks from Qatar, an ally of Iran, and from pro-Iranian militias based in Iraq and Syria. All these increasing hostile fronts against Saudi Arabia were strengthened and optimized by a complicit Obama administration, for a future war against the Saudi Kingdom. Obama is using his back-channel political connections that he forged as president and his continued connections to various intelligence agencies to eventually have the Shiite Islamic sect control Mecca. One of the major nuclear threats facing the world is Iran's possible use of nuclear weapons against Saudi Arabia in any future Sunni – Shiite conflict. Saudi Arabia has finally recognized this threat and has started to increase the diplomatic pressure on Qatar.

8. Whether in 2020 or 2024, the Democratic presidential platform presented at the DNC convention will contain explicitly anti-Israel resolutions. Anti-Semitism will continue to increase on liberal college campuses.

9. Anti-Semitism, anti-gay attacks, female genital mutilations, Islamic based terrorism, no-go zones and honor killings will increase in Western Europe and the United States, mostly in part secondary to increasing Muslim populations and increasing Muslim immigration trends. Studies indicate there are probably over 60,000 women in Germany who have undergone female genital mutilation. In Great Britain, there were about 6000 new case of FGM between 2015 – 2016, without any prosecutions. Some European authorities have accepted this barbaric custom as the norm.

10. The stock market will peak in 2017, which will be followed by a major correction of at least 20%. If the correction is less than 10-20%, there will be a stock market crash of at least 50% in 2019.

11. There will be a physical fight on the floor of the House of Representatives before the end of the Trump presidency.

12. Anti-Sharia political movements will increase in the United States. Any Muslims who are not critical of the Quran, who do not distance themselves from all the hate speech that is present throughout most Islamic religious doctrine, and who do not declare that the Muslim Brotherhood and all its subsidiary groups are enemies of the United States and the West – should be viewed as enemies of and subversives to the West. These Muslims and any other Muslims who believe in a future caliphate or Sharia law, should not be able to seek public office in the West and should have their citizenships revoked. You cannot support Sharia law and the Quran and still be loyal to a Western democracy that seeks to protect the rights of all citizens, when these Muslims view infidels as second-class citizens who should all be targets for submission to Islam. These Muslims, like Obama, will practice taqiyya, and use the power of their office to allow Islam to dominate over all infidels, and will silently support the "drip genocides" that accompany all societies dominated by Islam. Examples of seditious Muslims in Western politics include Keith Ellison, deputy director of the DNC and former member of the Nation of Islam, and Sadiq Khan, the mayor of London. Under Khan's leadership, London has had multiple Islamic terror attacks to which Khan responded that there is "no reason to be alarmed" and that terror attacks are "part and parcel of living in a big city." Later, Khan refused to support a Hezbollah ban in London. With these neutral statements after his countrymen have had their throats slashed, were run over by vans, and eight-year-old girls were blown up with nails, Khan, a radical Muslim, has proved his allegiance is to jihad and not to the citizens he has promised to protect. It is not a coincidence that under his leadership as London's first radical Islamic mayor, acid attacks by Muslims against non-Muslims have hit record levels, with London now being referred to as the "acid-attack" capitol of the world. And, of course, he is for unlimited Muslim immigration to the West, as are most Muslim politicians, since it advances hijrah and jihad. Muslim British Member of Parliament (MP) Naz Shah retweeted in regard to Muslim men raping and abusing non-Muslim British girls, "Those abused girls in Rotherham and elsewhere just need to shut their mouths. For the good of diversity." If religious Muslims get elected in the West, their policies and sentiments will most likely reflect those of Khan, Shah and Obama, and their loyalty will not be to protect the welfare of their non-Muslim constituents, but to support the advancement of Sharia law, hijrah, jihad, and the ultimate domination of Islam over all other faiths and cultures.

13. Future Black Swan events leading to a stock market crash and possibly World War III – listed in order of decreasing probability.

    a. War encompassing the Gulf states with Iran sends oil past $200 per barrel. Nuclear weapons may be used in a future war between Iran and Saudi Arabia. World economies will not be able to tolerate such high oil prices, and a worldwide economic depression will follow.

b. A war / confrontation between Israel and Hezbollah spreads to a conflict between Israel and Iran. Israel may be forced to use nuclear weapons against Iran if Hezbollah launches its advanced missile arsenal provided by Iran against major Israeli cities or IRGC troops along with Hezbollah troops invade northern Israel.

c. North Korea invades South Korea preemptively in fear of a future U.S. strike against North Korea ordered by Trump.

d. North Korea launches an EMP attack against the U.S. electrical grid. The nuclear weapon (s) could originate from a satellite based platform, a container cargo ship, a submarine, or from their new ICBM capabilities. Since North Korea has military alliances and shares nuclear technology with Iran, Russia and China, the U.S. president will need to decide whether to retaliate against these parties with nuclear weapons, besides destroying North Korea. Even Secretary of State Tillerson stated on July 28, 2017, "As the principal economic enablers of North Korea's nuclear weapon and ballistic missile development program, China and Russia bear unique and special responsibility for this growing threat to regional and global stability." Trump could solve the North Korean nuclear dilemma quickly by instituting a trade embargo against China, since it supports the North Korean regime economically. The embargo or severe sanctions would be lifted once North Korea's nuclear program has been verified to be decommissioned. If North Korea launches an EMP attack against the United States, it would secure China as the dominant economy and superpower in the world, thus its interests are aligned with North Korea. Russia and Iran would also benefit from an emasculated United States. Trump may need to decide if he will protect the world economy which would be hurt significantly with trade sanctions against China initiated by the United States and its NATO allies, or take the risk that North Korea will not try to destroy the U.S. electrical grid with nuclear weapons and their increasing offensive capabilities.

14. Europe is very close to the point of no return and is committing cultural and political suicide by permitting unrestricted Muslim immigration from Africa and the Middle East to its continent. Central Europe, excluding Germany, will impose strict limits on Islamic immigration to their countries, and will maintain their cultural heritage. Unfortunately, Germany, France, Great Britain, Spain and Scandinavia will be overwhelmed by Islamic immigration and will become states eventually dominated by religious Muslim leaders and Sharia law. One generation of Europeans who despise their cultural and Christian heritage have destroyed over 2000 years of European history which has safeguarded their freedoms and allowed progressive movements such as the Renaissance and the Industrial Revolution to bring forth advancements that have benefitted all of mankind. As Islam becomes more of a dominant factor in these countries, the political and sociological trends there will disintegrate to those paralleling most Middle Eastern

countries, where non-Muslim residents are viewed as second-class citizens whose rights exist only at the pleasure of the Muslim leadership. Rapes, continual harassment, forced / coerced conversions, and drip genocides will be inflicted upon the Christian communities in Europe by the Muslims, and over the next centuries, the Christians will be slowly eliminated from Europe as they have been erased from the Middle East. In the German state of Baden Wurttemberg, the number of sexual assaults committed by Muslim asylum seekers doubled from 2015 to 2016, which reflects German appeasement and increased aggressiveness by the new Muslim residents. These statistical trends are not unique to Germany but follow Muslim immigration and are an integral part of jihad. By initiating conflicts in Syria, Iraq, and Libya, Obama may have succeeded in fundamentally transforming the future of Europe. For the third time in 100 years, Germany and its socialist leadership, have managed to bring Europe to the brink of destruction with its open unlimited Muslim immigration policy. Germany is now embracing the Muslims instead of their own citizens as exemplified by the German government allying themselves with Sharia law enforcement patrols on the streets of Berlin. Radical Muslims from Chechnya are now enforcing Sharia law in Berlin with the blessings of Chancellor Merkel. History is repeating itself since the German Nazi regime led by Hitler allied themselves with Muslim forces in southern Europe when implementing the Final Solution against the Jews. The Jewish population of Europe will steadily decrease as Islamic influence in Europe increases. Over the following decades, the aggressive Muslims in Europe will slowly destroy cultural, historical, religious and artistic evidence of Western civilization, and then falsely claim that Europe has always been an Islamic continent, as Obama has claimed that Islam has always been part of America's story. By the summer of 2017, authorities estimated that there were over 17,000 Islamic terrorist suspects in France, over 24,000 Islamic radicals in Germany, and over 23,000 in Great Britain.[394] *(Gatesone Institute, August 2017)* Civil war is coming. Within the next decade, major Western cultural and historic landmarks in London, Paris, Berlin or other major Western cities, will be attacked and destroyed by Muslim terrorists. Germany, along with Scandinavia, France, and Italy, have decided to sacrifice their youth, culture, and future to the barbaric tenets of Middle Eastern Sharia law. The majority of European leaders are chosing submission over freedom, and are sentencing their grandchildren to a future dominated by fear, brutality, and a world devoid of ethics which were developed over millennia by the greatest philosophers and politicians raised in the West. These weak, greedy, and treasonous politicians are chosing Muhammad over Aristotle, the ayatollahs over Pope John Paul II, and Osama bin Laden over Churchill. All of the worlds's greatest artists, philosophers, and the military victories needed to sustain real freedoms which are indispensable to developing true human potential are being sacrified at the alter of political correctness and the ignorance and rejection of G-d, country and family.

Footnotes

1   "So You Mean Hilary is President After All?" Leonard Pitts, Jr., *The Miami Herald*, January 24, 2017.

2   "Trump Is Right: Sweden's Embrace of Refugees Isn't Working," Jimmie Akesson and Mattias Karlsson, *The Wall Street Journal*, February 22, 2017.

3   *Project Veritas* undercover video interview with CNN producer John Bonifield. Released June 27, 2017.

4   "Framework One Pager Benghazi," posted by Jim Hoff on Scribd, released by Guccifer 2.0 from Nancy Pelosi's computer.

5   "Why So Many Critics Hate the New Obama Biography," David Greenberg, *Politico*, June 19, 2017.

6   "FakePrez.con," Lloyd Billingsley, *FrontPageMag.com*, January 13, 2017.

7   "So When Exactly Did Bill Ayers and Barack Obama Meet?," Jack Cashill, *American Thinker*, May 18, 2017.

8   Ibid.

9   "Interview with State Sen. Barack Obama, Cathleen Falsani, *Sojourners*, March 27, 2004.

10 "Row Erupts over Turkey's 'Legalization' of Sex with Children as Young as Twelve," Rasheem Kassam and Chris Tomlinson, *Breitbart*, August 14, 2016.

11 "Obama, the Anti-President," David Solway, *American Thinker*, May 4, 2017.

12 "Writing on the Wall: Replace Obamacare, Stat," *The National Review* editorial, October 27, 2016.

13 "Obamacare's Meltdown Has Arrived," Andrew Ogles and Luke Hilgemann, *The Wall Street Journal*, October 6, 2016.

14 "ObamaCare Suffers Three Major Blows [higher premiums, higher dropout rates for participants, major insurers refuse to write policies] in One Week," *Investor's Business Daily* editorial, April 22, 2016.

15 "Fact Check: 'Obamacare' Hasn't Yet Reduced Health Insurance Costs," Noam N. Levey, *Los Angeles Times' Politics Now,* October 3, 2012.

16 "Some Health Plan Cost to Increase by an Average of 25%, U.S. Says," Robert Pear, *The New York Times*, October 24, 2016.

17 "If Trump is Liar-in-Chief, What of Obama's Lies?'" Larry Elder, *World Net Daily*, June 14, 2017.

18 "Senate Report: Illegal Immigrants Benefited from up to $750 million in ObamaCare Subsidies," *Fox News*, February 8, 2016.

19 "FACT CHECK: Presidential Debate Missteps," Calvin Woodward, *The Associated Press*, October 3, 2012.

20   "National Academies: Immigrants Cost State and Local Taxpayers $57.4 Billion per Year," Neil Munro, *Breitbart*, September 21, 2016.

21   "Sean Hannity: Trumps Path to Economic Success Blazed by Kennedy, Reagan," Sean Hannity, *Fox News, Hannity FNC*, December 15, 2016. Opening monologue talking points and slide presentation.

22   "America's Shrinking Middle Class: A Close Look at Changes within Metropolitan Areas," *Pew Research Center*, May 11, 2016.

23   "How America Changed During Barack Obama's Presidency," Michael Dimock, *Pew Research Center,* 2017.

24   "Obama's Whopper of a Claim on Tax Cuts," Glenn Kessler, *The Washington Post*, September 7, 2011.

25   "The Lessons of the Hamas War," Caroline Glick, *The Jerusalem Post*, March 3, 2017.

26   "U.K. Condemns Muslim Brotherhood, While White House Hosts It*," IBD editorial*, December 29, 2015.

27   "The Obama Doctrine," Jeffrey Goldberg, *The Atlantic*, April 2016.

28   "Jerusalem Post's Glick: Iran Deal 'Betrays' US Allies," Bill Hoffmann, *Newsmax*, November 25, 2013.

29   "U.S. Approves Deal to Ship Iran Enough Uranium for 10 Nuclear Bombs," TheTower.org Staff, January 9, 2017.

30   "Iran Using U.S. Cash to Fund Unprecedented, Massive Military Build Up," Adam Kredo, *Washington Free Beacon*, May 3, 2017.

31   "Exclusive: Arab Intel Source: Obama Ignored Warnings About Qatar's Ties to Terrorism," Aaron Klein and Ali Waked, *Breitbart,* June 24, 2017.

32   "Sen. Jeff Sessions Highlights 20 'Vetted' Terrorist Refugees as Obama Ramps Up Admission from Terror Hot-Spots," Caroline May, *Breitbart*, August 10, 2016.

33   "The Russian Stooge," Rich Lowry, *The National Review*, April 11, 2017.

34   "Exclusive – Immigration Expert: Obama's 'Catch and Release' Policy Allowed Illegal Alien Rape Suspects into the U.S.," Katie McHugh, *Breitbart*, March 21, 2017.

35   "President Obama: Accessory to the Crimes Committed by Illegal Aliens," Michael Cutler, *FrontPage Magazine*, April 26, 2016.

36   "Obama Admin Knew Gang Members Were Part of Illegal Immigrant Surge: Whistleblower," Stephen Dinan, *The Washington Times*, May 24, 2017.

37   "Border Patrol Agent: 80% of Illegals the Agency Apprehends Are Released in U.S.," Caroline May, *Breitbart*, May 19, 2016.

38   "Jan Brewer: 'Absolutely Shocking' for Obama to Suggest Illegal Alien Voter Fraud Will Be Ignored," Katie McHugh, *Breitbart*, November 6, 2016.

39   Comey Got 'Steely Silence' after Confronting Loretta Lynch About Clinton Email Probe," John Solomon and Sara Carter, *Circa*, June 13, 2017.

40   "Sen. Charles Grassley Requests State Dept. IG Investigate Clinton – Podesta – Kadzik – McAuliffe Conflicts of Interest," Neil W. McCabe, *Breitbart*, November 3, 2016.

41   "J. Christian Adams: Protecting Clinton Is Latest Scandal for Obama's Politicized Justice Department," John Hayward, *Breitbart*, November 3, 2016. Documented at *The Gateway Pundit*, "Flashback: Obama and Deep Sstate Bugged House of Rep's Cloak Room – Why Wouldn't Obama Wiretap Trump?" March 8, 2017.

42   "Exclusive: FBI 'Granted FISA Warrant' Covering Trump Camp's Ties to Russia," Louise Mensch, *HeatStreet*, November 7, 2016.

43   "Congressman Devin Nunes (speaking to Hugh Hewitt): No, I absolutely do not, especially after this wiretapping incident, essentially, of the House of Representative. I don't think people are focusing on the right thing when they talk about going after the AP reporters. The big problem that I see is that they actually tapped right where I'm sitting right now, the Cloak Room."

44   "Former Bush Attorney General: Trump Likely Right About Surveillance," Mallory Shelbourne, *The Hill*, March 5, 2017.

45   "How Many Countries Conspired Against Trump?," John Hinderaker, *Powerline Blog*, April 13, 2017.

46   "Dennis Kucinich on Trump's Wiretapping Charge: 'It Happened to me,'" Joe Concha, *The Hill*, March 14, 2017.

47   "Did the Government Spy on Trump? Of Course. It Spies on All of Us," Ron Paul, *Ron Paul Institute*, March 27, 2017.

48   "Nunes Must Ask FBI's Comey About Montgomery Mass Surveillance Case," Larry Klayman, *Newsmax*, March 19, 2017.

49   "Israel and Obama's Political War," Caroline Glick, *Frontpage Magazine*, April 10, 2017.

50   "Did the Obama Administration's Abuse of Foreign Intelligence Collection Start Before Trump," Lee Smith, *The Tablet*, April 5, 2017.

51   "Evidence: Supreme Court Justice John Roberts was 'Hacked' by Obama Officials," Patrick Howley, *Big League Politics*, July 12, 2017.

52   "Obama Intel Agency Secretly Conducted Illegal Searches on Americans for Years," John Solomon and Sara Carter, *Circa*, May 23, 2017.

53   "Newly Declassified Memos Reveal Extent of Improper Obama – Era NSA Spying," John Solomon, *The Hill*, July 25, 2017.

54   "Top Obama Adviser Sought Names of Trump Associates in Intel," Eli Lake, *Bloomberg News*, April 3, 2017.

55   "Susan Rice Requested Unmasking of Incoming Trump Administration Officials," Mike Cernovich, *Medium*, Aril 2, 2017.

56   "White House Logs Indicate Susan Rice Consumed Unmasked Intel on Trump Associates," Sara Carter and John Solomon, *Circa,* April 3, 2017.

57   "Former U.S. Attorney: Susan Rice Ordered Spy Agencies to Produce 'Detailed Spreadsheets' Involving Trump," Richard Pollock, *The Daily Caller*, April 3, 2017.

58   "Susan Rice: When the White House Twists the Truth, We are all Less Safe," Susan Rice*, The Washington Post*, March 21, 2017.

59   "Emails Show Susan Rice Prepped to Lie by White House," *IBD* Editorial, April 29, 2014.

60   "Obama Adviser Susan Rice Cites Syrian War as Biggest Disappointment," *NPR Morning Edition* interview with Rachel Martin, January 16, 2017.

61   Ibid.

62   "For Susan Rice, Benghazi was Kenya 1998 Déjà Vu," *IBD* editorial, November 20, 2012.

63   "Senate Report: Illegal Immigrants Benefited from up to $750M in ObamaCare Subsidies," *Fox News*, February 8, 2016.

64   Email for Cheryl Mills to John Podesta, "Fwd: POTUS on HRC emails," March 7, 2015.

65   "Obama White House Knew of Russian Election Hacking, but Delayed Telling," Emmarie Huetteman, *The New York Times*, Jun e 21, 2017.

66   "Obama's Cash Payment to Iran Was More Than a Ransom – It Broke Criminal Law," Andrew C. McCarthy, *The National Review*, August 6, 2016.

67   Ibid.

68   "Impeach Obama for Smuggling Cash to Iran," Daniel Greenfield, *FrontPage Magazine*, August 11, 2016.

69   "Seven Years Later, Recovery Remains the Weakest of the Post-World War II Era," Eric Morath, *The Wall Street Journal*, July 29, 2016.

70   "Merkel Must Face Trial for War Crimes," Daniel Greenfield, *FrontPage Magazine*, July 15, 2016.

71   "10 Major FBI Scandals on Comey's Watch," *Grabien News*, May 10, 2017.

72   "Fast and Furious Hearing Rips Holder, DOJ for Deception in Gun-Running Scandal," William La Jeunesse and Andrew O'Reilly, *Fox News*, June 7, 2017.

73   "Fast and Furious Whistleblower: ATF Still Broken Five Years After Scandal," John Dodson, *The Washington Times*, September 29, 2015.

74   "Indict Eric Holder," *Investor's Business Daily*, October 4, 2011.

75   "How Much Did HealthCare.gov Really Cost? More Than the Administration Tells Us," Veronique de Rugy, *The National Review*, October 1, 2014.

76   "PRY: North Korea EMP Attack Could Destroy the U.S. – Now," Peter Vincent Fry, *The Washinton Times*, December 19, 2012.

77 "Four Pinocchios for Obama's Claim That Republicans have 'Filibustered About 500 Pieces of Legislation," Glenn Kessler, *The Washington Post*, May 9, 2014.

78 "AP: Obama Administration 'Sets New Record' for Denying Records," Erik Wemple, *The Washington Post*, March 18, 2015.

79 "11 Times Barack Obama Abused Press Freedoms," Joel B. Pollak, *Breitbart*, February 17, 2017.

80 "Feds Blow Off House Subpoena for Obamacare Co-Op Docs," Kathryn Watson, *The Daily Caller*, April 20, 2016.

81 Senator Tom Cotton, *Fox News Sunday* interview, August 7, 2016.

82 "New Documents show the Obama Admin Aggressively Lobbies to Kill Transparency Reform in Congress," Trevor Timm, *Freedom of the Press Foundation*, March 8, 2016.

83 "Obama's Final Year: US Spent $36 Million in Records Lawsuits," Ted Bridis, *AP*, March 14, 2017.

84 "Obama Administration Packed with Lobbyists He Vowed Not to Hire," Timothy Carney, *The Washington Examiner*, July 23, 2013.

85 "Stop Blaming the 'Rogue Agents,'" Eliana Johnson, *The National Review*, June 10, 2013.

86 "Busted! The IRS Used Donor Lists to Target Conservatives for Audits," *Progressive Today*, July 23, 2015.

87 "An Un-American Decision," Dov Lipman, *The Jerusalem Post*, December 29, 2016.

88 "Race Relations Are at Lowest Point in Obama Presidency, Poll Finds," Giovanni Russonello, *The New York Times*, July 13, 2016.

89 Ibid.

90 "Conservatives Outraged Over Obama Transgender Directive to Public School," *Fox News*, May 13, 2016.

91 "An Empirical Analysis of Racial Differences in Police Use of Force," Roland G. Fryer, Jr, PhD, Professor of Economics, Harvard University, Working Paper 22399, *National Bureau of Economic Research*, July 2016.

92 "Surprising New Evidence Shows Bias in Police Use of Force, but Not in Shootings," Quoctrung Bui and Amanda Cox, *The New York Times*, July 11, 2016.

93 "Secret CIA Assessment Says Russia Was Trying to Help Trump Win the White House," Adam Entous, Ellen Nakashima and Greg Miller, *The Washington Post*, December 6, 2016.

94 "Top U.S. Spy Agency Refuses to Endorse CIA's Russian Hacking Assessment Due to 'Lack of Evidence,'" *ZeroHedge*, December 13, 2016.

95 "Final Numbers: Obama is the Most Destructive Leader of Any Political Party Since WWII," Joe Hoft, *The Gateway Pundit*, March 2, 2017.

96 Obama 2008 campaign speech, transcript of *You Tube* video

97   "Muslim Brotherhood "Massive" Government Infiltration While Stigmatizing Government Employees With 'Islamophobia,'" Capt. Joseph R. John, *Combat Veterans for Congress website*, June 29, 2016.

98   "DHS Ordered Me to Scrub Records of Muslims with Terror Ties," Phillip Haney, DHS 15 year employee, *The Hill*, February 5, 2016.

99   Ibid.

100   "DHS Secretly Scrubbed 1000 Names From U.S. Terror Watch Lists," Adam Kredo, *The Washington Free Beacon*, March 1, 2016.

101   "Judicial Watch: Homeland Security Records Reveal Officials Ordered Terrorist Watch List Scrubbed," *Judicial Watch*, March 01, 2016.

102   Catastrophic Failure: Blindfolding America in the Face of Jihad, Stephen Coughlin. Washington, D.C.: Center for Security Policy Press, 2015.

103   "Muslim-American Involvement with Violent Extremism," Charles Kurzman, University of North Carolina – Chapel Hill, February 2, 2016.

104   "Dangers Rise as America Retreats," Dick and Liz Cheney, *The Wall Street Journal*, September 9, 2016.

105   "Retired Navy, Marine Corps Officers to Congress: Deployment Rate Unsustainable," Douglas Ernst, *The Washington Times*, November 12, 2014.

106   "An Indefensible Defense Budget," Ed Feulner, *The Washington Times*, March 14, 2016.

107   "Barack Obama Says Congress Owns Sequestration Cuts," Molly Moorhead, *Politifact*, October 24, 2012.

108   "Once Again, Woodward Takes on All the President's Men," *Investor's Business Daily* editorial, February 28, 2013.

109   "Mike Pence: 'Obama Era of Weakening our National Defenses is Over,'" Adelle Nazarian, *Breitbart*, December 7, 2016.

110   "Study: Obama issued $743 B in Regs," Tim Devaney, *The Hill*, August 8, 2016.

111   "Former Obama Official: Bureaucrats Manipulate Climate Stats to Influence Policy," Chris White, *The Daily Caller*, April 24, 2017.

112   House of Commons Foreign Affairs Committee Report – Libya: Examination of Intervention and Collapse and the UK's Future Policy Options, Third Report of Session 2016 – 17.

113   "A Conversation with Michael Flynn," Elise Cooper, *American Thinker*, July 26, 2016.

114   "Larry Elder: Obama Claimed 'All' of Syria's Chemical Weapons Had Been Eliminated," Larry Elder, *IBD*, April 13, 2017.

115   Ibid.

116   "Duterte Vows to 'Forget About Human Rights' if Islamic State Attacks Philippines," France Martel, *Breitbart*, November 14, 2016.

117   "General McChrystal: As World "Melting Down" US Is MIA, *Newsmax* interview, May, 12, 2015.

118   The Obama Doctrine, Jeffrey Goldberg, *The Atlantic*, April 2016.

119   "The President Gratuitously Damages American Alliances," Elliott Abrams, *Pressure Points, CFR Blog*, March 10, 2016.

120   The Obama Doctrine, Ibid.

121   "An Epiphany on the Road to Tehran," Clarice Feldman, *AmericanThinker.com*, May 8, 2016.

122   "Obama's Hiroshima Visit Epitomizes His Failed Foreign Policy," Tom Rogan, *National Review*, May 26, 2016.

123   "How Barack Obama's Foreign Policy De-Stabilized the World," Victor Davis Hanson, Hoover Institution, Stanford University, *National Review*, May 19, 2016.

124   "French Intel Chief's Stunning Warning: Europe is 'ON Brink of Civil War' due to Migrant Sex Attacks," *Zero Hedge,* July 13, 2016.

125   "4 Reasons Your Obamacare Healthcare Premium is Going Up by at Least 10% in 2017," Sean Williams, *The Motley Foot*, August 14, 2016.

126   "Aetna's Bertolini Predicted ObamaCare's Demise Four Years Ago," *Investor's Business Daily editorial*, August 16, 2016.

127   Ibid.

128   "Obama Seeks to Pave Way to Mideast Deal After He Leaves Office," Mark Landler, *The New York Times*, March 8, 2016.

129   "Is Obamism Correctable?," Victor Davis Hanson, *The National Review*, September 15, 2015.

130   "The Aspiring Novelist Who Became Obama's Foreign – Policy Guru," David Samuels, *The New York Times Magazine*, May 5, 2016.

131   "Obama's Foreign Policy Guru Boasts of How the Administration Lied to Sell the Iran Deal," Lee Smith, *The Weekly Standard*, May 5, 2016.

132   "White House Admits It Played Us for Fools to Sell Iran Deal," John Podhoretz, *The New York Post*, May 5, 2016.

133   "New York Times: Iran Nuclear Deal was Based on a Lie," Daniel Greenfield, *FrontPage Magazine*, May 6, 2016.

134   "Iran Deal Lies Have Consequences," Jonathan Tobin, *Commentary Magazine*, May 9, 2016.

135   "Obama's Master of Deceit on the Ian Nuke Deal," Joseph Klein, *FrontPage Magazine*, May 11, 2016.

136   Henry Kissinger and George Shultz, previous Secretaries of States, "The Iran Deal and Its Consequences," *The Wall Street Journal*, April 7, 2015.

137   "Obama Said Iran's Nuclear Program Was Frozen. Then This New Report Slapped Him HARD," *Western Journalism*, June 2, 2015.

138 "Obama's Claim that Iran's Nuclear Program has been 'Halted' and its Nuclear Stockpile 'Reduced,'" Glenn Kessler, *The Washington Post*, January 22, 2015.

139 Peter Vincent Pry, executive director of the Task Force on National and Homeland Security, a congressional advisory board, *Arutz Sheva Israel News*.

140 "US Gave Away Better Options on Iran," Alan M. Dershowitz, *The Boston Globe*, July 16, 2015.

141 "Ex - White House Aide Ross: Obama Made Conscious Decision to Distance Himself from "Problematic" Israel," Deborah Danan, Breitbart, May 23, 2016.

142 "Israel May Need to Take Out Iranian Bases in Syria," Herb Keinon, *Jerusalem Post*, July 17, 2017.

143 Assessment of the JCPOA: Strategic Consequences for U.S. National Security, *JINSA Iran Strategy Council,* Ret. USMC General James Conway and Ret. USAF General Charles Wald, September 2015.

144 "Former Official: Obama Admin 'Systematically Disbanded' Units Investigating Iran's Terrorism Financing Networks," Susan Crabtree, *The Washington Free Beacon*, June 8, 2017.

145 "Obama's Master of Deceit on the Iran Nuke Deal," Joseph Klein, *FrontPage Magazine*, May 11, 2016.

146 Iranian Fars News Agency, Iran DM Rejects Report on Inspection of Military Centers Based on Lausanne Understanding, April, 8, 2015.

147 "The Aspiring Novelist Who Became Obama's Foreign – Policy Guru," David Samuels, *The New York Times Magazine*, May 5, 2016.

148 Henry Kissinger and George Shultz, previous Secretaries of State, "The Iran Deal and Its Consequences," *The Wall Street Journal*, April 7, 2015.

149 "The Obama Doctrine," Jeffrey Goldberg, *The Atlantic*, April 2016.

150 "The Aspiring Novelist Who Became Obama's Foreign – Policy Guru," David Samuels, *The New York Times Magazine*, May 5, 2016.

151 "Iran: Follow the Money," Shoshana Bryen, *American Thinker*, August 5, 2016.

152 "Iran: We Can Mobilize Nine Million Fighters Against the U.S.," Deborah Danan, *Breitbart*, October 5, 2016.

153 "Iran Claims It's Sending Elite Fighters to Infiltrate US, Europe," Adam Kredo, *The Washington Free Beacon via Fox News*, November 2, 2016.

154 "UN Chief Concerned Iran May Have Violated Arms Embargo," *Reuters, The Jerusalem Post*, January 9, 2017.

155 "The Outrages of Sharia," Eileen Toplansky, *American Thinker*, April 23, 2017.

156 "Mossad Chief Warns Iran Taking Over Territory Relinquished by ISIS," Herb Keinon, The Jerusalem Post, August 13, 2017.

157 "Top Saudi Columnist: Obama's Gulf Visit Did Little to Mend Rift with Kingdom," Saul Loeb, *Breitbart*, April 24, 2015

158   "The Obama Doctrine," Jeffrey Goldberg, *The Atlantic*, April 2016.

159   "The Obama Doctrine," Jeffrey Goldberg, *The Atlantic*, April 2016.

160   "Report: Saudis May Purchase Pakistani Atomic Bomb," *Times of Israel*, May 18, 2015.

161   "Iran Tests Ballistic Missile in Defiance of U.N. Sanctions, John Hayward, *Breitbart*, January 30, 2017.

162   "Report: Iran Violating Nuclear Deal with Secret Development Near 'Off Limits' Parchin Site," Adelle Nazarian, *Breitbart*, April 22, 2017.

163   "Sanctions to be Lifted on Iranians Suspected of Nuclear Weapons Work," Jay Solomon, *The Wall Street Journal*, July 21, 2015.

164   "Nuke Deal Won't Clear Up Questions About Iran's Past Weapons Work On Day 1," Bradley Klapper, *Associated Press*, June 11, 2015.

165   "Into the Fray: POTUS vs US," Martin Sherman, *The Jerusalem Post*, September 17, 2015.

166   "Dangers Rise as America Retreats," Dick Cheney and Liz Cheney, *The Wall Street Journal*, September 9, 2016.

167   Benjamin Weinthal and Emanuele Ottolenghi, "Iran Made Illegal Purchases of Nuclear Weapons Technology Last Month," *The Weekly Standard*, July 10, 2015.

168   "Iran Still on the Hunt for Nuclear Weapons Technology Across Germany," Benjamin Weinthal, *The Weekly Standard*, July 7, 2017.

169   Obama, Statement by the President on the Framework to Prevent Iran from Obtaining a Nuclear Weapon, April 2, 2015.

170   Emanuele Ottolenghi, Senior Fellow, Foundation for Defense of Democracies, "The Central Pillar Supporting the Iran Deal Has a Big Crack In It," *The Tower Magazine*, Issue 28, July 2015.

171   "Snapping Back Sanctions Won't Prevent a Nuclear-Armed Iran," *IBD editorial*, July 16, 2015.

172   Former Israeli Ambassador Oren, "Former Israeli Ambassador: Iran to Get $700 Billion in Sanctions Relief," *www.freebeacon.com*, July 22, 2015.

173   Assessment of the Joint Comprehensive Plan of Action (JCPOA). Strategic Consequences for U.S. National Security, Retired General James Conway, USMC and Retired General Charles Wald, USAF, *JINSA's Iran Strategy Council*, September 2015.

174   "Sanctions to be Lifted on Iranians Suspected of Nuclear Weapons Work," Jay Solomon, *The Wall Street Journal*, July 21, 2015.

175   "AP Excusive: Document Shows Less Limits on Iran Nuke Work," George Jahn, *Associated Press*, July 18, 2016.

176   "Obama Gave Iran a Faster Route to a Nuke – And Didn't Tell Us," *IBD editorial*, July 19, 2016.

177   Jose Maria Anzar, former president of Spain, "Confrontation with Iran Is Inevitable," *The Wall Street Journal*, August 5, 2015.

178   "Iran: U.S. Encourage Islamic Republic to Keep Illicit Missile Tests Secret," Adam Kredo, *The Washington Free Beacon*, May 16, 2016.

179   "Obama Admin Secretly Facilitated Iranian Ballistic Missile Program," Adam Kredo, *The Washington Free Beacon*, October 4, 2016.

180   "U.S., Others Agreed 'Secret' Exemptions for Iran after Nuclear Deal: Think Tank," Jonathan Landay, *Reuters*, September 1, 2016.

181   "Obama's Iran Deal is a Fraud on the American People," Andrew C. McCarthy, *The National Review*, September 3, 2016.

182   "Iran Received $10 Billion in Cash and Gold as Sanctions Relief – Obama Admin Denies **Direct** Role," Sarah Lee, *The Blaze*, December 30, 2016.

183   "Iran: US Surrendered More Than $10 Billion in Gold, Cash and Assets," Adam Kredo, *The Washington Free Beacon*, January 9, 2017.

184   "Israel Seeks U.S. Backing to Avert Permanent Iran Foothold in Syria," Matt Spetalnick and Mark Hosenball, *Reuters*, April 26, 2017.

185   "U.S. Payment to Iran Could Mean Over $1 Billion to Support Terrorism," Rachel Hoff, *American Action Forum*, September 14, 2016.

186   "U.S. Wire Payments to Iran Undercut Obama," Louis Nelson, *Politico*, September 18, 2016.

187   "The Iran Deal – More Shameful Than Munich," Martin Sherman, *The Jerusalem Post*, September 3, 2015.

188   "Patraeus: The Islamic State Isn't Our Biggest Problem in Iraq," Liz Sly, *The Washington Post*, March 20, 2015.

189   "White House Making Up Iran Data?," Michael Rubin, *Commentary*, March 6, 2016.

190   "Russia Arms Iran As Kerry Refuses to Use U.N. Veto," *IBD editorial*, February 26, 2016.

191   "The Fictional Iran Deal, Adam Turner, *American Thinker*, May 21, 2016.

192   "Defense Ministry Slams Obama Statement, Compares Iran Deal to Munich," Yaakov Lappin, *The Jerusalem Post*, August 5, 2016.

193   "U.S. Held Cash Until Iran Freed Prisoners," Jay Solomon and Carol E. Lee, *The Wall Street Journal*, August 17, 2016

194   "Senior Justice Official Raised Objections to Iran Cash Payment," Devlin Barrett, *The Wall Street Journal*, August 12, 2016.

195   "Obama Admin Paid Iran $1.7 From Taxpayer Funds – Iran says money was ransom payment," Adam Kredo, *The Washington Free Beacon*, January 21, 2016.

196   "U.S. Sent Cash to Iran as Americans Were Freed," Jay Solomon, Carol E. Lee, *The Wall Street Journal*, August 3, 2016.

197   "Obama's Ransom Payment to an Outlaw Regime," Joseph Klein, *FrontPage Mag*, August 4, 2016.

198 "US Payment of $1.7 Billion to Iran Made Entirely in Cash," Richard Lardner, *Associated Press and ABC News*, September 6, 2016.

199 "Cruz: White House Orchestrated Money Laundering Operation for Iran," Adam Kredo, *The Washington Free Beacon*, September 8, 2016.

200 "U.S. Wire Payments to Iran Undercut Obama," Louis Nelson, *Politico*, September 18, 2016.

201 "Politico Investigation: Obama's Hidden Iran Deal Giveaway," Josh Meyer, *Politico*, April 24, 2017.

202 "House Oversight Panel to Investigate Iran Deal," Josh Meyer, *Politico*, May 5, 2017.

203 "Guess What Else Obama Gave Away in the Iran Deal," *New York Post editorial*, April 24, 2017.

204 "More Disturbing Revelations on Obama's Disastrous Nuclear Deal with Iran," Joseph Klein, *Front Page Magazine*, April 26, 2017.

205 "Leading Saudi Cleric: Daesh ISIS Have the Same Beliefs as We Do," *Integrity Media*, January 22, 2016.

206 "13 Percent of Syrian Refugees Support ISIS: Poll," Ryan Mauro, *The Clarion Project*, November 1, 2015.

207 "ISIS Planning 'Nuclear Tsunami,'" L. Todd Wood, *The Washington Times*, September 28, 2015.

208 "ISIS Nuclear Attack In Europe is a Real Threat, Say Experts," Kim Sengupta, *The Independent*, June 9, 2016.

209 "Could ISIS Reiplicate Tokyo Chemical Attack in New York or London Subway?," *2Paragraphs*, Hamish de Bretton Gordon, March 20, 2015.

210 "First on CNN: ISIS Suspected of Mustard Attack Against US and Iraqi Troops," Barbara Starr, *CNN*, September 21, 2016.

211 "Not 'Lone Wolves' After All: How ISIS Guides World's Terror Plots from Afar," Rikmini Callimachi, *The New York Times*, February 4, 2017.

212 "Qatar, Trump and Double Games," Caroline Glick, *The Jerusalem Post*, June 9, 2017.

213 "Saudis to Qatar: Stop Supporting Muslim Brotherhood, Hamas," *Breitbart*, June 8, 2017.

214 "Memo Received by Clinton: Obama Admin Aided Group that Became ISIS to Control Area Where ISIS Formed Caliphate," Patrick Howley, *Breitbart*, June 15, 2016, and excerpts obtained from the complete original memo from the DIA.

215 "Letter: I Have Seen First-Hand The Abuse and Fraud in the U.S. Refugee Program," *Mary Doetsch*, The Chicago Tribune, February 7, 2017.

216 "FBI Director Admits US Can't Vet All Syrian Refugees for Terror Ties," Chuck Ross, *The Daily Caller*, October 21, 2015.

217 "IS Jihadists Stole 'Tens of Thousands' of Blank Passports: Reports," *AFP*, December 20, 2015.

218 "Study Reveals 72 Terrorists Came from Countries Covered by Trump Vetting Order," Jessica Vaughan, *Center for Immigration Studies*, February 11, 2017.

219 "Flashback: 3 Somalian Immigrants Stabbed 24 People in 3 Terrorist Attacks on U.S. Soil in 2016," Ryan Saavedra, *The Gateway Pundit*, February 11, 2017.

220 "Here's a Short List of Foreign-Born Terrorists Reporters Can't Believe Exist," Kyle Shideler, *The Federalist*, January 30, 2017.

221 Ibid.

222 "UK Officials Admit There are 6,000 – 10,000 Jihadis Loose in the Country," Rick Moran, *American Thinker*, April 30, 2017.

223 "Kurdish Opposition Leader Demirtas: 'Erdogan Wants a Calilphate,'" *Der Spiegel* International interview, April 19, 2016.

224 "Islamic State Fighter: 'Turkey Paved the Way for Us,'" Ariel Ben Solomon, *The Jerusalem Post*, July 30, 2014.

225 "ISIS Made $1 billion in Revenue in 2015: US Treasury," *Deccan Chronicle*, June 12, 2016.

226 "Meet the Man Who Funds ISIS: Bilal Erdogan, The Son of Turkey's President," *Zero Hedge*, November 26, 2015.

227 "Captured ISIS Fighter Says "Trained in Turkey," *RT*, December 28, 2015.

228 "Terror Task Force Chair: Obama Limiting Airstrikes on IS to Protect Environment," Edwin Mora, *Breitbart Interview*, June 23, 2016.

229 "New Counterterrorism 'Heat Map' Shows ISIS Branches Spreading Worldwide," William Arkin, Robert Windrem and Cynthia McFadden, *NBC News website*, August 3, 2016.

230 "Christianity is Being Driven Out of the Middle East," Perry Chiaramonte, *The New York Post*, April 14, 2017.

231 "IS Buried Thousands in 72 Mass Graves, AP Finds," Lori Hinnant and Desmond Butler, *AP*, Aug. 30, 2016.

232 *Fox News* Special Report, June 14, 2016.

233 "Obama Brags About Killing Bin Laden As He Frees Bin Laden's Bodyguards," *Investor's Business Daily editorial*, January 14, 2016.

234 "Why We Hate You and Why We Fight You," *Dabiq*, official ISIS publication, The Clarion Project pdf, Issue 15, 1437, p. 30 – 33, 2016.

235 "Confirmed: Islam, not Grievances, Fuels Muslim Hatred for the West," Raymond Ibrahim, *Front Page Magazine*, August 19, 2016.

236 *"Farook Family Values," Carol Brown, American Thinker, December 7, 2015.*

237 *Unexpected Treason*, James McCormack, 2016, self-published, Amazon.

238 "Barack Obama's Muslim Childhood," Daniel Pipes, *FrontPage Magazine*, April 29, 2008.

239 "Obama – A Muslim Wolf in Christian Wool?" www.arkpw.net, March 27, 2008.

240 "Jeremiah Wright: I 'Made it Comfortable' for Obama to Accept Christianity without Having to Renounce Islam," *The Gateway Pundit*, May 15, 2012.

241 *Unexpected Treason*, ibid.

242   Ibid.

243   Ibid.

244   "No Higher Power: Obama's War on Religious Freedom," Phyllis Schafly and George Neumayr, *Regnery Publishing*, 2016.

245   Ibid.

246   "Interview with State Sen. Barack Obama," Cathleen Falsani, *Sojourners*, March 27, 2004.

247   "Libyan Leader Gaddafi: People in Arab and Islamic World, Africa … May Have Been Involved In Legitimate Contribution Campaigns [To Obama]," *MEMRI website*, June 16, 2008.

248   "Obama Admires Bush," David Brooks, *The New York Times website*, May 16, 2008.

249   "Top Cardinal: Islam Want to Dominate the World," Nick Hallett, *Breitbart*, July 23, 2016.

250   Ibid.

251   "Dr. Ahmed Al-Tayeb: Meet the World's 'Most Influential Muslim,'" Raymond Ibrahim, *FrontPage Magazine*, August 24, 2016.

252   Sheikh Muhammad Abdullah Nasr, graduate and scholar of Islamic Law at Al-Azhar University, television interview discussing al-Azhar University and ISIS, early 2015. "Al-Azhar and ISIS: Cause and Effect," *raymondibrahim.com*.

253   "The Real Bomb is in Islam's Books," Raymond Ibrahim*, Front Page Magazine*, May 3, 2017.

254   "Paris Cardinal: Islamists Worship a 'G-d of Death,'" Thomas Williams, PhD, *Breitbart*, July 20, 2016.

255   "America's 'Arab Spring,' Nonie Darwish, *Gatestone Institute International Policy Council*, November 3, 2016.

256   "Ben Carson in CAIR's Crosshairs," Robert Spencer, *FrontPage Magazine*, September 21, 2015.

257   Ibid.

258   Ibid.

259   Ibid.

260   "Wear a Headscarf or be Raped," Ted Thornhill and Sue Reid, *The Daily Mail*, July 19, 2016.

261   "America's 'Arab Spring,' Nonie Darwish, *Gatestone Institute International Policy Council*, November 3, 2016.

262   "The Outrages of Sharia," Eileen Toplansky, *American Thinker*, April 23, 2017.

263   "Nonie Darwish's Wholly Different," Danusha Goska, *Front Page Magazine*, May 11, 2017.

264   "Jesuit Scholar: Islamic Extremists are the Extreme Muslims," Thomas Williams, PhD, *Breitbart*, June 16, 2016.

265   Ibid.

266   *Catastrophic Failure: Blindfolding America in the Face of Jihad*, Stephen Coughlin. Washington, D.C.: Center for Security Policy Press, 2015.

267 "Are Islamists Conducting a New Jihad Against the West," William DiPuccio, *The Gatestone Institute International Policy Council*, May 12, 2017.

268 Europol, European Union law enforcement agency, EU Terrorism Situation and Trend Report (TE-SAT) 2014.

269 "Israel's Arrest of Christian Aid Director Imperils Palestinian Charity Missions," Asma Jawabreh and Jacob Wirtschafter, *The Washington Times*, August 7, 2016.

270 "Muslim refugee, 20, who raped a boy, 10, in his Sydney home says what he did 'is not a crime because it is acceptable in his homeland'," Belinda Cleary and Belinda Geary, *The Daily Mail*, August 31, 2016.

271 "The West of Finally Fighting Back Against Militant Islam," Rev. Peter Mullen, *Breitbart*, November 19, 2016.

272 "The Invalidity of the Moderate Muslim Concept," Atlas Shrugs website, December 16, 2015.

273 "France Has 5 Million Muslims and Only a Few Hundred Attended 'Solidarity' Mass after Normandy Attack," Raheen Kassam, *Breitbart*, July 31, 2016.

274 "Ex-Islamist Leader: 'Stop Saying Violence has Nothing to do with Islam," Simon Kent, Breitbart, June 6, 2017.

275 "Leaked Police Report: There Are 23 Muslim-Controlled "No Go Zones" in Sweden: Plagued with Violence, Sexual Assaults and Gun Crimes," Marc Slavo, *SHTFplan.com*, June 23, 2017.

276 "The Acid Attacks of London's Muslim No-Go Zones," Daniel Greenfield, *Front Page Magazine*, July 17, 2017.

277 Obama, "President Obama: Our Fight Against Violent Extremism," *L.A. Times* editorial, February, 17, 2015.

278 "Poll: At least 44 Million Arab Youths Potential supporters of ISIS," Sierra Rayne, *American Thinker*, April 14, 2016.

279 "Little Girl Sings ISIS Song – Beheads Doll," *MEMRI TV*, August 4, 2016.

280 "Swedish Pediatrician: Some 'Children' Nearly 40," *The Loca*, September 3, 2016.

281 Islam: Has It "Always Been Part of America?," *FrontPage Magazine*, Joseph Klein, February 9, 2016.

282 "Nations Seeking to Ban Islam Keep Growing," Raymond Ibrahim, *FrontPage Magazine*, June 24, 2016.

283 "Obama Uses Mosque Speech to Subordinate All Religion to the State," Neil Munro, *Breitbart*, February 4, 2016.

284 "Is Obamism Correctable?," Victor Hansen, *The National Review*, September 15, 2015.

285 *No Holds Barred: Torrent of Anti-Israel Advice Found in Hillary's Emails," Rabbi S. Boteach, The Jerusalem Post, February 1, 2016.*

286 Caryle Murphy, "Facing New Realities as Islamic Americans," *Washington Post*, September 12, 2004. Wikipedia biography of Esam Omeish.

287 *"Favorite Hillary Clinton Pundit Cheers Hamas Attacks on Israel,"* Daniel Greenfield, *FrontPage Magazine, April 4, 2016.*

288 "EXCLUSIVE: How Hillary Clinton Mainstreamed Al-Qaeda Fundraiser Abdurahman Alamoudi," Patrick Poole, *PJ Media*, July 29, 2016.

289 "Stop Smearing Keith Ellison," Jeremy Ben-Ami, *The Washington Post*, December 6, 2016.

290 "J Street: For Sale to the Highest Bidder," Shmuley Boteach, *Times of Israel*, May 26, 2016.

291 "Watch: Abbas' Fatah Party Posts Video Instructing Palestinians to Stab Israelis, Become Martyrs," *Breitbart Jerusalem*, April 21, 2016.

292 "Palestinians Paid Terrorists $1B in Past Four Years, Knesset Panel Hears," *Times of Israel*, May 29, 2017.

293 "Taxpayer Support for Palestinian Terrorist Salaries Becoming Impossible to Defend," Edwin Black, *FrontPage Magazine*, July 14, 2017.

294 "The Aspiring Novelist Who Became Obama's Foreign – Policy Guru," David Samuels, *The New York Times Magazine*, May 5, 2016 – interview with former Obama Secretary of Defense Leon Panetta.

295 "Why Does Obama Call ISIS 'ISIL,'" Amil Imani, *American Thinker.com*, December 10, 2015.

296 "Obama's Sneaky Last Slap at Israel," Editorial, *The New York Post*, January 24, 2017.

297 "Our World: Israel's Moment of Decision, Caroline Glick, *The Jerusalem Post*, January 26, 2017.

298 "Why So Many Critics Hate the New Obama Biography," David Greenberg, *Politico*, June 19, 2017.

299 "Anti-Semitism in Chicago: A Stunning Silence," Eugene Kennedy, *The New York Times*, July 26, 1988.

300 The Religion of Peace website, Quran section, What Does Islam Teach About … Violence. Some of the following quotes originated at this website.

301 "The Quran's Deadly Role in Inspiring Belgian Slaughter," Nabeel Qureshi, *USA Today Editorial*, March 22, 2016.

302 "War Room," December 27, 2008, *Salon website*.

303 "Do Palestinian Arabs Want a Peaceful State Alongside Israel," Morton A. Klein and Daniel Mandel, *Front Page Magazine*, May 3, 2017.

304 Report of the High Commissioner on the Administration of Palestine 1920 – 1925, Jerusalem, April 22, 1925, p. 24-25.

305 "Israel Official: Obama Administration Secretly Worked with Palestinians to Craft 'Shameful' UN Resolution," Aaron *Klein, Breitbart*, December 23, 2016.

306 "Transcript Claims to Show US Worked with Palestinians on UN Resolution," *Times of Israel*, December 27, 2016.

307 "White House on Defense After Being Exposed as Architect of Anti-Israel U.N. Action," Adam Kredo, *The Washington Free Beacon*, December 29, 2016.

308   "Right from Wrong: Kerry's Moral Turpitude," Ruthie Blum, *The Jerusalem Post*, January 1, 2017.

309   "Ex-Defense Chief: Erdogan is 'Deliberately Islamicizing' Europe in Bid for World Domination," Raphael Ahren, *The Times of Israel*, June 6, 2017.

310   "No Holds Barred: Ignoring Aleppo, Obama and Power Target Israel," Shmuley Boteach, *The Jerusalem Post*, December 26, 2016.

311   "Chief Rabbi: US has Forsaken Israel, We Can Trust Only in the Lord," *Times of Israel*, December 28, 2016.

312   "Candidly Speaking: Responding to Obama's Malicious Betrayal of Israel," Isi Leibler, *The Jerusalem Post*, December 29, 2016.

313   "An Un-American Decision," Dov Lipman, *The Jerusalem Post*, December 29, 2016.

314   Ibid.

315   "U.S. Spy Net on Israel Snares Congress," Adam Entous and Danny Yadron, *The Wall Street Journal*, December 29, 2015.

316   "Obama Admin Rejects Funding for Israel's Security, Defense," Adam Kredo, *The Washington Free Beacon*, June 15, 2016.

317   "Column One: Obama's Money and Israel's Sovereignty," Caroline Glick, *The Jerusalem Post*, June 23, 2016.

318   "Australian PM Condemns 'One-Sided' UNSC Resolution," *Jerusalem Post*, December 30, 2016.

319   "Obama Sided with the Forces of Darkness," Thane Rosenbaum, *Times of Israel*, December 26, 2016.

320   "Candidly Speaking: Responding to Obama's Malicious Betrayal of Israel," Isi Leibler, *The Jerusalem Post*, December 29, 2016.

321   "Democratic Congressman: Jews are Like Termites," Adam Kredo, *The Washington Free Beacon*, July 26, 2016.

322   "DNC Expels Chairman Candidate from Race for 'Disgusting' Criticism of Islam," Ben Kew, *Breitbart*, February 1, 2017.

323   "Black Lives Matter Must Rescind Anti-Israel Declaration," Alan M. Dershowitz, *The Boston Globe*, August 12, 2016.

324   "Obama: 'Israel Doesn't Know What Its Best Interests Are,'" Jeffrey Goldberg, *The Atlantic*, January 14, 2013.

325   "ADL Chief: Kerry Speech Pushes Peace Away," *The Jerusalem Post*, December 29, 2016.

326   "Column One: Obama and Israel, Strike and Counter-strike," Caroline Glick, *The Jerusalem Post*, December 29, 2016.

327   "John Kerry, Those 'Illegal' Settlements, That 'Two-State Solution', Part II," Hugh Fitzgerald, *Jihad Watch*, January 4, 2017.

328 Ibid.

329 Ibid.

330 Ibid.

331 Ibid.

332 Ibid.

333 Ibid.

334 Ibid.

335 "The U.S. and 'Defensible Borders': How Washington Has Understood UNSC Resolution 242 and Israel's Requirement for Withdrawals" by Dore Gold, PhD posted at www.defensibleborders.org

336 "Obama Under Fire for Comment on Palestinians," *MSNBC website*, March 15, 2007, as printed in the Des Moines Register.

337 "Another Tack – A Delegitimization Called Nakba," Sarah Honig, *The Jerusalem Post*, May 14, 2015.

338 "9,000 Photos from 1800's British Mandate of Palestine – With No Trace of 'Palestinians,'" The Palestine-Israeli Conflict, February 13, 2013.

339 "Obama: 'Israel Doesn't Know What Its Best Interests Are,'" Jeffrey Goldberg, *The Atlantic*, January 14, 2013.

340 "Editorial: Jerusalem Attack Exposes Israel's False Peace Partner," *JPost Editorial*, January 10, 2017.

341 "Palestinians Use Deception for Greater Acceptance," Noah Beck, *Front Page Magazine*, May 11, 2017.

342 "Abbas Advisor: Western Wall Can Only Remain Under Muslim Sovereignty," Adam Rasgon, *The Jerusalem Post*, June 10, 2017.

343 "Trump 'Disrespects' The Intel community? What About Obama's Iraq Bug-Out?" Larry Elder, *FrontPage Magazine*, January 20, 2017.

344 "Study Claims Up To 2.8 Million Non-Citizens Voted in 2008," Peter Hasson, *The Daily Caller*, January 24, 2017.

345 "Voter Fraud Redefined," Matthew Vadum, *American Thinker*, November 8, 2012.

346 "Eighteen Issues That Help Define Barack Obama in the 2008 Presidential Campaign," James McCormack, Plagiarism and Other Ethical Issues Chapter, *Willowbrook Publishing*, 2009.

347 Ibid. "Voter Fraud Redefined."

348 "Hillary Clinton Received over 800,000 Illegal Votes, Research Claims," Ben Kew, *Breitbart*, January 27, 2017.

349 "Study: 1.8 Million Dead People Still Registered to Vote," Pam Fessler, *NPR*, February 14, 2012.

350   "Half of Detroit Votes May Be Ineligible for Recount," Chad Livengood and Joel Kurth, *The Detroit News*, December 5, 2016.

351   "More Than 7 Million Voter Registrations Are Duplicated in Multiple States," Joe Schoffstall, *The Washington Free Beacon*, May 18, 2017.

352   "One Third of Noncitizens Found Voted Illegally," *Public Interest Legal Foundation*, May 29, 2017.

353   "Study Supports Trump: 5.7 Million Noncitizens May Have Cast Illegal Votes," Rowarn Scarborough, *The Washington Times*, June 19, 2017.

354   "America May Have 3.5 Million More Voters Than Eligible Adult Citizens," Deroy Murdock, Dallas News, August 11, 2017.

355   "Russian Foreign Ministry: 'Obama Still Has a Few Days Left to Destroy the World," *ZeroHedge. com*, January 15, 2017.

356   "Woodward: Trump Dossier Is a 'Garbage Document' — Intelligence Chiefs Should 'Apologize' to Trump," Pam Key, *Breitbart*, January 15, 2017.

357   "CIA's Brennan Conspired with Foreign Spies," Matthew Vadum, *Front Page Magazine*, April 21, 2017.

358   "US Intel Sources Warn Israel Against Sharing Secrets with Trump Administration," Ronen Bergman, *YNetNews.com*, January 12, 2017.

359   "NSA Gets More Latitude to Share Intercepted Communications," Charlie Savage, *The New York Times*, January 12, 2017.

360   "Mark Levin to Congress: Investigate Obama's 'Silent Coup' vs. Trump," Joel B. Pollack, *Breitbart*, March 3, 2017.

361   "How Obama is Scheming to Sabotage Trump's Presidency," Paul Sperry, *The New York Post*, February 11, 2017.

362   "Obama, Organizing for Action, and the Death Throes of the Democratic Party," Scott S. Powell, *American Thinker*, March 3, 2017.

363   "Exclusive: Barack Obama's Close Confidante Valerie Jarrett Has Moved Into His New DC Home, Which is Now the Nerve Center for their Plan to Mastermind the Insurgency Against President Trump," Leon Wagener, *The Daily Mail*, March 1, 2017.

364   "Spies Keep Intelligence from Donald Trump on Leak Concerns," Shane Harris and Carol Lee, *The Wall Street Journal*, February 15, 2017.

365   "Insiders: Obama Holdover 'Shadow Government' Plotting to Undermine Trump," John Hayward, *Breitbart*, February 17, 2017.

366   "Fake News: Media, Democrats Distort Remarks to Target Jeff Sessions," Joel B. Pollak, *Breitbart*, March 1, 2017.

367   "Obama Administration Rushed to Preserve Intelligence of Russian Election Hacking," Matthew Rosenberg and Adam Goldman and Michael S. Schmidt, *The New York Times*, March 1, 2017.

368 "Obama Admin Loyalists, Government Insiders Sabotage Trump White House," Adam K
    The Washington Free Beacon, March 22, 2017.

369 "Gaffney: Rice's Unmasking Scandal part of Obama's 'Political Warfare Operation' to Destro
    Trump," Dan Riehl, *Breitbart*, April 5, 2017.

370 "Israel and Obama's Political War," Caroline Glick, *Front Page Magazine*, April 10, 2017.

371 "Trump Under Siege: More Than 60 Percent of NSC Employees Placed by Obama," Kristina
    Wong, *Breitbart*, May 17, 2017.

372 "Krauthammer: There's 'A Loyalty Problem Inside the White House,'" Ian Hanchett, *Breitbart*,
    May 19, 2017.

373 "Fmr. U.N. Amb. Power Emerges as Central Figure in Obama Unmasking Investigation,"
    Adam Kredo, *The Washington Free Beacon*, July 19, 2017.

374 "Former Obama Aide Ben Rhodes Now a Person of Interest in Unmasking Investigation,"
    Sarah Carter, *Circa*, August 1, 2017.

375 "What I See in Lincoln's Eyes," Barack Obama, *Time Magazine*, June 26, 2005.

376 "Iran's Prez Assails "Bullying Powers," *CBS News website*, September 23, 2008.

377 "The Other Obama," Lauren Collins, *The New Yorker Magazine*, March 10, 2008.

378 "Newspaper Shows Obama Belonged to Socialist Party," Aaron Klein, *World Net Daily*, October
    24, 2008.

379 "Disclosure: Another 41 Foreign – Born Individuals Snagged on Terror Charges," Adam Kredo,
    The Washington Free Beacon, January 8, 2016.

380 "Police: Refugee Children Behind at Least Four of the Five Sexual Assaults at the Bathhouses,"
    Mattias Albinsson, *Friatider*, May 18, 2016.

381 "Fake passports for ISIL Terrorists 'Found in Greek Refugee Camps,'" Josephine McKenna,
    Telegraph, August 21, 2016.

382 "Meeting Obama's 10,000 Syrian Refugee Target, No Matter What," Nayla Rush, Center for
    Immigration Studies, June 2016.

383 "The Map the Media Doesn't Want You to See: Nations with the Most Refugees Have the Most
    Terror Attacks," Mac Slavo, *SHTFplan.com*, May 10, 2017.

384 "The Obama Doctrine," Jeffrey Goldberg, *The Atlantic*, April 2016.

385 "Arab States issue 13-Point Ultimatum to Qatar: Cut Ties with Iran, Close Al-Jazeera, Shutter
    Turkish Base," *Zero Hedge*, June 23, 2017.

386 "The Aspiring Novelist Who Became Obama's Foreign – Policy Guru," David Samuels, *The
    New York Times Magazine*, May 5, 2016.

387 "Obama's Foreign Policy Guru Boasts of How the Administration Lied to Sell the Iran Deal,"
    Lee Smith, *The Weekly Standard*, May 5, 2016.

388 "The Aspiring Novelist Who Became Obama's Foreign – Policy Guru," David Samuels, *The
    New York Times Magazine*, May 5, 2016.

Apology Tour Lands in Hiroshima," John Bolton, *New York Post*, May 26, 2016.

al Claims Obama Sees NATO as a 'Threat,'" Rich Moran, *American Thinker*, 10, 2016.

a in Laos:; 'Stressed Americans' Typically Turn to Racism," Charlie Spiering, *Breitbart*, ptember 7, 2016.

"In Laos, Obama Repeatedly Calls Americans 'Lazy,'" Bre Payton, *The Federalist*, September 7, 2016.

393 "Why the Obsession with Giving Away Control of the Internet," Senator James Lankford, *The Washington Examiner*, October 6, 2016.

394 "Remarks by President Obama and Chancellor Merkel of Germany in a Joint Press Conference," Berlin, Germany, *The White House – Office of the Press Secretary*, November 17, 2017.

395 "UK: 23,000 Terrorists and Counting," Denis MacEoin, Gatestone Institute, August 3, 2017.

Made in United States
Orlando, FL
27 January 2022